# BEFORE THE WIND CHANGED

## People, Places and Education
## in the Sudan

# ORIENTAL AND AFRICAN ARCHIVES

The purpose of this series is the publication of materials from private (i.e. non-governmental) archival collections relating to oriental and African countries, and dealing in particular with British contributions to the history of those regions.

Materials for publication are selected in the first place from two collections: the Sudan Archive in the University of Durham, which consists chiefly of the papers of British officials of the Sudan Government during the Condominium (1899-1955); and the Private Papers Collection at St. Antony's College, Oxford, containing the private papers of individuals with a Middle Eastern connection from the early nineteenth century onwards.

Each volume of materials will be edited by a scholar with a specialist knowledge of the country or the subject with which it deals.

P. M. HOLT
*Chairman*
*Oriental and African Archives Committee*

# BEFORE THE WIND CHANGED

## People, Places and Education in the Sudan

*by*

INA BEASLEY

*edited by*

JANET STARKEY

*Published for* THE BRITISH ACADEMY
*by* OXFORD UNIVERSITY PRESS

*Oxford University Press, Walton Street, Oxford OX2 6DP*

*Oxford  New York  Toronto*
*Delhi  Bombay  Calcutta  Madras  Karachi*
*Petaling Jaya  Singapore  Hong Kong  Tokyo*
*Nairobi  Dar es Salaam  Cape Town*
*Melbourne  Auckland*

*and associated companies in*
*Berlin  Ibadan*

*Published in the United States*
*by Oxford University Press, New York*

© *The British Academy, 1992*

*British Library Cataloguing in Publication Data*
*Beasley, Ina, b.1898*
*Before the wind changed: people, places*
*and education in the Sudan.*
*I. Title    II. Starkey, Janet, 1948–*
*370.9624*
*ISBN 0–19–726110–8*

*Typeset by the editor at the Oxford University Computing Service*
*Printed in Great Britain*
*at the University Press, Cambridge*

To the women of Sudan, and especially the schoolmistresses.

'The wind of change is blowing through the continent. Whether we like it or not, this growth of national consciousness is a political fact.'

*Harold Macmillan, Speech, South African Parliament,*
*Cape Town, 3 Feb 1960*

# Contents

# List of Photographs

# List of maps

# Editor's Preface

**J.C.M. Starkey**

*'Sudan ... an empty limbo of torment but that there never was an Englishman who went there but was eager to go back' (Steevens, G.W.).*

Dr Ina M. Beasley (née Girdwood) was born in 1895. From 1919 to 1922 she was an internal student at University College, London where she obtained her B.A. (Hons). She also gained the Teacher's Diploma from the Institute of Education. After two years' teaching she was married and then worked at the University of Nottingham, in the Adult Education Department on W.E.A. and Miners' Welfare. In 1930 she went to Burma with her husband. She obtained an external Ph.D from University College, London on July 16, 1931. From 1935 to 1939 she was a part-time English lecturer and Tutor to External Women students at Rangoon University. Dr Beasley joined the Sudan Government Service on 4.11.39 as Superintendent, Girls' Education until 1941. From 1942 to 1949 Dr Beasley was Controller, Girls' Education in Sudan and member of Council of Gordon Memorial College. In 1950 Dr Beasley retired from the Sudan Government. From 1951 to 1961 she held the post of Lecturer in English at the Maria Grey Teacher Training College, and Lecturer in the Institute of Education; in 1960 and 1961 she was a Lecturer at the Summer School, Portland State College, Oregon.

Dr Ina Beasley's book gives a penetrating insight on daily life at the grass roots in the Sudan during and just after the Second World War for British and Sudanese alike. We can glimpse the emotional and physical hardships endured by British employees of the Sudan Government throughout the War, cut off from news of family and friends back home. One can only admire the way they 'just got on and did their job'. It is not just a memoir of a great educationalist but one which is full of human warmth recounted with an excellent sense of humour. Her energy to engage on gruelling journeys in pursuit of her work, her single-minded persistence to pursue the improvement of girls' education are themes which dominate this book. Yet her work was not without its pleasures and rewards, often in most unexpected forms and in unusual places.

The book not only gives an account of girls' education and the many social issues that a developing country has to face, but also gives insights on educational practices in the broader field. Nowadays in Britain we are concerned to impose an education system with a National Curriculum which excludes many subjects which were considered basic in the 1940s— domestic science, manners, needlework, drill, handiwork ... Perhaps there is a lesson to be learned for the creators of curricula.

Dr Beasley's pragmatic approach to the development of girls' education in the Sudan, using the limited resources of money, facilities and staff was commendable. The achievements by the Department of Education were often due only to the sheer will-power of officials like Dr Beasley, Miss Sylvia Clark and Sitt Medina Abdulla. They had a vision of hope, to create educational light and liberate women from horizons bounded by domestic drudgery, seclusion and 'female circumcision'. Their determination to reach beyond these limitations shines on every page.

The text which follows is that of Dr Beasley's book *Before the Wind Changed, People, Places and Education in the Sudan*. In a book concerned not only with the establishment of girls' education, but also the way of life of people and places in the Sudan (as the subtitle suggests) in the 1940s, I have provided biographical footnotes for Sudanese and British officials whom she met in her travels. B.D. Dee's book *Sudan Political Service, 1899-1956* provides some relevant information, but is limited only to those serving with the political service. I have supplemented information provided in this book, which is, in any case, in limited circulation. Where I have described a person as 'Author'in a footnote, the title of his principal book is given in the Bibliography. In addition I have added footnotes and headings throughout the text, to clarify the text, for which, as editor, I am solely responsible. Much of Dr Beasley's text was based on her diaries and letters which are now all lodged with the Sudan Archive, University of Durham. However, Dr Beasley omitted most names and dates from the text, perhaps with an aim to be episodic. However, unless one is of her generation and experience of the country and people, much of the relevance of her comments is lost, unless the reader knows of whom and when she is writing. In order to redress this balance, I have researched dates and names to give a rounder, more complete memoir. Many of those serving in the rural areas had a significant role in promoting and securing the development of the work of the Department of Education, without whom much of Dr Beasley's work would probably have been in vain.

Small excerpts from her diaries are also included, particularly to illustrate her expertise on the education of girls in the Sudan. These appear in smaller print throughout the text and should add to, rather than detract from its content. The selection is mine. Any material given in square brackets has been added by me for clarity.

Appendices I and II were written by Dr Beasley. Unfortunately I have been unable to trace the sources of quotations in them. The footnotes in Appendix I and II are by the editor. In addition, I have added several appendices which the reader might find useful—on the history of girls' education in the Sudan, on officials working in the field, and further excerpts from her diaries which illustrate the operation of girls' schools in the 1940s. Apart from these additions, I was requested by the Chairman of the British Academy Committee, not to make any alterations to the text, which has been left totally 'as is'.

I have also added a glossary, bibliography and indexes of personal and place names. I have retained Dr Beasley's forms of personal names as they occur in the text of her book and diaries. The form used for Sudanese officials' names in *Government Lists* has also been retained. In the footnotes, an exception is made for the names of the two holy men, Sayyid 'Alī al-Mirghanī and Sayyid 'Abd al-Raḥmān al-Mahdī. This makes it easier to maintain consistency with the names of other members of their two families in the footnotes. For other personal names, I have followed a strict transliteration. It was useful to retain Dr Beasley's punctuation and spelling of Arabic words to reflect their use in the 1940s. I have therefore retained Dr Beasley's spellings of Arabic words in the text but these are cross-referenced in the glossary with consistent transliteration.

The great expansion of girls' education in the post-Independence era was based on the solid foundations established by such hardworking and indefatigable pioneers as Dr Beasley. Perhaps the immense contribution of Dr Beasley to the development of Sudan is best summed up in the Annual Report of the Department of Education of 1949. 'Girls' education suffered a loss by the retirement in August of Dr I.M. Beasley who had been Controller since 1942. During her seven years of office, Dr Beasley had shown herself an able and energetic champion of women's rights in the Sudan, and under her leadership girls' education made immense strides'. The book is dedicated to all those ordinary women, both British and Sudanese, who have helped to develop girls' education in the Sudan and expand the horizons of ordinary women and girls throughout the country.

# Acknowledgements

**J.C.M. Starkey**

I should like to record my thanks to the British Academy in agreeing to publish the book, and to James Rivington in particular; to Professor P.M. Holt, for all his support and encouragement; to Dr Lilian Sanderson and Albert Hourani for reading the manuscript and for their helpful comments; to Mrs Sheila Connelly for the design of the cover; to the Geography Department, University of Durham for their help in preparing the photographs and maps, and to Arthur Corner in particular; to Mrs Jane Hogan, Dr Peter Sluglett, Dr Martin Daly and Miss Lesley Forbes for their encouragement; to Dr Paul Starkey for his editorial and computer expertise, and to him and our children Katie and Gavin for their patience during the preparation of the book for publication.

The photographs used in this book are from a variety of sources, including Dr Beasley's own collection (nos. 3, 5, 6, 7, 9; no.4 taken by E.H. Nightingale; no.10 taken by Mrs Sheila Connelly); J.C.M. Starkey (no.2); the Sudan Archive, University of Durham—no.1 from the J.F.E. Bloss collection (S.A.D. 705/3/2); no.8 and no.12 from the Bright collection (S.A.D. 729/22/9, 10). No.11 is from Mrs Elizabeth M. Hodgkin's collection. I should like to thank all those who helped to select these photographs, especially Mrs Jane Hogan of the Sudan Archive, and all who gave permission for their use.

# Glossary of words and phrases employed in the book

**compiled by J.C.M. Starkey**

The glossary is arranged alphabetically according to the spellings used by Dr Beasley. These spellings are not always very accurate, for example she uses *ab rahman* instead of al-raḥmān so the inaccurate forms are marked with an asterisk, viz. [*]. I have added the corrected, transliterated form, where relevant, in square brackets. In addition words and phrases in Arabic which I used in the footnotes are also defined below. The following abbreviations have been used, (Ar.) Arabic, (col. Ar.) colloquial Arabic, (T.B.) Tu Bedawie, the language spoken by the Beja. In addition to standard Arabic dictionaries, sources used include Captain H.F.S. Amery's *English-Arabic Vocabulary for the use of officials in the Anglo-Egyptian Sudan*, Cairo, Egyptian Army, Intelligence Department, 1905 and Dickins, James, *A Dictionary of Sudanese Arabic: Arabic-English, English-Arabic*, forthcoming.


*aaref* [*'arīf*], prospective teacher.
*abri* [*abray*], a thirst-quenching, non-alcoholic drink produced by soaking dried *kisra* or *dura* pancake flakes in water; a drink based on millet or sorghum dough treated with yeast and flavouring, and allowed to ferment slightly before being rolled out into flat pancakes which are then baked and dried; the dough is baked into thin wafers, dried and stored; the drink is prepared by soaking the wafers in cold water, straining and sweetening with sugar; drunk especially in Ramadan.
*adab*, manners.
*afreet* [*'ifrīt*, fem. *'ifrīta*, pl. *'afārīt*], a supernatural being supposed to be made of fire and to dwell underground; ghost.
*Allah* [*Allāh*], God.
*angareeb* [*'anqarīb*, *'angaraib* or *'anqarayb*] (T.B.), an indigenous type of bedstead comprising a wooden frame strung with palm fibre twine laced with rope or leather thongs.
*Ansar* [*Anṣār*], lit. supporters; the followers of the Mahdī and his successors.
*arab* [*'arab*], of Arab descent, nomad.
*ardab* [*irdabb*], measure of capacity: 198 litres—1 *ardab*.
*Ashiqqā'*, political party supported by the Mirghanists.

*asida* ['*aṣīda*] (col. Ar.), a dough cooked into a porridge made from *dura*, *dukhn* or wheat, and a very common article of food in the Northern Sudan.

*baggara* [*baqqāra*], cattle people, Arab tribes of Southern Wadai, Darfur and Kordofan.

*bakhor* [*bakhūr*], perfume used in smoke-bath *dukhān*; incense made from seeds and resins.

*baksheesh* [*bakhshīsh*], tips.

*baladī* (Ar.), relative adjective from *balad*, a village; used to describe the common variety of crop, a coarse locally woven cloth; rural.

*balilla* [*balīla*], seeds of *lubia 'afin*, Dolichos lablab *Linn.*, a boiled green.

*bamia* [*bāmiya*] (col. Ar.), fresh lady's fingers or okra, Hibiscus esculentus, *Linn.*

*baraka*, a heritable quality of grace linking a spiritual leader with his followers; a blessing; healing virtue; good luck.

*batikh* [*baṭṭīkh*], water melon, Citrullus vulgaris, *Schrad.*.

*batūl*, virgin.

*Beni* [*Banī*], people, sons of, part of a tribal section e.g. *Banī 'Āmir.*

*bersīm* [*birsīm*], lucerne, Medicago sativa.

*bikr* [(col. Ar.) *bikir*], a wake; period of mourning and attendance at the house of the deceased.

*Bimbāshī*, Egyptian Army rank equivalent to Major.

*birsh* [(Ar.) *bursh*, pl. *abrāsh*] [(col. Ar.) *birish*, pl. *birūsh*], palm frond matting often used for making containers for marketing agricultural produce, floor covering, and dwellings.

*bismillah ab rahman*[*] [(col. Ar.) *bism-i llāh- i l-rahmān al-rahīm*], In the name of God the Merciful, the Compassionate.

*bunn* (Ar.), coffee powder, locally means coffee, either Coffea arabica *Linn.* or Coffea canephora *Pierre.*

*al-Buṭāna*, the plain between the River Atbara and the Blue Nile.

*Butn al Hujar* [*Baṭn al-Ḥajar*], lit. belly of stones, the Nile valley immediately south of Wādī Ḥalfa'.

*cannaba* [*kanaba*], a wooden sofa with hard cushions, from the French *canapé.*

*dabita* [*ḍābiṭa*], schoolmistress entrusted with discipline in a school, often a separate post to headmistress.

*Dā'irat al-Mahdī*, the estate office of S.A.R.

*damur* [*dammūr*], cloth woven in the villages by hand-loom from hand-spun, locally grown cotton.

*damur baladi* see *damur.*

*dar* [*dār*], home, homeland, tribal centre, house. A house may also be called *bait, ḥawsh* and *manzil.*

*nimitti*, a small and troublesome fly, Simulium griseicollis. There is the tiny 'Khartoum' *nimitti* which does not bite and also the 'Dongola' *nimitti*, a black insect which bites hard.

*nuss sa'a* [*nuṣṣ* (col. Ar. for *niṣ*) sā‘a], lit. half an hour, often means sometime soon.

*omdah* ['*umda*], a local tribal administrative official, subordinate to a *nāẓir*, having lesser *shaykh*s under him; headman of a village or a number of villages. The post was abolished in 1969.

*omodia* ['*umdiyya*], the area or tribal group for which an '*umda* is responsible.

*Pasha* [*bāshā*] (Turkish), title of honour; highest ranking title conferred on military personnel and civilians during Turko-Egyptian rule (1821-1885) and the early period of the Condominium (1898-1956).

*piastre*, P.T. for short, a unit of money, 100 P.T. = £E1.000, 97.5 P.T. = £1 sterling [1948].

*qadi* [*qāḍī*], a judge applying the Muslim religious law, the *Sharī‘a*; one who draws up marriage contracts and who arranges divorces; a magistrate.

*quaadin sakit*[*] [*qā‘idīn sākit*], 'sitting quietly', 'just there', 'hanging around' translated as 'just sitting' by Dr Beasley.

*qubba* [pl. *qubab*], the mausoleum of an eminent Muslim holy man or saint, generally conical or domed.

*rahat* [*rahaṭ*], a skirt made of a leather fringe attached to a band of woven hair or with belt of hide; bridal skirt.

*rais* [*ra'īs*], chief, leader, ship's captain.

*rakuba* [*rakūba*], temporary shelter.

*rotana* [(col. Ar.) *ruṭāna*, (Ar.) *riṭāna*], non-Arabic language e.g. Nubian, from *raṭana*, to speak an unintelligible language.

*sagia* [*sāqiya*, pl. *sawāqī*] (Ar.) from the word meaning to irrigate, the Persian water- wheel. The water-wheel motivated by animal power, usually an ox, by which water is raised from the river to irrigate crops at the top of the bank; hence the plot so irrigated.

*sala* [*sāla*] (Italian), open air central room surrounded by cloisters or rooms.

*sarraf* [*ṣarrāf*], paymaster, treasurer.

*Sattal Sitt*[*] [sa‘ādat al-sitt], the excellent lady, similar to *janāb as-sitt*, honoured lady, used in Egypt.

*Sayed* [*Sayyid*], form of address to a venerable religious leader; a person who claims descent from the prophet Muḥammad and his family.

*semn* [*samn*, (col. Ar.) *samin*], clarified butter with the water driven off by boiling, used for cooking.

*shaduf*, [*shādūf*, pl. *shawādīf*] (col. Ar.), a hand-operated water-hoist suited for watering plots of vegetables. It is on the seesaw model with the water container counterbalanced with a lump of clay; bucket-lift.

*shāi* (Ar.) tea, a subject frequently mentioned in the text!

*shamla*, large, rough, locally woven rug.

*shammadan* [*sham'adān*], candle-holder.

*sharia* [*sharī'a*], the Muslim religious law.

*Sharīf* [fem. *Sharīfa*, pl. *Ashrāf*], descendant of the Prophet Muḥammad.

*sheikh* [*shaykh*], a village headman and the leader of a group of nomads or Sufi order; also *shaykh ṭarīqa*, leader of a religious sect; *shaykh al-sajjāda*, leader of a religious brotherhood, rather than its paramount head.

*sherifa* [*sharīfa*], a female religious leader who claims to be able to be descended from the Prophet, see *Sharīf*.

*shillukh* [(col. Ar.) *shalikh*, pl. *shulūkh*, also known as *faṣāda*], tribal scarring. *Shalikh*, the action of tribal marking, a single line of scarring; *shallakh*, verb, mark, scar; *mashallakh* (fem. *mashallakha*), a person with tribal scars. Tribal markings are a means of identity and are considered to be beautiful. The custom is probably dying out.

*Sirdār*, the Commander-in-Chief of the Egyptian Armed forces, a post originally held by the Governor-General of the Sudan.

*Sitt*, form of address meaning lady, mistress, Madame.

*som*, (Fur) which was used in Darfur, meaning 'school, meeting place'. This was within the *fāshir* where the *soming dogala* 'cadets (i.e.children) of the school' were educated under the *abbo soming dogala* or *malik soming dogala*. One of the Sultan's wives, *umm soming dogala*, supervised the school.

*sudd* from (Ar.) *sadd*, a barrier, a block; locally the vast bog or water prairie between Lake No and Bor.

*suffra*, a species of *dura* (cf. Brown and Massey, *Flora of the Sudan*, pp. 444, 445).

*Sufi* [*ṣūfī*], Islamic mystic.

*Sultan* [*sulṭān*], ruler.

*sunna*, customary law, usage of the Prophet.

*sunt* [*sunṭ*], Acacia arabica, also general term for Acacia.

*suq* [*sūq*], market.

*sūq al-ḥarīm*, the women's market.

*tagia* [*ṭāqiyya*], man's skull cap.

*taht raqaba* [*taḥt raqāba*], under supervision.

*tarha* [*ṭarḥa*], large kerchief for covering small girls' heads.

*tarifa* [*ta'rīfa*], a coin, half a piastre.

*tariqa* [*ṭarīqa*, pl. *ṭuruq*], religious brotherhood or order.

*tasliya* (Ar.), diversion, amusement.

*tebeldi* [*tabaldī*], the baobab tree, Adansonia digitata *Linn*.

*tisht* [*ṭisht*, (col. Ar.) *ṭishit*], a large shallow metal tray on which to wash clothes.

*tobe* [*tōb*], (col. Ar.) from *thawb*, a garment; locally a winding cloth of soft material that will not crease, about 3 metres long and 2 metres wide, worn by women, usually over ordinary European cotton dresses; also a long piece of cotton cloth which men sometimes wear, especially nomads. It is worn over a short shirt and long pants and may be used as a cover when sleeping.

*toich, toitch* [*toic*] (Dinka), the annually flooded lands along the watercourses draining into the Sudd, which affords good grazing in winter after the flood subsides. *Toic*s are a feature of Equatoria Province.

*tukl* [*tukul*, pl. *takala*], cylindrical grass hut made of a framework of poles with a thatched roof, and usually surrounded by a thorn fence to protect penned animals at night, also called *quṭṭiyya*.

*tulkh* [*ṭalḥ*, (col. Ar.) *ṭaliḥ*], a variety of Acacia, Acacia gummifera, or the red-barked small tree *ṭalḥ ḥamrā’* Acacia seyal *Del.* used commercially for firewood, not to be confused with *seyal* the small tree Acacia raddiana *Savi.*; or *ṭalḥ bayḍā’* Acacia fistula.

*turmus*, lupins.

*ulema* [*'ulamā’* sing. *'ālim*], Muslim scholar, a man learned in the religious law of the Muslims, the Sharī'a.

*al-Umma*, a political party supported by the Mahdists.

*'uṭfa* see *hawdaj.*

*wad al-Mahdī*, son of the Mahdi.

*wadi* [*wādī*], a shallow water course, dry except immediately after rain.

*Wahabi* [*Wahhābī*], religious follower of a puritanic movement found mainly in the Hijāz in the early nineteenth century; followers of 'Abd al-Wahhāb.

*wajd* [(col. Ar.) *wajid*], spiritual ecstasy.

*wakil* [*wakīl*], agent or deputy, estate steward.

*walud* [*walad*], boy.

*waqf*, religious endowment.

*weika* [*wayka*], the dried fruit or pods of *bamia*, Hibiscus esculentus *Linn.*; also applied to a semi-wild form of *bamia*.

*worrall* [*waral*], a monitor lizard.

*Ya* [*yā*], O (introducing the vocative).

*zaf* [(col. Ar.) *za'af*], palm-fibre, handicraft in fibrework.

*zakāt*, Muslim alms-tax.

*zamzamia* [*zamzamiyya*], canvas water bottle.

*zar* [*zār*, pl. *zairān*], evil spirit, a religious non-Islamic ceremony performed by and for persons possessed by these spirits to exorcise them, usually practised by women.

*zarāq*, the cheap cotton cloth, dyed blue, which the older women commonly wear.

*zareeba* [*zarība*], enclosure in the form of a hedge of thorny bushes, often used for cattle, sheep or goats.

*zāwiya*, pl. *zawāyā*, religious lodge.

*zeer* [*zīr* pl. *ziyār* or *azyār*] (col. Ar.), a large, baked porous earth pot mounted on a stand used for cooling the domestic water supply; It can also be used as a filter; (infrequent) 'whoring tosspot'.

*zikkr*, *zikr* [*dhikr*, (col. Ar.) *zikir*], 'remembrance', a Sufi gathering; a religious dance; a particular method of worshipping God in order to obtain spiritual ecstasy; a constant repetition of God's name.

# Abbreviations

| | |
|---|---|
| 4N. | Order of the Nile, Fourth Class, similarly 5N., 3N. etc. |
| A.D.C. | Assistant District Commissioner |
| ARDE | Annual Report of the Department of Education |
| ADC | Aide de Camp |
| Bp | Bishop |
| C.M.S. | Church Missionary Society |
| D.C. | District Commissioner |
| Fr | Father |
| G-G | Governor-General |
| G.M.C. | Gordon Memorial College |
| G.T.C. | Girls' Training College, Omdurman |
| P.E.O. | Province Education Officer |
| R.C.M. | Roman Catholic Mission |
| Rev Fr | Reverend Father |
| R.I.I.A. | Royal Institute of International Affairs |
| S.A.D. | Sudan Archives, University of Durham |
| S.A.R. | Sayyid 'Abd al-Raḥmān al-Mahdī |
| S.D.F. | Sudan Defence Force |
| S.G.A. | Sudan Government Archives |
| S.M.S. | Sudan Medical Service |
| S.N.R. | Sudan Notes and Records |
| S.P.S. | Sudan Political Service |
| V.F.M. | Verona Fathers' Mission |
| [date] | date (day.month.year) of an excerpt from Dr Beasley's diaries or correspondence. |

# Preface

Ina M. Beasley

An article and correspondence in *The Times* some months ago moved me to turn up an old letter and records and I found at the end of one of these, noted down after years of strenuous trekking: 'I never quite get over the wonder of doing these trips. Mentally I am always a little agape, when they're over.'

The substance of the article was a lament that the older generations of officers from the overseas services were passing and leaving scant records of the knowledge they had acquired in distant places. There was lacking too an understanding of their aims and achievements, the foundations in fact on which the developing countries were building. History books may give an overall examination of the beginnings of states and their rise to independence but they contain few pictures of the actual daily life which concentrates on the politicians.

It was stimulating, therefore, to light so early in my desultory reading on the above sentence. Reports of conferences and policies of international bodies trying to help the new countries give an impression of cold remoteness; they appear detached and impersonal. Perhaps the expatriate men and, I am sorry to see less often, the women who are sent abroad by these organisations may recapture something of our involvement. Usually their time is short and thus not conducive to being committed in the way we generally became. Most of us were strikingly unsentimental and given to exaggerated understatement of our feelings but there was a great depth of real affection for the people we served and a genuine enjoyment of the work despite many hardships, both physical and mental, and frequent disappointments.

The following then is a personal account of a period which is fast blending into history. It is in no way an *apologia* for the appeasement of anti-colonialists nor an attempt to prove anybody in the wrong. Taken as a whole, however, the results of this particular type of contact have been of overwhelming importance and can, no doubt, be argued over indefinitely.

Mine is only a small corner of that vast canvas but, if I can make explicit something of that sense of wonder, it may fill in one of the gaps in a chronicle often amusingly caricatured but frequently unhappily distorted. If I, at any point, appear to make fun of things or people, it is in no spirit of malicious mockery. It will be a sad day, when we are forbidden to laugh at what rightly or wrongly amuses us. The nature of comedy does not negate earnestness of purpose; rather it sweetens our endeavours.

# Chapter I

# The First Few Weeks

## 1. Arrival

Whichever way one approaches Khartoum, it is the desert which forces itself on all the senses. Today's frequent air travel by rushing at speed increases rather than lessens this feeling. I came first by the leisurely route of the Nile Valley in boats and trains, and was able to absorb the flavour more gradually. Desert, however, was still the abiding impression.

Otherwise what stands out most clearly from that original voyage was my good fortune in being able to see Abu Simbel in all its remote dignity appearing then a symbol of man's challenge, for centuries successful, to the mutability of Time. I tend now to think of it as a symbol of the changes that have followed with bewildering rapidity and in which people like myself strutted our little parts.

In the world of the 1930s, now merely a quaint background in fashions and the sphere of entertainment, service overseas was an accepted career in the professions and regarded as a commitment for one's working life. There was nothing remarkable, therefore, in my joining the Sudan Government with the prospect of ten years' service at least and an early retirement.[1] I should perhaps add here as sufficient explanation of my reason for doing so, that I had weathered a crisis in my personal affairs[2] and needed a secure appointment. I had been overseas before[3] and thought I should like the opportunities offered. Also, another feature of the thirties often forgotten, employment was not easy to find even with adequate qualifications in the summer of 1939. The Sudan was not so far from England as Burma which I had just left, and, although the salary was not high, annual leave was allowed on account of the difficult climate. This, I planned, would give me the chance to spend summer holidays with my daughter,[4] at boarding school in England. That was why I was on the Nile steamer in October 1939

1. Dr Beasley joined the Sudan Government Service in October 1939 and was appointed Inspector of Girls' Schools from 4.11.39.
2. See Sudan Archive, University of Durham (S.A.D.) 657/5/1-134, 657/6/1-59.
3. Dr Beasley was previously working in Burma from 1930 as Lecturer in English at Rangoon University and Tutor to External Women Students.
4. Ruth.

but the rest of my private history can be omitted as of no relevance to the far more exciting tale of girls' education in the Sudan.[5]

The contrast between the golden air of Egypt and the murk of a London autumn meant more in this year[6] than to the thousands of voyagers up the Nile who escaped there in the fashion of Victorian and Edwardian days. We had come from the utter blackness of the city with the heartbreak and tension of the early weeks of the War to this smooth sailing through the peace of an empty landscape. The barrenness of the country above the Aswan Dam has a certain awe-inspiring quality, for the range of the colour in the rocks and the distant mountains is offset, particularly at sunset, by a backdrop of rapidly fluctuating lights and shades and a startling vividness in the sky. It was on the morning of the third day after embarking at Shellal that we reached Wadi Halfa, an attractive little town which I grew quite fond of in the years to come, and I set off by train on the last twenty four hours to Khartoum.

This is the part of the journey which stamps on the mind the idea of the perfect desert. All I had ever read or seen of deserts was brought to its ultimate here. Kitchener[7] built the railway for the campaign of 1898 to avoid the great loop of the river in the Dongola Reach and the cataracts there.[8] The immensity of the task without the mechanical equipment of today staggers our modern conceptions of work but the pace of the nineteenth century was not the hustle we know and the trains still run across that uncompromising 232 miles to Abu Hamed[9] with something of that same leisurely flavour. From the windows the view in all directions is sand, gravel, piles of stones, large rocks, humps that are hardly hills, and nothing at all that grows. There is no hint of an oasis and not even the many-hued

5. Dr Beasley was encouraged by Sir Christopher W.M. Cox (b.1899-d.1982), British academic and administrator; Educated Clifton and Balliol College, Oxford; Fellow, then Dean, of New College, Oxford; 1937-39 Seconded to the Sudan Government as Director of Education and Principal of Gordon Memorial College; 1938-39 member of the Governor-General's Council. She was in contact with him before she went to Sudan and he encouraged her to write periodic reports of her findings.

6. In October 1939.

7. Sir Horatio Herbert Kitchener, First Earl Kitchener of Khartoum and of Broome. (b.1850-d.1916); 1882 joined the Egyptian Army; 1886 Governor-General of the Red Sea Littorial; 1888-89 Adjutant-General of the Egyptian Army; 1892 He was made Sirdār of the Egyptian Army; From 1896 he led the reoccupation of Sudan campaign; 1899 Governor-General of Sudan; 1899 Chief-of-Staff to Lord Roberts in Boer War; November 1902 he officially opened the Gordon Memorial College; 1902-09 Commander-in-Chief in India; 1909-11 Commander-in-Chief Mediterranean; 1911-14 British Agent and Consul-General in Egypt; 1914 he was made Secretary for State for War in Britain. In 1916 he drowned at sea while going on a mission to Russia.

8. In December 1899 the railhead was brought to the Blue Nile opposite Khartoum.

9. 232 miles from Wadi Halfa to Abu Hamed.

splendour of the banks along the river reaches. Stations have no names.
How could they? What is there to call them after? They perform their
necessary functions as places for the needs of engines and as passing places
for trains, but no villages have collected round them. How could anyone
have a beloved homestead at no.6?[10] Just that and no more. Yet the very
immensity of the desert fascinates and generally there is a brightness and for
half a year a crisp, enlivening atmosphere. Even when the sand blows hard
enough to force long stoppages, it is not the gloom of fog, although such
storms provide irritations enough to the temper and the body. At Abu
Hamed the track returns to the river and by then the two features which
determine the Sudan have been indelibly stamped—the desert and the Nile.

## 2. Omdurman

Omdurman, where I was to have my home for the next ten years, lies on the
river some seven miles from Khartoum[11] but it belongs to the desert,
partaking of its good and evil features; yet able to inspire a very real
affection not only in its own nurslings but in alien residents like myself.
With houses built mostly of mud brick and sheltering behind high walls,
often with rather crazy gates, there was little of orthodox beauty in its
architecture. Trim lawns or even untidy hedges were not possible where
rainfall is scanty and water supplies closely regulated. Official data seemed
to suggest that every pint of the Nile waters had to be measured and
controlled on its long journey to the sea. A garden of sorts was obtainable
in Omdurman but the cost in money and struggle was quite high and most
people could not afford to cope with it.

Along the river bank, however, was much of interest; birds, insects and a
small fringe of crops as the floods subsided. Boats of romantic aspect
abounded, built on the shore by skilled craftsmen with traditional
understanding [of] the tall-masted vessels which swept along rapidly, when
the North wind blew. But the heart of the town lay apart from the river in
the business centre, where two cinemas, cafés and the post office drew
always a large and noisy crowd. At first I missed the colour of the gaily
dressed Burmans, for here the majority wore the long *gallabiya* and
turban[12] in varying degrees of whiteness. Some preferred European clothes

10. There is also a lack of water at stations such as No.6 [raqm Sitta, al-Maḥaṭṭa].
11. Omdurman, the capital, was where the Mahdi Muḥammad Aḥmad established his military
camp in 1884, and was the Khalifa's base from 1885 for 14 years.
12. *Jallābiyya*, a long, plain, usually white men's garment like a night shirt and *'imma*,
turban.

and here and there the dark caftan and little red cap of a conventional schoolmaster would stand out among the monochrome impression. Further to the edge of the town, where the animal market was compelled to stay, nomadic camel drivers wandered in straight from the desert. Women were seldom seen at all. A few elderly dames, often of forceful character and probably of slave ancestry, carried on a paltry trade in the market.[13] Sometimes a Greek or Syrian might have occasion to pass by but the crowds as in many Eastern cities had an overwhelming quality of maleness. It is in no sense a hostile force nor in anyway impeding but at times a woman may be intensely conscious of it, as if the world were in its essence a man's affair, and women of no account in it at all. Yet, as I came to know the place, I always felt it friendly. The shopkeepers in the stores or the craftsmen in their small booths were affable. I might meet some official or clerk to pass the time of day or a *sheikh* who wanted to discuss the schooling of his daughter.

### 2.1 Location of Dr Ina Beasley's house

My own house was further south of the town[14] near the great square where stood the Mahdi's tomb and the Khalifa's house, (now a museum), the hospital, and close by the chief mosque. According to the older inhabitants this great gravel stretch had been the scene of many sinister happenings which they had witnessed in the days of the Khalifa's tyranny but it was chiefly used now as a playing field by the boys or for celebrations on the big feast days. The Girls' Training College had been built[15] on the site where the Khalifa's women used to be lodged, and the stables next to this were turned into classrooms for a school. Across the road was a shining new brick building for the first post-primary stage[16] and adjoining this was the house (also red brick and with wide verandahs) which I shared with the British headmistress,[17] although we each had our own quarters.

13. *Sūq al-ḥarīm*, the women's market.
14. Dr Beasley's house was in the Mulazimiyya quarter of Omdurman. The mosque in Omdurman is supposed to be a copy of al-Azhar mosque in Cairo and designed to have much the same function. The large mosque square surrounded by a brick wall was the place of prayer and assembly under Khalifa 'Abdallāhi al-Ta'āishī, whose own house was a complex of buildings, now a museum. Ruined and desecrated by the British at the Reconquest in Autumn 1898, the Mahdi's tomb was rebuilt in the last years of the Condominium (in 1947) by the Mahdi's son, Sayyid 'Abd al-Raḥmān. The original domed tomb had been built by Khalifa 'Abdallāhi al-Ta'āishī.
15. 1921.
16. The Intermediate School was opened 6.1.40.
17. Miss K. Sylvia L. Clark. 1.1.39 Mistress, Girls' Training College, Omdurman; 1.1.40-Aug 1949 Headmistress, Girls' Intermediate School, Omdurman (See Appendix IV).

## 2.2 Gardening

Fortunately we had in common too much else. One interest was a devotion to gardening, which was a strenuous matter, as nothing could be planted unless a hole had been dug in the hard earth and filled with soil brought up from the river. Once established and adequately watered, trees and shrubs and even a small lawn flourished in a great surround of gravel. It was heart-breaking when twice in one season the locusts ate everything including a young eucalyptus. The electricity had failed at this point and we had to sit on the verandah with a dim lamp and listen to the crunching. The effort, however, was well worth while for the general refreshing of body and spirit we found coming back to a patch of green softness away from the dust and harshness among which we spent so much of our time. As the place was free from malaria I used always to sleep on the lawn and, when the *neem*[18] trees were in full flower, their fragrant whiteness above my head rewarded any toil and trouble we might have had in making a garden.

That 'always' needs qualifying. There were nights, particularly in the summer, when the bed would stagger from a sudden violent gust of wind.[19] The frame was made of light wood strung with rope, which made excellent springing under a thick mattress. Sometimes I would lie for a few minutes hoping for a lull, which I did not really expect, but the sensible course was to roll up the bedding at once and go indoors. Occasionally I could make shift to put my *angareeb*[20] in a comparatively sheltered spot on the large verandah, but mostly it was quicker to give in at once and retire to the shuttered stuffiness of the bedroom. Nothing could keep out the dust, once it had started to blow, and in the morning the only white spot would be where my arm had lain outside the sheet. On the credit side there were far more clear skies than otherwise and one night lying in great comfort I had a magnificent view of the moon's eclipse for my bedtime story. My companion would have endured an equally restless night on her side of the garden, for the wind came round all corners with the same force. Appearing at breakfast both gritty-eyed and unrefreshed was not the kind of sharing which I meant to stress.

18. *Neem*, Azadirachta indica.
19. The violent gusts of wind indicated the arrival of a duststorm, *habūb*.
20. *'anqarayb*, bed with a wooden frame strung with rope.

## 3. Need for education

The most important conviction, which we both held unshakably, was that
life for Sudanese women could have small measure of fulfilment without an
education to match the level of their menfolk. Whatever the pattern might
have been in the past, the conditions of modern life were making this
necessary. We therefore believed in schools. Later in this book I shall
discuss this question in more technical detail but looking back over my
years in Sudan, this was the basis of all my reactions. All my journeyings,
however fortunate I was at times from the traveller's point of view, were
centred round the schools I went to visit or places where we hoped to start
one. The physical hardships of a difficult trek would be alleviated by finding
a school in good working order. Always there was the friendliness of a
welcome from the mistresses and the contacts with other people in a village,
which made me not just a visitor but a part of the life all around.

We were not sitting on the side-lines but were deeply involved, trying it
seemed to guide an explosive force bursting out all about us. Some of the
Sudanese were sympathetic, others doubtful and we judged them all by this
yardstick. Educated men who could rank as progressive in the spheres of
politics or officialdom would be known to us as hopelessly backward, where
their wives and daughters were concerned.[21] The comments and tales which
came from the schoolmistresses could be most illuminating and were not
part of such men's reputation in the outside world.    Happily there were
others helpful and zealous for every opportunity that could be given to girls
and taking a genuine pleasure in each step that could lead them away from
the dulled mentality which the practice of seclusion tended to perpetuate.

## 4. School visits

My first acquaintance with Omdurman was thus through the schools and it
was my constant visits to these during my period of initiation which made it
all too familiar to me.[22] The town possessed several, as originally the idea of
girls' education had been more readily accepted here than outside and men

---

21. 'A widening of education might increase the tendency for prospective husbands to prefer
educated wives ... custom of early marriage brings about a large wastage in the profession
which is tiresome from an administrative point of view ... in any really long term policy of
education the ideal of the tidy-minded little housewife is most inadequate'. Sudan Government,
Department of Education. *Note on Girls' Education in the Sudan*, Dec 1940.
22. See Appendix V for Dr Beasley's comments on the schools she visited when she first started
inspections in Sudan.

*mastaba* [*mastaba*], pl. *masatib*], a raised hard earth platform built against the wall of a house, used as a seat; a raised terrace in a grand house.

*meglis ahli* [*majlis ahli*] (Ar.), a local Sudanese council.

*mek* [*makk*] pl. *mukūk*], originally a title given to the vassal-kings of the Funj Sultan; the chief or ruler of a small political unit in the Nuba Mountains; it was also the title of the Funj Sultan himself.

*Melk ed-Dar* [*Malikat ad-Dar*], lit. 'queen of the home' — a girls' name.

*melukhiyya* [*mulūkhiyyā*], leaves and tender shoots of young plants of the jute plant, Corchorus olitorius *Linn.* used widely for making thick soup.

*menzig* [*manzig*], weaving, by extension craft lessons; from *mansij*, loom.

*merissa* [*marisa*], beer made from various grains, but chiefly millet (*dura*), in the central and southern Sudan; a valuable protective food.

*merkaz* [*markaz*], a district headquarters.

*merkoob* [*markūb*], slippers.

*millième*, a unit of money, 975 millièmes = 97.5 piastres = £1 sterling, 48.75 millièmes = 1 shilling, 1,000 millièmes = £E1.000 [1948].

*Mirghaniyya*, a religious brotherhood, owing allegiance to the Mirghani family, see also *Khatmiyya*.

*mu'allim*, teacher.

*mu'allimat kibār*, adult education women teachers.

*mudīriyya* [*mudīriyyā*], province headquarters (or the province itself).

*mufti* [*mufti*], the senior lawyer in a Muslim state responsible for expounding the application of the *Shari'a* to cases, a deliverer of legal opinions in Islamic law (sing. *fatwā*).

*muhafza* [*muhāfaza*], the government headquarters in Suakin. This was an anomalous term in the Sudan. It was actually a survival of old Ottoman administrative terminology.

*mulid* [*mawlid*], pl. *mawālid*], festival, [*Mawlid an-Nabi*], the Muslim festival commemorating the Birth of the Prophet Muhammad; the tradition in the Sudan is to hold public celebrations in the largest of the town squares for twelve consecutive nights.

*mustaba* see *mastaba*.

*naam* [*na'am*], yes, general affirmative.

*nazir* [*nāzir*], the chief of a tribe, who were given administrative and judicial powers and responsibilities by the Government. The *nāzir* was part of the system of Native Administration which was abolished in 1969 except for the position of *shaykh*, village headman. Dr Beasley spelt it as *nasr* which was misleading.

*neem* [(col. Ar.) *nīm*] (Indian), a type of tree, Azadirachta indica.

*keffyah* [*qafiyya*], a square of cloth, Arab head-dress for men.

*kerkade* [col. Ar.) *karkaday*], a drink made of an infusion of the roselle hemp, Hibiscus sabdariffa *Linn.*

*khalifa* [*khalifa*, pl. *khulafa'*], lit. successor, title of son nominated by the reigning Sultan to succeed, the successor to the Mahdi; leader of a *tariqa*.

*khilafa*, the era of the *khalifa*, caliphate.

*khalwa* [pl. *khalawi*], lit. a place of seclusion, a Koranic school where religious precepts and literacy are traditionally taught by rote learning taught by a *faqih*, also a guest chamber, a private room.

*Khatmiyya tariqa*, religious brotherhood, founded by Sayyid Muhammad 'Uthman al-Mirghani. The name is derived from *Khatim al-Turuq* 'the Seal of the Paths'.

*khor* [*khawr*, pl. *khiran*], a water course with deep sides, dry in the rainless period, also a backwater of the Nile or a narrow inlet of the sea.

*kisra* (col. Ar.), lit. morsel, very thin, flat cakes of unleaven bread made on an inverted metal plate over a fire, usually made of *dura* flour and the foundation of the diet of central and northern Sudan.

*kitab al-atfal* [*kitāb al-aṭfāl*], a children's textbook, a reader.

*Koran* [*Qur'an*], Muslim holy book.

*kuttab* [*kuttab*, pl. *katatib*], elementary school.

*kyda*, really!

*libas* (Ar.), the baggy trousers or drawers of the Arab.

*libia* [*lubia 'afin*] (col. Ar.), the bean Dolichos lablab *Linn*, grown for human food but mostly for forage, in the northern Sudan and a most important crop.

*limoon* [*limun baladi*] (Ar.), the lime, Citrus aurantiifolia Christm. *Swingle*, from which a pleasant drink is made.

*loofah* [*lif*], a cucumber-like plant.

*lugma* [*lugma*] (Ar.), morsel of bread, locally boiled *dura* porridge.

*Mahad, Ma'ahad*[*] [*al-ma'had al-'ilmi*], Islamic seminary in Omdurman, now the Islamic University of Omdurman.

*Maarif* [*Maslahat al-ma'ārif*], Department of Education.

*madresa* [*madrasa*, pl. *madāris*], school in secular education; historically, a religious boarding school associated with a mosque.

*magdum* [*maqdum*, pl. *maqādīm*], a commissioner or viceroy appointed for a fixed term or purpose, responsible for a district, a title dating from the late eighteenth century, used in Darfur. The office tended to become hereditary.

*Mahdiyya*, the Mahdist movement.

*mahragan* [*mahrajān*], festival, celebration.

*mamur* [*ma'mur*], Egyptian or Sudanese administrative officer serving under a British Inspector or D.C.

*darb al-arba'īn*, the 40-day camel road from al- Fāshir to Assiut in Egypt.

*Demanyai*, local ruler in Dār Masalīt.

*dewan* [*dīwān*], men's quarters of a house.

*dik-dik* [*umm dig dig*], a small deer.

*doleib* [*dulayb*], a species of palm, Palmyra palm, Borassus flabellifer.

*dom* [*dōm* or *dawm*], the common branching palm, Hyphaene thebaica Mart., its palm-fibre (*līf*) used for making mats and baskets.

*dubbān* [sing. *dabbāna*], flies.

*dukhn* [col. Ar.) *dukhun*], the food grain bullrush millet, Pennisetum typhoidium, the main crop in sandy areas.

*dura* [*dhura*], the great or common millet, Sorghum vulgare *Pers.* from (Ar.) *udhra*, millet.

*effendi* [*afandi*], a member of the Western-educated classes (the term is now banned in most Arab countries); a clerk.

*effendia* [*afandiyya*], the educated class.

*fellata* [*Fallāta*], West African ethnic groups who moved east towards Mecca but settled in Sudan.

*fantass* [*fintās*], a large tin to carry water.

*farikh* [*farīq*], section of a tribe, a group of nomads.

*farrash*, household servant.

*fasher* [*fāshir*], the area in front of the Sultan's compound in Darfur where he gave audience, by extension the whole court, and finally al-Fāshir.

*fellah* [*fallāh* pl. *fallāhīn*], peasant.

*felucca* [(col. Ar.) *fallūka*], rowing or sailing boat with tall mast.

*fetwa* [*fatwā*], religious ordinance.

*fiki, fikki* [*faki*, a Sudanese dialect form of *faqīh*, pl. *fuqarā'*], a religious teacher in a Qur'ānic school, a person who recites the *Qur'ān* and who is a jurist, more or less versed in the religion and law of Islam; also plays the role of a healer.

*forsala*, from the context this appears to be a kind of marrow, not *fasuliyya* beans.

*ful medames* [*fūl madammas*], horse beans, a staple element of Egyptian *fellah* diet.

*fūl*, (Ar.) bean, *fūl sudāni*, the ground nut, Arabis hypogaea *Linn.*

*fula* [*fūla*], a reservoir to collect rain-water.

*fulan* [*fulān*], so and so, someone.

*gallabiya* [*jallābiyya*, pl. *jalalīb*], a long plain, usually white, garment like a night shirt, traditionally without a collar, worn by men.

*gammēz* [(col. Ar.) *jummēz*] pl. *jimmayz*], wild fig tree, Ficus sycamorus *Linn.*

*gebenna* [*jabana*], an earthenware coffee pot, with a round body and long neck.

*ghaffir* [*ghafīr* (col. Ar.) for *khafīr*], a watchman, guard.

*goz* [*gōz*] (col. Ar.), stabilized sand- dune. *gōz* country means any part of that vast area of billowy continental sand occurring in Darfur and Kordofan and Northern Province. In the Baraka Delta near Tokar the dunes (*debba*, perhaps from *dabba* to creep) are mostly composed of silt and are for the most part active.

*gulli-gulli*, Egyptian conjuror.

*gussab* [*qaṣab*] (Ar.), cane, the straw of *dura*, maize or *dukhn* and a very important animal food in the northern Sudan.

*Habashiyya*, Ethiopians, by extension in Sudan this may be used to mean prostitutes.

*haboob* [*habūb*] (Ar.), locally a strong wind, not the trade wind, usually accompanied by thick dust; a strong convectional duststorm.

*haj* [*hajj*], pilgrimage to Mecca and Medina.

*hākim ʿāmm*, Governor-General.

*haraz* [*harāz*], the large forest tree Acacia albida *Del*.

*hareeg* [*harīq*] (Ar.), for conflagration, applied locally to a type of cultivation based on firing the old stand of grasses just prior to sowing.

*hareem*, harem [*harīm*], women's quarters in a house, a group of women, and, by extension, seclusion of women.

*hashab* [*hashāb*], the shrubby tree Acacia senegal *Willd.*, the source of the best kind of commercial gum.

*henna* [*hinnā*], a red dye made from the leaves of the shrub, Lawsonia inermis, used for decorating hands and feet, and dying hair.

*hawliyya*, anniversary of a saint's birth or death, cf. *mawlid*, often a great village festival; *hawliyyat al-Khatmiyya*, a religious festival held annually at Sinkat by the Khatmiyya.

*hosh* [*hawsh*], compound; a domestic courtyard where most day to day activities take place.

*howdah*, howdah, a carriage for women and children to ride on top of a camel.

*id* [*ʿīd*], religious festival and holiday; *al-ʿīd as-saghīr* or *ʿīd al-fiṭr*, the little festival; *al-ʿīd al-kabīr* (*ʿīd al-qurbān*, *ʿīd al-adḥā*), the Great Festival, festival of Sacrificer.

*Imam* [*imām*], a religious title, usually associated with a mosque, prayer leader.

*immah* [*ʿimma*], turban.

*ingle* [*injīl*], a green bush found in West Sudan.

*jallāba*, merchants from the riverain areas of central and Northern Sudan in Kordofan or Southern Provinces, travelling petty traders.

*jebel* [*jabal*], pl. *jibāl*], a hill, a mountain.

*kadi* see qadi.

*Kaid* [*qāʾid*], leader; *Qāʾid al-ʿāmm*, is the g.o.c. of the S.D.F.

of substance had given houses as a charity to foster the good work. Ten years before these had been adequate. A few small girls being taught in ordinary surroundings had been an easy beginning to a new venture.

## 5. Girls' Training College, Omdurman

The Training College[23] had opened in 1921 with exactly five students and for this reason as well as doubts on its advisability progress of schools at first had been slow.[24] The experiment, however, had been so successful that by 1939 the Omdurman schools were full to overflowing and disappointed parents and children had to be turned away every year.

This enthusiasm was of the greatest interest to a newcomer, for on the face of it the girls must have been extremely cramped in these inadequate quarters and the work varied to a degree that bothered me considerably. As all the teaching in the Training College and schools was in Arabic, I could not pass judgement on the content of the lessons, but it was easy enough to decide which teachers were energetic and making the children work and which were more likely to be found gossiping over coffee cups in the middle of what should have been lesson time. The pupils were too well behaved unfortunately to make life difficult for any member of staff who chose to be slack and careless. Some years later we counted it a sign of progress, when older girls began ragging an inefficient mistress.

## 6. 'Female circumcision'

During the first days there was much that daunted me and I began to wonder if I had made a mistake in coming. The harsh ugliness of the landscape distressed me and it needed a great deal of patience to accept an attitude which could so callously shut the women behind high walls. I was lost among the work in the schools despite all the friendliness of the Sudanese mistresses and this feeling of inadequacy dropped to rock bottom one morning. When I returned to lunch, I found my colleague[25] much distressed and just back from a talk with the Principal[26] of the Midwifery

23. Dr Beasley's first impressions of the Girls' Training College are given in Appendix V.
24. From Omdurman Girls' Training College, the higher schools, the Omdurman Girls' Intermediate School (1940) and the Omdurman Girls' Secondary School (1949) developed.
25. Miss K. Sylvia L. Clark.
26. Miss Elaine Hills-Young, D.N. A Nightingale Nurse trained at St Thomas' Hospital; 1.12.29. First appointment; 1929/30-37 Matron of Khartoum Hospital; 1931 Helped to start the Sudan Branch of the Red Cross, Vice-President for 10 years; 1935-40 Lecturer in nursing at

School across the square.[27] She had been in service for a year but the Headship was new and, taking her duties seriously, she thought she ought to find out all she could about a ritual mutilation practised on all small girls as a religious custom and known as female circumcision.[28] Some hours later I decided I did not want to stay and work for people who could indulge in such barbaric cruelty but wiser councils ultimately prevailed.[29] After the first shock this new friend and I settled on a less cowardly course and before much longer we both became zealous crusaders against the practice. Re-adjustment came gradually but this strand lay always as a shadow at the back of our endeavours, influencing our opinions of people in all walks of life. Even in later years, when I was accustomed to much that I had originally thought would be unbearable, there were times when the forces of ignorance pressed round like some tangible evil lurking in the darkness.[30]


## 7. Work routine

Arriving in November, I was fortunate in that the North wind was blowing, tempering the heat and leaving the sun pleasurable, if the day was managed sensibly. The general pattern was to drink tea on the verandah soon after sunrise and then work either in the office at the Girls' Training College or in a nearby school until breakfast, about half past nine. Work possibly further afield for me went on until 1.30 p.m., when lunch was followed by an afternoon rest. There might be more supervision or office work or Arabic studies[31] in the afternoon or evening and somewhere after four o'clock mild

Kitchener School; 1937-43 Principal, Midwives Training School, Omdurman. She took over from Miss G.L. Wolff and was succeeded by Miss P.M. Dickens in 1943; 1943 Retired to do war work in Europe, having declined the newly created post of Principal Matron; 1944-45 British Red Cross, U.K.; 1945-48 Principal Matron, N.W. Europe with the British Red Cross Commission for Refugees; 1949- British Red Cross Divisional Director in Hertfordshire.

27. The Midwifery Training School opened in 1921.

28. For further details about female circumcision, see Appendix I.

29. She discussed the subject with the Director of Education, R.V.H. Roseveare, as early as 13.2.40. 'He seemed at first to think it unlikely that much could be done in the schools but agreed subsequently that it might be useful in the same way that they are taught to wash their faces. He thought that at any rate no harm could be done by subtle propaganda. There was nothing very concrete from the talk.'

30. Dr Beasley campaigned vigorously against 'Pharaonic circumcision', found in Sudan and elsewhere, even after she retired to England (See S.A.D. 657/4/1-274).

31. Dr Ina Beasley started learning Arabic almost as soon as she arrived, on 11.11.39, and took her first Arabic exam 15.3.41, after which she was confirmed in the post, given a rise in pay, with the promise of promotion to Controller in October 1942. All Sudan Government teachers were expected to pass the first (Lower) Government Arabic examination to qualify for their annual salary increment.

exercise of some sort, tennis, sailing, walking, if only a mile or two to the market and back. Naturally there were variations but it was a routine more or less observed from which to deviate when necessary.

## 8. School stores and inspections—Need for Arabic

Work for me was bound to be limited, as an Inspector without Arabic could only deal with concrete matters. I was first shown round the schools by a Syrian mistress[32] from the [Girls'] Training College, who spoke English, and had an unrivalled understanding of the girls' attitude and that of their parents. Being introduced by her was most valuable but I soon found, that even with my few sketchy phrases of this new language, it was easy to make contact with the Headmistresses and my opinion of their possibilities was correspondingly high. It was stocktaking time[33] and we[34] counted the stores together making out requisitions for next year's needs. From my point of view it was an excellent example of the 'direct method' and the way to a school vocabulary not to be found in orthodox textbooks.

> I went there[35] to count the stores which are sent out from College. These are mostly, I imagined, things which boys' schools would not use. The Controller[36] thought it useful for me to understand the organisation and that it would help my Arabic [4.2.40].
>
> It was a big school[37] and the headmistress seemed to me to have very little idea of discipline and probably was incompetent to run a school of that size. When I started to count the stores, all the staff came to help and left the classes to their own devices, which were extremely fidgety ones. They were only half-hearted attempts to go on with the classes, even in the case of needlework. There was also a certain amount of confusion about the stores. It all seemed so slack that I very much doubt if any good work is done or possibly any at all.

The Arabic language, as it was presented to me by my male teachers, was

32. Sitt Negiba Kronfli, a Syrian mistress from the Girls' Training College. She was also active in the anti-circumcision campaign.
33. It was stock-taking time when Dr Beasley returned from her first trip to Blue Nile Province and Bakht-er-Ruda 14.1.40-19.1.40 and again in February 1940 (See Appendix V for details).
34. Sitt Negiba Kronfli and Dr Beasley.
35. Khartoum North Girls' Elementary School.
36. Miss L.Y. Pode. 1.10.35 First appointment; 1935-1938 Controller of Girls' Education and Principal of Girls' Training College, based Omdurman, succeeding Miss Dora Evans; 1938-42 Controller of Girls' Education, based in Khartoum. Miss Pode was taken ill and retired in 1942, and was succeeeded by Dr Beasley in October 1942.
37. It was also a chance to view the schools in operation on an informal basis. For example, see Dr Beasley's comments on Osman Saleh School which she visited on 14.2.40.

always rather grand with little interest in the needs of small girls trying to deal with the four rules of arithmetic. The unending patience of the mistresses with my inadequacies was of the greatest help to me and also made me realise how mistaken their menfolk were. 'Women are so stupid' they said at all levels and dismissed on those grounds any attempt to give them a chance to prove the contrary.[38]

It was obviously untrue and there is no need to dilate on the general proposition. Living in the conditions which had grown up in the settled communities, it was a marvel that so many had retained any flicker of liveliness and could respond to new possibilities, once they were opened up to them. I do not mean that as soon as it started the progress of women's education was one rushing torrent of uninterrupted success. Yet in later years when evening classes were arranged for adult women their deep gratitude for the opportunity was touching in the extreme. To balance this comes the memory of a respectable *sheikh* gazing in amazement at a display of work by a class of this sort. 'To think,' he exclaimed in awe, 'that our women can do this. Our women!'

## 9. Seclusion of women

In the girls' school therefore it had always been obvious that the potentialities were there but the handicaps were heavy. One of the chief of these was that the seclusion of women was regarded as the mark of respectability. The rules about this and the men to whom a woman might or might not speak and in what circumstances were too complicated for me ever to fathom completely and I had to depend on the guidance of the Sudanese for unravelling many little tangles. Broadly summed up, however, only the very poor were free to come and go. In the West, the Baggara[39] nomads wandered with their women unveiled and ready of speech but the 'Fuzzies'[40] in the East even when travelling generally hid their women in crazy looking erections[41] on their camels. The custom in the towns, as explained to me at the beginning, was that, as soon as a girl approached puberty she should not be seen by other men and it was better therefore that she should be married early. For the first three months after marriage she must stay in the house, for the rest of the year in the yard. Thereafter she might attend family ceremonies, if closely veiled and remaining in the

38. See Holt, P.M. *Modern History of the Sudan*, 1961, p.202.
39. al-Baqqāra group—These are cattle-nomads.
40. Beja group, usually Hadendowa, Beni Amer, Amarar or Bisharin.
41. A howdah or *'utfa*, a carriage for a woman and children to ride on top of a camel.

women's quarters, or she might go to gossip with a friend if, again closely veiled, she did not go out until after sunset. All the marketing was done by the man of the house or by servants, if he could afford them. Most of the Sudanese were not rich and their houses were small, their yards close. What saved this confinement from being intolerable was that women had grown up with the idea over the centuries and they had accepted it knowing no wider horizons. Moreover in most of the towns and large villages I visited, although the outside gates opened on to the streets, there were also communicating doors and gaps into the yard of a relative or perhaps a close friend lived next door. It must have been possible in some places to wander through whole labyrinths. The advantage was that a woman seldom had to be alone. She could always find someone to sit with and talk to, if it was not too hot and there was anything to talk about. To go at any time into the women's quarters of an establishment meant finding several women just sitting about at any time. What else was there for them to do? '*Quaadin sakit*'[42] was a phrase that cropped up frequently and translated that is what it means—'just sitting'. The saddest aspect of this was to see bright little girls from school marry early and come all too soon to this state of apathy. The most hopeful signs came from the number of girls who were not content with such a future and the cautious approval [of girls' education] of their husbands and fathers. It was a slow process but cumulative.

My lasting impression of Omdurman therefore is of a maze of sandy ways between high walls of the same colour and substance. Behind these would lie the houses of both the poor and those of more substantial means. A small number of wealthy merchants had warehouses here but some of these were Syrians or Greeks with homes elsewhere and only business connections in the town. The crooked streets twisted and turned presenting a bewildering sameness in this fawn façade. In fact the sameness of it all could be depressing in some moods, particularly at the end of a hot morning spent watching a lot of bad teaching. Yet there was never the utter dreariness of Northern industrial towns in England with their rows and rows of back-to-back houses. The sun may be an enemy in some ways but it has an inherent quality of gaiety: the tone of the mudbrick is not so disheartening as stucco grimed with factory smoke. Frivolous though it may sound I am sure that childhood holidays building houses and castles on the beach always lay at the back of my mind awakening an echo of long hours of happiness.

This barricade against the world never seemed to me especially sinister and I doubt if then many women questioned their confinement. In a country

---

42. *Qā'idīn sākit*, 'sitting quietly'.

where the wind can blow so fiercely these outer walls gave some measure of protection, even if nothing could keep out the dust.

One great mystery to me now is how we ever found our way about, because the schools themselves lay behind exactly the same high mud walls as the houses. To start the schools at all concessions had to be made to local opinion and on this matter of the seclusion of women feeling was strong.[43] Small girls could be allowed to walk to school provided their heads were decently covered by a large kerchief known as a *tarha* but when they reached the age of nine or ten, one *sheikh* explained they should not be seen out, as men in the market might look after them with lustful desire. No attempt apparently to alter the attitudes of the market place; just to deprive the girls of education. In passing I may note that in spite of all the talk of chastity and the measures to enforce it, there appeared to be as much adultery and illegitimacy as elsewhere. Educated young men confessed to amorous adventures which were probably quite exciting among the labyrinths of the backyards, while every town, particularly Khartoum and Omdurman, had its red light district.[44] There seemed a lot of talk and effort rather ill-directed.

Encouraging education, however, means playing with the cards dealt to you. One of these was to demonstrate that girls' schools could carry on behind high walls and custom not much infringed. Respectability was a firm ideal, even if it rang hollow at times, and could be used as an aid rather than a hindrance. Gradually the girls would find their own way out when they were ready. All the same, to an Englishwoman whose other experience had been among the liveliness and freedom of the Burmese, these were among the things which, as I mentioned earlier, rather daunted me at first.

## 10. Introduction to Omdurman schools

As a general proposition, however, it remains true and was re- inforced here by the privilege of going to school at all. Boys' education had been started by the Government in 1900 immediately after the occupation but girls for

---

43. 'In a country where so much lip service has been paid to respectability, the first profession open to women has won its laurels without a bitter struggle against ingrained prejudices ... there is plenty of room for immediate development within the existing framework without a sudden breaking away from the traditional ideas of seclusion' (Sudan Government, Department of Education. *Note on Girls' Education in the Sudan*, Dec 1940).

44. However female circumcision no doubt limited premarital intercourse. Many of the prostitutes came from tribes originating outside Northern Sudan—Eritreans, Southerners, Fellata etc.—on whom Pharaonic circumcision was not customarily performed. In colloquial Arabic, *Ḥabashiyya* (Ethiopians) can mean prostitutes.

various reasons, which I explain later, had had to wait until 1921, apart from one or two private ventures of varying efficiency. By 1939 opposition to girls' schools was still wide-spread but more in the way of non- co-operation rather than actual hostility and it was noticeably decreasing. There were, however, few schools[45] and, where the idea was accepted, competition for places was fierce. Enthusiasm tended to wane on the way up and, although the younger classes were uncomfortably squeezed together, the numbers at the top had often fallen to half the original entry. This is not a problem peculiar to the Sudan and only needs a comment here in that for me it presented an obvious duty. There was clearly no lack of good material among both teachers and pupils. Concern for higher standards and better buildings was my objective. A nice, large, overall target, easier to write about than to achieve.

Later in this book I have described in some detail the school system and what was actually taught and this for the following reason. When I was studying the beginnings of girls' education in West Africa it was difficult to find out exactly what did happen in the classroom. From 1806 apparently teachers went out from England and names are given with the number of schools. Writers such as the 'Lady of Quality' in Sierra Leone (1840) praises the work of the missionaries but gives no description of the schools. Conditions are changing so rapidly this century that our work is already past history but may at some future time be of interest to the diligent researcher, who wants to know about Nafissa's arithmetic or Zenab's needlework.

I may often have come back from my early visits hot and cross but I was aware of it then and what remains my most persistent memory is the quick friendliness which always greeted me and survived even adverse criticism. It was a relationship of trust that had grown up from the beginning and we never lost it. After all these years I still find it, when young women in England, whom I had not known before, come to tea with me and talk of their schooldays. Most Sudanese have delightful manners and as one of their own contributions the schoolmistresses encouraged proper behaviour as part of the mark of a girl who was lucky enough to go to school. At times this conception of a 'nice, little girl' seemed a trifle Victorian but it was very charming. Whenever a visitor entered, a class would rise, place their right hands on their chests, bow their heads and chant a little greeting in unison. Their little brown faces would be rather solemn but the mistress would probably be all smiles and eager to talk. Someone coming in from outside was always a welcome break in a cloistered life and someone coming from

---

45. The school system and syllabuses are described in Chapters 8 and 9.

the Training College, which they all held in such affection, could bring news of happenings elsewhere which they were avid to hear.

Just as with children everywhere classes would be made up of all shapes and sizes and all imaginable variations of intelligence, temperament and behaviour. One monotony, east of Suez, that has always forced itself on my attention is that hair is always black. It may be short, long, straight, coarse, frizzy but the colour is the same. This was true of these girls, who wore theirs plaited into dozens of tiny braids. It was the fashion too among the women and I thought it very becoming, as it brought out the lines of the head, which was often nobly modelled. Differences, however, there were in plenty both in the cast of feature and in the colour of skin. The Sudan is the meeting point of the Arab and Negro worlds and in a centre such as Omdurman all manner of strains had been mingled. Some familes still retained the paler shades and more delicate formation of their Arab forebears, while others showed definite signs of a slave ancestry from further south. Unlike the men there was nothing distinctive about their clothes except for the *tarha* or headkerchief of the children, and the *tobe* worn as soon as a girl began to grow up. A *tobe* is a piece of some soft material that would not crease, two metres in width and seven in length. It was worn over ordinary European cotton dresses and was wound round the body in a manner peculiarly difficult for the uninitiated to manage. The whole of the body was covered and the head, although the arms were left completely free. On venturing out, the *tobe* could be pulled over the face in such a way that only the eyes showed. The schoolmistresses mostly wore soft white muslin which fell in graceful folds round their slim figures.

Also in the school yard I met generally one or perhaps two of the *farrashat*. These were women, probably of good character but of no social standing, who served the double purpose of sweeping the school and acting as a sort of guardian and being in touch with the outside world, if a messenger should be needed. They wore *tobe*s of dark blue muslin, a colour which in that dusty climate invariably looked shabby and uncared for. Some of these women were feckless creatures not particularly useful in even the simple cleaning they had to do; a few, however, had determined views and were earning money to bring up their daughters to a better way of living than they had known themselves. This road they saw through the schools.

## 11. Sheikh Babikr Bedri[46]

There were other visits of a more sociable kind, even if not entirely unconnected with our official position. A week or two after my arrival,[47] came an invitation to tea for the five British women[48] then working in the Department. This was from Sheikh Babikr Bedri, affectionately known as 'the Father of Girls' Education'.[49] His exact contribution I have described in the history of the schools but it is as a personal friend that I chiefly remember him now. From time to time later on, when I took over the post of Controller, I found him always ready to encourage, to push us on to further ventures, while he showed an immediate understanding of problems which sometimes distressed me. Even now the photograph which he signed and sent me after my retirement hangs over my desk, recalling not only his friendliness but acting as a reminder of the faith he must have had to start a girls' school five years after the Occupation and in the face of much opposition.

This was almost like a link with a storybook past, since one of my earliest recollections was being given the little statuettes from my grandfather's mantelpiece and playing with Gordon and Kitchener. Babikr Bedri claimed to have been in Khartoum when Gordon was killed on the Palace steps and he had certainly served with the dervish army in the Battle of Omdurman.[50] After this he began early to work with the new administration and the reports[51] of those years pay tribute to him as a useful and trusted official. Now[52] he was no longer in Government service but running a large private school for boys and had become a revered figure but by no means a person from the past. I came away from the party in a bewildered haze but with two or three people standing out clearly from the

46. Sheikh Babikr Bedri (1864-1954). Born 200 miles south of Abu Hamed, at four years old his family moved to Rufaa. He was educated in traditional schools and was a supporter of the Mahdist cause. He was taken prisoner and spent a period in captivity in Egypt. After the Mahdist wars he was a merchant in Rufaa. He opened the first elementary school for boys in the Blue Nile Province in 1903 and the first girls' school in 1907. He later served as Education Officer. See Bedri, Yusuf and Scott, George (Ed), *The Memoirs of Babikr Bedri*, Vol 1, 1969.
47. 9.1.40.
48. Probably Miss L.Y. Pode, Miss E.M. Harvey, Miss Joan Pellow, Miss E. Hills-Young and Dr Ina Beasley.
49. Sheikh Babikr Bedri started the first girls' school in Rufaa in 1907, after applying to Sir James Currie, the British Director of Education, in 1904. In 1930 he moved from Rufaa to Omdurman where he opened the Ahfad Colleges for girls and boys [See the *Afhad Magazine* (in Arabic), Omdurman, 1955 and 1961]. He was still teaching in 1940, although he was about eighty.
50. Battle of Omdurman (1898).
51. Sudan Government, *ARDE*, 1900-14, 1928-1949.
52. In November 1939.

crowd, who had been introduced to us, and my whole impression dominated by the personality of the bearded little old man with an enormous *immah*, who received us so kindly but he was doubtless summing us up keenly.

I had forgotten that polygamy was still a tenet of Islam[53] and may not have expected to meet it in advanced Sudanese circles. Therefore it was not until afterwards that I realised that the two ladies who looked after the serving of the tea were both wives. They were introduced to us as 'mother of Sittana' and 'mother of Medina'[54] but, as I did not know the family ramifications this meant nothing to me.[55] English speaking sons helped to carry the party along smoothly, for our host spoke only Arabic, and one of these was a tall, handsome doctor who eventually became the first Minister of Health;[56] others were schoolmasters or in Government service. They were mostly married with children and even grandchildren of their own but a very small boy[57] of about two years or so leant up against the patriarch's knee. He was the youngest child and between him and the doctor stretched an age range of girls and boys whose number I never discovered. There was one point a few years later when the family claimed, that the *sheikh* had achieved ninety eight descendants, although he still took an active part in his school and public affairs generally. On this particular afternoon there seemed to be a constant coming and going in a most happy atmosphere, as we sat on a *mustaba*[58] inside one of the mud-brick walls that are my perpetual remembrance of the streets of Omdurman.

It was the first of many such tea-parties in this house and in plenty of others. As a social gathering in this climate the tea party had much to commend it. By four o'clock the heat of the day had always begun to fade a

53. Up to four wives are allowed concurrently under the tenets of Islam, though husbands are enjoined to treat co-wives equally. See Coulson, N.J., *A History of Islamic Law*, 1964, pp. 18-19, 207.
54. Umm Sittana, the third wife, Nafisa bint Ibrahim Madani and Umm Medina, the second wife, Nafisa bint Ahmad.
55. For genealogical table of the Babikr Bedri clan, see Bedri, Yusuf and Hogg, Peter (Ed), *The Memoirs of Babikr Bedri*, Vol 2, 1980.
56. Dr Ali Bedri, M.B.E., D.K.S.M. 1.1.28 First appointment; 1928 In the first batch of students who qualified from the Kitchener School of Medicine. 1928 won a prize in clinical medicine. 1937 First Sudanese doctor to visit London for post-graduate work. 1948-54 First Sudanese Minister of Health, when the Ministry of Health was formed to include the Sudan Medical Service. Of sound judgement and high intelligence and integrity, he occupied the post of Minister with distinction. 1952 He had the honour of being elected a Fellow of the Royal College of Physicians of London. He also took a keen interest in the campaign against Pharaonic circumcision.
57. Babikr Bedri's youngest child in 1939. 'A little boy and a little girl came down and were given a cake and an apple.'
58. *Mastaba*, a raised hard earth platform against the walls of a house or a courtyard.

little and a feeling of relaxation set in. Lunch was always a meal taken after an exhausting morning, to be finished off speedily in time for the afternoon rest. Dinner presented difficulties, to me at any rate, because I did not like asking the Sudanese men without their wives and, in those days, wives were firmly relegated to the women's quarters. There were very few other places, apart from the Bedris', where mixed parties were arranged but we had an uncounted number of cheerful women's tea parties and at times were entertained by the men of a household without their women. I never had the courage to attempt a mixed tea party in my own house, although schoolmasters visited us. Mostly our parties were for the mistresses who did not have so many opportunities for going out.[59] Once I could manage even ungrammatical [Arabic] conversation, these could be great fun, although in one or two houses decorum was apt to be a little burdensome.

## 12. Transport

On the afternon of this first party we were taken to the house in the Training College station waggon and until after the war, when private cars were at last obtainable, this was our general means of transport to and from the schools. We were shepherded by a fatherly old driver, who had long since identified himself with the College and was a tower of strength. His daughter had been a schoolmistress[60] but had recently married a wealthy import agent at least twice her age. We went to tea with them and found this most likeable husband and his young wife appeared to be very happy together.

For purely frivolous affairs we used the battered taxis which could be found in the market but it was a precarious business, not lightly to be engaged upon. Otherwise the only other form of transport from Omdurman was the tramway. The trams were a real feature of the place. A strip of tarmac had been flung across the desert between the town and the bridge across to Khartoum and the rails ran alongside this. There was a glorious abandon about the way in which the driver clanged his bell all the time, but

---

59. The Director of Education 'seemed anxious that we should go into the children's homes as much as possible' [13.2.40].

R.V.H. Roseveare (Dick), M.C. 4.9.39 First appointment. 1939-45 Director of Education and Principal of Higher Schools, following C.W.M. Cox. In 1942 he was asked by Douglas Newbold to review progress since the De La Warr Commission and submitted a report on higher education to the 501st Council meeting (5.9.42). In 1943 he held a series of conferences on girls' education; 1945 succeeded by C.W. Williams. He later became a teacher at Winchester College.

60. See Chapter 9.

sense lay behind it. Goats, sheep, camels, dogs, donkeys wandered about, and at certain times of the year, great herds of thirsty cattle might be driven down to the river. With all this there might be people straying in from the desert and unused to city habits. The trams did not run frequently enough for the bell to be an annoyance and it seemed to fit in wit the clamour and bustle of the market, as they clanked down the high street joining in the evening with the sound of two open air cinemas at full blast, radios at the top of their pitch from the cafés and the babble of people's voices in a place, where talking is a pleasure to be enjoyed with full-throated vehemence.

## 13. The first trek, to Berber

Discerning guides introduced me to all of this and I was equally fortunate in being taken early[61] to see schools in the provinces, where much of my future work was to lie. My first trip was to Berber, where a new girls' school was to be opened at the request of the inhabitants, ashamed now of the failure of a former attempt.

> We arrived about 4.30 to be met by the Theobalds,[62] MacPhail[63] and Walker.[64] We stayed in the empty house of the D.C.[65] who was at present at Atbara, and therefore needed full trek equipment.

This was a day's journey North by rail along the route by which I had already come. Berber lay near the river, not a large place but a good centre

61. Dr Beasley was taken to Berber from 10.1.40-12.1.40 (the day after her first visit to Sheikh Babikr Bedri) by Miss L.Y. Pode, the Controller of Girls' Education. Mahgoub El Dawi, Assistant P.E.O., Northern Province in 1940 was probably also in attendance.
62. Alan Buchan Theobald. b.19.7.06. Educated Varndean School, Brighton and University College, London; 2.9.29 First appointment. originally appointed to the Sudan Political Service; 1929-36 seconded to the Education Department, 1935-36 Tutor, Gordon Memorial College; 15.10.36-39 Seconded from the Education Department as Province Education Officer, Northern Province, based in Ed-Damer, 1938 Transferred to Education Department; By Sept 1941 at Bakht-er-Ruda; 1940-41 Inspector, Northern Province, based in Khartoum, temporary duty; 1944 Principal, School of Arts, Khartoum; 1946-52 Vice-Principal, Gordon Memorial College, following G.C. Scott's retirement; 1953-55 Dean, School of Arts, University of Khartoum. Author.
    Mrs Theobald used to work with the American Missions.
63. James Gordon Stewart Macphail, 4N. (1935). b.19.2.1900; Educated Edinburgh Academy and University College, Oxford; 27.11.22 First appointment; 1923-24 Berber; 1925 Red Sea; 1926- 29 Bahr el Ghazal; 1930-33 Kordofan; 1933-39 Upper Nile; 1939- 42 Northern Province, by 1.7.41 D.C. for Berber-Atbara, based in Atbara; 1943-47 War Supply Department; 1946-47 Assistant Deputy Sudan Agent in London; 1947 retired.
64. Possibly D.F. Walker. 23.9.39 First appointment; 1939-41 Tutor, Gordon Memorial College, Khartoum; July 1941 joined the R.A.F.
65. Probably J.G.S. Macphail.

for tracks from the east or west by camel and it had had much significance in the 1898 campaign, exuberantly described by G.W. Steevens.[66] A row of ruined buildings remained as some sort of momento but they were apart from the town where the school had been built and I doubt if they represented much to most of the people there.

At 5.0 pm we went to the school for a formal opening.

This visit was memorable to me for the enthusiasm of the village notables, about fifty of whom gathered in the large school yard for a tea party. I was new to all this and distressed to find no women, not even the schoolmistresses or pupils. The speeches, as translated to me, were full of good resolutions, and one in particular caught my fancy. It was made by a young merchant who had completed his secondary education [at Gordon Memorial College] in Khartoum and he followed up comments made by other speakers on the discrepancy between the mental equipment of men and women, by praise of equality. Men and women used to have this equality because neither had education but now they must work for equality again at a different level.

> Fathers and mothers used to have equality because neither had education but now they must work for equality again at a different level.

This young man impressed me most because in the case of some of the others I was troubled by the unworthy suspicion that they were actuated more by civic pride than any real zeal for girls' education and I wondered if they had any vision of the ultimate strength of the forces being unloosed.

At the end of the party, when the light was growing very dim, a short, very subdued procession of small girls emerged from the wall round the Mistresses' house in the far corner of the extremely large yard. We were sitting right at the other end. They walked quickly and quietly to the big gate in the outer wall and disappeared from view. This was their part in the opening celebrations and was regarded as a concession to the new ways. Concessions were to move fast in the next ten years. The scene was not so quiet and orderly in the morning, when the yard was besieged by mothers, pushing and shouting, demanding places for their children. Eventually eighty seven year olds were selected

> but a number of attractive little girls had to be turned away. Again I had the impression that they felt dimly that they were missing something but were not sure what. I objected to the confusion which ensued on this first meeting—due to slackness by staff or committee, but it was not impressive. In addition, the

66. Steevens, G.W., *With Kitchener to Khartoum*, pp.85-88, 165-167.

stores did not turn up until 12 January. I felt that there was something
inefficient in not making sure that a school has its stores before it starts.

The school settled down this time to a very creditable existence.

> The first morning consisted of games in the yard with Miss Pode, learning bits
> of Koran, and a gift of boiled sweets from the D.C.[67] The teachers, Harim
> and Nafissa, seemed very capable girls, in addition to their external
> attractiveness.
> The building was good. Mud walls, a rush ceiling and a cement floor and
> verandah, a large piece of ground for the children to play in, a house for the
> mistresses, eventually to accommodate four teachers.

Two other social occasions stand out from this visit. Tea and tennis with
half a dozen of the *effendi*s at their club was the first.[68] The word *effendi* has
been banished these days but it was in my time a term of respect and polite
address almost equivalent to our use of the word *Mr*. It did, however, imply
discrimination in that it designated men who had been educated by
European methods and usually wore European clothes but it could include
officials and non-officials. Other men one generally addressed as *sheikh*. The
local D.C. had brought along a bottle of champagne and a packet of
Bourbon biscuits for the launching of the school, the only time such an
event was thus glorified in our subsequent period of austerity. But the Sub-
Inspector[69] thought it demanded a proper feast and he swept off all five
British officials[70] to one of the largest dinners I have ever faced. He was the
son of the notorious Khalifa, but he and his brother had entered
Government service in the early years and had by then risen to posts of
responsibility. I came to know him well in time as an earnest and
hardworking official but it was some years before I was allowed to meet his
wife.

67. Probably J.G.S. Macphail.
68. 'I met educated Sudanese in their own setting for the first time ... They seemed unfailingly
cheerful, managing to avoid servility without lack of deference.'
69. Daoud el Khalifa Abdulla, M.B.E. 17.8.13 First appointment; 1.11.39 appointed to Northern
Province and by 1.1.40 Sub-inspector based in Berber; 1.11.46-48 Kassala Province, D.C. Kassala;
1949-51 Blue Nile, D.C. Sennar; 1951-52 Chairman, Sennar District Council; 17.10.52 retired. A son
of the Khalifa. Dr Beasley later met his brother, Abdel Salam Abdulla, at that time a Sub-Inspector in
Kordofan Province. Another brother was a Bimbashi in the Eastern Arab Corps (Gedaref in 1947).
On some Government Lists last name Abdullahi.
70. Probably Dr Ina Beasley, Miss L.Y. Pode, J.G.S. Macphail, A. Theobald and Mr Walker.

## 14. The 'phoney war'

During this period of the 'phoney war' in Western Europe with Italy sitting on our frontier but not yet a declared enemy, life had a strange remote quality so far away from home. All that could be done was to concentrate on the work in hand. Overseas governments in those days were not assisted by 'aid' programmes from the Great Powers and were accustomed to regulate their spending according to their own budgets. Thus it was quite logical to carry on with ideas of improving education within the closed circle of the Sudan itself.

## 15. Khartoum to Bakht-er-Ruda[71]

For some years a determined effort had been made to improve education in boys' primary schools and there was no need to slacken it now.[72] I was therefore taken down to Bakht-er- Ruda[73] that I might be stimulated by the work going on there.

> An interesting journey. The countryside was not much more luscious than the country to the north of Omdurman on the way to Berber. Near the village where we stayed for lunch there was no cultivation at all, certainly no long

71. Bakht-er-Ruda was five hours from Khartoum by car and two days by steamer, approximately 120 miles. On 14.1.40 Dr Beasley made her first trip to Bakht-er-Ruda, the Boys' Training College, and the surrounding area. She visited Bakht-er-Ruda again 21.1.41, having left Kosti by Province steamer for Dueim. She had 'a pleasant feeling of a return welcome at Bakht-er-Ruda, which has created such a definite character for itself that it is very fascinating'.
72. Although the early 1930s was a period of great financial slump, Bakht-er-Ruda was opened in 1934, with 39 students. By 1938 there were 85 boys and in 1941, 162. The Principal, V.L. Griffiths, was especially concerned with teacher-training lectures, curricula, supply of equipment and books, as well as the spread of trained staff.
73. Dr Beasley was taken down to Bakht-er-Ruda on 14.1.40 by W.B. de la M. Jamieson and G.H. Bacon.

W.B. de la M. Jamieson, O.B.E., 4N. 2.9.29 First appointment; 1930-36 lecturer at Gordon College, Khartoum; 1937 Inspector, Khartoum Province; 1937-43 Chief Inspector of Northern Province schools, based in Khartoum; By 1944 he was Chief Inspector of Education; 1946-47 Assistant Director for Education; 1948-53 Deputy Director of Education; 15.3.53 retired.

G.H. Bacon, M.A., Dip.Agric.(Cantab). 3.6.28 First appointment; 16.2.35-1937 seconded to staff at Bakht-er-Ruda and was, at that time, one of the most influential figures in primary education in the Sudan, along with V.L. Griffiths; 1940- Principal, school of Agriculture, based at Shambat; 1944 Senior Inspector of Agriculture, Khartoum, Dura Purchasing Commission; 1946 Senior Inspector of Agriculture, Blue Nile, based in Wad Medani. Secretary, White Nile Schemes Board. 1947-48 Manager, White Nile Schemes Board; 1949 Gezira Liaison Officer, Blue Nile; 1950-53 Assistant Director of Agriculture; 1953-55 Sudan Agency, London as Agricultural Adviser to the Sudan Government.

green strips of fields as at Berber. On the whole, despite the irrigation and the pleasure of seeing things growing, the countryside is barren and away from the river, where there are beautiful little corners like small beaches in front of sand dunes, it is very unlovely [14.1.40].

We crossed the river in a small ferry boat in company with a camel and several donkeys and innumerable people, some of whom were interesting—the real West African, walking across the country for cotton picking. A surprising number of spears seem to be carried in these parts. Sometimes only one, sometimes a whole quiverful. It was dark when we arrived in Bakht-er-Ruda but I was impressed by the comfort of the principal's house—a real comfort and obtained by simple methods.

In the morning I saw the buildings but was prepared for them. The mud walls are very unlovely and the general setting of the place is barren but I have found during the week that it has a real facination ... The boys are housed in conditions which are not too far removed from their everyday life ... The boys are in houses of six or eight, not giving much scope for individual expansion[15.1.40].

The main gain from the visit was the general heartening and the infectious enthusiasm.

Stimulating it was indeed, a most interesting experiment, and my one abiding resolve from this visit was that the girls must be helped to the same level as the boys but in their own way. Much has been written about this men's Training College elsewhere, its aims, achievements and disappointments.[74] It was not so much an experiment[75] in education as an attempt to make use of tried educational principles in adapting schools to the background of Northern Sudan.[76]

---

74. Much has been written about Bakht-er-Ruda, the Men's Training College, for example: Griffiths, V.L., 'A Teacher Training Research Centre in the Sudan' *Oversea Education*, Vol 16, 1944, pp.1-6; Sudan Government, *Guide to Bakht-er-Ruda Institute of Education*, Khartoum, 1949; Griffiths, V.L., *An Experiment in Education*. London, 1953, reprinted by London Institute of Rural Life, 1957; Sudan Government, *Bakht-er-Ruda Twenty years Old*, Khartoum, 1954; Griffiths, V.L., 'An experiment in Education in the Sudan' *Overseas Quarterly*, 1958, pp.1-6.
75. Griffiths, V.L. with Taha, Abdel Rahman Ali, *Character Training*, Khartoum, 1945; *Character Aims; Some suggestions on Standards for a Rising Nation*, London 1949; Griffiths, V.L., *Character, its Psychology*, Khartoum, 1949; Griffiths, V.L., *Teacher Centred. Quality in Sudan Primary Education 1930 to 1970*, Longman, 1975.
76. Dr Beasley visited the *kuttāb* at Bakht-er-Ruda. For her comments, see Appendix V.

## 15.1 Staffing

Apart from the Principal,[77] on whom the whole institution depended, the men in charge were not in essence trained educationalists.[78] This made for a lively and original approach very often but also wasted time in finding out things which experienced teachers would already have dealt with. Perhaps the atmosphere had crept in from the desert, but there was a feeling of working in eternity; every comma in a textbook had to be chewed over. Nevertheless the text-books which were being prepared were most valuable in a country starved of appropriate material.[79]

## 15.2 Simplicity

While on the subject of shortcomings the other two that struck me were first the attempt at simplicity. This was a very worthy effort to counteract the pull of the towns and relate the standards of the schools in physical conditions to what existed in the villages. 'One stage above their homes' was the Principal's slogan but to me one stage was not enough and the boarding

77. V.L. Griffiths. 1931-32 First appointment as Inspector of Education, after teaching experience in India; 1934 Set up the Elementary Teachers' Training College at Bakht-er-Ruda near ed Dueim; 1934-50 Principal of Bakht-er-Ruda and Assistant Director in the Department of Education. In 1950 V.L. Griffiths left the Sudan.

He was a firm believer in character training. 'What would Bakht-er-Ruda be like without such a sane and balanced head as Griffiths? If the institution could survive a mediocre or even peculiar personality, the argument in favour of being away from social contacts is strong' [1942].

78. Dr Beasley spent some time with Mr Greenlaw, the man in charge of art and handwork. She was particularly struck by the tremendous enthusiasm of Legge and Greenlaw for their hobbies and their work and the amount of labour they were prepared to put in. Mr Greenlaw had just finished writing a handbook on drawing and design whichwould be of real guidance to teachers. She saw the boys enthusiastically constructing a kiln. Despite his apparent lack of system, he managed to convey his own enthusiasm to the boys and to get good solid work out of them. Mr Greenlaw also made helpful suggestions about handwork for girls.

Jean Pierre Greenlaw. 16.8.36 First appointment; 1936-44, Handwork Officer, Bakht-er-Ruda; By 1946 Master, Omdurman Secondary School, Art Teacher Training Section; Sept 1946 Master, Hantub Secondary School, Wad Medani (seconded to Northern Province); 1947-49 Central Town Planning Board; By 1947 he was head, School of Design, Gordon Memorial College. One of his close colleagues was Osman Waqialla, a calligrapher.

79. Book production became a principal activity of the staff, to supplement the narrow range of Arabic books that was available. However staff at Bakht-er-Ruda were not just experimenting and producing books but were responsible for training course lectures, supervising teaching practice by aarefs, prospective teachers. In their vacations staff were expected to spend their time visiting schools.

By 1939 Bakht-er-Ruda had seven books published and two in the press. The Publications Bureau was established in 1946 and moved to Khartoum in 1947. For further details see Hodgkin, R.A., 'The Sudan Publication Bureau Beginnings', *Oversea Education*, XIX, no:3, April 1948, pp.694-8.

houses were displeasingly squalid. Raising the intellectual level first is a hazardous enterprise.

> The attempt is to find the best adaptation for village boys in order that they may live a fuller life in their villages and not be divorced from their normal circumstances ... I wonder if one stage is far enough. It seems so difficult to attain any real cleanliness in these mud-brick houses with their soft sandy floors. One of the boarding houses had made a special effort to beautify the building and plant a garden ... In addition to difficulties connected with water supply, the soil is poor and only cartloads of river silt could help to give beds where any sort of flowers could be grown. Despite the handicaps the boys had raised a bright patch of sunflowers [15.1.40].

## 15.3 Attitudes to girls' education

The great objection from my point of view was the attitude that girls' schools need not be thought about until the boys' education had been satisfactorily arranged. The Principal did not know anything about girls and was not really interested. In a country where strict seclusion still operated this dichotomy did not seem peculiar but it always enraged me. It enraged me still more in later years, when doubts arose about boys' education responding according to plan. Perhaps, it was suggested, there might be more success on the boys' side, if the level of development could be raised among the women and girls. No suggestion, I fumed, that the girls would profit.

## 15.4 Adult education

This note came early in my visit and gave me a valuable lesson in checking my tongue and, as I said before, playing with the cards that were dealt. Two of the senior Sudanese masters[80] had me to their house one evening[81] to meet their wives. They had realised the enormous gap between educated Sudanese and their women folk, and turned to me as a newcomer and a woman with personal understanding of family life. 'Give us better wives and mothers' was their cry. One swallows the obvious counter about better husbands and fathers. They were offering a way in and it was not to be despised.

80. Abdel Rahman Ali Taha and Osman Mahgoub.
81. Dr Beasley visited Osman Mahgoub's house on 19.1.40 to discuss adult education. 'Their suggestions included a schools' shop. It was also suggested that emphasis should be laid on experimenting at home.'
'I was shown Abdel Rahman's house' on 23.1.40. it was very similar in type to Osman Mahgoub's, 'except that there were no strings of dried meat hanging up'.

As a social gathering I found it rather pathetic, as I still had close memories of the easy and pleasant manners of the Burmese. The women did not come in until after dusk, when I had already had a talk with their husbands about the inadequacies of home life.

> I put forward the idea of mothers' meeting together occasionally ... The *effendis* were insistent on the value of demonstration, including First Aid, Ways of Amusing Children or teaching them to amuse themselves, Food charts, Odd Jobs in the House, more efficient methods of cleaning the house ... This general raising of home comforts would be pleasing to husbands and that cleanliness is commanded by their religion [19.1.40].

We agreed that change must be gradual and were not in any doubt about the size of the task. An educated Sudanese woman who could be a Welfare Worker at Bakht-er-Ruda and who could spread the gospel of better homes from this focal point was what they wanted me to produce. We tried very hard but it was not until after the war that we started such a scheme and then in a rather broader way.[82]

Meanwhile I was saddened to notice how the women slunk in and even here with two such admirable friends they had to keep their faces covered and had little to say. The wife of the older man[83] giggled feebly and received such a sharp rebuke from her husband that I was rather shocked. I never came to know her at all. When her husband rose to dizzy heights in the Education Department and later became Minister, I was always put off, if I suggested calling and my invitations were never accepted.[84] The wife of the other master[85] had much more character. I had tea with her a few days later[86] and although I had to talk through her husband translating, it was a

---

82. In February 1941 Dr Beasley was actively seeking a suitable Sudanese to be a welfare worker based at Bakht-er-Ruda and eventually Dar al-Gilāl was appointed (See Appendix V). After the War, Bakht-er-Ruda was also active in community education for village men and women.

83. Abdel Rahman Ali Taha (b.1903-d.1973). Educated at Gordon Memorial College; Sudanese educationalist and member of the Umma Party; 15.11.22 First appointment; c.1936-c.1947 Vice-Principal, Bakht-er-Ruda where he worked for 12 years; 1948 Assistant Director (Personnel), Khartoum H.Q; 1948-53 First Sudanese Minister of Education.

'... slight build, erect carriage, of the old school, emphatic, authoritative, sense of humour; belief in manners, strong religious principles and loyalties, sensitive to personal relationships and public opinion, sincere' (Griffiths, V.L., *op. cit.*, p.42).

84. Abdel Rahman's wife, although of high intelligence, has not yet [1991] learnt to read or write, but his children attained high levels of education.

85. Osman Mahgoub. 13.9.27 First appointment; By 1940 a Master at Bakht-er-Ruda, by 1.3.46 headmaster, Bakht-er-Ruda school; 1948-50 Supervisor, Dilling Teacher Training Centre; By 1953 Vice-Principal and Supervisor, Teacher Training, Bakht-er-Ruda; From 15.3.55 Principal, Bakht-er-Ruda and Assistant Director of Education, after R.A. Hodgkin retired.

86. 23.1.40.

much more enjoyable meeting than the earlier one. Her household seemed
well run and she was an expert with a sewing machine.[87] In the yard I saw
two, plump, black girls in cotton frocks who were her servants. They were
children of slaves who had belonged to Osman's father, and had asked to
stay on in the house where they were born and where they were contented.

### 15.5 Visits to surrounding villages

Osman was determined to be helpful and I was grateful to him for all his
information. To further my understanding he took me out into the
countryside to give me a quick glimpse of villages nearby and the way in
which the people lived in two different sets of conditions.[88]

The first was a cultivators' village not far from the river and about five
miles from Bakht-er-Ruda. Their sole crop was *suffra* and, as this had been
harvested, the place had a rather dreary appearance. We were shown into
the *sheikh*'s guest room,[89] where a carpet was hastily laid down and chairs
put out for us. On the shelves were a large number of solid books, probably
commentaries on the Koran, since our host was a man of learning with a
number of followers, some of whom we met and who looked rather fanatic.
Osman was evidently on friendly terms with everyone and was able to
discuss the value of girls' education and suggest that I might like to see the
womens' quarters. The *sheikh*'s view on a school was that, if it were started,
it should be right in the village.

> The old *sheikh* said that he approved of the Bakht-er-Ruda type of education,
> because it did not divorce the boys too much from their ordinary life. He had
> no objection to girls' education provided that they were taught in the village
> or at Bakht- er-Ruda.

Children should not be sent to Dueim, the nearest town, because he did not
approve of the habits of the people there.[90]

I was then taken into a nearby house through an outer to an inner room,
where all the women of the family seemed to have gathered to welcome me,
giving a somewhat scared impression, but whether because of me or the
*sheikh* I did not know. He was a serious minded sort of man but the women

87. 'They were an enterprising family but with no children.' They later had two sons, the
younger being the Cultural Attaché at the Sudan Embassy, Cairo in 1989. The two servant girls
are still part of the family. This information was given to the editor in 1990 by Abdel Rahman
Ali Taha's daughter, Fadwa, Ph.D., Department of History, University of Khartoum.
88. Dr Beasley visited villages before she had tea with Osman Mahgoub's wife on 23.1.40.
89. 'The house of the *sheikh* was larger than the others.'
90. Dueim was the old river port on the White Nile which declined after the railway reached El
Obeid via the Gezira, Sennar and the new town of Kosti. For comments on Dr Beasley's visit
to Kosti on 16.1.40 see Appendix V.

did not appear so much serious as dispirited. Their relationship to him and to one another was not explained to me, nor those of the masses of very dirty children who crowded in to stare. The room was none too clean either and its general untidiness suggested considerable discomfort. There were *angareeb*s, cupboards, chests and cooking utensils all jammed together.

I did not know where one would start trying to educate a girl from a home like this. Probably cleanliness and hygiene would be the only necessary things.

No cooking was in progress at this point but I was told that their staple diet was boiled grain[91] with occasional variation of dried goat's meat and dried lady's fingers (*bamia*),[92] a certain amount of milk and *samn*,[93] which was a fat somewhere between butter and lard. Tea and sugar came in the category of prized luxuries. After the talk we had had the evening before, I could appreciated Osman's point in wanting me to see the sort of conditions he deplored.

It made the work of the school seem rather hopeless. I doubt if many of our girls came from homes quite like that as we had no schools in quite such small villages.

True the sight depressed me but I was not feeling quite so weak in resolution, as I had been during the first few days in Omdurman.

In the evening we went further away to a village of semi-nomads who divided their time between a patch of cultivation by the river on the falling flood and pastures for their cattle to the West, when they had gathered their crops. Alternative livelihood schemes made necessary by the Jebel Auliya Dam[94] have been described in detail in the appropriate technical journals. I was to meet the other end of the process soon after in the actual settlements. These people were an example of those who were to be dispossessed, when the reservoir had filled up completely. As the water storage was entirely for the benefit of Egypt, officials had some difficulty in reconciling the cultivators to this disruption. I remember one old man[95] just upstream from the Dam who lamented in bewilderment that the river had not fallen for two

---

91. *Lugma*, boiled grain pudding, is made from *dura*, the great millet, Sorghum vulgare. Millet was also stored in pits in this village.

92. *Bamia* is used for fresh lady's fingers; dried and powdered lady's fingers are called *wayka*.

93. *Samn*, clarified butter. The product might be light in colour but was *not* a form of lard as no Muslim would eat pig's fat.

94. For further details on the Jebel Auliya Dam and the Alternative Livelihood Schemes see Mackinnon, E., 'Blue Nile Province', in Tothill, J.D., *Agriculture in the Sudan*, London, 1948, pp.789-809.

95. 'He brought us a bowl of milk (good milk but a dirty bowl) and later cups of coffee and was very pleased that his hospitality was accepted. His generation appear unable to grasp the essentials of the difference in their future life made by the Jebel Auliya Dam.'

seasons now. It was as if the sun had failed to rise one morning. The Agricultural Inspector[96] explained patiently that he had been warned of this but still the old man could not understand. The fixed rhythms of nature could surely not be disturbed by irreverent technicians in such a way.

On this sunny evening in the village we visited such a situation had not yet arisen and there was a more open and friendlier atmosphere about the place than in that of the learned *sheikh*. The houses were spread more apart and some, particularly the *omdah*'s, were clean and tidy.

> I found these people much friendlier and the *omdah*'s son and one old man, who was very wealthy in terms of cows and grain, were very good fun. They all stood or sat round while Osman drank coffee and chatted. They were sophisticated enough to suggest I should take their photographs and asked why I didn't take notes [23.1.40].

A nomadic life does have the advantage of not piling up a lot of clutter. The shape was the round mud hut in two parts common to so much of Africa. We sat on *angareeb*s covered with attractive straw[97] mats,the making of which from the fibre of the *dom* palm was a traditional occupation among the women. While we were there an old crone, so withered as to be almost like a monkey, crawled in on hands and knees to kiss our hands. She said she was the oldest member of the family and I thought her a pitiful spectacle. The *omdah* ordered her away but it was comforting to reflect that she would always have a place, even if unhonoured, among her people.

I went into a number of round huts, where the women were cooking the evening meal of boiled grain and *kisra*,[98] with which a good bit of milk was drunk morning and evening. That might have accounted for the sleek and healthy appearance of the children playing in the open spaces between the houses. Inside there was little furniture except one large bed for the whole family and a cupboard and generally there were some interesting pieces of leather work, saddles and ornaments for camels and hangings ornamented with cowrie shells.

Two small vignettes remained with me. One was a scene inside a hut, where a plump and pretty young woman was reclining on an *angareeb* gracefuly doing nothing, while an older woman cooked the *kisra* over a charcoal fire with a certain amount of scolding that I could not understand. I could only assume that these were two wives not on the best of terms. The fact that the women did not cover their faces was refreshing and seemed part of their greater freedom.

---

96. G.H. Bacon, the newly appointed Principal at the School of Agriculture at Shambat, was with Dr Beasley on this occasion rather than an Agricultural Inspector.
97. *Dōm*, (Hyphaene thebaica) palm fibre rather than straw, according to the diary.
98. *Kisra*, very thin unleavened bread, made on a flat metal plate over a fire.

A hole in the floor surrounded by hard baked clay in the form of a dish, which I noticed in every hut, was explained as the place for a pot of smoke[99] over which a bride had to sit. This was merely referred to as 'a custom' and I could only suppose that its exact purpose was for relaxation by means of the heat and the sweet smelling woods.

More picturesque was the sight of a man threshing with a flat beater on a long stick. The grain was then thrown in the air for the wind to blow the chaff away, before it was stored in pits, which I was shown on the other side of the village.

All this was most valuable for a newcomer and, as I had at the same time contacts with schools not far away, the discouraging aspects of these glimpses of home life were not overwhelming.

Some miles from Bakht-er-Ruda on the bank of the White Nile an enterprising landowner[100] had started a pump scheme at Gulli. With his blessing, a girls' school[101] had also come into being and was in very good working order, when I made an unexpected call.[102] Obviously there were many more problems unlike those of the town schools I had been visiting in Omdurman but rural schools were an important part of our policy and I was impressed by the serious attitude of the two schoolmistresses there towards their commitments. Among the usual lessons in the three R's were very practical cookery classes,[103] and an outdoor session[104] with the younger children fashioning various objects in clay.

> I liked the atmosphere very much. The children were obviously being well-trained ... as far as I could tell the level of the arithmetic was above that of Dueim. All the exercise books were far in advance for general tidiness. I should think a good school, however rural it may be [17.1.40]
>
> The headmistress is efficient and a good teacher and there was a general air of orderliness about the place. The girls all had their *tobe*s off all the time, folded up on their desks. This gave a much brisker look to the whole proceedings.
>
> The school was well situated, with plenty of light and air and looked delightfully clean. The reading lesson by the headmistress to the second year

---

99. *Bakhor*, perfumed smoke bath.
100. Sheikh Yacoob.
101. 'The inhabitants are not entirely stationary. A number of them move in the rains away from the river to their raincultivation plots. This means that a number of the children are away from school in July and August. Nevertheless, this was the only place in the Sudan where there was a full girls' school but only a subgrade boys' school' in 1940.
102. 17.1.40.
103. 'The cake looked good and everything was clean. It had to be cooked in the *suq* as they did not seem to have facilities there for same.'
104. 'The younger children were modelling coffee pots and cups on a tray from clay.'

class was bright and full of instruction. The girls appear rather solemn after some of the masters at Bakht-er-Ruda.[105]

It was all the more striking as a contrast to life in the house of Sheikh Yacoob himself. I was received in a pleasant room with a view of trees and green things growing, although I do not remember exactly what these were. I was still in the unfortunate state of not having enough Arabic to carry on a reasonable conversation outside classroom matters but my English escort bridged the gap. After a little, however, the *sheikh* asked if I would like to meet his wife and I therefore lost my interpreter. My host guided me to a door at the back which he unlocked with a large key. We walked down a passage into a small room, with a window high up but none of the views as from the front room. Reclining on an *angareeb* piled with cushions was a beautiful young woman, her coppery skin set off richly by the soft draperies of a pink, silk *tobe*. Her husband introduced us and went away, and I heard the key click in the lock at the end of the passage. I was grieved that our talk had to be so limited because she appeared an intelligent girl and the kindly expression of her face suggested an amiable disposition. Perhaps my limitations may have saved me from asking indiscreet questions, as I was still unused to the seclusion of women and this new bride was probably undergoing the customary first three months indoors. For that reason despite my inadequacies of language a visitor may have been welcome and we both did our best. She regaled me from a large box of excellent chocolates but mostly I remember the pleasurable sight of her grace and beauty as she lay on the *angareeb* in her soft draperies while I sat stiffly on a wooden chair dressed in a short cotton frock rumpled from a long, hot drive in the front of a lorry. When, after about quarter of an hour, we heard again the key in the lock, [this] was rather a relief to us but we could genuinely assure her elderly husband that we had been glad to meet, as I was led back to the outside world.[106]

---

105. Dr Beasley visited Gulli again on 20.1.41 from Kosti. For her comments on Gulli school, see Appendix V.
106. After visiting Gulli, Dr Beasley made her first visit to Kosti on 17.1.40, when she stayed the night with Mr and Mrs Bernard James Chatterton, A.D.C. Kosti District, based in Kosti from 1937 to 1940.

## 16. Return to Omdurman

I had been less than two months in the country, when all this assortment of new impressions had flooded in on me and, as we drove back to Omdurman,[107] I had a great deal to ponder. The idea of giving up had somehow slipped away but I still found the ungracious countryside drained off a certain amount of mental reserves. For hours there was little to see but flat, dun- coloured earth and one stretch of apparently endless telegraph poles, that could have become a nightmare. No doubt they helped to prevent wayfarers from losing the ill defined track, which counted as a road, but they could have a dizzying effect. One had to brace oneself against the dreary vista as well as the ordinary physical hardships of this kind of travelling. Happily my next trip[108] presented a less forbidding country and was the last on which I was escorted[109] before being allowed to go trekking on my own.

## 17. Kordofan

Kordofan will always be to me a euphonious word and leaning slightly on the last syllable it can be made to sound quite romantic. This first trip was full of pleasurable discoveries and I always returned to the province with enthusiasm. To begin with we left in the evening and settled down in comfortable little sleepers to pass through the arid part of the journey in the dark. I could not resist the fascination of the halts. The train stopped often with a jerking and a grinding to add to the clamour of the passengers dismounting and embarking. From behind the shutter of my window I could see knots of white clad men and a few women in blue *tobes* gathering up their bundles and discussing in their ordinary vigorous way the details of their movements. They always appeared to be much more excited than they really were. By the light of a hissing petrol lamp the station seemed cut off from the great waste all around and the lively scene by the rails to have no connection with the limitless darkness. Sometimes a donkey or two was standing impassively at the edge of the circle, and occasionally a camel was ridden close to the track. It was not a night of restful sleep but this was of no importance set against the interest and strange beauty of the black and white pictures at the halts.

107. By 4.2.40 'I was again back in Khartoum at work counting stores', see Appendix V.
108. Dr Beasley's next trip was to Kordofan, from 3.3.40.
109. Dr Beasley was escorted by Miss Elizabeth Harvey. 14.10.34 First appointment; 1934-38 Assistant Principal, Girls' Training College, Omdurman; 1939-42 Principal, Girls' Training College, Omdurman. In 1943 she left to be married to W.B. de la M. Jamieson.

## 17.1 Kosti

When the sun rose it was still over a flat, drab plain but before long we came back to the river, and to the exciting junction of North, South and West which begins at Kosti.[110] We crossed the river on a long bridge over the marshes. I was delighted with the water hyacinths growing in profusion but was frequently reproved at other times for such unpractical views by irrigation engineers who struggled against their entangling. So much further south were we by now that even early in March we had lost the benefit of the North wind, and the air lay heavy and humid by the river.

Kosti had probably never been a lovely place to gaze upon and recent developments had hindered any chance of natural growth.

> Kosti has all the sordidness of a railway junction without the usual teeming life. It reminds me of the Midlands particularly when I try to find a walk and have to search out little bits of green among the heaps of rubble which are admittedly being levelled and used as an embankment against the river [19.1.41].

Afraid of malaria from the backing up of the stream behind the Jebel Auliya Dam, the Government was moving the town away from the bank to a piece of higher ground a mile away. Thus the old mud houses decayed, and mud does not decay picturesquely, while the new buildings, many of them of brick, still stuck out raw and unmatured in the new township. To add to this there hung over the place an indefinable taint of the old slaving days, since here was the boundary of the preserves, where the Arab traders went hunting in the unruly days of the last century.[111] It was not until the nineteen twenties that the settlement of former slaves had been completed and the freed man given land and sometimes rather arbitrarily a wife and children.[112] This mixture of tribes could still be seen in the population and

110. Kosti developed after the railway to El Obeid was built in 1911 at the expense of Dueim. From an administrative point of view it lies just inside the Blue Nile Province but topographically Korodfan has really begun (S.A.D. 657/6/6-8). Kordofan lies across the pilgrim route from West Africa to Mecca between the old kingdom of Sennar on the Blue Nile and the western Sultanate of Darfur. It was the battleground for centuries of these two powers.

111. 'Definite traces of old (or rather comparatively recent) slaving days, when Kosti was a clearing centre for the Arab traders, could still be seen in the local population. Apparently it was only about fourteen years since the Government tried to clear things up, in a necessarily high-handed manner' [1940].

112. 'D.C. Arkell gave a man a plot of land to cultivate and then asked if the man were married. If he were not he then picked out a healthy looking wench and handed her over to the man ... ' (S.A.D. 657/6/5-6).

This was Antony John Arkell, M.B.E., M.C., 4N, B.Litt, D.Litt (b.29.6.1898-d.1980). Educated Bradfield and Queens, Oxford; War Service 1916-18 R.F.C., 1918-19 R.A.F.; 13.11.20 First appointment; 1921-26 Darfur; 1927-29 White Nile; 1930-32 Blue Nile Province; 1932-37 Deputy Governor, Darfur; 1937 Civil Secretary's Office; 1938-48 Commissioner for

the history of the place remained to hang over it.

Down by the landing stage, however, all that merged into the perennial interest of boats coming from distant parts, for me an unknown world. The river steamers were clumsy craft, as they had to be a very shallow draught and supported by barges but even so there were sometimes accidents in a high wind with a barge blown over and someone lost in weed infested patch of water. On this sunny morning they had all the fascination of the journey, moored to the bank and busy discharging their cargoes. After a short and sticky scramble to watch them we were glad to come back to the comparative shade of the train, where a *farrash* had prepared breakfast for us. As the trains to the West did not carry the same amount of traffic as the Wadi Halfa or Port Sudan lines there was no dining car but a servant managed to produce very adequate meals.

## 17.2 Kosti to El Obeid

By the middle of the morning we were in fresh country and reddish sandy soil began to replace the dull colours of the plain between the two rivers, which we left on crossing at Kosti. Any rise in the altitude was imperceptible as a whole but the land was more broken and the vegetation less sparse. Here and there as at Tendelti there was a large village with trees of some size, while at Um Ruaba, which we reached in the early afternoon, there was a glimpse of large *neem*s, although the station was some distance from the houses. Here we also saw a large, grey smudge against the horizon, which was my first view of a district of never failing interest and also stormy discussion—the Nuba Mountains. As the heat subsided a little, there was more and more activity to claim our attention.[113] Birds came in increasing numbers to perch on the telegraph wires or on the branches, for the *sunt*[114] and *tulkh*,[115] if not mighty, were definitely trees. Their colours were vivid and every few minutes the quick brilliance of an Abyssinian roller [took] flight with that intensity of blue as clear as the sky behind cloud. I was told

Archaeology and Anthropology, based in Khartoum; 1941-44 War Supply Department (Chief Transport Officer); 1948 retired to become Curator of Flinders Petrie collection of Egyptian Antiquities, University College, London; 1948-53 Archaeological adviser to the Sudan Government and lecturer in Egyptology, U.C.; 1953-63 Reader in Egyptian Archaeology, U.C.; 1963 ordained, Vicar (Bucks). Author.

113. 'When the trees started, albeit rather small trees and not very close together, the change from the wastes of Omdurman was really refreshing to the spirit' [September 1941].

114. *Sunṭ*, Acacia arabica var. nilotica.

115. *Tulkh*, probably *ṭalḥ*, a species of acacia (Acacia gummifera), *ṭalḥ ḥāmrā'*, Acacia seyal, or *ṭalḥ bayḍā'*, Acacia fistula.

that they do not sing but they were exquisite to watch either in movement or sitting among the mimosa-like foliage.

At this time too it was almost to come into a new country to get down at the stations and watch the crowds. Sudan trains were always full partly because they only ran once or twice a week, and partly because all the Sudanese thoroughly enjoyed travelling. They enjoyed seeing people off and meeting them to a degree that the most kindly relatives in England could never envisage. Add to this the fun of trains which arrived infrequently and one could understand the concourse at all the stations.

There was a marked difference, very easy to notice, between the people here and those to the North of Khartoum. They were by no means purely negroid but the paler Arab faces were in the minority and the skins more of a deep, rich bronze approximating to copper, which from a visual aspect toned in handsomely with the ruddier shade of the earth. Darker they may have been but not black, for real black is rare, and does, as the Arabs say, verge on deep blue. The brown was richer and warmer and the thin Arab features had given way to broader types, perhaps a little more earthy in appearance, but certainly rather jollier. Also they were less swathed in voluminous robes and a few women were to be seen unmuffled.

### 17.3 El Obeid

The end of our journey, El Obeid, the capital of the Province,[116] fitted in happily to the expectations raised so far. There was an improvement in temperature which was always welcome since the town is 1,800 feet above sea level, as opposed to Khartoum's 1,200 and even this rise made a difference. We stayed in a furnished resthouse[117] which had the luxury of a proper bath. Our own servant looked after us but the hospitality of the British officials[118] was profuse, especially that of the Governor, as we were

116. El Obeid, Kordofan Province, was an old Egyptian garrison town, first reached by railway in 1912 via Gezira and Sennar. 'It was a large town with a very big market and one or two large European shops.'
117. Dr Beasley visited El Obeid on 3-11.3.40 and stayed in the church resthouse.
118. British officials in El Obeid included Governor Ewan Campbell and his wife Evelyn, Deputy Governor and Mrs F.D. Kingdon, C.A.G. Wallis and Mrs Molly Wallis.
   Frank Denys Kingdon, M.C., 4N. (b.4.9.1898-d.1971). Educated Bradfield and Hertford College, Oxford; 13.12.20 First appointment. 1916-17 War Service, London Regiment; 1917-18 R.F.A. 1921-24 White Nile; 1924-28 Bahr el Ghazal; 1924-35 Blue Nile; 1935-44 Kordofan (1938 Deputy Governor); 1944-45 Deputy Governor, Upper Nile; 1945-48 Governor, Upper Nile; 1948 retired; 1949- General Manager, Eton School Stores and Hon. Treasurer, Sudan Diocesan Association.

living at the bottom of his garden.[119]

> The Governor told us interesting tales of the Nuba Mountains, including miracles with aeroplanes and eclipses of the moon.

This was an even more difficult district for gardening than Omdurman but valiant attempts and the use of indigenous plants for hedges, gave a little grace to the patches immediate to the houses.

This is not the place for inspection reports but our visits to the school[120] left me with the same impression of a richer atmosphere and a less restricted way of life.

> The school was impressive. The buildings, though not as palatial as Kosti, were definitely good. There was a very large playground with a number of trees in it and a small vegetable garden which the children had planted ... They showed me round and told me the names of the vegetables [3.3.40].

The Headmistress would probably have been a remarkable girl anywhere, and she also had a well-sounding name—Melk ed-Dar, Queen of the House.[121] She had the coppery skin I had been admiring and was a comely and strongly built person with a keen, clear eye. I saw her once focussing attention on something in a far corner of the yard and was reminded of all the old tales of the far-seeing people of the desert. On this first acquaintance I was delighted with her vigour and the schemes she had devised and the way she had made for herself a position in the town. She was serving on a committee arranged by the D.C.'s wife in connection with war work.[122] It was such hopeful indication compared with the depressing conversations I had had at Bakht-er-Ruda and some of the dispirited women I had seen.

119. Ewan Campbell, M.B.E., M.C., Ufficialato Corona (Order of Crown of Italy), 3N., C.M.G.. (b.13.8.1897-d.1975); Education Edinburgh Academy and Oriel College, Oxford; 1919-21 Oxford University R.F.C. (1921 Captain); 1915-19 R.F.A. (France, Flanders, North Russia); 20.12.21 First appointment; 1922-27 Kassala; 1928-34 Darfur; 1935 Deputy Governor, Kassala; 1935-36 Assistant Civil Secretary; 1936-38 Deputy Civil Secretary; Aug 1938 car accident near Hounslow; 1.11.38-47 Governor of Kordofan, succeeding D. Newbold; Jan 1943 on Advisory Council for the Northern Sudan; 1947 retired; 1948-62 Secretary, South-East Regional Hospital Board, Scotland; 1970-74 Council, British Red Cross Society; member, Queen's Bodyguard for Scotland.
120. In 1917 the inhabitants of El Obeid started a petition for a school, which opened in February 1948, under the supervision of the Headmaster of the boys' school (S.A.D. 657/1/10).
121. Sitt Melk ed-Dar Mohamed (b.1922-d.1969). See Appendix IV for her life history.
122. Sitt Melk ed-Dar Mohamed had been asked by the Deputy Governor's wife, Mrs F.D. Kingdon, to represent her community at a meeting of women of the various communities of the town, including Greeks and Armenians, to co-operate about Red Cross and other war work. 'I think the Governor wanted the committee to bring the various communities together, but it failed to do this' [3.3.40].

Here was something to build on.[123] After the war when we had started some special campaigns, Melk ed-Dar was among the first who was not afraid to go on tour in the villages.[124]

El Obeid had much to offer in addition to professional interests. It was at that time a town of some 27,000 inhabitants and fairly shapely as a place. Like all the country, however, walking there was never easy. I did walk. I have always liked walking and I have memories of plodding through miles of soft sand, tracks of uneven gravel and only once any sort of turf and that was in the Nuba Mountains. Here I walked across a sort of recreation ground with a bandstand in the centre, which might have come from any English seaside resort. As the Western Camel Corps had a station here, it was used at times. Beyond this was a very large *suq* with the usual arrangement of whole streets for different wares. Lying as it did on the edge of the great cattle country, where the nomads wandered with their herds in thousands, it was, of course, an important resort for large and small trading. Red shoes hung in long strings along both sides of one turning; in another each booth was full of camel saddles, while some shops displayed gaily plaited thongs and whips. Dressmaking and sewing of all kinds was a feature in another corner, while some rather dull looking stalls nearby held, nevertheless, all the spices of the East, some of them unknown to British cooks.

More impressive than this petty trading, however, was the enormous animal market outside the town, where hundreds of beasts were exchanged. One picture which has always remained with me is of a girl about nine years old I should think with a pretty, but surly face. She was perched on a high camel, which was somewhat restive but which she was controlling expertly, while she held also the rope of another camel, unwilling to stay still. Camels were roaring noisily too just behind the large *suq* where travellers gathered to set out on the three hundred mile road of sand to Darfur. Strings of beasts were prepared there and stalked off at sunset and, when dusk came, the newer caravans started also, the convoys of two or three great lorries, which made regular journeys from El Obeid to various centres of relative importance.

In contrast as well to the old fashioned animal market was the gum auction,[125] one of the real attractions of the place. It was rigidly controlled

123. 'The faint beginnings of adult education showed in El Obeid ... Women are encouraged to come and meet one another. Some of them are merely wanting to be amused and played with the treadle machine as with a new toy' [3.3.40].
124. See Appendix I.
125. They were taken to the gum auction one morning by the Governor. The gum auction was ' ... complete with up to date weighing machines and comptometers ... A most outstanding example of the British desire for tidiness in idea as well as in detail' [3.3.40].

to avoid the trickery that had been rampant in the past and was one of the quietest auctions that I have ever attended. The buyers sat in rows at tables and everything was done by numbers. I could not discover whether the merchants preferred this bit of tidy administration to more picturesque chaffering. Certainly outside we were back in the old world with lines of camels bringing sacks of raw gum and melon seeds from the wilderness,[126] while nearby stood the sheds, where the gum was cleaned and graded by West African women making a colourful picture with red and yellow handkerchiefs tied round their heads.

This large influx of West African labour congregated in the Fellata village which we went to look at after watching the gum auction. On the edge of the town the mere appearance of the place with its round huts and open spaces between emphasised the divergence between this and the typical Sudanese aspect of El Obeid with high walls around to shelter the dwellings. The difference, of course, was particularly true in the women's sphere, as the Fellata go about untrammelled and are used to hard labour. Most of the villagers were Muslim and many of them had arrived in the Sudan on their long pilrgimage across the Continent, often on foot, hoping eventually to arrive in Mecca. Thus some had stayed for a time, where work could be found and some had settled permanently, forming a sort of colony apart because of a way of living entirely unlike the Sudanese culture and its Arab foundations.

Despite the feeling of greater freedom here [than in central Sudan] the schoolmistresses told me that they would not be allowed to visit the gum market even with their fathers, but they thought it would be quite in order, if the D.C.'s wife[127] would take them, which she promised to do. Although in the women's quarters, they heard much of what went on outside and were eager to see for themselves the life around them, from which they had been debarred. For the purposes of a lesson they might know that Kordofan has most of the country's gum trees but some of them had never seen one.

Since Sudan produces about 80% of the world's supply of gum its value in the economy of the country need not depend on its appearance and

---

126. Little clumps and gardens of gum trees (*hashāb*, Acacia senegal) grow east of the White Nile where rainfall is between 12 and 16 inches p.a.

127. Mrs C.A.G Wallis (Molly) who was wife of Claude Anderson George Wallis, 4N. (b.13.3.1902). Educated Christ's Hospital and Wadham College, Oxford; 6.12.24 First appointment; 1925-27 Education Department; 1927-30 Bahr el Ghazal; 1930-33 Halfa; 1933-34 Berber (P.E.O.); 1935-36 Education Inspector, Northern Province; 1.12.1936-42 Kordofan (D.C. Central District based in El Obeid); 1942-44 Equatoria (D.C. Torit); 1944-45 Assistant Civil Secretary (Departmental); 1945-50 Assistant Civil Secretary (Local Government); 1950 retired; 1950-66 Colonial Office (African Studies Branch) and Local Government Adviser. Author.

indeed it is not a particularly glamorous plant. The little clumps and gardens, however, to be found in the province do make pleasant, shady corners in a land where green shade is often rare.

## 18. Back to Omdurman

This was the last of my escorted treks and after a few days at home[128] I was off on my own, the beginning of ten years constant and varied travel of intense interest, which is somehow difficult to convey. It is not easy to explain how soon I became attached to Omdurman. I said 'at home' for this indeed was what I felt it. However far away I might go during my period of service this was the centre to which I always returned. After living for a short time on borrowed furniture, my colleague[129] and I acquired some pieces of our own and continued in adequate comfort, though by no means extravagantly. Each of us had a personal servant[130] and we shared a cook and part-time gardener. Servants were no unmixed blessing but despite occasional storms and changes we had a fairly smooth background from which to operate. In order to explode the Collector of Boggley Wallah image, which dies hard when people in England think of overseas officials, I may mention that my starting salary was £400 a year. I am not grumbling. It was roughly the market price. We did, however, join a service, once the probationary two years had been successful, with the prospect of a pension and security. There was security also in the work we were trying to do with every prospect of seeing some results from our labour.

### 18.1 Associates

Work, of course, had to be the main consideration that ordered our days but it would be wrong to give the impression that I was so wrapped up in it that there was no time for some lighter diversion when opportunity offered, but these lesser matters such as tennis, sailing, [bridge], dancing, parties and picnics have naturally faded with the years, although at the time they helped to give some balance to the very exacting conditions of our working life. There is no room in this narrative to say much of the British officials, although I made many excellent friends among them, some of whom

128. From 11.3.40. Dr Beasley was in Omdurman where she continued inspections of nearby schools.
129. Miss K. Sylvia L. Clark.
130. Dr Beasley's servant Sayed accompanied her on many treks to the provinces, as did her cook Mahomet (e.g. Kordofan in 1945).

happily I treasure to this day. Compared with the size of the country, they were few in number, scattered over the million square miles and engaged in all kinds of activities, from the Jack of all trades of people like D.C's or agricultural inspectors in remoter stations to fiscal and political experts in the Secretariat. Small commercial communities were also to be found in the few larger towns. They gave me generous hospitality as I travelled round the country and I can think of innumerable instances in which they advised me to everyone's profit from their knowledge of a district and through their contacts with the people there.

## 19. Trip to Rufaa and Hillaleia

On this my first unescorted trek[131] I was fortunate in being asked to stay with the D.C. and his wife[132] while I inspected the two girls' schools in Rufaa[133] and one in Hillaleia. Going to investigate the home of girls' education was an inspiring thought but the contrast between the scenery of this large village on the Blue Nile and that I had recently admired in Kordofan was not uplifting. In March the crops were all finished and the flat, dun-coloured earth, radiating heat, showed only a few remnants of stubble with no trees to add a semblance of grace.

> Country very dull as far as Rufaa. I went through a little of the Gezira before crossing the river and saw evidence of much cotton but it is flat and cheerless [6.4.40].

I came often to stay in this house and could never understand why it had been built in so much more cramped a style than many others, since it was of mud-brick of which there was plenty round about. The remains of previous failures to make a garden had made even more desolate the path

---

131. 6.4.40.
132. Dr Beasley was to encounter C. de Bunsen in many different locations on her inspection tours. Charles de Bunsen, 4N. (b.13.10.05-d.1969). Educated Marlborough and Trinity College, Cambridge; 1926 member of Cambridge University Arctic Expedition. 12.12.28 First appointment; 1929-36 Kordofan (A.D.C. Soderi); 1.12.36-41 Gezira then Blue Nile Province (1939 Medani, 1940 D.C. Rufaa); 1940-41 Governor-General's Temporary Commission as Bimbashi in the S.D.F. (attached Coldstream Guards and Frontier Battalion), S.D.F. Abyssinia; 1941 Major, General List; 1941 reseconded to Staff of Minister of State Middle East; 1.1.1942-44 Kassala (D.C. Sinkat for Beja District); 15.11.44-46 Khartoum (D.C. Khartoum District); 1946-51 Darfur (1946-47 Dar Masalit Resident, based at el-Geneina, 1948 Deputy Governor, based el-Fasher); 1951-52 Deputy Governor, Equatoria; 1952-54 Governor, Khartoum; 1954 retired. 1954- Century Insurance Co.
133. One girls' school in Rufaa was that which had been established by Sheikh Babikr Bedri and the other was at Deims Rufaa.

by which I passed from the little round hut, where I slept, to join the
welcome of family meals.[134]

### 19.1 Tea-parties in Rufaa

Plenty of tea-parties among the women of the village marked my visit.

> Mrs de Bunsen and I went toa tea-party at Rufaa school. The mistresses from
> both schools were there and the important ladies of the town, all beautifully
> dressed [11.4.40].

I was a little disappointed to note that, despite the fact that Sheikh Babikr
Bedri had started the first girls' school here in 1905, the women were in
many ways more restricted than [they] appeared to be in El Obeid.
Conventions bulked large and the idea of schools for 'little ladies' came to
mind. Osman Mahgoub was on leave from Bakht-er-Ruda and I was
summoned outside the school one morning[135] to discuss with him a centre
for these 'better wives and mothers' which was his sincere desire. In no
circumstances would he enter even the schoolyard and we stood outside the
high [school wall] in a dust-laden wind to plan what might be done, and
who would be the best schoolmistresses to undertake such work. He had
exchanged his European clothes for the loose and undoubtedly more
comfortable Sudanese robe and turban and enthusiastic though he was for
the project, he was full of warnings about local opinion, and certainly the
women were not to be allowed to kick up their heels and do anything they
liked. 'Better wives and mothers' was to be held firmly before our eyes. In
fairness to Osman I must acknowledge that he was advanced and
progressive in this matter far beyond most of his generation and his advice
and information was of the greatest use to us all then and later.

---

134. Dr Beasley also met Dr C.B. Drew, a medical doctor, at the de Bunsens' house at lunch on
6.7.40.
   Dr C.B. Drew, M.R.C.S., L.R.C.P., M.B.E., Abyssinian Military Medal. 1928 qualified
from St Thomas' Hospital; 9.9.29 First appointment, Province Medical Inspector, Blue Nile
Province. By 1.1.40 Senior Medical Inspector, based at Abu Usher; 1940 Commissioned in the
R.A.M.C. and rose to rank of Lt-Col; Aug 1940-Nov 1943 Served in Abyssinia during which
time he was in charge of Menelik Hospital in Addis Ababa and was A.D.M.S. British Military
Mission; 1944, 1945 East African Division in Ceylon and Burma; then Assistant Director
Hospitals; 1951-53 Director of Medical Department/Service succeeding Pratt; 1953 retired.
135. On 8.4.40 Osman Mahgoub called to arrange a meeting at Deims Rufaa. Osman would
not enter the schoolyard because of the younger mistresses, whereas Sheikh Lutwi could come
to the school 'because he has a beard and is old'. The headmistress could come to the meeting
but not the younger mistresses.
   Sheikh Lutwi was possibly Sheikh Mohammed Lutfi Abdalla, listed as senior Arabic
Inspector, based in Khartoum, on the 1.1.44 Government list.

The meeting was eventually held on 10.4.40. Although the women appeared to expect me to produce something out of a hat and were overawed by the presence of the two men, Sheikh Lutwi and Osman Mahgoub, they did ask for cooking and sewing lessons, first aid and home nursing. I then went to tea with Sheikh Lutwi ... He has a house in a good position overlooking the river. We were joined by a delightful old *qadi* [10.4.40].

A Women's Dispensary was already in operation in Rufaa and it was suggested that this could be joined up with the movement we wanted to start. It was staffed by a nurse and a superior sort of dispenser and judging from my visit[136] and an inspection of the books it was well patronised.

## 19.2 Hillaleia

Less encouraging was a hot drive[137] through the barren countryside to Hillaleia, where my unannounced visit was not at all welcome to the headmistress.

She had not marked the registers for two days and on this particular day half the school was absent ... it was not a very pleasing school—everything rather grubby ... it is a very real problem to keep the work of rural schools up to standard when it is so difficult to keep in touch with them.

To me the visit emphasised the problem of rural schools, where the staff, feeling themselves cut off from the main stream and not liable to inspection without notice, might very well sink into this type of grubby inefficiency. In one class the children kept crowding so to the end of the bench that any girl there was constantly being pushed off and going to the other end to start again. It reminded me of Bill the Lizard[138] but the poor victims did not regard it as at all funny. This was always a depressing village, although, when I came to know it better, it could offer a great deal of other interest.

Most of the district round about Rufaa belonged to families of a rich and influential tribe, the Abu Sinn.[139] Whether the important man we went to call on belonged to this I do not know but the visit stays in my memory. We drove upstream for some miles, the country just the same and entirely opposed to my romantic notions of the Blue Nile, until we came to a biggish semi-fortified settlement. A large [gate] in a high wall was opened to us and

136. 11.4.40.
137. 11.4.40.
138. Carroll, Lewis, *Alice in Wonderland*, Chapter IV.
139. The tribe in the Gedaref area to which Dr Beasley refers was the Shukriyya. Abu Sinn is the name of the ruling family. Dr Beasley visited the Abu Sinn *hosh* with C. de Bunsen on the first afternoon she arrived in Hillaleia.

we came into a great courtyard all cleanly swept

> ... with one or two trees and shrubs here and there and so attractive in the
> evening light.

It was empty at the time but a small table and chairs were soon set out for
us and *limoon* were brought for our refreshment. Our host and the D.C. had
matters of business to discuss and there was no impoliteness in studying the
layout of the buildings. There was a hint of fortification in the high wall and
the great yard into which a large number of animals could have been driven
[for safety in times of war] but it could not have been necessary for many a
long year. It did, however, serve the useful purpose of keeping out the wind
and there was withal a pleasant lordliness about the scope of it. No
suggestion was made that we should meet the women of the household and
I was too unsure of myself at this stage to bring up such a request.

> Then he took us to his garden a mile or two away near the river, where he
> grows fruit for the market. It was mostly bananas, two miserable papayas, an
> odd fig or two, some good lemons and limoons and one excellent mango. He
> had herbs, a few vegetables and *kerkede*. There were also some tall trees down
> by the river, making a delightful shady walk. We had more *limoon*, tea and
> biscuits and more coffee with the holy man and the local *nazir*.
>
> Went sailing in the afternoon with Legge[140] and the Luces,[141] the D.C. in
> Hassiheissa. There was a brisk wind and it was very good fun [7.4.40]

It was at Rufaa that outside events firmly laid hold on my future. I came
back from school one lunchtime to find two or three Sudanese officials
sitting in the lounge talking to the D.C.,[142] who handed me a telegram in a
mood of exhilaration. I forget his exact words but they were to the effect
that now we could get to grips with them. The Germans had invaded

---

140. M.M. Legge. 12.9.37 First appointment; 1937-44 Master, Rural Studies Bakht-er-Ruda;
By 1946 Master, Wadi Seidna Secondary School; 1947-54 Assistant Headmaster, Wadi Seidna;
By Mar 1955 Headmaster, Agricultural Training School at Yambio (seconded to the Ministry
of Agriculture); 1955 retired.
141. Sir William H.T. Luce (Bill), O.B.E., C.M.G., K.B.E. (b.25.8.1907-d.1977). Educated Clifton
and Christ's College, Cambridge; 7.9.30 First appointment; 1930-34 Berber; 1934-36 Darfur;
1.12.1936-41 Blue Nile Province (1940 A.D.C. Hassiheissa); 1941-47 Private Secretary and
Comptroller to the Governor-General; 1947-48 Imperial Defence College; 1948-50 Civil Secretary's
Office; 1950-51 Deputy Governor, Equatoria; 1951-53 Governor, Blue Nile Province; 1953-56
Adviser to the Governor-General on Constitutional and External Affairs; 1956 retired; 1956-60
Governor, Aden Protectorate; 1961 H.M. Diplomatic Service; 1961-66 Political Resident in Persian
Gulf; 1970-72 Personal Secretary of State's Representative for Persian Gulf, Director for Eastern
Bank, Chartered Bank, Inchcape and Gray Mackenzie; 1968-70 Chairman, Anglo-Arab
Association.
142. C. de Bunsen.

Norway;[143] the phoney war was over. It always seems out of proportion to speak of one's own troubles in relation to the immense horrors of those years but the effects on us as individuals remain. My personal griefs at this time centres mainly on the fact that all leave was cancelled and my plan to spend the summer holidays with my daughter could never come about. It was in fact five years before I saw England and my family again.

I did not therefore share the zeal of the active young D.C.[144] anxious to take part in the struggle and returned home[145] in a very gloomy mood. It was not as a journey trying since I had only to cross the river to catch the train. The ferry was a most remarkable craft built on the lines of a rowing boat but almost as large and heavy as a barge. It was propelled by a pair of enormously rough-hewn oars needing much strength to manage. Delay was caused not so much by the number of passengers, but by the refusal of a couple of camels to tuck themselves tidily into the stern of the boat. Eventually, however, they were persuaded and, although still noisy, made no further objection. We were pushed off some distance upstream from the opposite landing place and the vessel was guided, rather than rowed, with the help of the current to the right spot on the other side.

## 20. Work in the Censor's office

During this period of distress educational matters were rather at a standstill[146] and the general uncertainty of the position was underlined when Italy, sitting on our frontiers, declared war in June.[147] Schools would have been shut anyway for the vacation but this was indefinitely prolonged and I, knowing some French and half a dozen words in Russian, was sent to one of the dreariest jobs imaginable in the Censor's Office. Necessary no doubt but arduous and tedious and, if we did ever catch a spy, we did not hear about it. I cannot, however, imagine any intelligent spy allowing himself to be stranded in the Sudan from which all means of exit were so sparce and difficult.

143. 9.4.40.
144. C. de Bunsen.
145. Dr Beasley returned to Omdurman on 12.4.40. having set off at noon to Hassiheissa. 'It was one of the hottest trips I have ever had to make.'
146. The staff of the Education Department, as in others, was depleted as men joined the War effort. Dr Beasley's leave was stopped; then she stayed a week or two in the Education Department.
147. 10.6.40 Mussolini declared war on France and Britain and his troops invaded Sudan, occupying the Kassala district and Gallabat in July 1940. On 12.8.40 a small British mission crossed the Sudan-Ethiopian frontier to gain the collaboration of the local chiefs in harrassing and ultimately defeating the Italians.

Morning and evening we drove across the White Nile Bridge to the office in Khartoum and, against all the tenets of our upbringing, opened other people's letters and pried diligently into the affairs of business firms, particularly the gum merchants. In a small community such work could be an embarrassment, as we might meet socially someone whose correspondence we had been examining that morning.[148] The evening work was the most wearing, since a black-out had been enforced and, as the sun normally sank about six o'clock, the crowded office had to be closely shuttered. There are few days in a Khartoum summer, when the maximum shade temperature is less than 100°F.,[149] and it frequently varies between that and 112°F. Every degree after 112°F. is a distinct and noticeable burden.

Two of us went back one night in July[150] after an exhausting session and drove out to Jebel Kerriri[151] to try to find some relief in open country. We had eaten quite well at a small Greek restaurant, for rationing had not been introduced and in a cattle country like this we were never short of meat. But normally meals were served out of doors or in this place on the roof. A stuffy room lit only by a candle had been no improvement on the office. Kerriri is the spot where the famous Battle of Omdurman[152] really took place, which features dramatically in the stories of the lives of Kitchener[153] and Winston Churchill.[154] We climbed a short way up the stony hill and sat down to look over the desolate expanse of gravel waste, where the Khalifa had met his final defeat.[155] There was little moon and the air was hazy with the dust hanging in it.

From the town not far away came no sound nor glimmer of light.

---

148. 'During my time in the Censor's office I read a lot of missionaries' letters ... and I was coming to the rather cynical conclusion that, however great might have been their enthusiasm in the beginning, they were settling down to a quiet and placid country existence and ... sustaining sense of doing their duty' (S.A.D. 657/6/24). 'The work was certainly not educational.'
149. Mean daily temperature reaches 34.1°C (93.4°F) in June.
150. July 1940.
151. Jabal Surkab in the area known as Karari, 6 miles north of Omdurman, on the left bank of the Nile.
152. 2.9.1898.
153. Sir Herbert Kitchener had 22,000 men against the Dervish army of 45,000. Possibly 11,000 Sudanese were killed and 16,000 wounded. The Anglo-Egyptian losses were 49 killed and 382 wounded.
154. Churchill, Winston, *The River War, an account of the Reconquest of the Soudan*, London, 1899, pp.269-300.
155. The battle marked the end of the Mahdist state in Sudan though the Khalifa managed to survive for a further year before he and his close colleagues were killed in the Battle of Umm Diwaykarat on 24.11.1899.

All around was just the rough surface of piles of stones building up to the height of a considerable hill. It looked like the old imaginary pictures of the moon and we felt as cut off from England and the world we belonged to, as if we were indeed on there. From out of the East planes might come at any moment to rip open the sleeping scene with the evil crash and flare of gunfire but fortunately we were always spared that particular horror.[156] What has remained with me for ever from that night is the lonely and bleak hopelessness of it all,[157] that the setting seemed to symbolise.

156. It was not until November 1942, with Montgomery's victory at El Alamein, that the prospect of a German occupation of the Nile Valley was destroyed.
157. At the beginning of September 1940, Dr Beasley asked to be sent back to the Department of Education. Owing to Miss Harvey's non-arrival from leave, Dr Beasley helped to run the Training College from 11.9.40, and continued school inspections in Omdurman. Like many of her colleagues at the time of increased pressures of war, Dr Beasley felt despair about the possibility that they might never get home [8.10.40].

# Chapter II

# The Nile in the North

## Trips North, 1940

That long, melancholy summer of 1940 did draw to a close. News from home was black and our own position appeared extremely precarious with the Italians over the frontier at Kassala and only a few hours away. Yet, despite all the tragedies in Europe, Hitler had not finally triumphed, whilst the tip and run campaign of bluff played by the local police and D.C.s supplementing the Defence Corps seemed to bewilder the Italians.[1] Our despair at this period, however, began in me a sort of Rider Haggard imagining.[2]

### 1.1 Reflections at Shambat

At Shambat, just across the river, was the School of Agriculture.[3]

> It is an attractive building which manages to be dignified without being pretentious. It strikes one as very luxurious after most of the educational buildings here ... admirably adapted for working in, in that it gives scope and space and comfort without excessive grandeur [16.2.40].

We reached it by a noisy steam ferry that chugged from Omdurman to meet the last descendant of the Puffing Billies, which drew an open string of coaches to Khartoum North. That the estate was rich, green pasture would be an exaggeration but there was the sight and smell of crops growing and the gardens had trim lawns and huge clusters of sweet-scented jasmine.

---

1. With 1,200 miles of frontier and only 2,500 British and 4,500 (later expanded to 9,000) S.D.F. troops, with few planes and little armaments, against the Italian forces of 250,000 men and over 200 aircraft. The fear was that they would move against Khartoum, Atbara and Port Sudan. Imaginative ways were used by the British to deceive the Italians, including nocturnal troop movements near the Front. (Woodward, Peter, *Sudan 1898-1989: The Unstable State*, 1990, pp.59-61).
2. Sir Henry Rider Haggard (b.1856-d.1925) wrote 34 adventure novels, most notable being *King Solomon's Mines* (1886) and *She* (1887), set in Africa, which 'vividly conveyed the fascination he found in its landscape, wild-life, tribal society, and mysterious past' (Drabble, Margaret (ed.), The Oxford Companion to English Literature, 1985, p.426).
3. Dr Beasley 'attended the quiet opening' on 16.2.40.

There was also a hedge round the [tennis] court which added to the flavour of 'tea and tennis at the vicarage'. I remember one wretched afternoon, when I had a vision of explorers in the future trying to track down the legends of a remote, white tribe lost in the deserts, who continued a strange ritual of tossing spherical objects over plaited string.

### 1.2 Return to the Education Department

Even these moods of dejection, however, found respite eventually, for by September [1940] Indian Regiments[4] were arriving to reinforce the local efforts and the general feeling was that as much normality as possible should be encouraged. I asked therefore if I might return to education and was soon back in the work which I had come out to do and finding life that much more satisfying. After this I was probably out on trek for more of the time than I was in Omdurman, and thus had the privilege, which I shall always cherish, of sampling the aspects of all the provinces and making friends in all communities. So rich and varied were these experiences that, although the thread of my particular work strings them together, I could never manage to set down adequately the quality and depth of this kind of service. Much of it remains with me as a vast store of visual impressions, which are meaningful to me, but which might be to others no more than a stranger's collection of colour slides. The significance behind them all, of course, was the schools and even a dreary-looking village gained my affection, if there was a keen and willing attitude to girls' education.

## 2. Dongola Reach

Yet the worst schools could not destroy the strange and austere fascination of many parts of this vast country. My first trip, for example, after returning to the Department, was northwards to the Dongola Reach.[5] Since the heightening of the Aswan Dam is planned to drown this stretch, my good fortune is unbounded that I had the opportunity to visit that isolated bend of the river, with its groups of date palms beside pleasing tawny pinkwashed villages. Pink is perhaps a slightly misleading word, as the local earth which colours the wash verges on a tawny shade, but the general effect is uncommonly misleading. In the great flood of 1946 these were mostly

4. British, Indian and Sudanese troops under General Platt took part in the decisive battle at Keren on 15.3.41, which essentially ended the danger on the Sudanese-Ethiopian border.
5. Dr Beasley's trip to the Dongola Reach was from 15.10.40.

destroyed and replaced by much superior buildings;[6] now, I presume they are to disappear below the waters for ever.

## 2.1 Inspection at Berber

I did not start on the reach but went to inspect the school at Berber,[7] which was always for me the beginning of outside work. Even in those few months it had made much progress[8] and owed a great deal to the continued enthusiasm of the local officials.

> The school is promising. The faults, I fear, are due to faulty training. The teachers are keen and careful and showed a surprising amount of energy for Ramadan. The school building is rather a joy after some of the others and was beautifully clean ... I thought at first that the discipline was exemplary but after the children got used to me they became perfectly natural.
>
> Nafissa, although the junior, is probably better at this [discipline] than her sister [Haram]. She does not allow the pernicious Training College habit of answering all together. The amount of actual work achieved is interesting ... Nafissa took a rather dull reading lesson and did rather too much for the children ... In arithmetic the work was careful and the results seemed adequate. The books were very neat and clean. The difficulty here again is the labour imposed on the teacher in making up enough examples for each lesson ... The needlework is really quite good for little girls but as usual there is too much attention to embroidery and neglect of plain sewing. Some of the older girls ... have made frocks which are quite creditable. The designs were good and symmetric. The drawing, as usual, is terrible [10.10.40].

The D.C.[9] and the Sudanese Sub-Inspector[10] came to see me in the school,[11] and I had the impression that I in my turn was being inspected, which for the newcomer I was seemed fair enough.

> I also saw Nafissa take a nature study lesson on a cat. This was the usual stuff but as I persuaded her to obtain a real cat it didn't seem quite so deadly ...

6. In August 1946 Dr Beasley returned from leave and went through the biggest Nile flood for a century. 'Below Wadi Halfa there was again an enormous amount of water and practically the whole of Debeira village destroyed. In Wadi Halfa itself the people were building a very strong earth-work as the level of the water was higher than that of the streets. Everyone joined in and the day we were there was the peak and they managed to keep the water out ... After Atbara we had to make a detour which took four days instead of one night'.
   In 1946 some exceptional damage was done to monuments at Jebel Barkal and Meroe by this flood (*ARDE*, 1946, Antiquities Service).
7. The date of this visit was 9.10.40-12.10.40. Dr Beasley first visited Berber from 10.1.40-12.1.40.
8. Berber girls' school attendance IA 38/42 IB 36/40 in October 1940.
9. J.G.S. Macphail.
10. Sub-Inspector Daoud el Khalifa Abdulla.
11. 12.10.1940.

Haram's arithmetic is not bad but ... the tendency to avoid the issue and deal with tens and units by a cunning process of never having to carry or borrow seems rather widespread ... I must find some better method of teaching reading than this constant hurried repetition of the same lesson ... Haram was a little too lady-like and was somewhat too shy to give a good drill lesson ... I feel the children definitely profit from coming to school [12.10.40].

The weather was overwhelmingly hot and sticky.[12] I had the comfort of an empty house, once used by a British official, but, as in all but about six main towns, there was no electricity and no fans. I put in my journal the record of an unsuccessful experiment. I was lying in a bath of perspiration during the afternoon with all the shutters closed, and I wondered if movement of any sort might cause enough disturbance of the air for this to act as a slight current on my damp skin. I started walking rapidly about the rooms to create a draught but the result was more exhausting than lying still. By four o'clock the tension always eased a bit and I could put on some clothes and sit outside in the fresh air as it gradually became cooler. On this afternoon a graceful little *dik- dik* wandered in through the open gate and up the path towards me looking just like a Tenniel[13] drawing from 'Alice'. Unfortunately it behaved in exactly the same way, when I spoke to it, bounding off across the garden and down to the river.

## 2.2 Dongola Reach

After this[14] came a day's journey north to Abu Hamed and then south west across the desert round the loop of the river to Kareima. The train which ran on this track was but a poor relation of the grander types on the main routes with their sleepers and dining cars. This morning too there was a struggle against a sandstorm, which not only slowed down our speed but sometimes made visibility so low that the driver stopped to make sure he would not be running into a drift. The steamer to Dongola connected with this train and waited for us at the terminal, when we were free of the cramped dusty compartments and could sit happily on a deck, however small, and feel the gentle rocking of flowing water instead of the jerks and jolts over a difficult permanent way.

Quarters in the first class were not spacious but there were only two other passengers, both officials, one Englishman and one Sudanese. Aft

12. 'I was not bored, merely dissolving with heat, a concentration which leaves no thought for boredom.' The house was probably that previously used by J.G.S. Macphail who had moved his base to Atbara.
13. Sir John Tenniel (b.1820-d.1914), illustrator, noted for his illustrations for *Through the Looking Glass*, 1871 and *Alice's Adventures in Wonderland*, 1895 by Lewis Carroll.
14. The train was also half a day late on 13.10.40 after Dr Beasley's stay in Berber.

there was much cargo and a number of passengers travelling second class, while the barges, attached to hold the ship steady, were thronged with people and bundles. Journeys of this kind provide a never failing source of interest in watching the comings and goings at the village halts. The markets surprised me, as one could hardly dignify them by that name. Vegetables, for example, were unprocurable [except for carrots from Merowe] and we had to be content with a few grapefruit. Looking at the way in which the wares were set out, I began to realise that perhaps the cliché about living on a handful of dried dates in the desert was no mere fiction.

There were plenty of trees in parts and healthy-looking cultivation on each bank of the river, which at certain times of the day produced a strip effect of startling and unusual beauty. In the centre the river reflected the light, appearing intensely blue; the young crops bordering it were a vivid green; and a sharp edge of golden sand closed them in, with the bright yellow stretching away to the horizon under the clearness of a pearly sky. At night the change was to an equal precision. The moon was full and one evening, when we tied up on the right bank, the effect was of a black-and-white definiteness in which the shadows showed lines of almost geometric acuteness. Because of wartime regulations no lights could be allowed but they were in fact hardly needed. Men in white robes clattered noisily over the planks and then squatted in groups against the dark trunks of the date palms. Moonlight flooded down through the spaces and was turned on to the steamer in an almost theatrical effect. Here and there the brilliance lay on the dark water under a cloudless sky suffused with a radiance that belonged to this superb contrast of black and white.

## 2.3 Dongola

Dongola, as my port of disembarkation,[15] was a fitting terminus for such a refreshing voyage. Scenically it was a very attractive town set on a lovely curve of the river among a wide belt of cultivation. Everywhere the streets were lined with avenues of large trees, and little channels of water ran alongside them. My quarters were arranged at Dongola Palace, which I mention with some pride, as the first time I have occupied a Palace by myself. The building lived up to its name. I do not know its date but it might well have gone back to Turkish times.[16] It was vast. The ground floor

15. Dr Beasley arrived in Dongola on 16.10.1940.
16. In 1811 the Mamlūks escaped from the control of Muḥammad ‘Alī in Egypt and established the petty state of Dongola (al-‘Urḍī), a dependency of the Shayqiyya confederation. This was defeated by the Egyptians in July 1820 and this marked the beginning of the Turko-Egyptian régime in Sudan. Dongola was Kitchener's base in September 1884. Under ‘Abd al-Raḥmān al-Nujūmī, the Khalifa's expeditionary force remained in its advance base at Dongola

was entirely given over to stores and a certain number of bats, who gave me no trouble. Upstairs some rooms were kept as a residence for the D.C. but at this time the appointment was vacant. Visitors like myself had the rest. I have seen village halls in England smaller than my bedroom but the effect of my scanty furnishings in one corner hardly mattered, as I lived on the enormous verandah which ran right round the building. Somebody had praised the place once as having the flavour of friendly ghosts. So many houses in the Sudan were too new and utilitarian to have acquired the patina of other people's living. This was indeed true and I wondered, although I could find no reference in *The River War*,[17] if Winston Churchill had stalked about this verandah. Certainly the atmosphere was most welcoming and, even when the servants disappeared for the night, I could settle down comfortably in my splendour.

Next morning early I explored a large garden full of healthy citrus trees and bananas with a sprawling, unkempt vine. The schoolmistresses came one [Saturday] afternoon to wander in it, but as it was Ramadan, I was not allowed to arrange a tea party and felt rather inhospitable in consequence. They were delighted with it all, as they had never seen it before, and could not come without my chaperonage. They did, however, have some friends in the town and did not appear to be quite so isolated as the teachers in Berber. For my part strolling about the garden was a real joy, or sitting on the *mastaba* by the river bank and listening to the melancholy but not entirely mournful creak of the *sagia*s.[18] By this time the North wind had reached us and after the oppressive summer the air had a tonic quality. The temperature was probably never above 90°F[19] and the sun was brilliant without being overwhelming.

My enthusiasm for the place was moderated by a school of unequal merit[20] and a first superficial impression of rather gipsy-like children in dingy red shawls, instead of the white muslin *tarha*s customary in Omdurman. After the Friday holiday, there was a general improvement in cleanliness and on the whole the prospect was not unhopeful. The mother, of one of the girls came to see me to discuss her daughter's future, arriving with her face uncovered and certainly none of the 'little lady' ideas, which I

from November 1886 to May 1889. Dongola was handed over by the Mahdists on 23.9.1896, at the end of the Dongola Campaign.
17. Churchill, Winston, *The River War*, 1899.
18. *Sāqiya* (Ar.), from word meaning to irrigate, the Persian water-wheel.
19. 90°F (30°C). 'I felt that if the weather were always like this, it would be a remarkably good spot to vegetate in for a bit.'
20. Dongola girls' school attendance figures in October 1940 were Kindergarten 26 present of 30, Class I 21 present of 40, Class II 15 present of 23, Class III 5 present of 7, Class IV 9 present of 14 in register.

feared elsewhere. I gathered that she sold vegetables in the market and this was my first contact with the realisation of some of the women, that education might have something to offer girls as a secure livelihood. The 'better wives and mothers' theme was never mentioned.

> Poverty need not make the children dull but it might account for their rather dirty and bedraggled appearance ... The school is not so good. I feel it has all the background of town slums. There is an entirely different atmosphere from the school in Berber. The rather flashy clothes of the mistresses suggest the glittering allurements of a town ... I think that they probably work quite hard but their standards are low ... The idea of establishing a kindergarten was a good idea. I suggested that it should be put into a larger room, where Sitt Afifa would have more scope for kindergarden methods, rather than have the children crowded together on benches all the time.
>
> Class I (Sitt Fatma). I thought her first lesson was religion and did not therefore interrupt, thinking she was keeping the Arabic till later. The third lesson was really religion and was exactly the same as the first. The arithmetic consisted of two miserable problems, the numbers lost in a deluge of Arabic. Class III and IV cooking good. Needlework here and in class II indescribably dirty. Zenab has neither the skill nor the patience to let the children learn for themselves. Drill in III and IV taught by Afifa was definitely good ... also true of drawing which Afifa took in III and IV ... Afifa a tribute to Joan Pellow's[21] enterprise [20.10.40].

## 2.4 Tangassi Island

My next call was to be at Tangassi Island and the rather tricky time-tables on this route were avoided by the fortunate arrival of an Agricultural Inspector in a Province steamer. It was smaller than the ordinary mail boat but had generous accommodation for two people.[22] Dealing with the paperwork of administration in these conditions was a luxury, deepened by the colourful views that I could gaze on, whenever I looked up from writing reports.

## 2.5 Khanduq

As the *rais* did not wish to continue until the moon was up, we stopped at dusk at Khanduq[23] and went on shore to examine the place. It was a small, straggly village superimposed on the countryside long ago and once used as

---

21. Miss P. Joan Pellow. 21.10.39 First appointment, teacher at the Girls' Training College, Omdurman until 1942/43.
22. 21.10.40.
23. Khanduq [al-Khandaq] is about 40 miles from Dongola.

a fortification. All this had decayed, leaving a dead impression made more eerie by the complete blackness. An occasional shrouded figure slinking close to the high walls, which bounded the narrow streets, added to the macabre presentation, while the heavy silence was broken only by a sudden voice or the cry of a child. From the dark mosque at the top of the rise came the monotonous sound of small boys chanting the Koran loudly and, although I knew this to be religious education, it did nothing to detract from the sinister feeling of all the evil that might be hidden behind the closed doors. Down on the landing stage was an additional picture in the shed, for the *rais* had to discuss business with the local official by the very dim light of a shaded lantern. There was, of course, nothing underhand about this; it was just the last in a series of visual impressions. As far as I know the villagers of Khanduq were citizens of the same calibre as most people. It was all part of the rather theatrical effect of this part of the river. Even after we set sail I remember staying very late watching from the rail the strange fascination of this empty landscape under a gibbous moon.

Our call the next evening was a complete contrast. We tied up early at an open cultivated island where we wandered among pleasant cool green fields of tall *dura* and inspected plump and glossy cattle. Down on the river bank a few small boys had made a fire and were boiling a pan of water for a picnic of some sort.

## 2.6 Tangassi Island

My destination, although a larger island,[24] looked much less promising, when I arrived in the middle of a hot morning with much dust blowing about. Arrangements appeared to have been strangely muddled but were eventually sorted out by the kindness of the local schoolmaster, who allowed me to use an empty room attached to the corner of his house. It had the disadvantage of sticking out into the village street and having only one window and that with a wooden shutter. If I closed this I could not see, and if I opened it, all the schoolboys very understandably found my various activities of absorbing interest. For the two or three days that I was here dust seemed to be blowing the whole time, but not in sand-storm proportions.

It is easy enough to say sympathetically that one realises how difficult it must be to struggle against dirt but one afternoon when I returned from a walk along the shore, I knew what D.H. Lawrence meant about [complete] believing through the solar plexus. I was sticky with sweat mixed with a

24. Dr Beasley arrived at Tangassi Island on 22.10.40. The next day the Province launch came to take her to the mainland.

light grime and everything in the room was covered with this thin coating of dust. According to the routine a walk was immediately followed by a bath or sponge-down, as the facilities dictated, and clean clothes. This evening I sat down on my folding chair and looked round the dark, dusty room with its earth floor and thought, 'What is the point? I shall be just as mucky in half an hour.' And this temptation was only on one day for me, whereas for the women of Tangassi Island and many other places it was every day. For the record I may add that habit and upbringing prevailed and the temptation did not occur again but the memory remained as a moment of deep revelation.

I had been warned that the place would be difficult. The *omdah* drank heavily; the school was in bad shape and the children wild. As to the *omdah* I cannot pass judgement. Contrary to the usual cordial welcome there was no call from him and at a brief meeting, almost accidental, we exchanged only a few words. Certainly the school needed some re-organising but the teachers were only too ready to take advice and some of the work was most commendable. Still under the influence of my previous evening's insight I wondered how they had managed to accomplish as much as they had in these demoralising conditions.[25] The children were most rewarding and there was always a very strong bond between schoolmistresses and the pupils. The girls were by no means so unapproachable as I had been led to believe.[26] It was not good manners anywhere for girls to take the initiative but these were at once friendly and responsive, when a conversation was started and there was the usual mixture of bright and dull.

> The school was not as bad as I expected but it was by no means good ... The real reason for the appearance of inefficiency lay mostly in the bad arrangement of the school ... the younger class was larger than the other two classes put together. The first year was divided into A and B ... each mistress tried to teach the same subject to two classes at the same time. Instead of handiwork in one and arithmetic in the other, they tried to do arithmetic in both. This might account for the neglecting of IB ... IB was not taught so often as A ... Nevertheless the method of letting children learn by themselves is not a fruitless one ... Sitt Saddia Adam is by no means a bad teacher and she wrestled manfully with the two classes ... the children were sufficiently interested to work together in IA when the headmistress was dealing with IB.
>
> Pleased also to note at least one sum involving carrying, which the children coped with without effort ... A tremendous amount of work on slates ... the

---

25. Tangassi Island school had 70 pupils, 2 teachers in 1938. In 1946 there were 102 pupils, 2 teachers. In 1948 Tangassi school re-opened after being shifted to Debba by the Flood Relief Fund, after flood damage in 1946.
26. Miss L.Y. Pode said that at this school the girls 'were wild—suggesting something rather farouche'.

paper shortage may make this valuable later ... reading good, also dictation. Quite advanced in comparison with Dongola, for example. But composition not good. I think they were writing from memory something written before. I do not think I was supposed to notice this ... A good, well-kept building ... A lovely kitchen but I saw no cooking. The headmistress said II and III were doing cleaning just now ... suggest there should be more cleaning. Admitting all the difficulties of the place, the children were unnecessarily dirty ... possible the headmistress feels cut off here and possible also Tangassi regarded as a bad school to be sent to. Lack of contact with other schools and mistresses must be a definite set-back [22.10.40].[27]

## 2.7 Mansurkoti by lorry

All the same I had no regrets, as at Dongola, when the launch arrived, and I watched my servant packing all my goods for the next stage by lorry through Debba[28] and Gushabi.[29] I was grateful to the schoolmaster for his hospitality in an emergency and could appreciate how valuable was this slow type of inspection in obtaining in some measure the feel of the countryside.

Like all roads in the Sudan the road was a rough track but it crossed slightly undulating country and allowed for some very fine views across great stretches of yellow desert to the broad strip of green by the river, sometimes even a glimpse of the water and then pink, rocky but small hills on the other side. Interesting though it was, it was a tiring form of travel compared with the steamers, and it was a relief in the evening to have reached Mansurkoti. Here I was almost startled by the look of the house, as we drove up. It was a large, one-storey, building, well-proportioned and made of reddish brick and situated in the middle of an excellent garden. Inside, a large lounge with a great fireplace needed little but a couple of spaniels on the hearth and a tea trolley to have been found in the Home Counties. The place had in fact been the home of Colonel Jackson,[30] where he lived for twenty years hoping to retire here after his service with the

---

27. Tangassi Island girls' school attendance figures in October 1940 were Class IB 18 present of 22, Class IA 17 present of 21, Class II 9 present of 13, Class III 6 present of 7 on register.
28. Debba is an important trading point with the Kababish, who bring salt from the desert and the starting point of a caravan route to El Obeid.
29. Dr Beasley went to Mansurkoti on 23.10.40.
30. Ernest Somerville Jackson Bey. (b.1872-d.1943). British lieutenant- colonel, and mīrālai in Egyptian Army; 1892 commissioned to the Welch Regiment; 1898-1914 served in the Egyptian Army; 1899 took part in closing operations against the Khalīfa 'Abd Allāhi and spent most of remainder of service in the Sudan; after fighting in the First World War, he returned to the Sudan where he farmed at Mansurkotti. See Hill, R. *Biog. Dict.*, 1967, p.188.

administration in the early years. He was driven away by the tiniest of menaces, a peculiar type of *nimitti*.[31]

This was a blood-sucking insect which appeared in swarms, when the delightful, weather in these parts was at its best. The local description, and I do not vouch for its scientific reliability, was that this plague had not always been an annoyance but that during the thirties at any rate it recurred most years and that it tended to be unpredictable except within certain broad limits of time and place. Its origin had not been traced but the Government entomologist[32] had started research on the problem and this was intensified after the war. When I was there [in October] it was too early for the insects to have arrived, but when they did, it was impossible for people to be out of doors during the day unless all the skin was completely veiled. Weakly infants and poultry had been known to die from the biting and irritation and for everyone it was an infuriating and debilitating struggle. When I woke at sunrise on the roof of this pleasant house and looked out over the expanse of trees, I could only feel how grievous to be distressed by something so minute and so unaccountable.

I lingered in the garden, while the lorry was prepared and the manager, a capable Sudanese agent of one of the important holy men, Sayed Ali Mirghani,[33] talked very sensibly about practical education. He was not in favour of too much bookishness. Judging by the acres of well-tended date palms, citrus and mango trees he must in his own case have been very skilled in applying his practical knowledge. I was told elsewhere that in addition to being so pleasant a house and garden, the fruit market was a very profitable business.

31. probably Simulium griseicollis, a small and troublesome fly (though this may be the Khartoum *nimitti* and not the Dongola biting *nimitti*). These insects attack when the cool winter weather is at its best. 'They swarmed round people's heads and got in their eyes, ears and noses.'

32. Lewis, D.J., 'The Simuliidae of the Anglo-Egyptian Sudan', *Trans. Royal Ent. Soc.*, London, Vol 99, 1948.

33. Sayyid Sir 'Alī al-Mirghanī, K.C.M.G., K.C.V.O. (b.1879-d.1968); hereditary leader of the *Mirghaniyya* or *Khatmiyya ṭarīqa* (religious brotherhood) who are followers of his ancestor, the orthodox leader, Sayyid Muḥammad 'Uthmān al-Mirghanī (b.1793-d.1853) from Arabia. 'Alī's sphere of influence was Kordofan, Khartoum, Berber, Dongola and Halfa. 1916 he was regarded as the 'Senior notable' of the Sudan; 1919 leader of delegation to London; April 1922 headed a delegation of 40 notables when Lord Allenby visited Khartoum; Until early 1940s a firm (but often critical) supporter of the Government; later, following the apparent support by the British of S.A.R., he made an alliance with Egypt and the 'pro-Egyptian' Sudanese parties. His supporters formed the N.U.P. and he favoured close ties with Egypt (See Daly, Martin, *Empire on the Nile*, C.U.P., 1986, pp.394-395).

PLATE 1

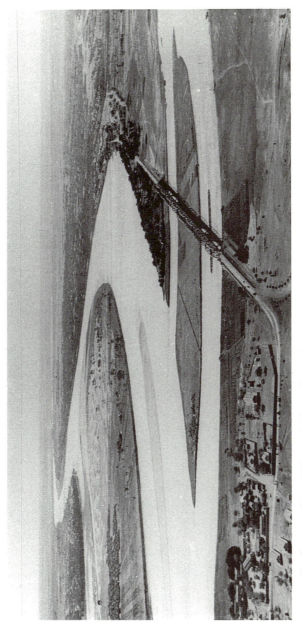

Confluence of the White and Blue Niles, Khartoum, 1930s. J.F.E. Bloss collection, S.A.D. 705/3/2.

PLATE 2

The Nile near Abu Hamed, in drought conditions, 1984. Taken by J.C.M. Starkey.

PLATE 3

Girls going to school in Omdurman. The Mahdi's tomb in the rear, 1940s. I.M. Beasley collection.

PLATE 4

A Fur woman hoeing her cultivation on Jebel Marra, with her baby asleep on her back, 1940s. Taken by E.H. Nightingale, from I.M. Beasley's collection.

## 2.8 Merowe

There were no schools in the villages we passed, although in subsequent years they were started in most of them. The high point of my visit was at Merowe, opposite the quay from which the mail boats started for Dongola.[34] Here I was lodged in a small rest house near the river built on the Sudanese model and thus with a wall keeping out any view but it was easy to stroll along the shore and to follow a tree-lined path to the school. Rest houses had no set plan and I noted with satisfaction that this one was not only fully furnished but provided several shelves of books.

My morning walk to school was to another English-style house set in extensive grounds. In this case it had been the property of General Jackson Pasha, one of the first Governors in the Province,[35] [from] 1902 [to] 1922,[36] who, as it happened, was no relation to his namesake at Mansurkoti. He had built this large, white house with a wide verandah in a particularly attractive setting, on a slight rise near the river and surrounded with lawns and shady trees. Here he had retired, fortunately too far south to be plagued by the *nimitti*. The house had been left as a legacy for a girls' school and this far-sightedness had produced excellent results.

Resisting the urge to dilate on the influences of environment, I must mention that it was the cleanest and most energetic school I had yet visited.

> Arithmetic in III and IV seemed able. The children, after a brief discussion, were left to do the sum by themselves and they did seem to know the four rules and be able to apply them. Fatma says they have done all that is set down in the syllabus but I am a little doubtful of this. Nafissa was taking arithmetic in II. A very good teacher, painstaking and thorough. Easier for these people who have to deal with small classes.

The children were even lively enough to be giving disciplinary troubles to the old *sheikh* who taught religion and Arabic.

> Arabic in IB (as taught by Sitt Shama) was careful but very slow. I think they should know more than their letters. A difficult class at many different levels ... He [the *sheikh*] is very old-fashioned and pleased with too little. Might be

34. Dr Beasley arrived Thursday 24.10.1940 and inspected school 26-30.10.1940.
35. Dongola Province.
36. El-Lewa Brig-Gen Sir Herbert William Jackson (Bey), C.B., 2N., 2M., 4O., K.B.E. (b.5.2.1861-d.28.1.1931); Educated at Rugby and Sandhurst, also France and Germany; 1899 Seconded from Egyptian Army to Sudan Government; 7.2.1899 First appointment, Commandant Fashoda, appointed by Kitchener; 1899 Province Governor, Berber; 1900-01 Civil Secretary to Governor-General (Wingate) and Deputy Governor-General; 1902 Governor, Berber; 1902-22 Governor, Dongola Province, based in Merowe; 1922-23 Inspector-General, acting Governor-General in Stack's absence; 28.1.31 Died Merowe. No relation to his namesake at Mansurkoti.

> better to keep him to the higher forms except that he is so deadly dull. A nice old man but discipline atrocious ... I wonder if his superior Arabic is useful. Certainly most of the school read well—which is not true of all the schools I have seen ... he just makes them read the same piece over and over again.

He had been dumped here, I suspected, because he could not control boys, for I had never before seen any difficulty with order in the classroom, the girls in general being too docile. Everything looked much more businesslike too, since *tarha*s were removed om arrival and the mistresses taught without their *tobe*s. They may have lacked the grace of the falling draperies but there was no bother about constantly hitching up long yards of muslin in going about the ordinary affairs of the classroom. Over the years this sensible practice gradually spread.

The headmistress[37] made a sudden and memorable impression. Although still comparatively young she was enormous both in height and girth and this was made more apparent by the lack of a concealing *tobe*, but her vigour matched her size. Her pride in her school too was unbounded and her feeling of involvement in the work never diminished.

> One of the best schools I have seen ... Eagerness sometimes apt to lead to noisiness but with mistresses class never out of hand. Nafissa without effort kept IB perfectly orderly. More inclined than many schools to let children work on their own without neglecting them. The whole place deserves much praise [26.10.40-30.10.40].

Some years later, when Fatma was transferred to a school in Atbara, she came into my office one day and burst into tears. I was sure that some heart-breaking family tragedy had occurred. When at last she could speak, the sad story was sobbed out. 'My new school! My beautiful new school! They promised I should have it in September and it isn't built yet.' Explanation about builders' customary dilatoriness re-assured her a little but could not completely overcome her disappointment. When finally the school was finished, her delight was channelled into making it, as far as she could, a model of its kind.

Those days lay ahead, however, but here in Merowe she stood out as one of the women who would go further than being just a 'better wife and mother', although from all the signs she would help her pupils that way. It was a stock lesson which she put on for a demonstration but her competence in showing how to bath a baby was notable. What was more, some trusting mother had lent a real baby for the occasion.

As in Dongola, Ramadan restricted sociability to mere calls but what with the satisfaction from the school, the cooler air and the general

---

37. Fatma Mahmoud. 1940 headmistress at Merowe; 1945 Berber, later in Atbara.

surroundings, Merowe was a pleasant place in which to linger. School had to continue despite the fast and the great majority of the pupils were too young to take part. It was interesting to notice that the two or three at the top, who had reached the appropriate age, regarded it as a sort of promotion. At the break in the middle of the morning, when everyone rushed to the great waterpots, they would stand by with a certain amount of ostentation watching the little ones gulping down their drinks. Being grown up [they] could evidently withstand even the hardship of thirst in a hot climate. For the benefit of the mistresses the morning sessions were shortened but some chose to come back in the afternoon for needlework and embroidery. Having something to do, they said, took their minds off the desire for food and drink.

How long Ramadan will survive in the modern world as a discipline in its original design can only be a matter of conjecture. Fasting no doubt is a very salutary exercise but, judging by the effect on the girls, we thought that the feeding at night to make up for the day's abstention tended to upset their digestion unduly. Unexpected problems also needed decision. Was an injection to be considered an intake of fluid? How ill did a girl have to be before she would allow herself to claim exemption? Few, if any, of the schoolmistresses ever went to the extreme length of refusing to swallow their saliva, a practice which was adopted by men claiming strict religious principles, but which appeared to this infidel exhibitionist as well as unhygienic.

No doubt by now all the picturesque details of these rites have been scientifically decided but it must have been an anxious time, when men really did wait for the first glimpse of the new moon to know that Ramadan was ended. In theory, I believe, this still holds good but whether or not modern calendars are used it is a moment of rejoicing, when the word comes that life can take on its ordinary rhythms. This glad event had occurred on my last night in Merowe and the general gaiety the next day was really infectious.

I was sorry to leave. It was one of a number of places in the Sudan— Dongola was another, but not Tangassi Island—where I never felt lonely, even although I was spending the evenings on my own. But I left it in the splendour of a glorious sunny morning with a fresh breeze driving across the river the tall masted boat in which I was sailing. On the right bank was a great party going on with a large concourse of men sitting in circles. Nearby was a much smaller group of women, mostly arrayed in bright dresses of a style I was to see more often further downstream. One or two sheep were tethered close to the crowd, waiting for the ritual slaughter which would precede the feast.

## 2.9 Trip to Jebel Barkal

For my part I had a little expedition planned for my holiday,[38] the kind of
tourist ploy I always delight in. Jebel Barkal[39] can boast a pyramid whose
date is estimated as belonging to the nineteenth dynasty.[40] It was not as
large as those at Gizeh,[41] which I had visited on my way through Cairo, but
it had all the added attractions of its situation in this empty land, far away
from the meretricious trappings of a greedy city. The few people who
followed me into the tomb had no thought of *baksheesh*.[42] It was just a bit
of friendly companionship, as they looked at me looking at the pictures on
the walls. Even through all those centuries there still emanated a feeling of
enjoyment from the frescoes also, as if the men doing the work had found
the subjects congenial. The actual craftsmanship was not as high as in such
a splendid place as the Temple of Tiy[43] but the indications of the way of
living there, derived from the far off centres of culture in Ancient Egypt, can
never fail to set one philosophising about the long history of this stretch of
the river.

## 2.10 Home in Omdurman

After a month of movement I found much satisfaction in settling down at
home [in Omdurman] if only for a short period. One of my renewed
comforts was a small and silly matter but it had forced me to certain
observations I might not have otherwise made. On the morning I was
leaving home, my last minute packing was interrupted by a caller. My bags
therefore were whisked away by my servant and I was hurried into the
waiting car in order to catch the train. When I came to unpack I discovered
I had combs, a clothes brush, very useful in a dusty country, but my hair
brush had been left behind. With Burmese bazaars still in mind I expected
to pick one up in one of the larger *suq*s. I have already described those I saw
on the river bank and even in a place the size of Dongola there was nothing
but large strong combs. Subsequently I looked around and came to the
conclusion that brushes were not in common use. The women, of course,

38. Probably between 30.10.40 and 6.12.40.
39. Jebel Barkal, site of the ancient city of Napata at its zenith in 8th cent. B.C. Dr Beasley
called the site Jebel Barka in the text.
40. 1350-1200 B.C.
41. c.2690 B.C.
42. *Bakhshīsh*, tips.
43. Teye—either the temples at Luxor and Karnak associated with Queen Teye, or the ruinous
Temple of Sedeinga about 13 miles below Soleb, built by Amenephis III 1411-1375 B.C. for his
wife Teye, who was venerated as the patron goddess of Nubia.

plaited their hair in tiny braids and when the men aspired to nice straight partings they did so by means of a razor.

## 3. Shendi[44]

Between the Dongola Reach and Khartoum lies another important centre, which I visited often. Shendi is situated close to the river but it always recalled to me a sort of intermediate atmosphere. It was not the utter desert of the district further north; it certainly had none of the unique qualities of the villages I had just left; and lacked the self-important values of the Three Towns. Here I always stayed in great comfort with the D.C.[45] and from my first visit remember it as a friendly place with one or two outstanding Sudanese families[46] who were very welcoming in their hospitality.

> The school[47] is mediocre but not as bad as I expected ... As they were not expecting me, things weren't too bad. Every girl had at least got something to do ... In IB there was the usual discrepancy between half the class who knew a little and the other half, whom no-one worried very much about ... In IB Arabic some were still at the end of the year—learning their letters while the others were in the early part of *kittab al-atfal* and found simple dictation too

44. Dr Beasley had a long talk in the train to Shendi on 6.12.40 withAbdel Aziz Amin Abdel Magid. 'Was glad to assure him of my desire for co-operation. I hope I haven't done wrong in agreeing he should visit some of the girls' schools ... He is really keen and might be helpful ... Discussed an idea for sending Sudanese girls for a visit to an Egyptian Training College. Would undoubtedly raise much opposition' [6.12.40].

Abdel Aziz Amin Abdel Magis. 27.6.39 First appointment; Master of Arabic Studies at Bakht-er-Ruda; In the 1960s he became a Director in Egypt. He had a German wife.

45. Maxwell Frederick Arthur Keen, O.B.E., 4N. (b.27.11.1903-d.1971); Educated at Haileybury and St John's College, Cambridge, 1926 Cambridge University Rowing Club; 12.12.26 First appointment; 1927-30 Darfur; 1931-32 White Nile; 1932-34 Darfur; 1935-39 Northern Province; 1938-46 he proposed a plan for the development of adult education; 1939-1940 seconded to the Education Department as Adult Education Officer; 1939 Seconded to Civil Secretary's office as Broadcasting officer for 6 months (SGA/GENCO/3/42, also SGA/DAKHLIA/17/5/File 17B8); 18.6.40-42 Northern Province, D.C. Shendi District, based Shendi. The previous D.C. John Noel Richardson, was killed on Atbara bridge in July 1940; 1.11.42-47 Equatoria; 1944 experiments at Bakht-er-Ruda in adult education; 1946 D.C. Moru District, based Amadi; 1947-48 Assistant Civil Secretary (Councils); 1948-53 Clerk of the Legislative Assembly; 1954 Clerk of House of Representatives; 1954 retired, conservation interests in Scotland. Farming in Kent. Settled in Australia.

46. For example, Adam Awad, father of the headmistress and the junior mistress, entertained Dr Beasley on 6.12.40.

47. Shendi girls' school attendance in December 1940 was Class IB 40 present of 40, Class IA 28 present of 32, Class II 26 present of 30, Class III 17 present of 18, Class IV 16 present of 16 on register.

difficult ... Apparently III and IV had received high praise from Sitt Medina[48] ... Decent building, quite well kept [6.12.40].

    ... once again caught the school unawares.[49] The headmistress had a bout of asthma and cleared off for four days. Transfers of other two mistresses had caused much weeping ... Fawzia Ibrahim is probably the most hopeful. Nur had undone some of the worst of the needlework and we started again. A poor school ... Mrs Scott[50] might help with the after-care idea [10.12.40].

### 3.1 Metemma

Just across the river lay Metemma, which like Berber figured strikingly in the history of the Mahdist troubles.[51] There still remained some ruins in the centre of the village as a memory of the brutal massacre here of al-Ja'alin by the Khalifa's lieutenants at the end of his reign.[52] There was no talk of these atrocities to me and anyone interested can find it all in *The River War*.[53] It was just the sort of village where we wanted to foster a strong desire for girls' education in order to balance the disproportion, which could come from the towns' more ready acceptance of the idea. Both the *nazir* and his brother[54] were interested and had demonstrated this by sending daughters to the new Girls' Intermediate School [in Omdurman].

    I stayed[55] in the guest room in the *nazir*'s house. I had an opportunity for a long talk with the brother Haji Omar, when he called one evening[56] to have tea with me. He was much easier to get on with than the *nazir* himself, who invited me to tea in a long room covered and hung with good rugs.

---

48. Sitt Medina Abdulla, B.E.M., O.B.E. Her son was born in 1924 son born, later divorced; late 1920s attended a government school in Omdurman; persuaded to enrol at the Girls' Training College; ten years later she was teaching at the Girls' Training College; First Sudanese Inspectress of Schools; 1970 decorated by the Sudan Government in recognition of her services.
49. On 10.12.40.
50. The wife of J.R. Scott, Agricultural Inspector, Northern Province based in Shendi. 5.12.37 His first appointment, for Berber area; 1939-40 Inspector of Agriculture at Gurier.
51. Metemma was captured by General Wolseley on 17-21.1.1885, after the battle of Abu Klea. This was the final act in the campaign to save Gordon (Churchill, *op. cit.*, pp.61-67).
52. Metemma was the capital of the Ja'alīn during the Mahdīya on which the Khalifa's cousin, Amīr Maḥ,ūd Aḥmad marched from Omdurman in May 1897. Although the Ja'alīn, under 'Abd Allāh wad Sa'd, fortified the town and appealed for help from the Sirdār, this did not arrive in time. The Mahdists stormed the town on 1.7.1897 and massacred the inhabitants (See Theobald, A.B., *The Mahdīya, a history of the Anglo-Egyptian Sudan 1881-1899*, 1951, pp 212-214).
53. Churchill, *op. cit.*., pp.188-189.
54. Haji Omar, brother of the *nāzir* of Metemma.
55. From 7.12.40-10.12.40. Dr Beasley visited Metemma again on 5.4.43.
56. 'He spoke well of the Intermediate School and was sure that the teaching was very good' [7.12.40]. Dr Beasley felt that Haji Omar's daughters and those of the *nāzir* were 'definitely the type wanted'.

Conversation languished but I heard afterwards that the poor man suffered cruelly from some digestive trouble, which must therefore have put a considerable strain on him. In this he was in marked contrast to the famous old man of the district, who had documents from his service with the Turkish Army proving him to have reached the age of one hundred and twenty eight. I never met him but according to report he was hale and alert, running his own affairs but refusing to grow excited about changes in local government.[57] *Nazir*s may come and *nazir*s may go, so to speak.

A better school[58] than I anticipated ... after a bad start. Apparently the newly married headmistress went off with the keys and when the D.C.[59] arrived, a week after the school had started, they were all sitting doing nothing. They were bright but very subdued. There has been some stern discipline somewhere either in school or home.

The headmistress, Amna Taha, seems energetic. Sekina Mahdi was working better than in Omdurman and her sister Khadiga has equal possibilities ... The trouble with these constant transfers is that responsibility can be shelved ... and teachers do not know just how much the children really know [8.12.40].

Zenab Abdul Halim may be all right if looked after. Zenab sitting down rather a lot. She was wearing smart new blue *merkoob*s which probably hurt ... Zenab's hygiene as disgraceful as her arithmetic. Gave demonstration of a blanket bath which consisted of washing patient's face with corner of dirty *tarha*.

Drill lesson ... children rather unintelligently crowded at end of verandah ... Arithmetic in IA, III and IV—seemed to be trying to keep abreast of the syllabus. I think they are making a real effort with needlework ... I went to see the *menzig* in the afternoon ... rather indifferent except for the *omdah*'s niece who was doing a gazelle in cross stitch [6.12.40-7.12.40].

On one occasion, when I was there, an experiment was being made in the crops on the irrigated land just outside the village and while taking my

57. Early in 1940 the authorities were irritated by a direct appeal for financial assistance by the Graduates' Congress to the P.M. of Egypt, 'Alī Māhir Pasha. its founder, Ismā'īl al-Azharī (b.1900-d.1969) later became leader of the *Ashiqqā'* and the Unity of the Nile Valley party. The Government refused to recognise the Congress' claim to speak for all Sudanese people which led to the resignation of the committee of 15. The followers of S.A.R. gained control of the Congress which led to boycotting of broadcasting and statements that they should not volunteer for war service without the consent of the committee which provoked warnings from D. Newbold (See Henderson, K.D.D., *The Making of the Modern Sudan, the life and letters of Sir Douglas Newbold, K.B.E.*, 1953, pp.537-538). In January 1954 Ismā'īl al-Azharī became the first Prime Minister of Sudan until 1956 when he was overthrown by a coalition of political followers of Sayyed 'Abd al-Raḥmān and Sayyid 'Alī al-Mirghanī.
58. Metemma school attendance figures for December 1940 were Class IB 30 present of 30, Class IA 21 present of 21, Class II 19 present of 21, Class III 11 present of 17, Class IV 5 present of 7 on register.
59. Probably M.F.A. Keen.

evening walks I would be hailed by satisfied cultivators. 'Come and see our wheat,' they would say with justifiable pride, delighted in the change from the usual planting of beans or millet. It was easy to praise the healthy looking plots and admire their fertile aspect, set against such a barren background.

Among the houses the friendliness was a little more distracting and I was reminded of C.M. Doughty's experience in Hayil.[60] To stroll along the main street was to collect a tail of small boys who did not come to talk to me but trailed along behind. Occasionally also the inquisitive face of a woman would peer out from behind a half-opened door and, if I waved, she would too. Goats wandered everywhere, in through the gates, into the school yard, into the *nazir*'s court but not, as far as I remember, actually into my guest room.

When they came one morning[61] to a cookery lesson in the school, the mothers seemed rather more shy. These unofficial gatherings were as much a social meeting as an actual time for instruction and were arranged solely at the discretion of the headmistress. They fitted into the line of development which I had discussed with the two Sudanese masters[62] at Bakht-er-Ruda but in many cases in these early days it was better to keep them informal and not try to force the pace. Generally the headmistress could gauge the possibilities fairly accurately but a great deal depended on her initiative and some heads were much more energetic than others.

This particular meeting confounded me a little. The women drifted in during the last lesson period and we sat in the school kitchen, where a savory-smelling stew was prepared over a charcoal burner and the headmistress gave the demonstration. It was all very free and easy and I tried to join in with a little small talk to my nearest neighbour. But my remarks were passed on down the line like a game at a Christmas party. 'She says ... ' going along from one to another. Casual remarks treated in this way sound so different after several repetitions that they tend to wither and die. On all counts, however, Metemma was an amiable place, far more friendly than the landscape round about.

60. Doughty, C.M., *Arabia Deserta*, Vol II, 1888, Chapter IX.
61. 'The children cooked an abundance of food which wouldn't have been so bad, if they hadn't cooked it so long' [9.12.40].
62. Osman Mahjoub and Abdel Rahman Ali Taha at Bakht-er-Ruda.

# 4. Ed Damer

North from Shendi was Damer, in my time the capital of the [Northern] Province, and a few miles north from there was Atbara, which was, and probably still is, a sufficiently unusual place to deserve a special note. It was some years before I visited Atbara for inspections, although I frequently passed it on the train, generally descending there for a stroll on the platform as a relief from the stuffy train. Air-conditioning had of course been invented at this period but the Sudan was not a wealthy country and it tried in those days to live within its means. Therefore we had only fans in the compartments. We had a girls' school at Damer of no particular distinction, but at this time[63] none at Atbara, with its population of nearly 20,000 people. The excuse was that there was a good school run by the C.M.S.[64] and we should be wiser to deploy our limited resources in places like Metemma.

> The school [at Damer] has been in rather a bad way but looks as if it might pick up. The headmistress is a vigorous person full of pride in her school as an extension of her own personality. The attendances were better[65] and she had had the wisdom to start again from earlier stages all through ... I saw a hygiene lesson[66] in which Kultouma made the members of IA wash and clean

63. 11.12.40-12.12.40.
64. 1938 C.M.S.(1) school had 143 girls (including 31 intermediate and 6 secondary) and 19 boys, 28 girls at the C.M.S.(2) Police School and 103 at the C.M.S. Town school. By 1946 C.M.S.(1) had 122 girls (52 boys), C.M.S.(2) had 56 girls (20 boys) and C.M.S.(3) 31 girls (33 boys). In 1946 C.M.S. decided that the Atbara school had no place in C.M.S. missionary planning and should logically be taken over by the American Mission from 13.4.46. A Roman Catholic girls' school was founded in Atbara in 1930 and by 1938 had 203 pupils. The Government girls' school in Atbara had 113 pupils by 1946.
65. Ed-Damer girls' school attendance figures in December 1940 Kindergarten 24 present of 28, Class IB 17 present of 19, Class IA 25 present of 27, Class II 22 present of 22 on register.
66. On Friday 12.12.40 'the Governor came and I did not see many lessons'.
   The Governor of the Northern Province at the time was Major General Maurice Stanley Lush, 4N., C.B., C.B.E., M.C. and Bar, Legion of Merit, U.S.A. (Officer), Order of Knight of Malta (Commander). (b.23.11.1896- ); Educated at Tonbridge and Royal Military Academy, Woolwich; 17.10.19 First appointment; 1919-20 seconded from the Egyptian Army to the S.P.S.; 1920 appointed to the Political Service; 1919-22 Secretary to H.B.M.'s Minister in Ethiopia; 1923 Deputy Assistant Director, Intelligence (Sudan); 1923-25 Kassala; 1927 Khartoum; 1928-29 Assistant Civil Secretary (Personnel); 1929-30 Private Secretary to the Governor-General; 1931-32 Deputy Governor, White Nile; 1932-35 Deputy Governor, Upper Nile; 1935-38 Sudan Agent, Cairo; 1.6.38-1941 Governor, Northern Province, based in Ed-Damer; 2.7.40 seriously injured when run into by a shunting engine while walking at night on Atbara railway bridge during a dust storm; 1941 seconded to B.M.A. of Occupied Territories in Africa with rank of Brigadier, as Deputy Chief Political Officer, Ethiopia and assembled a small group in Khartoum, for entry into Ethiopia; 1942 Military Administrator, Madagascar; 1942-43 Tripolitania, D.C.C.A.O.; 1943-46 Executive Commissioner and Vice-President, Allied

the heads of the babies. Drill in babies good, religious ablutions by Um Salama interesting and attractive. A very practical and enjoyable business ... Glad to see that local clay and *gussab* were being used. Terrible desire to show off ... Nafissa, the headmistress, is not scholarly but a good organiser ... old-fashioned.

In the evening I went back to see the women's class. Nafissa is teaching 40-odd women three times a week.

## 5. Atbara

I went to Atbara[67] to see the C.M.S. school run by Miss Jackson[68] ... They read to me well in English and Arabic ... they do rather a lot of embroidery. Miss Jackson denies this but the D.C.[69] contends wasteful to teach children what they can learn in their own homes ... The upper part seemed quite good.

Much of the reason [there was no government girls' school in Atbara] was that no-one really loved Atbara. I do no think that Kipling ever visited it but it was the spiritual and actual home of his 'Sons of Martha'.[70] They [the people of Atbara] may have developed a firm loyalty to the place but to most people there was a feeling of incongruity that a small imitation of Crewe should have been set down in the limitless desert, where the Nile receives its last tributary.[71] Everyone who lived in Atbara was connected with the railways and their interest in and devotion to this most important work gave to outsiders the impression of a local patriotism and a guild fidelity jealous of interference. No doubt it was all the romantic stuff about the desert which made Atbara seem an uninspired place with its rows of neat bungalows and tidy gardens. Yet Kipling came, as so often, far nearer to the heart of the matter in his praise of the sons of Martha. I travelled up and down the country, investigating, encouraging and discovering material for composing high sounding policies for girls' education. The work in

Commission in A.M.G.O.T. Italy; 1946 retired; 1946-51 International Committee on Refugees and Relief in the Middle East; 1951-55 Adviser to several oil companies.
67. 12.12.40.
68. Miss L.V. Jackson, Headmistress, C.M.S. girls' school, Atbara in 1930s and 1940s; Retired 30.9.47; Her brother-in-law was possibly Dr A.C. Hall from Old Cairo C.M.S. Hospital, who died in 1903; the C.M.S. hospital in Omdurman was built as a memorial to him. His widow and her sister, Miss Jackson, remained on to work in the Sudan for many years.
69. Either J.G.S. Macphail or H.R.P. Harrison.
70. '... But the Sons of Martha favour their mother of the careful soul and the troubled heart.
    And because she lost her temper once, and because she was rude to the Lord her Guest,
    Her Sons must wait upon Mary's Sons, world without end, reprieve or rest.'

Rudyard Kipling (b.1865-d.1936), *Sons of Martha*.
71. The Atbara River.

Atbara made this travelling possible and often comfortable. The Sudanese manager in the garden at Mansurkoti talked of the values of practical education. In the workshops in Atbara men and boys were trained in the actual making of all manner of things from engines and rolling stock to knitting needles.

There was plenty of talk, especially after the war, about Sudanisation. By the end of the thirties trains, stations, steamers were staffed entirely by Sudanese. The central administration in Atbara retained British staff but Sudanese had been trained to take over the actual running of the trains.

The knitting needles meant a great boon to us, since we were very short of all supplies during the war. Knitting, however, had been introduced into the schools in 1939 and was soon a very popular skill. The economy of the country, of course, floated on cotton and we had no lack of that. The girls all learned to use a hand spindle, which was one of the few crafts practised by some of the women, but we had no needles. A kind engineer in Atbara arranged to turn out quantities of smooth wooden needles to knit the coarse cotton thread, which the girls had spun. Still further some inventive genius designed a spinning wheel from memories of one at home and the workshops at Atbara produced some for the Training College students to speed up their work.

Efficient, helpful, of great value to the country as the hub of the complex of docks, railways, steamers, even hotels and catering services, but Atbara never won my heart. This stayed, as far as the Northern Province was concerned, on that last loop of the river between Merowe and Wadi Halfa.

## Trips to Wadi Halfa, 1941 to 1945

After Khartoum, [Wadi Halfa] is probably one of the places best known to casual callers in the Sudan, as towards the end of the forties it was a night stop for planes en route further south, but this did not last long and I have few recollections of it as a staging post. It was the frontier end of that secluded world which lay along the river. In December 1941 I found myself, after thirty hours needed for the train journey,[72] in a different climate from

72. On 30.11.41, Dr Beasley travelled to Wadi Halfa 'with the Traceys, a number of aircraftsmen were only too pleased to have some women to talk to. Loneliness becomes quite starkly apparent here'.

Christopher Birdwood Tracey, 4N. (b.9.5.1898-d.1954); Educated at Monkton Combe and St John's, Cambridge; 1917-10 Royal Artillery (France); 25.12.22 first appointment; 1923 Khartoum; 1924-27 Upper Nile; 1928-30 Blue Nile Province; 1931-32 Inspector, Finance Department; 1932-33 Secretariat for Economic Development; 1934-38 Khartoum; 1939-40 Equatoria; 1.12.40-44 Deputy Governor, Gezira (later Blue Nile Province); 14.7.44-1948

that I had left in Omdurman and there are times, when this can be one of the most inviting imaginable. In the winter the sun is without glare and the light settles with a vivid sparkle on the bright colours of the broad river with the yellow sand dunes opposite, groves of green palm trees and in the British gardens by the waterside all the flowers of spring and summer. Wearing a tweed skirt and a woollen jumper, I could relax in the sunshine and admire beds of roses and carnations, while nearby in the herbaceous border, stocks jostled violets and *linaria* and there was a promise of splendid sweet peas.

> Apart from the trees the country was sand and dunes and howling wind ... The hotel was a joy ... I had a room overlooking the river and rose garden. It was bliss to have a properly fitted bathroom and W.C. all to myself after the makeshifts I sometimes get. There was also a small electric fire and what I had not seen for two years, large coal fires in the lounges.
>
> Social life was brightened up by a large cocktail party given for the Governor General[73] and his wife—and by the presence of an R.A.F. squadron who were again effusive in their welcome to women visitors [1.12.41].

In a small way there was much that was reminiscent of Egypt just across the border and this individuality was just another strand in the fascinating diversity of this vast country. The town itself, grouped round the dock and the railhead, was not symmetrically planned and its double-storeyed houses were placed with a fine idiosyncracy which showed itself in sites as well as in architecture. There were none of the carefully carved balconies of the Cairo palaces but here and there an attempt at a latticed window suggested the tradition of the magnificent Arab houses from the Mediterranean region. The inhabitants added to the picture too by those subtleties of dress and feature which are difficult to define but which help to make distinctions, when seen often enough. It is, for example, inadequate to say that a man glimpsed in the street looked Egyptian, when perhaps all that one could point to would be the winding of his *immah*. It was easier with the women; they wore the trailing, black robes which were an exact replica of the

Governor, Northern Province, based in Ed-Damer; 1948 retired; 1949-52 British Administration, Tripolitania.

73. Governor-General Maj-Gen. Sir Hubert Huddleston, K.C.M.G., C.B., D.S.O., M.C., and Lady Huddleston.

Sir Hubert Huddleston (-d.1950); Former soldier, served in Sudan from 1914; 1916 led the reconquest of Darfur; by 1940 Commandant of the Sudan Defence Force; August 1940 replaced Sir Stuart Symes as Governor-General because the latter was considered by Churchill not to have a strong stomach for war and to believe Africans should be kept out of European affairs; 1940-1947 Governor-General, based in Khartoum.

Constance E. Huddleston was also active in the anti-'female circumcision' campaign.

Egyptian. It was a very graceful dress, hanging in soft folds from the shoulders, with a covering for the head which fell straight and might on occasion be used to hide the face. But the skirt was long and dragged at least a foot behind the wearer. In this country of sand black was an untidy colour but it became definitely squalid when the skirt was allowed to trail and the interest in laundry was questionable.

Rather as in the Egyptian villages there were plenty of women in the fields, carrying jars on their heads from the well. They might veil a little in the town but here they went with their faces quite uncovered.

> There were three schools to see. The one at Halfa in rather poor fettle, the one at Degheim rather better and the one at Debeira quite good.

## 6.1 Halfa Degheim

To the south of Wadi Halfa was a fairly large tract of cultivated land in the middle of which we had a school. It was always a rather grubby effort and I was most distressed with it on my first morning. A fierce wind was blowing and the children sat huddled up in thin cotton frocks and light shawls. [Extremes in] temperature were a disadvantage we could never deal with adequately. It had obviously not been weather for washing; they all had colds and the use of the handkerchief was unknown, but of course shawls were useful. This last unpleasantness we managed to dispel with the hard labour of years but I am not sure that the pretty bright handkerchiefs which the children sewed in their first year were more than a symbol, which brought the matter to notice. There was a distinct improvement but I suspected that the clean little squares pinned on to dresses had not superseded more old-fashioned methods, but such operations were then conducted outside.

Halfa Degheim was an unlovely village in itself but down on the shore was a delightful grove of palms, where I could wander for a mile or so. Small houses appeared among the trees and there were generally a few goats in charge of a young boy or girl. Women came down with pots or petrol tins to fetch water; a man might be sitting on the bank mending his boat. Downstream there was constant traffic from shore to shore, cultivators often crossing every day in the tall masted boats[74] to the large island in mid-stream.

> There was one bright little teacher who enjoyed teaching so obviously as to be a pleasure. There was an enormous tea-party one day there with about a hundred women (all speaking *rotana*), in their awful black clothes. There was

74. *Felucca*, sailing boat.

one Sudanese woman amongst them and she looked such a pleasant contrast in her clean white *tobe*. The D.C.'s wife[75] also came.

## 6.2 Wadi Halfa and the War

This year[76] there was traffic of a different sort for in the complicated strategy of the Middle East a remote oasis named Kufra[77] was regarded as worth fighting for and frequent convoys of lorries set out across the sand dunes opposite Wadi Halfa to act as a life-line for the troops engaged there. It must have been a difficult and hazardous business, for all the supplies had to be ferried across the river, which here was wide enough to act as a flying-boat station, and loaded onto trucks, which then set out with nothing but sand for the limitless miles between the Nile and Kufra.

## 6.3 Debeira and wartime worries

The anxiety of the War lay very heavily on us at this time and for me the Rider Haggard fantasy reached its lowest depths one morning, when I was having an early beakfast in preparation for a lorry drive of about an hour downstream to Debeira.[78] An ill-conditioned wireless crackled out the news of Pearl Harbour[79] but could give us little but the bare facts and the involvement now of this fresh peril. It may have been the constant pre-occupation with the 'Jap menace' that I had heard so much about in Burma, that made me feel that, if we had to fight the Japs also, it might well be the end.

It was an unhappy morning climatically. Sometimes the brightness of Halfa could be clouded and this was one of the days, when the North wind blew bitterly through a dim haze of sand. I was using an elderly box car which had no sides by the seat and the wind whistled through. Wearing a fur coat and with a rug across my knees I still grew more and more numb

75. Mrs G.W. Titherington 'who knew all the girls personally and was quite prepared, most usefully, to take an active interest in the school'.
    Major Geoffrey Wrench Titherington, 4N. ('Bill', 'Tiths', 'Squire of Bum' (b.16.1.1893-d.20.10.51); Educated at Radley and Queen's College, Oxford; 31.10.19 first appointment, seconded from the Egyptian Army to the S.P.S.; 1919-28 Bahr el Ghazal; 1928 appointed to the permanent service S.P.S; 1929-31 Kordofan; 1.4.31-34 Upper Nile (1934 D.C. Malakal, Central Shilluk District based in Malakal); 22.10.34-42 Northern Province (1935 D.C. Merowe District, by 1939 D.C. Wadi Halfa District); 1.1.42 retired. Dinka expert, ornithologist, archaeologist, created a model cradle for Arab babies made out of interlaced palm fronds.
76. 1941.
77. al-Kufrah in the Libyan Desert 24.20°N 23.15°E. al-Kufrah is 1150 or more miles from Wadi Halfa.
78. 11 miles from Wadi Halfa to Debeira.
79. 15.12.41.

with cold. The surface of the road was bad but ordinarily it was an interesting drive within sight of the river all the way on the left. On the other side there were rocky hills, not very high and rather broken in shape with valleys leading off, that looked as if they might be rewarding to explore. About half-way[80] came a long straggling village, Ashkeit, built with its back to the hills, which afforded it some shelter from the harsh wind.

By this time I was in a state of hopeless imaginings. We had been very much cut off from England since March 1940; we had had no leave; and letters sometimes took months to arrive. It was all too easy to come back to this idea of being marooned for ever—a strange white tribe in the middle of Africa

> doomed to this for the rest of my life, never again the gentle fertility of England, always this bitter, hostile country with its extreme climate and this fight to obtain food from the desperately dry ground

away from all contacts. On this hard relentless morning passing by those barren hills, which bounded great expanses of desert, it did not seem so impossible a future. It was a fitting scene for some Twilight of the Gods, a perpetual diminuendo without a grand catastrophe to end it.

Happily even in these moments of bleak despair the never failing friendliness of the Sudanese came to my rescue. When I reached Debeira, I was taken straight to the *omdah*'s house,[81] an impressive looking building of mud-brick, one-storeyed as most of the houses are, but extensive. I was stiff with cold, as I climbed down from the car and his first words were very welcome. 'I expect you'd like a cup of tea.'

I was led through a well-swept forecourt into a long room furnished with chairs and sofas all round the edge and supplied with hard cushions. It was a type of furniture, not uncomfortable although not easy for complete lounging, but I found it restful after the hard seat of the lorry and the rocky bumps of the road. The room was dark, as the shutters had been closed to keep out the wind, but this respite [too] was welcome. It was the tea, however, that I always remembered.

The Sudanese drank a lot of tea but not in the way we like it. Sometimes they boiled it in the pot together with the milk, and sometimes they added mint and sugar but no milk. Sometimes they made it very weak and then added large amounts of hot milk but very seldom did they make an ordinary cup of tea. This *omdah*, however was one of the exceptions and the tea was perfect.

---

80. 6½ miles from Wadi Halfa.
81. 'The Governor-General had visited the house a few days before'.

He was a burly man in his prime with a solid reputation. During the period of rationing a great deal depended on the integrity of these local, native administrators, who could, if they really had the welfare of their villages at heart, ensure a reasonably fair share for all. My standard test, interest in girls' education, he passed with flying colours.[82] We talked a lot about the school, which he had been largely instrumental in getting started, and about the problems connected with attendance in a place, where the village was strung out along the river and the children had to walk a fair distance. As there were always plenty of young girls, and it was the older classes which were not full, this difficulty did not seem a very good explanation of absenteeism. 'Of course they ought to finish the four years,' said the *omdah*. 'Otherwise it is like getting up half- way through the meal'.

The sun was not yet shining but the twilight in my mind was fast receding, and very soon, all warmed and brisk, we were able to set off to the school. Straggly though the village might be, it had some very pleasant corners. The large date plantation near the *omdah*'s house was a sight of much beauty and probably full of grateful shade in weather other than this, while between the hills and the river a large tract of alluvial soil was being intensively cultivated. Canals led off from the river to small squares just beginning to sprout, in some cases with grain but mostly with leguminous plants. Grass lined the banks of the bigger waterways and at one junction a large group of ducks was swimming happily about.

I had a little difficulty in persuading the *omdah* to come in and discuss some necessary questions of repairs in a building, which was simple and adequate. Although he had a peep at the youngest class, he was very diffident about seeing any more of the school work. People had such evil tongues, he said, and it would be ill received, if it were known that he had been looking at the girls.

The Headmistress[83] was a local girl and under her guidance the school was becoming very much a part of the village community. She had been educated in Wadi Halfa and had come back to her home, but the other mistresses belonged to Omdurman and their feeling of exile did not express itself in any romantic nonsense about mystic twilights but in a real honest to God grumble about things of immediate import.

The weather. I could see for myself, they explained, how impossible it was to live in cold like this. They drew their thin cotton clothes round them and their teeth began to chatter. Dust swirled round the yard in clouds; the wind howled through the crevices of the mud house. There was not very

---

82. 'After the news of war, this conversation put my feet a little firmer on the earth.'
83. The headmistress was a niece of the *omdah* of Debeira.

much to say about the probability of weeks of sunshine to people, who seldom see anything else.

Then the food in this forsaken place. There was no market. The cultivators grew only peas for drying and horse beans.[84] Everything had to be brought in from Halfa, and how could a lot of lone women manage to get stores from there with transport so infrequent and lorries in the state they were, because of the war? Yes, it was true that the *omdah* helped with the rations but what use were two pounds of sugar a month to anybody? And the black market was dear enough in Halfa and Omdurman but in this outlandish spot prices were prohibitive.

Lastly the people. No-one, except the Headmistress had any relations here. How could anyone make friends with women who spoke no Arabic. There was no-one to go and visit and to sit indefinitely for one of those long, long gossips that must be part of any normal life. It was bad enough having the children come to school needing to be taught to speak a civilised language without ever being able to talk to a soul outside.

This seemed to me the most important grievance of the lot. The people on this part of the river, roughly from Merowe northwards into Egypt, called themselves Nubian and did in fact speak a language, which had no affinities with Arabic. The men in the course of their daily lives came into contact with affairs which demanded knowledge of the general speech of the country, but the women, tucked away in their villages and not expected to traffic with strangers, were in no sense bi-lingual. It was hard indeed for mistresses to be shut behind walls even in places, where there could be an occasional outing or at least visitors. To have no-one but one's three colleagues and their elderly chaperones to exchange a word with could not make for contentment.

The mothers [of the teachers] were as vociferous as the mistresses. I sat on an *angareeb* in the boarding house, which, despite the soft sand floor, was clean and tidy, and sipped their excellent coffee. Excellent it was and very sweet, black market notwithstanding. They too poured forth their troubles and I promised to see what exchanges I could make at any rate for the girl who had nearly finished the two years of her contract. The difficulty of staffing these outlying schools was always acute. Fortunately this one managed to keep its standards high enough to enter students for the Training College and to have back eventually teachers from local families. This desirable aim, however, was still some years away on that bleak and dusty morning and all that we could do was to work towards it. Being able

---

84. *Fūl mudammas*, horse beans, a staple element of Egyptian *fellah* diet.

to pour all this out to the person who could remedy their troubles seemed to cheer both mothers and daughters considerably.[85]

## 6.4 Wadi Halfa

For my part I felt quite normal by the time I got back to the hotel[86] with its comfortable chintz-covered furniture, electric heaters in the bedrooms and great coal fires roaring up the chimneys in the lounges. I had not seen a fire for two years and derived a most unexpected amount of satisfaction from the sight.

> There were two more teaparties in Halfa, one a big entertainment by the Boys' Intermediate School where there was some good acting in English and Arabic ... Was surprised to see them introduce a prayer into a comic play and make use of it as a trick for escaping.

There was a school in Wadi Halfa as well but that also was connected with the misfortunes of the war, since the army had commandeered the building. I had spilt a lot of venomous ink about the relative importance of education for one hundred and sixty girls and the comfort of twelve sergeants, who were, after all, on active service in a sunny climate. Unnecessary occasions for venom form one of the minor evils of war, not always in the balance against it.

The delay in re-opening had not improved the quality of the school and a very inefficient Headmistress had done little to prevent its deterioration. She was for a Sudanese woman quite unusually devoted to the practices of her religion and was determined to go on pilgrimage.[87] Someone had told her that unmarried girls could not do this, although I believe that the information was inaccurate. Nothing daunted, she declared her intention of getting married in order to go, and in this she succeeded, although I thought her plain, stupid if amiable. After a year or so therefore to my great relief, she left the service in the accomplishment of this double aim.

> Remember one fierce morning when I called in at the school unexpectedly and found chaos—also a superfluity of small children in Class I. Apparently 2 mistresses had gone to pieces when their mother died.
>
> The other party[88] I attended was a family affair in the girls' school. It was rather poor for them not to be ready when I arrived. Then the teachers from

85. When Dr Beasley visited Debeira in January 1945 the visit was much more enjoyable. 'The place seemed greener and looked as though the irrigation had been extended. The tall palm trees and the green lines of the canals make a very peaceful scene'.
86. In December 1941, in Wadi Halfa.
87. *Hajj*, pilgrimage to Mecca and Medina.
88. Dr Beasley attended this party with Mrs Titherington in December 1941.

Degheim arrived, one of them dressed in local dress and bursting with excitement at her joke.

When Lady Huddleston came to the school she was very kind and gracious but seemed a little nervous ... I felt definitely on home ground, as I had a well-cut costume as opposed to her rather ordinary coat, and could stand at the top of the steps to welcome her. She was also very kind about a *khalwa*[89] to which she promised slates ... [90]

## 6.5 Buhen

My memories of Halfa are not all as uneasy as this. There was one afternoon of pale sunshine and a cold wind, when I sailed upstream in a small dinghy[91] with almost scarlet sails, to visit an ancient Egyptian temple[92] on the west bank. Its building was attributed to Queen Hatshepsut[93] and it was thus probably older than Jebel Barkal[94] and still with a liveliness of drawing in the frescoes and the colours fresh and clear. Placed up there on a small bluff above the river it immediately evoked the same questions [as at Jebel Barkal] about the men, who had thought it worthwhile to labour with so much love and care. The walls of a Coptic church around it were standing as a protection now from the weather. What sort of community had needed a church of that size?

It was so fascinating we lingered longer than we should have done and the sun set soon after we started back. The wind was stronger than ever. Tacking was an exciting business. I've never been standing upright in a boat like that before. There were quite large waves and we got absolutely soaked. Then when it was really dusk we hit a sandbank.

89. *Khalwa*, lit. 'a place of seclusion', a place for religious instruction, nowadays the teaching of the Qur'ān.
90. ' ... stayed in Omdurman for Christmas which was ... rather second best especially as the war news continued to be so discouraging. 1.1.42 went to lunch at the Palace, rather dull and proper.'
91. Dr Beasley went sailing 'with Hilary Bell' in a 'very strong North' wind about four 'in the afternoon' in January 1945.
92. Probably at Buhen, an Egyptian colony established under the Middle Empire c.2100-1700 B.C.
93. 1495-1475 B.C.
94. Jebel Barkal was at its zenith in the 8th century B.C.

## Trip to Butn al-Hujar, 1949

This part of the river could provide stimuli for innumerable questions of that kind and, when I went upstream in the early part of 1949 on one of the pleasantest trips I ever made, I found plenty.[95]

### 7.1 Abka

Most arresting among these ancient monuments were the recently found rock drawings of Abka,[96] rather less than half an hour's drive from the town of Halfa itself. Leaving the river[97] for a little we crossed a piece of scruffy and uninteresting desert coming back to a new version of the Nile. Past the town the water swept along in a wide, clear stretch, impressive and full of power. Here it divided into a number of channels and for about three miles there were streams tumbling over rocks and wandering through little by-ways in a manner which was not characteristic of the dignified, palm-fringed waterway which is the normal picture of the Nile. A short way back from this cataract was the group of rocks on which primitive men had hammered these fawn-coloured lines on the black, polished surface, still vital and compelling, whatever the original impulse behind them. Some of the attempts were frankly crude but no doubt there were unskilful hands among the people of that age, wheras others wielded their rough tools with the sureness, that is the mark of artist and craftsman. There were human forms among the drawings but the most lively representations were those of animals. Many of these had long since been lost to the region, horned beasts of all sorts, some with their tails curled aloft with a real note of flourish, some rather odd-looking crocodiles, and, what made most impression on me, a herd of giraffe running. In these the line of the neck had evidently been noted with the head forward and the whole suggesting a sense of grace and movement, pleasing in itself and not merely a wonder of antiquity.

95. Dr Beasley requested Province transport to investigate a little trouble at Abri, and the D.C. for Wadi Halfa, A.E.D. Penn, also asked her to go to Delgo in January 1949. The D.C. and his wife met Dr Beasley at Angush, the station before Halfa on the Saturday [21.1.49].

The Dean of Gloucester, Costley White, previously headmaster of Westminster, and wife were staying to preach the sermon on Sunday, which Dr Beasley was obliged to attend. Dr Beasley visited Halfa Degheim on Sunday morning, with the Dean and his wife. 'It was a pity that it is one of our bad schools'. The following Sunday he was due to preach the Gordon Memorial Sermon in Khartoum.

96. 'Abka is near the Second Cataract, c.10 miles from Wadi Halfa and was excavated by the Department of Archaeology, Gordon Memorial College, December 1947-February 1948 (See Myers, D.H., 'Excavations in the Second Cataract area', *Sudan Notes and Records*, vol 29, 1948, p.129).

97. Saturday 21.1.49.

## 7.2 Trip to Sarras and Butn al-Hujar

I was travelling in company with the D.C.[98] and his wife, and we set off one cool sunny afternoon in January[99] in a comfortable station-waggon with a lorry behind piled high with servants[100] and luggage.[101] For a great part of the way we drove along the old [Kerma] railway line, which, now made into a bearable road, was very good going. This part of the country figures largely in *The River War*[102] and all the way were constant, often saddening, reminders of it. The rails themselves, however, had been put to good use and cropped [up] in all sort of places, the most noticeable being the cross-beams to support the flat house tops.

## 7.3 Migrant workers

At a place called Gemai there was a camp of Egyptian surveyors. They were prospecting for a place to build a dam to start a hydroelectric plant. The Cataract ended near Gemai but the river was interesting with rather uneven banks and small hills on both sides ... We drove fairly near the river all the way.

## 7.4 Sarras

The afternoons were short, with a rapid drop in temperature after sundown. As we approached our first stop [about 5.30] at Sarras,[103] what stood out most prominently was a long, white-washed building with pointed arches and a small dome. It was the boys' school. In all the villages round here the best building of all—in fact the outstanding feature—was the new boys' school. Much of the money for these had been contributed by people belonging to the village but working away from the place. From roughly

98. Albert Eric Penn, 4N. (b.6.6.1903-d.1988); Educated at Shrewsbury and Brasenose College, Oxford; 7.12.25 First appointment; 1926-29 Kordofan; 1929-33 Khartoum; 1933-35 Blue Nile Province; 1.11.1935-37 Equatoria/Upper Nile; 1.7.1941-46 Kordofan, D.C. Lakes District, based at Rumbek: 1.6.46-1951 Northern Province (1949 D.C. Wadi Halfa); 1951 retired; 1953-63 Administrator, Oxford University, Business School; 1963-73 Elected to Berkshire County Council.
99. 'The Dean left on Monday morning', 23.1.49.
100. 'We had in attendance the D.C.'s head-boy and assistant and his cook, my servant and two police drivers.'
101. 'One lot of pots did for all the cooking but we each needed our bed, bedding, chair, table and wash basin. The extra comforts were *shamla*s (large, rough native rugs), a portable wireless, a box of sodas, a good pressure lamp. Not excessive but they made a lot of difference.' This was all packed into a Chevrolet station-waggon.
102. 'During the long years of preparation Sarras had been Egypt's most advanced outpost and the southern terminus of the military railway' (Churchill, *op. cit.*, p.123-124, 164).
103. Sarras is about 32 miles from Wadi Halfa.

north of Merowe a remarkably large proportion of the young men went into domestic service all over the Sudan and in Egypt, where Sudanese servants were much sought after. There remained that curious balance of population, which in Europe we connect with war conditions. Few but elderly or middle-aged men were to be seen with a large number of women and children. It was not in fact so strange an economic system as it might seem, for the strip of land along the river was far too narrow to support a great number of cultivators. The tradition of domestic service had grown up and much of the district's revenue was from postal orders sent by absent relatives. The men encouraged one another by introducing friends to the employers, but they generally retained some stake in the village of their birth and retired in old age to a small plot and a date palm to sit under. When we were told that much of the money for these buildings had come from far-away sources, I thought of the gentle 'rake-offs', which my cook made everyday on the shopping. If the sum total of these 'rake-offs' were spent in so laudable a way, the housewives' loss was very much the children's gain.

Certainly there seemed very few men in Sarras and most of the schoolboys were boarders, as the houses were situated in a long string stretching for miles along the river. The children shivered, when they were called from their play to stand in a line and welcome the D.C. They were not quite so clean and shining as their beautiful school-house.

> The resthouse was another white washed building[104] with a verandah, just outside the village, situated on a high bank near the river ... There was a patch of cultivation all round the resthouse ... The river went burbling on, a marvellous air of peace and contentment.

The next day we had our early morning tea in the dark. Then, while the lorries were being packed, we set off walking down the road, exhilarated by the fine coldness of the thin desert air. The sun was just coming up over the hills on which we could see the remains of a ruined fort[105] from that long-forgotten small war at the end of the last century. A small war it may have been but those campaigns must have known many horrors in the long summers without motor transport and present day knowledge of suitable food and clothing. The frequent cairns and cemeteries we passed were

---

104. 'It had only two rooms and a kitchen, so we used one room for eating and took it in turns to undress or dress in the other. The Penns slept out and I in.'
105. The fort at Sarras is south-east of the resthouse. With the advance to Akasha in March to June 1896 'Sarras, deprived of its short-lived glory, became again the solitary fort on a crag' (Churchill, *op. cit.*, p.123, 126).

melancholy reminders enough.[106] It was easy for us on a bright crisp morning with a couple of cars in good condition. When these caught us up, we could bowl along through the Butn al Hujar[107] (the Belly of Stones) and admire its strange type of beauty but it must have been very different for the men who built a railway[108] in the eighties.

The place does indeed command admiration. There is no vegetation of any sort; the river is out of sight, although near enough for an occasional bird to be seen; one gazelle was the only living creature we met. Yet in some curious way the hills do not suggest anything dead. They are great blocks of stone, whose geological structure is beyond me, but it looked as if there were every type of rock imaginable, and the number and combination of colours was unending. On one side would be a mountain of dull purple, on another a pinkish beige; a lively grey would be intermingled with a red like Devonshire loam; there was orthodox golden sand. In places chunks of rock lay about beautifully layered in pink and green, and even blocks of what looked like alabaster, just about the size for small statues or vases and of very lovely shading from cream to brown. The landscape had the effect of more ordinary hill scenes in that between the slopes came rivers of sand. Whether they move at all I do not know, but the loose surface gave an impression of mobility against the massiveness of the coloured mountains.

In two places were small, flat plains between the slopes with tracks leading down through the gaps to the river.[109] They were quite barren but of much importance because posts had been set up for a local mail box. There was a regular service of mail lorries coming this way and this is how the villages on the river were served. Very lonely they looked, these few small letter-boxes, standing up bravely in all the wilderness.

106. 'At Akobo was a fort on an isolated hill.' Dr Beasley saw other examples 'all the way as memorials to British soldiers, and the grave of Major Roddy Owen [at the foot of Firket mountain] who won the Grand National in the eighties.' He died in the cholera epidemic in July 1896. 'The grave was two slabs of granite, with a [now broken] sword on it.' (See Churchill, *op. cit.*, pp.142-143 for details of the epidemic).

107. Baṭn al-Ḥajar, at the north end of which is the Second Cataract.

108. The Wadi Halfa-Kerma railway (See Churchill, *op. cit.*, pp.123, 140, 164, 167).

109. 'The road was marked by kilometre stones' [and on the slopes] 'one or two stunted thorn trees would be growing or some half dozen xerophitic bushes about a foot high.' In Akasha 'we saw the river tumbling through a cataract again'.

### 7.5 Akasha

It must have been about eleven o'clock, when we passed through a narrow defile with the mountains coming down close on either side. We were suddenly on a little [irrigated] plain with the village of Akasha lying before us and its new, white school, like that at Sarras, the most noticeable feature of the place. At the other end we had not been quite sure exactly where the Butn al-Hujar started but here the entrance was very clear. I had always heard it spoken of with so much dread that I was agreeably disappointed. Tales of men passing through on camels[110] were of a valley excessively grim but with their transport[, the journey took] several days not, as in our case, a few hours. There would probably have been all the time a feeling of enclosure, which might have become oppressive, for the hills stretched a long way. We climbed a smallish one on our way back and looked across to the east but we could not see the end. I have no doubt that in the heat of a July day travellers on any sort of transport would find it difficult to enthuse, as we were doing, about the lovely play of shade and colour.

On this day Akasha was full of bustle and excitement to greet the visitors who had come to share in their pride in opening such a splendid school. The boys were all lined up outside and the crowd pressed round to watch us inspecting them, a male crowd, of course, although a few bolder women looked on from a distance. After we had been shown the buildings in detail, we were taken into the largest room, where chairs had been set for the party. We all drank tea, but I thought from the number of glasses at the other end of the gathering, that there seemed to be a certain amount of rotation, glasses being collected up and then brought back, before some could drink. The great speech for the occasion was made by the younger schoolmaster but was, I regret, in far too classical and high flown Arabic for me to follow accurately. I was happier with some of the shorter efforts of the [two] cultivators, doubtless penned with much labour.

The Headmaster, a thin, nervous, earnest person, I had met before.[111] We smiled at one another and I had just begun to say, 'What about girls?' when he broke in eagerly, 'Please, we must have a girls' school. But that we cannot do without your help. If there are enough boys, there must be enough girls. And education for the boys needs education for the girls with it'.

---

110. The journey by camel from Dongola to Wadi Halfa takes about ten days. The road to Egypt was on the other bank of the river at Akasha.

111. 'The D.C. made a speech in Arabic to say how pleased he was.' The headmaster of Akasha, whom Dr Beasley had met before at a private school at Ashkeit, did not give a speech. She was rather surprised by his enthusiasm to set up a girls' school in the area.

We lunched in a little resthouse perched on a small cliff, which at the time of flood had the water washing right up against its base, and was a pleasant spot even in the depths of summer.

> The view towards the river was delightful with the usual little green fields but the view from the back over a Muslim cemetery was not so good ... I also remember the remains of a British port from *The River War*[112] and another memorial. There was also a very nice calf behind a *birsh* mat shelter.

On this particular morning, the North wind was so strong that there was no joy at all in sitting on the balcony that crowned the little cliff. It was much more enjoyable on the smooth, black rocks which jutted out into the river, where we could watch the tiny waterfalls and the odd ducks floating cheerfully on the strong current. Nearby in the patches of cultivation on shore, an old woman, dressed in black [in the Egyptian fashion], was hunting for a few ripe lupin pods[113] of which presumably she would make some sort of porridge. It seemed poor fare for such bracing weather.

> On our way to the school we were stopped by a bitter altercation. A man came up to the D.C.[114] with a fierce complaint. His people had been household slaves of a merchant who had recently died. He wanted to stay and work in the village, he said, but the *omdah* wanted to turn him out. The man himself, a singularly unlovely specimen, wanted the D.C. to intercede for him. There was a shouting match and the wife threw herself on the ground in front of the car and rolled in the dust.

The matter was not settled until after lunch, when D.C. sat on a kitchen chair and listened to the excited shouting of a crowd of villagers accompanied by the dramatic gesture of an unprepossessing old woman, who threw herself to the ground and poured dust on her head. He sorted out all their complaints with an unruffled patience, no doubt born of long experience, but the man's issue was complicated and could only have arisen in the social flux after the Khalifa's downfall. Slavery in one way or another often cropped up in strange prejudices and jealousies. Technically, of course, he had been free since the turn of the century, but he had always remained with his master and now, an unlovely misfit on the local routine, the villagers wanted to be rid of him. While he committed no offence, the D.C. firmly ruled, a free man could choose where he would live. I have sometimes thought that no-one in the Middle East ever gives in gracefuly and certainly dissatisfaction among this group went on rumbling, as we

112. Churchill, *op. cit.*, pp.108, 124-131.
113. *Turmus*, lupins.
114. A.E.D. Penn.

embarked again on our lorry. On the other side, however, we departed in a shower of happy blessings from the school authorities and all the pupils.


## 7.6 Beyond Akasha

After this the road followed fairly close to the river and there was a delightful and curious feeling of being shut away in a separate world. During the winter a continuous traffic of lorries taking dates [out of Dongola] to the railhead was noticeable but continuous traffic might mean two or three vehicles each day at most. This in no way interfered with the impression of seclusion which was probably enhanced by the precision of the boundaries. To our right was the small strip of cultivated land lying on both sides of the river with a sharp edge where the desert began and on each side too there were hills, not a continuous chain but enough to give the effect of a barrier. The green of the wheat, a few inches high in the small, irrigated plots, may have been strengthened by the bareness round about but its colour seemed more intense than in England. Trees and hedges do not make such a startling contrast as sand and rock, and the groves of palms have dullish fronds and are too high above the ground for any immediate comparison.

Under one of these clumps of palm trees on the other side of the river was an encampment of Arabs living in grass huts. In this case the word 'arab' would be used in its derogatory sense of people who wander about with no fixed place of abode. 'Just an *arab*', a cultivator would say scornfuly, although he would be at much pains to prove that his descent was Arab as opposed to negro.

In fact in this Northern Province parents often used to have a small cut made with a razor blade on a baby's forehead and on the nape of the neck, just where the hair begins. They hoped in this way to ensure that the shape of the head would not become negroid. Scars of this type could be plainly seen in adults and had nothing to do with the custom of *shillukh*.

These *arab*s from all accounts had been living there for generations but they still built themselves grass huts, that were little more than shelters.[115] Perhaps there still persisted the idea that they would some day move on, for quite close was the desert road[116] that led into Egypt.

Close to them also, although with no apparent connection, were some

115. *Rakūba*, temporary shelter.
116. *Darb al-arba'īn*, the 40-day camel route from El Fasher to Assiut in Upper Egypt and Darfur's main link with the outside world, by which slaves and ivory were sent to the north by Arab traders. In the nineteenth century, especially between 1800 and 1850, slave raiding increasingly provided the manpower with which the Sultanate was run. (See O'Fahey, R.S. and Spaulding, J.L., *Kingdoms of the Sudan*, 1974, pp.159-160).

warm, mineral springs among the rocks [upstream from Akasha], on the river bank. They were supposed to cure rheumatism and leprosy but the organisation, which was reputed to be in the care of a *fiki*, seemed a little sketchy. The local people did not receive at all well the suggestion, made by [the] D.C, that the springs might be commercialised and made into a source of revenue for the district. They said that the Turks had tried that, when they were in charge of the country, and the springs had dried up. *Allah* evidently intended that this should be a religious charity.

As opposed to the draughty shelters of the nomads on the west bank, the prosperous houses we passed, standing back from the cultivation, had less than usual of the appearance of outsize sand-castles. The mud was smoothed off to a clean, straight edge and some were bright with colour wash and simple designs or with plates let into the wall.

> The high walls and rooms opening into the protected courtyards provided shelter against the pervading winds. There was never any rain.

Most of them had been built after the high flood of 1946 and set further away from the river.

## 7.7. Amara

Our first stop was Amara where excavations were in progress on an ancient town on the other side of the Nile [at Semna West?]. Last year[117] the archaeologists, three British[118] and one Sudanese, had found a temple[119] probably of the eighteenth or nineteenth dynasty, but this season they had been obliged to concentrate on more ordinary things like the foundations of ordinary houses and the drainage system. No doubt a valuable and fascinating study, if approached in the right spirit, but it must lack the glamour and aesthetic joy of unearthing a Pompeii or a Tutankhamen.

117. 1948. Amara West was excavated in the 1947-48 season and Dec 1948, Jan, Feb and Dec 1949. It was the first time that the Antiquities Service collaborated with an outside body in an excavation (*ARDE*, Antiquities Service, 1949). See also Shinnie, P.L., 'Archaeological Discoveries During Winter 1947-48, Amara West', *Sudan Notes and Records*, vol 29, 1948, p.128.
118. The Commissioner of Archaeology, P.L. Shinnie, was Field Director, with H.W. Fairman as Field Director for the Egypt Exploration Society ... one with wife and child. The wife ran the mess and looked after the office side, for the four month period of the excavation.
    P.L. Shinnie; 9.12.46 First appointment; Until 15.7.55 Commissioner for Archaeology, Antiquities Service, succeeded by J. Vercoutter; he excavated extensively at c.1955 Meroe, 1963-64 Debeira West.
119. Amara West temple was built by Thutmosis III and Hatshepsut and dedicated to the Nubian deity Dedun. It was covered up again as protection against erosion in 1948. There was also the temple of Ramses II 1296 B.C. and a town, the earliest levels being from the reign of Seti I c.1314 B.C.

## 7.8 Abri

The modern village looked attractive enough in the soft, afternoon light but, as soon as the sun began to drop, it became colder than ever and it was with relief, that we descended at our destination, Abri, about half past five. Here again the resthouse stood on the top of a small cliff, which fell sheer for about fifteen or twenty feet [to the river bank] and had nothing to protect it from the fierceness of the wind. It was a large and pleasant building. [It] had tall, generous windows all round but the glass had long since fallen out and the shutters were rather decrepit. There seemed no corner in my room which was out of the draught and all the blankets and woollen garments I possessed could not suffice to keep me warm in bed.

> [The building consisted of] two rooms and a *sala*, and another block for the kitchen ... All the archaeologists came to dinner and I very much admired the catering of the D.C.'s wife. The D.C.'s wife, who had had a slight cold, began to look very ill, growing paler and paler as the evening wore on. She found it wiser to stay in bed all the next day.

Hopes for the morning were disappointed since the bitter wind was still blowing and from somewhere a lot of cloud had arrived to cover the whole sky and give the place a generally wintery prospect. There were a few buildings near the resthouse but the main settlement was about half a mile further on, where there was a large palm grove.

> The D.C.'s wife had a temperature and probably 'flu, so we had to abandon the prospect of going on to Delgo that night. I had hoped to go on the next day to Delgo and Argo, villages upstream where we wanted to start schools, but this plan had to be abandoned.

Plans were just being completed for an extensive pump scheme[120] which would go into operation within the next few months.

With this in view it was thought advisable to put the new building for the girls' school just near the road, as this ran right through the middle of the scheme and houses were to be put up nearby. It was most encouraging to see one of the delightful cream-washed buildings with pointed arches and a small dome being built for a girls' school. At the back of the courtyard was a very pleasant house for the mistresses and to my surprise there was a wall round this but none round the school. 'We don't need it', said the men of the village. 'There are no passers-by in these parts. We are all our own people. It would cost so much that we might not have been able to build the school. And we must have a girls' school'.

---

120. An extensive pump scheme was planned at Abri for up to four square miles.

It was a most unexpected point of view, for the people in the Northern Province were generally considered extra conservative, but it was a highly satisfactory and practical attitude to a very great problem. Elsewhere some *sheikh*s had once demanded a wall sufficiently high to obscure the view of a man sitting on a camel.

As there were still a few finishing touches necessary classes were being held in an old [sub-grade school] building in the middle of the village. It was not a favourable arrangement and, whenever they could, the pupils came to look longingly at their new building to find out when it would be ready for them. There were plenty of girls in the school but it was difficult to know how they managed to survive these cold mornings. None of them had any warm clothes and their diet by our standards was fairly scanty.

> There were two classes of forty and twenty, much more backward than they need have been because the two former pairs of mistresses had hated the place and there had been far too many changes ... The children seemed rather quick. There was none of the apathy that one meets in a bad malarious district.

The mistresses, two very pretty sisters, were most unhappy and sighing for the warmth and comfort of Omdurman. They had been appointed here, as their father's family belonged to a village[121] upstream, about a day's journey on a slow lorry. They did not, however, feel any affinity with the place. Their father's village was at the end of the post-boat route and no great distance from the town of Dongola, but Abri they regarded as complete exile. Like the girls at Debeira they grumbled bitterly about the weather and the trouble of getting food, as all the shopping they could do was by the little canteen boat, which the Sudan Railways service sent along the river about once a fortnight. There was no market at all. Once again it was a case of struggling on for some years with constant changes of disgruntled staff, until some local girls were ready to take over. As it took at least seven years to prepare a girl knowing nothing to be even a moderate sort of teacher, these schools needed infinite patience. It was only because the mistresses were Government servants and under contract to go where they were sent, that we could staff such schools at all, but it would have been unwise and unkind to keep teachers there longer than one or two years even with a three-months vacation.

It was always a problem in these outlying areas. Yet time and time again one comes across earnest articles in reputable journals and in White Papers with airy plans about village education to make all Africans literate in a generation—'if only we will conceive a bold and imaginative policy'. The little *sitt* Suads and *sitt* Amnas who have to run the village schools cannot

121. Argo.

yet be made to think in terms of bold and imaginative policies. And who else is to do the teaching?

I cajoled them a little, scolded them a little, praised this, condoled about that, promised them some better equipment and took them for a short drive. But I had to stand firm on the question of transfer. Someone had to teach these children and all mistresses had to take their turn of the difficult stations. Moral uplift about educating Sudanese womanhood did not go over well in such conditions but, of course, it was the principle behind these unpopular postings. They brightened up somewhat, as the sun came out and the day grew warmer but I knew they would never be content, until they were appointed somewhere else.

> After lessons ... I took the mistresses to see the new house and school. A lot of children came running over with us too.

### 7.9 Zwenko

During the afternoon I drove a few miles upstream in country, which maintained the same blend of green strip by the blue water and bright brown and yellow beyond. I stopped at a village opposite Say Island,[122] which is supposed to be full of ancient remains, but on this afternoon was covered with young, green crops. The air was a little softer here and the houses settled down in a comfortable corner in a bend of the river. While I stood in the shade of some palm trees marvelling at the blue of the water, the driver came to tell me, that the *sheikh* of the village would take me into the tomb[123] of Sheikh Idris.[124] I was rather hazy about what was expected of me in such a visit but it was obviously a great honour. Nothing was said, however, about my taking off my shoes and I stood just inside the entrance at the top of the flight of steps and did not go on to the actual burying ground. There was not a lot to see but the large tomb of Sheikh Idris was pointed out with some banners of no particular beauty hanging up. I asked what were his claims to fame but could understand none beyond the fact, that he had been a very good and holy man and, in this peaceful strip of earth it seemed a very appropriate reason for being remembered. The graves

---

122. 'As Mrs Penn was staying in bed, the D.C. offered me the car' ... 'The countryside began to remind me of the country between Dongola and Merowe.' She visited Zwenko village, oppposite Say Island.

123. *Qubba*, tomb of a holy man or saint.

124. The driver 'thought I should go inside [Sheikh Idris' tomb] and while he went for the caretaker, I wandered through the village to the river .... I did not go to the burial ground, but I doubt if there would have been any real objection ... The building was built very cleanly of mud-brick coated with cement' and contained tombs of 'both men and women' from Sheikh Idris's family.

of the other members of his family inside the tomb were also pointed out to me but their histories were no more colourful than the great man's, and all I could do was to express my admiration for the architecture and take my leave.

## 7.10 Abri

I excused myself from coffee, as so unexpected a visit in the middle of the afternoon could not have failed to be a nuisance to the *sheikh*. All the people here were of a most captivating friendliness. They did not thrust their attentions on a visitor but the response of their greetings was of a real and sincere pleasure.

I had hoped to go on the next day to another two villages further upstream, where we wanted to start schools, but for various, unexpected reasons[125] time was against us and we had to return at once by the road we had come. There were no clouds the next morning and I remember it as a bright day all through. We set out early in the cold, vivid sunshine and the road was busy with dozens of people in their best clothes tramping in for a funeral in Abri. A *bikr* in this country had much of the importance of an Irish wake and was probably just about as noisy. The shrill wailing of the women was a sound, which only they could make by some curious manipulation of the tongue and by pressing the finger against the outside of the top lip. They did not make this cry as they walked along the road but both men and women, moving generally in separate groups, had a slightly holiday air about them. It was evidently going to be a party of large dimensions.

## 7.11 Akasha

We stopped at Akasha for lunch and climbed out on to the black rocks sticking out into the river and watched the D.C. trying without success to shoot some wild geese. After the first shot the geese just went a bit upstream and floated around in a quiet corner as if they were in St James' Park. After the second they got out into midstream and looked as if they were enjoying being tossed on the rough stream.

Somewhere south of Wadi Halfa, probably near Akasha, the women stopped wearing black robes and appeared in coloured print frocks with a lengthened form of kerchief over their heads. The frocks were no frivolous

125. 'We went back to Abri and I went for a walk along the river until dusk ... The next morning the invalid declared that the rest and fast had worked a complete cure and we decided to breakfast and then go back to Wadi Halfa by easy stages.'

imitations of European fashions but cut all to the same pattern. They hung loosely like a smock about the knees and after this was a full sort of frill reaching right to the feet but not so far as to touch the ground, yet giving a pleasant swing, as the wearer stepped along. There was a faint suggestion of the Balkans about the general impression but I may have arrived at this conclusion, because I had read, that a number of Bosnians from the Turkish Army remained in the country and settled in these parts. Not only do some of the cultivators lay claim to such ancestry but a few bear unmistakable traces of their origin in the shape of feature, if not so much in colouring.

### 7.12 Butn al-Hujar

> Entering the Butn al-Hujar this way is more impressive. You plunge straight in through a defile and see no more green until just before Sarras. The entry from Akasha was between quite high steep hills like going through a gate. The sun seemed brighter than the time before and the warmer glow of the afternoon made it seem even more brightly coloured ... the hills to the South ... seemed to go on for ever.

It was sunny too, when we passed again through the Butn al-Hujar, where the colours were fuller than ever in the late afternoon light.

### 7.13 Sarras

At Sarras, where we stopped again for the night, we had for contrast the pure white-and-black of a full moon.

> Sarras seemed very homely and welcoming ... it was still cold but not as bleak as Abri. It was pleasant to think that only a couple of hours' run separated us from the comfort of Wadi Halfa, the pleasure of a fire in the evening but the joy of the rose garden in the morning. In actual fact it took us more than two hours.

### 7.14 Gemai

Then on the next morning to Gemai for breakfast, where there was another new [boys'] school building to be inspected.

> It had been put up by the efforts of the villagers. They promptly asked for a girls' school to go with it. It was all very encouraging.

The resthouse had been a fort and was the exact replica of the toys with which the Christmas shops used to be full.[126] One side was sheer down to a cliff and at the back came the bends of a road up a steep slope to a courtyard with rooms all round. It was a lovely place for a resthouse for it must always have caught every breeze that blew in the front rooms, but there was bound to be shelter in the sunny courtyard by the entrance. We sat on the roof of the rest-house. It did not perhaps seem such a retreat this morning as there were about 200 Egyptians investigating the possibilities of a dam at this point, where the cataract narrowed the river considerably. It constricted the channel perhaps but made the stretch that much more interesting. Enormous black boulders stuck up out of the water and eddies and currents swirled and in some places [were] a few little trees.

> We lingered after inspecting the new school, while the D.C. went again after more geese. I didn't mind. It was very pleasant wandering about near the water. There were enough rather small trees for there to be a number of birds and I watched a green bee-eater.

## 8. Wadi Halfa

Halfa welcomed us back about midday with flowers in the garden and fires to gather round after dark. There were more parties too but I am not sure on what pretext, although an incident from one reminds me of the general friendliness I associate with the place. When I came into the room, an old man took my hands and greeted me with such warmth that a Sudanese official standing by remarked, 'Anyone would think she was his daughter'.

### 8.1 Sheikh Osman and Halima

Sheikh Osman was a merchant of much consequence in the town, whom I had known for many years, and it always gladdened me, that we remained friends, although I had had to disappoint many years before over a sad, little story.

The daughter of a cultivator, whom I will call Halima, had come to the Training College when it was not easy to get recruits from this district. Starting as a rather scruffy, sullen student, she blossomed during her first two years into a bright, attractive girl, though not academically shining. I returned from leave in the Lebanon one summer to find a very difficult

---

126. 'The resthouse at Gemai was a really delightful retreat.' It was constructed during *The River War* and was built 'on a small spur commanding the road and the river'. There were 'a flight of stairs into' a courtyard, whilst 'the two living rooms faced the river and had long windows on to a *mastaba*.'

tangle. Contrary to all we had had thrust on us unendingly about Sudanese customs, Halima had been left by her mother alone in the house with a cousin. He had taken prompt advantage of this opportunity and, when Halima returned to the Training College after the vacation, she was pregnant. To inflame the scandal still further she tried to commit suicide but electrocuting herself on the dim lighting system was not likely to be very successful. There was great indignation against the girl among the students and the Sudanese staff. The old *sheikh*, who taught religion, managed to complicate the issue still further. Claiming to be related to the family, he assured everyone with much emphasis, that on no account must her father know. He would be obliged to kill her, since his honour had been tarnished. No action was to be taken against the cousin apparently. On the advice therefore of the *sheikh* and the other Training College staff, the Director of Education ruled that Halima should be sent home as unfit for teaching because of her eyesight, which was admittedly weak, and incipient asthma. The mother, whom I never met, must have been a woman of resource, for immediately after her return home, the daughter had a miscarriage.

It was at this point that I returned to duty to be importuned by Halima's father. Calculating that, as I had been away, I could start again and reverse the Director's decision, he promised to take his daughter to Egypt to be tested for spectacles and to see a doctor about the asthma. Meanwhile with the old *sheikh* repeating his solemn warnings in season and out of season, this pretence of ill-health had to be maintained. I was quite sure, that her father was much too fond of Halima to do her any harm, and it did not make sense to suggest he had not heard what everyone else knew. But we always tried not to ride rough shod over Sudanese opinion and the sorry fiction was kept up. I might have persuaded the Director to grant a pardon but feeling in the Training College was so strong that the poor girl's position there would have been untenable.

Soon after I had to be in Halfa for an inspection and Sheikh Osman invited me to tea, as he always did. He lived in one of the large, two-storeyed houses in the centre of the town and we sat in a great, cool room, closely shuttered, drinking tea and making conversation. Suddenly he said, 'There is a matter on which I want your help'. At this moment with wonderful theatrical timing, the door opened and in came his daughter holding Halima by the hand. They made a charming picture Halima especially, with her sad, pretty face framed in spotless, white muslin making a most appealing figure. 'You see', said the old man, 'she is quite better now. She is a good girl and my daughter loves her dearly. They have always been together like sisters. The doctor says she is quite strong now'.

It was obvious that the health fiction had to be continued but the whole scene was so unexpected, that I was completely at a loss. I just stammered a few commonplaces and then asked, if I could talk to Halima alone. This was a great relief to both of us, since we no longer had to pretend, that we did not know what had happened. At first there was little to say. The unhappy girl just laid her head on my shoulder and sobbed bitterly, and I was distressed that I had no means of comforting her. She realised, however, far better than her family the hostility she would have to face at the Training College, and it would have been unkind and pointless to talk about discipline.

I felt myself a failure in not being able to devise some third way out of the difficulty and went back to Sheikh Osman with a very heavy heart. There was no doubt that he had heard the whole story and, although not a relative, had interceded from his general benevolent attitude. The best thing, I suggested, would be for her father to find a husband for her, but the old man appeared to think that this would not be easy. He did not urge me much more and I felt that in his kindness he understood my dilemma and was sorry for me too. It was this that increased my affection for him. There was no question of taking offence at my refusal but he always gave this friendly welcome, whenever we met. The end of Halima's story is fortunately not tragic. She did eventually marry some undistinguished person but not the dastardly cousin, who was sheltered by all this pretending from any punishment.

I have told this story at some length, because, in my recalling of the Sudan, people recur as readily as places and matter much more. The sight of Halfa I can always conjure up but with it comes memories of the schoolmistresses, the kindly *omdah* at Debeira and the warm heart of Sheikh Osman. He died some years ago and thus will never have the grief of seeing engulfed in the rising waters from the Aswan Dam the town of which he was so much a part. At the time of the high flood of 1946 I remember him, despite his age, actively directing the sand-bagging which saved the place from destruction. Now modern technology and Egyptian desire have frustrated all his efforts and will soon have laid waste all these peaceful villages, exiled the friendly people and ruined the historic treasures. I count myself fortunate that I was in time to have even so small a share in this remote, unhurried life.

# Chapter III

# The West

## A. Kordofan

## Trip 1

### 1.1 West to El Obeid

I had gone early to Kordofan[1] and the fascination of these more colourful parts always gave a special flavour to journeys to the West. The first trip to El Obeid had been something of an adventure; now it seemed rather like home ground and was generally a stage to a more remote spot. Yet I always enjoyed the journey and remember with particular vividness going there one September[2] during the war. I pulled up my shutters after supper and slept through the flat monotony of the Gezira. Looking eastwards at dawn was a cheerful start to the day, for about a dozen ostriches, startled by the train, were hurrying towards the rising sun with all the comic awkwardness of gait, that the cartoonists have led us to expect. Unfortunately as they moved with great speed directly away from us, they were soon lost to view.

Shortly after, the country showed a very different aspect from my original sight of it. Intensive grain[3] cultivation had been going on in these parts to ensure supplies against a food shortage, since, cut off as we were, there would have been no possibility of enlisting help from outside. It had been no easy task, as labour was difficult to obtain. Unemployment as such was relatively unknown, although there were often a lot of vagrants hanging about the towns, where the tradition of hospitality generally meant a casual meal could be found somewhere, or food of some sort for those with few standards regarding quality. To press these unhandy types into service may be the only means in an emergency but it made hard going for those in charge of the cultivation. The men were well paid but had no incentive to

---

1. 3-11.3.40.
2. September 1941.
3. *Dura*, millet. 'Kordofan has a surplus, which it was sending to the eastern provinces and to the clamourous towns. The lorries incidently belonged to Italians in Eritrea and our late enemies were being provided with a comfortable livelihood by using their vehicles to transport these extra loads of corn'.

strenuous toil. Sugar and tea were rationed, cigarettes and tobacco very scarce and there was little else of luxury in their limited ideas. Making a plan for the starving poor to grow food was appropriate enough but the starving poor were more interested in the lack of tobacco than non-starvation. Nevertheless the effort had been made and for acres round tall plants of *dura* raised heavy plump heads to a cool damp morning. It was a most encouraging sight.

We had been travelling almost due south between the two Niles but, as we came back to the White Nile, there was the contrast from a rainfall[4] heavier than that in Omdurman. Instead of dry, gravel wastes the ground was covered with lush, green grass [near Kosti] besprinkled with odd flowers and, crossing over the causeway, I could see the marshes below bright with the red and white of the water-lilies and the purple of the water hyacinth.

This extra luxuriance continued all the way [to El Obeid] with the grass high and plentiful.

> It was sufficiently tall for the enormous droves of cattle strolling in leisurely fashion to be almost smothered in it but not entirely covered.

They were under the guardianship of remarkably few herdsmen. Cattle on the move are difficult for the inexpert to number but these appeared to be well beyond the thousand mark. Docile beasts they were but collected together like that they were not easy to control. There was one unhappy incident, when a herd suddenly divided and half strayed across the railway line. One wretched man darted off, shouting wildly; the cattle began to run, with more and more following their leaders over the track. The train whistled furiously but it was too long to pull up quickly. At least three beasts were hit and rolled to the mud at the bottom of the embankment. Whether their backs were broken or whether they were just unable to pull themselves out of the mud, I could not tell, but it was a sad finish to the exciting spectacle of hundreds of cattle forging through the tall grass.

### 1.2 Visit to Sheikh Ahmad in El Obeid

Behind the romantic sights in El Obeid, the strings of camels bringing in the gum, and others setting off with much stamping and roaring, as the sun went down; the busy *suq* with its tailors and saddlers and cobblers sitting among their wares was the prosaic section of the town settled in bourgeois comfort inside their mud walls. The houses of the Syrian and Greek traders were sometimes a bit grander than those of the middle class Sudanese, but a

---

4. Rainfall for El Obeid 14.21 inches p.a. compared with Khartoum 6.30 inches p.a. (*Sudan Almanac*, 1941).

visit to one of the latter showed how in this particular case social habits were changing. Sheikh Ahmed was immensely proud of the fact, that he had taught in the Girls' Training College, when it had first opened. This was indeed much to his credit and a real matter of faith and courage, since even twenty five years later there were men who objected to teaching girls as being beneath their dignity. He spoke excellent English and at his stage of promotion in the Education Department many of his colleagues had adopted European dress but he preferred his robes, which were much like those of a judge. A loose garment of striped silk, which fastened on the shoulder and had wide sleeves, was girdled with a silk sash. Over this was worn a flowing gown open all down the front; this was the real caftan and was usually made of very fine gaberdine. Navy and black were the most common colours but maroon and brighter blues were quite popular and I once had a visitor who was resplendent in a most exquisite cloth of pale lime green. A small red cap with a button in the middle was worn on the head with a white cloth, known as an *immah* wound tidily about it.

His choice of this becoming costume was no symptom of conservatism on the part of Sheikh Ahmed, as we found when he invited another English woman and myself to his house. Tea parties tended to divide into two groups. In one, the visitor, often myself as the only woman, sat solemnly in the outside court with the host and some male guests. I appreciated the compliment but the atmosphere was generally more free and easy in the back- quarters with the women, with the master of the house absent. This, however, was different, for we were introduced into the family in the most homely way and the atmosphere was delightful. His wife was a shrewd, intelligent woman of much good-nature, who had taught needlework in a mission school before her marriage. Even at Sheikh Ahmed's level there were plenty of officials with illiterate wives and he was justly proud of this other link with women's progress. She had now settled down to be a capable housewife but her contacts outside her home were still wide and there was evidently much companionable gossip between her and her husband. Among other descriptions of household management she gave is a long dissertation on the uses of spices, which we had seen in the market place, and their various uses.

The children did not sit down with us but they were allowed to come and talk for a while but not to be a nuisance. There was a difference of about a year between the ages of the two daughters and their education was to be an experiment. One was to go as far as she could on the Government system, while the other attended a non-Government school which used Egyptian syllabuses and took Egyptian examinations. Their father wanted to discover which would produce the more satisfactory result. Both girls were very promising and the failure of the plan was only because the Egyptian school in El Obeid closed down.

> El Obeid was not very different from my previous visit except that the country round about was so much greener and pleasanter. I was a little worried by the problem of shows put on for my benefit. Suspected, for example, that the adult education work was not always as I saw it. I suppose the only way, as inspectors are so few, is to try and get some conscience into the headmistress. The Governor very kindly invited all the mistresses to tea. They were very pleased to come and all behaved quite nicely but seemed just a little over-awed.

## 1.3 El Obeid to Bara

After a few days for a brief inspection of the schools in El Obeid itself, I set off for Bara early one morning, after a night of rain had washed the air clean and fresh and left a delightful temperature for travelling. To add to this was the firm surface of the road, where the damp sand presented much easier running than the usual dusty progress. Once out of the town we were in open country, where the tall grass by the roadside had not yet wilted. The land undulated very gently and at times we came to the top of an incline and could look round at a gently rolling landscape with sufficient growth of small trees to give an appearance of greenness.

> One of the prettiest roads I have been on for a long time, at that time of year but very possibly unpleasant when the weather gets dry and sandy later.

There were sudden corners of delight. At one point there might be great stretches of ripening corn, which bordered the road and hid the view. *Dura* is not a crop with the flowing beauty of wheat or barley, but its tall full-headed magnificence with each plant set a foot or so from its neighbours has a glory of its own. Another picture I recall was a bend in the track where some moderate-sized trees leaned over a pool left by last night's rain. A little further along, the deep cart ruts in the sand were also filled with water rippling slightly in a fresh breeze. The washed earth was a clean, bright red, the puddles the soft reflected blue of the sky except where the shadows of the branches moved backwards and forwards across the larger pool. The thorn trees still in leaf were a palish green. In a country were so many of one's days are spent in a sand coloured atmosphere, if nothing more drab, such moments of variegation remain.

## 1.4 Bara

The two hour journey along a road of this sort [by lorry] had been pleasing all the way and the sight of Bara itself was a fitting ending. It was a very wide village with broad streets, planted irregularly with many well-grown trees.

> Bara is a slightly odd place, having been an Army Headquarters, and not like Shabarqa ... The resthouse was a small mud building, two rooms, verandah and fortunately a proper bathroom.

The fences, mostly made of grass, surrounded extensive enclosures in which were a number of round huts according to the needs of the family. Grass was used for thatching also and the general effect was a satisfying contrast to the square mud houses and walls that I was accustomed to further east. After the over-crowded old houses with which we struggled in so many places, the school itself was a joy. There was an enormous yard of at least an acre, plentifully besprinkled with shady trees, and placed under these trees were two long cream-washed buildings with gaily painted green shutters and deep thatched roofs sloping out over the verandahs. Similar houses and an equally generous provision of space had been allowed for the mistresses' living quarters.

These, however, were enclosed within the high fence and, although the mistresses were very appreciative of the excellent and comfortable arrangements, they were withal a little restless, as they did not belong to the district. When the usual friendly greetings and politeness was over, one of them smiled broadly and said, 'We are so glad you have come. Now we can go out'.

This was [the beginning of] October and since their arrival in July, such was public opinion locally, they had literally not set foot outside the gate. I had with me a box car and an amiable driver and we quickly made arrangements for some expeditions. The first was a short drive in the evening towards the hills in the west. We were travelling towards a vivid sunset made glorious by many clouds and spontaneous cries of pleasure from the girls made the evening still more enjoyable. 'Oh, what a lovely view,' said one, whose home was in Khartoum, as soon as we emerged from the village street.

Before us the country rose gently in a series of softly sloping ridges still green with the grass of the rains. Here at one time had been a station of the Western Camel Corps [to the west of the town] and the old barracks and groups of houses presented the orderly and workmanlike appearance of cantonments in most places. Occasional mishaps such as sticking in the sand only added to the fun and gave my policeman-driver a chance to show his skill. Away from prying villagers and with me as chaperone, the girls could uncover their faces and exchange a few little jokes with him at these points. I was only sorry that they had not seen what I had the night previous. I had been walking in this direction rather slowly, because the going is heavy, when the sand is soft all the way, but my attention had been diverted from the discomfort of my feet to a disturbance overhead. The sun had gone and in the grey dusk it was a little difficult for the ignorant to see what birds they were but, I think, storks. As I stood there looking up, they passed over in hundreds, one flight after another. While one group whirred over my head, another appeared faintly against the dimming horizon. I had read of the orderliness of migrations but could never have expected to be so close to such a superb example. For about a quarter of an hour I waited in wonder and curiosity and still there was no end, as the cohorts followed one after another, as far as I could see, in perfect formation. As the light falls so quickly, I felt I must go before the darkness was complete, and I might lose my way. Yet all the way back to the resthouse the air was full of the swish of their rapid flight.

> I enjoyed staying here. It was cooler than Omdurman and very restful to be quite alone for two or three days, alone in the sense that my only social duty was to have the mistresses to tea at the resthouse. One brought a very spoilt small sister, another an aunt.

There was a teaparty at the resthouse, another at the school and a less unsuccessful call on the *nazir*'s wives. These dowdy looking women sat in a badly lighted room and appeared most uncomfortably over-awed. There was, I understood, a tradition of jealous seclusion. As a striking contrast, the mistresses were wearing their usual crisp, white muslin *tobe*s; the little braids of their hair were clean and smooth; their skins shining and healthy. They chattered away, full of gossip and any small tale they could find for amusement, while the ladies of the house, closely wrapped in dingy cotton, had little to discuss, shut in within the limits of their house and yard. Evidently I was not the only one to make the comparison. After a year or two when girls' schools began to spread in the West, it happened, not infrequently, that a wealthy *nazir*, perhaps owning much land and many cattle, married the local schoolmistress, who might have even been a girl of quite humble origin from elsewhere.

It was a pity that in a district like this, seclusion should have been such an important issue in the village itself. The morning after our drive the Headmaster of the boys' school came down in the middle of lessons to tell me, that it was quite all right for me to take the schoolmistresses out. By this time I was learning to hold my tongue and I just let him continue. He understood, however, that the geography syllabus included studying the district and making maps of the village. The District Education Committee, all male of course, objected to these walks and so far there had been none. They were not regarded as proper for girls. 'Traipesing about the streets,' he said, scandalised at the mere prospect, 'instead of staying in and learning their lessons'.

The staff were present at this discussion, as the argument had evidently been started some time before. In the course of it the teacher from Khartoum exclaimed, with some heat, 'Who are the Local Education Committee that they should object to what the Girls' Training College and the Controller of Girls' Education think is right for the children to do?'

This comment was very ill-received, but we made a compromise. A walk as far as the Post Office should be tried; it would not be a long one and it would avoid any busy streets.

I was not surprised that after an interval that was not too blatant, there came a lot of vague talk against this particular mistress. She and her aunt went out visiting, the village tale tellers said, and stayed out late.

> The subsequent news, according to village gossip, that the aunt (who came to tea with me) had been taking her niece and another teacher gallivanting about late at night makes me wonder ... She seemed a well brought up and pleasant creature whom I liked when she came to tea with me earlier.

Feeling grew so high that we had to transfer her. The aunt, whom I had met and liked, was a woman with some force of character and the girl herself was a bright and useful teacher with a most pleasant disposition. She was, however, known to have slave blood and that joined to an enterprising outlook and a general forthrightness resulted in all sorts of people taking opportunities for slandering her; but she weathered the storms and did well in the service, particularly when she came back to the Three Towns, and started learning English on her own initiative.

## Trip 2

### 2.1 Um Ruaba

The following January,[5] I was able to investigate yet other parts of Kordofan. This time I left the train some hours before El Obeid at Um Ruaba among the red sand and the great *neem* trees. It was about two o'clock and I was taken to the resthouse, a very comfortable European style building, where I had a proper bath and a pot of tea sent across by the

---

5. 11.1.42 onwards. See also S.A.D. 657/6/8 for Dr Beasley's visit on 22.4.45.

Sudanese Sub-Inspector.[6] This was all set out on a most elegant tray with fine china and glittering silver, very much more splendid that the peasant pottery that lumped around in my trek box.

I waited for the lorry to Tegale which arrived an hour late.

I was bound for a village on the edge of the Nuba Mountains and was to travel on the public lorry, because, among other reasons, transport was becoming too scarce during the war to spare a vehicle for one person, if any other arrangement were possible. For my part, I was interested in finding out how people did travel and was fully rewarded, when I discovered that it was rather like the carrier's cart in a Hardy novel. True this was a very heavy lorry, but it performed much the same function.

We set off just [after] five, which is the routine pattern for most of these journeys. The drivers preferred night work, since it was manifestly cooler and the sand was firmer and the lorry less likely to stick. I have no reliable data on this last point. I only know that I could never induce the driver of a public lorry to alter his timing, even if all the passengers and freight were ready. This vehicle was typical of all the others I ever saw. It was piled so high that to a casual observer it looked most unsafe and extremely hard on the engine. Passengers were allowed to lie on top of the goods and, as far as I know, managed to cling on over the roughest of tracks. I always expected a cry that Ahmed or Mohamed had been jolted off but I never remember one. Privileged persons paid extra to sit in the front with the driver, where the seat had been extended to jut out over the wheels and accommodate as many as five persons. Extra privileged persons, like myself, shared the front seat with the driver only, although in this case we had a young woman too for a couple of stages.

It was not as cold as I had hoped but nevertheless very pleasant setting off in the freshness of the evening to drive towards the faint line of the mountains with the great ball of the sun alongside them. We crossed the railway line and journeyed vaguely south-west and soon floundered into wide patches of soft sand, through which we went grinding along in bottom gear but without mishap. I noticed particularly one of the joys of evening in other countries, which was rare here with seldom any dew—that was the faint scent of some aromatic plant, which rose up from the ground. As we went along, the vegetation increased, for, although there had been trees of a

6. Abdel Salam Abdulla, O.B.E., 5N. 1.7.15 First appointment; 15.12.38 appointed to Kordofan; 1942 Sub-Inspector then A.D.C., Eastern Kordofan District, based in Um Ruaba; 1.7.45-47 A.D.C., Berber; 1948 D.C., Dilling; By March 1949-1954 Under Secretary for Interior; 1955-1956 nominated as Senator to the parliament of Sudan. His brother was Daoud el Khalifa Abdulla and his father was the Khalifa.

xerophytic type scattered sparsely from the beginning, during the journey they became larger and shadier, sometimes occurring in fair-sized clumps big enough to be classed as copses.

Twilight was just finishing, when the foot-brake gave way and we sat for half an hour or so in the complete stillness of the empty countryside, while the driver and his assistant tinkered about inside the bonnet.

> There were not many passengers, one or two old men and a policeman with a musket who may have been looking after the mail.

I understood later, when we came to the hills, why so much care had been necessary. After it was all safely repaired, the driver explained to me that he was always quite happy, if his lorry was going well, but he did dislike having anything wrong with his engine—a sentiment which I heartily applauded. Apparently he made a weekly round, spending most of his life on the road. I asked him if he never got tired of it all, but he repeated that he was perfectly happy, as long as the engine was going well. I wondered if this were some of the much-discussed Arab *Wanderlust* but in a mechanised version.

For the remainder of the journey it was completely dark and the fascination of driving at night was enhanced by the strangeness of the place and not knowing what would appear in the headlights. Occasionally people, generally carrying spears, would be focussed in the white glare of the lamps, as they walked along at a steady pace, looking very black in contrast to their robes. Odd hares or rabbits scurried across the path or little jerboas skipped along in front of the light and once a gazelle bounded out. Then my attention was suddenly caught at one spot, where we had to cross a dry water course. A large number of these, which had very steep sides, lay across the track and must have been quite creditable streams when in spate. As we rose out of one of these beds, the [head]lights picked out a group of mounted men clustered together on the high bank under the trees. Actually they were on donkeys and were no doubt weary cultivators going home, but in this strange setting the first impression was of some 'ambush by the ford' in a cloak and dagger drama with riders shrouded in white robes. Getting in and out of gullies like this one made me understand why the driver had been so concerned to have his foot-brake in order.

A less dramatic but more intrinsically beautiful wayside scene was formed by the glow and shadows on a *rakuba* projecting from a grass hut, where a family was squatting round a fire cooking a meal. The movement and colour of the burning wood as one bright point in the darkness was arresting enough but added to this loveliness were the changing silhouettes of the half-naked black bodies moving against the glow.

I was surprised that there were not more vignettes but the country was thinly populated anyway and the people settled near their cultivation, away from the road. The one or two villages we did pass through thoroughly roused my curiosity, for the driver always had some business to transact which meant quick glimpses into other people's lives. Here he had bought something for one of the inhabitants; there he was given a small commission to discharge at the next stop; somewhere else was a bill for him to pay on a client's behalf, when he returned to Um Ruaba; at another place there was more merchandise to be loaded on to what I had thought too much already; finally he was to take charge of a woman who had to travel to another village.

## 2.2 Abbassia Tegale

Fascinating though these transactions proved to me as an onlooker, they used up a considerable amount of time and progress was slow anyway, for we were mounting gradually all the way and the track was very rough. It was, therefore, about half past nine, when we reached the village, which was my destination at Abbassiya, but the driver was going on until morning, as his round through the mountains would take two or three days. He deposited me, with my servant and my luggage by a building, which would have looked uninviting at any time but viewed by the light of the caretaker's hurricane lamp fitted all too well with the 'ambush by the ford' motif, especially as there were no other houses near to radiate a friendly glow. This old resthouse had been condemned and soon after was superseded by a much more comfortable one, but it was to be my shelter for the next few days. It consisted of a low, mud room, very roughly shaped many years before and whitewashed at some distant date. Several seasons of rain had given it rather a streaky look and in the unending struggle with white ants it had not always resisted successfully. To guard against these the great thatched roof, which came almost down to the ground in some places, had been propped up on a double row of piles, set in the earth outside

to prevent the wood from touching the walls. They were roughly hewn and the whole structure looked rough.

My consolation was that I need only use it as a dressing room, for all my sleeping and eating could be outside.

Even then I was more ready for bed than food and, content with just a bowl of soup, soon realised again how comfortable a good camp bed could be after the hard bench of the lorry. As I lay there in the darkness, however, I was kept awake until midnight by the noise from the market place.[7]

7. 'I was actually unlucky because this was *suq* day and there was not another while I was there.'

Judging by the drums and pipes, the singing and clapping of hands that suggested dancing, it must have been a party of some considerable size and great hilarity. It was tempting to wonder if anybody might join in, but much as I should have liked at least to watch all the gaiety, I was a bit diffident about going down on my own in a place, where I did not know anyone. This was not quite the ordinary Arab village, where the *sheikh* or *omdah* might have been an old acquaintance. I had never met the *Mek* of Tegale and did not want to start my visit with a breach of manners. A solitary white woman was bound to be conspicuous and might find her presence difficult to explain, since the general merriment suggested there might be more of Nuba than Arab in the company.

I turned over and slept soundly in the end and, as so often happens, the morning prospect was much more pleasing. At one end of the resthouse, the roof did not hang down so far and I could sit on a sort of verandah to drink my early morning tea and look over the valley to the higher peaks, where trees grew, if not in profusion, yet in sufficient number to soften the stony appearance of the surface. Abbassiya was just at the beginning of the Nuba Mountains but already some 2,000 feet up.

> The village was practically all round grass huts with one or two brick houses for *effendia* and the schoolmaster.

It was just the kind of scenery to tempt me on exploratory walks. Perhaps it was as well that I had to spend my time in the school, if one listened to local gossip. People said that strange things happenened to those who went walking in the mountains, the implication being that the spirits did not want intruders. Look at those two D.C.s who would wander about and then had peculiar illnesses that no-one could diagnose but they had to leave the district. I had not heard all this and a little regretfully walked down the road to school.

There were no regrets, however, when I got there.

> The school buildings were good ... It did not appear to be overwhelmingly popular.

The schoolmistresses were so genuinely glad to welcome me first as a visitor, and then as an official with whom to discuss their problems. It was another difficult school to run and for many years was only about half full. Most of the children were the daughters of merchants or officials or cultivators of rather mixed origin; there were no real Nuba among them. Nevertheless they were somewhat backward compared with the school at Um Ruaba and the Headmistress said she had to deal tactfully with parents. By the time the girls had reached the Fourth Year they would listen to her, but she dared not be too strict about cleanliness in the early stages, or the children would not come to school at all. I appreciated her point, when I met some of the villagers in the fields later, and for a few minutes I pondered the idea of whether I should not be doing these women a greater service by peddling soap than by trying to spread education. Certainly it seemed arguable that a Government's duties should provide access to soap and water as easily as to justice.

That each of the schoolmistresses should ask to be transferred to her own home was part of the routine which we all accepted. Once that was over we were very merry together with a tea-party either in their house or in the resthouse every day. Two of them were particularly lively girls with a great deal to say for themselves. There was much giggling generally and a lot of tittering especially, when I mentioned the party in the market place on the night of my arrival. This was due to what one might see on a market day. Naked Nubas apparently strolled in from the neighbouring hills and the effect on these *harem* bred girls was to cause a snigger rather than a display of moral disapproval such as was voiced by the educated men of the towns.

Whatever the difficulties of rationing schoolmistresses usually managed to look well-dressed and these four were no exception, although very different from one another. The Headmistress was a girl of much charm, intelligence and intrinsic worth with features that were almost European and a warm skin approximating to the tan to be seen on Mediterranean beaches. Another was a fat, jolly girl rather darker, whose intellectual abilities were not high, but who always had her class under perfect control despite the frequent gusts of laughter which came floating out. One was a pretty small, child just out of College, and the fourth was a rather black young woman,[8] royal in manner, who gave herself airs, because she was [niece] of the local *mek* and thought she might marry his son, although no-one else agreed. Altogether she was a troublesome person, who had to be constantly moved, since the villagers did not take kindly to her superior manners. At the moment they were all living very happily together and had made friends in the village.

> They giggled a lot, especially as the arm of my camp chair would not hold and every time Melk ed-Dar made an emphatic gesture, the strap gave way amid much laughter.

On one of the afternoons when I went [to tea] in the [mistresses'] house, some of these friends arrived, and one woman was introduced to me as the

8. Sara Ramadan, niece of the local *mek* Adam; 1942 teacher at Abbassiya school. Tegale was a hybrid kingdom which had been strong enough at one time to wage war successfully against the sultans of Sennar. It survived in semi-independence through the Turkish regime and was resuscitated in a new guise as a local government unit. *Mek* [*Makk*] was a title given to the vassal-kings of the Funj sultan.

wife of an official in the Agricultural Department. And she has been to school, the mistresses announced proudly. From our point of view it may be an odd way to introduce one's friends but the idea of the educated women in a village immediately getting together was an encouraging one.

> I used to have another visitor in the afternoons when I was trying to work. The *ghaffir* from the school, a gnome-like man with one leg, used to come and lean on the verandah and talk.
> None of the notables came to see me ... I should have liked to meet a *mek*, although I believe they are rather spurious royalty.
> ... I was taken round the boys' school by the headmaster ... The school had an agricultural basis but their fields were some distance away. The boys shouted poems at me in each class and the band was brought out to play for me ... They played very well, about a dozen pipes and a large and small drum. As I did not meet the schoolmaster until the day I was going away, I couldn't visit him, which might have been interesting. I had already met him in Gedaref ... He and his assistants came to see me off the next day and he made arrangements about the lorry, which I thought very kind of him.

Although this time I saw little of the place beyond the road between the school and the resthouse, I enjoyed my first glimpse of Tegale and, as I was able to return to Um Ruaba in the afternoon, I had a good view of the country in the daylight on the way back. It may not have been quite so romantic as seen by the headlights against the darkness but it was an interesting road with the changing shapes of mountains, for about half the way and the dry water courses with trees lining their banks.

### 2.3 Um Ruaba

> I liked Um Ruaba, the red sand and the rows of green *neem* trees, the wide streets and the grass houses give it a colourful look. I never remember so many flies. The people were friendly and the school was good.

Um Ruaba seemed very civilised in its well-appointed resthouse.

> It had a garden with trees in it, with the hills faintly visible on the skyline. The first evening I had dinner with the Sub-Inspector[9] who spoke English which made a welcome change ... He talked a lot and I think he thought it rather an exciting experience. We had a thoroughly English dinner ...

in his garden by the light of red shaded candles [which] was a touch of sophistication I had not expected. It was an excellent, if rather over-abundant meal including fish and turkey. I knew it was not the custom for wives to eat in front of their husbands and that in this particular case

9. Abdel Salam Abdulla.

doubtless the wife would have felt embarrassed, but I could never get used to a situation in which the husband so flagrantly pushed his woman on one side. His wife was very shy in front of him, although I think she would have talked more, if we had been left longer on our own.

'You see, she isn't educated', he explained with a wave of the hand and so back she retired to the probable squalor of the back quarters [leaving] her husband and the foreign woman to the spotless linen and silver of a European dinner table. The other contrast, which I could not avoid, having read the country's history, was that this clever and able Government official was also one of the sons of the Khalifa and like his brother,[10] whom I had met in Berber, rapidly rising in the service.

> The school was good. The headmistress was not a Kordofan girl but from Giteina ... with a strong personality, who seemed to justify so firmly girls' education ... There were faults in the school but it was such a vigorous institution that I got a lot of pleasure out of it ... There was a tea-party on the last day of my visit and the girls acted the usual Pied Piper extraordinarily well. There were quite a few mothers about and interested spectators.

I was given hospitality of all kinds while I was there, including an informal tea drinking with the *mamur*'s wife after an experience, which, I devoutly hope, will never be repeated.

Finding the resthouse stuffy, I went for a walk a little before four o'clock. It was pleasant country, slightly rolling with a fair amount of green still about in the trees, although mostly sand underfoot of a red and cheerful colour. There were no very definite landmarks and I wandered idly along, getting off the path as being somewhat easier to the feet, since what little grass that remained had been worn away in the track, making the going very soft. After about an hour or so I thought I had better go back before sunset. There was no sign of the path on which I had started and, when I turned, I realised with a horrible sick feeling that I had not the least idea within a half circle where Um Ruaba lay. Never even in London in 1944,[11] when fly bombs cut out overhead, have I known such acute and devastating panic. I wanted to run, just to run somewhere, anywhere. It was unbelievable, that I should be alone, really lost in this unending wilderness and all through my own stupid fault. There was not a sound, except the occasional chirrup of a bird, hardly even a breeze to stir the branches of the thorn trees. I tried to keep control of myself and, once the effort was made, I was able to plan a little. I knew that I should be looked for in the morning

---

10. Daoud el Khalifa Abdulla.
11. Dr Beasley went on went on leave to London in 1944.

but I also knew that there was no moon and the thought of a night out there in the darkness was not the least of my horrors.

> I even forgot I had matches and cigarettes with me. I found that I was praying really sincerely, which startled me.

I had an idea, mistaken as it happened, that the railway ran north-west here. In actual fact it ran due west and the turn was much further on. I decided that if I walked due west I was bound to strike the railway eventually but the sun was sinking very rapidly and I could not calculate what sort of a detour I had made. I headed therefore in that direction trying to focus on the faint smudge of the Nuba Mountains. Then just when the sun had really gone, I stopped short, for, although the surprise took my breath for a minute, it was a definite uplift in my present state of mind. Just at my feet was a path, not a very wide one but quite distinct and running vaguely south-east, north-west. It did not seem to my erroneous ideas that I wanted to go either way but the track had been trodden so often and so recently by the feet of a number of donkeys, that I was sure it must lead to some biggish place. I chose the north-west direction for no particular reason but that I had west in my head, and I stepped along it as briskly as the soft sand would allow. By this time the ordinary palpitations of fear had a considerable mixture of real anger with myself for being such a fool as not to notice some kind of point for a bearing, and for not telling my servant what I was doing. I had seen no-one since he cleared away my lunch.

Suddenly I thought I heard a noise in the greyness ahead of me, a noise that was neither birds nor trees but might have been someone gently urging on a beast. On this rolling countryside it was quite easy for anyone to be out of sight until really close. Because of this and the shadows thickening all round and no doubt my own mood it would have been simple to imagine that the little donkey with a great rustling load of straw[12] on his back was coming towards me out of the ground. And the little brown peasant who followed him might have been conjured up too; he would have made a very good gnome. I was not, however, thinking in terms of folklore at the time and, as I uttered the usual salutations of peace and blessing, I realised how heart-felt mine were. 'I want the Um Ruaba road', I then said. 'This is it,' he answered. I exclaimed with joy but obviously sounded amazed. 'Yes,' he said. 'I am going there. But you are going the other way'. 'I don't care where you are going,' was my prompt reply. 'I am coming with you.' He was obviously going home for the night and at least there would be people. Food and shelter did not matter as long as I did not have to spend the hours of darkness alone in the wilderness. Conversation was a bit restricted, since

---

12. 'Gussab' [qaṣab], straw.

my rescuer could not understand at all what I was doing wandering about in the dusk. For a man who probably had to walk five miles to his cultivation, just going for a walk did not make sense, nor could he find any reason for me to be heading in the opposite direction to where I wanted to go. Afterwards I wondered if he might have taken me for some sort of *afreet*,[13] appearing suddenly, all white against the gathering gloom. My explanation of my presence in Um Ruaba and my connection with Government Service appeared to reassure him.

We were probably not more than two or three miles from the town but tramping back through that sandy waste the road seemed interminable. As it soon grew quite dark, all sorts of queer fancies came, but the plodding of the little donkey, who evidently knew the way, had a stabilising effect. How long all this took I do not know; there are many ways of measuring time. [After about half an hour] the donkey began to quicken his pace; then there was the bray of another in the distance; and lastly the very faint hum of an inhabited place. Quite suddenly, as if it too had risen from the earth, the beginning of the town was there in an extra blackness, as we stood under the great trees. Here we met friends of my guide and after calling a greeting, he shouted, 'I met her on the road. She thought she was going to Um Ruaba and she was walking right in the opposite direction.' At that, they all roared with laughter, as if it were the funniest joke they had heard for years.

'Arabian Nights' humour has never appealed very much to me but I had no objection to providing a subject for mirth now that I was safely back. I thanked my cultivator effusively, and, as I shook his hand, I poured into it all the silver which I had in my purse. I was glad I had silver, because it seemed a proper gesture. Paper would have been unfeeling. 'There is no need,' he protested. 'There is no need. But thank you.'

The friends then took charge of me and led me to the *mamur*,[14] who by his very presence neutralised my recent nightmare sensations. He was an immense man in girth and well over six feet in height. In company with a number of elderly *sheikh*s he had been sitting on the ground among a circle which had evidently been discussing something very earnestly. They made

---

13. *Afreet* [*'ifrīt*], evil spirit, ghost.
14. Ibrahim Yusuf Bedri, son of Yusuf, brother of Babikr Bedri. Babikr Bedri stood *in loco parentis* after Yusuf's suicide in 1923. Yusuf was a merchant in Kosti who shot himself because he was bankrupted over the Government sugar contract. Ibrahim was a founder member of the Sudanese Union Society (1923), the pioneer organisation of educated political opposition. In 1924 he scarcely troubled to conceal his sympathy with the White Flag League militants, with Ahmed Bedri (Babikr's son), which led to some delay in his appointment, as sub-*mamur* in 1925; 1942 *mamur* Um Ruaba.
    Ali Awadalla was *mamur* Um Ruaba, Northern Kordofan District from 1.1.48.

an impressive array under the big *neem*s in the harsh light of a petro-max lamp.

He took me straight into his house to drink tea with his wife, telling me that I knew her father, and this indeed was soon established, for Sitt Sara[15] was one of the many children of my good friend, Sheikh Babikr Bedri, and had herself been a schoolmistress many years ago. There was no undue formality here. Drinks were brought and she and I gossiped over a pot of tea, while a very charming small daughter clambered over me and wanted to be played with in the manner of small children everywhere.

I came [to this house again the next day] to a different and in some ways less enjoyable visit to drink tea with all the wives of importance in the town. The schoolmistresses had been invited as well and they spoke with much gratitude of the kindness of Sitt Sara, who always welcomed them and saw that they were not shut away and lonely. The officials' wives, with whom I had tea here and almost every other day that I was in the place, may not have risen to the dizzy heights of rose-shaded candles but they were perfectly at home sitting on chairs and sipping tea from European cups and saucers and chatting away, in an endless tide of cheerful conversation. In fact I received so much hospitality during my week in Um Ruaba, that I had to have a couple of days fasting, when it was over.

## Trip 3 The Nuba Mountains

Two years later[16] I was able to penetrate right through the Nuba Mountains and this time I had the good fortune to be accompanied by an Englishwoman,[17] whom we had recently appointed for the post of Province Education Officer. With the easing of the war effort in 1944 we had been allowed to recruit five British staff[18] and after the times, when there had

15. Sitt al-Sara Babikr Bedri (b. 24.11.1899, m. 1915). One of the first pupils at her father's school in Rufaa.
16. 21.4.45, before the roads became impassable in the mountains during the rains. (See Dr Beasley's Report to the Director of Education, 3.5.45. (S.A.D. 657/3/5-73). Also Dr Beasley's letter to her sister Mrs Sheila Connelly (S.A.D. 657/6)).
17. Miss Elizabeth M. Hodgson; 27.9.44 First appointment; 1945-46 mistress at the Girls' Training College, Omdurman; 1.1.47 Kordofan, P.E.O. (Girls), based in El Obeid; with the resignation of the Principal, Girls' Training College, Miss L.M. Witherspoon in March 1947, she took over the post in Omdurman, until September 1950 when the post was taken by Mrs H.M. Wibberley (née Parkin); by 1948 she was married to Robin A. Hodgkin.
18. New British staff recruited around this time included Miss M. Beevers, Miss M.P. Burns, Miss M.D.G. Edwards, Mrs H.M. Glass, Miss M. Irish, Miss N.B. Stewart, Miss M. Butcher, Miss K.M.E. Challis, Miss H.M. Parkin, Miss M.B. Brown. See Appendix IV for further details.

been only two of us, the Headmistress[19] of the Girls' Intermediate School and myself, to do everything and then some part-time help, this was luxury. My companion was an ardent geographer and enthusiastic about being posted to the West with headquarters in El Obeid.

## 3.1 El Obeid

The journey to El Obeid was by no means as bad as we feared and El Obeid at night was blanketworthy.[20] We started from there one April morning immediately after breakfast[21]

> ... after gloomy forebodings by the Governor, regarding the state of all transport and the prospect that we might easily come roaring back on camels the next day.

## 3.2 El Obeid to Dilling

The road ran through typical Kordofan country, a light sprinkling of smallish trees, sandy roads and untold quantitites of vividly coloured birds. It was a comparatively populous district and we met groups of peasants, mostly on donkeys, jogging peacefully along, and saw clusters of huts at frequent intervals or even fairly large villages away from the road. By this month [April] the harvest had long been finished and the fields were bare, but near to the settlements last season's cultivation showed roots and stalks of *dura* over a large area.

Our transport was a rather poor lorry from the *suq* and belonged to a fairly stupid driver, who managed to get stuck in the sand more often than most people, sometimes from sheer carelessness. Admittedly the highest skill can be defeated, when even the most perfect timing of gear changing and acceleration can fail, but this man was the sort who floundered and hoped for the best. It did, however, give us the opportunity to appreciate the helpful good nature of the local people, who pushed and dug and unloaded

---

19. Miss K. Sylvia L. Clark.
20. 'The Governor of Kordofan was on the train and the Deputy Governor had come to meet us all.' The Governor was Ewen Campbell and the Deputy Governor was G. Hawkesworth.

Geoffrey Hawkesworth, 4N., C.M.G.; Educated at St Bees and Queen's College, Oxford. 12.12.26 First appointment; 1927-28 Nuba Mountains; 1929-35 Kordofan; 1935-40 Blue Nile; 4.9.45-50 Kordofan, Deputy Governor, based in El Obeid; 1950-54 Governor, Kordofan; 1954 retired; 1954-56 Sudan Service Re-employment Bureau, London. His twin brother Desmond Hawkesworth was also in the S.P.S.
21. 8.00 a.m., on a Government lorry, 'with my cook Mahomet and Miss Hodgson's Nuban servant Osman'.

and carried our luggage[22] with the utmost readiness. During one of these halts two elderly *sheikh*s asked for a lift.[23] One of them laid claim to relationship with a schoolmistress and had decided that this was reason enough for travelling with us as far as Dilling, although there was a post-lorry not so far behind. There were two theories on the subject of passengers. One was that there was less danger of sticking, if the lorry was not overloaded. The other was that the more men there were on the back, the more quickly the lorry could be pushed out of a rut. The old couple were of no help on that score but their bundles were small and it seemed unkind to refuse them.

As usual we had plenty of requests, one of which was particularly interesting. Where we stopped for lunch, there was a well field at the bottom of a slope, with a very primitive resthouse at the top. The day was warm but there was ceaseless activity with people coming and going from all directions with no thought of an afternoon *siesta*. We had just finished a rather elaborate meal which the cook had prepared before leaving El Obeid, when two girls wandered in and started to look at our belongings. The folding chairs and the table were the greatest attraction. Chairs were always packed at the top of a lorry. Then, if a stop had to be made for any reason, engine failure or sticking in the sand, out came a chair for me the *Sattal Sitt*[24] (The Excellent Lady) to wait in comfort. Servants frowned very sternly on any suggestion of sitting on a stone or a log or an occasional piece of turf.

It was not merely curiosity about our furniture which had brought the girls; they had come to ask for a lift to a hamlet not far down the road. Baggara girls were famed throughout the whole country for their beauty and repartee and with their nomad traditions they wandered freely and unveiled. One of these, the more intelligent, who did all the talking, was also the more ordinary but the younger might have been moulded by a most meticulous sculptor of bronzes. Her face was stupid and she did little but giggle but the proportions of her slim and supple body were perfect and so lightly draped in a piece of dark blue cotton, that their grace was easy to see. She had pulled her *tobe* just over the back of her head but the upper part of her body was practically uncovered, revealing small firm up-pointing breasts, one of the special features of their charm, often discussed.

22. 'Two campbeds, rolls of bedding, two chairs, two tables, two suitcases, two trek boxes, a bundle of mosquito net, poles, bundles of bedding for the servants ... a *zamzamia*, a canvas water bottle, a briefcase with my papers, odd bags in which the cook had put food, a canvas water bucket, two enamel basins with lids for our ablutions and a folding canvas bath' (S.A.D. 657/6/14-15).
23. The elderly *sheikh*s asked for a lift to Kadugli (S.A.D. 657/6/18).
24. *Sa'ādat al-Sitt*.

It was a sad, if commonplace reflection, looking at the women round about, to think how soon this real loveliness would disappear and to wonder how much appreciation it would know. Since they were not going very far, we decided that the two old *sheikh*s were enough passengers for our decrepit lorry.

## 3.3 Dilling

The road continued through much more wooded country after this and we did not glimpse the mountains until we were almost in Dilling. As it is only about 400 feet higher than El Obeid, we had not much opportunity to think of climbing, and the Nuba Mountains had a rather special configuration on this side. They were more like very large stony lumps, perhaps two or three hundred feet high, rising up from a plateau. Among these queer collections of boulders the Nubas clustered their huts, either at the foot of the hill or a short distance up, but, tucked away as they were, they were rather difficult to distinguish. It was a strange, divided sort of country with a different tribe on almost every hill, [each] speaking a language incomprehensible to the others. Raids and forays between the hills were known to occur infrequently. There were Roman Catholic missionaries in Dilling in the days of the Egyptians, but during the Mahdia the place seems to have been completely cut off and even after the reconquest little notice was taken of the district until the 1920s. Then extending the administration meant small military expeditions before normal government could be established. As soon as the district was pacified, missionaries were allowed to set up schools[25] and clinics and the education of the people was entrusted to them.[26] I have discussed the implications of this policy in a later chapter. Here it is sufficient to note that this journey had been undertaken, because one of the missionary societies had requested a Government grant for a girls' school and naturally the place had to be inspected, before public money could be spent.[27]

Our first stop was Dilling, where we unloaded for the night.

Dilling is very attractive. There is a village on the flat and a small *suq* and hospital and of course cantonments with pleasant straight roads bordered

---

25. The missionaries were given more or less a free hand. 'The political service here included in its ranks a greater number of parsons' sons than I had ever expected to exist. It went against the grain for them somehow to let the Nubas be delivered over to Islam and yet the Government could not press on the Nubas an official religion and say that they must be Christian.'
26. 'They could convert what Nubas showed any signs of wanting to be converted. After 20 years the missionaries had uncommonly little to show for their zeal.'
27. For a note on Government policy in the Nuba area, see Appendix V.

with green *ingle* and here and there a gold *mohur* in flower at that time—all on
a very small scale ... This market provided all our needs on our first evening.

It was the District Headquarters, which up in these cool hills had been made
into an attractive village with a large market serving the country round
about.[28] A Sudanese official[29] stationed at Kadugli had nevertheless
travelled up specially to greet us, as the D.C. was on leave. Two of the local
inhabitants also came but in their case mainly to ask us to start a girls'
school, which a couple of years later we were able to do.[30]

> It was a very pleasant furnished resthouse and we used the D.C.'s bathroom.
> We did not have any contact with the local people really[31] ... There was an
> encampment of a fair size, possibly Baggara Arabs ... nomads who wander
> round sometimes camping near the larger settlements with part of their herds
> and supplying milk to the townsfolk. The tents of these people were very
> remarkable to look at from outside ... The tents are made of mats of various
> sizes woven by the dwellers themselves from the strong grasses found in these
> parts. When finished they have a silky texture and are wonderfully light and
> supple, fine and delicate pieces of work. They are placed over a wooden
> framework, so that there is a general rounded effect, but withall a somewhat
> precarious appearance as if they were not very strongly fastened. Some of
> them are small and one can only just about get inside bent double at that, and
> perhaps turn round to get out. Some of these were very large. One I can

28. Dilling was also the location of the Girls' Education Conference held 21.1.47. Those
present were Canon C.E. Arnold, Nuba Area Superintendent, C.M.S Sallara; J.W. Kenrick
and Mrs Lunn, Field Superintendent Sudan United Mission, based at Abri; Rev. and Mrs
Edwards, United Mission; Ewen Campbell; Miss E. Hodgson; H.R.P. Harrison and Dr
Beasley.
29. Abdel Rahman El Agib. 15.7.13 First appointment; 13.12.42 Kordofan, By 1946 A.D.C.
Kadugli.
   The D.C. who was on leave was Herbert Reginal Polhill Harrison, 4N. (b.18.5.1906- );
Educated at St John's, Leatherhead and Jesus College, Cambridge; 13.12.28 First appointment;
1929 Khartoum; 1930-34 Darfur; 1934-36 White Nile; 1936-38 Equatoria; 1.11.38-45 Northern,
D.C. Ed-Damer; 1.1.1945-50 Kordofan, D.C. Western Jebels, based Dilling; 1950-54 Deputy
Governor, Khartoum; 1954-55 Governor, Khartoum; 1955 retired.
30. The school opened in 1948. 'Although the school at Dilling was mostly attended by Nuba
girls, it was in a Muslim area and did not need special arrangements' (*ARDE*, 1948, see
657/6/21).
   Miss K.S. Jays was appointed mistress, then Principal of the Girls' Training College, Dilling
from 1949 to 1955.
31. On the evening of the second day Dr Beasley and Miss Hodgson walked to the *khor* to
watch water being drawn from a hole dug in the stream bed. 'It was a most lovely sight with
great trees on either hand, some acacias and some *haraz* with a light foliage, some still bare and
waiting for the rains to come ... To be walking in a watercourse which twisted and turned and
was so full of promise was more than ordinary pleasure ... Here and there among the trees on
the bank the ground had been cleared for small patches of cultivation' (S.A.D. 657/6/30).

remember particularly because it had great stripes of black woven into it as a pattern with a very striking result.[32]

### 3.4 Dilling to Sallara

As we had not any news and we were very comfortable at Dilling, we decided to stay there and go to Sallara each day.[33]

As we drove to Sallara the next morning, we were often reminded of the arguments one meets [in England], generally from people who have never left their comfortable homes, 'Why do you interfere? They are happier without education'.[34]

Such criticism could have found ample justification on this fresh April morning. All the people coming along the road to market turned with bright smiles to wave in the friendliest way to us. The women, many of whom were very comely, wore nothing but a girdle of four to six rows of large, vivid [Oxford] blue beads with a sort of tasselled apron in front and behind but at the back this was sometimes replaced by a curved gilt tail. At one point there were three of them, supporting water-pots on their heads and walking in step across a field with the rising light at the back of them—a perfect frieze. A little further on we came across a warrior sitting under a tree with a spear beside him. His hair was cut into an elaborate coxcomb and there were dabs of paint here and there and an odd bracelet. Otherwise he wore nothing at all. He was probably not actually whistling but that was the attitude he suggested, one of complete contentment, as if he had not a care in the world.

A man dressed like that has only to stand on one leg, leaning on a spear and the effect is perfect.

Others we met were also quite naked but some had bits of garments thrown on, giving the impression than an odd piece of cloth was flung round on the way to market and then taken off on the way home. There were a few in ordinary Sudanese dress riding on donkeys, but these could have been settlers from outside.

The actual road into Sallara twists down through rocks ... beyond the country opens out into more usual ideas of mountain ranges. The rocks were rather a drab colour and the whole place very dry.

32. See S.A.D. 657/6/30.
33. Sallara was half to three-quarters of an hour's drive away from Dilling.
34. Dr Beasley's view was rather 'Simplicity is the last refuge of the complex' (Oscar Wilde).

### 3.5 Sallara

It took us under an hour to reach the mission station, which was beautifully situated in a space between the hills with a view far into the distance, where the mountains rose higher in great ranges of a more orthodox type than the lumpy hills round about.

> At the top of the hill were two long, low mud buildings, one the courthouse and the other the office of the local *sarraf*.[35]

Some years before it had been a very flourishing medical centre but changes of personnel had left it without the admirable doctor[36] and efficient matron who had ensured its success. Now the clinic was in charge of a very elderly woman with some nursing qualifications,[37] whom we had known in Omdurman as always living, no doubt quite happily, in an uncontrollable muddle. Here things were no different and trying to talk to her in her sitting room was made all the more difficult by a collection of poultry on the verandah, to which had recently been added a young ostrich.[38] While she chatted away to us, the patients waited but there were very few of them and this added to the general feeling of a place in rapid decay. Depression settled on one from the beginning for the water supply was difficult at this time of year and the dryness was that of the desert.

To add to the initial confusion the news she delivered to us in her usual

---

35. Ṣarrāf, paymaster.
36. Dr Catherine Macdonald, a medical officer and wife of the missionary Rev. R.S. Macdonald. They served in Omdurman from 1926. In 1939 they moved from Juaibor to Katcha and Sallara, Nuba Mountains for C.M.S., Northern Sudan Mission. In Katcha they were joined by the linguist Roland C. Stevenson in January 1940. In 1944 Reverend Macdonald was ordered on medical advice to return to England.
37. 'There did not even appear to be many people using the clinic, which I should have expected to be a great centre.'
    Before coming to Sudan Miss Helen A. Norton had been a keen and experienced nurse in Jaffa; c.1936-1944 nursing sister, Abu Ruf Dispensary, Omdurman, where she gave devoted service. She (and before her Miss Hall) had for many years had a few girls boarding in her compound in Abu Ruf and kept in touch with the houses of the children coming to the school and clinic; 23.11.44 she made a spontaneous offer to continue the work of Rev. and Dr R.S. Macdonald at Sallara; By April 1945 running clinic at Sallara, C.M.S. Northern Sudan Mission. After her retirement she edited letters about Sudan. See also S.A.D. G//S 992, O. Allison, C.M.S. Mission Nuba Mountains file.
38. The menagerie also included 'hens, geese, rabbits and orphans whom she had adopted (many transferred from Omdurman) ... Poor old Miss Norton looked more tired and vague than ever.' Some of the orphans were Peter, Mariam and Aziza (who was ten years old in 1945), who all came from Omdurman. In 1956 Aziza was engaged to an officer in the Sudanese army (S.A.D. G//S 992).

vague manner was that the school was not functioning that day, because the missionary[39] who ran it was unwell and had no assistant.

> I firmly asked to see Miss Hassan ... She would not be able to teach that day. After my first quiver of annoyance, the thing that struck me most was the general lack of grip on anything. It did not seem to matter very much if one worked to a timetable or not.
>
> We ate what supper did eventually arrive with crested silver. She [Miss Norton] was an odd-looking woman with untidy, wispy grey hair and one eye that wanders round the wrong way. Some people regarded her as a saint ...

We were taken to see her after a time,[40] sitting up in bed with a large bandage round her throat, because her companion had diagnosed tonsillitis. We thought it was more likely overwhelming nervousness, although we never found out whether or not she had been told, that the grant depended on the impression she made. I could only hope that this was because of what I represented as a Government official and not from rumours of my formidable personality. It is a sobering thought that the news of one's coming might prostrate an ordinary healthy woman. The day, however, was not entirely wasted, as we feared on our arrival.

> We saw the domestic arrangements for the girls which were quite simple to primitiveness. 21 in 2 small *tukl*s and four to a bed.[41] A diet of grain and water with a few dried dates.[42]
>
> The children wore no clothes except actually in the classroom, where they were issued with rather rubbishy bits of cloth to tie round their waists.[43]

---

39. Miss Rachel Hassan who had only been in the country five months arriving 27.10.44. Before she came to Sudan she had 9 years' teaching experience in L.C.C. elementary schools; National Froebel Union Certificate; one year study at L.S.O.S; Woman educationalist on probation to Sallara to initiate girls' education in the Western Jebels from January 1945 (S.A.D. 657/3/3). She was originally allocated to Omdurman for one year; October 1944 joined C.M.S., teaching for three months at the Society's girl's school at Medani. At Wad Medani she proved an excellent helper to Miss Parker, who had waited for 5 years for assistance; 1945 Teacher, C.M.S. School, Sallara Mission; 1945 passed first Arabic exam; 1947 second Arabic exam. By 1954 she had moved to C.M.S. Katcha. Miss Dale and Miss Hall succeeded Miss Hassan at Sallara. In 1956 she moved to the Three Towns.
40. Dr Beasley went first to see the Martins and had a tour of the boys' school. After tea she was eventually taken to see Miss Hassan. 'I thought we might have been spared the bandage, especially in these temperatures. An unmistakable smell of throat paint would have been a rather more intelligent hint, if one were needed.'
41. '21 girls between 6 and 14. None were the children of baptized parents or professing Christians' (S.A.D. 657/3/10). 'It contributes nothing to the problem of educating the Nubas for the Government to pay for an expensive kindergarten under missionary supervision for 21 little girls' (S.A.D. 657/3/3).
42. 'A diet of porridge made from grain and water, the next day of dried beans, *asida, ballila*, a few dates, dried meat once a week, water for drinking' (S.A.D. 657/3/6).
43. S.A.D. 657/3/6, 657/6/31.

The children were there and were a real joy; jolly little girls. We did not see them, when we came into the yard, but then [the next day] there was a sort of twittering noise in some stunted trees near the gate and about a dozen or more little bodies came tumbling down with shouts of mirth. They gambolled all round us with no self-consciousness, like a bunch of young puppies at play. Despite all their friendliness communication was difficult, as they had not had time to learn much Arabic. One girl of about thirteen was an exception, as she had attended the boys' school at Kadugli and was so determined to be educated that she was prepared to go to any school whether Government Muslim or Christian Mission.[44]

There were two boys' schools in Sallara, one a Government school and one in the charge of the resident clergyman,[45] who gave us an interesting morning by showing us all he could and explaining a great deal about the customs of the Nubas. He was a scholarly man, who really preferred the Evangelical side of the work but was conscientiously struggling with a school here and two bush schools, which were offshoots from his Mission school, to which he had to walk several miles twice a week.

> There was very little to the evangelical side, although we were shown the church, where the boys from the Mission and the Government school come at their own option. I gather they all come!

He also gave an impression of defeat, although too loyal and earnest to make complaints.

> I remember that morning in terms of one long 'drift'[46] ... We went to see the Mission boys' school. After tea we drifted across to the Government boys' school. Mr Martin then took us to the village ... just a few houses round an open space, a Government office, a very small room and a longer one with a dais in it, where council meetings and Native Administration affairs are dealt with ... more tea with Mrs Martin. We eventually finished up with tea with

44. On 29.1.47 form IA 30 pupils, IB 30 pupils and form II 9. The school closed from mid-1946 to mid-1947, for six months as Rachel Hassan was ill. There were 3 teachers, one trained at Katcha and two others either semi-trained or untrained, from Sudan United Mission. There were also 3 sub-grade schools attached to the school, Tindia 18 pupils, Fassu 30 pupils, Kermitti 35 pupils.
45. Rev. A.H.M. Martin, M.A. Educationalist; Arrived 1939 and after 4 months Arabic in Omdurman moved to Sallara, C.M.S. Northern Sudan Mission. He temporarily returned to the U.K. to take his Diploma in Education. 24.3.1939 appointed Principal at the boys' school, Sallara (opened 1935). April 1945 left to U.K. to take up post as a vicar in Essex.
46. S.A.D. 657/6/26. Even in February 1949 'things seem to be just drifting at Sallara' (Director of Education, C.W. Williams to Rev. J.S. Trimingham, Secretary of C.M.S. (S.A.D. 657/3/50-56)). On 20.2.49 there were 38 girls at Sallara—15 Kindergarten, Class I 9, Class II 7, Class III 7. There were two teacher trainees with Miss Hassan and Miss Drinkwater and one mission-trained Sudanese. Miss Zenkovsky was also working in the area in 1947. It was 'continuing with much the same problems they started with' (S.A.D. 657/3/52).

Miss Norton. Mr Martin did not seem to have any duties that could not possibly be left.

On our way back to his house,[47] we were startled by a great column of black smoke. 'Oh,' he exclaimed mildly, 'my kitchen'. It seemed almost symbolic for indeed a charred heap of embers was all that was left of this grass *tukul*.

> The cook in a frenzy of bread-making had been unintelligent about the heating. Both Mr Martin and his wife bore their loss with great equanimity.
>
> This was followed by a rest in Miss Norton's room at the other house, where pictures and literature about the Royal Family were much in evidence and about half past three I went to inspect the handwork class.
>
> We started off rather earlier the next morning [from Dilling to Sallara] and there was much misgiving in my heart. I had decided that, if Miss Hassan considered herself still too unwell for work, I should come back to D[illing] straight away and spend the morning in the boys' school. I could not endure the thought of frittering away another morning in the exasperating futility of that first day. We pinned our hopes on recovery, however, and were justified. The lady in question met us and without the bandage.[48]

Despite this, we were given lunch [the next day] by his pretty, blue-eyed wife, who was very cheerful, although again without complaints, at the prospect of going home almost at once, as her husband had been appointed to a country living in Essex. There, no doubt, he would have a chance to forget the disheartening lack of response he had been wrestling with and they would both be less anxious about their two attractive children, who did look rather sickly.

> I feel he will be more usefully employed as a country parson ... Mrs Martin was a disappointment to the C.M.S. Once a teacher in [the mission elementary school in] Omdurman, she refused to work after marriage.

Our lunch had one unexpected accompaniment.[49] There was a great babel of men's lusty voices shouting and singing. 'Only a funeral', said the missionary, as calmly as he had mentioned the ruin of his kitchen.

For us it was more exciting, as our meals were not often interrupted by the sight of a couple of hundred naked men swinging along the road and

---

47. The Martins' kitchen caught fire when Dr Beasley was on the way back to the house after visiting Miss Hassan on her sick bed.
48. S.A.D. 657/6/30.
49. S.A.D. 657/6/32.

uttering wild chants, while they bore the body down the hill.[50] Our other glimpse of local colour was a visit to the *Mek* at the Courthouse, but he and all the businessmen around [the tax collector] were dressed in ordinary Sudanese clothes and there was no particularly Nuba aspect, even here in the heart of the mountains.[51]

> I felt that any yearnings for so-called progress came from this line of contacts. Those who came in contact with Government and merchants had probably a dim idea that education was a good thing and were prepared to try it, especially if it was free.[52]

With the missionary family gone, the outlook for the two women at the school and the clinic was going to be even more bleak.

> No-one knew who his successor was to be. I could only imagine how dreary the place would be when the Martin family had gone and wondered how Miss Norton and Miss Hassan would cope even for a few weeks quite alone.

It must need an unshakable sense of vocation to struggle on alone in such dispiriting conditions, two days' journey from the railhead and no assured transport. Certainly no telegraph or telephone. The teacher's general attitude was that 'The Lord will provide'. This is no doubt very laudable for a missionary, but Government Departments are at a disadvantage in trying to make budgets on that assumption. Heroic though her effort was personally, it was no contribution to the main question of education for Nuba girls. When one adds to the normal discomforts of tropical life those of a place where to obtain food and water takes a great deal of planning, it is just superfluity of worry to throw in a few extra difficulties like the clothes ethos, language problems and little girls who run away. After its first session the school was closed for nearly a year, because the mistress was ill and no-one could be found to replace her. I asked her what had made her think of working among the Nubas. It was apparently not her idea. All she knew,

50. 'Ever since the riots of my Rangoon days I have disliked collective native noises and I looked up with some apprehension. No-one else seemed at all interested except that Miss Hodgson thought she might be present at a bit of local manners and customs' (S.A.D. 657/6/32).

51. 'He [The *mek*] had consented to send his daughters to the school. Unfortunately when the *mek* learned on the first night that the children had had their clothes taken away and were running around naked like other common children who do not go to school, he decided that this was a step backward, probably a deliberate one to impede what he regarded as progress. He sent for his girls forthwith and they have not been allowed to come back.'

52. 'We all behaved like perfect ladies. I managed to suppress my most acute moment of irritation, when Miss Norton started to give me excellent reasons for educating Nuba girls, which were the ones I had written in an impassioned note some six months before. We parted, however, on the best of terms with expressions of good will and promises to be mutual friends. I was much relieved when it was all over' (S.A.D. 657/6/32).

she said, was that she had to come to Africa and the Mission had sent her there.[53]

> She had very little apparatus and that rather poor. She learnt Arabic while waiting an exit permit—which took a year—and had been posted to Medani, which she enjoyed ... at an ordinary, satisfactory school. At the end of the year she had been told to come to the Nubas. She did not know why. Miss Hassan was just a good teacher under ordinary conditions and was finding difficulty adapting herself to the strange ones.

It was heartening to learn that after a time she went back to Wad Medani where her very real ability and experience were not thus wasted.

I have discussed the implications of this in more detail in examining special problems later in the book. I need only mention here that the next day she had sufficently recovered for us to see something of the working of the school. An accurate description of this would be too unkind, for cynicism about other people's failures can, in such cases, be altogether too facile.

> I can't believe that there was anything there to attract the Nubas to come to the place ... The general dispiritedness might give them a poor opinion of the white man's way of living and no desire to be interested in anything he had to say.

Nevertheless this pathetic attempt cast quite a gloom over this side of our trip and we were lucky that the district and the scenery had so much to offer.

> ... A school like this this isn't leading anywhere—a very amiable appendage to the station if the Mission likes to run such but the Government shouldn't be expected to support it.[54]

The atmosphere of defeat, which had brooded everywhere in the station, re-inforced the tempting nostalgia for things unchanged. Even in the dryness of April many of the small trees had covered themselves with a sort of spring green and the grass had not gone from all the pastures. The women came smiling along the roads with their water pots. The straw huts sheltered cosily along the boulders at the foot of the hills. Sometimes a turn

---

53. Daily school work consisted of $\frac{1}{2}$ hour drill ('in English for Miss Hassan to be spontaneous'), $\frac{3}{4}$ hour Arabic reading, $\frac{1}{2}$ hour Writing, $\frac{3}{4}$ Arithmetic in Arabic, $\frac{3}{4}$ hour Scripture in Arabic (Miss Norton), $\frac{1}{2}$ hour English, 1 hour Sewing, Games, Handwork. Between 3.30-5 nature study, walks, gardening, drawing, painting, stories, acting (S.A.D. 657/3/5). For further details on Sallara school, see Appendix V.
54. She did not recommend the renewal of the Government grant nor the provision of further buildings. 'I regard this purely as an amiable experiment on the part of the C.M.S. and cannot see it offers any prospect for the development of Nuba education' (S.A.D. 657/3/7, 657/6/31).

of the road brought a wide vista of a great range in front, with all the interplay of light and shade and colour, that is never absent in mountainous regions. It all plays havoc with earnest convictions about girls' education.

> We left Sallara with some relief. What a theme for a depressing, naturalistic novel of the more malicious type.

### 3.6 Delami

> It was our first driver and lorry who came to take us on the next stage of our journey to Rashad. He had been down to Kadugli he said and had the lorry mended ... the A.D.C. had been round the night before to say goodbye ... we acquired some passengers [including] two soldiers on leave[55] ... We set off early from Dilling and went through pleasant country.

We found the road managed to skirt all the hills and, rather to our disappointment, we never had to climb to any height on our way round to Delami.

> As we went along the prospects improved ... great ranges of mountains on all sides of the type we had expected. Everything was still very dry and all the brooks empty. But the trees were getting new leaves of a delightful fresh green ... bulbs, we were told, came up in all directions ... bright red lilies ... There had still been a few naked Nubas on the road but their number seemed to have decreased considerably this side of Dilling.

As far as we could see, this [Delami] was just an Arab village in a delightful setting. It was situated on a patch of very fine gravel, giving an appearance of cleanliness, that was very striking, and a sense of order by a number of traffic signs.[56] There were roughly carved wooden heads which added a note of fun to the whole. They fitted in too with the murals in the comfortable resthouse, where we had lunch.[57] A local constable with

---

55. S.A.D. 657/6/33.

56. 'As we approached the centre of the village, we came to a large and modern-looking roundabout with small flat wooden figures ... these were variously intended to represent policemen and soldiers and were serving as signposts to point the way to the *merkaz*, or the *suq* or, in our case, the resthouse' (S.A.D. 657/6/34).

57. The D.C. from Talodi, came in for lunch with his wife. 'A very tall young man in uniform and an unusually tall young woman bride ... They were going to Rashad also' (S.A.D. 657/6/34).

J.C N. Donald was D.C. Talodi until 1.5.44. The post was then vacant until John Fleetwood Stewart Phillips, C.M.G. was made A.D.C. Talodi from 25.11.45. (1946 A.D.C. Eastern Jebels, based in Rashad). This was probably therefore J.W. Kenrick, A.D.C. Rashad.

John Wynn Kenrick., O.B.E. (b.22.1.1913- ); Educated at Wellington and Trinity College, Cambridge; 29.12.36 First appointment; 1936-41 Equatoria; 1941-43 Aide-de-Camp and Assistant Private Secretary to the Governor-General; 1941-44 Governor-General's temporary Commission as Bimbashi in S.D.F.; 20.4.44-49 Kordofan, 1944-46 A.D.C. Eastern Jebels,

aspirations as a painter had been let loose to express himself with the result that the walls were furiously decorated with modern primitives. There were spirited scenes from village life, including dances and journeys by every kind of transport, and very nearly the whole of the railway line from El Obeid to Um Ruaba.[58]

### 3.7 Delami to Rashad

For the rest of the day the scenery grew increasingly impressive. Until about four o'clock a twisting bit of road led through a small gorge onto a pleasant plain, surrounded by noble hills of varying shapes with plenty of trees.

> It was wooded in parts and there were one or two wide places for corn-growing .... [The hills] certainly invited climbing. We went up a certain distance of one easy slope but could not get to the top in the evening period ... It was as pleasant a place as I have seen in the Sudan.

### 3.8 Rashad

Rashad was certainly an inviting spot and my companion[59] wished she were a missionary, as she was sure that then she would have 'a call' to Rashad. After this trip I investigated the possibilities of a 'College of the West'[60] here but, when we were ready for education among the Nubas, this particular official was married and no-one else was so attracted to the place. The little town stretched out comfortably on the flat expanse with Government buildings, a few European houses, a busy and active market and the dwellings of the ordinary Northern Sudan type, where traders and settlers from outside lived. Although the huts of the Nubas were still clinging to the slopes, primitive simplicity was much less in evidence. There

based Rashad, Sept 1946 D.C. Rashad; 1949-53 Khartoum; 1953-55 Asst. Adviser on Constitutional and External Affairs to the Governor-General; 1955 retired; 1955-62 Mullard Ltd; 1963-73 personnel manager, Philips Industries; 1971 member of Cunningham Inquiry into Fire Service; 1973-74 member of National Industrial Relations Court (Donaldson); 1973-76 Home Secretary's nominee to Advisory Council for Probation and Aftercare; 1976 member of Army Welfare Inquiry Committee; 1977- member of A.C.A.S. Arbitration Boards.

58. The painting included '... hunting scenes, local officials, a woman driving pigs, children in school... There was also a kind of primitive (geometric) decoration which had spread to the W.C.'

59. 'I just gazed at her [Miss E. Hodgson] in dumb horror'.

60. There was a plan to establish the 'College of the West' at Rashad, starting in 1949, especially if the works at Abu Habl could provide an all-weather road. 'We might think of a build up from the West, probably healthy girls with less cloistered ideas..It might do quite a bit to hasten this tearing of the veil' (See *Report to Director of Education*, July 1945, also S.A.D. 657/3/8-29, 57, 58).

were fewer women in blue beads, and warriors with just daubs of paint and elaborate hair styles.

> We were taken to an empty house in Rashad which was commodious but not quite so well arranged as the resthouse ... very soon after we arrived came a charming note from the D.C.'s wife asking us to tea and dinner. The D.C.[61] I had known for some years ... There was rather a party for tea because the tall D.C. from Talodi and his wife had caught us up by this time and we all sat on a high *mustaba* and gazed at the lovely views.

On the other hand the sense of decay which had depressed us so acutely after Sallara was soon displaced. An enterprising boys' school had admitted twenty girls, even up to the age of eleven, and their clamorous demand was to help both boys and girls.[62] They were put through their paces.

> We went one [Friday] morning to the boys' school ... There were a lot of little girls all carefully dressed in little cotton frocks and white headkerchiefs sitting in a row and looking very interested in this novel event.

It would have been wrong, the schoolmaster insisted, to refuse the girls but giving them places deprived an equal number of boys. Therefore they must have schools for both.

> It seems to be getting quite popular for the girls in the Jebels here to go to boys' schools and the D.C.s who are really keen[63] think that they thereby deserve preferential treatment in the matter of schoolmistresses.
>     We then went along to see the D.C. at the *merkaz* buildings [which] were strange and wonderful[, a fort] with towers ... [after a walk] ... the evening's amusement was drinks with the D.C. There were fresh visitors, an Australian missionary girl with a stiff neck going to hospital in El Obeid and the Director Designate of the Medical Service. Dinner ... in the garden by the light of the moon and went to bed early, as we wanted to get to Tegale before breakfast.[64]

---

61. D.C. Rashad was then N.M. Innes. 'The D.C. had his family here, 3 children 5-10 living in a house of their own in the gardens and having a real story book existence'.
    Neil McLeod Innes, 4N. (b.17.11.1903- ); Educated at Royal Naval Colleges, Osbourne and Dartmouth. Haileybury and Trinity Hall, Cambridge; 12.12.26 First appointment; 1927-30 Berber; 1934-35 Kassala (P.E.O.); 1935-36 Blue Nile; 1936-46 Kordofan, 1944 D.C. Eastern Jebels District, based in Rashad; 15.2.46-48 Blue Nile, Southern Gezira, D.C. Wad Medani; 1948-50 Asst. Civil Secretary (Prisons); 1950-52 Commissioner for Prisons; 1952 retired; 1953- Minister for Foreign Affairs, Sultanate of Muscat and Oman.
62. The school only had first and second year classes.
63. Especially the D.C. Rashad (N.M. Innes).
64. S.A.D. 657/6/45.

### 3.9 Abbassia Tegale

> The driver turned up at quarter to six. We swallowed a hasty cup of tea, cursed rather because the prisoners had not put enough water in the tank ... and once again pushed all our possessions on to the lorry.
>
> The road from Rashad to Tegale was equally entertaining, especially in the first stretches. There was another steep bit on the way out through the basin and then woods with lots of rocks in which we saw two kinds of monkeys[65] and one or two gazelles. Then a wide flat plain among the hills ... with hills all round, fairly well wooded. And so to Abbassia. This was a great improvement on my last visit, when I arrived alone in the dark. There was a good new resthouse, which was very comfortable.[66]

Equally encouraging was the growing interest in the school in Abbassia Tegale, where we finished our round.

> The village itself is not very attractive. It is rather scattered, a bit scruffy-looking and with nothing peculiarly Nuba about it ... The headman is known as the *Mek* of Tegale (nicknamed 'Slim Adam' by the D.C.). After some persuasion from the D.C. Rashad he had sent one of his daughters to the Training College entrance exam the year before. It was held in El Obeid for the Western provinces at the same time as the Kordofan Province Council. Unfortunately both Slim Adam and Princess Amna developed relapsing fever ... She was advised to try again next year but she turned haughty apparently and told the D.C. she had had enough of schooling ... The younger sister ... told us emphatically that she wanted Intermediate education and not in El Obeid but in Omdurman, so that she could see a bit more of the world. A most advanced remark from a Sudanese girl.[67]
>
> While the servants unloaded and prepared breakfast we went to look at the school ... There was a definite improvement in the school too, although the headmistress had a bad foot and didn't want to work ... (We persuaded her that with a little arranging she could manage to teach sitting down and once she lost her nervousness, she did in fact manage quite creditably).[68]

It was still very much the centre of the village as far as the women were concerned, and they attended in large numbers, when the girls gave a concert.

> The number of mothers who came, admittedly very late, was gratifying in a place which had at one time rather boycotted the school. The *Mek*'s wife came and sat in solitary state and Princess Amna turned up in a beautiful apricot *tobe*.

---

65. 'Red hussars?'
66. 'I had been before but had approached it from the other side.' See also S.A.D. 657/6/48-49.
67. See also S.A.D. 657/6/46.
68. S.A.D. 657/6/49-50.

There was a new Headmistress[69] but the tact of the former one was definitely paying dividends to the extent that a successful boarding house for twenty girls was having full support.

> There was a boarding house for over 20 girls and the difference between this and the Mission one was most marked—a largish house with room for each girl to have her own *angareeb*. All very clean and the children, considering the tradition and water problem, surprisingly clean. There was a concert to which a lot of mothers came ... some of the girls in the 3rd and 4th year just wore neat petticoats which they had made themselves. A very sensible, inexpensive form of dress. It might be the answer to the clothing problem in Sallara.

It was a satisfying ending to our tour, as we sat in the shining new resthouse,[70] carefully wired against flies and mosquitoes, and watched the great lines of hills all changing colour, as the day passed.

### 3.10 Um Ruaba and back to Khartoum

> The car duly arrived in the middle of the morning and the 2 D.C.s in it ... [another inspection and a rest] ... The drive down to Um Ruaba was pleasant but hot but we did it in about two and a half hours.
> We had another kind invitation to dinner from the D.C.'s wife and arrived there looking rather mangled ... Our host[71] met us in evening dress plus monocle. Sudan evening dress for men is rather sensible, a short sleeved white shirt with soft collar and white trousers, a black cummerbund and a black bow. Our hostess, just out from home, had a pretty, long housecoat and naturally curly hair.
> We had promised to spend a half hour or so in the local school, partly for our own information and partly because the D.C. was rather proud of it ... This certainly justified the D.C.'s praises and it was a great relief to find one of our institutions working up to standard.[72]

69. The headmistress was 'a divorced woman about 35 previously teaching in El Obeid on temporary terms ... knowing that school scholastically she was a bit out of date. I sent her two of the brightest students [from the Training College] from last year's batch, although I had to threaten the father of one of them with a law suit before he would let her go. There was already one quite passable mistress there and she stayed' (S.A.D. 657/6/50).
70. 'The tall D.C. from Talodi had had a new resthouse built while D.C. Rashad, his senior, had been on leave and he had been in charge' (S.A.D. 657/6/49). i.e. J.W. Kenrick had built the resthouse while N.M. Innes was away. Nevertheless basic conveniences were not provided but had to be carried on trek—'After a bath in a collapsible canvas contrivance brought along by Miss Hodgson, we sat outside the house reading.'
71. D.C. Um Ruaba in October 1948 was John Miller Hunter (b.15.2.16- ); Educated at Glasgow Academy and Christ's College, Cambridge; 26.12.38 First appointment; 1938-42 Blue Nile; 1942-48 Equatoria; 8.8.48-55 Kordofan, D.C.; 1955 retired; 1956- farming in Aberdeenshire.
72. See also S.A.D. 657/6/55-59.

# B. Darfur

The most westerly Province of all, marching for much of its border with French Equatorial Africa, was Darfur,[73] literally the home of the Fur. When I made my various journeys around it, it shared in the ordinary Government routine of the rest of the country, but it still managed to retain a special identity.

## 1. History of Darfur

Except for a brief period during the 1860s and 1870s,[74] it remained a separate kingdom until 1916. Surrounded as it was by a great belt of deep sand it was nevertheless known for centuries to travellers and appears in a surprising number of memoirs. For one thing it lay on the *Arba'in* Road of ill repute by which slaves were sent to the North by Arab traders. Perhaps it was this that brought it to Napoleon's notice for, while he seems to have ignored Khartoum during his brief spell of glory in Cairo,[75] he addressed one of his celebrated manifestoes to the Sultan of Darfur.[76] During Turkish times[77] the Mahdia had some following here[78] but after the Khalifa was overthrown,[79] the Sultanate was left alone until during the First World

---

73. 'Darfur was like the Fung, rather a kingdom on its own' although it came under the Sudan administration from 1916. 'I have never met anyone who served in Darfur and disliked it' [October 1948].
74. In February 1874 the Khedive Ismā'īl declared war on the Sultan. Sultan Ibrāhīm Muḥammad al-Ḥusayn was defeated on 23 October 1874. He was killed on the orders of al-Zubayr Raḥma and was buried in Manawāshī at the Bornu mosque. A week later al-Zubayr entered El Fasher where he was joined a few days later by Governor-General Ismā'īl Ayyūb Pasha (See O'Fahey, R.S and Spaulding, J.L., *Kingdoms of the Sudan*, 1974, pp.179-186).
75. Napoleon occupied Egypt in 1798.
76. The Sultan of Darfur, 'Abd al-Raḥmān, was asked by Bonaparte to send him able-bodied slaves to be used as soldiers in Napoleon's eastern schemes.
77. The Turko-Egyptian regime continued in Darfur between 1874 and 1883, under the influence of Slatin Pasha.
78. Unlike the Baqqara, the Fur were largely unresponsive to the Mahdist message. Indeed the Fur under the Keira were fighting for their own conception of freedom.
79. When the Khalifa was defeated at Karrari in September 1898, 'Alī Dīnār b. Zakarīyā Muḥammad al-Faḍl (1865-1916), a grandson of Keira Sultan Muḥammad al-Faḍl, hurried from the battle to Darfur and declared himself Sultan and ruled from 1889. From 1898 until the First World War the Sultanate was an independent state based in El Fasher, when 'Alī Dīnār revived the old administrative system. The newly established Condominium in the Sudan had no immediate plan to annex Darfur. His relations with the Condominium deteriorated during this period, as 'Alī Dīnār was nervous of the French advance to the west.

War.[80] Then the Germans egged on the ruler to invade Sudan and the Condominium sent a military expedition against him. He was soon driven out[81] to the hills, where in a dawn attack according to local legend he was hit while at his morning prayers. With his death the movement collapsed and the Sultanate became a province of the Sudan, evoking in the British officials[82] who served there a degree of local patriotism even more intense than that found elsewhere.

## 2. Transport to Darfur

There was a time when nothing but a camel could take the road to Fasher, the attractive capital built on sand dunes some 300 miles from El Obeid.[83] One or two intrepid people have been known to complete the journey on horseback, but it was the coming of mechanical transport in the 1930s which really opened the way to the Province. Ten years later a plane route had been developed, of greatest importance during the Second [World] War, while the Mediterranean was closed. With this over and the large American Air Force base at Fasher closed, air services remained but on a much more limited scale. When I knew it, however, the main bulk of the traffic in goods as well as pssengers went on the great lorries, which nightly swung out into the desert and lumbered on through the darkness. It took three days by this means from the railhead at El Obeid to Fasher; first roughly one hundred miles to Nahud, a stretch of track with some bad patches intermixed; secondly another hundred including the Seventeen Gozes, sand hills which appeared to go unendlingly until at last the hills of Um Keddada were reached on the borders of Darfur; finally, another hundred miles and a weary day of sand still stretched between there and Fasher.

For my first trip I flew to Fasher[84] on a service plane of some small type quite out of fashion now. Its size, however, had made my timetable uncertain, for, although I was very much a light-weight, everything

80. Influenced by the Pan-Islamic propaganda of the Turks and the Sanūsīya of Libya and urged by the Germans, 'Alī Dīnār invaded the Sudan by declaring war on the British. The Condominium sent a military expedition to invade Darfur. His army was defeated at Birinjīya near El Fasher.
81. 'Alī Dīnār was driven out of El Fasher to the hills where he was killed in a dawn attack by the British some months later. It was the usual story of modern weapons versus ancient. There had to be a military occupation in Darfur for some years after.
82. About 45,000 square miles were administered by about eight white men in 1943.
83. 'It takes about a month from Khartoum to Fasher on camels and the road is chronic' [March 1943].
84. Dr Beasley flew in a 'big four-engined, old-fashioned' service plane, in March 1943.

depended on the size of the aircraftsmen being transferred from Asmara to Lagos.

> I was not a priority passenger ... Until the last moment B.O.A.C. would not decide whether the weights were right. At 10.30 am one Wednesday morning it was decided that I could go. Apparently the aircraftsmen were not very large but there was a lot of cargo on board ... In the end we were told the plane was not leaving and I was taken back to the Grand Hotel [in Khartoum] ... I was told 5.00 a.m. was the time of departure ... it was rather exciting down on the aerodrome in the dark.

Eventually we were all taken to the airfield outside Khartoum and that chill moment just before dawn, as we waited there, gave an extra tinge of excitement to starting out for the centre of Africa. Flying over those apparently featureless expanses was to have a rather frightening impression of the country below. I knew that west of El Obeid there were trees and villages, but in the dry season from above they looked like small black dots, until nearer Fasher the lie of the land altered and the hills on the way to Um Keddada appeared.

## 3. El Fasher

Fasher itself would be an interesting spot even without the romantic legend of Ali Dinar, which still clings to it. The palace of the late sultan had been built on one steep *goz* and the buildings were afterwards used as Government offices and for the Governor's house, but the real town was situated on another *goz* with a great *wadi* in between, which in most years was half filled by a lake, locally known as a *fula*.[85] It was always pleasant to sit in the Governor's garden and look across this stretch of water to the houses opposite, climbing up the slope which was crowned with the minarets of an impressive mosque near the top. At sunset it was particularly attractive, when everything was partly veiled by the smoke from the evening fires and the dust from the movement of many animals, while the call to prayer and all the muted noises of a busy place wafted in a gentle murmur over the valley.[86] Between the *gozes* there was constant activity, with lorries arriving from all directions, camels singly or in files, to finish at the market and the coffee houses spread along the foot of the hill.[87]

Most years there was plenty of water in the *fula* and then the town end

---

85. *Fūla*, reservoir.
86. February 1948.
87. In March 1945 on her second trip to El Fasher she found 'nothing new at Fasher except a lot of Americans and a cinema'.

was a resort for all, drawning water for men and beasts. At the far end of the lake[88] the birds came and sportsmen could bag a few wild duck almost from their doorsteps. There was one unhappy year, however, when the rains failed and no water came down into the *fula* at all. Activity was, if anything, greater but less kindly.

All day, from early morning strings of little donkeys, laden with water-skins, went trotting through the dried-up [water] course from the water bores on the opposite *goz*. Water was a source of pre-occupation all over the Province for, although there was a reasonable amount of rain in the summer, approximately twenty inches at Geneina, the other months could be very difficult.

According to report, which I did not myself verify, water drinking was not one of the local habits. *Merissa*, the native brewed beer, was reputed to be the staple article of diet, and, so the tale went, by late afternoon the majority of the population had reached a happy state of mellowness. Dietetically *merissa* could be very nourishing, as it often retained the consistency of thin gruel, but it used to be argued that its excessive use was one of the factors keeping Darfur a backward province. My normal contacts being mostly among the better class women I had little opportunity to test theories of this kind at first hand. I remember being surprised at the mother of a school-mistress, who objected to her daughter being transferred from Fasher nearer home. She burst into my office one day, a tall, buxom figure, and shouted, 'What's all this about Zenab being transferred? Fasher's a lovely place. The air is good and the food is wonderful.'

We did not go into details. It was true that mistresses and their chaperones always seemed to grow fat at Fasher but no breath of scandal had ever reached me and the school maintained a persistently upward course.

### 3.1 El Fasher school

In 1943 [the school] was just struggling to maturity and needed rather careful handling, the Headmistress said. Cloth was desperately short at this time and soap none too easy to come by; as at Tegale parents might very well be discouraged by too heavy an insistence on personal cleanliness. Five

---

88. In 1947-48 the rains failed. 'More wells were being dug in the vicinity and pumps being used to supply the town' [February 1948]. In October 1948 when the rain was plentiful, wild fowl were shot over the lake, ' which seemed odd in the middle of a sandy town. [In that year the] lake stretched right between the two hills, the one on which the *suq* is built and the cantonment one. There had probably been more malaria in Fasher but the town is twice as attractive'.

years later[89] the lower classes at the school were full and the town demanding another.

It had improved a lot since I first went there in 1943. One of the first questions asked in the Legislative Assembly was by the local *mek* to enquire why they hadn't a second girls' school in Fasher. I conducted an examination for 13 girls wanting post-elementary education. It is quite striking really when one thinks it is only thirty years since Ali Dinar was defeated [February 1948].

Most of the top class were clamouring for further education in the intermediate schools or in the Training College, while a small company of Girl Guides was active through the helpfulness of the D.C.'s wife.[90] She was an outstanding example of the unofficial work generously given by the wives of British officials and of the greatest value. Schools always prospered, when there was a British woman to take an interest in what was going on. In these distant stations the teachers found unfailing support by having someone to whom they could pour out grievances and worries, which were often too small and immediate for officialdom.[91]

---

89. In February 1948 'it became imperative to do a little inspecting as Sylvia Clark had diptheria, one P.E.O. had an operation and the other had to stay in bed for months with acute kidney trouble'. According to Lilian M.P. Sanderson, Miss Mary D.G. Edwards was P.E.O. (Girls), Kordofan, but when she had recovered from kidney illness, she was stationed at El Obeid. Another Province Education Officers for Girls at this time was Miss A.M. Ravaisou (Blue Nile Province), see Appendix IV. 'Then another [Mrs K.M.E. Wood] who had been destined for inspecting had to go to run the Girls' Intermediate School at El Obeid, where the headmistress [Miss M. Beevers] had a breakdown in September [1947], which had involved us all in a lot of strain and stress'.

90. D.C.'s wife, probably Mrs E.F. Aglen.

Edward Francis Aglen (b.30.5.07- ); Educated at Winchester and Magdalen College, Oxford; 7.9.30 First appointment; 1930-31 Civil Secretary's office; 1931-35 Kordofan; 1935-39 Upper Nile; 1939-44 Blue Nile, A.D.C. Medani District, based Wad Medani; 1.3.44-48 Darfur, D.C. El Fasher District; 1948-49 Civil Secretary's office, D.A.C.S. (external), Political Section, based Khartoum; 1948-49 Secretary to Executive Council; 1949-53 Assistant Director, Department of Economics and Trade; 1953-55 Director; 1955 retired; 1955-71 Secretary, National Association, Scottish Woollen Manufacturers; 1957-70 Governor, St Denis Girls' School, voluntary work e.g. Scottish Episcopal Church, Prison Visitor, Housing Associations.

91. In October 1948 'all the mistresses asked for transfers. I think it is immediate reaction to the sight of me ... The girl whose home is there said that she should like a transfer just for a change.'

During the same trip she 'met a nursing sister, who really went round the Province inspecting clinics and looking after midwives ... a new departure ... she seemed keen ... and likely to be of great value. She was sure that Pharaonic circumcision was being practised ... We went to a party one afternoon to which about a dozen wives of notables had been invited. The headmistress made a speech against Pharaonic circumcision in which she was supported ... by the ex-headmistress ...' Possibly either Miss M.E. Shepherd (13.4.47 First appointment; By 1948 Province Nursing Sister, based in El Fasher) or Miss N.G. Reilly (25.12.47 First appointment, by 1948 Nursing Sister, based in El Fasher) [October 1948].

## 3.2 'Alī Dīnār's Palace

To add to the satisfaction of beginning schools in what had been regarded as a difficult province was the fun of staying in a story-book atmosphere. Behind Ali Dinar's outbuildings, now used as Government offices, a small gate led into the Governor's garden, where he lived in the original Palace, modernised enough to make it comfortable but in no way detracting from the flavour.[92] The dining room was the show-piece,[93] repainted in bright red and yellow and with a large number of Arabic texts over the doors and round the walls. Each corner had a strong, triangular shelf fitted into it above the heads of the guests, and, during banquets, the Sultan used to station a beautiful slave girl up there to tend the lamps.

Across the garden lay the guest house, which had formerly been the audience chamber and in its vastness still suggested a worthy judgement hall. Like the house it was constructed with enoromously thick mud walls, which may have been intended for defence but had in the upshot the happy result of neutralised extremes of climate. I found it a delightful place in which to stay; the tremendous pillars, about the diameter of fair-sized oak trees, supported the roof and divided the whole very comfortably into study and sleeping quarters; through the small, low windows there were glimpses of bright flower-beds, which had been made to flourish despite the ceaseless struggle with the sand.[94]

It was while I was staying here[95] that a slight misadventure occurred,

92. When she first arrived in El Fasher on her way to Nyala in March 1943 ' ... it was the Governor's house where I went for breakfast. There was a horrid little mongoose (Pooh) with deformed feet, who would nip my calves. He ruined breakfast always by fussing till he got his poached egg and spoilt tea by slipping down unobserved from any place of safety and coming up behind me and giving me a nip.'

The Governor in March 1943 was Philip Ingleson, C.M.G, M.B.E., M.C., 3N. (b.14.6.1892-d.1985); Educated at Rossall and Queen's College, Cambridge; 1.11.19 First appointment; 1920-21 Darfur; 1922-25 Blue Nile Province; 1926-31 Kassala (1927 Deputy Governor); 1931-33 Halfa, Governor; 1933-34 Berber, Governor; 1934-35 Bahr al Ghazal, Governor; 14.12.35-1944 Governor of Darfur based in El Fasher (December 1941 visit to Fort Lamy, Chad); 1944 retired; 1944 Ministry of Production; 1944-49 Board of Trade; 1949-54 U.K. Trade Commissioner, Queensland; 1954-56 U.K. Trade Commissioner, Western Australia and Commercial Adviser to the High Commissioner.

93. The dining room, had a beamed ceiling which was repainted in red and yellow '... and the walls [were] decked out with all sorts of weapons.'

94. On her return from Um Keddada to El Fasher in October 1948 'I went to the house of the D.C. and was given a very charming *tukl* at the end of the garden. It was all blue and white, very simple, but most inviting.' This was probably E.F. Aglen's house.

95. On her first stay at the palace in El Fasher, after her return from a trip to Nyala, March 1943. During this stay 'two Americans came to dinner, one an engineer who boasted of their comforts when travelling round in air-conditioned caravans ... I teased him..but he took it quite well.'

which was never repeated in all my years of trekking. I was, in fact, sleeping on the roof but there were two beds made up in the big room below. One morning, when the servant went in with my tea, the beds had been stripped. Nothing else had been touched, neither my money nor any of my personal possessions. Cloth rationing was very strict during the war years and sheets, blankets and bed covers must have made a good haul.

Mrs Ingleson took it very well, being mostly concerned for my safety. I had not heard a thing but was rather startled at the idea of a theft in the middle of the Governor's garden.

### 3.3 El Fasher to Nyala

From Fasher I went several times[96] south west to Nyala, where there were other attractions that the mixed cosmopolitan centre with its efficient Greek grocers' shops could not offer. It was impossible to leave the town without more sand to cross but after a time the country grew continually richer.

I had to go on to Nyala immediately after breakfast[97] at the Governor's house in Fasher. I was lucky and was taken in a comfortable B.O.A.C. shooting waggon because the airways representative wanted to go and the D.C. Fasher[98] came too. The first part of the road was rather dull and sandy [March 1943].

During the whole journey I think I was more nervous than I ought to have been about the car, particularly when it was going over sand [February 1948].

Whatever the vehicle, driving through sand was always an experience I found wearing. Even the most skilled of police drivers made a wild rush at a *goz* slope; the wheels would slip and he would wriggle the steering. There would be a sudden, violent change-down, sometimes calculated to a split second; then the breathlessness until all was over and a firmer piece of ground had been reached. Yet the golden ridges with their covering of coarse grass were a most pleasing sight so that it seemed niggardly to be anxious to be done with them.

When this stretch lay behind us, it felt like the first obstacle overcome and I could relax to enjoy the sight of increasing numbers of trees, not just

96. March 1943, March 1945, February 1948.
97. They eventually set off at one o'clock.
98. William Thomas Clark, O.B.E., 4N. (b.19.5.1905-d.1987); Educated at Reading and St Catherine's College, Cambridge; 14.12.27 First appointment; 1928-30 White Nile; 1930-31 Port Sudan—Suakin Administration; 1931-33 Berber; 1933-37 Kassala; 1.4.37-42 Equatoria, D.C. Moru District, based at Amadi; 1942-46 Darfur, 1943-44 D.C. El Fasher; 1946-48 Khartoum; 1948-53 Commissioner of Port Sudan; 1953 retired; 1953-60 Director, U.N.W.R.A., Amman; 1961-62 Development Secretary, Muscat and Oman; 1962-66 Adviser to the Ruler of Abu Dhabi.

thorn but *haraz*[99] and *gemaiz*,[100] and the useful *tebeldi*,[101] in which people stored their water all through Darfur. In some of the lower undergrowth the bright- hued birds perched and fluttered, beautiful and fantastic, while on the ground partridge and guinea fowl.[102] As in Kordofan this was country with enormous herds of cattle with which the tribes wandered constantly, and at intervals we would pass a large well field,[103] with the cattle standing patiently, while water was poured for them into a trough.

> Presently we stopped for an excellent sandwich lunch (airways packing). I hadn't had a ham sandwich for years. At this point the D.C.[104] remembered his suitcase and wondered if it had been put in the car. It hadn't. No pyjamas, no toothbrush and what he stood up in was a rather old pair of shorts and a faded navy shirt. I was told later that this was an accident that had happened to him before [March 1943].

There were some favourite spots[105] where I liked to eat my lunch, one in particular, which had lovely groups of tall trees along a dry water-course. It must have been a hundred yards wide and, although rather shallow, must have been an arresting sight, when the river came down in full spate. Even in the wet season the flow of these streams was intermittent. Perhaps for two or three days after heavy rain they would run and then subside for a time until another cloud-burst. Yet even without water I sat happily under the trees in the heat of the day and felt at peace. It was so quiet one afternoon[106] that I could imagine the gazelles, occasionally seen from the road, stepping daintily from behind the bushes but my only visitors were half a dozen engaging black and white kids, their fat, little bodies as tight as a drum.

99. *Ḥarāz*, the large forest tree, Acacia albida *Del.*.
100. *Gammēz*, lit. sycamore-tree, locally the common wild fig-tree, Ficus sycamorus *Linn.*.
101. *Tabaldī*, the baobab tree, Adansonia digitata *Linn.*.
102. '... Occasionally the greater bustard ran to safety. The B.O.A.C. man shot some guinea fowl and a hare.' Ground partridge—possibly Harlequin quail, Coturnix delegorguei; Guinea-fowl, probably Numida meleagris; Greater bustard, probably Denham's bustard, Neotis denhami or Senegal bustard, Eupodotis senegalensis.
103. The wellfield at Musho, for example, which she visited in March 1943 and February 1948.
104. W.T. Clark.
105. Dr Beasley stopped at Munnawashi to picnic under the trees which were mostly *haraz*, on her treks in March 1945, February 1948.
106. One afternoon in March 1945.

## 4. Nyala

We were very late arriving. Well after dark (about 9 o'clock) we met a lorry which had been sent to look for us. We were just in Nyala and rather tired [March 1943].

... among others [in Fasher in February 1948] were two mining engineers going down to the south of the Province to investigate some old copper workings. There were also two water engineers ... These outside places are amazingly social ... Travelling by air, we could not pile up the whole array of paraphernalia that was pushed into the back of a lorry. This we had to borrow in Fasher, plus a temporary servant, as recommended by someone ... I was sent to Nyala straight off the plane without kit or servant, since a car was leaving that morning ... I had rather a lot of trouble as the mining engineers had pinched the servant who had been engaged for me. I fixed up with one about 8 a.m. on Tuesday and we set off about 9.30. I arrived about 5.30 [in Nyala] desperately tired. I really should have gone to bed but felt that impolite in someone else's house, as I had only met the D.C.[107] and his wife in passing. So I went through with all the sociability including the mining engineers and the local British S.D.F. officer to dinner. [Throughout my stay] I could not help noticing the sociability. There were four others (and myself) to dinner on Friday, on Saturday the Director of Education,[108] and yet another on Sunday.'

Nyala itself was a scattered settlement without charm which Fasher had acquired through being centred on the slopes round the *wadi*. It had wide contacts with the grazing lands to the south and west and had become the hub of a flourishing cheese industry. A great boost was given to this by an enterprising D.C., who enlisted the help of the schoolmistresses, but could not understand why his cheeses always turned out pink, until he noticed the *henna* on the girls' finger nails.

107. William George Ranald Mundell Laurie (b.4.5.1915- ); Educated at Monkton Combe and Selwyn College, Cambridge, 1934-36 Cambridge University Boat Club; 19.12.36 First appointment; 1936-40 Kassala; 1940 Governor-General's Commission as Bimbashi in the S.D.F.; 1942-44 seconded to O.E.T.A. (Cyrenaica);1.1.45-50 Darfur, 1945-1947 A.D.C. Nyala; 1948-9 D.C. Southern District, based Nyala, 1948 Gold Medal, Olymic Games, Coxwainless pair with Jack Wilson another D.C.; 1950 resigned; 1954 graduated M.B., B.Chir. (Cambridge); 1955 G.P., Oxford; 1969 Service with Save the Children Fund and Methodist Missionary Society, Kenya; 1980-81 Service with U.N.H.C.R., Somalia.
108. C.W. Williams (Billy), C.M.G., M.B.E., 4N. (b.1899-d.1957); Educated at Wellington and Oriel College, Oxford; 2.9.20 First appointment; 1920-28 Gordon Memorial College, 1923-35 Tutor, by 1927 Senior Tutor; 1929 Inspector, Department of Education; 1930-37 Warden, Gordon Memorial College; 1937-44 Assistant Director of Education; 1944-50 Director of Education, succeeded by D.H. Hibbert.

I was staying with a D.C., Matthew Wordsworth,[109] son of the Bishop of Salisbury, who was a nephew of the poet. A large bearded man, rather a character and full of the most marvellous stories which he had been told by tribes like the Baggara ... He took a great interest in the girls' school, which was not doing too badly. He had been trying to teach the schoolmistresses to make good cheese but they wearied a little at the idea of sticking to it every day [March 1943].

So devoted was he to the pastoral side of his duties that he kept a herd in his back garden. D.C.'s usually had some particular hobby, that they were eager to discuss and generally it was very stimulating to hear them do so. I can remember, however, racking my brains furiously to find something fresh to say about the trees, which so many of them used to plant.[110] One orange tree was apt to look rather like another. But cattle were different and I had a peculiar and irrational aversion to them.

He invited me into the middle of his herd to admire his spot beasts ... Matthew Wordsworth took the mistresses and myself for a picnic to a vegetable garden some miles away. They enjoyed it immensely. Saw bulls raising water using a great skin. Certain amount of desperate courage from the mistresses giving food to the bulls at arms length [March 1943].

I could not, however, let the side down by confessing. I therefore allowed myself to be led among the closely packed beasts and did my best to concentrate on what I was told were their merits. I was relieved beyond measure when the wife of one of the [Baqqara] herdsmen came along and pointed out her particular bull, and then led me away to her house to show me all the *impedimenta*, which it carried while on the road. It was an amazing array including an *angareeb*, pots and pans, rolls of matting and any number of odds and ends. It is possible that, with the woven ropes of the *angareeb* to cover the bull's spine his broad, cushioned back might make quite a comfortable resting-place, for they were very gentle beasts and slow of gait.

---

109. Matthew Charles Wordsworth, C.B.E., 4N. (21.9.1905- ); Educated at Marlborough and Oriel College, Oxford; 14.12.27 First appointment; 1928-32 Education Department; 1932-38 Kordofan (P.E.O.); 1933 D.C. Um Gabralla or Talodi; 1.11.38-44 Darfur, 1942-44 D.C. Southern District, based in Nyala; 15.6.44-1947 Equatoria, D.C. Torit District; 1947-54 Commissioner and Registrar of Co-operative Societies; 1954 retired; 1954- Adviser on Agricultural Credit and Co-operation, Development Division, British Middle East Office, Beirut; Son of Bishop of Salisbury.
110. 'I thought of Browning, 'Your ghost will walk, you lover of trees" [March 1945].

## 4.1 Visit to the Beni Helba

Very properly in such a district, cattle figure largely in my memories of Nyala. There was another occasion,[111] when one of the D.C.s[112] arranged for a visit to a nomadic Baggara tribe, who were encamped nearby for a season. When I asked the schoolmistresses, if they would like to accompany me, and if there would be any impropriety in such an expedition, they were unanimous and enthusiastic in its favour. They were all girls who belonged to the West, and thus more accustomed to free- er ways than in the Northern Province, for example, but they had been brought up in the town of El Obeid, and the idea of a visit to a nomad, cattle tribe was as enthralling to them as it was to me.

Matters were arranged through the son of the *nazir* of the tribe, the Beni Helba. This young man worked in some ill- defined position at the hospital in Nyala and probably ranked as an *effendi*, because he spoke some English, but he still seemed to retain considerable authority among the tribesmen.

We drove out in a tourer as far as Jebel Nyala, slowly because the road was rather sandy. Suddenly out of the bushes rode a man on a black horse, waving wildly at us. He had only been lying in wait to make sure that we did not miss the way, but we felt it an appropriate gesture to begin what we all regarded as an adventure, however mild a one. Then we met the *nazir*'s son, who rode on ahead of us at a gallop. I thought it rather a nice piece of horsemanship, for his girths were broken and dangled; he had no stirrups; he was having a lot of trouble with a sunhelmet, that would not stay on; and his jodhpurs fitted so badly that they too must have been very awkward. The Darfur tribes had very little to learn from anyone about riding horses.

As we drove right into the heart of a most delightful wood, the Beni Helba gathered round in a crowd to meet us. With much exuberant friendliness they adopted the suggestion of the *nazir*'s son that we should look round some of the little *birsh* houses, which though small, were impressively clean. No-one had a lot of gear to litter up the place and, as I noted often, constant moving avoided the accumulation of much junk. The mats, which formed the walls of the houses were beautifully woven and delightfully soft to the touch. Weaving was one of the local crafts and some

---

111. Dr Beasley visited the Beni Helba with three schoolmistresses, including Banouna, the Headmistress of Nyala Girls' School, on her visit to Nyala in March 1945. 'The mistresses were really enthusiastic about their outing.'

112. Edward Christopher Haselden, C.M.G., 4N. (b.14.8.1903-d.1988); Educated at Cheltenham and Pembroke College, Cambridge; 7.12.25 First appointment; 1926-28 Kassala; 1929-32 Khartoum; 1932-35 Public Security Intelligence; 1935-42 Kassala; 1940 Temporary Commission as Bimbashi in the S.D.F.; 1942-45 Darfur, D.C. Southern District based in Nyala; 1945-53 Sudan Agent, Sudan Agency, Cairo; 1953 retired, Chairman, Anglo- Egyptian Aid Committee.

of the coloured food-covers, which the women made, would be a decoration in any home.

One elderly woman, rather tall and good-looking, welcomed us to her hut with the dignity of a lady of the manor and then brought us a bowl of milk to sip and a present of eggs to take away. Quite a number of the women were attractive but she stood out as a personality, whom I should have liked to know better.

I was a little nervous about the mistresses, fearing that they might be townee, coy and giggly, which I had seen happen elsewhere,[113] but I need not have worried. Once they took stock of the situation, they uncovered their faces, seeing that the other women were all unveiled, and asked innumerable and intelligent questions about all they saw around them, wanting to find out at first hand what really did happen in such a community. As usual they looked pleasing in their white *tobes*, compared with the Beni Helba women, often wrapped negligently in a bit of faded, navy calico and with large, pale beads of amber. But neither group was stand-offish. The mistresses were genuinely interested and met with a most friendly response.

There were not as many cows as I had expected, but apparently these had been taken nearer to the town, because the milk was required in the afternoon for the cheese-making. The tremendous number of horses, I was told, was due to the fact that every man owned one.

After a while they offered to dance for us and started off with evident pleasure both men and women together. I am sure that there is much more skill in this than I shall ever know, but even now, when I have seen a lot of African dancing, I cannot truthfully say that I really like it. There were times when I have felt the excitement of it and could have readily joined in, but as a spectacle it was too unco-ordinated for my tastes. So much of it was a monotonous shuffle with unrelated leaps and bounds, or muscular wrigglings and liftings, which have their significance but which I do not find beautiful. Somehow the African figure tends to be lumpy and cannot compare with the supple posturings of the Burmese, for example, nor the grace even to their fingertips of dancers from Bali. I was, therefore, perhaps unfair to the Beni Helba, who danced for us on a sunny afternoon in their lightly wooded glade. The mistresses obviously understood the finer shades of it all, and commented on the performers, as they moved up to select their partners, although not in the orderly way in which we now move through our country dances. 'Look at her,' Sitt Zenab would whisper, 'the second from the end. Isn't she good?' To me she was just like the others. When a woman did us the honour of shuffling right up to us with a rhythmic lifting

---

113. For example on a geography trip at Gedaref.

of the breasts, I could only decide, that it must have been very difficult, but it was also rather unsightly.

The dance looked as if it would go on for a very long time and, as it seemed to be the same all the way, we decided to leave after some time. The D.C.[114] had very thoughtfully provided me with tea and sugar, then strictly rationed, which I was able to present to the *nazir*'s son and ask him to give it to the women for a drink. We were waved away with the greatest friendliness but did not go far, because the schoolmistresses evidently had a feeling of being footloose and suggested that, while they were there, they would like to wander about in the woods for a bit. This we did, until one of them recalled that she had never seen the river bed, which bordered by trees, swept in a noble curve round the back of the town, a fine sight when full of water, and by no means bereft of beauty at any time.

> We therefore piled into the car and waved goodbye to the Beni Helba. There were a number of wells near the edge. Across the *khor* was the house of the second D.C.[115] where I stayed in 1943.

We finished up in the fruit gardens[116] on the other side of the river drinking ginger beer out of bottles, again thoughtfully provided by the D.C.

## 4.2 Nyala schools

As a centre of girls' education, the various mistresses seemed to make the school at Nyala colourful and interesting, although the level of scholarship was never high.

> I took one class for a geography walk one morning, which consisted of a short walk to the native court and the making of a map of the route ... it was the old men in the court who were most embarrassed.
>
> Went to tea with one of the mistresses, daughter of an Omdurman merchant, now making much money in Nyala. Was rather shocked at the way they discussed black marketing—not that the principle was wrong but that prices were so high—this particularly surprising as father was just out of prison for profiteering. He was leader of a *tariga* and just out of prison in time to instruct his following at the *mulid* [March 1943].
>
> Various people came to see me in school including ... an enterprising young

114. E.C. Haselden.
115. Matthew Wordsworth's house. On Dr Beasley's visit in March 1945 she stayed with another D.C. in Nyala, E.C. Haselden. Michael Ernest Christopher Pumphrey was also D.C. Southern District, based in Nyala from 1944-46.
116. On Dr Beasley's visit in March 1945 she 'enjoyed it very much but everyone would take me to see gardens. The D.C. [E.C. Haselden] took me, the children took me to the *magdum*'s garden for a geography walk the day after their trip to the Beni Helba. The mistresses took me to gardens.'

Sudanese doctor. The schoolmaster brought in all my visitors. I couldn't help
wondering what was happening to his own school ... The two new teachers
were doing well but the headmistress had got fat and lazy and the inevitable
clash occurred [March 1945].

I was asked to tea by the mistresses and met the headmaster's wife, a
friendly soul, and the wife of another master, she being a direct descendant of
Ali Dinar. I was not much more impressed with her than with the other
descendant who used to be a teacher at El Obeid, a sloppy minded girl ... who
got into trouble in the orthodox way and then wasn't made an honest woman.
The *magdum*'s daughters, in frocks evidently lent them by the young teachers,
did some wonderful character sketches and some amazing acrobatic dancing. I
always find these tea-parties rather a strain but they are part of my job [March
1945].

The school was going well but the top classes were very thin. There was a
boarding house with girls from districts round about.

It helped the place extremely when the *magdum*'s[117] daughter was accepted
in the Training College and subsequently went back to teach in her home
town. Another fillip was given when a Headmistress had arranged
expeditions, first for a couple of days to the Beni Helba, and then for a week
to Buram, a place of some considerable distance, to demonstrate to the
*nazir* and his wives the benefits of learning Domestic Science in schools. She
enlisted the help of the D.C. for transport, as they had to be away for
several days during a public holiday, but the initiative and the work were
entirely hers. All the mistresses went and a number of the older girls.
Apparently it was not regarded as flighty or forward in any way; there was
nothing but praise for the ability of these educated women. If there were
doubts, they did not come to my ears and the little party returned with two
hundred pounds for the school chest and five new girls entrusted to the
boarding department of the school.

The headmistress here I had known as a cheerful and energetic assistant
at Tegale and her rather flamboyant personality gave an exciting touch to
the whole idea of schooling. I remember going out for a picnic[118] with her
and the two top classes to garden at Gandua, a few miles away. When the
business of eating and drinking was over, the fun was fast and furious. With
a few bits of cloth the children soon transformed themselves into any
characters they wished to impersonate. Some of the girls were born actors
with an abandon to clowning which was uproariously amusing. True their

---

117. *Magdum* [*maqdūm*], was a native official responsible for a district (a type of local inspector), a title
dating from the time of 'Alī Dīnār.
118. The headmistress 'took great pride in her school'. Dr Beasley went on the picnic with the
mistresses to the Government garden at Gandua after examining the girls in February 1948.
'Thanks to the kindness of the D.C. they all had tea.'

songs, dances and recitations may not have all been in the best possible taste, but the lack of squeamishmess was concerned rather with matters of food rather than innuendo about sex. The latter might be included in such a way as a small sketch in which the jester steals the donkey of a woman who is six months pregnant, and out of this women and girls seemed to be able to make a tremendous joke. Nor was there any false delicacy on the part of the actress who was made up to represent the unfortunate woman. But what the children chiefly loved to portray were elderly *sheikh*s with paunches and enormous appetites and the variations on this theme were endless. I was rather struck by one item in which the soloist walked up and down in front of a line of chorus with the loose limbed gait and action, which was reminiscent of what we used to call Christie Minstrels.

It may not have been very elevated but they all enjoyed it immensely, and so did some thirty or more herdsmen who gathered round to listen—to the complete unconcern of everyone. The girls went home in the lorries singing lustily like children from a school treat anywhere. I had sometime been afraid that our educational aims might become distorted and we should begin to produce a class of 'little ladies'. For that evening at any rate my fears were allayed.

Life in Nyala always ran on for me as easily and pleasantly that I forgot the difficulties of the road. I used to stay in a round, thatched hut at the bottom of the D.C.'s garden in Nyala where I was very comfortable.

Haselden[119] had a piano which was in poor condition. I played a couple of Chopin's noctures to him, as if in a Victorian drawing-room.

Once when I had a couple of days sickness[120] and was lying there in peace, I was visited by *two* schoolmistresses, who were horrified to find me alone in the room. I assured them there was nothing to worry about, as the Sudanese doctor had examined me and I should soon be recovered. 'But we never leave an invalid by herself', they exclaimed. 'Someone always sits beside her to chat to her and keep her cheerful'. And they shook their heads over my strange preferences.

I can't imagine anything more horrible than not being left alone when I am unwell.

119. E.C. Haselden.
120. 'After the school trip to Gandua I disgraced myself and I was very sick all night. The doctor and the D.C. said it would be unwise to go on to Zelingei ... an accumulation of strain and fatigue. I felt so much better after two days in bed, although ... thinking Nyala would be a horribly remote place to be buried in. I want to leave on record ... the kindness of the Lauries to such an awkward guest.' The mistresses 'expressed surprise that neither Mrs Laurie nor her mother sat with me'.

Being ill in someone else's house always produces a sense of guilt and especially here, as, when we came from Khartoum, we had to rely so much on the kindness of local officials. Travelling by air, we could not pile up the whole array of paraphernalia that was pushed into the back of a lorry. This we had to borrow in Fasher plus a temporary servant, whom someone could recommend. On one occasion[121] I was sent to Nyala straight off the plane without kit or servant, since a car was leaving that morning.

### 4.3 Nyala to El Fasher

Transport back[122] was more precarious and the D.C.,[123] not trusting the lorry, which was going to Fasher for repairs, was careful to provide me with a large bundle of food and to put a mattress and folding iron bedstead with the rest of the load.

This particular load consisted of the household goods of a *merkaz* clerk who was being transferred. They were personal possessions rather than furniture but the company included both his wives, one of whom had two very young children.[124] When we stopped for lunch a nice point of etiquette arose for me. We were in a long, straggling village[125] with a white bridge over a deep *khor* anda big well nearby, where large herds of cattle and flocks were being watered. Small tobacco plantations[126] bordered the road and there was the usual sprinkling of shady trees. I had assumed that we should all have a meal together in an informal way. But the clerk went off to the village with the driver and Each of the wives gathered up her brood and chose her own tree to sit under and eat her own food at some distance from the other. Whether they were not on speaking terms or whether this was a variant of the rule that wives must all be treated alike, I could not tell. I had been used to situations, where each wife had her own house within the

---

121. In March 1943.
122. March 1943.
123. Matthew Wordsworth.
124. In March 1945 'I started back one morning after breakfast with a large lunch and a bundle of tangerines to keep me amused. As the car was old and untrustworthy the D.C. made arrangements for two lorries to follow later in the day and pick up bits if anything went wrong. One meets with so much kindness travelling round this country that even the most jaded cynic ought to have his or her faith in human nature restored. Mr Haselden was the first person to express surprise at my travelling around alone and think it a brave thing to do. As a matter of fact it isn't really, when everyone makes such careful arrangements for one's welfare. I have always in secret been a little surprised at myself but that is because I was brought up to be afraid of things and never take risks.'
125. Probably Shingeltabaye, also visited February 1948. In March 1945 'I stopped here again to lunch on the way, only this time I was taken into the resthouse, a mere grass *tukl* but cool and tidy'.
126. The tobacco is used entirely in the Sudan and mostly for chewing.

women's quarters and I had known them visit in one another's houses but this was outside my experience. It seemed less embarrassing for me to choose myself a tree under which to eat my sandwiches and make polite overtures afterwards. These were rather apathetically received, and I can only conclude that the wives were as tired and worn as I was, since it was an extremely hot day and the ancient lorry was very bumpy.

> We arrived [in El Fasher] at 4 o'clock and, as there was no-one about, I went to my room for a bath and a rest. Subsequently I went across to the [Governor's] house and was writing a letter, when I heard voices in the garden, the Governor's wife and the youngest D.C. from Nyala[127] whom I had met at dinner one night. He was saying I expect she is all right. There aren't any lions after ... so I made myself known ... Certainly his remark is the nearest I have ever been to a lion [March 1945].

### 4.4. Nyala to Zelingei

Going out of Nyala in the other direction[128] on asubsequent visit[129] I turned north west towards Zelingei.

> I went off from Nyala amid friendly choruses of goodbye, well equipped for the journey and full of admonitions.

Anyone who had worked in these parts usedto assure a newcomer that it was a beautiful road. One would assent politely thinking it probably only comparative by Sudan standards and that anything in Darfur is likely to be an improvement on the White Nile. Nevertheless the road to Zelingei was beautiful in its own right and by all ordinary standards of nature lovers. To begin with the road surface was better and the way was not just a track to be followed at will but a definite high road running between grazing land and plots of cultivation with still more of the tall grass and trees which characterise Nyala. The skyline was always interesting with the changing shapes of high mountains and in the distance the renowned Jebel Marra, 10,130 feet above sea level. This particular peak was famous in a country like Sudan, because it could boast running streams, cool breezes and an abundance of fruit from strawberries to apples. Unfortunately it was very difficult of access and few people have the time to spend a week in solid travelling to taste its strawberries. Admirable though it might have been for a hill station, it still remained uncontaminated in my day. On this particular morning there was a certain amount of hazy cloud, which was pleasant for

127. W.G.R.M. Laurie.
128. The road to Zelingei is in the opposite direction to El Fasher from Nyala.
129. In February 1948.

driving but toned down the landscape until the afternoon, when it was radiant with colour.

From here onwards the character of the country altered becoming very much more the Home of the Fur. Although nominally Muslims theyput no restraints on their womenfolk and both men and women could be seen on the roads or working in the fields without even the pretence of veiling that village women often made in other parts. They were reputed to be rather a backward people but industrious above the normal degree. To look at they were not attractive, as for example the Fuzzies[130] can be in their wild way, since they were rather short and rather black, lacking any of the fineness of feature to be found in the Arab races. In their own way they made good cultivators, although their methods were often stigmatised as primitive.

**Kass**

Apart from the odd worker who waved in a friendly way and one or two villages the roads were empty. I was surprised therefore, when I came to Kass, where I stayed for lunch, to see a collection of grass huts sufficient to house probably two thousand people. It was situated among a sweep of rolling hills, part in a hollow and part on the slopes and generously spread out over the grassland. Near the beginning of the village was a boarding school for boys, which appeared so successful that I immediately began to canvas on behalf of the girls. The Headmaster, an able person of the unpretentious type, offered to give any help he could. The second offer I had was of another kind, a baby gazelle, which two boys brought along hoping I might want it. The tiny creature was enchanting but I had to decline, for I was sure that it would not survive the varied hardships of a journey back to Omdurman.

> The rest-house where I had my lunch was more of a brick *rakuba* than anything else but it was at the top of a slope and had a lovely view.

I had caught up here with a *Kadi*[131] who was supposed to be holding courts in various out of the way places. He was obviously town-bred and not at all happy travelling round the country and therefore seemed unusually anxious to accompany me to Zelingei. I suspected that this was more for his own loneliness than for my protection, especially as I learned later that he had

---

130. Beja in the East of Sudan.
131. Sheikh Magzoub Malik, worked with Mohammedan Law Courts, Legal Department; 1.2.20 First appointment; 1939-42 *Kadi*, based in Port Sudan; 1944 *Kadi*, based in Berber; 1946-1947 *Kadi*, later Kadi First Class, based in Dueim; 1947-1951 Province *Kadi*, First Class, based in El Fasher; 1952 *Kadi* First Class based at Omdurman; 1953 Judge of the High Court *Sharia*, based in El Obeid; 1953 retired. Married Ali Bedri's daughter.

hurried back to Khartoum[132] and the local people felt that, however profound his knowledge of Mohammedan law, he was sadly out of touch with rural inhabitants.

Col. Boustead's description of him as 'straight off the cement' seemed a good one. He was fiftyish, grizzled and fat and I was shocked to hear that he was married to the sixteen year old daughter,[133] prettiest of four daughters of the Sudanese Deputy Assistant Director of the Sudan Medical Service.[134]

As we went further into the mountains, there was unending pleasure in watching the country. The haze had cleared after lunch and the lengthening rays of the sun caught the colours of the grass with varying brilliance; it shaded from a pale straw to a deep rust or almost flame colour. One hillside, where the grass was in seed, glowed with a soft red brick hue. It looked the sort of place to harbour innumerable lions and in fact in this part of Darfur lion were rated as vermin and could be hunted at will. The British woman,[135] with whom I had toured the Nuba Mountains once saw a leopard near here lying at ease by the road but, intently as I watched, I never saw anything at all. Gazelle occasionally skipped across the track and enormous numbers of fat partridges strolled unconcernedly in the undergrowth.

The tidiness of the villages impressed me, the houses carefully clustered under the big trees with straight well-made [*birsh* fences. At intervals too we came across old discarded huts which had been pulled down and burnt. I learnt later that this was part of the local hygiene methods employed by the D.C. Whenever necessary he gave orders that such and such a village should burn its old huts and build new ones. Making a straw hut is not a lengthy business and the order was not as harsh as it might sound, as there would always be plenty of room for people near to their cultivation.

It was a generous district, not exhausting its beauty spots after a couple of miles. The richly coloured country with alternating grassland and forest went on until about six o'clock in the evening, when we descended to a broad valley with great trees, but with the usual dry water-course. There must have been a certain dampness coming from the heavy, green crops and

132. According to Dr Beasley's diaries Sheikh Magzoub Malik went back to El Fasher 'in someone else's company the next day. He should have been spending at least a full twenty-four hours in a number of lonely places'.
133. Adela Ali Bedri.
134. Dr Ali Bedri, a son of Babikr Bedri.
135. Miss E. Hodgson.

the general shade for the air was struck with a sudden chill. Then the road curved steeply up the opposite hill leading at last to Zelingei.[136]

## 4.5 Zelingei

> I slept in the house of John Owen.[137] John had always talked at such length about the beauties of Zelingei and his house and garden. It was great fun to find him so abundantly justified.

The officials' houses, surrounded by bright flower gardens, were sited on a slope and looked out across the valley, by which I had come, to a long range of mountains with foothills in front. Some of the highest peaks had trees right up to the summit instead of being the barren bumps of rocks which muster for hills near Omdurman. One of the nearer hills was outstanding in being shaped like a pink pyramid, giving thus extra variety to the play of lights, always a feature of morning and evening in the Sudan, but which here—nearly 3,000 feet up—was more arresting than ever.

Zelingei was at an interesting stage of development, administered as it was by an autocratic and benevolent D.C.[138] and an important, local ruler, although there was nothing in the regulations to differentiate this district from others. It was just a long way from Khartoum. Outside the residence of the ruler was a native court, which sat in an attractive building, constructed as a long room, open in front with white-washed walls and with a large thatched roof. A square in front of it had been cleared and a place allotted for the erection of Local Government [Headquarters] Offices in the same style. Seeing Local Government was just beginning to take shape, the

---

136. 'We reached Col. Bousted's house about 7.00. he was having tea on the verandah enjoying his view ... We used to drink our lunchtime soup on the verandah while Col. Bousted absorbed the view' [February 1948].

Col. Bousted was no doubt Lt-Col. J.E. Hugh Boustead, D.S.O., O.B.E., M.C.; Gordon Highlanders; climbed Everest to 27,000 feet; 1933-34 Camel Corps Commander in El Obeid; 16.2.35 First appointment; 16.2.1935-36 Darfur, Western District based in Zelingei, 1935-36 Resident, 1937-41 D.C.; 1939 Eritrean Campaign, army; 1941-42 Commanded the S.D.F. Frontier Battalion in the Gojjam, whilst D.C. Zelingei remained vacant; 1942 D.C. El Fasher and S.D.F.; 1944 not on Government lists; By Mar 46-1948 D.C. Zelingei; 1948 Darfur, Western District, D.C. El Fasher; his god-daughter was a great friend of Ruth's.

137. John Simpson Owen, O.B.E. (b.13.12.12- ); Educated at Christ's Hospital and Brasenose College, Oxford; 29.12.36 First appointment; 1936-42 Darfur, based Zelingei; 1942-1945 Khartoum, D.C. Omdurman,; 15.3.45-47 Civil Secretary's office, D.A.C.S. (Internal) based Khartoum; 1.10.47-52 Equatoria, D.C. Torit; 1952-55 Seconded to Department of Agriculture as Commercial Manager; 1955 retired; 1955-59 Courtaulds; 1960-72 Director, National Parks, Tanzania; 1972-75 Consultant, East African National Parks.

138. 'Col. Boustedwasaccusedofwantingtobealocal T.E. Lawrence' and ruled Zelingei district in an independent manner.

D.C. had built schools, a hospital and police-lines while the going was good.

> The fourth side of the square was open and looked across the wide valley, full of trees, across which I had come on my arrival ... [The school] was the other end of the village. It was a nice red brick building with proper outhouses and a good [enclosed] house for the mistresses.

Whatever arbitrary methods had been used, I had nothing but praise for the girls' school, when I saw it. The D.C. said that in his opinion people, who were not used to education should have good school buildings, as then they would realise how important it all was. This was the opposite view to those who believed in fitting schools into the existing African background—a dispute which can wrangle on indefinitely. Sometimes therefore the beginnings of a school were all too painfully near the home conditions and rarely, as in this case, they sprang from nothing to a flourishing, well-housed institution in two years.

> Much of the orderliness and cleanliness of the school was due really to slave labour. There is no other description of the system. A number of women prisoners had been allotted to the school by the D.C. as cooks and *farrashat*. To give the D.C. his due he had not consigned his prisoners to work which they found burdensome. They were probably quite happy living in the schoolyard instead of prison. Certainly they were singing away that morning we went round, as they knelt in a corner grinding corn with a stone. They smiled very cheerily and had a saucy word for the D.C. ... I don't feel that this is such a good system as Medani where the children do all their own work but it may make a useful beginning ... The children were concentrating on other things to their obvious gain.

Both classes were full and thirty girls were living happily in a long, brick boarding house with no fence round it.

> To my surprise one side of the boarding establishment was open to the hills, the grass coming right into what would have been the *hosh*.

No-one seemed to worry about this lack of seclusion and, as the children had probably been used to a good deal of freedom in their ordinary lives, it may have been one of the factors which kept them happy. For they certainly appeared to find school a thoroughly enjoyable place. On the whole they were very black and rather uncomely, although there was a mixture of merchants' and officials' daughters of more noticeably Arab blood, but they had vitality, brightness which were very marked. Most of them spoke no Arabic at all before they came to school. Learning in a strange language and withal coming from an illiterate background should have made school very remote to them but they gave the impression that trying to cope with the three R's or taking part in a geography lesson was all rather fun and they were quite prepared to bring to their lessons the industry for which the Fur are noted. Certainly girls and mistresses thought it a great joke when the D.C. brought his gramophone down to play to them some records of *Oklahoma*, which he had just received. They beat time quietly to the rhythm and laughed whole-heartedly at the queer inflexions in some of the singers' voices.

> I think, however, that the Director of Education,[139] the D.C. and myself as part of the audience was just a bit overwhelming for them. It was typical of the D.C.'s affection for his parishioners that he was constantly thinking of odd things of that sort to give them pleasure.
>
> In the afternoon we went to tea at the boys' school. This afternoon we were to watch a gym display. The instructors were from the police and they gave the boys one hour every morning before breakfast. Ordinary sort of tea-party and then we were shown the hospital and the police-lines. It was all very paternal and one can't help wondering what happens next and how soon this paternal despotism ought to go. It works at the moment and that is what makes it so attractive.

We went to call one morning[140] on the district's most important leader and drank a glass of tea in what he was pleased to call his garden. This was a bare yard planted with a few, very young citrus trees.

> He was full of ideas about pulling down a fence at the back and making a garden from which he could sit and look out across a little valley to the boys' school and the hills beyond ... He was very feudal in outlook but a kind host.

What chiefly interested me was the intricate series of courtyards, separated one from another by wattle doors through which we came, as by a kind of maze, to his rather ordinary-looking brick house. He said the arrangement was to discourage thieves; it did not appear a very firm protection, although it was probably confusing. I was soon given to understand that the idea that I should greet his women-folk was not acceptable. I was told that he had a large number of wives but, as they would not be likely to speak Arabic, such a meeting would not be very profitable. Although in my heart I did not agree, I was obliged to let it pass. I imagine he felt they would hardly do him credit but what was important was, that he did have some daughters in the school and was prepared to back the venture whole-heartedly.

Unimpressive though fruit trees were, there was a Government fruit garden at Zelingei of considerable dimensions, producing among the usual trees bananas, and an attempt at coffee growing. In this case the bananas

---

139. C.W. Williams, Director of Education.
140. On the third morning of Dr Beasley's visit to Zelingei in February 1948 she visited the local leader, the *Demanyai*.

surprised me, for they had suffered from frost early in the year, and a number of experiments were being tried to find out, if they could be protected. I personally never came across a frost in the Sudan, so the idea was sufficiently novel to register itself strongly.

Not all of Darfur was as beautiful as Zelingei. There were places, where at certain times of the year the women had to walk for a day and a half to fetch water, others where for weeks there was nothing but *batikh*, the large, green water melon whose pale pink flesh remains crisp and cool even on the hottest day.

> After visiting the Government garden, Col. Bousted wanted to show us where he was going to have his tribal gathering and horse show the next week ... I should have liked to have seen the 3,000 horsemen coming down the hill.

### 4.6 Zelingei to Geneina

> It must have been after 10. 00 when we got off. The Director of Education wanted to visit two schools ... as my driver[141] did not know the way we followed the Director of Education.

The first part of the way out led down a wide valley,[142] where water was always a few inches only beneath the surface of the dried-up river, and there were many fields in which a great deal of activity was going on. The dampish heat lay heavy, for the mountains came down fairly close on the Northern side and shut off any breeze, and it felt very different from travelling in the desert. Despite this both men and women were working steadily in the fields, although it was not easy to see exactly what they were doing, except using hoes and probably just cleaning in readiness for another crop. Most of them wore very little, the women's attire being a piece of stuff tied round like a short skirt but with no attempt at any sort of head covering. Some of them had babies tied on their backs with their heads lolling in what looked an extremely uncomfortable manner and exposed to the full glare of the sun. Nevertheless most of them were sleeping sweetly with the most contented expression on their faces.

> The school where the Director of Education stayed was rather like the one at Zelingei and had been 'administered' by Col. Bousted in his direct way. I went on, my driver having instructions about the road.

For about two hours the road led through this country crossing and re-crossing the river-bed, where often parties were gathered busily digging up

141. A policeman, Badawi, also took Dr Beasley to Nyala in February 1948, and to Um Keddada in October 1948.
142. The heat in what was probably Wādī Azūm 'made me think of Burmah'.

water. Eventually on the western bank we came to a fork in the way with one large and important-looking branch leading towards the West. The driver confessed at this point that he did not know the way but considered that, as Geneina lay in that direction, we had better take the wider road. We drove into splendid country, the mountains becoming higher and wilder and more varied in shape with alluring prospects ahead at every turn of the road, as the settled river-bed with its numerous inhabitants was soon left behind. The driver began to worry. He called two men busy about some indeterminate chores but they came unwillingly and apparently could not answer his questions. As we went on again, the scenery became more and more impressive, but eventually I agreed to the driver's suggestion, that we should turn back to the fork in the road, since it would save time in the long run to make sure. While returning we came across a [guard] in some sort of uniform, that I did not recognise, which included an *immah* adorned with ostrich feathers but he, like the men we had accosted before, and could give no help. My driver, perhaps because of his police uniform, probably frightened him since he always thought it necessary to address strangers in a really brusque manner, and his annoyance with this man's stupidity turned to downright bullying. Abruptly he started up and set off again, with a long and scornful discourse to me about these miserable peasants, who could speak no Arabic. Other people's degrees of pride are always a surprising revelation.

The smaller fork of the road led along the valley again and this was so much more populated that we soon found some Arabic-speaking cultivators to assure us we were going in the right direction. The road we had abandoned presumably led into French Equatorial Africa, and my chief grievance at this point was, that it was not there, that we had to go.

> The village where the school was, was large with a very busy *suq* and enormous crowds of people most interested in our arrival ... The Director of Education was looking very perturbed, was wondering, he said, what he ought to do. I thought it a bit obvious, as they knew I had taken the wrong road but accepted it all as a tribute to my self reliance and he was so delighted that I wasn't lost that we just pushed on to a better place for lunch. As the Governor-General[143] had recently been around, there were some rather superior halting places.

From here, though we were able to stop and lunch in a pleasant wood.

*Birsh* huts only but a lovely clean encampment away from all the noise and

143. Sir Robert G. Howe, K.C.M.G., G.B.E. (b.1893- ); Educated at Derby School and St. Catherine's College, Cambridge; 1920 entered the Diplomatic Service; 1942-45 Minister in Abyssinia; 17.4.47 First appointment; 1947-55 Governor-General of the Sudan; 1955 retired; 1955-68 J.P., Cornwall.

flies of a village. Lunch was really rather grand—tinned kraft cheese, Vitaweat, Lyle's Golden Syrup with lime squash and tea. None of this living off the country today.

Soon after this the richer country ceased. We came to high ground, rather barren and uninteresting, from which we eventually looked down towards a wide dull plain—what, I regret to state, I should be inclined tocall a real Sudan view, and as usual an enormous stretch of it. There were certainly some tall mountains showing dimly in the North, but they were a very long way off and only made the piece in between look more dreary. As it happened, it was not even a plain, but just one wearisome sand-dune after another with seemingly no solid ground beneath the wheels at all.

I thought there had been a lot of sand on the way to Nyala but it was nothing compared with this. There seemed to be no solid ground anywhere.

## 4.7 Geneina

About five o'clock, when I was reaching the stage of feeling that I could bear it no longer, we saw a *wadi* lying below us thickly set with trees and a cloud of dust rising from among them, like trails of smoke coming from an English village but not quite so welcoming.[144] This was indeed Geneina and we made our way to the Resident's[145] house, situated on a small hill about three miles from the town.

It was a pleasant house ... situated in a very sandy *hosh* which had, however, beds of bright flowers, mostly petunias. Inside the house was full of roses, carnations and large marigolds.
    I had a small room (with no water supply) tucked in between a large hall (an unnecessary room) and the main bedroom (where the Governor[146] and the Resident were sleeping), and which lay between me and the bathroom and all the other out of date conveniences. A silly house I thought. The Director of Education was sharing the rest-house at the bottom of the garden with yet

---

144. 'I think it was the accumulation of this [strain] which made me funk the road to Um Keddada.' Dr Beasley eventually went to Um Keddada in October 1948.
145. Charles de Bunsen; 1946-47 Dar Masalit Resident, based at Geneina who succeeded Eric Armar Vully de Candole (in Darfur from 1936 to 1944).
146. Graham Dudley Lampen, C.M.G., C.B.E., 4N. (b.7.4.1899-d.1960); Educated at Merchant Taylors and Queen's College, Oxford; 1917-19 Royal Field Artillery (Salonika and Caucasus); 24.7.22 First appointment; 1922-23 Finance Department; 1923 appointed to Political Service; 1923-24 Blue Nile; 1924-32 Darfur; 1933-34 Blue Nile; 1935-35 Civil Secretary's Office; 1936-37 Blue Nile; 1937-39 Kordofan, D.C. Eastern Jebels; 1939-44 Deputy Governor, Kassala; 1944-49 Governor of Darfur, based in El Fasher; 1949 retired; 1950-51 member of Sudan Terms of Service Commission; 1951-54 Deputy Sudan Agent, London; 1954-56 Governor-General's adviser in London; 1956-57 Foreign Office (Middle East Section). Author.

another vet. The Governor had come for a tribal gathering [parade and horse races] which we had just missed.

The next day was Friday ... almost immediately after breakfast the Sultan called.

In theory Geneina was the headquarters of Dar Masalit, an independent principality ruled over by a Sultan,[147] whom the Resident advised. There was little doubt that the Sultan, a man of very strong character, did in fact do quite a lot of ruling but independence was rather a misleading word. For example, there were a number of minor officials who belonged to the [Sudan] Government Service and were liable to transfer and appointment by their Departments, and not according to the whim of the Sultan.

> There really was not enough for some of them to do, particularly the aerodrome officers and they just took to the liquor which crept licitly and illicitly across the frontier from French Equatorial Africa ... The Government was trying to get [the Sultan] to name one of his sons as successor but he in turn was trying to put the burden of choice on the [Sudan] Government.

Although the latter[148] was providing the buildings, the girls' school he was so anxious to have would be staffed, equipped and inspected by the Government like the elementary schools in the Sudan proper.

His desire for a girls' school had been very sudden and, the Resident thought, one of his crazes which were apt to pass rapidly. So definite and vehement was he on the subject, however, that it seemed wise to take advantage of the opportunity for, if it could once get started with his blessing, it might thereafter be carried along on its own momentum. Nevertheless I should very much have liked to discover what lay behind this insistence, for I found it difficult to believe, that he understood what would evolve, when once his women-folk became educated even to the degree, which we knew in Omdurman. People[149] said, that at a parade of two thousand horsemen the day before I arrived, he recognised all the horses,[150] but they also said he would have difficulty in remembering the names of his wives or counting the number of his daughters.

> The Sultan was not such an impressive man as S.A.R. ... He was older, smaller and not so good looking, nor so well dressed. He was wearing much cleaner clothes than when I saw him before [October 1948].

147. Sultan Muḥammad Baḥr al-Din, O.B.E., Sultan of Dar Masalit. He was granted special terms in 1916 when his country was occupied. In a boundary agreement with the French in 1919, Dar Masalit remained part of Darfur.
148. The Sultan Muḥammad Baḥr al-Din.
149. In Dr Beasley's diary the Resident, C. de Bunsen, made this statement.
150. 'About 3,000 horses.'

It is not easy from two or three meetings and much second-hand discussion to arrive at an estimate of people's motives, but I was led to much speculation on this point because his character was of so much interest, and because in some degree a thread of the same colour ran through the attitude of so many Sudanese towards the education of their women. The Sultan belonged so obviously to a disappearing world, a world in which he took part in terrific skirmishes along the French border

> ... until the frontier was delimited. I noticed he had lost the middle finger of his left hand. Apparently in his youth he had been a great fighter.

Another rumour was that, being personally responsible for the death of a number of French officers, he was more or less proscribed across the frontier. Was he in his old age settling down to the arts of peace and forcing schools on his people, because education brings in its train such comfortable results as electric light and refrigerators? I thought I detected in him a hard core of arrogance, the sort of quality which made the medieval theologians rank pride as one of the seven deadly sins and because he was sure of himself and his power, he could not be less than others. Everyone has girls' schools now, therefore there must be one belonging to the Sultan of Dar Masalit.

About the practical details he was most helpful. We could not start it next week, as he wished, and the Resident was afraid that the fad might pass. Fortunately it did not.

> I met the Sultan again later in the morning in a rather less imposing position ... We went to see the boys' school ... a good stone building ... We then turned to the really serious business of looking at the boys' former buildings to see if they would serve for a girls' school ... The [former] school was in the square near the Sultan's palace ... The buildings could [and were] be made use of for a year or so, although by no means ideal. Building being such a price now ... As it was then time for him to go to the mosque we went home and I spent the rest of the time writing out a plan for the new girls' school.

The school was started in some disused rooms belonging to the boys' school.

> There were a few even in the third year and one who wanted to go straight on to an intermediate school. There were two girls directly from the Sultan's household, the daughter ... younger than the granddaughter.

On my next trip some months later I went down to make enquiries about proper buildings. The Sultan insisted that the school should be near his palace, as he could then give rightful protection to the mistresses and the girls. After all Geneina was on the main road across Africa and no doubt plenty of undesirable types found refuge there. One thing that struck me was the trust which the schoolmistresses definitely accorded him. They came with me to investigate the possibilities of a new site and, when the Sultan and the Resident joined us, stood there with their faces uncovered discussing the position and the amount of ground required.[151] They made a pretty picture in their dainty draperies, especially as the Sultan, who was an old man, rather short and stocky, as usual was wearing crumpled white cotton robes, which were none too clean.

'This would really be the best site', I said weighing things up. 'But we ought to have a good-sized yard. It's a pity those houses are there. Is there another site we could look at?' 'You think this is best?' answered the Sultan with a wave of the hand ... Then the houses can be removed. They can go and live round the corner.'

Admittedly they were rather tumble-down *birsh* huts and little but good would come of the inhabitants having new ones. It seemed, however, a little arbitrary, because the Sultan wanted the view of his girls' school from his front-door.

The Palace itself was an unlovely building, unimpressive, rather squat collection of mud rooms with a high wall round with a plan of a fortress.

There was a white building with verandahs and a thatched roof for Local Government offices which was much more impressive [February 1948].

On this particular evening, as we stood there talking, a small herd of cows came along making a tremendous cloud of dust and evidently by habit filing straight into the Palace [courtyard]—a nice, rural touch.

Very shortly afterwards the modern age intruded. The Director of Economics and Trade[152] had been holding a meeting with notables of the

151. In October 1948 Dr Beasley eventually flew to Geneina from El Fasher, to look at the girls' school and discuss the new site with the Sultan. 'A number of girls at the boys' school at Geneina were transferred to the new girls' school and were making an excellent beginning' (*ARDE*, 1948).

'The Director of Economics and Trade was on board. Gins before lunch. We didn't get away until well after four o'clock for the school.'

152. Ronald Johnstone Hillard, C.M.G., 4N. (b.6.5.1903-d.1971); Educated at St. Paul's School and Christ Church, Oxford, 1924-25 Oxford University R.F.C., 1925 represented England at Rugby Football; 7.12.25 First appointment; 1925-29 Kordofan; 1930-34 Assistant Civil Secretary (Administration); 1934-38 Blue Nile; 1938-44 Khartoum; 1944-46 Assistant Controller, War Supply Department; 1946-1949 Director, Department of Economics and Trade, and Controller of Supply, based in Khartoum; 1947 member of Sudan Government Delegation at hearing of Egyptian case, Security Council; 1949-53 General Manager, Sudan Railways; 1949-52 member of Governor-General's Executive Council; 1953 retired; 1953-54 Director, Tunnel Portland Cement Co. Ltd; 1955 Chairman and Managing Director, East African Portland Cement Co. Ltd, Nairobi; President, Chamber of Commerce, Nairobi. Author.

town, who now began to emerge from the gateway. The mistresses,[153] who had been talking to the Sultan without embarrassment, immediately took alarm. They muffled up their faces and walked off with a hasty farewell.

> I left the next morning at dawn—had breakfast in Fasher. The Governor came down to the aerodrome and I told him about the school at Geneina and the decision regarding the site [October 1948].

I went to visit them[154] later in the house which the Sultan had lent them, an ordinary mud house of the Northern Sudanese pattern and they said they were very comfortable there. They were genuinely enjoying the excitement of getting the school going.

> The school was doing surprisingly well ... There were two odd classrooms but a few trees in the *hosh*.

As several of the girls had been in the boys' school as far as the Third Year, they had a reasonable amount of help from these older pupils. The children were very mixed, the daughters of officials and merchants from the East and representatives of all the tribes around. Like the mistresses they all appeared very happy. In the house, however, I found the mistresses' mothers, two poor old souls, one from El Obeid and one from Omdurman. They stood up, when I came in and shook hands, returning my greeting politely but dispiritedly. Unlike so many others they did not complain but the Omdurman one remarked pathetically, 'Yes, it is a nice house. But it is such a long way from home.'

I tried to tell them how much the women of the future would owe to them, in that their efforts were making it possible for schools to be opened up in these distant places. Their daughters followed up my remarks, but I doubt if they really understood. Nevertheless high praise is certainly due to these middle-aged and often elderly chaperones, who left their homes to perform these prodigious journeys for the benefit of their daughters. Financial considerations might not be absent, but without them to give respectability to their daughters' sojourn, girls' education would never have become so firmly poised. Quite often chaperones came into the office and railed at me and I was insistent with them but, when I saw these two standing there dejected yet uncomplaining, strangers in a scruffy town with a vaguely foreign atmosphere, I deeply wished I could have made them understand the magnitude of their service and of others in their situation.

Being a border town gave Geneina a slightly unusual flavour, because it had mud[-brick] buildings for the majority of the inhabitants like many

153. One mistress was from El Obeid and the other from Omdurman.
154. 'The Sultan had not altered the buildings as he promised,' but he had given the mistresses a good sized mud-brick house nearby.

another place, with a few superior brick houses for the rich merchants and for the sons of the Sultan, while hangers-on were in *birsh* huts on the outskirts.

> There is a lot of thieving and roguery as one might expect in a frontier town [October 1948] ... I should have liked to poke around the ordinary looking *suq* as some of their leather work is interesting ... poking around a *suq* is not possible with a couple of males ...
>
> The officials live apart from the rest of the town. There was a bakery, a very well stocked grocery store and a little mosque. The mosque had been built by the cook of a former Resident and no-one ever seemed to use it but the donor.

Three miles away from the Sultan's palace was another settlement, where officials lived near to the police-lines and the fort. This last, was a relic of troubled times, feared but never realised

> but less than twenty years before the authorities had thought these precautions necessary.

Now the Post Office functioned in it; and visitors climbed up at sunset to gaze at the truly magnificent view, the great mountains on the frontier, the *wadi* with its line of trees, the flat tracts of the airfield, lonely then but of vital importance when the Mediterranean was closed during the war. It was a brick building in the veritable 'beau geste' style, which made me realise that such a situation was not, in time, so far away.

### 4.8 Geneina to El Fasher

> Sudan Airways had started a weekly service. The Director of Education planned to go back to Khartoum on it. Unfortunately Sudan Airways chose that week to cut down their service at a couple of days' notice and enraged telegrams did no good at all [Feb 1948].
>
> I hoped to get to Fasher and thus catch up on my two days' illness. I set off early after breakfast but the Director of Education wanted to inspect the school thoroughly and was staying until after lunch. Also he has a pleasant habit of looking up former students such as clerks at the *mudiriyya*. He is incredibly good at remembering them ... one senior District Commissioner said he was the most popular British official in the service [Feb 1948].
>
> ... It was a sandy road down to the town from the Resident's house. The road followed the *wadi* [where] in places it had been built up like a causeway [Feb 1948].

From Geneina eastwards I followed[155] the main trunk road across Africa, not a very impressive highway. I was told, that it was better on the other

---

155. In February 1948.

side of the frontier, because the French have no divergent opinions on forced labour. I had used another part of it on an earlier trip[156] from Fasher to Um Keddada and, although I had heard lorries rumbling through in the night, I had not seen enough traffic, not enough possibilities of valuable merchandise, to feel that heavy expenditure on the road would be justified. That did not make parts of it less painful for the traveller.

'Don't lose heart', said the Resident when I set off. 'It's only the first two hours that are so depressing'.

There were as many *goze*s to leave Geneina in this direction, as there had been coming from the South. Happily there were a lot more people to lighten the way. I thought it probable that many of them were returning in leisurely fashion from the tribal gathering of a few days before. There were groups of horsemen with spears trotting along or cantering about and looking very picturesque and all with a friendly greeting.

True to report, the road and scenery did begin to improve after midday. The sand was left behind and, even if the surface was bumpy, it was firm. There were mountains in the distance and tree-lined *wadi*s at fairly frequent intervals. I halted for lunch in the middle of a lovely stretch of wooded country. The light-leaved trees [were] sufficiently far apart for there to be sun and cheerfulness as well, while here and there patches had been cleared for grain cultivation. Many of the trees were *haraz*, which grows to noble proportions and a most pleasing symmetry, while the tall grass between, although yellowish in colour, softened any bleakness which might have comefrom lack of undergrowth. It is the English 'carpet' which one misses so much in the Tropics. Seldom in uncultivated parts does one walk on turf sprinkled with flowers.

For the centre of Africa I had picked on quite a populous place. At least a dozen people must have passed by, while I was eating my lunch, mostly sturdy Fur cultivators, very dirty and earthy-looking andextremely ill-clad. One group provided quite a spectacular little scene. There were a couple of men with two camels and a donkey. My driver in his officious way thought that they were going too near me and ordered them to the other side of the road. The lorry was standing there with its bonnet up but perfectly quiet. All the same one of the the camels seemed to take a dislike to it, roared loudly and gave a shrug. Just one shrug and all his load fell off and he was away into the forest before anyone could hinder him. I was amazed that a load could be so completely and easily jettisoned by just one heave from the camel's back, but I remembered Gertrude Bell's comments on the way in which Arabs load camels. There had been wild confusion of animals for a

156. March 1943 or March 1945.

few seconds with the camel kicking and plunging and, after he had run off, I thought I saw a dead goat near the car. There was a babel of uplifted voices, which I hoped would not develop into a fight. I soon realised, however, that it was mostly shouting at the animals and, of course, ordinary Sudanese conversation always sounds excessively violent. Then one man ran after the straying beast and the other gathered up the pieces and led the animals on. To my great relief the goat proved to be only a stiff skin, lying in the shade with its feet in the air. Peace descended and I sat under my tree looking at the road stretching away, as far as I could see, between a tangle of grass under the big *haraz*.

We passed quite a few Fur cultivators during the afternoon and, although their villages were not very obvious, I could see clusters of huts occasionally and ordinary labourers trudging home after a day in the fields. In some places where bushes came down to the edge of the road, there was a suggestion of a lane with hedges. Meeting two or three men with hoes over their shoulders, I almost expected to come round the corner to a village green.

One hillside between Geneina and Kebkebiya, where the grass was in seed, glowed with a soft red-brick hue. It looked as if it might harbour many lions, and indeed in this part of Darfur lions were rated as vermin and could be hunted at will. The British woman[157] with whom I had toured the Nuba Mountains once saw a leopard near here lying at ease by the road. I never saw anything, however intently I watched, except gazelle which occasionally skipped across the track and enormous numbers of fat partridges which strolled unconcerned in the undergrowth.

## 4.9 Kebkebiya

Kebkebiya, where I was to spend the night, boasted a large open space in front of a *wadi* and the resthouse, but it was anything but green. It had been drastically cleared and in the evening light with the mountains a great mass behind this helped to make the place look rather forbidding.

As the Governor-General[158] had recently stayed here there was a lot of spit and polish. Whitewashed stones marked all the directions.

The main village was further along the road [to El Fasher from the resthouse] and I could not see any houses from here. A strong wind, rapidly becoming chilly, swept across in a desolate way. Nor was it any more cheering to find the place securely locked. I sat outside the house and

157. Miss E. Hodgson.
158. Governor-General Sir Robert G. Howe.

wondered what it must have been like, when it was a D.C.'s post,[159] This night it seemed extraordinarily lonely, but perhaps it was different when one knew the district. While I was still meditating, the driver returned with the *ghaffir* who was fairly mellow and quite certain he had not been warned of our arrival. 'No occupation except *merissa*', grinned my servant, as he looked at him, and we all greeted one another very amiably. I understand that *merissa* leaves no hang-over the next morning, so that there was always an air of geniality about these drinkers, even if their reactions were somewhat vague.

> I went in as soon as the sun was down ...I had an odd feeling of horror while sitting writing before my meal, not a new thing but one which has usually preceded something disastrous. Shadows of this hung about me until I decided not to go to Um Keddada ... The Director of Education[160] did not arrive until after 8 o'clock by which time I had fed on my own.

I spent a very comfortable night there, although the wind howled and birds and rats rustled in the thatch. While the servants were packing up inthe morning, I went across to an old fort[161] to see, if the buildings could be used for a boys' school. To my surprise I found a [sub-grade] school in progress. There were thirty of the dirtiest and most uncared for boys possible with two teachers, one a cheerful young man in an apple green *gallabiya* and the other a creeping old*fikki*, but even at that level did not seem to be serving a very useful purpose. I asked about the prospects of a girls' school but received merely evasive answers.

> He had probably run the place as a *khalwa* in the old days ... Very different from the sub-grade schools in Col. Bousted's domain ... Later, when the Director of Education asked him, he said he thought it unlikely that girls would be sent to school.

It was all so different from Zelingei or Kass or even the sudden craze of the Sultan. Until he had retired a couple of years before, the district had been

---

159. The editor has been unable to trace when Kebkebiya was a D.C.'s post. The area was probably administered by D.C. Kuttum.
160. C.W. Williams.
161. 'I had promised to look at the fort for the D.C., Kuttum.'
By 1948 the D.C. Kuttum was Arthur Eber Sydney Charles, C.B.E. (b.6.1.1910- ); Educated at Sherborne and Worcester College, Oxford, Oxford University R.F.C. 1932, Rugby Fives 1930-32; 24.12.33 First appointment; 1933-36 Kordofan; 1936-38 Civil Secretary's Office; 1938-41 seconded to Govt. of Palestine; 1941 Temporary Commission, British Army, General List; 1941-43 Equatoria; 1943-46 Finance Department; 15.6.46-51 Darfur, D.C. Kuttum; 1951-52 Finance Dept.; 1952-53 Asst. Director of Establishments; 1953-55 Director of Establishments; 1955- Establishments Adviser.

run by a D.C.,[162] who believed quite sincerely, that his people would be happier without schools. Girls' education was firmly discouraged. We had much to contend against. Apart from this reminder of different opinions about happiness, that morning I felt the complete joy of just wandering, for the rest of the journey was wonderful sightseeing. We were soon right in among the mountains and, although the road did not apparently climb much, we must have been fairly high. There was still the vivid red and yellow grass with an occasional hillside almost scarlet and the dark rock from the slopes coming through in grey and blue tones. The shapes of the hills were a little fantastic but not terrifyingly so, as in Kassala. Perhaps it was the softening effect of the vegetation and the clear quality of the air, which made the countryside something to be so actively enjoyed.

At one corner a green field had cattle watering at the well and a line of them following a zigzag path up the hill. Strange though it may sound to have noticed it, here I saw some cows lying under a tree. I think the reason that this seemed such a pastoral idyll was because in my mental pictures of cattle in the Sudan they were always on the move, large herds crossing the Kordofan pastures, or coming down to the river at Omdurman, or gathered round the wells at Musko.

When the mountains closed round, rather more stony than before, we came to a hill, a haunt of baboons. Some of them, sitting by the roadside, gazed at the car with much interest, some stopped to look after us, whilst others continued running on their various ploys. From that distance, they are not frightening although in fact they are always offensive-looking beasts. The few monkeys, red hussars, which scampered across the road now and again, were much more pleasing, but they did not often pause long enough to be seen closely. The baboons were far more insolent.

We had left most of the high country behind and come to flatter, arable land, which was comparatively populous.

> The resthouse, a grass *rakuba* or less, had been taken over by some locals, so I picked a spot under a tree for my lunch. The Director of Education arrived half an hour later and we had the same sort of lunch as the day before. It was—for the centre of Africa—rather like a highway, although ours were the only vehicles.

162. 'I rebel against people like that ... Education could not be held indefinitely from Kuttum.'
Major Guy Morton Moore, M.C. (b.12.3.1896- ); 28.11.28 First appointment; 1928-46 Darfur, 1928-34 A.D.C. Central District based El Fasher, 10.8.34-46 D.C. Northern District, based at Kuttum; In December 1940 he led a tiny Anglo-Egyptian expedition to Merga Oasis and in 1941 he had contacts with Chad; 1946 retired. 'In Khartoum early December one year Guy Moore announced with glee that he was setting off to Kuttum by camel all the way and his next bath would be on Boxing Day; He used to fast in Ramadan as it was so hard on the servants.'

Near the place where I stopped for lunch[163] there was an interesting experiment in water catchment being carried out. A kind of dam had been constructed across a wide *khor* made of large stones and wire netting. As far as I could gather from one of the neighbouring cultivators the idea was to prevent the rains rushing away and thus by sinking through the stones, where the stream was canalised, the wells would be filled. My informant was immensely proud of the dam and in no way superstitious about a new fangled contraption. After this the country stopped being grand but with the mountains in the north and the bright dunes at our feet it was never uninteresting.

> More *gozes*—although with some hard flat bits between ... on one of the *gozes* trying to cut across out of the track we stuck ... with the help of the other driver and servant and some tin contraptions we were off in about a quarter of an hour. Director of Education's driver remarked that he was surprised that in 'that car' we hadn't had trouble before. The A.D.C.[164] in Fasher enquired anxiously when we got in ... and said he too was surprised. People do seem a little casual the way they push a poor, unsuspecting woman out into the wild.

Nevertheless it was sand to the end and the sight of Fasher mosque on its hill in the distance was very welcome.

> The sand was with us to the end, even in the 'Valley of the Trees'—an appalling road and very cut up.
>
> I went back to the same delightful room in the Governor's[165] house, feeling rather exhausted. The great news of the day was that Sayed Siddiq (son of Sayed Abdel Rahman) was making a visit to the West. This had not been allowed since the days of the Khalifa and was causing a certain amount of concern to the authorities. The Mahdi had drawn a lot of his supporters from fanatics of the West and the Khalifa's tribe, the Taishi, belong to Darfur. I didn't personally notice any intense feeling in Fasher the day before his arrival nor was there any apparent commotion the day he arrived. We heard a certain amount of drumming as he came to the town ... I wonder if people are to some extent losing interest in this combination of holiness and secular good living dependent thereon.
>
> Then came the *Kaid's*[166] plane unexpectedly and had no objection to taking Director of Education and me back to Khartoum. I am not sure that the D.C. will ever forgive me. The School at Um Keddada is his pride and joy and he feels I have failed them ... I had a most disappointed letter from the mistresses, followed by one from the D.C. saying couldn't anybody go? It was

---

163. At Tawila, 'a large well-field'.
164. El Fateh Mohamed El Bedawi, M.B.E. 1.10.35 First appointment; 11.2.40-1947 Northern Province, *mamur*, Atbara; 15.3.47-52 Darfur, A.D.C. El Fasher District, based at El Fasher; 15.4.52-53 Blue Nile, A.D.C. Fung District based Singa; 18.5.53 retired.
165. G.D. Lampen, Governor of Darfur.
166. *Kaid*, i.e. *al-Qā'id al-'āmm*, the British G.O.C. the Sudan Defence Force.

only 1 ½ days from Nahud. He didn't add that Nahud is a day from El Obeid and El Obeid 24 hours from Omdurman, with trains only twice a week. I wrote back in sorrow.

## 5. El Fasher to Um Keddada

I kept my promise and went to Um Keddada in October 1948.[167] I flew to Fasher.

Journeying eastwards from Fasher to Um Keddada there was little of scenic grandeur and my memory is mostly of deep ruts in the sand.

Because of the petrol shortage I was travelling there by *suq* lorry and I was to come back with the *mamur* in a 'box'. I know that I am entitled to a tourer and lorry all to myself, by virtue of my rank but those days are gone ...

As I was travelling by *suq* lorry it was in some ways a slightly uncanny experience, like some modest link with the great desert trade routes and I could not fail to marvel at the enterprise which had built up this kind of mechanised caravan organisation.

We left Fasher about nine in the morning, rather to the driver's annoyance I gathered later, as it did not fit in with his regular hours.[168]

I was provided with equipment and an excellent servant who used to be a cook of the D.C.,[169] just transferred. Having seen me before, he treated me like one of the family.

His lorry was an odd-looking conveyance, piled high with sacks of tobacco on which my luggage and my servant reposed along with two youths, who assisted the driver. There was a very broad cab in the front of the vehicle not entirely closed in but with a little door of flimsy design. The end place, where I sat, had been built out but there was a large empty space in front of

167. Dr Beasley was supposed to go to Um Keddada after her return to El Fasher in February 1948 but 'repairs on the car, combined with stress and fatigue meant that my courage failed me especially as everybody told me tales of the awful road'.
168. 'The driver had been ready as usual at 7 o'clock' in the morning.
169. E.F. Aglen's cook. E.J. Bickersteth was D.C. El Fasher after Aglen. Edward Jelf Bickersteth (b.27.4.1915- ); Educated at Haileybury and Christ Church, Oxford; 1937-38 Private Secretary to High Commissioner of Palestine; 26.12.38 First appointment; 1938-40 Kassala; 1940 Equatoria; 1940-41 Governor-General's Temporary commission as Bimbashi in S.D.F.; 1941-43 Equatoria; 1943-46 Northern; 1.2.46-51 Darfur, El Fasher District, based in El Fasher; 1951-53 Blue Nile; 1953-55 Assistant Director of Establishments; 1955 retired; 1955-75 Reckitt and Colman Co.; 1976- Member, Chairman's Panel, Civil Service Selection Board; 1969- Treasurer and Vice-President, Royal Commonwealth Society; 1968- Council Member, Missions to Seamen; 1976- Governor, Salisbury and Wells Theological College.

my feet and between the extension from the dash-board. It made for coolness and flexibility but did not give me an over-riding feeling of complete security.

To go back along the road through the countryside I had flown over previously was to view the place from another dimension. The hills I had noticed from the plane were still not very impressive but then Fasher is already 2,500 feet above sea level. A fairly ordinary road with fields bearing a lot of grass and stretching up the slopes started the drive and here the going was not bad, as at times there was a flat, firm valley bottom of some width. There were some very sandy bits with ruts up to 18 inches deep. To prevent any monotony, however, some wicked little dry water courses kept crossing the track and in these the lorry stopped and groaned but the engine possessed a wonderful gear below the ordinary bottom one, which seemed to give the vehicle almost the climbing properties of a tank. They were interspersed with patches of sand that gave its character to the strenuous journey.

The sandiest piece I remember was at a well-field, a strange place with the hills coming down on every side to a wide stretch of soft sand. To the North there was a little grazing but the water-holes, a score or so, had been sunk right in the sand and were being used by a large crowd of people for the flocks and herds standing by the troughs. Another lorry was drawn up near the track, as some vital part had broken, and the crew were awaiting the arrival of a kind of portable crane to tow them back to Fasher.

Our lorry stuck in the sand nearby and it was then I realised the function of the young boys up on top. They jumped down from the sacks and dug furiously to free the wheels. Then they flung down in front the sand channels, shallow troughs of iron perforated with large holes, on which the driver revved up loudly and the lorry slowly pulled out. I expected him to stop then to allow the boys to climb back, but not at all; he went steadily forward. On subsequent similar occasions I looked round to see what happened to the boys. As soon as the lorry was clear they made a wide dash, throwing up the spades and the sand channels, and then scrambling up the sides, while it was moving. It had all been reduced to a very skilled technique and, despite the cumbersomeness of the lorry, we were never stuck for more than a few minutes at a time. I was much impressed also by the skill of the driver, as he twisted the steering wheel when navigating the more difficult ruts, although I disliked the perilous way the lorry swayed as he twisted the steering wheel when navigating the more difficult ruts.

## 5.1 Khoreit

About one o'clock we arrived at the resthouse at Khoreit, where I was to
lunch and have an afternoon rest. This again was a centre with a well-field
but the houses were few. The most noticeable feature was a certain amount
of machinery connected with the wells, which were much less primitve than
the holes in the sand. The more modern equipment struck no jarring note in
a spot with so much unspoilt natural charm. Exactly in what this lay I could
not analyse, although I had plenty of time in which to meditate the subject.
The driver had said that we would start at four, but it was after half past
five, when he actually arrived. My fancy had been caught by the shining
fields and pale gold of the grass on the gently rounded slopes, which lay still
and bright in the clear mountain air. It was one of those scenes which
lingers without any clearly defined reason.

Watching this and a little desultory conversation with the caretaker,[170]
filled in the gap until we were ready to start. He had a tale to tell of how he
had lost his arm in a fight with a leopard—'over there'—pointing vaguely to
my shining fields.

> While I waited for the driver, I sat by the door and was intensely aware of
> Tennyson 'Go not, happy day, from the shining fields'. After a time I got
> restive and sent my servant down to find the driver ... another long pause and
> I was just on the point of sending the caretaker's son when I saw the lorry
> coming.

When the driver arrived he explained airily that he preferred driving by
night. Usually he slept all day but he had made an exception in my case. I
calculated that a hundred miles could hardly take more than eight hours
and that, as we had already done four, we should presumably be in Um
Keddada by about nine o'clock.

At this point I did not agree with the driver in his preference for night
journeys. I thought I should find the sandy tracks even more nerve-racking
than by day but in point of fact I re- affirmed my Tegale discovery that
driving by night had a fascination all its own with aspects of the 'romance
of the road' which I had not expected. One of these was that, although the
day had been warm, after the sun went down, I needed to wear a top coat.
That in itself was a plus value in the Sudan, where most lorry travel was a
matter, if not of tears, certainly of sweat and blood occasionally as well.

When it was quite dark we halted on top of a *goz* to cool the engine. The
way had been such deep sand all the time that we had hardly been in top
gear at all and the boys had been constantly jumping down to lay sand

---

170. 'A queer old man, rather frightened, slit eyes and only one arm ... he gave me some
marrows (*forsala*).'

channels for the wheels. While we waited on this bleak, inhospitable upland, the men all said their evening prayer devoutly[171] except, I noticed the driver. I felt a little lonely. The servant was not my own but one I had borrowed in Fasher the day before and instead of support from a police driver there was a tough-looking lorry- owner with his active little myrmidons.

All these lorry drivers had a hard-bitten appearance and a Governor[172] of Darfur once described them as a race apart.

> [The Governor] thinks that the first man who dared to do this lorry route was a Greek. It cannot have been so very long ago ... not much before 1930 that the traffic began ... The fathers of the drivers lived in a world of camel transport.

Certainly there must have been some strange philosophy of life for a man to take to a job demanding so much endurance. Undoubtedly there was an element of adventure about it and perhaps a freedom that appealed, but the going was so difficult that there could be none of the pleasures of movement as in a fine car on a good road.

> Driving all night through the dark and sleeping by day in shoddy coffee houses in the sandy desert needs a little explaining.

True it was an extremely profitable enterprise but most of all I wondered, as the first time I went to Tegale, if this were a modern form of nomadism. Perhaps too it was the challenge of difficulty, the appeal of a strong man's job. It was not an easy subject to discuss with the driver himself. Apart from his concentration on the road, which I had no wish to disturb, he was not much disposed to conversation and certainly preferred light gossip to any analysis of motives.[173]

So we went on following the deep ruts through the sand, grinding along in first or second gear or sometimes in that fierce lowest of all, which gave the impression of a triumphant reserve, when it screamingly pulled us out of our troubles. The lorry had formidable lamps but our world was enclosed, It was only the next few yards that mattered; the vast blackness outside was nothing to do with us. Coarse grasses showed by the roadside, some scrubby bushes and occasional trees, but only once do I remember any houses.

Nevertheless it was by no means so empty as one might expect, driving by night across the sand in the heart of Africa. At one point we came across some fires and there was a big lorry like ours drawn up beside the track, and

171. 'I suppose in a way I did too.'
172. G.D. Lampen.
173. The driver preferred 'to talk about the other *sitt* [Miss E. Hodgson] whom he had transported a couple of years previously'.

people busy in household chores nearby. The stranded driver said he had a puncture and wanted a spare wheel. Had we got one? No, said my driver hastily and emphatically. He was asked the question once or twice more during the conversation, just to make sure he would not change his mind. We did, however, leave behind a large tin[174] containing perhaps about 10 gallons of water, and promised to send help.

> I was a little shattered by his bland negative assurance and could only hope it wasn't true. Anything might have been hidden under those sacks.

Then we continued with that feeling of timelessness which crept over me so often on these journeys. But there was another meeting awaiting us before long. This time on a flat hard piece of ground two or three lorries had been drawn up, since one of these had broken down and had been pulled to one side with the crew making preparations to sleep in it. The others were travelling in convoy and were waiting for another couple whose lights could be seen gleaming about a mile away. Unlike my conveyance with its one pampered passenger, these lorries had several people squeezed in alongside the driver, while one or two hardy souls of less adequate means perched on the sacks at the back. It appeared the extreme of discomfort but there were always a number of people waiting their turn for a place to travel along this road. The schoolmistress and intermediate schoolgirls with their chaperones had to go this way and, although they did not take it as a matter of course, nevertheless they did go and made a virtue of it by discussing the adventure afterwards with some relish.

### 5.2 El Abyad

Our first real stop was at El Abyad. It was half past nine and I was ravenously hungry, but there was no time to dig out any food, only some scalding hot tea, which the servant had procured from a kind friend.[175] We drew up in the village square and could see little save the inviting glow of firelight shining out of some of the houses. The buildings themselves were indistinct, just black stains against the dark sky, but the odd gleams of the fires and the sounds of people talking inside or passing by in the road gave it all a homely feeling which I was sorry to leave. The wind was cold and strong, as I stood by the lorry and watched the boys saying their prayers again. This driver like the others declared that the cold air at night hardened the sand and made driving easier. On this I can pronounce no judgement

---

174. *Fantass*, a large tin to carry water.
175. The caretaker at the resthouse prepared the tea. Dr Beasley saw the resthouse on her return journey.'It was not very inviting ... round *tukls* joined by a roofed-in space.'

but certainly for the passenger the cool air was an advantage over the glare and heat.


## 6. Um Keddada

The rest of the way was deep sand again, although we passed some attractive corners with clumps of trees and huge rocks showing up here and there, but by this time I had lost all count of the hours and was absorbed into the incessant movement grinding along the track, lost to all sense of beginning and ending. It must have been well after eleven o'clock, when I was suddenly shaken by the realisation that we were moving between long, straight *birsh* walls in a kind of street and we had come to Um Keddada at last.

> No-one was about and I opened a couple of doors [in the resthouse] and saw a man asleep on a bed in one of the rooms. I retreated hastily thinking it might be the *mamur*[176] but my servant had no such scruples. He advanced and shook the figure heartily, called out Ahmed [the caretaker] in a loud voice ... I insisted on using my own mattress on a bed in the other room.

At least I had come, for the driver demanded a certificate to say that I had arrived intact with all my goods. I protested that it would surely do in the morning but he was justifiably insistent. This was not a halt for him, as he was going on until daylight, when he would stop at one of the small coffeehouses on the way and sleep till night again.

Darfur is by the sun three quarters of a hour later than Khartoum but it used the same time. It was, therefore, dark when my morning tea was brought, and I had that indefinable excitement which can come from getting up at dawn, when the day seems more full of possibilities. It was a large and pleasant resthouse with deep, thatched roof over a wide verandah and with airy rooms, the whole set in a clean, sandy yard with clumps of trees and beyond a view of fields sloping up to small, kind hills. I was made most comfortable there, for my borrowed servant proved a very capable provider, zealous for my well- being and quite unscrupulous about borrowing to enhance it.

> I could not agree with Elizabeth Hodgkin that Um Keddada was the nicest place in the world but it was extremely attractive and I very much enjoyed

---

176. *Mamur* Muzzamil Abdulla. 9.12.14 First appointment; 1945 Blue Nile, *mamur* Kosti; 24.2.45-46 Northern Province, *mamur* Wadi Halfa; 1.9.46-47 Khartoum Province, *mamur* Khartoum North; 15.3.47-48 Darfur, El Fasher District *mamur*, succeeded by Ramadan Abdel Rahman; 1.8.48 retired.

being there ... I felt it would be easy to get sentimental about Um Keddada.

The *mamur* was in the next guesthouse and I went to see him [after breakfast]. He was an enormous man, about 6 foot and 18 stone at least. A friendly person of the 'old school' and just about to retire ... He took me to see the local garden which produced a little fruit and vegetables for the local officials ... He also pointed out the boys' school which was next door and took me along to the girls' school.

Mornings in school tended to a similarity, which would not be of much interest outside official reports. This school was so remote, that the mistresses rapturously welcomed any visitor, even one with the right to scold. Happily, scolding was not needed, only a little advice. It was a good school and a pleasure to be in, particularly as the village was so isolated, with the sand stretching away on all sides.[177]

Each mistress had a little round hut of her own, with proper doors and windows. The boarders were [a maximum] of six [per hut]. The headmistress complained that their rations were inadequate—mostly porridge with stew two or three times a week ... as the Sudan Medical Service has presumably approved the diet, there was nothing to do on the spot.

To the east lay the houses of the village, where the road led to the Seventeen *Goze*s. In the evening I went out to wander along this road and to look at the place generally. The houses were mostly of grass and not very prepossessing but the people were friendly. Half-clad women busy about their evening chores smiled shyly at me but a burly man in ordinary Sudanese clothes took me under his wing to show me the sights. He was a butcher by trade and it was the meat stalls that we first inspected, empty then but quite clean. Then there was the post office and the native hotels, where travellers could sleep, though hardly in luxury, and the eating houses with rows of benches for those who could not afford more.

He walked back to the resthouse with me and we parted with many expressions of friendliness.

This corner was very much like a version of a posting station. On the morning I left I was with the *mamur* who wanted bread from the baker here, and we waited for a few minutes, while it was brought. It was a striking scene, the sun just coming up in front of us, the desert stretching limitlessly towards it and here on the edge of the village, where a large lorry had just stopped and passengers, very much muffled up, were dismounting stiffly and standing about. One man went to find water to drink, another was buying cigarettes from one of the shop boys. Others were interested in a

---

177. 'At Um Keddada they managed to erect a most suitable building of mud-brick, plain but adequate for the scheduled £E1,000.'

wonderful tray of crisp, brown loaves which had suddenly appeared from the cavern at the back of the coffee-house. There were people of all kinds including one or two obvious strangers, just different enough for one to know that they belonged to French Equatorial Africa.

I felt it would be easy to grow sentimental over Um Keddada from the general feeling of friendliness, which pervaded it. Probably this had grown up because it had been a welcome to so many travellers at the end of that weary road. Certainly on this fresh, bright morning it looked inviting with the rows of benches and tables and the glow of a fire coming out of the darkness of the shop.

One afternoon[178] I took the schoolmistresses for a drive in the other direction. It was a lovely evening with just a few small clouds to make the sunset even more interesting. I borrowed the *mamur*'s truck and police driver and we drove out for about five miles on the way towards Fasher, as two of the teachers had never seen that part of the journey. There was a slight consternation at the beginning, because, although the Headmistress could sit with me at the front, the others would have to sit at the back without screens. Once this objection was over-ruled, perhaps a little brusquely [by me], they were perfectly happy. When the driver, probably showing off, managed to get stuck, they all jumped down and strolled along the road with the greatest enjoyment. When we got back to the truck, they all offered the driver plenty of advice about getting the wheel free, apparently quite oblivious of their original qualms about being seen. This was not caused by any sort of hypocrisy, just sheer inconsistency of thought.

> On our return journey to Fasher, Badawi did not stick anywhere, which made me wonder if the school mistresses had distracted him.
>
> I think that the mistresses enjoyed it. I left them at their door and went back to my bath. The servant had borrowed, among other things for my comfort, a *tisht* (tin basin) into which he poured a tin of hot water. I could just about bath in it.

Expediency and interest in work were gradually breaking down the niceties of seclusion but they had then and probably still have much to struggle against. I had an example of this later that evening, while I was reading on the verandah and the Headmaster of the boys' school came to visit me. He was a short, round man, with a fierce little glitter in his eye, which made me wonder if he had an extra spark of that hard Islamic faith, which has carried Mohammed's creed so far for so long.

---

178. The day after Dr Beasley arrived in Um Keddada, she took the three 'mistresses out in the opposite direction from the market place, after the usual school inspection in the morning'.

He began to criticise the girls' school in the light of what he had learnt at
Bakht-er-Ruda ... It is sometimes difficult to discriminate between it and
officiousness but I gave him the benefit of the doubt.

His chief criticism of the girls' school was that they did not have enough
religious lessons, and he would not be put off by any arguments of mine,
that the girls' curriculum included Domestic Science subjects and the boys
had nothing comparable to take up so much time. I had to give a definite
promise to re-organise the timetable, before he would go. I was not quite
sure of the propriety of a village headmaster being so dogmatic to the
Controller of Girls' Education, that the syllabus proportions were wrong,
but genuine interest was never an attitude to be discouraged and the
headmaster in a village could often be a tower of strength and support to
the mistresses. I could not help reflecting that it seemed rather the same all
the world over, as soon as women start being educated. They have to be as
good as men on the scholastic side and do well in the extra matters of the
domestic sphere also.

I was interested, therefore, even if prejudiced, when I went into the boys'
school the next morning to find that they were by no means ahead of the
girls in their ordinary lessons. Moreover, although presumably from the
same level of society as the girls, they looked lumpier and dirtier. For a
remote village school it was undoubtedly a most creditable institution and,
when one thinks what the country was like thirty years before even, there
was something remarkable in these rows of large boys accepting meekly the
idea that they should sit in the classroom and learn their letters.

Mostly they wear the undershirt and knickers and a *tagia*, or were bare-
headed ...

After this I went across to the *mamur*'s office to meet the Local Education
Committee. In some places the Committee asks to see me but here I had taken
the initiative. It seems a proper contact if one can manage it, but some of the
old *sheikh*s wandered in looking a bit bewildered, probably at being called to
meet a woman.

The Local Education Committee had nothing to ask me except, prompted
by the headmaster, for more religion for the girls.[179] Compared with the
elegant *sheikh*s of Omdurman some of the notables in these outside districts
used to look a bit scruffy, but many of them had a very real dignity and
were most worthy and public-spirited individuals. When I attended their
meeting here I could wholeheartedly praise their enterprise in starting the
school and making sure that it was well attended. They had brought heavy

179. 'I repeated my promise and did actually manage to put in one lesson [on religion] per class
per week.'

pressure to bear on the Education Department in the beginning and now after three years of existence enthusiasm was as lively as ever. My only regret was that I could not come more often to visit them.

> I finished my morning in the girls' school in the usual way and had tea with the mistresses in the afternoon, in the shadow of the schoolhouse ... largely ... the mistresses asking for transfers. All three were anxious to get away and each thought her reasons most pressing. I have grown very weary of this control over peoples' lives.
>
> I had another visitor that evening. I was again sitting reading when a very English voice came out of the dark. 'Excuse me, do you mind if I use the other half of the rest- house?' It was an S.D.F. officer on his first trip to Fasher. It was strange to have someone blow in like that in the middle of a remote village ... after a few polite remarks we retired each to our own quarters ... I was [down to] drinking whisky in my tooth mug or Thermos top, so couldn't have been lavish.

## 6.1 Um Keddada to El Fasher

> We were off early the next morning to drive the 100 miles to Fasher along the same road I took the mistresses earlier. The *mamur* put a mat on the seat, rather like a small prayer mat in design and said *bismallah abrahman*[180] before he stepped into the Bedford truck.
>
> I was tucked in between the large *mamur* and a fairly solid driver ... I got a bruise on the thigh every time we went into bottom gear.
>
> We caught up the army officer at El Abyad where he was breakfasting. The *mamur* and I breakfasted standing, from biscuits and sardines. There was a nasty sandy slope out of it and the army lorry had got well dug in already.
>
> We made good time and were in Khoreit before noon. It was getting warmer ... so when the *mamur* considerately suggested I ought to have a good rest, I was only too pleased to retire to one of the rooms, eat my bread and cheese and lie on my bed. The lorry arrived punctually at 4 o'clock ... There were some bad patches of sand where lorries had evidently stuck before but the driver raced across any intervening flat pieces at a pace I found rather harassing. A little later Melit was pointed out in the distance with the mountains behind it. This is the next site for a school in Darfur but I am afraid that I shall never see it.
>
> About 10 miles or more out of Fasher we saw a village lying back a bit and one or two donkeys labouring up to it. The *mamur* said that in the rains they had plenty of water but for the rest of the year had to fetch all their supplies from Fasher ... By this time I was getting very tired and stiff and was greatly relieved to see the lights of Fasher. The *mamur* was a delightful person ... it

---

180. *Bismallah abrahman*, i.e. *bism Allāh al-raḥmān al-raḥīm*, 'In the name of God the Merciful, the Compassionate...'

was nice to have someone to chat to. But he did not leave a lot of room on the
seat and no air at all from the window.[181]

Wearying though the road might be, the sight of those yellow *gozes* and
shining coloured fields of grass still lingers, merged into a mellow
background of an unhurried world apart.

181. When Dr Beasley flew back to El Obeid from El Fasher she '... tried to retrace the Um Keddada
road ... it looked more desolate than ever.'

# Chapter IV

# The Blue Nile

Like every other geographical feature in the Sudan, the Blue Nile is so vast in length, that one can only talk of it in sections. Perhaps much of the romance of its name comes from the fact, that its origins were so eagerly sought by early explorers fascinated by that strange land of Abyssinia, where it has its source. Certainly it can indeed be as blue as the Mediterranean, when the afternoon sun catches it at just the right angle, as I saw it at Kamlin. Even immediately downstream from Khartoum, where the two Niles meet, the dividing line is clearly marked. As the two streams rush together, the eastern one is dark with silt against the more leisurely flow of waters of the White Nile. By the time they have reached Omdurman they have blended for their two thousand mile journey to the sea.

Exciting though the river may be in its further reaches, the part I came to know first demanded a different response. Rufaa and its district had been one of my earliest inspections, and it was sufficiently near Omdurman for fairly frequent visits[1] to be arranged. I find an aside in my diary about the place: 'I cannot understand why the people at Rufaa are so nice, when the district is so ugly'.

## 1. Khartoum to the east bank of the Blue Nile

I would travel[2] in the Training College station waggon the first part of the way and then be left in a village, hoping that a couple of days later some local official would remember to send transport for me to go on to the next school. To get to the east bank of the Blue Nile was simple. We crossed the swing bridge out of Omdurman, followed the embankment road past the hotel and the Governor-General's Palace, the Secretariat, Gordon College and then to the double bridge for road and rail across the Blue Nile to Khartoum North. After that matters were not so easy as they might sound. I wanted to go south to Eilafun, Hillaleia and Rufaa, all villages on the river but the track, which we grandly called the main road, ran inland for most of

1. Visits included 11.11.41, 18.3.41, 26.11.41, 29.1.42, 22.3.42.
2. Dr Beasley often made this trip from Khartoum to the Blue Nile Province, as on 22.3.42.

the way and was indistinguishable in parts from the stretches of sand and gravel through which it led. To find Eilafun, for example, one had to know where to turn off this track to go nearer the river. Sometimes there might be a cultivator in sight who would know, but the odd traveller might not belong to the locality and would therefore be of little help. Moreover in this expanse there were so few features, that it was difficult to talk, for instance, about turning right by the third clump of trees. Once, however, we were delighted with a small boy, who found a stick and drew a beautiful map in the dust, exactly, he said, as he had been taught at school.

I do an injustice, perhaps, to the district in an overall generalisation about ugliness. It just happenend that it was always more convenient to inspect there at a time, when the crops had been harvested, and this gave the impression of unending stretches of barrenness.

## 2. Eilafun

Even then Eilafun itself was by no means lacking in picturesqueness. It was close enough to the river for trees to reach their roots down for water, and shade a large open space in the centre of the village. No doubt I was influenced, as so often, by a well built school, cream-washed and pleasantly thatched and efficiently run by two enterprising sisters. I have too a happy memory of breakfasting there after a hot and sandy journey,[3] which had started at dawn. This must have been some time after the war because I was a little overwhelmed by their lavish hospitality which included fresh pineapple (a local product), and tins of sardines

> ... rather extravagant and all from Khartoum ... the mistresses should not spend their money on quite such elaborate meals for me ... bread, butter and cheese, olives, tea or coffee.

It is this which fixes the date, as we had no tinned food during the war.[4] Probably the impression has lingered since, although I was accustomed to

---

3. On a journey from Rufaa. On another trip [16.3.41] 'I started for Eilafun [from Hillaleia] taking Mrs McCrell in the car. Not quite so much sand about, not so depressing, particularly thinking one would get away'.

There are references in Dr Beasley's diaries to Mrs McCrell and Mrs MacCrell. This is probably the wife of John Edmund Colborne Mackrell, 4N. (21.4.1906-1978); Educated at Haileybury and Oriel College, Oxford; 8.9.29 First appointment; 1929-32 Darfur; 1932-35 Khartoum; 1935 Bahr el Ghazal; 1936-41 Equatoria; 15.10.41-1945 Gezira, later Blue Nile, D.C. Rufaa; 1.8.45-49 Northern, D.C. Merowe; 15.3.49-53 Deputy Governor, Bahr el Ghazal, based in Wau; 1953-55 Governor, Bahr el Ghazal; 1955 retired; 1955- flower cultivator, Plymouth. Listed in official lists as Mackrell or Colborne-Mackrell.

4. A journey from Rufaa on 22.3.1942.

generous meals, this was laid out in style, with embroidered cloths, good china and glass, with evidently much thought and effort. I owe it to the schoolmistresses to repeat that, even without the influence of the breakfast, I should have been satisfied with the work in the school.

> The school had only been in existence a few months and the children had learnt rather more than usual and seemed exceptionally bright and interested ... Sometimes these pairs of sisters [as teachers] seem a particularly good investment. It worked at Gulli and later at Abu Guta and at Berber: these two originally did well at Tegale.
>
> Eilafun was itself a better village and by no means lacking in picturesqueness. It may have been the contrast from al Hillaleia but it seemed more promising. It didn't seem just one large garbage heap [16.3.41].

This, however, was towards the end of my journeyings and memories of most inspections were more like one I undertook in 1941,[5] before the school at Eilafun was started.

> There were the right number of children all looking scrupulously clean. One of the spare rooms had been turned into a sitting room with a clean white cover on an *angareeb*.

The month was March with the comparative coolness of the winter fading but the wind was restless and blew quantities of sand for the whole fortnight that I was away. It was not the fierce onslaught of a complete *haboob*, the sort of storm which can have the visual effect of a London pea-souper. I have looked out of my windows in Omdurman and been unable to see the garden wall, some twenty yards distant, for the orange-coloured cloud sweeping over it. Not that the cloud was always of that hue; it might be black or grey or any number of drab shades. There the resemblance with fog or mist ends. Tiresome though it may be, a fog does give one the chance to merge with its still secrecy, as it creeps over the land on stealthy cats' feet, and quickly envelops the whole. But a *haboob* hits with sudden violence, tossing up any small objects that lie in its path and bending down the tops of trees in anguished movements, until its fury is spent. On this particular journey we never had a complete storm but only the unending restlessness of a little sand blowing over everything and dimming slightly the brilliance of the sun. Always travelling through this dun expanse in the middle of the day, the world seems drained of colour, although the heat is fierce, and away on the horizon the hot shimmering is indeterminate, giving strange proportions to man or beast or tree within its compass.

> We got back to Khartoum before lunch. Not an aesthetically enjoyable trip

5. 16.3.41.

but I am glad I finished with Eilafun. It did cheer things up a bit but what extra bitter things I should have said of Hillaleia in contrast.


## 3. Um Dubban

On this particular morning[6] we suffered not only from the climate but from war shortages, which had rapidly affected our supplies. Within the first hour we had had a puncture and before we came anywhere near our destination had had to stop twice to cool the engine. Just to give the first part of the journey an extra twist of unpleasantness we had to pass through a famous holy place known as Um Dubban (Mother of Flies), which justified its name. The legend was that a holy man on his way back from Mecca had a vision in which he was told to go on until he found a tree full of flies and there he was to abide. One is tempted to remark that he could not have needed to go far, unless conditions were very different in those days. The tree was still there and a number of *qubba*s had been built round it. Unfortunately, the place gradually acquired a reputation for curing or at least dealing with lunatics. The brutal methods employed by *fikki*s for driving out evil spirits are the province of medical science and need not nauseate anyone here, but they were known to be in use at Um Dubban. As the reverence accorded to the place was so intense, it was difficult to get rid of the institution in one grand sweep. Whenever, therefore, the D.C. tried to arrive unexpectedly to investigate stories of mad men chained and mercilessly beaten, news of his coming had preceded him and not a sign of a chain was to be found.

A *khalwa*, a school run by a holy man for teaching religion only, was conducted along the same lines. The teaching of religion in a *khalwa* generally meant learning the *Koran* off by heart and sitting for hours chanting in unison the ninety nine names of God. Sometimes the boys finished by being literate, more often they did not. Mostly they were often extremely dirty. We had to stop here for water for the car and I wondered how many of the unhelpful people about were patients, for they certainly looked very unattractive.

They were definitely in contrast to the majority of men to be met on the road, who would push a lorry out of sand or mud or assist in the changing of a wheel with the utmost readiness. Once even on another occasion, when our lights had gone wrong, a lorry-driver stopped and improvised a connection, which I did not understand, with silver paper from a packet of

6. 'It was a dull, hot drive' to Hillaleia from Khartoum, on 22.3.42, 'with a lot of sand blowing about'.

cigarettes and it lasted until we reached home. Happily therefore everyone else we encountered gave us the usual friendly greeting, although after our enforced halts, we had no time to stop and chat. My various journeys were always carefully plotted and the police posts informed to look out for us in case of breakdown.

## 4. Hillaleia

As we came nearer[7] there were a surprising number of people on the road, mostly on donkeys or camels but some walking behind the loads carried on their beasts, making their way to the village just before Hillaleia. Here was evidently a regular market but, apart from the animals, there appeared to be little else to traffic in. Away from the few houses and congregated on a flat spot completely bare of trees, it had a casual, extempore look, dumped down in a wilderness away from everything.

Hillaleia presented a shabby aspect, although no more so than many such places, but on this sandy morning[8] the monotony of the colouring obtruded itself.

> It was as dirty as ever, particularly in a sandstorm. There are immense fields which have been full of grain [but now there was] a drabness, where nothing was growing at all [20.10.42].

The houses were just irregularly-shaped blocks fashioned from the soil on which they stood, a lifeless shade between dun and grey and set down at random for the streets to straggle where they would without plan or order. Yet the remark in my diary, which I quoted at the beginning of this chapter, was as true here as anywhere.

> There are one or two good houses in the village but most of it is very squalid.

As a guest in the *nazir*'s house, I could not have been given a warmer welcome.[9]

> I appreciated his hospitality and the fineness of his residence, comparatively speaking.

I was allotted two rooms, and a small recess for bathing, the main one with a verandah which gave on to a large courtyard. It was all made of mud-brick but of ample proportions. A *nazir* was not strictly a Government

7. Dr Beasley visited Hillaleia on various occasions including 16.3.41, 20.10.42, 22.3.42.
8. On 22.3.42.
9. 16.3.41, 22.3.42.

official, although his responsibilities were considerable in the large district, where his power and influence predominated over the lesser charges of *omdah*s and *sheikh*s. Yusuf was held in high repute for the handling of affairs within his bailiwick, and gave me the impression of being a man of action rather than a scholar. I wondered at times if his insistence on having a girls' school had grown out of rivalry with Rufaa, because he was not very well versed in the standards needed for even the most simple of village schools. In fact so welcoming and hospitable was he, that I felt rather ill-mannered to see how put out he was, when I could not lavish praise on his school. It was this disarming friendliness everywhere, which was of the utmost value but on occasion demanded enormous reserves of tact.

Although a busy man he had waited to greet me, despite our unpunctuality and assured me, that he had had everything prepared for me and plenty of food ordered for his honoured guest. By then it was the middle of the morning, through our various mishaps, instead of nine o'clock, as we had hoped, when we left Omdurman just before dawn. He then had to leave me to two elderly *sheikh*s, who came into the sitting-room with a servant bearing a jug of sugared water and glasses. I had a few sips of this suspicious-looking liquid but could not go on indefinitely with civilities, as I knew the school would be waiting. As this was only half a minute's walk away, I made my excuses and went across.

> I went to see the school as soon as I arrived after a tiring journey. The school was bad, the buildings clean but inadequate and children very dirty [22.3.42].

The wretched servant found this all too difficult to understand and kept appearing, following me from classroom to classroom with drinks in the order considered proper for honoured guests—some kind of flavoured water, then a tray of tea, weak and very milky, then a pot of Turkish coffee, strong, black, sweet and laced with subtle spices.

> After my own tea , I went to sit in the *hosh* and was promptly regaled with coffee by a large black slave. The *nazir* came to drink with me and then an old *sheikh*. They talked about the quarrels among the staff. The mistresses share a very small house with their chaperone. I feel anyone would quarrel under such conditions [22.3.42].

It was not only to me that the *nazir* was hospitable.[10] There always seemed many guests about the place with a camel or so usually tied up outside the gate and stir and movement in the outer court. I never appeared on the verandah but someone rushed up and shook me by the hand and a cup of coffee arrived from the back immediately. A cup of coffee in the Sudan was

10. 16.1.41.

as in most Arab countries a very small bowl about the size of a standard coffee cup in Europe, generally made of quite fine china but without handles. Surreptitious investigation brought me the pleasing information that a large number of them bore an English trade mark. The coffee, when made, was poured into an earthenware pot called a *gebenna*, a vessel of comely proportions with a spherical belly and a long, thin neck with a spout. This would be kept hot on a fire and brought to the guest on a cushioned stand. it was probably more customary to be asked 'to have a *gebenna*' than to use the word coffee. Very often the drink was so hot that it was difficult to do other than sip it noisily, as it was none to simple to hold the little bowl. Since it was good manners too show appreciation in this way, I used to try but my upbringing was against me. The Sudanese were very kind about our strange ways and I never felt they minded my different manners.

The question of visitors can become awkward when staying in someone else's house. The courtyard where my rooms were situated led to various other quarters at the back. On my first afternoon[11] I lay down for the usual rest on my camp-bed in the room further from the gate, where I had installed my sleeping apparatus. No doubt a truly grateful guest would not have noticed that all the corners looked somewhat neglected. Grateful or not, it seemed wiser to use my furniture rather than the *nazir*'s, as a sharp attack of relapsing fever was gathering strength in the village, and relapsing fever is carried entirely by vermin bites.

The afternoon was hot and I was tired from a strenuous morning. I took off most of the few garments that I ordinarily wore and prepared for sleep. Soon I was aware of a pleasant little girl,of about nine or ten propped up against the door and gazing in with much interest. I asked her if I could do anything for her. '*Naam*' she replied. I continued more definitely, did she want anything? But *naam* was all she would say. *Naam* is a sort of general affirmative, which can range over varying degrees of positiveness from a definite yes to a half-hearted assent. It can also mean 'I beg your pardon. What did you say?' Or in some tones of voice simply, 'I am aware that you have spoken but I have no idea what you have said and I don't want to know'. It can be the most exasperating word in any language.

I asked the girl if she had a message, whether the teachers had sent her, or her mother. Where had she come from anyway? And again what did she want? Finally I suggested that she went away and came back later. I was hot and tired from my journey and wanted to sleep. The last type of *naam* was all her answer to any of it. I therefore illustrated my purpose and firmly shut

11. 22.3.42.

my eyes. Eventually she disappeared. Had she come a little later it would have been quite fun to talk to her.

With the cool of the evening[12] there were all sorts of other visitors including the Headmaster of the boys' school who sat down for a long chat and was very helpful about the problems of the school. The mistresses quarrelled so much, he said. Their house was too small, which was indeed true, and he had a definite scheme for housing two of the four elsewhere. As a rule I liked a visit from a schoolmaster, since we shared much common ground and that meant a common vocabulary, which was no light matter in making social conversation.

After he had gone,[13] the *nazir*'s two wives came to see me and here we were hardly on any ground at all. One was a woman about his own age, a dignified person with an attractive, patient face, and the other a more energetic girl in her teens. Each, very literally, had a baby at her breast; other children up to about the age of twelve came and hung about or tumbled round on the floor. The very small ones did not take kindly to advances from a strange woman but the boys and girls who were at school were easier to talk to. The daughter, for example, who had had three years' schooling was much more alert in her bearing and quicker of understanding than the uneducated wives. To begin with she did not find my foreign Arabic so difficult and here again we could talk of schools. With the women one could say a few words about the children but I had been warned, that in order to divert the attention of evil spirits one should say, 'That's a nasty, undernourished looking brat you've got there, but, please God, he'll improve'.

I was never able to bring myself to do it. Sometimes the mothers beamed with gratification but if my pleasant remarks about a child did not seem well-received, I tried to talk about something else. But to women who sit in the yard all day, what else? There is the weather but mostly it was hot and dusty in Hillaleia, as on that day. When it rained in the summer, women as respectable as these would just sit indoors. There were servants for what little housework might be done. Fortunately they were close to the school and the mistresses visited them; we could therefore exchange a little desultory gossip about *sitt* So and So.

The name of the headmistress' father was favourably mentioned by reason of the house he gave for the women's welfare work.

12. On the 16.3.41 Dr Beasley met the headmaster 'an elderly bearded man with a kind face and an ability to understand my level of small talk'.
13. On another evening, 22.3.42.

There was a minor diversion as the younger wife brought with her a tray with a great bowl of fresh milk and some queer drink resembling diluted pear-drops. Not to be outdone in honouring the guest the other woman fished up her skirt until she found a purse tucked away; then she sent the small girl to the back regions with a key. Presently another tray appeared with mint tea and some saw-dusty biscuits. Not to offend anyone I kept sipping all round but nobody joined in. What was most depressing about it all was not merely sitting there and not being able to find anything to talk about but the realisation that this was the ideal of respectability to which every man would wish to attain, if he had the means—to keep his women shut away without thought that they might atrophy in squalor. It was small wonder that even sensible men said, 'Women are so stupid'. What else could happen to them? They would not envy the peasant women I had seen at the well near the school that morning, women so poor that they had to work and could not be shut up. And in some ways the *nazir*'s wives would be right for there is little to envy in a life of grinding poverty.

> The conservatism and apathy of the people, combined with the ugliness and dirtiness of the place makes one feel very hopeless.

After about an hour and a half of this I began to fidget but it is a bit unmannerly to try to turn people out in their own house. I pleaded the excuse of work and my hostesses collected their joint brood and departed with obvious reluctance. I had the matter on my conscience afterwards, as I realised, that it was probably a rare event in their lives to be released from the dingy back-quarters to sit in the wide, lighted yard of the guest house and dispense hospitality to an Englishwoman. Compared with this dispiriting session there was much hope in the thought, that there was a girls' school in the place and that the daughter was attending.

> The D.C. then came from Rufaa to suggest plans for rebuilding the place. After this I went back to find Mrs MacCrell and lots of people at the *nazir*'s house—trays of tea etc ... we then bathed and went in the car to a tree about one mile from the ferry. Then got on donkeys in order to cross the sand, very stretching on a native saddle. Then a dirty ferry. Then quite a long car drive to Abu Usher where we played bridge with the hospital doctor, an interesting man. Then back the way we had come, only we first lost our way on the donkeys and then couldn't find our way into the village in the car.

It was a very different party I had the next day[14] with the mistresses. An ordinary tea was served with the restrictions of war-time allowed for; this meant a sort of plain sponge cake, biscuits and sugar bought on the black

14. 23.3.42.

market. It was arranged in one of the classrooms, as their house was too small for entertaining. Whatever stresses there may have been in private, there was no sulking or quarrelling at the party. Two of the teachers were naturally bright and lively talkers and they chatted away on all manner of subjects. With schoolmistresses as with schoolmasters there was always much to talk about, schools failing any other topic, but they also had plenty of little tales to tell about their pupils, bits of information about other mistresses, especially when these left to marry. They had the good taste as a rule not to indulge in scandalous comment on these occasions nor in any backbiting. Complaints would come in plenty and personal vindictiveness but officially through my office, a procedure which was fair enough, as I could deal with such grievances officially. But unkind remarks about others, not present, would have embarrassed us all. Their natural good manners seldom failed in this particular but they were not slow to expound their likes and dislikes, having very definite opinions on such subjects as food, clothes, prices, or places where they had been.

On this occasion they had one or two guests, the schoolmaster's wife, a relative of one of them and so on. The *nazir*'s wives did not come, since they were not allowed out although the house was so close. The schoolmaster's wife had a bright eye and a cheerful disposition and had brought with her a little boy. When we were being shown some of the pupils' charts she asked him his numbers and letters. I enquired, where she had been to school and she replied no school but that her husband had taught her since their marriage. It raised still more my former good opinion of the schoolmaster and I thought what a pity it was, that there were not more like him. Most of the educated men who married early were merely ashamed of their women-folk. They appeared only too glad, that tradition allowed them to keep their wives in the background as much as possible, whereas many of these women might have amply repaid a little care and attention, if given time.

I was not sorry to leave Hillaleia, although I had been very appreciative of the general welcome and kindness. Its ugliness had depressed me so, that at one point I tried to escape for a short walk by the river which proved to be further away than I expected, being before the arrival of the floods. A genial old man discouraged [gangs] of boys from following me but I had to buy off the village idiot with a *tarifa* or so. What, however, did not sweeten my views on life was rubbing the skin off my heel through blisters, that occurred from the constant dust in my shoes.[15]

> The sand still blew a bit the next day. I didn't like the school any better even going after a good night's sleep. The school is in better condition than last

15. The evening of 16.3.41.

year. The new headmistress, Sitt Khitma, has energy and character. There is still a long way to go in reaching the desired standard but it should pick up. I felt a little annoyed when I have to start and teach the new mistresses their job but Asia Saeed is sufficiently quick in the uptake. Apart from the usual attempts at eyewash, some good drawing and handwork, some very good *menziq*. Arithmetic in class I very bad but may do better with a little solid concentration. Khitma talks about starting a mothers' class, if she can have a kitchen built, an excellent idea in a place like this [16.1.41].

When, therefore, my three days were ended, it was a relief to see the lorry from Rufaa arrive according to schedule,[16] because there was always the chance, especially with transport so precarious, that arrangements might fail through the lorry breaking down. Camels and donkeys were always available, of course, but that would have meant a complete re-drawing of plans, and fortunately was never necessary.

# 5. Rufaa

About an hour's drive through more empty spaces of sun-parched earth waiting to be fields of grain, took me to this larger village,[17] for such it really was, although administratively and commercially it was equivalent to a small market town. Mud-brick for the houses was the general feature here too but, although it had many streets which were almost replicas of Hillaleia, there was something more spacious about its lay-out, which included a large market place with a few trees and a number of houses above the average in cost and construction. Snob value though this might be, they did improve the look of the place.

## 5.1 Acquaintances in Rufaa

Again through most of the year the river is a long way from the settlement [except at flood time] and almost always a hot wind blows. On this particular visit[18] it continued to lift the sand in even heavier amounts than in the previous few days, with sudden gusts and a perpetual dulling of the light. Trying to relax in the netted verandah in the D.C.'s[19] house after the sun had gone down gave me the impression that living in a blast furnace

16. 22.3.42.
17. Rufaa.
18. 22.3.42.
19. The D.C. in March 1941 was Charles de Bunsen. On 29.1.42 Dr Beasley made her third trip to Rufaa. She stayed with the D.C. and his wife who were very delightful people. The D.C. in March 1942 was J.E.C. Mackrell.

must feel somewhat similar. The Sudan had never developed the *punkah* system of India and it was only in the few large towns that electric fans might stir the air to a pretence of coolness.

> Once my foot was better came a really foul sandstorm, a dirty one with a wind that felt like a blast from an oven. It was so stuffy indoors with the windows shut that I could not bear it. I could understand on a day like this how living in the houses they do, they lose interest in their apprearance and clean bodies and clean clothes.

My good fortune in being lent the D.C.'s house, outweighed most other inconveniences, since I had the luxury of well-stocked bookshelves and a lovely wallow in an orthodox bathroom.[20] Piped water again was for the pampered few in towns but from my point of view in a place like Rufaa I had only to turn on the tap. Each morning prisoners from the local gaol filled a tank half way up the outside wall and after that the plumbing was no problem. This was an arrangement to be met with all over the country but the D.C.'s house had two less charming details peculiar to itself.

Some years ago a former occupant had tried to make a garden by filling small holes with river silt and planting flowers in them. To counter the hot blast he had fashioned little mud walls at the back of each bed, but the plants had long since disappeared and only the wind breaks remained, giving the effect of a graveyard of irregularly shaped head-stones. An addition to this ghoulishness had been left by my absent host,[21] just then taking part in the Abyssinian Campaign. No doubt he had been zealously training his police and there remained, swaying in its frame in the garden like some primitive quintain, a stuffed sack which had been used for bayonet practice. At Rufaa the frontier was easily two hundred miles away and the terrain between was rough-going for any vehicle. Admittedly such a distance might seem small to a mechanised army but I do not remember that any of us were particularly disturbed about it. After the first shock of losing Kassala[22] and places like Gallabat,[23] we accepted the position with possibly some of our Moslem friends' fatalism and told one another the sort of funny stories that go the round at such times.

> Went to polo at Messelamia, rather an effort owing to [lack of] transport. There were very few people there and it seemed again like a few lost souls 'keeping up the old tradition', quite out of touch with the things going on in the outside world [29.2.42].

20. 16.3.41. Dr Beasley was in Rufaa after visiting Hillaleia.
21. Charles de Bunsen.
22. Kassala was occupied for a few months in 1940.
23. Gallabat episode during 1940.

## 5.2 Rufaa School

I have mentioned elsewhere the claim of Rufaa to be the original outpost of girls' education and it would be pleasant to record that henceforward all was sweetness and light. Indeed allowing for occasional lapses there were always two schools[24] overflowing and of high standard, although in some other villages of comparable size there was difficulty in filling one. As a town no doubt it was composed of much the same mixture as many but, personal prejudice apart, it did suggest qualities which to a visitor offset the weather and the drab aspect, and helped it to compare favourably with other places with much the same natural disadvantages. I felt I had real friends of my own here but everyone wanted to be helpful. One afternoon when I went down to the market to do some shopping, I had a delightful small boy for companion, who talked about football and asked me if I knew the words 'goal' and 'shoot', and would not be persuaded that they were anything but Arabic expressions. At the stalls the position became embarrassing, because everyone wanted to assist my purchasing and in the end the *omdah* came to my rescue to keep the crowd back a bit. In the morning he sent for my servant and gave him as a present for me sheep's brains and tongue, which were esteemed a special delicacy, and they indeed make very good eating.

## 5.3 Tea parties in Rufaa

Of tea parties there were, of course, the usual round and the one I had at the D.C.'s house[25] was a notable success, as two of the mistresses were vivid talkers and infected with their teasing and banter, even drawing out some of the ladies who had joined us but who tended to be more reserved.

> Sittana Khidir was the life and soul of the party but all talked fairly freely and had their little jokes, making Zenab drink a lot of sugary tea because she is already so fat and so on.

Some of us went to a smaller and more intimate but equally enjoyable party[26] with the *mamur*'s wife, and an interesting invitation[27] came from a schoolmistress[28] who, though she had recently married a wealthy merchant, was still working.

---

24. For details about Dr Beasley's visit to Deims Rufaa school 9.4.40-10.4.40, see Appendix V.
25. 20.3.41.
26. 29.2.42.
27. 29.1.42.
28. Sitt Esh Shol, daughter of a schoolmaster.

She herself was by no means a bad investment, as she had been earning a high salary from the Government for about fifteen years, out of which she had managed to buy some land and build a good house on the edge of town. Moreoever she would receive a dowry of upwards of £S50 on retirement. Rumours were also rife, that she had been speculating in grain and hoarding many tons of it. The house indeed was a good one and scrupulously clean. Most of the living room was occupied with a large, brass four-poster bed, which glittered resplendently and was covered, like everything else with a shining white embroidered cloth.

> We had tea on the verandah sitting up to table, a sensible tea wth just biscuits and fruit.

As a hostess she was polite and punctilious and almost aggressively ladylike; a distinct contrast to one of the other mistresses[29] of her own age, who was inclined to sprawl over the table and talk loudly, trying to be admired for her wit and daring. She too would have to marry a merchant, she declared, simply in order to have enough sugar, about which she was definitely greedy, taking five lumps in each cup, although this was a time of shortage, and eating lots of sweets. Curiously enough some of the educated young men in Rufaa thought a schoolmistress to be demeaning herself by marrying a merchant but I did not hear such aspersions from the girls themselves, who were sought by bridegrooms from all ranks. In contrast to these two, the *mamur*'s wife, who was also a guest, was a gentle, motherly soul, talking a lot about her children, one of whom was an officer in Libya and another a translator in Asmara.

After tea our hostess danced the bride's dance in my honour and, making all allowances possible for my prejudices, I still remember it as interesting but aesthetically unpleasing. Removing her *tobe* she appeared in all her gold regalia, a cap-like net of gold coins, a string of gold coins from the right nostril to the ear, large crescents of beaten and patterned gold thrust through the tops of her ears, quantities of gold beads and bracelets, a necklace of gold coins and heavy silver anklets. Her lips and gums had been tattooed dark blue. All these ornaments could be worn effectively against the graceful folds of a *tobe*, with its softening effect, but they made a slightly repellant contrast against a bright pink satin frock of European cut and close-fitting. The basis of the dance was a curious shuffling step which looked very intricate, and the other movements of particular difficulty were one which resembled a 'League of Health and Beauty' exercise for a double chin, another which involved much arching the chest and various significant wrigglings of the breasts and buttocks. The bride's hair was plaited with silk

29. Sitt Maymouna.

at the end to make it long, and she flung this about with little jerks. As a gesture of honour she would shuffle up to a guest and flick the hair at her. All this took place to the gentle accompaniment of singing and clapping by young girls, who were not allowed to dance, as they were maidens, but in private they would practice carefully in order to perform well, when their great moment arrived. At real marriage ceremonies, which I attended later, there was drumming and music for the dance. This was the first time I had seen it in its entirety and I could only decide that here the East and West were not well blended. Danced under the moon without any clothes at all, it might have had significance; in that tight pink satin frock I found it vulgar. But I was judging by inappropriate standards; and nevertheless we all enjoyed the entertainment thus provided. I ought to add at this point that the other side to the bride's character was that she had been an excellent headmistress, who had had the initiative to run classes for adult women and to help with ante-natal clinics, and had given a distinctive character to her particular school.

## 5.4 Rufaa schools and staff

The original school,[30] which Babikr Bedri started in 1905, was situated in the better residential part of town.

> The first girls' school in the Sudan ... The buildings, after Omdurman, seem adequate, but would be improved by being a couple of metres larger all round and the yard is rather small.
>
> I had a good opportunity of estimating the value of my former judgements on Rufaa [17.1.41]. A pretty good school although not as solid as I had hoped. The attendance I think is regular and the children bright and well cared for ... it has a personality and is alive and energetic ... I was interested in the headmistress' attitude to the idea of nursing as a career. She was one of the pioneers of teaching and said that they were only a few to begin with but now the profession had grown. She thought nursing might be the same. Apparently the mothers' cooking club each week is a great success.
>
> I don't know if my standards are dropping or if it really has improved a bit. The arithmetic is still not sufficiently thorough ... Sakina is not much good, her arithmetic was bad. The children were dealing with numbers far beyond their capacity ... did not understand that subtract means take away and had no idea what to do with counters. In needlework all the class sat still while she put in a couple of stitches for each in turn. Wondered what means had been taken to keep them all quiet. In geography was using a new book and not getting things right (IVth year) ... one or two girls understood better than the teacher. Approve of habit of bringing live things for nature study lesson although a duck and two large turkeys clutter up the place. Admire Sittana's

---

30. The next morning, 7.4.40, Dr Beasley went to the famous school in Rufaa.

ability in dealing with them but Sittana could be pushed further to something better ... The new one Zenab Osman is plump, pretty and generally delightful but lacks drive. Haram is still teaching well and in her class the girls do really good needlework [19.3.41].

At this time, its Headmistress,[31] was a woman who had been among the students of the first year of the Girls' Training College in 1921. This may not seem very long by British standards but the historical was close here in the Sudan. Partly by temperament but a bit also by training and tradition, the Headmistress encouraged a curious, old-world flavour which she had imparted to the atmosphere of the school. The children, in class at least, all had beautiful manners and this was obviously insisted on despite the quiet voice and demeanour of the Head. It may have been a little prim but was by no means unattractive.

The subsequent history of Sitt Haram throws an interesting sidelight on the force of accepted social custom. This small, compact little figure used to stand demurely talking about the marriages of women we both knew and their children. Then she would look at her school and with a smile of the most real affection to the pupils she would say, 'These are *my* children'.

It appeared to be a school for 'little ladies', with all their conventions ... Nice children, nice manners, nice mistresses, things like needlework good but very little genuine instruction [8.4.40].

When she had been teaching for twenty years she was awarded the Meritorious Service Medal of the British Empire. She was the first woman to complete so long a period of service and her work had been of that unobtrusive but valuable type that carries on with the foundations and has no ambition towards glory.[32]

[She] is number one on the list of teachers, has been teaching since 1923 and, although probably not more than 34 or 35 gives the impression of being elderly. She is quietly competent in her own work but does not exercise sufficient supervision over the other mistresses to keep them up to her own level. She reminded me of an old-fashioned head at home, who didn't mind very much provided the girls were ladylike. The tone of the school was excellent but a little subdued. I am sure that the younger teachers took advantage of the excellent discipline to conduct their classes carelessly, as the children were not in the habit of giving trouble. I was rather disappointed in the school as I had expected so much. I felt it compared unfavourably with El Obeid, where there was so much vigour [7.4.40].

31. Sitt Haram. c.1923-40 headmistress at Rufaa; first mistress to receive the B.E.M.
32. 'I discovered that she is a property owner, having had a very good house built for herself' [10.4.40].

It came therefore as a shock to learn that a few weeks later she had married and left us. A first marriage at that age was most unusual in a country where girls were still taken away from school and married at any time after twelve years old. Her husband was a merchant and apparently willing to pay a large price to marry the first Sudanese woman to be awarded the British Empire Medal. I never saw him but I remember that their little daughter at the age of two was one of the loveliest little girls I have ever seen anywhere and, needless to add, beautifully brought up and always in exquisite clothes of her mother's own making. The great tragedy was that the child died young and the inconsolable Haram had no others.

## 6. Shabarga

Had it not been for the hope of a better wind elsewhere, I could have stayed longer in Rufaa with much pleasure and profit, but the time-table was still functioning efficiently and I duly set off one dusty afternoon[33] to continue south along the east bank. For some two hours we drove over a medium sort of road for this country, that is to say there were no patches of deep sand, where one was likely to stick nor bad areas of rock in the way. The surface was solid, although bumpy enough to make me hope that I should not be pitched through the windscreen. Anyone light in weight does not sit very firm over tracks of this sort, but this old-fashioned type of box was much better than the more elegant ones we had in later years with sprung and cushioned seats, which shot up to the roof. We passed through very lightly wooded country with xerophytic vegetation and, although we were among the same dry fields, the suggestion of small copses here and there made the road interesting. At one point we came to a fairly wide *wadi*, where some fine trees meant plenty of water at a depth.

---

33. 'Mr Watts, a new young D.C. came to lunch. [He was] earnest and religious but quite human and with a sense of humour. He was very young but found I had no difficulty in exchanging ideas with him. I probably seemed very talkative after a week devoted entirely to Arabic conversation.' Dr Beasley left Rufaa after tea with Mr Watts on the same day, 20.3.41.

Ian Harold Watts (b.18.12.1915- ); Educated at Sutton Valance School and St. Peter's Hall, Oxford, 1937-38 Oxford University, R.F.C; 30.12.39 First appointment; 1939-43 Gezira, A.D.C. Wad Medani; 1943 Kordofan; 1943-46 Equatoria, A.D.C.; 1946 resigned; 1946-47 Diploma of Education, Oxford University; 1947-48 Master, Sedbergh School; 1948 recruited by C.M.S.; 1948-53 Master (headmaster by 1951) at C.M.S. 'Old Nugent' school, Loka, Equatoria Province; 1953-57 Master at William Hulme's Grammar School, Manchester; 1957-62 Winneba Teacher Training College, Ghana; 1963-68 Lecturer, Department of Education, Ahmadu Bello University, Nigeria; 1965 ordained, later Chaplain, Uppingham School; 1973-79 Holmfirth High and Batley Grammar schools; 1979- Chaplain, International Church Society, Cannes.

About dusk we arrived at Shabarga[34] and, although the village was no more beautiful than the others, it differed in having less square, flat-topped houses and more of the *tukl* variety, a feature of the parts of the country with heavier rainfall. The type with slight differences had various names in other parts but they all approximated to the same kind of building. Here the walls were made of mud and the roof thatched. The *nazir*'s guest-house, in which I was staying, was of this shape but of quite unusually large dimensions. As a shape it has much to commend it. I have stayed in similar rooms in people's gardens, when they were furnished in European style and the effect was wholly charming; it may have something to do with the softness born of no corners or angles.

The strangeness of my shelter here was not what disconcerted me but the extreme publicity. If Rufaa was friendly, this was like an unending triumphal procession. The resthouse was near to the *nazir*'s compound but set in a large yard, probably an acre or so, with other houses scattered about. There seemed to be people in all of them but I never fathomed their especial functions. They did not interfere with me but there was no knowing who might be walking past the window, while I was bathing inside. As it continued blowing sand all the time, the only thing was to bath, when I wanted to and chance the immodesty. Specific bathroom there was none and the pit latrine was sheltered by a *birsh* mat only.

The concourse was not only the menial staff about the place but a ceaseless stream of cordial and interested visitors. The *nazir* was there to offer me hospitality, as soon as I arrived; a strong and capable man, he did not leave so definite an impression as Sheikh Yusuf of Hillaleia. One or two *sheikh*s came to call during the evening and when it was completely dark, the schoolmistresses, very carefully shrouded in clean muslin *tobe*s, drifted in accompanied by an old serving woman with a bit of dark blue drapery, which did not conceal her face. Somehow they looked a bit grand in this setting, for they were Rufaa girls still clinging to their training in what was ladylike, but the rather theatrical note, which their difference emphasised, might very well prove a valuable advertisement for girls' education. In any case their dressing-up for parties did not really matter, since they were not afraid to soil their hands while working. The next day I saw the Headmistress getting down to a strenuous cooking and cleaning lesson, even making *kisra*, which was regarded very much as menial work.

The *nazir*'s kitchen must have been like that of a Yorkshire housewife, with the pot always on the hob. Whenever women called to see me, small glasses of tea without milk were brought round. And they came at all times. There were two or three to greet me, when I had my early morning tea. Two

---

34. Shabarga was about two hours drive from Rufaa.

or three more, when I came back from school for the breakfast interval. More for lunch and about twenty, while I was having a quick cup of my own brew at four o'clock before going to a party at the school. As this seemed in the manner of a really definite visit, we sat and chatted, until I felt I could not keep the children waiting any longer but I wanted to comb my hair and put on some walking shoes before going out. My callers were so intensely interested in all my sayings and doings, that they repeated my intentions to one another, as they trooped into the *tukl* with me. They sat on the *nazir*'s *angareeb*s or my camp-bed, or leant against the wall, making comments, watching my toilet operations and taking note of all my belongings.

It[35] provided a good opportunity to talk about school problems, particularly the old stagers, unpunctuality and irregularity of attendance.

> The various harvests and fieldwork, despite the attempt to regulate the holidays, interfere with regular attendance. The school is not an unpleasant building, apart from the first year classroom which is entirely *gussab*.

The Headmistress had said in the morning that the latter was due to lack of clothes. People who live by subsistence farming never have much in the way of ready cash and the rationing of material made things extra difficult during the war. There had been one or two quite big girls in just check knickers and *tobe*s wrapped closely round them. It was cramping attire for any active sort of lesson. Some of the small girls obviously wore clothes belonging to some adult member of the family and some were in such rags, there seemed little point in pretending that they were coverings.

> The clothes of Class I were frequently very disreputable.

As on other occasions I urged the mothers to put their younger girls at least into *rahat*s, a most becoming dress for them and one which could easily be kept clean. A *rahat* looks very much like a grass skirt, except that it is not quite so full, and is made of a leather fringe attached to a band of woven hair. 'Most unsuitable', insisted the mothers. 'Oh, not for girls who go to school. All right for the children of *Arab*s wandering in the desert.'

It was part of a recurrent problem which could not be lightly brushed aside on grounds of expediency or common sense, and it cropped up with similar variations in the pagan areas.

> Things began well with a very good drill by Khadiga Yousif ... arithmetic poor throughout. In I Khadiga was lost in a whelter of rather unruly personalities and was not quite to grips with the work ... Good vigorous lessons by Miriam and Nafissa Abu Zeid in nature study and geography and

35. A tea-party.

careful by Fatma Abu Zeid especially in arithmetic ... I should think a hard
working school [21.3.41].

After this we all walked across to the school and watched the children
playing organised games, [rounders and skipping], with much zest.

I was used to being a public figure inside the school-yard but what I
never became used to at Shabarga was being a public figure everywhere. I
wondered if this was what it felt like to be Royalty. Between the school and
the resthouse was a well where women were drawing water or coming and
going at all times. They would call to me loudly. 'We are so pleased you've
come', 'We do like you', 'You are very nice', and so on. I could only wave
and try not to look as embarrassed as I felt.


## 7. Wad Medani

Having spent the morning[36] in school I left Shabarga after lunch one day.
There was more sand blowing than ever, after a restless night, in which I
had dragged my bed from place to place in the yard in search of a sheltered
spot, which I never found. It was too hot indoors, and I was not quite sure
what the things were that kept falling off the roof. There is no need to
expatiate more on this perpetual discomfort, only to remark that after a
fortnight such as this one, the never escaping from the dun-coloured dust
and the restless wind did tend to fret the temper.

It was largely this that made me glad to move on, for I had been very
much welcomed. Once again the [lorry] arrived according to schedule and
we drove down through the same lightly wooded country with sandy soil
and occasional patches of cultivation and *wadi*s with larger trees. In one of
these we stayed for quarter of an hour or so, while the driver made enquiries
about the ferry,[37] which had been commissioned to meet us. To while away
the time I sat watching a number of monkeys swinging about in the trees or
sitting looking at us in their intent way.

Eventually the driver discovered the place to which the boatmen had
come and, rather to my consternation, he drove the laden lorry down an
extremely steep bank of loose earth onto a sort of barge, which had just
enough room for it. Although I found the procedure alarming and would
rather have walked, I had to conceal such base ideas, as I gathered that he
was very proud of his skill in judging the distance. I know that vessels afloat

36. 23.3.41.
37. 'The ferry was a dirty large boat with its terrific oars made of great planks, roughly hewn ...
camels and ... people mixed up together' [February 1942]. Dr Beasley's comments on
Hassaheissa school are given in Appendix V.

are not so heavy as they appear but being pulled upstream by a gang of boatmen looked a strenuous effort. There was a ferry service, which operated on a chain and pulley, but owing to a lack of spare parts it was not functioning. As in the case of most of these crossings, when we had gone upstream for some distance we were propelled into the middle of the river and glided across, finishing up at the required point downstream.

> I felt unpleasant about being tugged upstream by human labour on such a hot afternoon.

It must have needed very experienced calculation, although it seemed such a basic method.

Compared with explorers and officials who used to go out on tough, camel treks, I knew I had been enduring very little, but I had a pleasure, which it is difficult to estimate, to go into a freshly painted, cool, white room in the Governor's house in Wad Medani,[38] and people to talk English to after my Arabic fortnight.

> We arrived in Medani very hot and dirty and tired ... after the *nazir*'s quarters in Shabarga, ... [to] rest in cleanliness and without disturbance ... I stayed with the Deputy Governor[39] and wife and made some very good new friends. Apart from work in the morning, life was a round of pleasure with swimming, tennis, pictures, bridge. Met some stock types including the lady I offended by not liking her cheetahs in the drawing room.[40]

Wad Medani would have ranked as a town by any standards even if only a small country town. Its great claim to attention was, that it was the administrative centre for the cotton-growing plantations from which the

38. J.W. Robertson was acting Governor, Blue Nile from 1.9.40-18.5.1941 and was succeeded by G.R.F. Bredin.

Sir James W. Robertson, K.T., G.C.M.G., G.C.V.O., M.B.E., 4N. (b.27.10.1899-d.1983); Educated at Merchison and Balliol College, Oxford; 1918-19 Gordon Highlanders and Black Watch; 27.11.22 First appointment; 1923-25 Blue Nile; 1926-31 White Nile; 1931-34 Fung; 1934-36 kordofan; 1936-39 White Nile (1937 Sub-Governor, White Nile Sub-Prov.); 1939-40 Blue Nile, Deputy Governor; 1.9.40-18.5.41 Acting Governor, Blue Nile; Civil Secretary; 1941-42 Assistant Civil Secretary; 1942-45 Deputy Civil Secretary; 1945-53 Civil Secretary following Douglas Newbold's death in 1944; 1953 retired; 1953 Hon. Fellow, Balliol College, Oxford; 1953-54 Chairman, British Guiana Constitutional Commission; 1954-55, 1960-61 Director, Uganda Co.; 1955-60 Governor-General of Nigeria; 1961-71 Barclays Bank; 1961-69 Chairman, Commonwealth Institute; 1962-67 Royal Overseas League; 1961-71 Overseas Pensioners Association; 1961-79 Britain-Nigeria Association; 1965-68 Deputy Chairman, National Committee for Commonwealth Immigrants; 1961-74 Governor, Queen Mary College, University of London; Author.

39. C.B. Tracey, 4N., Deputy Governor, Blue Nile.

40. 12.10.41. 'I stayed in Hantub with the Headmistress and her husband and we had to cross the river each day. With the full moon in the evening it was delightful and from school to home under half an hour' [8-11.12.41].

Sudan drew so large a part of its revenue, the life blood of the country. Cotton plantations immediately call up the old world image of 'Uncle Tom's cabin' and deep-voiced choruses of tuneful syncopation. The Gezira, as the district was called, was not at all like that and Wad Medani, although its English population was large, had nothing of the Deep South flavour either. Anything over a hundred would count as a large white community and very few places approached such a figure.

> On the surface life was rather a whirl of social engagements beginning with people to tea on Saturday and then to dinner parties on Saturday, Monday, Tuesday and to breakfast on Tuesday [23.3.41].

The town itself had some very attractive stretches on the road by the river, which was flanked by lovely public gardens on the embankment and by administrative buildings and houses. There were further back narrow streets bordered by the usual high mud walls, an untidy market and some rather messy quarters but plenty of trees offset this with gardens and much loveliness in the actual sight of the bend of the river. I was to come here often, as we decided to make it one of our strong points for girls' education.

> I visited two schools and a *khalwa*. The new school ('A' school) was in a magnificent building but the work was very uneven. I thought the headmistress rather an old soldier. Apparently there had been trouble between the girl appointed to her place, when she married.
>
> 'B' school had that pleasant atmosphere which suggests someone is interested in the work. The headmistress and the other staff were still young and seemingly enjoying the work. The Welfare Worker was attractive and willing.
>
> The *khalwa* was curiously enough a matter of pride to the local inhabitants. It was run by a hunchback, who might ... have been a bad-tempered wench ... I felt there was a danger that the girls might be exploited to do needlework under poor conditions for profit of the hunchback. With all their faults, the Government schools are at least disinterested [23.3.41].
>
> The schools were in good order. A tea-party was difficult as until the sun set I was the only one who could eat ... I thought the mistresses rather abstemious ... possibly there were further orgies after my departure. I was glad to notice they fed the driver. One girl had not been fasting, on health grounds ... She had composed some recitations about tropical events, kicking Hitler out of the Sudan and so on. It seemed rather enterprising in a *hareem* girl [12.10.41]
>
> I went to Medani for the Domestic Science School Open Day. Very satisfactory to see it going so well. It rather had to be forced on the Sudanese ... perhaps they are beginning to see part of its point. The mothers loved seeing their daughters performing. The headmistress clever in allowing every girl a small share in some part of the performance ... the girls scamper about, a joyful activity [8-11.12.48].

I went with the P.E.O. (Girls) to see the site of the new school in the Gezira at Wad Namman near where the Adult Education women are going to operate. We had breakfast with the local Syndicate inspector and wife. The houses of these inspectors, set among trees and floweres are rather oases in the middle of the dreadful black soil of the Gezira. The schoolchildren were clean, the others uncommonly dirty. I cannot get up any enthusiasm for the Gezira, although I acknowledge its efficiency and usefulness and I like to see things growing.

## 7.1 Wad Medani to Khartoum

To travel back by road to Khartoum was to obtain a firm impression of irrigation values.[41] At this particular time of year, that is March, most of the plots were as brown and empty as the fields on the east side of the river. The very formal lay-out with the mathematical precision of the grid suggested farming turned into industry and made me wonder, if it would become dull and utilitarian like a manufacturing town. Just then the main canal would come into view, the straightness of its course softened by vegetation, which no amount of clearing and dredging ever completely dispelled, tall trees shading the water, which was generally a gently reflected blue. At the junctions of the canals there was usually a lock-keeper's house and another group of trees. The flatness of the country was mainly responsible for the depressing effect it could have on a visitor, for there did not seem to be a hill anywhere within sight. People who worked there, however and had an interest in the social and agricultural development of it all, found much real happiness and often those sudden, unexpected moments of beauty which can redeem the most unlikely places.

When the crops were growing well, the sight of vast acres was impressive to even vague and unpractical lovers of rusticity. Cotton in great extent can never have the charm of fields of corn in appearance but it was the life-

---

41. In October 1941 'I was sent back from Medani in the Governor's car which was coming to Khartoum'. Dr Beasley appreciated 'the size of the irrigation scheme, miles and miles of it, cotton and *dura*'.

The Governor at this time was George Richard Bredin, C.M.G., C.B.E., 3N. (b.8.6.1899-d.1983); Educated at Clifton and Oriel College, Oxford; 1917-18 Royal Engineers (France and Flanders); 20.12.21 First appointment; 1922 White Nile; 1922-26 Kordofan; 1927-29 Assistant Civil Secretary (Administration); 1930-31 Darfur; 1932-33 Assistant Civil Secretary (Administration); 1934-35 Deputy Governor, Kordofan; 1935-39 Deputy Governor, Blue Nile; 1939-41 Deputy Civil Secretary, but ill in June 1940; 18.5.41-28.8.48 Gezira, later Blue Nile, Governor based at Wad Medani; Sept 1943 on 'Special Committee to investigate the question of an advisory council for the Northern Sudan'; 1945-48 member of Governor-General's Council; 1948 retired; 1948-49 Assistant Registrar, University of Liverpool; 1950- Fellow and Bursar of Pembroke College, Oxford; 1951- Church Commissioner; 1967-72 Chairman, Governing Body Abingdon School; Governor, Gordon Boys' School.

blood of the country and such comparisons were irrelevant. This, the Gezira Scheme, was not the only one in the Sudan but it was by far the largest, then [1941] covering over a million acres and by now much increased. It proved also an interesting experiment in sociological development, as Sudanese tenants farmed the land rather in the manner of small-holders, a proportion of their land being given over to cotton, the rest to subsistence crops. The history of this has been well-documented elsewhere but such development naturally demanded co-operation with the Education Department in a number of special schemes, which are described later in the book.

Whatever one may think about industrialised crop production as opposed to less stereotyped methods of agriculture, to come out to the untended waste [of the Kamlin road] which lay immediately outside the scheme, was to be filled with admiration for the vision and enterprise responsible for this tremendous undertaking. There was nothing beautiful about the drab, empty land with its occasional stunted bushes. This was not a desolation made by man but a natural one. I was for ever quoting Browning: 'I never saw such starved, ignoble nature'. It soon became easy to understand the fascination of the ordered richness, which had been won from a similar forlorn land by the application of care and scientific method.

Although Gezira literally means 'an island' it was here applied to the expanse of country between the Blue and White Niles and specifically this large scheme irrigated from the Sennar Dam.

## 8. Jebel Auliya scheme

There was also a smaller one with a particularly interesting origin, which in its way could claim too to be a sociological experiment. For me it linked up with the semi-nomad villages I had visited near Bakht-er-Ruda during my first weeks in the country. I mentioned that the building of the Jebel Auliya dam to give Egypt more water had deprived these cultivators of the land, which they had habitually sown on the falling flood.[42] Instead of cash compensation[43] they were offered holdings on a new irrigation scheme, between the rivers at Abdel Magid. The success of the venture was affirmed by the speed with which these semi-nomads adopted this more secure way of

42. Until 1939, semi-nomads were used to wandering between their plots of land, made possible for cultivation by the short rainy season, and their plots down by the river, which were available when the river went down. 'The expected development is that a static peasantry may grow up where before there was a migratory population without fixed dwellings'.

43. Alternative Livelihood Schemes made necessary by the Jebel Auliya Dam have been described in detail in Richards, G.E., 'Adult Education amongst Country Women; an Experiment at Um Gerr', *Sudan Notes and Records*, XXIX, 1948, pp.225-7.

living and soon became versed in making the appropriate calculations for their water supply, and telephoning them to the regulating official.[44] Some three years after its beginning[45] came murmurs about the need for a girls' school and an enthusiastic D.C.[46] pressed on with the project, sweeping aside all objections about war-time restraint. It was planned for the administrative centre at Abu Guta and would draw its pupils from the villages around, which had been arranged in groups of thirty houses.

## 8.1 Giteina and Abu Guta

He[47] arranged to fetch me one morning after I had been inspecting at Giteina, a village on the east bank of the White Nile about two hours by [lorry] from Omdurman.

> Two hours there, a morning's rather intense inspecting and two hours back in the heat of the day pretty exhausting.

It was refreshing to visit something new and promising, as Giteina was already suffering from the rising of the waters, since the Jebel Auliya dam for good or ill coloured developments in all this part of the country. The [Government] decision to move houses away from the river had been put into effect but, although a new school had been promised, it had not yet been built and classes were still functioning in the old and shabby one, among the dreadful derelict remains on the river bank. Mud- brick does not make for picturesque ruins and I was not surprised that this depressing atmosphere of ugly decay had had a disheartening effect on the school.

> The school is in a bad way. It is too far away from the new village. Much of the teaching was bad ... how many girls go to school regularly and how can

44. The following year Dr Beasley found 'something impressive about Abu Guta—so many tilled fields and crops grown in the desert by what were nomads three years ago. Some of them can calculate the amount of water needed for their fields, a very tricky business, and telephone to the pump for same' [22.2.42].
45. In 14.1.1940 'there were no girls' schools for the migratory population but it was possible that they might be required in time, if in a few years permanent villages took the place of the straw shelters which seemed then to be the only habitation'.
46. Bazatt Annesley Lewis (b.4.6.1907- ); Educated at Haileybury and Jesus College, Cambridge, 1927-28, 1930 Cambridge University Lacrosse XII, 1950 Exeter College, Oxford; 9.12.30 First appointment; 1930-31 Dongola; 1931-33 Khartoum; 1933-35 Inspector, Secretariat for Economic Development; 1935-38 Upper Nile; 15.3.38-41 Blue Nile, A.D.C., later D.C., Dueim District, based at Abdel Magid; 1941-45 Upper Nile; 1945-46 Service in the Sudan Agency in London; 1946 Finance Department; 1947-48 Civil Secretary's Office; 1948-52 Darfur; 1952-53 Deputy Governor, Equatoria; 1953-54 Special Duties, Ministry of Interior; 1954 retired.
47. B.A. Lewis came from Abu Guta and took Dr Beasley back there on her second visit to Giteina [2.2.41].

one be sure in these outlying districts that the attendance is what the mistresses say it is.

There was something sinister about these deserted piles right away from the village proper, that weighed on the spirit even on a bright morning. In a thick *haboob*, of which there were plenty, it must have looked like a setting for a horror film.

Accompanying the D.C. was the wife[48] of the Agricultural Inspector who was in charge of the experimental schemes. She was one of the British women, whom I mentioned earlier, whose personal sympathy and support was of untold value to schoolmistresses, who might be lonely, and would work with zeal, if given encouragement from someone interested in the school and the progress of the children. Unrecognised and unsung, they added their mite to the development of the whole.

Everything was naturally raw and unfinished at this early stage of the scheme and one could not expect the matured order of the Gezira plots, but in this bleak, flat landscape with the inevitable drab hues prevailing there was the excitement of something beginning, which was already showing progress. Regarding the girls' school the Government was responsible for the staff and equipment but the local cultivators themselves had erected a temporary building.[49] True it was of thick straw but was thus not out of keeping in the present stage with the villager still moving to a different way of living.

All very primitive ... The stores of course did not arrive in time. Picturesque inefficiency is all very well in the country but not at Headquarters.

Money had been raised by various means but principally by a concert given by the boys' school, which had brought in £S20 and thus sufficed to meet their simple needs. Apparently the greatest success of the evening was their version of an ever-popular theme. Some boys impersonated the *sheikh*s who were having trouble with their irrigation demands. One obviously stupid man, however, always had his calculations and his accounts in order, and no-one could understand how he managed it. 'After all you can't read and do sums', they told him. 'No', he replied with a cunning smile, 'but my daughter has been to school and she does it all for me'.

48. Dr Beasley felt that girls' education was greatly encouraged in the Sudan by some official's wives who were often 'energetic and enthusiastic ... particularly if they happen to be practical too.' Mrs Graves was the wife of H.A. Graves, 4N., Dip. Agric (Wye); 12.11.21 First appointment; 1941 Inspector of Agriculture, Gezira Province, based at Abdel Magid on the White Nile Alternative Livelihood Scheme; 1944-46 Senior Inspector of Agriculture, Kordofan based in El Obeid; 1946 retired.
49. *Rakūba*, a temporary shelter.

The roars of laughter which this elicited were enough to launch a girls' school very strongly on course. This is no place for a record of its subsequent ups and downs[50] but it maintained itself through many vicissitudes and progressed with the general development of the district.

Whatever the interest and usefulness it remained unlovely as a place, a criticism difficult to avoid in the part between the two rivers.

## 9. Kamlin

Further east actually on the west bank of the Blue Nile, Kamlin was a little more rewarding for that very fact, that part of the village was close to the river and large *neem* trees stood round the open space enclosed on three sides by Government buildings.

> The first part of the journey was just scrubby country. We came fairly close to the river about 4 o'clock.

It was here on more than one occasion that I remarked the real blue of the water in the late afternoon and it was under the trees, that I camped once through a rare breakdown in the arrangements.

> We came at last to the river and what had once been the D.C.'s house, now a heap of ruined mud and a tennis court nearby, making things look all the more desolate.

Round about also there were both rain cultivation and irrigation plots, which in such a month as October gave fullness and character to the place. My first visit[51] was in the middle of Ramadan, never a good time to travel. As it was difficult to distinguish between the tracks, the driver stopped to ask the way on the few occasions, when we met anyone, and to show his devoutness he had to spit before speaking, in order not to swallow his saliva. Ramadan does present the pious with a lot of problems. By the time we did arrive, it was almost dusk and both he and my servant must have

---

50. 'I went a second time when the school should have started but it seemed rather a muddle. I understand eventually 43 girls turned up out of the 74 written down.'

'There was no D.C.' on Dr Beasley's next visit [22.2.42], and 'the original enthusiasm in the school seemed to have waned. The new headmaster had helped by riding round the villages on a horse to encourage the children to come to school. The local Medical Inspector was also working hard to keep the children clean ... some of the girls had their heads shaved ... as he wanted to prevent relapsing fever from spreading.'

51. On 6.10.41 Dr Beasley found the Kamlin area 'with good tall corn and the beginning of good cotton. The great canals and orderly fields were much as I had seen them at Abu Guta ... The day had been very hot.' Whilst the men broke their fast Dr Beasley 'sat there, wet through with perspiration'.

been desperately thirsty. We drove to the old *merkaz*, since the only man about at this time knew nothing of a resthouse.

> This was very pleasantly situated on the river, built round on three sides of a square and rows of great shady *neem*s between the *merkaz* and the river.

Under the cool trees I was given a chair while the two men settled down at once to break the day's fast. Everything [in the *merkaz*] was firmly locked and it was only fair to wait until their meal was finished.

After this, which took less than quarter of an hour, my servant turned a corner of the verandah into a kitchen, while the driver went to look for the keys. In the end the *sheikh* of the village turned up, with profuse apologies and the courtroom was unlocked for me to use, as it suited me. I did turn the seat of justice into a dressingroom but found it more pleasant to be eating and sleeping under the trees, especially at night when the full moon was radiant over the river.

> The *sheikh* also unlocked the iron gates into the prison yard in order that I might use the latrine but a bucket between tall iron footrests—wide apart— was worse than the usual inconveniences.
>
> I objected to the *sheikh*'s suggestion that no-one knew I was coming. I had just drunk my tea and was thinking of changing, when the *nazir* appeared to assure me I hadn't been forgotten. He sat and talked for a long while, during which my clothes dried and I caught cold. He sent round a table and a comfortable chair and a lamp. The place looked better by the light of a full moon. I used the square in front of the *merkaz* for eating and sleeping and Sayed cooked on a primus there and the servants slept a little way off. All very matey.
>
> The school was pretty poor.[52]

Going home, we had other Ramadan troubles. Our one Sudanese inspectress[53] had been helping with the school but staying in the *nazir*'s house, but she and her chaperone were to return with us in the station-waggon. When we went to pick them up, I was amazed at the number of women, who came out from the gate to assist in the send-off, or at any rate to have a look. Sitt Medina was a woman of many sterling qualities and enormous courage in important matters but she was no Stoic in small things. I grew more and more attached to her, as the years went on and she grew in stature with her responsibilities. But this evening as a travelling companion I needed all the sympathy I could muster. She decided that the middle seats would be best as giving more air, for the heat (which was

52. 1911/12 26 in attendance at Kamlin Government School, by 1913 there were 50 (S.A.D. 657/1/20).
53. 'Only the oldest crone came to kiss my hand. The journey was rather a nightmare.' with Sitt Medina Abdulla.

considerable) and the smell of the petrol made both her and the old lady feel sick. Since they would not have tasted food or drink of any sort for the last ten hours this was very understandable, and however helpful I might want to be, there was nothing I could do. Even my suggestion for a little water poured on the wrists was waved aside, making me feel definitely infidel and sacrilegious. At intervals therefore she called to the driver to stop, while she descended and retched for a time, and then lay prostrate by the road, until the spasm has passed. My servant, who was right at the back perched up on the luggage, was quite unaffected by the rigours of the fast and sang lustily all the way home to the accompaniment of the belchings and gurglings of the two unhappy women in front of him.

> ... having done the end of the journey in a rush, the driver tried to beat the railway crossing. We retreated just in time. However we arrived home just before the gun and Medina wallowed on the roadside while the luggage was removed.

Life had to go on in Ramadan and Medina, despite these trials, never made it an excuse for not going on trek. As it was calculated by lunar months, it could come at any time of year, and it was impossible, therefore, to plan not to travel during that month, whatever minor complications might result.

## 10. Fung

Much further upstream, the Blue Nile does indeed live up to its reputation. A trip I made to Fung, also in October,[54] rivals my favourite excursions to the Halfa and Dongola Reach.

> Recalling Fung brings the temptation to linger over the sudden glorious colours of the area.

I was equally pampered in the matter of transport. Knowing that I was planning an inspection of the schools the D.C.[55] suggested that I should make my visit co-incide with one he was making on the Province steamer. There was not a great deal of room on the ordinary mail boat, which only

---

54. The Blue Nile 'had a romantic flavour about its very name'. Dr Beasley's Fung trip began 20.10.42.
55. Geoffrey Maberly Hancock, O.B.E., 4N. (b.5.11.1901-d.1985); Educated at Tonbridge and Magdalene College, Cambridge; 6.12.24 First appointment; 1925 Blue Nile; 1926-27 White Nile; 1927-28 Upper Nile; 1928-32 White Nile; 1932-35 Upper Nile; 1.11.35-42 Blue Nile, D.C. Fung District, based at Singa; 1940-42 Governor-General's Temporary Commission as Bimbashi in the S.D.F.; 1942-45 Assistant Civil Secretary; 1945-46 Deputy Civil Secretary; 15.11.46-50 Governor, Kassala and also Director of Gash Board; 1950 retired; 1952-60 Adviser to the Ruler of Qatar; 1960-70 J.P.

ran to the end of the rains, while there was plenty of water on the river; otherwise one had to wait until a very bumpy road was re-opened in the dry season. Rhythms in many spheres were dominated by the Sennar Dam, which let its full spate of water through during July to September, and was then regulated from the reservoir backed up behind it.

On this occasion I did not stop at Sennar but went through in a train that ran once a week round a line linking Khartoum with Gedaref and Kassala and then completing the circle by joining up with the Atbara to Port Sudan line. It was not one of the show trains but not very uncomfortable. As I, however, had to change at Suki in the early hours of the morning, there was no prospect of really settling down to sleep.

> The D.C. had said that I should be met and taken to the boat and that we should set sail at once and that he would meet me at Singa for breakfast.

When we arrived, a brilliant moon had set and left a world of utter blackness. At this period,[56] the Abyssinian and Eritrean campaigns had pushed the invasion dangers further east but this small junction had been swollen to a disproportionate importance by the unusual amount of traffic routed this way. Probably on military orders no lights were showing and I felt quite bewildered as I climbed out from even the shaded compartments of the train. A policeman had been detailed to meet me and to bring some prisoners to carry my luggage. This was whisked away before I remembered that my electric torch was packed in a case. Consequently I went stumbling round the piles of stores and equipment and tripping over the railway lines and the ditches and general rough patches guided by the restraining hand of my escort. When we did eventually reach the bank, the boat was in darkness too, waiting for the dawn before it started off.

> However, just as I got on board the D.C appeared, looking very tall in a dressing gown. I suddenly realised that I had only met him once before, at the bridge table, and now we were to spend ten days on a boat just the two of us. I wondered if my conversation would last out. It did ... I induced the D.C. to talk about the Campaign against the Italians in which he had taken a prominent part ... one of the men who had been particularly notable in tricking the enemy with his few dozen of police ... dispassionate way in which the tale was told.

An inviting camp bed under a mosquito net had been set up for me near one of the sleeping cabins at the stern. These boats were very adequately planned with two sleeping cabins, a bathroom and a sitting room. We did, in fact, have our meals in this but it was too hot to stay in more than

56. 1942.

necessary and both for sleeping and sitting, even writing reports, we were much happier out of doors.

This first night, however, there was not much sleep, for at sunrise with a great clanking of chains and rumbling of engines we set off. An hour or two later, when I did emerge, all the dusty dryness of the Omdurman summer was transformed into a soft, melting temperature with lush green banks on both sides of the broad river.

## 10.1 Singa

Soon in a great curve [of the river] Singa appeared with the D.C.'s house standing up white on a little bluff with a garden in front fairly blazing with colour. There was another garden in the town alongside the river, more in the manner of a public park with tall trees and this arresting impression of rich, luxurious growth. Otherwise the place had no striking features, being mostly a collection of grass huts with a mixed looking population, many of whom showed obvious traces of negroid stock. After a couple of days in a mediocre but acceptable school. I was told to re-embark in the afternoon.

## 10.2 A naturalist's paradise

We were not, of course, travelling in great luxury in the sense that there was no electricity or fans and certainly at this time air-conditioning was unheard of in the Sudan. Food was adequate, although such little pleasures as tea, sugar, butter and whisky were rationed, and there were times, when the bread was soggy with more beans than flour. Packets of biscuits or tins of any sort had long since been consumed. Nevertheless I could not but make the facile comparison between my lot and that of earlier travellers down this magnetic waterway. The essential difference was being part of the accepted scheme of things, even though we were of an alien race. We had work to do which belonged to the recognised order of people's days and the villagers never questioned our coming. It is only on looking back from this distant point in time, that that particular aspect occurs to me. Then it seemed perfectly natural, that I should go to inspect schools under the conditions which existed, since that was part of my job. I always recognised the added value for me, that I did have this link and was not merely a sightseer.

Between the villages, therefore, I lay in a deck chair rather lethargic from the damp heat, reading or knitting or watching the unending stretches of forest revelling in the fresh green of it all and confused with delight at the number of birds. I could never remember the names of half of them but the sand banks were fringed by hundreds at a time: duck of all kinds, geese, [blue-jays], plovers, storks including the unsightly marabou, ibis, all the water birds I had ever heard of except flamingoes. They sat in lovely patterns or played on the edge of the water or set off in flight in yet another beautiful pattern, or came two or three at a time gliding and dipping across the water. Then, when we went on shore, there were others of a brilliance of plumage, that sometimes meant pausing in wonder every few steps. The Abyssinian rollers flicked their radiant blue; two bee-eaters one morning looked as if their feathers had been coloured by a child using all the tubes in a new paint box. I still preferred the more common bronze and greenish bee-eaters but these two sitting on a low branch invited long, almost unbelieving, attention. Another afternoon in a dense, bamboo thicket a bird about the size of a starling and scarlet all over perched unmoving, a startling red against the light green background. It was a durra-bird[57] in full plumage, I was told afterwards. I never saw another, although I often came across rollers and the bee-eaters, but not in such numbers.

> I have never seen so many birds at once in my life ... We sailed all the next day most of which I spent lying in a deck chair ... The pleasure of sailing along despite the perpetual sweatiness ... Occasionally the D.C. had a pot at a crocodile.

For even the most ordinary naturalist it would have been paradise. At one point, when we stopped to take on fuel for our wood-burning engine, it was too hot to go on shore immediately[58] and I stayed in my deck-chair engrossed with the busy movement on the bank. I woke to realise that the bank was alive with all manner of small creatures going about their own affairs from insects hopping and crawling, climbing in and out of holes, balancing on sticks, to a *worrall*[59] clambering carefully along, and always the graceful swooping of the bee-eaters. Other inhabitants of the banks were not so treasured, even just to look at. An apparently inert log might be lying on the shore or sandbank. Without warning there would be a slight flurry of water and the crocodile had disappeared. Sometimes they did not move and I tried one day to decide what there was in their appearance, that produced so much aversion, since other beasts kill in secret and are not so universally detested.

We had occasion for our hatred, for on the way home we took on board a man and his little daughter to land them to their village. They were dazed and inconsolable, the girl in particular quite bewildered with grief. Coming to the river for water one evening the man's wife had been seized by a

57. Durra-bird, Euplectes orix Linn.
58. According to Dr Beasley's dairy, 'after visiting the saw-mill I came back to lie in the coolest spot possible for an afternoon rest. I went to sleep despite the thumping as the logs were thrown into the store'.
59. *waral*, monitor lizard.

crocodile and, although she managed to escape, she had been so badly bitten that gangrene had set in. They had taken her to hospital in Roseires but she had not recovered and both father and child were overwhelmed by their loss and the manner of it.

For the first part of the journey we had no such shadow and went ashore, whenever the boat refuelled, theoreticaly for exercise but for my part for the joy of being amongst the soft, warm richness of growth. About four o'clock one afternoon, a magic hour in the Sudan when the hot peak of the day has lowered, we pushed our way through some thick undergrowth and found we were on the edge of a great swamp, where the green had all the vividness of a marshland and enormous trees stood with their feet in the water. Here again birds of all kinds were bestirring themselves for the cooler evening but the most noticeable were large quantities of snipe swooping down to drink. We had no gun, which was perhaps fortunate, as it would have been unseemly to shatter the quiet peace of the retreat, although our dinner was the poorer. The undisturbed stillness of the country was what made the most lasting impression. Soon after sunrise another day we came across a second swamp behind the fringes of trees on the river bank. A moist, steamy penetration was beginning already but it was still fresh enough to enjoy pushing along a path that led us gently up and down. The ground had hardly attained to the status of hills but it was starting to lose its absolute flatness. Through a wealth of bushes under tall trees we came at last to a wide sheet of water lying motionless without a ripple to break the reflections and shadows at one edge or to disturb the shining of the centre. There was a little chirping from the birds, already wanting to seek shelter from the growing heat, but no breeze to stir the leaves. It was a world of soft green and blue, where a complete peace was an integral part of the whole, not superimposed and to be shattered at any moment. The empty stretches of the Northern desert can be lonely enough but they never enfold one in this all-absorbing peace. Solitude there is harsh and hostile and demands that a man should pit himself against its forces. Nor is there ever the same stillness; something is always fidgeting, even when there is no fierce wind; the stones shift restlessly and the surface of the sand is disturbed for no reason. There may be birds but they are likely to be kites or vultures. Never is one lulled to be part of the beguiling beauty as with this soft scene of probably over-fecund growth.

We walked along by the river pushing through thickets which reminded me of Burma. We also saw quantities of large fish just at the edge of the water. We had, of course, no line, so we caught grasshoppers and threw them to the fish, who gobbled them up.

Most of the forest was of *sunt*, a colourful tree with its reddish trunk and light foliage and mimosa-like flowers. There was plenty of evidence, when we penetrated the borders of the swamp, that the forest was regenerating itself without any human assistance. This, I was told, could be completed within a man's lifetime.

It formed therefore a valuable source of timber and the saw-mill, which was our next expedition ashore, did not appear such a destructive feature. The tall piles of logs gave off that clean, slightly acid smell of freshly sawn timber and glowed with a rich, full red which suggested a gleaming surface, if oiled and polished. Designing rose red furniture was out of the question, because, my informants said, the wood splits too easily for this purpose, although it has its use in straightforard building.

Recalling the Fung brings the temptation to linger over these colour slides, as it were, of sudden scenes of glory. To add even more to the series [of memories] it was the time of a full moon and we had also the startling silver and black of the nights in almost theatrical contrast. Despite the brilliance of the light the *rais* insisted on tying up at dusk for the river was becoming shallower and he feared the rocks and sandbanks. This brought a disadvantage since, while we were moving, the mosquitoes did not trouble us and however rapturous I might wax about the blue and green and peace of the swamps in the morning, mosquitoes bred there with alarming fury and spread malaria far and wide. It was too stuffy to sit in the cabin after dark and a lamp, of course, attracted even greater quantities of insects. There was nothing to be done therefore but to put on mosquito boots and long sleeves and sit in the mooonlight at any point, where we could detect a slight quiver in the air. All of us have our peculiar forms of luck, I suppose, and one of mine is that, although I always suffered intensely from the irritation of bites, I never contacted malaria in any of the various tropical stations, where it prevailed, despite the fact that the prophylactics, introduced during the war, were unknown at that time.[60]

### 10.3 Karkoj

> We also did a certain amount of work at intervals ... we arrived at Karkoj the second morning after we set off ... It was not quite as depressing a village as I expected ... The country here is slightly undulating ... still a lot of grass about but turning a bit yellow.

Nevertheless life was not all an idyllic communing with Nature and had to be real and earnest, whenever we reached a village. Our first stop brought

---

60. Prophylactics according to Dr Beasley's diary, 'were not available to us', rather than unknown in 1942.

me a distasteful problem that happily seldom recurred. There had been a school at Karkoj for some years but it had dwindled to the point of extinction although no-one could be sure of the reason. Contrary to the usual custom the notables of the village did not come to welcome me and everyone very definitely kept out of the way except the boys' headmaster and an assistant schoolmistress. As the master did not belong to the district and had only recently been transferred there, he did not feel involved in the humiliation, with which public opinion regarded the closing of the school through lack of support. The schoolmistress was a local girl but she was a poor, miserable little creature, with not the force of personality to make an impact on parents or to counter the general apathy. Having given up the struggle she was looking forward to going elsewhere to play her modest part, for we were extremely short of staff all over the country and could profitably use her services in a more responsive village. Nothing remained but for me to give the official death warrant to the school's gentle demise but it grieved me much to think of neglecting the children of Karkoj and also to compare the overcrowded conditions of some of the old town houses, where we worked, with this pleasant wooden building now left empty.[61] For at this time of year against a background of green fields it was an attractive place of adequate size and appropriate design roofed with a picturesque thatch.

### 10.4 Abu Hujar

On the other side of the river, however, Abu Hujar was clamouring for its girls to be educated. So far from being avoided we were greeted by all the important persons of the place. Followed also by a string of hangers-on we went first to look for a suitable site, to be ear-marked for the time, when we could make arrangements to start. It was a rather more barren district than the east bank with the lie of the land somewhat broken, but we managed to find an even place with one or two trees on it and decided this would be fitting. Rivalry with Karkoj was evidently keen and one or two people expressed considerable scorn for the other village, which had so manifestly failed. There need be no bother about buildings, one large man suggested, since the villagers there did not want theirs. He would take a few equally strong men across, dismantle the school and set it up here. It would only be a matter of a couple of days. These precipitate methods were resisted much to his disappointment. Decay we might admit in Karkoj, but no such

---

61. Karkoj Girls' School reopened at the beginning of 1946 under an energetic Headmistress and made satisfactory progress (*ARDE*, 1946).

absolute defeat as to give up all hope for the future. In fact after two years'
closure, Karkoj did return to the fold.

Having made this definite choice we then trooped into a *rakuba* erected
just outside the village. Two local guards were pacing up and down outside
carrying rifles looking as if they did not feel their best in European-style
uniform. The *nazir*, the *omdah*, members of the Local Council sat on chairs
near the D.C., who was at a table, but the rest of the company were
comfortably seated on *birsh* mats on the ground. To me the scene was an
exact replica of drawings I had often known in the geography books or tales
of adventure in my childhood. The members of this local assembly were
very mixed in type, partly no doubt because the Kingdom of the Fung at the
height of its glory in the seventeenth century was inhabited by a black race,
and partly because there has been a large infiltration here from West Africa.
Pilgrims trekking across to Mecca often stayed to work in the Gezira and
then they might drift down to this softer atmosphere on the more southerly
reach of the river. People of Arab stock had been settling in the region for
over a century and what I saw that morning was a noticeable array of very
different types. It was certainly not the Northern snobbery perpetuating the
tradition of Arab master and black slave, since, although the *nazir* was of
ordinary medium colouring, one or two of the most important men were
very black indeed.

I sat on a chair slightly apart as, no doubt, there were matters of
precedent in all these arrangements, and the question of the girls' school
was the first item for discussion among a long list. One or two were most
enthusiastic and a number murmured assent to their strongly-voiced
opinions; no-one definitely opposed the idea; and the result was a general
promise to make sure that a school would prosper. Out-doing Karkoj was
evidently going to give a vast amount of satisfaction and to their credit,
whatever the motives, they kept their word, when the school was started.

While the Local Council discussed other affairs with the D.C., I went to
call on some of the women, beginning with the *nazir*'s wife. He may have
been a competent and useful leader but to look at he was rather a grubby
old man and his wife was much the same. My welcome was extremely warm
both from her and from the various other women who gradually gathered
round. It was not a particularly well-built house and rather squalid in
upkeep but the women's quarters did not give one the feeling of such close
confinement as many I have visited. The women who came in might veil
their faces but in a rather haphazard sort of way. Conversation dragged a
little but nobody really minded. I think that the mere fact of my visit was a
sufficient break from ordinary routine to be thoroughly enjoyed and the
new topic of a girls' school was definitely stimulating. None of them had
been to school and I gathered they had little idea of what would be involved

but the novelty of the idea was enthralling. When it was started, it was reckoned rather fun to be in on this fresh thing, and anyone who was excluded on grounds of age was going to be bitterly disappointed at the thought, that she was missing something. The talk mostly revolved round this subject with a good bit of personal details in between. As usual there was compassion for me and scorn for the small size of my family. Only one daughter and no sons! During all this I was given quantities of *abri*, one of my favourites among the native drinks. It was made from a solution of *kisra*, the ordinary millet bread, and has a slight bitterness that was most refreshing in this thirsty land. I do not think that it was alcoholic, except that the millet paste is allowed to ferment slightly, before it is rolled out into the flat pancakes, which are then baked. As a more signal honour my hostess came across to me and without warning poured on my head a particularly pungent scent, which, to be truthful, did not appeal to my sense of smell as the *abri* did to my palate. Judging by the picture on the bottle it was probably imported from Egypt or Asmara and did not therefore have even the significance of a home-made product. Then to complete the ritual the palms of my hands were anointed and I did thank her genuinely for what, I was sure, was a very real tribute to a guest. There were, however, no facilities for washing my hair on board and I had the idea, that people kept to windward of me for a few days.

After about an hour a messenger arrived to take me to the *omdah*'s house, which was not, like the *nazir*'s, put up casually behind a grass fence but was an orthodox mud[-brick] building, where his women-folk could be firmly shut away. I had wondered why his wife had not been down to join the first party but at this call I understood. Partly no doubt the *omdah* wished to do me the honour of having me in his own house, but also I feared that his wife was too much of a lady to go out. Also I suspected that she despised the *nazir*'s wife as being a dirty, uneducated old woman, which indeed she was, though a certain innate liveliness had persisted. My host here had made an attempt to emulate the *effendi* type of refinement according to the taste of the Egyptian middle class. The guest room was crowded with shabby chairs and a large table filled the centre; photographs were stuck all over the walls and scattered around were a lot of cheap and ugly ornaments of various kinds. My hostess was certainly much more presentable than the other women in the village, and much easier to talk to. She politely made a point of informing me that she had had a little schooling and discussed the purpose of my visit with interest, but otherwise she appeared rather subdued. Here I was given *limoon* and some very black tea, since I was not attracted by the look of the milk provided. In the cause of hospitality there was an enormous amount of gastric adventuring, and on this count my immunity was not so well-developed as my resistance to malaria. The pleasantest part about all this was the number of bright little girls around and the hope that they might be helped to steer between what I judged as two dull ways of life; the snobbish seclusion of the *omdah*'s wife and the squalid, probably less dreary, life of the *nazir*'s.[62]

## 10.5 A Fellata village

At our next call there was a cheerful openness about the whole village. I tend to call most of these settlements Fellata, but whatever the actual tribe they were people of West African origin, who had not adopted the customs of the surrounding districts. Our visit was brief but the more widely spaced *tukl*s, often with *loofah*s thrusting their brilliant yellow flowers over the roofs, impressed me as brighter than the stolid, hidden mud houses I was accustomed to.

> It looked comparatively clean. Somehow not so squalid as Abu Hujar.

As they spoke no Arabic there was no chance to talk to anyone and at this point we could not contemplate a scheme for educating the friendly children, who returned our greetings.

## 10.6. Roseires

Roseires was our furthest port of call. Here I settled down to the routine of an ordinary school inspection, with the pleasant variation of the boat to live on instead of a resthouse. As I walked to and from school I had little paths to follow through something approaching a dell and not far away were small hills and beyond them the promise of foothills and mountains leading into Abyssinia. Everywhere was covered with longish grass turning to a pale gold and along the roads and in the yards were trees of all sizes among them fine specimens of *kapok*. Harnessed now by the zeal of a new nation to build more dams, the river, when I saw it, was obviously a mountain stream dividing in its rush into two turbulent sweeps among the scattered rocks. It seemed odd after such a long stretch of country with little but green vistas and grass villages to come to this pleasantly laid out small town with some good European houses, empty because of depleted staff, and a centre with tidy shops of Greek traders.[63] From a brief glance I could not be sure what

62. 'I doubt she [the *omdah*'s wife] mixed much with the *nazir*'s wife. This urban snobbishness again! ... I was glad when Mr Hancock came to fetch me back to the boat, even if he did tease me about keeping to windward.'
63. 'Some of the Greeks here had a bad time during the War.' Dr Beasley noted the European houses in Roseires, 'particularly the old double storied one with a wonderful view from the verandah'.

they stocked but they looked fairly prosperous, although some of them had suffered much, when the campaigns were at their height. By this time[64] the war had ebbed much further east and there was an atmosphere of calm over the place. No halt had been called, however, to the constant coming and going across the frontier, but during the days I was there I did not see any wild Abyssinians. Tales of lawlessness were plentiful and it was in fact a routine and by no means infrequent part of the D.C.'s work to deal with slaves with their chains still on escaping over the border to obtain freedom.

## 10.7 Suki

After this, my companion[65] had work at Singa and I was allowed to use the boat to the other end of the reach and live on it in Suki. This I found a great comfort, since the depressing little rail and river junction was so congested by manifold duties thrust on it by the war effort. Grazing and cultivation lay quite close but all vegetation seemed to have been cleared away from the village itself and the general memory of the ground recalls cinders. Fuel for the engines was one of the shortages of the war years and to overcome this a small factory had been set up to make brickets out of charcoal. I have no doubt that it was a most valuable piece of work but Fung had made me rural- minded and I wanted it hidden.

Although limited in numbers, the girls' school was the most inspiring point of interest, run under difficult conditions by three bright and energetic mistresses with an unexpected ally from outside. The junction was virtually governed by a British engineer, who lived on a boat, and had the reputation of being a surly recluse and was accused by the vernacular press of being a reactionary dictator. As his dictatorial habits included insisting that his workmen sent their daughters to school, I took little exception to them. Over lunch to which he invited me he talked with genuine concern about the well-being of the school and the mistresses praised him as being of unfailing support in some of their small troubles.

One of the teachers came from Kassala and, although she had been in [the Girls' Training] College in Omdurman, she had never been near the river nor seen a steamer. We therefore arranged an entertaining expedition one day, in which they and about a dozen of the older girls walked along the river bank to the landing place. On the way the children made quite creditable little maps under the supervision of one of the mistresses. The Boat they found immensely interesting but all rather bewildering and did not know quite what questions they wanted to ask, especially about the

64. October 1942.
65. G.M. Hancock.

engines. The laughed a lot over the 'vacant' and 'occupied' lock on the lavatory door, which very much caught their fancy, and I thought they might be playing with it to breaking point. As a school visit as as a social occasion it was a most successful party.

I was not, however, sorry to leave, as the weather was very warm and sticky without the delight in greenness to offset it, as there had been upstream. I was introduced to yet another form of transport on my way from the boat to the station. This was a hand-worked trolley on the railway line. Standing up on this with the feel of rushing through the air was a most agreeable form of propulsion even in the middle of a hot and dusty afternoon.

> I decided there was much to be said for mechanical propulsion ... I wonder if I will ever go there again.

## 11. Sennar

Compared with all this Sennar was based on very different standards. Whenever I went there, I realised how strongly it dominated all the activities and way of life in the Blue Nile Province. Not that it was either the administrative or the commercial head, but it was from the power of the Sennar Dam,[66] that the great experiment of the Gezira Scheme drew its substance and thence flowed the revenue to provide most of the finances for the rest of the country. Upstream the Fung was a corner of the world cut off by the dam but nevertheless dependent for its communications on the rhythms of the river, which this vast work regulated. By no means outstanding now for sheer size among more recent constructions it remained an achievement to inspire admiration by an impressive dignity and for some inexplicable reason it was not at variance with the landscape. I never liked Jebel Auliya, which stretched for about three miles across the flat desert and the sluggish flow of the White Nile, while its design always reminded me of a long expanse of seaside promenade with lamps at regular intervals.

> It is a rather prettier view from there than Jebel Auliya Dam; the banks are closer; there are more trees ... Sennar is full of gardens ... The whole thing looks more colourful and the reservoir is not so large.

66. On 5.11.41 Dr Beasley first crossed the Sennar Dam by night, *en route* to Kassala, reflecting it was exactly two years since she had come to the country. In August 1946, owing to the great Nile flood that year, the train from Wadi Halfa to Khartoum was diverted via Kassala. 'The water was booming through Sennar Dam. It was quite indescribable. Millions of tons per second. The whole journey had been uncomfortably hot but Sennar was most evilly sticky.'

At Sennar the reservoir lay among its green surroundings with a frieze of birds standing in the reeds and a wild cascade of water poured over the sluices to run between banks, where rocks and boulders piled up. Fishermen spent happy hours angling for Nile perch in the sparkle and flurry of the stream and the deep pools. Seen from below it was most exciting but even looking out from the railway, which ran across it beside the motor road, was one of the spectacular moments of an otherwise monotonous journey. In a country where one sees so little running water and so seldom hears the splash or gurgle of a brook, there is sheer joy in the rush and movement through the sluices and the roar of the water's passing, with all the pleasant subsidiary noises of the eddies round the stones by the edge of the river.

For travellers Sennar can pander also to the creature comforts.[67] During the construction of the dam a very comfortable resthouse had been built for the use of engineers engaged on the project and it had been retained for officials and the occasional tourists, who liked the place for fishing.

> There were two fishermen in the rest-house—syndicate inspectors, one a baronet with no money—who gave me their views on education.

It may have been because of its sudden contacts with modernity, but I never found the town to have the recognisable entity of such a place as Rufaa. Having read something of its former history[68] I expected it to be more deeply rooted in the past but the traces of former glory were not to be seen on the surface and I did not have much time or adequate information for any exploring. The most satisfying parts of a stay there were to wander in the public gardens, where in the close, lush atmosphere belonging to the tropics something of the faraway perfection of English gardens had been transplanted.[69] Shady walks led to green lawns and beds of well-tended

---

67. 'My first impression' arriving at night in Sennar from Gedaref, 15.11.1941, 'was the comfort of the rest-house ... A long building all glistening with clean white paint, a row of brightly lit rooms each with electric light and a white suite of furniture, proper bathrooms, with a wide verandah and a pleasant garden—in short a white painted palace of luxury after mud-brick and grass *tukls*.'

68. In the sixteeth century the Muslim Fung kingdom, the Sultanate of Sennar, known as 'The Black Sultanate' (1504-1821), was founded after the Kingdom of Soba succumbed to a coalition of Arabs and negroid Fung from the Abyssinian foothills and the Upper Nile. This alliance with the Arabs led to the final demise of the weak Christian Kingdom of Nubia and completed the process whereby the Northern Sudan became Arab and Muslim. This led to a revival of learning and prosperity with the centre at Sennar. The Sultans claimed to be descended from the Umayyad caliphs of Damascus. In the eighteenth century wars against Abyssinia and the Sultans of Darfur led to anarchy. By 1821 the North was still nominally subject to the Sultans of Sennar but was dominated by powerful Shayqiyya.

69. 'There is a fairly settled British community here and the general friendliness was not so aggressive as in remoter parts. I was, however, asked to an excellent dinner. Nor was the native population so friendly. I met the schoolmaster but there was no attempt at friendliness.'

roses, surrounded by long, flower-covered pergolas. All the luscious savours of the East were added from the fruits, pawpaws, custard apples and some of the best mangoes I had tasted since I left [Mandalay]. True a veritable serpent lurked in this Eden, for during one of my visits my servant came excitedly to tell me of a python, which had been caught in the banana plantation.

> Saw one or two monkeys also and someone killed a python among the bananas ... crocodiles can sometimes be seen lounging about.

From the river to the resthouse the path led across a sort of green common fringed with trees but the local irrigation did not stretch much farther and down by the school the dust and barrenness took over. My first visit has perhaps reinforced an idea of dusty chaos, because in this debilitating temperature the staff were struggling to carry on in one half of the school while building went on in the other.

> In November 1941 the school was a mess. The fault lay partly with the authorities, who had not finished building extensions during the holidays; but mostly with the staff who were not bothering to teach the children more than the most superficial things. How to instil a conscience into these girls ... and the idea of responsibility?

The Headmistress, a soft voiced girl with a pretty heart-shaped face, seemed quite broken in spirit and helpless to control little invasions of small brothers and sisters, who wandered in from the building site from time to time. Officially ejected at the front gate they promptly re-appeared through holes in the fence, strayed about in the classrooms, until they were bored and created general confusion. For me humiliation was added to the muddle, for one of the mistresses produced a version of a lesson, which I had tried to teach at a refresher course at the Girls' Training College. At that time we had no Domestic Science specialist and I was anxious to overcome the complaint of Sudanese husbands about perpetual hard-boiled eggs. I had therefore given a demonstration of six different ways to cook an egg. Made slowly and with the wrong materials and left to congeal on cold plates, nothing can look less appetising than an omelette and I could well understand the disgust on the faces of the pupils, who held the plates at arm's length, with their heads turned away.

> All that sticky climate could hardly fail to produce slackness. It was interesting to notice how distressed they all were when I expressed my displeasure ... they have a genuine desire to please.

Despite the resthouse and the river walks, Sennar was never one of my favourite haunts, possibly because I did not come to know anyone there as I did in Rufaa or Wadi Halfa. Yet the name still carried the special overtones of that lost, historic kingdom, whose greatness was submerged now in a modern fame of economic and financial significance.

# Chapter V

# The East

## 1. 'The East'

To passengers from liners voyaging through the Red Sea the Sudan is largely represented by what they can see in a brief call to Port Sudan, or in pre-war years by a rapid excursion to Suakin. Kipling made the 'Fuzzies'[1] famous: 'Who broke the British Square' and 'The Light That Failed' helped to build up a picture, which persists, even if rather vaguely. Yet the riverain people often spoke of 'The East', as if they regarded it almost as a foreign country. Certainly like all the other Provinces it had a character of its own and could boast, if that is the right word, more enormous expanses of harsh, bleak landscape than the others.

### 1.1. Sennar to Kassala

Coming from Sennar to Kassala, as I did on my first trip,[2] this impression was definitely modified in November,[3] for, when the line turned east after the junction, it ran through a countryside covered with tall grass and smallish trees and again innumerable birds.[4] I had been told that in these parts the grass grew so high, that it would hide a man riding on a camel.

1. Beja.
2. 'There are usually no sleeping cars on this line. The first class compartment can sleep four when the backs of the seats are raised to make the top bunks ... no wash basin but plenty of room. There is no dining room but the *farrash* cooks meals and serves them in the compartment ... I managed to get a sleeper, a new departure for the Kassala line, but intended for the benefit of Eritrean travellers. I had to induce Basil Lee of the Education Service (then a Captain helping to administer Eritrea) to give up his double cabin and share one. The train was mainly military and I was the only Englishwoman on the train, but he grumbled incessantly afterwards about the discomfort of being two in a compartment. I played hectic and talkative bridge most of the way. Some of the people on the train were interesting—a South African Jew going up to organise Red Cross work in Asmara, a curious major, suddenly promoted, because of his knowledge of Italian.'
3. Dr Beasley went from Sennar to Kassala on 4.11.41, after the Eritrean campaign; but the Anglo-Ethiopian agreement which re-established the Ethiopian Government administration and ended the danger on the Sudanese border did not take place until 31.1.42. Her letters home indicate a visit to Kassala 19.9.41 '36 hours by train if you are lucky'.
4. ' ... different kinds of bee-eaters, Abyssinian rollers and once in Kassala I saw a shrike.'

Struggling at much expense to produce even the smallest patch of lawn in Omdurman, I was apt to smile a polite assent, as with most of these tales, but they were no exaggeration. On either side of the railway there were yellowing stretches of grass, which occasionally at some point would waver with an alien disturbance. Nothing could be seen at first until gradually there would emerge a camel with a rider swaying on its back. There were, however, none of the great herds of cattle, that I had seen in the grasslands of Kordofan, but much more frequent were wide fields of grain, either of *dura*, an attractive plant with its round ruddy heads about the size of a woman's fist, or *dukhn*, which is graceful like a thin bulrush. Water lay in rivers we crossed, the Dinder and the Rahad, but it was the wrong time of day for animals to be drinking at the pools, although this was in fact a game reserve, where herds of giraffe sometimes appeared and raced beside the train.

## 1.2. Gedaref to Sennar

Villages were mostly hidden but the tops of thatched roofs peeped up here and there. By day there was less colour than in Kordofan but at this season the nights could produce their own vivid spectacles. This particular year,[5] the School of Agriculture was trying an experiment to control the *hareeg* cultivation, which was a feature of these parts. The method ordinarily employed by the local people was to wait until the new weeds had reached the right stage of growth and set fire to last year's dry grass; then old and new weeds were burnt together and the land was clear for sowing. There were obvious dangers about all this, not the least being the control of the fire, once started, and the equally common one of an accidental fire at the wrong time ruining later cultivation.[6] Many poignant stories also were told of families trapped down-wind of the blazing grass. What the Agricultural students were arranging were fire-lines, passages about a hundred yards wide being burnt around blocks a mile square. Knowing the flames to be regulated, I could enjoy a display finer than any show of fireworks, since at night the sky would be lit up by intense glows varying from red to white, while, if seen close to, the line of fire ran brilliant and sparkling through the blackness. '*Afreet*s running away' shouted one of the labourers laughing gleefully at the flames chasing in and out of the dry grass.

5. Gedaref was the centre of a large *dura* producing area. In order to increase yields of *dura*, and for other experimental crops such as sunflower seeds and groundnuts in the Gedaref area, there was a big government agricultural scheme at Ghadambalya where they used fire-lines to increase production. 'On the train from Gedaref to Sennar I saw one of these burning some distance away' [15.11.41].
6. 'There also seemed much difficulty as to whom the land really belonged.'

## 2. Kassala

For some reason, which escapes me, the train was delayed and we did not reach Kassala until nearly midnight. As no-one had come to meet me, I gathered that something had gone wrong with the plans or perhaps the police driver, whom I normally expected, had fallen asleep somewhere out of call. In a place this size there were a few taxis and the easiest remedy was to take one to the resthouse on the other side of the river. At this time of the year the Gash was dry and one could drive across a causeway from the station on one bank to the town on the other near to the Eritrean border. During the [Eritrean] Campaign, not so long ended, the Italians had captured the town but the Sudan Defence Force had retained the station. When at another point[7] I saw the method of crossing the river in full spate, I wondered if this had helped to deter the invaders.[8] I was passing through on the train[9] and to while away a long halt sauntered down to look. I never had to undertake the risk and a bridge, built in 1949, put an end to this picturesque peril. Until then all goods and persons were carried across on *angareeb*s borne by groups of four, strong black porters, all of whom were apparently descendants of slave families. They started at a point higher upstream than their destination and waded into the water, being then forced by the current into making a diagonal path. Sometimes they were obliged by the unevenness of the river-bed to disappear below the surface of the water, although the *angareeb* was always held aloft to the manifest discomfort and terror of the unfortunate passenger. The price of this hazardous crossing was ten piastres (roughly two shillings) but perhaps twice this amount, if the current was running strongly enough to be definitely dangerous. It was not unheard of for bearers and load to be washed away, but it was not a frequent occurrence. During half the year, however, the river did not run and one could cross dry-shod. Most people therefore arranged their journeys accordingly. On this occasion,[10] it did not take long to reach the resthouse, which was firmly locked and no caretaker to be found. An impressive but rather forbidding place it looked, especially in the circumstances, as it had been built for a regimental mess by the Egyptians [in the] last century. It was planned with a large, central hall leading to three rooms at each end. Eventually we roused somebody's servant, who told us, that all the gentlemen were sleeping on the roof, but that he could let me

---

7. During the great floods of 1946 Dr Beasley's train for Khartoum was detoured via Kassala.
8. The Gash flood was also one of the factors which held the Italians in Kassala during the summer of 1940.
9. In 1946. Dr Beasley also made school inspections in Kassala in November 1946.
10. Most travellers tried 'to avoid the terrific floods of July and August'. 'As I arrived after dark [4.11.41] and we also left after dark, I never really saw the Gash.'

into the bathroom. While I was gratefully removing the grime of the journey, my bed was put up in the yard and I could settle down to sleep in peace. Troublesome though the Sudan climate may be in some ways, there are few nights in the North, when one cannot be independent of shelter, and rest in comfort, provided a bed has been included in the luggage.

As I lay there, even the high wall could not obstruct the view of Jebel Kassala, dominating the town and standing out in all its grotesque relief, while the mountain range behind was barely a smudge on the dark background. It was not the beauty of black and white, which had been so arresting on the Dongola Reach or in the Fung, or even at moments in the angular shadows in Omdurman. It loomed sinister and ugly in its twisted shape and therefore might have invited the appropriate screaming of the hyenas in the distance, a loathsome sound, which came closer and closer, until they were running through the town itself. In the morning I was greeted by a most striking skyline, as the peaks began to appear out of the mist, but these volcanic structures were cruel, tortured blocks with no bush or growth to clothe their nakedness, a veritable Devil's landscape, suggesting a world in disruption, where, however fitting the haunts of hyenas, the rocks alone conveyed an atmosphere of horror.

Jebel Kassala itself from below looks absolutely smooth but it has been climbed by two British officials,[11] who managed to leave a cairn on top to mark their success. It never inspired me with the friendly recognition one normally accords to familiar mountains and, although it could fascinate by a play of light and constantly changing colours, mostly it seemed to catch and radiate so much heat, that the temperature was seldom at an enjoyable level. There was, however, water at its foot and gardens responded to a little tending. In fact bananas were so prolific, that at one time a scheme was discussed to make this part of the Gash into plantations operating on a commercial scale, but as in so many of these plans transport and distribution presented formidable obstacles.

Right under its shadow, there is a delightful green spot full of little huts and

---

11. Jebel Kassala 'is a bundle of tall candle rocks'. None of the Italian alpinists had been able to manage to climb Jebel Kassala but in December 1941 two Gordon College tutors, Robin A. Hodgkin and Lewis W. Brown got to the top by means of ropes.

Robin A. Hodgkin; 11.1.39 First appointment; 1939-c.1944 Tutor, Gordon Memorial College, based in Omdurman; By 1947 managing editor, Publications Bureau, Bakht-er-Ruda; By 1952-55 Principal Bakht-er-Ruda and Assistant Director of Education; 1955 retired. Author and academic.

Lewis W. Brown. 2.1.35 First appointment; 1935-38 lecturer, Gordon College; 1939 tutor, G.M.C.; 1940 Senior Tutor, G.M.C.; 1941-44 Assistant Warden, G.M.C.; 1945 Principal, Junior Secondary School, Bakht-er-Ruda; 1946-55 headmaster, Hantoub Secondary School.

palm trees ... In this spot lived a very famous holy man who appeared to make his living giving advice to people. My servant borrowed money from me in order to go and see him [4.11.41].

There are pleasant gardens round the officials' houses as there is no lack of water. The Governor's[12] garden ... A lovely old-fashioned place, spacious and solid, with six or seven acres of garden with wide lawns and flowering shrubs and beds of annuals. Masses of fruit trees round a little swimming pool, where the swallows sweep down and drink while you are swimming. I had meals with the D.C. like the rest of the visitors of whom there were a large number coming and going from Eritrea or just staying there. There was, for example, the old judge from Iraq who had been interned during the bothers there ... he lodged with the manager of the oil company, who had a habit of passing out and needed reviving with champagne.[13]

There was a general brightness of the company. This was partly due to a very amusing and energetic D.C.[14] with an amazing zest for life. They also told many exciting tales of the occupation. I remember the excitement when it was suddenly discovered that the Italians had painted a red cross on what had been their battery control room ... The D.C. and another man went to explode an old bomb [4.11.41].

Apart from the coming and going of officials working in Eritrea and various Army people, the war had receded rapidly and people were

12. John McNab Humphrey, M.C., 4N., Croix de Guerre (avec Palme) (b.12.2.1897- ); Educated at Winchester and New College, Oxford; 13.11.20 First appointment; 1921-22 Kordofan; 1922-27 Berber; 1928-30 Police Magistrate, Khartoum; 1930-34 White Nile; 1935 Khartoum; 1936-37 Kassala, Deputy Governor; 1938-1940 Assistant Civil Secretary—Auxiliary Defence Force staff officer; 3.3.41-1946 Kassala, Governor; 1946 retired.

13. 4.11.41, and January 1947 when Dr Beasley arrived in Kassala by train from Gedaref about 9.30 p.m. and went to stay at the Governor's house. He also came from Gedaref, by car, after meeting the Governor-General there (Letter to Sheila Connelly, March 1947, S.A.D. 657/7/55-94).

The Governor-General was still Sir Hubert Huddleston the predecessor of Sir Robert G. Howe. By 1947 the Governor of Kassala Province was Geoffrey M. Hancock.

14. This was either E.D. Arbuthnot or P.J. Sandison. According to Dr Beasley's letters home [21.11.41] she found the D.C. Kassala 'a particularly entertaining person'.

Ernest Douglas Arbuthnot, 4N. (b.15.9.1905- ). Educated at Blundells and Balliol College, Oxford, 1926 Captain Oxford University Boxing Club; 14.12.27 first appointment; 1928 Nuba Mountains; 1929-31 Kordofan; 1931-32 Blue Nile; 1932-35 Bahr el Ghazal; 1935 Mongalla; 1935-39 Kassala; 1939-40 Khartoum, D.C. Omdurman; 1.8.40-45 Kassala, D.C. Kassala Province Headquarters, based in Kassala; 1945-49 Equatoria; 1949-53 Northern; 1953 retired.

Paul James Sandison, O.B.E., 4N. (b.1906-d.1970); Educated at City of London School and St. Edmund Hall, Oxford; 13.12.28 First appointment; 1929 Mongalla; 1930-35 Darfur; 1935-39 Mongalla; 1939-42 Kassala, D.C. Kassala, including the Gash District; 1942-45 Governor-General's temporary Commission in S.D.F.—Mentioned in Despatches; 1945 seconded to B.M.A. Tripolitania; 1946-48 Deputy Chief Secretary (Lt-Col); 1948 British delegation to International Commission on the Future of the ex-Italian colonies; 1948-50 Civil Secretary's Office (Assistant Commissioner of Labour); 1950-54 Commissioner of Labour; 1954 retired; 1954- farming in Dorset.

forgetting it. The girls' school[15] had been re-opened in simple mud buildings in a very large yard containing a line of shady trees, under which the children had a number of their lessons. It had definitely been affected by the gap, as we had considerable difficulty in recruiting adequate numbers in any except the youngest class. The Headmistress was working whole-heartedly, although originally I had had some difficulty in persuading the headmistress to accept the transfer. One of her assistants was causing us trouble on grounds other than teaching, [in] which she was eminently satisfactory.

She had greatly distressed one of the older pupils at the Intermediate School by sending her passionate love letters couched in a most improper strain. When these remained unanswered, the Headmistress[16] began to receive anonymous notes accusing the girl of immoral behaviour. Senior Sudanese mistresses declared that the handwriting was identical and were very indignant about the whole affair. *Hareem* conditions do produce an unwholesome atmosphere and more tendency than in other societies to perverted inclinations, although among the majority of the Sudanese these were roundly condemned. In my student days I had been advised to burn anonymous letters unread but in this case my hand had been forced, as they had not been sent to me. I had no option but to give this teacher a warning, that we should have to take action, if all this did not stop. Of course she strenuously denied everything and I assured her, that I did not require a confession but was simply informing her, that there must be no more such letters. She was a highly intelligent girl, who immediately understood the situation and all the letters ceased from that point. Although claiming to be Sudanese, she had some Egyptian connections and wore her smooth, slightly curly hair in a bob very becoming to her light-skinned, rather sharp featured face. Unfortunately a couple of years later she was caught up in a worse and proven scandal in which with three other mistresses she had to be dismissed. It should be emphasized here, that this second affair was the only one of its kind we had to deal with, but firm measures were necessary despite the distress it caused us all. As so often Sheikh Babikr Bedri gave us full and understanding support in contrast with one or two old *sheikhs*, who told me that the matter should have been hushed up. He advised me, 'If the branch is rotten, it must be cut off for the good of the whole.'

Some years later, when I was in Cairo, I was surprised that the girl from Kassala came to call on me. Surprised and very relieved, for discipline to

15. 'The school was going well.' In 1938 Kassala Girls' School had 120 pupils and 4 teachers, in 1943 96 pupils and 4 teachers and by 1946 Kassala school had 110 pupils and 4 teachers.
16. 'An awkward incident arose after I left.' The girl in question was 'a bright, intelligent wench'; the Headmistress of the Girls' Intermediate School was Miss Sylvia Clark.

such extreme lengths is always disturbing. She said that she had heard that I was in the city and had just come to greet me. By this time she was married and had a son but was still teaching. She was looking remarkably pretty, attractively dressed in European fashion and with a general air of well-being. Whether she had come in a spirit of forgiveness to me or whether to let me see that she had made good, hardly mattered from my point of view, since all she wanted was a little amicable conversation and gossip about old friends. To me it was a comfort to know that the prophecies of the more rigorous Sudanese about the end she would come to had not been fulfilled, and for her no doubt satisfaction, that I would go back and tell them so.

## 2.1 The Khatmiyya village

All this, however, was a long way off from my first visit[17] to Kassala, which included the question of another school about half an hour's drive away and even more under the shadow of the Jebel. The way[18] led through groves of *dom* palms to a village which gained in architectural dignity from being grouped round a mosque.[19] Instead of a ragged collection of flat, mud[-brick] houses, there was a sense of cohesion in the whole with the minaret acting as the centre. This was definitely appropriate, since the village depended on a relative[20] of Sayed Ali Mirghani, who claimed descent from the Prophet and was revered leader of one of the two great sects[21] into

17. According to Dr Beasley's diaries, it was on a visit in January 1945, not her first visit, that she investigated setting up a school in the Khatmiyya village at the foot of Jebel Kassala.
18. The way from Kassala.
19. The mosque was founded by al-Ḥasan b. Muḥammad 'Uthmān al-Mirghanī, and has gained great prestige from its miracle-working powers. It was rebuilt by the Government after it had been destroyed by Dervishes during the Mahdiyya outbreak, as the Mirghaniyya supported the Egyptian Government.

The village was founded by al-Ḥasan, son of the founder of the Mirghaniyya, who died in the Khatmiyya township in 1869. Today he is more revered by Mirghaniyya followers in the Sudan than the founder, Muḥammad 'Uthmān al-Mirghanī (b.1793-d.1853). None of the al-Mirghanīs is recognised as the paramount head, but the leader (*sheikh as-sajjāda*) in Kassala was responsible for the Kassala, Gedaref and Gallabat sphere of influence. (Trimingham, *Islam in the Sudan*, 1949, (repr. 1965), pp.203, 233-235).
20. 'Uthmān al-Mirghanī.
21. Al-Sayyid Sir 'Alī Muḥammad 'Uthmān al-Mirghanī was regarded as semi-divine by his followers, the Khatmiyya, the popular name for *Khātim al-Ṭuruq* 'the Seal of the Paths'. His sphere of influence included Kordofan, Khartoum, Berber, Dongola and Halfa. The other sect included followers of the Mahdī, the *Mahdiyya* or *Anṣār* under the leadership of Sayyid 'Abd al-Raḥmān al-Mahdī (Trimingham, *op. cit.*, p.235). In opposition was the *Ashiqqā'* political party, under its President, Ismā'īl al-Azharī, when it emerged in 1943, Sayyid 'Alī gave his support to the National Front Party when it emerged in 1950. Sayyid 'Alī died aged 98 in 1960 and was succeeded as leader of the Khatmiyya by his son Sayyid Muḥammad 'Uthmān al-Mirghanī.

which the country was roughly divided. The holy man of this village was not only a great support to his people in normal times but had been outstanding in his work for their protection during the Italian Occupation.

He was a man of very firm character, and had now decided on the need for a girls' school and asked for, or rather demanded, one from the Government immediately.

> Osman Mirghani was youngish but very sure of himself. He was a little shattered when told that he would have to wait his turn [Jan 1945].

When I reminded him of the difficulty of filling the top classes in Kassala, he eyed me coldly. 'My people will do what I tell them', was his reply. 'Girls will stay in school for the full four year course.'

He kept his word and the attendance throughout was excellent. What was more he had himself put up the school buildings, which were simple and suitable, in a wide yard covered by a coarse, light-coloured sand, that was easy to keep clean.[22]

> He would not accept the schoolmistress we suggested as people would not approve. I should have thought his reputation would have carried a little Nafissa. I wonder what he knows about her. I've had a few doubts too. But she has had a difficult time. Had to run for it when the Italians took Kassala. She had to escape on a camel and drink the puddles along the road. She was a problem child at College but she teaches in the house of the Sherifa[23] in the holidays [Jan 1945].

His unflagging interest stimulated parents and encouraged staff, who never raised objections to coming here. From the beginning the schoolmaster too was most helpful, since the mistresses were housed next door to him and were allowed to knock an opening in the wall between their yard and that of his wife, whose friendliness also helped in the general feeling of being in a community.[24]

22. On Dr Beasley's visit in February 1947 he was still 'very interested in the school' and she found 'it was almost a model for a simple village school'.
23. *Sharīfa* Maryam al-Mirghanī in Sinkat whose main sphere of influence as a Mirghaniyya religious leader was the Red Sea Hills. She was 'a direct descendant from the Prophet and very much holier than S.A.R.' (S.A.D. 657/7/19).
24. In February 1947 Dr Beasley attended large parties at both schools. 'Each school also visited the other. Things are moving when the mistresses without help from me, arrange a bus and transport the children on an outing. A few years ago there would have been an awful outcry.'

## 3. Gedaref

> When I took the train from Kassala to Gedaref I found the old judge had a
> carriage all to himself and there were three of us in another. He had told me
> he always got his own way in awkward situations [11.11.41].[25]

The other large settlement in the area was Gedaref, some 140 miles south-
west on the railway. Kassala was not a beautiful town but with its gardens
and trees against the background of twisted, barren mountains it had a
strange, arresting character of its own. Gedaref was just ugly, although the
country round about sloped in a gentle rolling fashion, and the dirty grey of
the soil was covered by long, yellow grass. It was important as an
agricultural and military centre but in itself was peculiarly unsightly. The
ground had been cleared and the roads marked out with white stones but
for the rest it was featureless.

> There is a mosque and a Coptic Church nearby, one or two villas belonging to
> the merchants, and a short way away is the headquarters of the army. The
> army buildings on the hill are all white-washed but the vast majority of the
> houses in the town are grass huts rather like beehives, set in large yards with
> grass fences around. The town sprawls on both sides of the railway line.
>     There was a furnished rest-house, rather mucky, and with no definite yard.
> It was very different from Kassala, where I had, after the first night, slept in a
> little walled-in yard.
>     [In February 1947] a stocky little D.C.[26] met me [off the train]. The rest-
> house was full of drillers who were making wells. The wife of the A.D.C.[27]
> had had a diptheria relapse so she could not stay with them, so [she] stayed in
> the D.C.'s dressing room.
>     Gedaref is a big market[28] and a place of importance.

Feelings, however, were most strongly differentiated by the keen rivalry of

---

25. In February 1947 on the train from Khartoum to Gedaref Dr Beasley opened her shutters
in the morning. 'There were about a dozen ostriches trotting away towards the rising sun.'
26. E.A. Balfour wrote to his mother, Lady Grace Balfour on 21.11.41, 'The girls' education in
this country seems to me the one bright spot in an otherwise murky outlook ...' (S.A.D.
606/7/34).
    Elliott Archibald Balfour (known as 'B') (b.29.5.1909- ); Educated at Edinburgh Academy
and Gonville and Caius College, Cambridge; 12.9.32 First appointment; 1932-33 Khartoum;
1933-34 Fung; 1934-36 Blue Nile; 1936-37 seconded to Education Department as tutor at
Gordon Memorial College; 1937-42 Darfur; 1942-45 Equatoria; 1.10.45-50 Kassala, D.C.
Gedaref; 1950-52 Civil Secretary's office (Local Government); 1952-54 Northern, Deputy
Governor; 1954-55 Northern, Governor; 1954 retired; 1955-68 Chief Executive Officer, Atomic
Energy Authority.
27. Mrs D.F. Hawley?
28. Gedaref had originally been called Sūq Abū Sinn. In 1947 'I was a bit dazed because after
all the wartime restrictions, I was able to buy a pair of sheets in the market without a permit'.

the two important families in the place, which made extra problems in the matter of schools. The town was divided between the influence of one *nazir*, head of the great Abu Sinn family,[29] whose connections stretched down to Rufaa, and another of the Bakr clan[30] who lived on the further side of the railway. The head of the latter had come into prominence in the war by raising an irregular fighting force,[31] which had played its part during the recent struggle in Eritrea.

Girls' education boasted that it stood neutral in sectarian issues, whether religious, family or political. In an attempt to deal justly with the girls of both families the school had been put down near the railway line on the other side of the *suq*.

It was a collection of pleasing, thatched buildings in a large yard with a number of trees, and surrounded by a tall grass fence.

The town was still full of talk about its war experiences ... An old shell of a bomb still lay near the school [November 1941].

It was really inconvenient for everybody and, although nearer to the Bakrs, in fact there were more girls from the other area. One valueless distinction was claimed for it; it was the only school to have a bomb dropped near it during one of the few Italian air raids.[32] Little damage was done but for a long time it made a lovely story for the mistresses to describe in detail.

Eventually we abandoned compromise and we decided on two schools[33] but, as building was difficult, the unfortunate result was, that we had to make do for many years with some picturesque erections of grass and plaster with thatched roofs. They looked very simple and fitting for a village school but were hot and noisy, and there were constant accidents. The roofs

29. Muḥammad Aḥmad Abū Sinn, 1941 *Nāzir* in Gedaref of the great camel-owning Shukriyya tribe in the Butana (see S.A.D. 606/8/1); c.1953 Councillor without Portfolio on Executive Council. The ruling family, the Abū Sinn, date back to Nā'il Aɓ 'Adlān c.1620 and rose to importance as Funj power declined in the eighteenth century. Followers of al-Mirghaniyya, the Shukriyya supported the Egyptian Government against the Mahdī dervishes.

30. According to E.A. Balfour, the Dar Bakr were 'the black western element which had settled in the south of the district during the Mahdiyya and was governed by the house of Bakr'. For further details of the rivalry between Bakr and Shukriyya see E.A. Balfour's papers (S.A.D. 606/8/1-11).

31. Sheikh Abdulla Bakr, O.B.E., *Nāzir* of the Dār Bakr. He was once a Bimbashi in the Egyptian army (S.A.D. 606/8/6). His military force which helped to harrass the Italians in the Eritrean campaign was known as the Banda Bakr.

32. The only significant Italian incursion was up the Blue Nile and cost 400 Italian lives. With problems of transport and supply, they withdrew (Woodward, *Sudan 1898-1989. The Unstable State*, 1990, pp. 59-61).

33. In 1938 there were 100 pupils and 3 teachers in Gedaref Girls' School and 135 by 1943, with 5 teachers. By 1946 there were 84 pupils and 2 teachers in Gedaref A school and 135 and 4 teachers in Gedaref B.

would catch fire; the rain would wash away whole walls; the fence would fall down. It was an unending struggle but the girls continued coming and the Abu Sinn *nazir* sent one of his daughters to the Girls' Training College in the hope of encouraging the inhabitants to give more active support.[34]

It was also a place for tea-parties, one of which I remember particularly. I was invited to the mistresses' house,[35] right in the centre of the town, where for once I was aware of neighbours close by and not the shut in feeling of so many walled yards. One of the mistresses was a Copt[36] who had adopted Sudanese dress and many of the local customs without changing her religion. She and her fat, cheerful mother, who reminded me of many an Anglo-Indian I had met, had settled down very happily here. They all came back to tea with me one day in the D.C.'s house and had no diffidence about noticing and commenting on everything they saw and enquiring about everything else.

> The only picturesque touch was going to a garden made by a *sagia* from a well. The owner gave me the one rose in the garden and some custard apples. The headmistress, a great fat lump, giggled so she embarrased us all. There was also a tea-party in the house of a *wahabi*, a dear old man who ran the post office.[37]
>
> ... had tea with the *nazir* of the Abu Sinn, *sheikh* Mohammad, in his garden, which some Turk or Egyptian had planted in the old days. Apart from the *sheikh* there were only the English people of the place, the 3 D.C.s, the Agricultural Inspector and his old Anglo-Indian wife. It was rather dull as we had all met before. There had been riotous dinner parties at [Balfour's] house every night, including two or three army officers training the S.D.F ... also arranged for the headmistress of the girls' school to entertain the Governor-General's wife[38] to tea.[39]
>
> Like Kassala there was a lot of European entertaining—a spare woman was an unusual visitor. Very riotous bridge once or twice, being shown over the hospital by a doctor who fancied himself as a lady-killer ... 2 vapid officers, one fierce and bristling and stupid, the other with a silky voice and long eyelashes who talked about the fighting he wanted to do. He had been an

34. By sending his daughters to Training College, the Abū Sinn *nazir* gave support to the school 'which is considered very enlightened of him' [11.11.1941]. One *nāzir* in Gedaref married three schoolmistresses, all of whom continued to work after marriage (S.A.D. 606/8/97).
35. 11.11.41, also 7.3.47 (Diaries and S.A.D. 657/7/55).
36. Nataliya Christoforos (Bibi); 1941 Gedaref; By 1945 Wad Medani B Girls' School.
37. In Jan 1945 Dr Beasley visited Gedaref after Kassala.
38. The Governor-General's wife, Lady Huddleston, had been in the Sudan for a long time twenty years previously, but did not understand Arabic.
39. Two of the three D.C.s in Gedaref in February 1947 were E.A. Balfour and N.S. Mitchell Innes, and the Agricultural Inspector was L.E. Humphreys. N.S. Mitchell Innes; 28.12.37 First appointment; 15.2.46-47 D.C. Gedaref. L.E. Humphreys, M.C., N.D.A., Dip. Agric (Lancs); 3.11.24 First appointment; retired by September 1947.

[Aide de Camp] at the Palace the first time I lunched there. I had forgotten him—to his manifest displeasure [11.11.41].

Each time that I was in Gedaref there were a number of British officials in the place, for, even when the war was over, there was movement to and from occupied Eritrea while throughout those years and afterwards the district proved useful for a 'swords into ploughshares' policy. The land was sufficiently level for experiments in mechanical crop production to utilise the wide, empty tracts for growing sunflower seeds and ground nuts.

## 4. Red Sea Hills—a trip to Tokar[40]

Fertile development might be planned in these parts, [the Butana], but further east the desolation of the Red Sea Hills suggested that only cacti, aloes and their kindred could rise up anywhere near. Oddly enough, however, between the mountains and the sea and some hundred miles or so south of Port Sudan the district around Tokar produced a particularly good type of cotton and in a settlement of some size with all the usual administrative offices a girls' school was required. Modern jargon would probably describe most of what we drove on in the Sudan as 'non- roads' and of these the way to Tokar reached the extreme of the type. I generally managed to strike other hazards also, of which one on my first visit was, happily, never repeated. This was March 1942,[41] when petrol was scarce and vehicles generally in rather poor condition. Before making a final plan there was some acrimonious telegraphing by the D.C.[42] to ensure that the Education Department would be responsible for the mileage account. When that was settled, I was told, that I could be fitted in with another official going from Suakin, and that I must therefore catch the Port Sudan train and go via Atbara to Sollum, where I could join a local train for Suakin.[43]

40. Dr Beasley made several trips to Tokar, in March 1942, and possibly in November 1946 and February/March 1947.
41. Dr Beasley began her trip to Tokar on 3.3.42.
42. Arthur Charles Beaton, C.M.G., 4N. (b.22.8.1904- ). Educated at Leeds Grammar and Keble College, Oxford; 11.9.27 First appointment; 1927-30 Education Department; 1930-35 Mongalla; 1935-38 Darfur; 1.11.38-1945 Kassala, D.C. Red Sea District, based at Tokar; 1940-41 Governor-General's Temporary Commission as Bimbashi in S.D.F. (Meadowforce); 1945-47 Equatoria, Deputy Governor; 1950-52 Director, Local Government; 1952-53 Deputy Civil Secretary; 1953 Acting Civil Secretary; 1954 Permanent Under-Secretary, Ministry of Interior; 1954 retired; 1955-61 Assistant Area General manager, National Coal Board; 1961-67 Civil Defence Officer, N.C.B.
43. The railway from Atbara to Suakin was built in 1904-5. Port Sudan was officially opened in 1909.

'Equally important', ran the message from the Commissioner,[44] 'was to bring all my trek kit,[45] as I should be staying in empty resthouses'.

This year the north wind had left us early and the journey was uncomfortably hot until at night, when we were up in the Red Sea Hills.

> The mountains are very barren, not perhaps quite so jagged and fantastic as the ones near Kassala, but very uninviting.

By the time we reached my destination, that relief was over and we were back on a flat, sandy plain with that smell of absolute heat, so difficult to describe but so characteristic of such country.

> It was too hot for dinner ... I spent the evening talking to a young officer I had met at Abu Guta. He had been in charge of a prisoners-of-war camp on the scheme, growing wheat, and felt it was the best kind of job to have, if he couldn't be with his regiment. He had been through the evacuation of Dunkirk and his right hand shook unceasingly.
>
> The next morning was better. I was interested to see the camps, prisoners, R.A.F. and so on, which had been tucked away in the hills near the railway. Samit(?) had been an R.A.F. camp much talked about during the Eritrean Campaign.

### 4.1 Sollum junction

Sollum was nothing more than a railway junction, with a dirty, untidy collection of huts away from the railway and made either of grass or petrol tins. While I was looking at this depressing prospect and still rather jaded from a night in the train, my servant arrived in a state of great agitation. All this trek kit of mine, which I had been told was so necessary, had been put off the train at a station in the heart of the Hills. Someone had mistaken Sinkat for Sollum. I went up to the signal box and broke all the regulations

---

44. Edmund Osborn Springfield, O.B.E., M.C., 4N., Order of Menelik, 3rd Class (b.2.7.1892- ); Educated at Uppingham; 1914-16 Middlesex Regiment; 1916-18 Norfolk Regiment and Machine Gun Corps (Belgium, France, Italy, Austria, Egypt); 14.4.23 First appointment; 1923-24 Red Sea; 1924-25 Assistant Private Secretary to Governor-General; 1926-27 Private Secretary; 1927-30 Khartoum; 1930-34 Comptroller, Palace; 10.10.34-44 Kassala, Port Sudan—Suakin—Tokar Administration, 1936 Commissioner, Port Sudan; 1944 retired; 1944- British Council.

45. For example, on Dr Beasley's trip to Gedaref in February 1947 her luggage consisted of '2 suitcases full of clothes and sheets etc., a briefcase with books and papers, an enamel bowl with leather case for washing, a roll of bedding, i.e. mattress, pillow, sheets, blankets, in a waterproof sheet, a camp bed, a folding table, a folding chair, 4 long poles for my mosquito net, 2 large strong wooden boxes full of pots and pans and food of tinned and dried varieties and candles and a primus stove, a pail with a lamp in it. My servant also had a bundle of bedding and a basket of odds and ends' (S.A.D. 657/7/55).

by a personal phone call to the D.C.[46] at Sinkat, who promised to try and find a lorry to bring my *impedimenta* direct to Suakin. It was fairly breezy in the signal box and I hung about there waiting for a message, but the Suakin train came and departed and still no news. I did not know the district and after the previous warning thought it would be imprudent to go further without more than my small night-stop bag and my servant's roll of bedding. As we waited, the breeze faded and the heat grew. There was one plain wooden chair in the signal box and the signal man and I took turns to sit on it.

> When I left the signal box, the signal man snatched it back. Sometimes he returned it to me, sometimes I sat on my case, sometimes on my servant's roll of bedding on the platform. The signalman took advantage of the opportunity to ask me to arrange for a school in his village, so that his son could teach there. I said, there was a war on: no new schools.

Outside the hot air shimmered up all round the rails, gleaming in the reflected heat, stretched tantalisingly to places, which we could not reach. About eleven o'clock, the D.C. phoned through from Sinkat to say he had found a lorry but it was in such a precarious state he doubted, if it could make the journey. We decided, that, as the Suakin train had gone, it would be better for him to put my baggage on the next goods train, which, [he said], was leaving Sinkat in about half an hour. I could then join it and go on to Port Sudan. That phrase 'half an hour' haunted me through one of the longest days I have ever spent. The D.C. had started it and then the stationmaster, the signal man and the booking clerk went on heartening me up, with me in a state of wishful believing to the end in their '*nuss sa'a*'. Afterwards I decided it was more fundamental than just encouraging me. On a line where a passenger train comes through only once a week, 'some time today' and 'in half an hour' could have very similar meanings.

In addition to this I made yet another discovery of considerable importance. I came to understand the process of 'just sitting', which had often made me impatient in dealing with people, when I forgot the moral of Kipling's poem about the man who tried to hustle the East. Having decided that the least uncomfortable position was to sit on my servant's bedding roll on the outside platform of the signal box but propped up against the door, I sat and looked over an empty landscape, where nothing moved except on two occasions, when a tribesman appeared out of the heat and loped across on his camel to the village huts, his lean figure and fuzzy mop of hair a dark silhouette against the fawn background. Gradually I came to a state of being I had not known before. I was neither asleep nor unconscious but it

---

46. C. de Bunsen, D.C. Sinkat 'would let me know' if he had found the luggage.

was as if any mental activity had been switched off and I remained passive in a state of timelessness. I had reached, no doubt, a valuable point of understanding but Western habits intruded in the end. By one o'clock I was very aware that I had neither eaten or drunk since a small breakfast about seven.

The Sudanese are generous to a fault with their hospitality but in such an out of the way place the entertaining of an unexpected guest was doubtless too much of a problem. My servant had long since disappeared but probably in consultation with him, the station officials had considered the matter, for my reverie was interrupted by the booking clerk, who asked me, if I knew there were some British soldiers encamped on the far side of the village. Such a thought had never occurred to me, although I might have known, that railway junctions usually have a guard. He escorted me to their tidy, wooden huts, still re- iterating the warning that the train might come in half an hour. Naturally, only a small number of men were stationed there and the sergeant-major, who met me, looked as if he might rush away to study the security regulations, which probably did not deal with the contingency of a stray English-woman wandering in from the desert with some tale of having missed the train. He never really relaxed, although he was very kind in coping with my needs. Their meal was finished but I was given cheese and biscuits and good N.A.A.F.I. tea. Remembering my instructions, I retreated soon to my perch in hope but still the train did not come.

Presently the palely Egyptian-looking checking clerk turned up again and pressed a couple of stale oranges[47] into my hand while enquiring diffidently, if I would help him with his English. This proved a much more effective way of forgetting the heat. Towards four o'clock a cheery soul of indeterminate nationality arrived from the [soldiers'] canteen and offered me some very welcome tea. Then one or two soldiers drifted down. 'They had heard,' they said, 'that there was an Englishwoman about'. They were very polite and friendly but, I am afraid, a bit disappointed. Yet even for something younger and prettier and snappier a day in a signal box in that temperature would hardly have been a beauty treatment. It was 6.15 p.m., when at length the train arrived and I then with my luggage in front of me jolted into Port Sudan in the guard's van,

> ... in company with a lot of Tommies who were going to Port Sudan to the pictures.

---

47. Oranges were not for sale in Sudan at the time. Only the Railway Catering Department had them.

## 4.2 Port Sudan

I made a half-hearted attempt to phone the D.C. when I arrived. Being unlucky, I went to the hotel.

I thought with joy of the luxurious night I should have in a comfortable room at the hotel after an excellent dinner and after that I would deal with authority. Authority, however, forestalled me. Just as I was stepping into the bath, the Commissioner[48] rang up to say that he had heard of my arrival and I must go on to Suakin that night. It is not policy for a woman official to plead fatigue or weakness.

The question of luggage and servants was awkward as I had been obedient enough to bring everything. Just as I was going down to dinner, he phoned again. My servant was not to be found and the luggage problem was too much for him.

My compliance this time was rewarded, for in the end through some devious hitches he could not arrange for me to go until the next morning. My curious day was followed by the common-place blessing of a wonderful night's sleep [in Port Sudan].

## 4.3 Tokar

The Governor's[49] lorry which took me right through to Tokar provided perhaps the most straightforward of all my trips along this stretch and from it my first view of Suakin was unforgettable.

I started about 8 a.m. Port Sudan was rather sticky, but it was nice to see ships in the harbour. Port Sudan's gardens looked brighter than I remembered [from 1937]. It had grown too. There seemed a lot more grey, shabby, wooden shacks. The big camps outside the town were new. We were checked out by the police on the edge of Port Sudan and about two hours later we reported to the police again in Suakin.

The road ran for an hour or more out of Port Sudan through a dreary waste on either side which was too salty to produce the meanest plant and was too far from the sea for there to be anything else to look at. Then, when I was beginning to feel a bit restive, Suakin emerged gradually out of the mirage.

It was delightful, but tumbledown. The village street had storeyed houses but rather poor-looking shops. There were glimpses of side streets with Moorish casements jutting out. Then we came to the end of the street and the rest of the

48. E.O. Springfield ('how he knew I was there I can't think'). wanted Dr Beasley to go to Suakin that night 'in order to go to Tokar in a car about 5 a.m.'.
49. J.M. Humphrey.

town was on an island ... We went through an old gateway past the police
post.

There was an uneven cluster of tall white houses against the blue of a sea of
which the colour itself seemed to be sparkling. Just near the causeway was a
solitary Beja woman in a bright red *tobe*. I did not have time to explore it
this time but, when I did come to stay there, it fully satisfied my
expectations of this impression at any rate from a visual point of view.

I do not remember so vivid a picture on other journeys but always the
road after this defied all standards of comparison. I was travelling on one
occasion[50] in a remarkable vehicle, hired in the *suq*, the body of which must
have been put together locally from odd pieces. It was of no accepted size
but small, as lorries go, and with ordinary wheels, not the balloon type that
plunge so surprisingly over the sand. One feature appealed to me strongly;
wooden doors had been fixed onto the cab, where I sat with the driver, and
this gave me something to hold onto without scorching my fingers.
Generally the metal of a door was too hot to grasp even over the bumpiest
tracks and one was tossed about. I once wore a patch of skin off my back,
when I had not taken the precaution to wedge myself in with coats or
cushions. This conveyance had another novelty in possessing neither crank
nor self-starter, as I had always thought of those mechanisms. The driver
pushed a tool which looked like a chisel or screwdriver through a hole in the
dashboard, pedalled a tune on the accelerator and with a roar and a splutter
we always managed to go.

The first part of this journey was deceptive, for after Suakin we sat down
by the roadside for breakfast. I was filled on this bright spring morning, as
so often, by the uplifting exhilaration of this outdoor life. There were a few
discouraging thorn trees and one or two dry plants on the ground but
enough apparently to attract several birds, who made a cheerful noise,
although nothing in these parts really sings. I could just glimpse the sea in
the distance and feel the freshness of the air, a bit softer than the desert.
After this things deteriorated. As the morning drew on, it clouded over. We
lost sight of the sea and for most of the way there was nothing to relieve the
dullness of the outlook but frightening barren mountains in the west, but
even these were left behind after a time and the landscape was empty. A
solitary inn sign, featuring a ship and swinging by the roadside, surprised
me at one point,[51] as it seemed to have no relation with anything round
about and led to my irrelevant imaginings of Chesterton's 'Flying Inn'.

---

50. In February 1947.
51. According to Dr Beasley's diary this sign was on a coffee-house between Port Sudan and
Suakin. The mountains to the west were 'some 5,000 feet high and where nothing ever grows.

Eventually I was able to make out a tumble-down coffee shop some distance away, built mostly of straw.

> There were two broken down lorries with the owners camped beside them. They could not mend them and were afraid someone else might steal the spare parts. I believe this happened all along this road.

Then I was conscious of the road only, for the result of the good cotton crop in Tokar had been to make a bad track still worse, since it had been ploughed up by the continual passing of the heavy lorries transporting the bales to Port Sudan.

> We sat under an umbrella tree for lunch. At least I did. The servants sat the other side of the lorry.
> The only saving grace was a breeze off the sea, which kept it from being too desperately hot. There had been a big tribal meeting of the Beni Amer and I met a group of them on their camels. One camel had a large *birsh* shade[52] over it sheltering a woman and child. Most of the women[53] wore vivid tobes, bright red, orange, sometimes green ... The sand was a more than usually fine quality which had drifted into small dunes.

There were also rocks and sudden bends and patches of unforeseen sand but the fun did not really begin until about twelve miles outside Tokar. It took us two hours to do this last bit.[54] For hundreds of yards in either direction, when we left what might claim to be the recognised track, there were ruts and wheel-marks of vehicles trying to find a firm footing. The lorries with their great balloon tyres just seemed to plunge straight in and sway through with a tremendous flurry of dust, like some clumsy bather splashing through the surf.

> We met quite a few of these lorries in 1947[55] which had its advantages, because it is a very lonely road otherwise.

But we had no such resources[56] and were obliged to attempt all the devices of going diagonally across corrugations or following someone else's tracks; in fact, when we rounded two *gozes* at an angle of 45° because the driver

---

52. *Hawdaj*, howdah.
53. 'A number of the [Beja women] have rings through their noses. Enormous things about the size of a finger and thumb closed in a circle. The piece through the nose is thin but the rest spreads out to an inch or more in width.'
54. February 1947.
55. On Dr Beasley's first visit [March 1942] she 'did not see any cotton growing. There was a certain amount being loaded on to the light railway which took it to the sea at Trinkitat for shipment.' In 1946-47 'suddenly the tugs and barges were not available and cotton had to be taken away on great lorries with enormous double wheels'.
56. In March 1942.

had accelerated too violently, I decided we had essayed every method except careful plodding.

> The second time I remonstrated and he replied 'That's all right. I'm very strong. I can hold on to the wheel'. It never seemed to occur to him that it would have been me who went through the windscreen.
>     The drill, when you get stuck in sand is to clear away the sand with a shovel or one's hands then everyone pushes as the driver starts the engine. If you give a lift to a number of chaps they will help you with the pushing. The other school of thought—if you keep your lorry light by not giving lifts, you are not so likely to stick. The little boy who was with us was small enough to get right under the car and clear away the sand there. We had, of course, no shovel [March 1947].

While we were very badly stuck at one time, a miserable looking herdsman with a few goats, appeared from nowhere in particular and asked for a drink, which we gave him from the *zamzamia* hanging beside the car. Having taken a good swig the old man moved off. There was only my servant, the driver and boy small enough to get right under the vehicle and scrape away the sand. They were all vociferous in their rage at this ingratitude. It is a curious and notable point that only in these parts did one meet with such unhelpfulness, and many stories told of the surliness and sometimes cruelty of the nomads of the East. Another time in almost identical circumstances the 'Fuzzy' merely replied, 'I have an appointment' and, having slaked his thirst, marched off into the desert, driving his scruffy beast ahead of him. Admittedly the Arabic phrase does not sound so grand but that is the literal translation.

The favourite tale about Tokar was, that it was so dusty, that one had to eat meals out of a drawer, closing it quickly after every mouthful. I was not reduced to these lengths but as a place it certainly had no visual charm. The D.C.[57] at that time had been valiantly trying to cheer it up by having the houses colour-washed. It made an astonishing difference to the place, which looked infinitely more drab when I visited it at a later date[58] and the idea had been forgotten.

> All the streets are nothing but sand ... The resthouse was furnished and comfortable.[59] ... I was sleeping in the rest-house, which had been very comfortably prepared for me and feeding with the D.C. and family. So apart from using my things for breakfast that morning, near Suakin, all the stuff I

57. A.C. Beaton 'kept a careful eye on the school' [March 1942]. It was he who tried to improve Tokar 'by hopefully planting trees' and colour-washing the houses—some 'attractive beige and green, a reasonable blue, or a horrible pink'.
58. In February 1947.
59. In March 1942.

had lugged from Omdurman was not wanted at all. I could well have eaten my breakfast in a simpler manner.[60]

The school in its beginning had a definite character of its own.

The school was not too bad. It was housed in two houses knocked together. They had round roofs, which was someone's bright idea for preventing dust collecting, but they looked a bit like tombs.

It had been started by an ex-schoolmistress, the wife of an [accountant] in the *merkaz*, and had been sufficiently successful for the Education Department to send another sister, who was a teacher, to help her. The Headmistress was old-fashioned and motherly[61] and there was a pleasant, muddly, dame-school quality about the place, which seemed to encourage the reluctant inhabitants of Tokar. Unfortunately the Headmistress died in childbirth a year later and the school, of which she had been so proud, became regarded as a punishment station by mistresses from other parts, who felt completely cut off there. They could never stimulate more than twenty or thirty children to attend.[62] They were bored and therefore the staff had to be constantly changed. The notables of Tokar wrote once and asked for a nice motherly woman to run the school and stay for some years. Their request was all too sensible but women of the calibre of the founder of the school were not easy to come by. Even on such small numbers it was worth continuing since gradually a few of the girls from the local nomad tribes began to attend, as their fathers took to cultivation in the Delta,[63] and this then provided a nucleus for spreading [education] over the region in the years to come.

I had had a terrific complaint from the notables of Tokar about the way the Government was dealing with the school. I arrived on Saturday and had to be back in Khartoum for a special meeting on 'female circumcision' on the Thursday and the only train which could do this left Port Sudan on the Monday. I therefore presumed the D.C. Tokar[64] who knew all this and knew my haste as well, would have arranged for me to see some of the *sheikh*s but

60. In February 1947.
61. The Headmistress had two small boys of her own.
62. The attendance in March 1942 was small but fairly steady. 1943 36 pupils, 1946 38 pupils, 2 teachers.
63. Baraka Delta.
64. Andrew Paul, 4N (b.19.1.1907-d.1985); Educated at Glenalmond and Peterhouse, Cambridge; 10.12.29 First appointment; 1929-31 Kassala; 1931-34 White Nile; 1935-36 Northern; 1936-38 seconded to Legal Department; 1.11.1938-45 Blue Nile, D.C. at Geteina (1940) and Dueim (1941), seconded for duty concerning Jebel Auliya compensation, 1942 D.C. El Hassaheisa; 1.4.45-48 Kassala, 1947 D.C. Tokar; 1948-50 Upper Nile; 1950-54 Deputy Governor, Kassala; 1954-55 Governor, Kassala; 1955 retired; 1955- editor, Sudan Diocesan Review. Author and authority on the Beja.

no. He did not think there was anyone I could profitably talk to but he asked the two mistresses to tea and he had arranged for a bridge party that evening, in the house of an agricultural inspector.[65] He said I must be off at the latest by eleven the next morning and as school didn't start till eight, I had come all that way for a social chat with the schoolmistresses and less than three hours in the school. Hopeful signs indicated that the school should not be closed (there were 21 children in one class and 4 in another which made it worth keeping open) but moved to better buildings. The two new mistresses were making friends with the mothers and one had relations in the town, which helped. We left matters for a fuller inspection in the autumn.[66]

On the whole the people there were not particularly interested but my rather unfavourable impression on my first visit[67] may have been due to their having other matters to occupy them at the time. There had been a big, tribal meeting of the Beni Amer, a very large clan,[68] which stretches over the frontier into Eritrea; a holy man had come down from there and parties in his honour were taking place everywhere. People had evidently gathered from near and far. I saw them trotting along on their camels, some with their women under plaited grass covers, others in little groups racing one another and apparently showing off. Seeing these wild men tearing round on their mounts, it was fairly obvious that they would not settle readily for the kind of education for their girls, which we had evolved in Omdurman. Their independence of spirit did not extend to their womenfolk, for they were probably more conservative on this point than any of the tribes in the country. Increasing contact with less harsh ways of living might tend to break up the nomadic pattern, since they were beginning to realise, that, when the rains failed, help could be brought from other provinces, and thus the advantages of permanent cultivation were manifest to people with no margin of security. There was no shortage of cultivable land in the Sudan, but it was not to be found among their rocky hills.

65. William Allan Porter, N.D.A., Dip. Agric (Glasg); 3.10.25 First appointment; By 1947 he was Senior Inspector of Agriculture based in Tokar, or S. Hills, B.A. Agric (Cantab); 9.12.46 First appointment; 1947 Inspector of Agriculture based in Tokar.
66. In February 1947.
67. On Dr Beasley's first visit in March 1942, the local *sheikh*s were not very enthusiastic about girls' education '... I was not invited to any tea-parties'.
68. The Beja group, the Banī 'Āmir, who occupy the areas of Tokar and south into Eritrea.

## 4.4 Suakin

On the way back from my first trip[69] I had the good fortune to stay at Suakin. I left Tokar soon after lunch in a smallish lorry, which was due in Port Sudan for repairs. The authorities were trusting, that it might stumble through the sixty miles to Suakin and, if it could be coaxed no further, I might find a place on some of the commercial transport, which plied more frequently along that last forty miles. Having this in mind made me hesitate, when we came upon a broken-down lorry about an hour after leaving Tokar. It was so crowded with passengers, that I felt very selfish being accompanied only by my servant and a police driver, but with our vehicle in parlous condition we obviously could not take them all. With the stranded company was another policeman with a leather bag, probably containing mail, and a rifle. He and my driver had a lengthy consultation and finally we arranged to take him and all the women, about half a dozen or more.

They made a gay and colourful load, for the women here did not favour the faded indigo prevalent among the village women over most of the country. A little higher in the social scale and, when able to afford 'best clothes', a white or cream material was used, which varied between the coarse homespun and the fine muslins and even silks of the rich and well-dressed. The coarsest homespun was obligatory for mourning and suggested a connection with the Biblical sackcloth. In these eastern districts vivid colours, green, orange and bright red predominating, were the normal wear for all the women I saw. Crammed into the back of my lorry they suggested a herbaceous border and some of the younger ones were in every way flowerlike. The tribes here[70] tended to have fine feature and a slim figure with practically no trace of negroid features. Some of the women wore enormous rings in their noses, made of thin gold admittedly but at least half an inch broad, and fastened through the septum by a tiny bar. Just before we reached Suakin, their companions caught us up and my responsibilities were over.

> Suakin is a very old port, dating back some centuries. It was used by the Arab slave traders and the houses were tall and built after the Moorish tradition with carved wood and balconies. It is falling rapidly into decay because it is much too expensive to keep it in repair for a showpiece.[71]

Even then[72] the empty, rotting Moorish casements were unpeopled and nothing more than a romantic backdrop to a drama that had ended, and

---

69. March 1942.
70. Mostly Beja, with some Rashaida groups living in this area of Sudan.
71. Beasley, Ina, *The Verandah at Suakin*, unpublished typescript, (S.A.D. Beasley papers).
72. By 1942.

today these remains of a former glory have fallen apart and left no substance. No doubt it was right, that the old slave port should lose its traffic but it is sad, that nothing should now be left of its 'Arabian Nights' flavour. Magnificent though it must have been in the days of its prime with the storeyed wooden houses designed on an expansive scale and beautifully proportioned, their carved balconies and shutters jutting into the narrow streets, but I was not to be translated into this decaying fascination.[73] I was housed in the *muhafza*, where Kitchener[74] had had his headquarters in the early days of the Condominium. This too was a most impressive building with wide staircases sweeping up both sides, as soon as one entered the gate [way from the street], and carved arches all round the landing.[75] It was not so vast as Dongola Palace but enormous enough to make me feel very small on my own, as I ate my dinner in a great dining room and wondered, if the mighty Victorian sideboard was really part of the furniture, which Kitchener was reputed to have designed for the place. Everywhere was full of cats and at night, when I chased some out down the wide passage, I suddenly came to an open door leading onto a roof with easy access down and, as far as I could see, across to most of the roofs in the street. The view really underlined the authentic note of Tales from the East. At [my] end of the verandah was a flight of stone steps leading down between the cellars to the water[front] and shut in by a spiked sort of Traitor's Gate. The moon, I may add, was gibbous.

I locked the door, not at all concerned as to whether it was my servant's way of re-entry. Servants usually went off after dinner was cleared away, unless they were required for any special duties. On leaving the lorry I had noticed a quick and surreptitious few words with one of the young women, we had had as passengers. I am not accusing him of making an assignation; she may have been giving him news of a prayer-meeting, if one may put a

73. Red Sea Province 1908 '... at Suakin there are at present two private schools where the daughters of the townspeople are taught and this might form the basis of a large school for female education.' In 1909 there were 15 *kuttāb*s in Suakin, also in Tokar, Akik and Adobana but they were of little educational value; of these 11 were for boys (185 in attendance) and 4 for girls (151 in attendance).' ... I venture to suggest that the time has now arrived when female education should be provided for'(S.A.D. 657/1/12). By 1943 there were only 317 pupils in four government girls' schools in Kassala Province.

74. Suakin, originally an Ottoman port, was at one end of the east-west trade route from Darfur and was an important port for slave trade and pilgrims to Mecca. In February 1891 an Anglo-Egyptian expedition from Suakin routed 'Uthmān Diqna (a Suakinese of part Beja descent who led the Beja forces for the Mahdiyya) but did not defeat him. He was eventually captured and died a prisoner in Wadi Halfa in 1926.

75. The *muhafza*, which was used as a rest-house for Government officials, had a landing 'with rooms and passages leading off in all directions. A long, wide verandah stretched round two sides of the building ... I had the rest-house to myself and at night the servants went out, I discovered.'

*zikkr*[76] into that category. Certainly there was no-one in the house to disturb my sound sleep on its big, cool verandah.

The unusual but wholly enchanting view of a gray day, soft sky and pearly sea was what I woke to. Over the railing I could look down into water so clear, that I could watch in detail enormous numbers of fish in every direction. There were ordinary-looking ones, glinting and flashing, as they swam slowly by or suddenly darted away; there were spotted ones of all manner of colours; others were brilliant in broad stripes; and at intervals came shoals of very small multicoloured ones like quick flights of butterflies.[77] Then unexpectedly but to complete my joy two flamingoes rose up from the edge of the harbour.

Across the water picturesque decay had to some extent been ousted by modern efficiency in the shape of the unsightly erections of the quarantine station

> where all the pilgrims have to stay in transit ... with its own noisy electric light plant ... On the way back my police driver stopped by two frightful looking vagrants to enquire if they had escaped from the quarantine. They pretended not to understand.

Thousands of pilgrims made their way to Mecca by this route, sometimes trudging across Africa for years before they arrived here, but all were obliged to undergo a medical examination at this centre. It seemed a far cry from the earlier [slave] traffic when the ships went out from this same harbour, not carrying the devout, who were realising the summit of their spiritual ambitions, but laden with human cargo for the markets across the Red Sea.

## 4.5 Suakin to Port Sudan

Nothing very remarkable ever happened on the last stage of the journey except that we stopped one hot afternoon[78] to buy a water melon from a 'Fuzzy' by the roadside. Considering how many excellent melons I must have eaten in the Sudan, I must have been especially thirsty to remember it so vividly. This time I had come back from Tokar in a battered old tourer

---

76. A *dhikr*, a Sufi gathering for a particular method of worshipping God in order to obtain spiritual ecstasy (*wajd*) by the constant repetition of His Name either mentally or aloud, and chanting of songs and prayers, which may result in an orgy of ecstatic excitement, trances etc. (Trimingham, J.S., *Islam in the Sudan*, pp. 212-217).

77. In March 1942 'I had missed a fishing trip the afternoon before. They had gone out in a rowing boat and caught twenty three large fish'.

78. The last stage of the journey was from Suakin to Port Sudan. On this occasion in February 1947, Dr Beasley was travelling in a vehicle with balloon tyres, which were particularly suitable for sandy terrain.

belonging to a Greek cotton broker. He was a rather seedy-looking little man but was probably very rich, and certainly was a most skilful driver. Nevertheless his particular style had its unnerving aspects. To begin with he smoked incessantly and drove nonchalantly over sand drifts and ruts dividing the work of his hands between striking matches and guiding the steering-wheel, while bending his head to light the cigarette.

We only stuck two or three times over the *gozes* on the first part of the road and then there was also a cotton lorry or two nearby floundering happily along the tracks. One of them would come up behind us and give a gentle shove, while the Greek engaged in some smart footwork on the pedals and we were off.

> My luggage came back in the lorry I had come in and this was to go ahead so we could pick up the pieces. Of course we soon found my lorry firmly stuck and the man on the cotton lorry also helped him off. I thought he would be in the sand all night but he raced us in the end.

He appeared to know all the lorry drivers on the route and our only stops after this were, when we met or overtook one of these, and he went for a quick talk presumably on his affairs.

> At one o'clock we stopped at a coffee house and I ate my packet of sandwiches. He insisted on giving me handfuls of chocolates and toffees, from an enormous tin of Macintosh he had bought in Tokar. Things like that don't seem to come my way ... About 4 o'clock we reported to the police post at Suakin.

We drove round to the sea-front, where a row of rather tumble down sheds lined the edge of the beach.

> We did not cross to the island itself but there was a great fawn coloured palace looking out to sea at the beginning of the causeway. The windows were all shuttered, the balconies broken and the carving falling away, but there was still dignity in its ruin and a certain amount of beauty in its line ... definitely evocative of past splendours, as we, in our less picturesque shabbiness hurried round to the battered and unbeautiful sheds [February 1947].

In the middle of the day they looked no worse than slightly disreputable but at night they could have taken on a very sinister aspect, and fitted admirably into the whole background of a cloak and dagger adventure, which Suakin suggested in all its corners. We picked up a friend, another trader going to Port Sudan, and it was after that we bought this very welcome melon. The 'Fuzzy' cut it for us with a great curved knife, probably used for skinning, which looked far too ferocious an implement for the flesh of such a mild fruit.

We arrived in Port Sudan soon after five o'clock and I stayed in the hotel. But the dirt. I could hardly bear to touch the clothes I took off ... I never get over the wonder of doing these trips. Mentally I'm always a little agape when they are over.

## 4.6 Port Sudan

In the days of its prime Suakin was a great trading centre and it was the foundation of Port Sudan,[79] which led to its lingering death. The comparison leapt to the eye and all other senses immediately. Port Sudan came under the administration of [Sudan] Railways and thus in its own way perpetuated the ethos of Atbara, to the financial benefit of the whole country. My first contact with it was many years before[80] I thought of coming to work there. Even in 1930 I was struck by the ordered efficiency, rather soul-less, compared to other ports I had known. Near the docks there was none of the warm, colourful life that exudes from La Joliette in Marseilles. I had been told that Port Said had been cleaned up, but the waterside had not in those days had the face-lift it afterwards received. Passengers going ashore in Egypt were a target for beggars, *gulli- gulli* boys and robed and specious vendors of amber necklaces 'straight from the desert'. No-one in Port Sudan importuned in this way. I remarked on the absence of beggars and was told by an indignant official that there were no beggars in the Sudan—'We look after our people'. To a large extent I found subsequently that this was true. Indeed during this first brief call no-one demanded gifts. On the contrary a convict working in the little public garden presented my small daughter[81] with a flower, which he picked for her.

Naturally the docks dominated the lay-out of the place, the railway coming to its terminal on the quayside and the houses placed some distance back from the harbour. Unromantic as it was, like many other bits of utilitarian planning, it had much to offer in the way of bodily comfort. By trekking standards the hotel was the last word in luxury with soft beds, private bathrooms, electric light and fans. One could eat on the verandah or sit with a cup of tea after a strenuous day watching the ships and enjoying the breeze which always sprang up about four o'clock. Sometimes it was only a heated blast but it was fresh and moved the staleness accumulated in the morning. The temperature was never bracing, but the climate was at its worst during such months as July and August, when the humidity, never

79. Port Sudan was founded between 1906 and 1909.
80. Dr Beasley visited Port Sudan *en route* for Burma in 1930 and again in 1937.
81. Ruth.

much below 70[%], felt as if it were at saturation point. There was, however, a large swimming pool on the edge of the harbour, where we could float in the very salty water and look right out to sea. Fishing and sailing were an extra delight. To turn the other direction was to have yet another glimpse of the drab contours of the hills, that backed the barren wastes around the town. I might admire the courage of an enterprise which had forced the success of an unnatural growth on such an inhospitable shore but it did not set my imagination aflame. Only by a stern concentration on its commercial statistics could one come to appreciate its value.

> On my return from Tokar I had lunch with the Commissioner.[82] His two storey house reminded me of a pleasant suburban residence, very comfortably furnished. All the people I was introduced to seemed to have heard of my Sollum junction adventure.[83]
> It was a sparkling day ... In the afternoon the Commissioner[84] and his French wife (in Brittany all through the war) came to take me for a drive to Flamingo Bay, where there were odd boats, and fishy smells and piles of mother of pearl and sea slugs (Chinese food) and one or two flamingoes.[85]

During the war, of course, education was at a standstill here but after the various small excitements in the Red Sea, the town returned to its original functions but it was never again the calm, ordered port of call with passengers from the liners amused by the leaping 'Fuzzies', who unloaded the cargoes, and not always so amused by notices requesting ladies not to go ashore in abbreviated costumes. I forget the exact wording. The 'Fuzzies' were still there after the war; in fact their numbers had increased and they constituted a special problem, which had to be tackled separately.

The ordinary girls' school made rapid strides once it started up again in a house which had benefited from Army occupation. It was a double storeyed building made of coral blocks and had large, airy rooms with verandahs upstairs and quarters downstairs for the mistresses. When commandeered by the Forces two bathrooms and electric light had been put in, additions much appreciated by the staff, when it was handed back. In fact compared with many Port Sudan was a popular posting, for there was plenty of

82. E.O. Springfield was Commissioner, Port Sudan in 1942.
83. March 1942.
84. By 1947 the Commissioner, Port Sudan was Edmund William Thomas, 4N. (b.11.5.1901- ); Educated at Edinburgh Academy, Clifton and Corpus Christi, Cambridge; 19.10.23 First appointment; 1923-26 seconded as Secretary to H.M.'s Minister at Addis Ababa; 1926-28 Red Sea; 1929-30 Fung ; 1930-35 Berber; 1935 Northern; 1935-39 Kassala; 1939-40 Kordofan; 1940-49 Kassala, 1944-48 Commissioner, Red Sea District, based Port Sudan; 1948-50 Deputy Civil Secretary; 1950 retired.
85. Dr Beasley started the next morning for Tokar in February 1947.

company in the town and a number of places such as the museum and marine gardens to be used for expeditions.[86]

The Headmistress who re-started it was uncritically enthusiastic about it but she was one of the girls who obtained unstinted satisfaction just from her work and position. By no means one of the most brilliant intellectually, she had so many of the qualities that parents required, that she was a great favourite with the mothers of her pupils and able to influence them considerably.[87]

I was talking to her one morning, when we heard a small demonstration outside by some schoolboys. 'The fools', she said scornfully. 'What good will that do them? They say they want to govern the country. They can't. They aren't fit. Not in a thousand years will they be ready'. Then she turned to me quite fiercely and went on in a really intense tone, 'Look at me! Would these men of ours have bothered to educate me? It was only the English who said girls should be educated. What would have happened to me, if the English hadn't come?' Her manner softened with a sense of pride and fulfilment, as she swept her hand out. 'Should I have been the headmistress of this lovely school?' Neither of us mentioned what we both knew, but she may not have been aware, that I had been told of her slave ancestry. 'When I say my prayers every night', she continued, 'I pray that I shall be under the ground before the English go'. This part of her wish was not granted to her and, when I last enquired, the news was that she was still happily teaching.

Her school was filled mostly with the daughters of merchants and others following the usual urban occupations and our hope that we might encourage some Beja children met with little response. Nevertheless her enthusiastic work won so much popularity, that it was easy to start another school in the west of the town nearer to the tribesmen's settlements. Since the War the number of 'Fuzzies' resident here had increased so greatly that the Municipality had taken firm measures to prevent encampments of tents near the outskirts. There was always a large and changing population engaged as dock labourers for whom provision had to be made but it was not easy to turn them into ordinary, peaceful citizens, since they were a proud, reserved community, difficult of approach. In their native setting of the hills there was nothing very picturesque about their small, frowsty tents. Pitched, as they were on completely barren ground they immediately

86. In 1948 'Port Sudan acquired the discarded Seaman's Mission and erected a delightful wooden structure with enormous rooms, wide verandahs and glistening green and white paint' (*ARDE*, 1948).
87. Port Sudan Girls' School had 80 pupils, 4 teachers in 1938. In 1943 there were only 50 pupils and 2 teachers; but by 1946 there were 113 pupils and 4 teachers.

suggested that here was the minimum needed to sustain human life, and that obtained through the most bitter struggle. In the mountains they took their goats and camels where pasture might be found, and during the brief winter rains managed to cultivate a little grain. The suburb[88] they inhabited in Port Sudan was not a replica of this, for the efforts of the authorities had resulted in straight, wide streets and a reasonable degree of conformity with surface cleanliness but the general aspect was of a bare, unlovely poverty. Happily there was no display of grand houses to underline this, although one or two of the merchants in the town were reputed to be extremely wealthy.

## 5. A School for Beja Girls

### 5.1 Sinkat

The problem of schools for Beja girls was an important issue in itself and it had, for me, the upshot of sending me to some remarkably interesting places. Sinkat had a number of advantages as a place to start,[89] as it took on a secondary role during the summer. Before the building of the bridge over the Gash[90] the Governor of [Kassala] Province and his staff moved up there, because Kassala in the rains was cut off by the river in spate. At first the school we began was a rather haphazard affair not without a certain degree of success,[91] although its chief defect from the point of view of its avowed aim was that only two out of the twenty pupils were Beja. The others were the daughters of merchants and officials of whom the *mamur* had contributed four.

The little Beja girls were charming. They had fine, rather sharpened features common to these tribes and this attraction was set off by bright red *tobe*s, wrapped closely round them. The younger of the two was evidently not very much accustomed to the garment and was constantly tripping over it. As they wore nothing at all underneath except a bust bodice, like an abbreviated waistcoat, there was nothing to do but wait until she learned to

88. Deim al-Arab.
89. Dr Beasley visited Sinkat from 26.5.45, thus visiting the two religious centres of the rival politico-religious factions in the North within a month. Dr Beasley went to Sinkat just after her momentous visit to Aba Island '... not in a *divide et impera* mood but to follow out the Department's tradition of inspecting the school there in the holidays'.
90. The bridge at Kassala was built in 1949.
91. 'The Governor opened the school in defiance of me so was run by a grant from Local Government funds for the Beja. The school was better than I expected.' The Governor was J.M. Humphrey. By 1948 the school was housed in standard school buildings (*ARDE*, 1948).

manipulate it. It must have been very inadequate covering for the cold weather in the mountains but appeared to be the normal wear for most of the women. Gradually the number of Beja girls increased, but remained small. This was a pity, for many of them were above the average for general intelligence and [had] a spirited enthusiasm which was most encouraging, even if more difficult to control than classes in a place like Fung, where the children were listless from chronic malaria.

To the first teacher the establishment of the school brought a settled career. She was untrained and had been married young and then deserted. When other staff were appointed, she was sent to Omdurman to the [Girls' Training] College and the immediate sequel was quite unforeseen. Her husband suddenly appeared and induced the police to arrest her, as soon as she stepped off the train. It did not take long to straighten matters out and in the end the *sharia* Court made an order for her maintenance by her husband. Meanwhile she worked hard to obtain her qualifying certificate and make herself financially independent.

> The teacher who had managed, quite unlawfully, to stay seven years in an Omdurman school had glimmerings of what a school ought to be like, and was only too pleased to be given a few hints. She is coming to Omdurman in September [1945] for a month to try and pick up some ideas [26.5.45].

The mistresses who took over from her had the unparallelled advantage of support from the *sherifa* Mariam,[92] who had asked for a Headmistress, whom she knew, and encouraged her and her assistants to visit at her house. In fact it was of greatest value that this revered lady had, even if belatedly, given her blessing to a girls' school and that, like the Sultan in Geneina, had decided to have it built practically on her doorstep, which gave it tremendous prestige.

The *sherifa*'s importance derived from her being the person in the Sudan in most direct descent from the Prophet. She was related to the family of Sayed Ali Mirghani and, had she been a man, might very well have taken precedence over him but even so in her own right the holiness of her lineage had given her enormous power. In a country where women had practically no status at all, it was amazing that even the teachings of the Koran about the subordinate place of women did not appear to have lessened the high [esteem] set on her prerogative of birth. She had been married but had no heir and in changing times it was difficult to guess, where the influence would turn. Unquestionably there was no other woman to take over her function. For the most part she lived in the Red Sea Hills at Sinkat or Gebeit, going down to Suakin at times or making an elaborate journey to

92. *Sharīfa* Maryam al-Mirghanī.

Eritrea, since her adherents were not confined within the artificial boundaries of modern states.

> I sent a message to say I would like to call on Sitt Mariam, but was told she was ill. She is getting old now and had been to some big festival in Gebeit. I should have liked to have seen her [26.5.45]. I have been told that she had a sister in Eritrea who was quite unsecluded, wore slacks, smoked cigarettes. I don't know Sitt Mariam's views on emancipation.

Naturally her affairs with the outside world had to be conducted by her *wakil*s (agents) who, I suspected, often spoke in their own person, when giving out what were said to be her wishes. This, however, was not always the case, for Sitt Mariam was very well informed and had a decided mind of her own. I remember during one visit[93] the *wakil* was explaining to me in her presence, the views of the *sherifa* on the siting of the new girls' school. She quickly interrupted and contradicted him; she was quite sure what she wanted and in a quiet but forceful manner would not allow him to misrepresent her. I had been much favoured in that she had received me without sitting behind a curtain, which was the way she usually talked with the D.C.s or male officials. Therefore I had the opportunity to admire an interesting face, light- skinned with large, dark eyes and a purely Arab cast of feature. Otherwise her *tobe* was closely wrapped round her and I saw only her hands and face but I estimated her age at well over sixty.

Unfortunately she was very tired that morning, as it was the day after a great religious festival,[94] which had been held in the mosque nearby. Special trains had been run from Port Sudan to Gebeit, bringing [not only] the [nomadic] tribesmen but also merchants, shopkeepers, clerks, doctors, and officials who had come to the *sherifa*'s headquarters for a special family party. Round the mosque thronged crowds of warriors in the scanty bits of cotton, which was all that the 'Fuzzies' wore, and in the outer court they chanted and leapt in their wild and energetic dances. Apart from this the entertainment at such times was generally sermons and speeches, and the feasting, coffee, lemonade and cakes. But most excitement of it to most people seemed to lie in the fact of just being together and rejoicing in

93. April 1947 when Dr Beasley stayed at 'Reggie's place ...In his late 30s he had recently married his wife Daffodil'. Reggie was Reginald George Dingwall (b.4.4.1908- ); Educated at Lancing and Christ Church, Oxford; 14.9.31 First appointment; 1931 Khartoum; 1931-32 Kassala; 1932 Halfa; 1932-36 Darfur; 1936-38 Civil Secretary's Office; 1938-41 Kordofan; 1.4.41-49 Kassala, 1944 D.C. Southern District, based in Gedaref, 1946 D.C. Beja District, based at Sinkat; 1949-52 Equatoria; 1952-55 Commissioner of Prisons; 1955 retired; 1955- Farming in Hants.
94. *Ḥawliyyat al-Khatmiyya*, a religious festival held annually at Sinkat by the Khatmiyya (See Milne, J.C.M., *The changing pattern of mobility and migration of the Amarar tribe of Eastern Sudan*, unpublished M.Phil thesis, S.O.A.S., 1976, pp.428-432).

company, for the spirit of festival was undoubtedly genuine and thoroughly noisy.

Admittedly it would be again a question of people being of more importance than places but I cannot honestly feel, that I should find pleasure in being a queen in Sinkat. The place was featureless[95] and seemed a bit deserted. Many of the houses were built of stone but a short distance away the 'Fuzzies' had placed their scruffy, black tents, untidy, insanitary and not even picturesque to look at.

> ... I went to the *merkaz* [26.5.45] where there were too many 'Fuzzies' for comfort ... The Governor's rest-house was a strong stone affair with a green painted corrugated iron roof, so different from Sayed Abdel Rahman's leaky sieve [on Aba Island]. It was well arranged inside, with an L- shaped room with fireplace, a wide verandah and *mastaba* where we had tea in the afternoons. The Governor had some flowers on his table, which he said came from Sitt Mariam's garden. It must have been the only garden in the place.

There was only one bourgainvillea in the village and that was to hide the policemen's latrines.[96] For the rest all that grew there were aloes. Perhaps it was the harsh, neutral tints, which made the view so much more forbidding than the golden deserts of sand round Wadi Halfa.

> There was a definite feeling of mountain air. The mountains have a certain sombre beauty morning and evening, otherwise nothing but barrenness. Only dark and shade where rain[97] fell in the mountains and from the banks of cloud.

## 5.2 Erkowit

> It seemed sensible while in the mountains, to take a few days local leave at the hill station at Erkowit,

some miles further on, about two or three hours' drive [from Sinkat].

95. In 3.3.42, when Dr Beasley passed through Sinkat on the train for Sollum, 'Sinkat did not look very exciting'.
96. The 'magnificent scarlet' bourgainvillea was 'planted by the D.C. I had recently met in Nyala', E.C. Haselden. There were also 'candelabra euphorbia, dragon trees and every kind of cactus in the grey gravel' of Sinkat.
97. In 1943 'there had been such a violent storm in Sinkat that the whole of the Governor's garden had been washed down to the railway and two visitors in the guest house were marooned for hours without food because the flood was so deep'. The Governor was then J.M. Humphrey.

The road from Sinkat was rather exciting driving along between the mountains. A certain amount of vegetation but mostly of the cactus and aloe variety and the famous dragon trees, with their odd clusters of fleshy leaves and white flowers. After the first bit of road we came to a wide, flat plain and some lights twinkling at the far side. This was Carthage, which had been an R.A.F. station during the war with Italy. It gave the enemy a lot of trouble because they could not locate it amongst these mountains. It was so-called because someone intercepted a message from the Italians saying that this aerodrome *delenda est*. It was now changed into a concentration camp. The particular political prisoners were reported to be the Stern Gang and other Palestinians. Report has it they were well-fed and housed and there were football fields.

My room in Erkowit was quite comfortable, a little stone house, simply furnished but the service was good and the tin bath big enough. The camp was arranged with little houses scattered about on winding paths and a large central block at the top of the hill, with the public rooms. I found Erkowit ungracious and not very full of opportunities. I also started to be ill again with dysentery which lasted the rest of the summer, evidently picked up on Aba Island earlier in the month [May 1945].

I looked out through a gap in the mountains[98] some 3000 feet up, and found the prospect frightening. Below me right away to the horizon in the north were enormous mountains; huge, barren ranges without a leaf, or a blade, or a stream to soften their invincible ugliness.

On my way back from this disturbing vista one day I strayed into a [Beja] camp just off the road and found this equally depressing. The black tents were most uninviting and hidden away out of sight of one another among the boulders. Dogs barked and very dirty, timid children just peered at us, while the women cowered away. It was quite different from the open friendliness of the [Beni Helba in Darfur with their fresh *birsh* houses] or the quick responsiveness of the Nubian cultivators by the Nile. Much of the apparent surliness was due to their not being Arabic speaking. This meant no chance of the casual greetings or interchange of small talk, which was common elsewhere. Officials working in these parts, however, had a great respect of all the various [Beja] tribes and found sterling qualities in them as a whole, despite some cruel and unsociable traits.

98. At Kitty's Leap, in Erkowit, which Dr Beasley visited during her 7-day stay in April/May 1945.

## 6. A Beja school near Kassala

Whatever the opposition and apathy we were determined to persevere and did eventually manage to start a school in a place called Wagar, where about half the fifty children enrolled were Beja, [especially] Hadendowa. The preliminaries to this were a little out of the ordinary and modified considerably my idea of unfriendliness.

While I was inspecting in Kassala[99] the D.C. of the Red Sea Hills[100] was there and was most anxious that something should be arranged for his district. I came back from school one morning and found him talking to a handsome old *sheikh*[101] with a white beard, whose name I never remembered, because he was always referred to as 'Old Frosty Face'. He had done such good work in caring for his people during the war in Kassala, that he had been awarded the C.B.E. It was planned, that I should have tea with 'Frosty Face' and a man living in Kassala, who was an agent[102] for some of the tribes. When I arrived for this meeting, I had already attended a large tea party and entertainment at the girls' school, and was therefore not feeling very fresh. The agent, Sheikh Ibrahim, was a tall, fine man with exceptionally good features and a small beard rather like a chin strap; he was a pleasure to look at but he made such long speeches about the benefits of education, that I became rather restive. It seemed a bit unnecessary to tell me, what a good thing schools were and I had difficulty in remembering that, in a place where girls' education was by no means acceptable to all, a man must show which side he was on, and that it was customary to be long-winded and pompous. As I came to know Ibrahim better, the pompousness was dropped and our friendship was firm, if brief. Both he and 'Frosty Face' complained that the hindrance lay in the women's attitude. Naturally I asked to go and talk to some women and this, to me, obvious rejoinder produced a surprised silence for a little. It had evidently not occurred to them that this time-honoured excuse, which had served well enough with male officials, could not be readily shuffled off on a

99. February 1947.
100. 'The D.C. [R.G. Dingwall] went on being earnest and reprimanded me once for trying to cut short the speeches.'
101. The white-bearded *Nāẓir* of the Hadendowa from 1927, known as 'Old Frosty Face' was Sheikh Mohamed Mohamed El Amin El Tirik, C.B.E. During the Italian invasion a formidable Hadendowa unit ('Frosty-force') in the Gash acted as scouts, intelligence agents, guides and counter-espionage corps (see Paul, A., *A history of the Beja tribes of the Sudan*, 1954, pp.127-128).
102. The D.C. planned that Dr Beasley should have tea in the Governor's garden with the Hadendowa *nāẓir* and his agent (*wakīl*) who had been a soldier. The agent had 'bright brown gentle eyes (though there was no fundamental softness in him)'. She visited the agent's house the next day 'in the Governor's luxurious saloon'.

woman. They soon recovered, however, and made arrangements for me to start next morning by a visit to Ibrahim's household.

He took me the next day to the edge of the town, where his mud- brick house was situated in the middle of a collection of grass huts, set in wide yards with grass fences or slight wooden ones. A young man, probably in his late teens, came to meet us and I imagined he was a poor relation in some dependent capacity, as he was not introduced. There was, however, nothing dependent about his bearing, for in his way he was as fine and upstanding as Ibrahim. Dressed rather after the fashion of the nomads with his *tobe* crossed in front and thrown across his shoulders he sported with a certain amount of pride, a large, rather ungainly sword in a leather scabbard. His head was swathed in the usual *immah*. Thus, although both belonged by tribe to the 'Fuzzies', they had not that wild look, that the wild, unkempt hair gave to the majority of them.

I was led into a pleasant yard, moderately tidy and with shady trees, but taken straight through to an inner one fenced off at the back, where there were two or three huts and a cow under a tree. A kindly but by no means fastidiously clean lady came to greet us and was introduced by Ibrahim as his father's wife, but, I gathered, not his mother. At this point he disappeared and she shepherded me indoors. Here was a large room with another leading off and we sat down on the *angareeb*s, the three of which constituted all the furniture. Very sweet mint tea was brought to me, while we tried to find some common ground for conversation.

One or two children hung around and an indeterminate woman or so drifted in to exchange a few words or just to have a look at me. They assured me, that all girls in the district went to school, when they reached the right age, which I knew was untrue, or else the population was very oddly distributed. Then Ibrahim's wife came in, a bitter disappointment. She was not very old but such a complete slattern, a faded, unhealthy woman in a grubby, muslin *tobe* with a baby, to which she gave suck every few minutes. The father's wife and one or two of the other visitors talked a little but I did not get a word out of Ibrahim's wife. I think that she was just stupid. After about an hour I said, I must go as it was then ten o'clock, and I had some work to do. The women were rather disappointed; they seemed to find it amusing to have an unusual stranger in the place, even if they had little to talk about.

Ibrahim was summoned and, as we drove back, I had a moment of inspiration and asked him, if he had ever seen a girls' school. After all he had been laying off some pretty heavy platitudes the evening before about the value of girls' education. He confessed that he had never been in a school, and was a little shy about the idea of a visit, but I assured him, that

PLATE 5

'Writing on the Sand' at the Girls' Primary School, Kassala, 1940s. I.M. Beasley's collection.

PLATE 6

Road to Yambio, Equatoria Province, c.1949. I.M. Beasley's collection.

PLATE 7

Sayyid ʻAbd al-Raḥmān al-Mahdī, 1940s. I.M. Beasley's collection.

PLATE 8

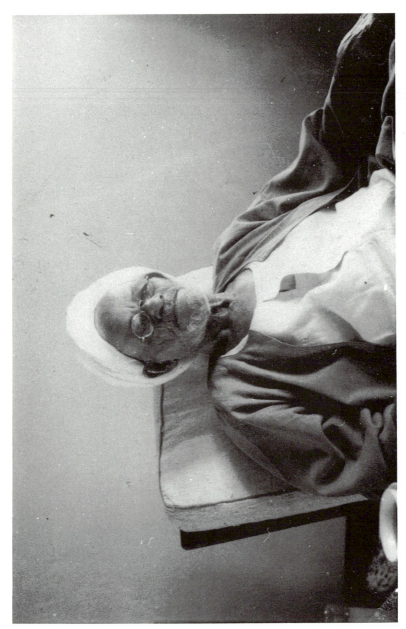

Sheikh Babikr Bedri, 'father of girls' education' in Sudan, 1940s. Bright collection, S.A.D. 729/22/10.

no-one's reputation would suffer, if he looked in for five minutes in my company. The spacious school-yard with its shady trees and simple but adequate mud buildings always made a pleasant impression and, I think, it did on Ibrahim. Then the four mistresses all looked attractive, as they came smiling to greet us, the Headmistress in particular being a very lovely, sweet-natured girl of about twenty. They were all very bright and active, but withal respectful, and such a striking constrast to the bundle of clothes, which was Ibrahim's wife. He was most impressed with the children in class and, although he did only stay about five minutes, there was no doubt, that he straightway became a complete and unshakable convert.

We set off the next morning, as soon as it was light, Ibrahim, the Province Education Officer,[103] and I. This official himself belonged to one of the local tribes, but he had received a secondary education and spoke English quite well. In person he was a thin, bony little man, rather ineffectual, who compared unfavourably with most of the tribesmen round about and was physically a very indifferent advertisement for education, seen for example alongside his uneducated relatives. The air was cool and fresh and the drive for the most part most enjoyable. After a very bad bit of road along by the railway we turned off and journeyed for a time through lightly wooded country, until we came to a great stretch of irrigated land, growing cotton. This had been made possible by utilising the flood waters of Gash, which were formerly wasted in the sand. Swinburne[104] seems to have been wrong about weary rivers, but this one anyway was being quite as useful now without winding safe to sea on this sunny February morning.

## 6.1 Aroma

The end of the Gash Delta was a most desolate, sandy plain and here at Aroma we breakfasted [with]

the Agricultural Inspector,[105] [who] had been there twenty years, a remarkable person, well over six feet in height and about two feet more in girth than most. He and his wife appeared to live in considerable comfort. I

---

103. Abdel Kadir Okeir; 8.1.24 first appointment; 1.1.45 Assistant P.E.O., based in Kassala, seconded from Education Department; He wrote 'Education amongst the Beja', *Oversea Education*, Vol 23, no.1, Oct 1951, pp.194-196.
104. A.C. Swinburne (b.1837-d.1909): *The Garden of Proserpine*, xi:
  'That even the weariest river

  Winds somewhere safe to sea.'
105. W.C. Young, O.B.E., M.C., M.M., 4N., N.D.A., Dip. Agric. (Glas); 6.11.19 First appointment; By 1947 Manager, Gash Board and Senior Inspector of Agriculture, Kassala Province, based in Aroma; 1947 retired.

had a terrific breakfast including apples (cold storage from Italy, via Khartoum, very rare).

[We] then discussed with the notables the possibilities of a girls' school. They were gathered at the Courthouse and consisted of a native judge, rather scruffy but admittedly taken unawares, a police officer looking very smart in uniform, and an odd *sheikh* or two. They were not, I regret to say, enthusiastic. The [police] officer had provided for his daughters by sending them to board in Omdurman and the others made excuses about water. The Directors of the Gash Board, they argued, were concerned about the increasing demands on the water supply and it might be advisable to wait, until this was better organised in a plan for starting a new well field. Both Ibrahim and the P.E.O. said a few kind words about the benefits of education, but we agreed that with this lack of support we should be wiser to push on to Wagar and find out if we could stimulate any keenness there, since we could only offer one school in the district in the next year.


## 6.2 Wagar

This place was an even more depressing spot than Aroma. There was nothing to see on the way except a few empty canals in ground that was being left fallow for a year or two, and some tidy brick buildings, where the cotton, brought in from the fields, was weighed and the Agricultural Inspector paid the cultivators for it. Quite a number of these cultivators belonged to the local tribes and were thus gradually coming to understand something more settled than their former nomadic ways. Wagar itself was an ugly, little settlement of the small market town type, which one would expect to spring up in a district, both pastoral and agrarian. We made our way through the streets, which were more or less at right-angles, and bordered by high, mud walls, irregularly-shaped with crude wooden doors set in them.

Our first visit was to the boys' school, where a Beja relative of Ibrahim's was a teacher. The wife of the latter had been in school for two years so it was suggested, that I should call on her to talk to her and her friends. While the master went to warn her, I had a chat with the boys in the top class, aged about twelve, and asked them, if they would like a school for their sisters. Five of them immediately and heartily applauded the idea but the others looked a bit blank.

Although the dirt and disorder in the boys' school reflected small credit on the schoolmaster, his house was extremely tidy, a tribute to his wife, for she had had very little time for preparation. I was shown into a tidy guest room, just inside the gate, and sat down in a stiff sort of armchair. She was a bright and cheerful young woman, probably in her late teens and her acquaintances, who drifted in, were a most varied collection. The first, who was very attractive, had a great deal to say for herself; she made herself very much at home, propped up on cushions on an *angareeb*. Both she and my hostess came from Kassala and were soon well away on a tide of harmless gossip about schoolmistresses there and elsewhere. Some other women were more elderly and there was one Rabelaisian soul with enormous teeth and a bony face, who was draped in a red *tobe*. She sat next to me and stroked me at intervals, saying, 'You are so nice'. She did not like my sitting straight up in the armchair and urged me to take off my frock and shoes and recline on the *angareeb*. Children as usual were an unfailing subject of interest. My one daughter they regarded as quite insufficient for a family and had a great deal of advice to offer about my future. High time, they said, that I started in and had a few more; my grey hairs meant nothing at all; I was patently good for another three. It was a pity that the daughter's father was no longer about but I could easily get another man. Wouldn't I like that? And so on with much repetition. It was not quite the high-minded line of talk, which 'Frosty Face' and Ibrahim had indulged in the night before, but it was all very matey, and may perhaps have been better propaganda, than it would appear written down *verbatim* in an official report.

One or two small girls peered in and I asked them how they would like a school. One cried and ran away but the others hung around and seemed interested. Most of the women said that they were in favour of a school and that there were plenty of girls to go. I wondered at the time, if their agreement was just politeness but on the evidence of the enrolment the following year they must have been voicing general opinion, and the school certainly prospered.

Presently a very pleasant elderly woman came in who was the schoolmaster's mother. I observed that the wife had muffled herself in her *tobe* and could not be seen at all. It seemed a strange thing to do and I wondered if she was unwell. After a little talk the newcomer went out and the wife re-emerged to join in the conversation again. The vivacious one, who came from Kassala, asked me if I had noticed this, and when I said I had, she replied rather scornfully, 'That's a Beja custom. We don't do that. But she may not look at her mother-in-law'.

> I was very much interested to come across such a prohibition, but I never expected to come up against one while quietly drinking mint tea among a group of women in a house.

After about an hour Ibrahim came to fetch me. Apparently he had been down in the market telling people what a good thing a girls' school would be and their reactions had been favourable. The idea was to start with the local children and gradually the wild tribesmen round about would be interested and want to send their girls. Then we could start a boarding school. It had been an entertaining meeting and I always meant to go back and have another chat with the women of Wagar. But time was short; the Sudan is large; and staff were few.[106]

### 6.3 Tementai

We could not stay longer that morning, as we were going to the tribal gathering of the Hadendowa at Tementai, where we were to make propaganda with the chiefs on this subject of the neglect of their girls. These tribal gatherings were arranged in order that nomadic people could come together at intervals to settle any complaints or difficulties which they might have. In the ordinary way it was hard to make contact with them to discuss, for example, any new laws and ordinances which had been promulgated, or to deal with legal or judicial matters, which even in these unsophisticated parts could be of importance. The gathering sometimes went on for about a month with people drifting in and out.

First of all we came to a great well field with enormous herds of cattle, sheep and goats all over the place. The country was not barren like Aroma but had small trees and bushes scattered about, which made a little shelter for the encampments of the tribesmen, who were sitting in groups in the shade, looking very wild and uncommonly dirty.

We went to a rough sort of shelter where the D.C.[107] was sitting haranguing the chiefs. He was a big man but many of them were a great deal bigger and the more important of them were dressed in ordinary Sudanese robes, which [seemed to] increase their stature still further. Some of the others wore only a pair of drawers and a bit of stuff across their shoulders and their hair just fuzzy. There were all types of face and all ages, some magnificent, some evil, some just vacant. 'Old Frosty Face' was sitting beside the D.C.. I thought the speech he made later on girls' education was a bit thin, but, as it was not in Arabic,[108] I had to ask the P.E.O. to translate it. It was by the general tone and manner that I felt it unconvincing. All round the discussion was not very spirited. Ibrahim said

---

106. There was an unexpectedly good start at Wagar with a number of Beja girls attracted into the school (*ARDE*, 1948).
107. 'Dick ... a handsome Empire type in his mid 30s.' Richard Vivian Macaulay Stanbury (b.5.2.1916- ); Educated at Shrewsbury and Magdalene College, Cambridge; 1937-39 Kassala; 1939-42 Equatoria; 1942-46 Darfur; 1946-48 Kassala, A.D.C. Beja District, based at Sinkat (in 1947, D.C., Hadendowa); 1949-50 Blue Nile, D.C.; 1950 invalided; 1950- Farming in Portugal.
108. His speech was no doubt in Tu Bedawie, the language spoken by the Beja.

his little piece rather diffidently, because he was only an agent and many of the others were important chiefs. As there were about forty people there I had expected a rather more exciting debate.

There is never active opposition, of course. Schools just are not supported.

It was only the D.C. and I who approached anything like a hot dispute. He asked me, in English, other people talking the while, if I realised why some of the back-benchers were laughing. They knew, he said, that their women were so conservative, that they would never entertain the idea of schooling and all this talk was a waste of time. I stoutly maintained, that they were grinning, because they had not the slightest intention of letting their women be educated and get out of hand. As his riposte was that he did not himself approve of independent women I thought it better to swallow hard and return my attention to the Arabic part of the argument. I felt that despite the apparent apathy we might have broken a little ground. The mere idea of my coming to discuss the subject might make the men start thinking.

The D.C.[109] took me to his tent where I had a wash and brush up, very badly needed, and he said lunch was ready ... But I was sure I hadn't time ... although he assured me it was only ten minutes' drive and we had half an hour. I was fidgetty. He assured me he wouldn't let me miss it [the train], so I consented to stop and drink a gin. It seemed so uncivil when he'd gone to all the trouble of preparing a meal in the wilds ... Eventually I managed to persuade him it was time to go and he said he'd come too, still assuring me there was plenty of time.

After this there was a wild rush to the railway, since I had planned to catch the one train of the week and my servant was on it with all my luggage. As we rounded a bend in the road, there it was a few minutes away standing at the halt. Fortunately there were a lot of sheep to be put on. By good luck also the Governor[110] was on the train travelling in a comfortable saloon.

... and the train was delayed or I should have missed it. 'Watch must have been slow', said the D.C ... When I explained what had happened he grunted, 'Probably did it on purpose. Very susceptible chap'. *Very* indeed, as I hadn't met him before and must have arrived covered in dust, no make up, hair all out of curl and blowing out from under a handkerchief ... I went aft to my carriage, where I found my servant and belongings all intact.

He generously offered me the use of his bathroom and to have a proper bath on such a dusty journey was an indescribable luxury. The trouble with the heat in these parts was that one could hardly bear to touch clothes, as

109. R.V.M. Stanbury.
110. G.M. Hancock, Governor of Kassala Province.

they were taken off. The sweat seemed to soak into the very fibres and then they dried stiff and caked. It was only a minor discomfort, that everyone accepted, but it always gave an added joy to a wallow in a deep bath.

# Chapter VI

# More People
## Including a Visit to Aba Island

## 1. Sir Sayyid ʿAbd al-Raḥmān al-Mahdī Pasha

People stand out more vividly than places but some of these are inseparable from a particular background. This was especially true of the Mahdi's son,[1] who invited me to visit Aba Island, which will always remain one of the highlights of my travels. Never before or since have I had the experience of being the honoured guest of a man, revered as holy by hundreds of thousands, and himself aspiring at that time to be King of a country the size of the Sudan. His hospitality to me was generous and considerate to a degree, that I heartily appreciated. That I enjoyed also the magnificent comedy of it all without reservation was my sincere reaction and I applauded my host as a superb performer; that I did not savour it all in quite the manner intended was no mark of ingratitude on my part. We approached life from different angles.

As with the other men I had met from the days of the Khalifa, I felt I was touching the real stuff of history, when I was first asked to tea by Sir Sayed Abd er Rahman El Mahdi Pasha, as he was then called, but known familiarly to all as S.A.R., except for his devout followers, who spoke of him reverently as The Sayed. There might be plenty of *sayed*s but to them he was the only one. In actual fact he was not the only surviving child of the Mahdi and had been born posthumously, but the mantle of his father had

---

1. Muḥammad Aḥmad ibn ʿAbdullā (b.1948-d.1885) of Dongolawi origin declared himself Mahdī in June 1881. He had over 400 descendants but his politico-religious heir was his posthumous son, Sir Sayyid ʿAbd al-Raḥmān al-Mahdī Pasha. He became the leader (*Imām*) of the *Anṣār*, i.e. the Mahdī's followers and their descendants. Initially in obscure outcast, by 1908 ʿAbd al-Raḥmān had been allowed to cultivate the Mahdī's land in Aba Island, but Slatin Pasha's continued degradation restricted his influence until Slatin's removal in 1914. By 1925 S.A.R. was probably the most powerful man, with both religious and political authority, in the Sudan outside of the government. S.A.R. was made Knight Commander of the Order of the British Empire (K.B.E.) on 1.1.1926. Sir Geoffrey Archer, the then Governor-General, paid an official visit to Aba in February 1926, much against the wishes of senior officials in his Council. This precipitated the early replacement of Sir Geoffrey.

fallen on him[2] and his rise to power had been encouraged by the Condominium Government as a focal point for the loyalty of the Western tribes.[3] All this early life was rather shadowy but, when I first met him in 1939, he was an established person, regarded as holy by many, of considerable wealth,[4] whose power lay in the spiritual realm of other men regarding him as holy. Politics was also mixed with this question of loyalties and British officials were often accused of their favourite 'Divide and Rule' intention with S.A.R. on one side and another religious leader, Sir Sayed Ali Mirghani,[5] on the other.

To most people, S.A.R. was by far the more colourful personality[6] and I met him often, as he took a spasmodic and, I suspected, spurious interest in girls' education.[7] Opinions differed wildly as to the essentials of his character but on one point all were agreed, both in himself and by reason of his supporters, he was one of the most important figures in the country. Opponents berated him as ambitious and scheming; some officials condemned him as a rogue but of an old-fashioned breed, but the power

2. Only 'Alī (d.1944) and Sayyid 'Abd al-Rahmān survived, the others, including al-Faḍl, Muḥammad, Bushrā, Ṣiddīq, al-Ṭayyib, al-Ṭāhir and Naṣr al-Dīn all died in battle 1898/1899 or from illness contracted during imprisonment (Rudolf C. Slatin's *Fire and Sword in the Sudan*, London, 1896 gives an intentionally dramatic account of those times).

3. Between 1898 and 1915 S.A.R. was under strict Government surveillance. The First World War 1914-18 gave S.A.R. the opportunity to use his influence in Darfur and Kordofan to support the Sudan Government and Britain, particularly in opposition to Sultan 'Alī Dīnār of Darfur, and thereby re-establish the Mahdists. Mahdist agents actively proselytized in the West in the 1920s.

4. By shrewd agricultural and commercial enterprises S.A.R. built up his position as a leader. In the 1920s he was given large government contracts in wood, for the construction of the Sennar Dam, for example, and was considered then to be one of the richest Sudanese. By his early recognition of the importance of cotton financed the Independence movement. He also received *zakāt*, the Muslim alms-tax, from many of his followers. Although he was extravagant and ostentatious, he also had numerous financial obligations to his dependants and followers.

5. Sayyid 'Alī al-Mirghanī.

6. See Thomas, Graham and Ismay, *Sayed Abdel Rahman al Mahdi, A Pictorial Biography*, 1986.

7. Nevertheless S.A.R. was an enthusiastic support of Babikr Bedri's efforts in girls' educational development. 'At intervals he made presents in the shape of old houses in Omdurman for girls' schools and after considerable difficulty, when these were condemned as unfit for the purpose, we persuaded him to put up some more suitable buildings' (S.A.D. 657/7/1-19).

and influence could not be lightly disregarded.[8] I should hesitate to call him complex by temperament, although there were plenty of turns and contradictions. What I always wanted to know, but it would have been impertinent to enquire, was just how he himself felt about this reverence that was accorded to him. It was not the power of great spiritual virtue, which explained the prestige of Gandhi. Mixed up with the religion was something like the Divine Right of Kings.

I once travelled in the same train and was much impressed by the way in which groups of white-robed figures crowded round at every halt to kiss the hand he extended through the window. Most of the way it was moonlight and this added to the romantic aspect of the scene with people pressing up to the carriage and shouting, while shaggy-looking tribesmen paraded about on camels to add a real flavour of wildness.

Mostly, however, our view of him was more ordinary. He used to bid us, the British women officials, to a lavish tea-party, where he made an admirable host. Either in his Omdurman house or in the grander one at Khartoum, where golden crested cranes ornamented the garden, he would receive us magnificently dressed but with no trace of flamboyance.

### 1.1 Preparation for Aba Island visit

Quite different was the proposal I received in May 1945, when I had just returned from a tour in the Nuba Mountains; this was a personal invitation to stay at the family seat on Aba Island to be present at the opening of an extension to the boys' school and a new school for the girls, who were employed there in spinning cotton. The Director of Education[9] had also been asked but, as he could not go, he allotted me the honour of representing the Department. Immediately after came a message from the Sayed for me to have tea with him in Omdurman to discuss arrangements.

> I thought I could go on Saturday night and return on Monday night. He pressed me to journey down on Tuesday 15th and return on following Sunday, and stay to give some advice about the school. I had an unworthy

8. In 1924 S.A.R. was leader of the more conservative elements who opposed the militant nationalism and pro-Egyptian sympathies of the White Flag League. In the 1920s and 1930s, in spite of his professed support of the Sudan Government he was often suspected of organising, both among his religious followers and Sudanese intelligentsia, a subversive nationalist movement. At best he was an over-mighty subject, more dangerous because he avoided open confrontation. In the 1940s the Sudan Government began to collaborate with him as the strongest opponent of Egyptian claims to sovereignty in Sudan, and those Sudanese who wished to end British sovereignty in the Sudan.
9. C.W. Williams.

suspicion that I was being asked for some purpose I could not guess and certainly never found out.

This was a very different reception from the formal tea parties with the Sayed, gracious but lofty. There were no other guests and, although we sat as usual on a sofa in the middle of the dais, he unbent considerably and later his youngest children came and played round our feet and were petted.

> We had quite a friendly *tête-à-tête* till after tea, when we went down to the other end of the garden where Madame Huldchinsky[10] was sitting with the children. She came and sat with us and the children played round our feet and scoffed the plum cake until the petted youngest son (two years old and in European clothes) wetted the good Persian rug.

### 1.2 Aba Island

### Arrival, Tuesday 15.5.45.

Aba is an island in the White Nile near Kosti and its fame among the Sudanese springs from its having been the point, where the Mahdi began his preaching and later spread his movement in those troubled years of the 1880s. For this hallowed reason S.A.R. had built himself a house there and developed a very profitable estate, while his followers regarded it as a place for reverent visits. As there were only two trains a week, the plan was for me to journey down on Tuesday and return the following Sunday.

> The more I thought over my promise to go the less I liked it but I did realise that it was a chance in a lifetime. I was nervous about what exactly was going to be expected of me. I was really quite glad when a terrific thunderstorm broke on the 15th and the train delayed till the morning.

I expected to be met on arrival but I was gratified by the courtesy of one of the family[11] coming to see me off. To my very great pleasure I discovered on the train S.A.R.'s cook, who had long been a good friend of mine. Like

10. Madame Huldchinsky, S.A.R.'s housekeeper. '50 or less, a wealthy German who had married a Polish doctor of Jewish extraction. They left Germany when the Nazis made life too difficult and found their way to Egypt. There the husband died and the lady took on a post as housekeeper to a hospital. Naturally when Rommel was at the gates of Alexandria [she] together with numbers of others of all nationalities came rushing down to [the] Sudan.' She tried to earn her living by dabbling in sculpture and painting. 'Meanwhile she obtained a post as housekeeper of the big British [Grand] Hotel.' Early May 1945 'she took over the job as housekeeper to the Sayed ... She always dresses in white or black ... I subsequently saw [her] report ... condemning the utter squalor of his back premises and suggesting a few improvements. I think her advice went unheeded ... ' Madame Huldchinsky planned to leave Sudan at the end of August 1945. (S.A.D. 657/7/2-3,10).
11. A member of S.A.R.'s family saw Dr Beasley off at the station. 'I could not understand all this concern.'

his master he was a tall, impressive man and in reality more of a major domo than just the maker of the excellent plum cakes I had eaten so frequently. Our acquaintance had ripened cordially, because he was the father of a large brood of daughters, whom he was anxious to educate at Government expense as far as they could go. Girls of some spirit, they did us all credit. He used to come into my office to discuss with me his schemes for them, and then go on to tell me what the 'best people' thought, assuring me, if it was something slightly progressive, that they were good solid citizens, who agreed with him. Having to deal with so many die- hards, I found him a great comfort and inspiration. On this particular trip I thought it a comfort to know, that he would be there, as I was a trifle uncertain of my place in what was reputed to be a centre of fanaticism. Moreover I was not sure, what I could do for five days, if the school had not actually come into being.

At this time of year, the island was joined to the railway by a short causeway and a luxurious car met me at the station. South of Khartoum there is always a little rain in the summer and this year it had come early, delaying the train to such an extent, that we did not arrive[12] until eleven o'clock at night. I was escorted to the car by one of the Sayed's men of affairs,[13] with whom I had often had dealings. He was a tall man with a thin, ferrety face, and about the biggest *immah* anyone wore. Somehow his appearance was reminiscent of an *Arabian Nights* illustration and I often thought, although our relations were always most cordial, that I should not care to cross swords with him.

I could not see much on the way[14] to the house[15] but brilliant electric light from a private generating plant lit up the garden, as we turned between flower beds at some gates[16] and drove down a long straight avenue of *neem* trees with a white, high-domed pavilion in the middle. This, which was much in the style of those one sees in Persian pictures, stood in the centre of a long terrace behind a balustrade of rather crude plaster. from the pavilion

---

12. Dr Beasley arrived 'at Rabak, the station before Kosti. Rabak is an unusual place. It is rather a wartime product as a junction when the military had to move up this way and Jebelein had to be the embarkation point. After the Mediterranean was cleared, Rabak reverted to an ordinary wayside station'.
13. S.A.R.'s *wakīl*, al-Zein Amin. 'He always dressed in Persil-white cotton robes.'
14. The road—'clumps of grass-roofed *tukl*s at intervals and beasts wandering about. There were fruit gardens.'
15. Sayyid 'Abd al-Raḥmān al-Mahdī rebuilt the Mahdī's home at Aba Island, which was subsequently destroyed by Nimeiri in 1970 (See Mohamed Ahmed Mahgoub, *Democracy on Trial*, 1974, pp.237-239).
16. 'I was surprised to see that the last one before we turned into the drive had barbed wire on it. I shouldn't have thought a holy man wielding all that power would have needed to take such secular precautions.'

a wide flight of steps led up to a deep verandah in front of the house, and a single room at each end of the balustrade flanked the terrace. The impressive simplicity of it all standing out clearly against the surrounding darkness gave an inviting welcome to a weary traveller.

At once I was taken to the left-hand room, a large and pleasant spot with plenty of doors and tall windows, comfortably furnished with an odd shabby collection, which was shabby more from shoddiness than any great age.[17] A tray of fruit and milk[18] was brought for me and I was told that the Sayed would receive me in the morning. That, I decided, was most considerate of him, since all I wanted at that point was to curl up on the welcome bed which had been prepared at my end of the terrace. A small bathroom under a covered way from the guest room completed my suite.

**Wednesday 16.5.45.**

After a cool and restful night it was no hardship to be up early, for although no-one came to disturb me, the bed was in rather an exposed position

> (on a very high *mastaba* in the square garden enclosed by the balustrade and the walls of the house and outbuildings)

and there appeared to be many preparations afoot.

> Next morning I could see the layout of the garden. Subsequently I went into the house which was not as grand as I expected. There was a largish room on entry which had some (oldish) good rugs in it and the usual type of easy chairs. There was an archway into a much bigger room, running the length of the house, which had a large dining table in it and groups of chairs by the windows at each end. Other rooms led out of this but I was not taken to them.

As soon as I was dressed our Sudanese inspectress[19] called, to talk to me about the school. Sitt Medina, whom I have mentioned before, was here now, because she belonged to the Sayed's household in a feudal way, which is not easy to define. I was delighted to see her, since I felt slightly astray in this masculine world centring its values on the religious eminence of the Sayed, and, although she subscribed to this unquestioning devotion to him, nevertheless she belonged also to the domain of girls' schools, where I was at home. We talked too the same kind of women's language. She was living,

17. 'A plain white painted bed, a dressing table covered with messy green baize, with a badly hinged three-faced mirror, also used as a wash stand. A common sort of desk in one corner and bookcase in the other. A round table in the middle covered with a green chenille cloth. There were two chests of drawers, pseudo-Jacobean. They looked old and shabby but were rather badly made.'
18. 'I did not like the milk much. I learnt later that it may have been buffalo.'
19. Sitt Medina Abdulla.

she told me, in the back premises. 'Now', she said with emphasis, 'if you want me at any time, any time at all for any reason, you must just send word. I will come at once.'

I thanked her warmly and suggested breezily, that I would come round to see her some time and have a good long chat. At this, however, she became a bit confused and said that might be very awkward, as she was staying in Hadi's[20] house, and it was not like being in her own. Obviously I should have been a great embarrassment and I had to accept my disappointment at not being let loose among the Sayed's women and to be glad, that she was within call, although I could not imagine why I should need her. Then she went back to [her] prayers and I sat down to my knitting.

About quarter to eight a servant came to say, that the Sayed would like to see me in his office at eight o'clock. To my surprise some ten minutes later, just as I was gathering up my work, I noticed S.A.R. dash across the garden to a splendid, grey horse, held by a groom. He presented a very fine sight, dressed in the Arabian manner with a loose over-garment, a flowing head-dress bound with a girdle and short boots but I did not see him mount. Rather at a loss I was just beginning again on my knitting, when the boy re-appeared exactly at eight o'clock and I obediently followed him to the [office][21] at the other end of the balustrade. Left on my own I wandered round it but there was nothing to investigate and, as it happened, no time to do so. Promptly at two minutes past eight the Sayed galloped up to the office door to dismount full of vigour from his morning exercise. We greeted one another warmly, as I thanked him for the arrangements he had made for my comfort. We would go into breakfast at once, he said, as the horse was led away. It had been such a pretty little bit of stagecraft I had not the heart to ask him how far he had been, nor let him know I had seen his departure.

Breakfast was not the family meal I had hoped. Although I did not expect any of the ladies of the household, since I knew that respectable women should never eat in front of their husbands, I had thought some of his sons might appear in the way they did at Sheikh Babikr Bedri's but there was nothing so informal. The vision of five days *tête-à-tête* meals was a bit intimidating but no-one could have been kinder and friendlier than my host nor more anxious to put me at my ease. I soon discovered that he could

20. *Imām* al-Hādī 'Abd al-Raḥmān succeeded his brother Ṣiddīq 'Abd al-Raḥmān in 1962; he was educated in Egypt and spoke a little English; he was killed in April 1970 at the time of the Aba Island massacre, when possibly 12,000 *Anṣār* were slaughtered by Nimeiri's forces and extensive holdings of the Mahdi's family were confiscated.
21. 'An ordinary sort of office with no manifest signs of unduly hard work.'

carry on a conversation at the rate at which I spoke Arabic with his mind
running on other things. He could turn to me and utter *kyda* ('really'), in a
deep oleaginous tone and in the same breath summon a servant to give him
instructions about some detail of the arrangements which had just crossed
his mind. Instead of hoary trusted retainers I was surprised to find how
young these attendants were and how much in need of appropriate training
[except Abdel Latif, the cook]. All the meals were enormous. Breakfast
consisted of porridge with cream and sugar, fried fish, fried eggs on liver,
toast and marmalade and piles of delicious local fruit (guavas, mangoes and
bananas). Lunch and dinner always included an outsize turkey, served
whole, while for tea a large, iced, plum cake appeared, a new one every
afternoon. In addition there were little bits of thoughtfulness, which I
warmed to. During some desultory conversation the Sayed expatiated on
the value of different kinds of milk, goat's, cow's, camel's, buffalo's, and he
learned that I had never tasted camel's. That night a glass of milk appeared
on my late tray, camel's milk, my servant explained, sent expressly by the
Sayed's order. On another day while being shown the fruit gardens I was
making small talk and suggested, that perhaps the orange was the nicest
fruit of all. Oranges on the estate happened to be out of season but from
somewhere a few appeared on the breakfast table especially to suit my
tastes.

Dinner the first night was a notable breach with custom, which, to my
sorrow, was not repeated. When I was summoned to the *mastaba*, where
only one faint candle[22] was set far away from the table, I heard a woman's
voice. This was S.A.R.'s youngest wife, of whom I had heard in Khartoum,
as she occasionally went riding with him in the *Sunt* Forest, albeit so
muffled up that no-one had seen her. Eating out there with her husband and
a strange woman must have been most indecorous and no doubt the dim
light was lest any skulker in the garden should see her face. The talk during
dinner was not of the most brilliant but it was all very amiable. She chatted
about Erkowit, the Sudanese version of a hill station in the Red Sea Hills,
where she could go out walking. She made little wagers with her husband as
to when the rain would come. After the meal was finished, she said she
would come to my room with me to make sure, that I was comfortable.

> I could not see her very well but she had a fresh, attractive voice ... I said I
> would sleep inside that night. I think she came to have a better look at me in a
> good light ... She was under thirty, I thought.

In the harsher electric glare we each had a good look at the other. If she had
not been so prematurely fat, she would have been extremely pretty, with a

22. *Shammadan [sham'adān]*, candleholder.

skin of a most attractive coppery colour but with her face scarred in the usual manner. Unfortunately this comeliness was not set off by the graceful folds of the *tobe*, for she was wearing a frock of some checked material ill-cut and badly fitting with European shoes and stockings. What amazed me most was a sort of bandeau round her head made of cheap red and silver lamé and giving a sort of coronet effect. I should have liked very much to have pursued the acquaintance but she never emerged again and, after Medina's confusion about my visiting the women's quarters, I felt it might be unmannerly to enquire too much. Medina was so loyal, that she never let fall a word of gossip and it would have been indecent to have pressed her about the Sayed's motives for producing the lady and then hiding her. But it was a pity.

**Thursday 17.5.45.**

Even though I was never permitted behind the scenes, my days were full of activity of an undemanding kind, since the Sayed was most resourceful in thinking of things to show me. The first day began with a parade of Boy Scouts from the Coptic College in Khartoum, who marched off to the sound of fife and drum. This seemed an unexpected piece of broadmindedness on both sides.

> There were also some Gordon Memorial College[23] students of whom Medina's son was one. I was introduced to him. He seemed a pleasant young man.

We were accompanied to the [girls'] school by S.A.R.'s son, Hadi, who has now, I learn, inherited the religious side of his father's duties. He did not figure largely in the rest of the visit but I remember noting at the time, that he had one of the gentlest faces I had ever seen in a Sudanese and was a particularly amiable person to talk to. As the [girls'] school was a private one to be financed entirely by the Sayed, my duties were only advisory but I soon discovered that, despite his wealth and proclamation of a desire for girls' education, he did not intend to do more than supply a cheap building put up no doubt by free labour on the estate.

> Sitt Medina came too. We turned to the right outside the flower gardens and drove on a few hundred yards ... A simple brick building with two class rooms

---

23. His mediation in the 1931 Gordon College students' strike meant S.A.R. obtained a hold over the *afandiyya*, according to the government's view. S.A.R. participated in the founding of the Graduates' own club in Omdurman in 1919 by graduates from the Gordon Memorial College.

and in each about 30 little girls sitting on *birsh* mats. As one might expect ...
only a few slates borrowed from the boys' school and a few readers.

[otherwise] there was no equipment of any sort and only one teacher,[24] who
had recently been dismissed from Government Service on a charge of
Lesbianism to which she had confessed. When I told her, that now she had a
chance to make good, she assured me that she was a reformed character,
and I felt that Medina would keep a stern eye on her. No doubt the Sayed
knew the whole story but it did not seem fair to the girl to discuss it with
him.

Just across the yard was a long, white-washed building with a thatched
roof which housed the twenty-five spinning wheels, the ostensible reason for
the venture, although about sixty other little girls had turned up in addition
to the spinners.

> Some of the girls could spin a really good thread. I wondered whether the
> quantity that they could spin, even given 25 wheels working four hours every
> day, is very important. I asked to see the weaving, and I was shown rather
> hastily a piece of *damur baladi* which might have been woven anywhere, I was
> never taken to see the weaving.

I promised to make out time-tables and schemes of work for them all,—a
promise which I faithfully kept and Medina's son translated my efforts into
Arabic for the Sayed to approve. As the school was not under my
supervision, that was the last I heard of it.

> I suspect Es Surra will teach a few of the brightest in the top class ... and the
> others will be left to take their chance.
>     I gathered that the sight of the forlorn little girls sitting doing nothing was
> supposed to touch my heart so that I would straightaway provide a teacher.

In the years to come, however, the girls of the Island were not neglected, as
an ordinary school was started there.[25] At this point just after the war
resources were thin.

> We were already twenty teachers short and I wanted a proper Government
> School on Aba Island and complete control of it.

---

24. 'To my surprise the mistress at the school turned out to be es-Surra Hassan dismissed by us
on a confessed charge of Lesbianism. Anyway S.A.R. knew all about it, so I decided the
responsibility was his. The girl was living in the *hosh* and presumably any fun and games could
be checked. Even Mekki Abbas thought I had made rather a fuss in 1943.'
25. The Sayyid's palace was taken over by the Government and in the 1980s was used,
ironically, as a girls' school.

It would have been regarded by politicians as favouring S.A.R.'s faction, if we had arranged a Government one there, when there were so many neutral places demanding girls' schools.

> Medina was told she could go home.[26] I had the system of fallow explained to me, saw the river, the pumps and the workshop. There was, however, trouble with the pump because the river was so low. There was therefore feverish digging, men at work deepening an irrigation channel to let the water in. The engineer in charge was an Italian, a pleasant, capable person, presumably an ex-enemy alien. He had a Yugoslav to help him. The workshop is linked up with the boys' school so that the boys get some idea of making and mending tools.

The rest of the estate was interesting in its general feudal atmosphere but had one unexpected feature. As we passed some cattle sheds, which were being put up, we came across a group of women and children carrying building materials, even the tiny ones toddling along with some little thing in their hands. Hadi commented that, when the children started young, they were able to learn the work. Admittedly no-one looked at all unhappy nor overburdened and there was no appearance of strain or hustle. Activity was more feverish down by the river, where a large number of men were digging channels for the irrigation pumps. The actual work in the fields we did not inspect, as it would have made the trip too protracted. What I could not in all good manners discuss with the Sayed and his son was the custom, whereby these labourers came for short periods to cultivate or to pick cotton[27] in return for the holy man's blessing.[28] The ordering of his husbandry in this way did not preclude S.A.R. from selling his cotton at the highest market prices he could obtain. There could be no reason for anyone to interfere with this arrangement, since the men concerned came voluntarily and received a spiritual satisfaction difficult for outsiders to appreciate. One could reasonably assume that in time the custom would die out of its own accord but, when Trade Unionism really becomes a force in Africa, the European brand may find problems of a nicety not expected. Who, for example, would be rash enough to weigh spiritual satisfaction of a blessing against minimum rates of pay?

26. After the visit to the school.
27. Aba Island cotton scheme established in 1928, which helped S.A.R. to meet his social obligations to support his followers and dependents. Dr Beasley felt 'that made one think of serf labour on Russian estates'.
28. *Baraka*, a heritable quality of grace, linking a spiritual leader with his followers.

Unfortunately the dairy plus dairy maid, next on our programme,[29] was not on show but we sat in its office for a few minutes, while S.A.R. began some high-flown talk about the value of education.[30] It seemed an odd moment to engage me in such a discourse, until I noticed some old chaps nearby listening intently and nodding sagely, until the speaker broke off abruptly, when the car returned.

> We then went back to the house and I escaped to write a simple programme of work for the girls' school. The main emphasis of the school was on arts and crafts—knitting, cloth, clothes, *birsh* mats and basket making. [She later sent a simple list of equipment to S.A.R. to the value of £10].

On the estate was also a museum, where I was shown in the afternoon [after tea] the holy relics of the Mahdi but apart from these there was nothing unique and only an expert could have decided whether the pieces of armour were really Saracen and the pots[31] and shards of any archaeological significance. What stands out clearly was that, as it was hot, the Sayed kept mopping his brow and then dropping his handkerchief or rosary and ordering Medina to pick them up, which she most willingly and dutifully obeyed. Outside the building was a light horse carriage reminding me of the sort used for trotting races. I asked if it had any special connection and was told none but it had come from Asmara. After this Medina was told to go away, while we two had tea in state on the terrace.[32] This too, I thought, was a pity.

Far more interesting than the objects in the museum was the ceremony which took place every afternoon about this time, when the *wakil*s presented a number of men for the Sayed's blessing. It was not a particularly spirited performance, as the old man just walked along the line and had each person's affairs explained by the *wakil* but it must have been of value to all of them. Some days S.A.R. then sat in the pavilion with his clients at his feet like an orthodox Oriental picture and one afternoon, when all the others had gone, an old man stayed on by himself and was evidently recounting some long tale, which gave vast amusement to them both. As it was

---

29. According to her diary, Dr Beasley visited the dairy before looking at the fields and irrigation scheme.

30. S.A.R. established or contributed to many *khalwa*s (*khalāwī*) both in the North and in the South and financially aided Southern scholars. He showed a lively interest in the traditional Islamic arts of literature and poetry. He, amongst others, supported the foundation of the Ahfad University College at Omdurman.

31. The museum was housed 'in a room on a raised platform rather behind my bedroom'. It also contained the Mahdī's camel saddle and 'a white metal basin in bas relief supposedly dug up near Jebel Moya'.

32. According to the diary 'At 4.30 the Sayed and I had tea in state on the terrace'. Then they went to the museum.

obviously no occasion for a foreign woman, I could only sit inside my door with my knitting, watching the play and hearing nothing.

The evening after the museum visit the little, carriage from Asmara drew up outside my door with the groom explaining, that the Sayed had thought I should like to try riding in it. A kind thought, which I much appreciated, even if we did not go very far. In fact we[33] went to inspect the preparations for the Flower Show,[34] which was for the great day on Sunday, when the school was to be officially opened, and then we returned to the open space outside the garden gate to watch the rehearsal for the victory celebrations [to be held] the next morning.

> There was an impressive troop of about 25 horses. Then came the Coptic Boy Scouts and some local troop in rather more highly coloured clothes. There were drums, fifes and bagpipes, not playing the same tune but playing all at once.
>
> I was then taken to see the buffaloes, the only ones in the Sudan, I was told.

As there was only one seat in the carriage beside the groom I wondered about the etiquette of returning but to my relief we both walked, certainly as far as the pavilion in the centre of the garden, where we rested, while the Sayed asked me a lot of questions about Burma. He appeared surprised to know that Burmans had only one wife, seeing that there was no obligatory marriage ceremony. I wondered what confused picture my laboured explanations had left, as no doubt his mind had also been running on other matters at the same time.

> I asked Sitt Medina to come to my room about 6 pm to explain the programme I had written for the school. Sitt Medina was waiting for me and we went through my little programme. She took the programme and said she would get her son to translate it. This she did and it was handed to S.A.R. She was not allowed to stay to tea.

Memorable among the other happenings was that night's storm, all of a piece with the unusual setting. I had decided to sleep indoors, as I did not want the hasty scramble of carting my bedding some distance, if the ominous-looking clouds should suddenly descend. Even with all the doors and windows open it was very hot and for about an hour or so thunder rumbled in the distance. By eleven o'clock, the electricity had been turned

33. Dr Beasley went with the Sayyid in the Asmara carriage to visit the Flower Show. 'I felt a little insecure but the groom was a nice, capable person.'
34. In the 1930s and 1940s S.A.R. made frequent visits to Egypt, usually to visit the Royal Agricultural Show of Egypt with contacts in Egypt's Ministry of Agriculture, the Egyptian Agricultural Organisation and the Royal Egyptian Agricultural Society.

off at the main [generator] and I lay in bed watching increasingly frequent flashes of lightning streaking round through the many windows. At one point, when a particularly violent crack burst, I wondered if anything had been hit and felt the storm a slightly sinister background in the stronghold of Mahdi-ism.

> It was too hot to close the shutters and even when I shut my eyes and tried to sleep the vividness of the flashes was disturbing.

Then the rain tore down suddenly, no warning drops, just a great wall of water, accompanied by a terrific gale. I tried to close the shutters, shouting meanwhile for my servant, although I had small hope of making anyone hear. He was certainly housed hundreds of yards away and safely battened down. As the heavy wooden shutters were fastened outside, I could not move them but after a frantic struggle I managed to dodge the curtains streaming out into the room and close the glass windows. By this time my nightdress was soaked and one side of the bed was damp. So vivid and so continuous was the lightning, that I was able by its aid to find a fresh nightdress and to take off the damp sheet and re-arrange the bedding. On the big round table, covered with a fringed chenille cloth, stood a perfectly good lamp but my cheap war-time matches had quickly become so damp, that the heads dropped off. Electric torches were one of the luxuries that had early disappeared from the shops during the years of scarcity.

I had not been lying down for long, when I heard a disastrous drip followed by others at shorter intervals and then a virulent stream on to the bed. The wooden roof had evidently shrunken during the dry weather and the rain was running down between the planks. I explored the possibilities all round and by dint of shifting about the heavy furniture found a spot into which I could push the bed and have half of it away from the most insistent splashes. When I had finished this, I needed a dry sheet and pillows from my bedding roll, luckily still covered up in one corner. As I tried to settle again, I thought I saw something darting across in the lightning flashes, by now almost without a pause. Away in the village at the end of the garden a loud and uninterrupted moaning sounded all through the rest of the night, but whether human or animal I could not be sure. I learnt the next morning that it was in fact a madman disturbed by the thunder. I curled up in the corner of my bed, where I hoped to receive the least splashes and took myself to task for harbouring wild fancies.

**Friday 18.5.45.**

Evidently I must have slept more than I expected, for I was wakened by the dawn call to prayer. Then came gradually growing in volume a most sonorous chanting nearby. Looking out from behind the curtain I saw a great circle of men squatting on the wet earth around the pavilion on the terrace. In rhythmic and musical responses they answered the deep voice of the leader, a most impressive service in its splendid simplicity, these solemn worshippers in the grey light on their day of religion.[35] A great peace lay over it all in the swiftly spreading dawn, made even more intense by contrast with the wild and noisy tumult of the night's storm. No breeze ruffled the stillness of the cool, rain-washed air, as these dignified figures knelt there chanting against a background of soft, pearly shadows. The whole effect was of strength and sincerity, which was deeply moving, and distilled a sure feeling of contentment and security.

As I picked my way among the puddles on my floor, re-assurance came to me on a lesser plane. Sitting on the bed rail its fore- legs crossed, its head cocked apparently watching me, was the largest praying mantis I had ever seen. Therefore something darting about in the lightning had not been a fiction of my disordered imagination or some kind of visual hallucination. In fact apart from the dampness and disorder life had quite a normal appearance in the daylight. Also I knew by now the wooden roof had probably swollen again and there would be no repetition of last night's dripping.

> About 8 o'clock I got a message from the Sayed. Would I like a turn in the garden? It was beautifully cool. We strolled down to the second pavilion in the middle of the drive and then chairs were brought and we sat talking.

S.A.R., coming back from prayers with a large and ornate book under his arm stopped to warn me, that breakfast might be late, as visitors were coming. He was very gratified, when I told him how impressed I had been by the dawn service, a special service, he explained, because of the Victory Celebrations. Fortunately the visitors arrived in good time, the D.C.[36] from

---

35. 'It was a special ceremony to begin the day of the festival.'
36. Donald Frederick Hawley, C.M.G., M.B.E. (b.22.5.21-). Educated at Radley and new College, Oxford; 27.12.41 First appointment; 1941-44 Governor-General's Temporary Commission as Bimbashi in S.D.F., 1941 Royal Artillery, 1941-43 S.D.F.; 1944-46 Blue Nile, A.D.C., Kosti; 1946-47 Kassala, A.D.C., Gedaref District, based at Khasm el-Girba; 1947 Legal Department; 1947 Police Magistrate, Khartoum; 1947-51 Deputy Assistant Legal Secretary (Lands); 1952-55 Chief Registrar of the Judiciary; 1955 retired; 1951 Barrister-at-Law, Inner Temple (called 1951); Subsequently, Britain's first Ambassador to Oman. Author and diplomat.

Kosti, some twenty miles distant, with a new British schoolmaster[37] and the Sudanese *mamur*.[38] The meal was still very stately but I enjoyed the bigger company.

> It was exactly the same food as the day before ... Mr Hawley's Arabic made me feel ashamed. That and the fact that he was talking of commercial matters made him really hold S.A.R.'s attention.

I was sorry to hear them say, that they could not stay to lunch, as they had already been stuck in the mud several times on the way, and they feared that the causeway from the island might soon be flooded. They remained, however, for the Victory Parade, where we all sat in splendour in a row of armchairs in a field at the bottom of the garden. I had, of course, been a spectator at the rehearsal and was sorry that an item, which had put the girls in the picture, had been left out. This had been a cart with girls sitting on it and spinning vigorously on the wheels from the school, the horse being led by a sort of King Cotton in a tall, pointed hat made of lint and with a very long beard and moustache of the same. He had really made such a good clown, that S.A.R. had laughed at him uproariously. It seemed a pity to cut it out and I enquired about the girls to receive a hasty answer, that the procession had been too long. This and many other small happenings during our acquaintance made me me wonder how far the Sayed could really initiate a forward policy among his followers and how far he had to take note of conservative views, if he did not want his position weakened. He might be deeply revered but it was very doubtful, if his lightest word was law.

Thousands of people milled around, however, and evidently enjoyed the show immensely. There were some long, flowery speeches, the marching band of the Coptic Boy Scouts, followed by a local band. These were boys in the age range from six to sixteen, dressed in a bright uniform—

> blue cotton shorts, khaki shirts outside these and neckerchiefs and *immah*s of pink (blotting-paper pink for preference, but any pink where this failed)—

and all stepping out most valiantly, although many had been put into canvas shoes several sizes too large [for all the smaller boys]. With their thin little legs they looked like a Micky Mouse cartoon and I found it very endearing but it was regarded as a serious business, I gathered, and did not raise a smile.

---

37. H.J. Dickinson, schoolmaster from Kosti; 9.2.45 First appointment; 1946 master, Wadi Seidna Secondary School, based at Wadi Seidna.
38. *Mamur* Kosti District based in Kosti in 1945 was Sedik Nadim; 1.1.18 First appointment; 24.2.45-c.1946 Blue Nile.

Nevertheless they had been very well drilled and they all kept in step ... There was a little more care about the bands too, so that they weren't both playing different tunes at the same time.

It would be all too easy in any affair like this to treat it in a 'Back Garden of *Allah*' spirit but that would hardly be fitting. I had, however, seen so many Sudanese entertainments that were excellent, that a poor imitation of little bits of European ways distressed me. But if the people for whom it was intended, were pleased by it, then that was the whole point of the party. Games by the schoolboys and a parade of horses finished the performance. Probably it was all followed by some kind of feasting but I was not shown that. In Omdurman we had roasted sixteen oxen whole but I did not remember smelling anything so succulent here.

> Then the crowd was told to come nearer ... horses were used to keep them back. I was most surprised that no-one was trampled ... nor any of the horses bolt. There were a number of other men in ordinary clothes with little badges sewn on ... appointed ... to keep ... order. The chief 'order keeper' who stood near us flourishing a stick wore a wonderful but ill-fitting uniform of *damur*—a sort of bush shirt with celluloid buttons of blotting paper pink—a rather large *immah* in white just the shape of a policeman's but with a lion rampant instead of a province badge. There was a general sloppiness about his garb which, like the scouts' marching turned him into a caricature instead of being a praiseworthy effort.

Then there was a visit to encourage the preparations for the Flower Show. With traces of the damage of the previous storm all round I could not imagine how they could be ready for Sunday, but I was wrong, for the feverish replanting then in progress was finished in time. A most enthusiastic Egyptian agriculturalist[39] was in charge of the proceedings, only too anxious to show us round again and to expound his hopes of founding a centre here to advise the local cultivators on better methods.

I was sorry to see the visitors go, for the Sayed and I were back to our dignified duet. He changed for lunch into a dazzlingly white version of the sort of clothes the ordinary *sheikh*s wear. In this he made such a handsome picture that it is sad to recall, that on one of his rare visits to London he turned up at Ascot in plus fours and *kefiyah*.[40] Dressed with the excellent taste in which I always saw him, he would have been an ornament to any

39. Hassan (Effendi) used to work for the Sudan Government at Miri, Northern Province and was a specialist on fruit farms.
40. In 1919 S.A.R. was included in a delegation to London (with Sayyid 'Alī al-Mirghanī and Sharīf Yūsuf al-Hindī to present an address to King George V and Queen Mary (28.7.1919). He presented the King with (supposedly) his father's sword (but the king returned it to S.A.R. to use in defence of the Empire). He was conferred with the honour of Commander of the Royal Victorian Order (C.V.O.). Sir Reginald Wingate translated at this meeting.

enclosure. At this particular meal[41] I glimpsed a side of him which was most attractive. During the turkey course by some maladroit movement he shot his portion into his lap and the pristine glory of his robes was disfigured by spreading stains of grease and gravy. Without too much flurry the boys helped him to remove the outer garment and with it he sent away the *immah*, retaining only the little skull cap. Then sat down again to finish his food looking like some homely, benevolent merchant.[42] When coffee arrived, we sat one at each end of a long *cannaba*, a kind of wooden sofa with hard cushions, and he slipped off his shoes, tucking up under him his feet in little white socks. In this garb somehow he quite unbent and dissipated the regal tension, not exactly by frivolous conversation but by a much more ordinary manner of talking. I had never liked him as much.

> [Fri] It did not rain [hard] that night and anyway I took the precaution of lighting the lamp before the electricity went off.

## Saturday 19.5.45

> [Sat] Once again I was invited into the garden before breakfast ... . After a lot of talk, the visitors were sent away and S.A.R. [and I] had another dignified meal perched in solemn state in the tall pavilion halfway down the drive. I decided that it doesn't improve a plate of fried eggs and liver to carry it quarter of a mile before consumption.
>   I was then packed off with Medina to see the fruit gardens and afterwards the school. The school was going rather as I expected, only there were no girls spinning. We explained the new plan to Es Surra. She looked a bit vague about the girls' clubs in the afternoons. She wrote it down but I don't suppose she'll do anything about it.

For part of the time I tried to do what I could for the school but it soon became clear, that walking anywhere was considered unsuitable and I was diffident about making claims on transport. I would not have pried where I was not wanted, but I did have the feeling of not being free to roam even as far as the village to talk to the girls and their teacher. But the Sayed kept thinking of little trips to amuse me; a visit to see his water buffaloes, a look at the stables, and, failing all else, to measure once again the progress of the Flower Show again.

> A lot of people came crowding around on the way. A schoolteacher from Khartoum North came and joined us. We then went to look at the exhibition in the boys' school—the collection rather scrappy and pointless.

41. Lunch consisted of 'soup, fish, a whole turkey, a white cornflour mould flanked by pieces of tinned peaches'.
42. In his *jallābiyya* and *ṭāqiyya* (skull cap).

Dr Pridie[43] came to lunch—a welcome break—and we all had tea on the lawn together with the Sudanese doctors. After tea we went to the tent and Hassan Effendi explained the agricultural show again.

Inspecting horses was not in my line at all but I gathered there was a rooted conviction, that all Englishmen and women were devoted to them and I must be burning to admire his various purchases. By this time a number of guests had begun to arrive and a select company of schoolmasters, doctors and minor officials came along to watch the animals led out or left to prance round the yard. Not being able to discuss a horse's points in English I found it difficult to respond adequately. The only Arabic word I could recall even remotely connected was hunting; I therefore suggested, to show that i was still awake, that one large beast might be a good hunter. This desultory pronouncement was taken up with such seriousness and passed on for the Sayed's consideration that I felt not a little foolish.

The position of these guests interested me, as they raised a point of etiquette, that, luckily, I did not have to solve. In my house such men would have sat down with me to tea but not here. They were entertained to tea but they sat below us, while the Sayed and I remained in state on the terrace. Moreover I noticed that they were given the plum cake, which we had had the day before, while we had a large, new one, which was sent down to them, when we had eaten what we wanted. This distinction may have been due to *baraka*, that subtle mixture of blessing and spirit, which among its many manifestations, goes into anyone who shares food with a holy man. In fact an awed Sudanese once told me, that even I must have been full of *baraka* after having tea with the Sayed, and that in a gradually diminishing degree it could be passed on to him and thence to others. What I thought a pity was that we could not join their circle, as they were a very merry party, and now that we were on show again the Sayed's homely relaxing at lunch-time never appeared again.

After tea S.A.R. went along to sit in the middle of the circle and talk to them.
Medina came in for a few minutes but wouldn't stay as there were special prayers. There were also more men for S.A.R. to bless. I stayed in my room

43. 'Dr Pridie refused to go to the stables.' Sir Eric Denholm Pridie, K.C.M.G., C.M.G., D.S.O., O.B.E., 3N., M.B., B.S. (b.1896-d.1978). First World War served in France and Mesopotamia, awarded D.S.O.; 2.6.24 First appointment; 1924-27 Medical Inspector, Port Sudan; 1927-29 M.I., Kassala; 1929-31 Senior M.I., Wad Medani; 1931-32 S.M.I., Khartoum; 1932-33 Assistant Director, Sudan Medical Service; 1933-45 Director of the Sudan Medical Service, based in Khartoum; 1934-45 member of Governor-General's Council; 1940-43 Brigadier R.A.M.C. in Sudan and organised military medical requirements to meet the threat of invasion from Eritrea by the Italians; 1945-49 Health Counsellor to the British Embassy in Cairo; 1946-49 Health Adviser to the British Middle East Office; 1949- Chief Medical Officer to Colonial Office.

reading and knitting. I began to feel there was a slight *harem* flavour about my room!

Sat. evening it was cold and we had dinner indoors.

Later in the evening we did sit round in the garden talking, while more guests arrived.

> The other son, Saddiq,[44] had arrived the night before by car with a party of guests for the opening of the school. The guests were some Sudanese doctors, the Head of the *Maahad*[45] and there was a dignified and I should think very observant old *sheikh* from the Hejaz ... They looked quite nice people, *kadi*s, *effendi*s, merchants.

Some of them I knew and we greeted one another in the usual way, but when the Head of the *Ma'ahad* appeared, his embarrassment was all too obvious. As the Principal of a theological school it was not surprising that he should have the reputation of being fanatically strict in matters of religion.

> He kissed S.A.R.'s hand, shook hands or embraced all the others but was obviously so much at a loss at what to do about me that he studiously avoided looking at me ... He turned a rather perturbed eye on me. So I waved a friendly greeting which received a rather sickly acknowledgement.

I was amused at his inability to deal with anything so unprecedented as a woman on this holy ground, sponsored apparently by the holy man himself. He resolved his problem by refusing to look in my direction and seating himself as far as possible on the other side of the group. No-one else seemed to mind and we had a very genial evening until the Sayed and I departed for our grand dinner on the terrace in full view.

During this we mentioned the arrangements for the next day including my departure and the Sayed said, that there was now between us—and he used some high-flown classical word unfamiliar to me. I had an idea that it meant something like a bond of friendship but was not sure of the exact implications. Remembering that I had come as a Government representative and aware of the political ferment connected with him, I took

44. *Imām* Ṣiddīq 'Abd al-Raḥmān (d. September 1961) S.A.R.'s eldest son, who succeeded him as *Imām* in March 1959. Ṣiddīq accompanied his father to London in September 1952. He was succeeded by his brother al-Hādī. Ṣiddīq's Oxford-educated son Ṣādiq was Prime Minister from July 1966 to May 1967, in detention in 1970, sent into exile to Cairo and then lived in Oxford. He master-minded a serious coup attempt against Nimeiri in 1976. He became Prime Minister again from 1986 to 1988 and is at present under detention.
45. *Al-ma'had al-'ilmī*, the orthodox religious college in Omdurman for the *'ulamā'*, with teaching strictly following that of al-Azhar in Cairo to train religious functionaries other than *qāḍī*s. It started in 1901 and was managed by a board of *'ulamā'* appointed by the Government under the auspices of the Department of Education. This is now the University of Omdurman.

fright and did not want in my ignorance to assent to some support for his schemes. His own fault it might be, but the Sayed had earned for himself the reputation of always hiding his real motives in anything he undertook and I had never understood why I needed to stay five days to advise on the 'school for girls who spin'. I replied therefore that I was always anxious to help girls to be educated, but that was obviously not the required answer, and we talked of other things, among which was S.A.R.'s unbounded admiration for Ibn Saud I.

> Secondary and Gordon Memorial College boys who were going to do a play were dashing around during the meal. I think it was to be staged the next day and we were having a private view. It eventually started at 10 o'clock.

By this time a screen had been set up in the garden and two chairs in front of it with a group of others some distance behind them, where the guests of the afternoon were seated. Women very heavily muffled crept round by the wall and sat afar off. I should have liked to talk to them, but I was so firmly conducted to the front seat, that I was just left again to the puzzlement of what was the correct behaviour in this situation. The first two films perturbed me still more regarding the proper response. We were shown a short piece of the coronation of George VI with the King surrounded by cheering crowds. Immediately there followed a scene, with S.A.R. descending from his car to be mobbed by larger and more vociferous throngs than in the former picture and the showing went on much longer.

> Himself addressing large crowds during Ramadan. The second reel was all S.A.R.; true it finished with his horses running a race but I hadn't got over the original juxtaposition of famous men, more especially as there had been much talk at dinner of Ibn Saud and what an astute and clever chap he was. I understood S.A.R. to say that he had a son with Ibn Saud.

Pertinent comment was hard to make but the old man was probably satisfied by the spectacle without my having to join in the admiration. Some good films on cotton followed; plays from some secondary school boys continued the performance but by midnight I was beginning to flag. I remarked on the fact that the women had all disappeared and the Sayed replied that it had been nice for them to have a little treat occasionally, as they were so secluded. In the country here surely, I protested, they could go out sometimes. His reply was a hasty 'no' and a complete change of the subject. I went to bed before the end but was not disturbed by any late rejoicing, for soon the rain came again. Not the sinister sort of storm of the early part of the week but a good steady downpour, appropriate for any Flower Show.

**Sunday 19.5.45**

[Due to the rain] all the arrangements for the morning were thus upset and I sat down again just inside my door with my knitting to watch the various comings and goings of servants, *wakils* and visitors and to listen to the growing hum of the crowds gathering round the centre of activities.

> I hoped there would be someone I knew. I got a message to say S.A.R. had gone to the mosque and would I start breakfast?

After prayers, S.A.R. came, very resplendent, although dressed with impeccable taste, a large copy of the scriptures under his arm, and sat down for ten minutes to discuss his changed plans. Cars had been sent to the station for the 'hundred and one' guests, whom he told me, he had invited, but so far they had not yet returned. Possibly the rain had caused some delay on the railway. I continued with my knitting but the ten o'clock arrived, the scheduled starting hour, and still no summons. At eleven a schoolmaster escorted me to the house, where the Sayed, was chatting comfortably to an old *sheikh*, whom he introduced as a cousin who preferred the 'old ways'.

> He looked to me a ribald old man who wouldn't care a toss for this person he had known as a boy and would probably laugh at his pretentiousness.

He seemed to me to have an irreverent twinkle in his eye and certainly not a particularly respectful manner of address to his grand relative. For half an hour we kept listening for the cars and then S.A.R. decided, that we ought not to keep the people waiting any longer. He was strikingly even-tempered about all this upset and remained so throughout the day, although the programme had to be revised constantly on the spur of the moment.

I did not actually see him mount and, as he was a heavy man, the process was probably not very agile, but once on a splendid horse the Sayed was far more impressive to my way of thinking than in his elegant primrose car. The groom brought round the light carriage for me and thus following on I was the tail as S.A.R. was the head of a very truncated procession. Against the gentle drizzle which looked as if it would go on for hours I had put on a tweed coat and a felt hat and perhaps because of this and the horse and trap for some strange reason I thought of Queen Victoria. This led me to the recollection that, representing the Sudan Government, I supposed I was an extended version of the British Raj; certainly representing women's emancipation, which seemed enough for the time being.

> At the end of the drive we waited until S.A.R. caught us up ... He rode in front through a lane between the populace and they were there in their thousands

standing ... and [I] smiled at any woman if I actually caught her eye. After all they had been waiting some hours in the rain.

[The men] had left a lane for us to pass through but they did not cheer, which rather disturbed me. Instead there came a low, constant growl, probably a muttering of blessings on their holy man but not the ecstatic acclaim I had expected. At me they looked with such surprise, that I felt a little out of my element, and uncertain whether or not I ought to imitate Queen Victoria and bow to right and left. Then by another silly trick of fancy I remembered 'The Woman Who Rode Away'. Suppose some of the heavy-looking fanatics took a dislike to me? Presumably my daughter would receive handsome compensation. All I managed to do was to gaze round with what I fondly hoped was a dignified and pleasant expression. Quite spontaneously the groom beamed at me and remarked how pleased everyone was to see me. A most comforting thought, as at the end of this strange quarter of an hour the crowd was even thicker near the marquee. Inside the enclosure were a number of *sheikh*s looking impressive, as they often did, and all the lesser visitors, who had been about the place since the Victory Celebrations. I was very sorry for the Egyptian agriculturalist in charge, when he realised that instead of all the distinguished guests he had expected, S.A.R.'s procession consisted of one woman, who had been along every day that week and watched things from the beginning. We had, however, to put up a show for the *sheikh*s and he bravely swallowed his disappointment and guided me round yet again. At least I did know what questions to ask and could congratulate him on having successfully finished all his planting. As we halted in front of one of the tables all set out with specimens of Aba products, a cheery old *sheikh* asked me, if I had ever seen such wonderful groundnuts. Nowhere else were such large ones grown and he handed me an extra big one as a proof. The Sayed then gave one to another *sheikh*, who kissed it reverently and put it away. Later when I found mine in my pocket I opened it. It was bad, hollow all through.

Outside the tent there was livestock to be noticed, chiefly in the sheds at the back. Not so admirable was a miserable little monkey, which had been placed among the *sunt* cuttings and was vainly trying to shelter from the weather. Equally wet and forlorn was a tiny gazelle crouching among the cannas.

Some of the craftwork—leather and birsh was really excellent ... An ambatch cart a boy had made drawn by a kitten and another by a mouse ... all rather wet and unhappy looking.

I wished I had offered to arrange the flowers, although I do not know whether the suggestion would have ben regarded as unfavourable criticism.

But handfuls of indifferent blooms thrust in a lump into half a dozen vases quite ruined the Village Flower Show effect, which the dripping tent had managed to create.

At one point we all sat down, while a schoolmaster read a lengthy speech about the progressive agriculture which was going on all over the island. We heard a car draw up outside and everyone began to look hopeful. All that happened was that a paper was handed in [to Saddiq] to say, that the train would not be arriving

> ... until 5.00 with all the distinguished guests. At this the wretched Hassan gave up the struggle and showed me round for at least the fourth time. It was probably very interesting for the *sheikh*s. I did feel sorry for him. I never quite decided at what stage it was arranged that I should open the girls' school.

A lot of whispering went on for a time and then I was asked, if I would perform the ceremony of opening the girls' school. I could hardly do other than consent, although I had never done such a thing before and certainly not in Arabic.

We went along to the school, where the girls, who had been drawn up in rows for hours, sang some little chants of praise and welcome. This was almost revolutionary for in the more conservative centres girls did not usually take part in an opening ceremony, even in their own school.

> Es Surra was ill, sick and vomiting they said. So Medina had come along to take her place. I wouldn't have believed it possible to put on a *tobe* and leave so narrow a slit for the eyes.

During this more whispering went on, because a green tape had been fastened across the door but nobody had thought to bring anything to cut it with. After a certain amount of confusion my groom handed up a very blunt clasp knife, with which I sawed away at the tape very solemnly while uttering a few pious hopes and wishes.

> I performed the same ceremony on the spinning room and then everyone crowded in to see the girls spinning.

Then someone said [that] there was a great mass of people waiting near the boys' school and we must not disappoint them. Up on the open space there they had pitched one of those lovely tall tents with the front flap upheld by long poles and brightly coloured hangings inside. By this time the rain had stopped but everyone was looking very bedraggled. The dull grey, cotton soil made such dirty mud. [*Sheikh*s'] robes and [*effendi*s'] trousers were all stained round the hem. The latter had been tucked into the men's socks which may have been more comfortable but not very smart.

Despite this it was a resplendent sight with S.A.R. and his visitors sitting under the flap of the tent and all his enthusiastic followers clustering in a crowd and this time cheering loudly. We had to listen to more speeches all in praise of the Sayed. A Byronic-looking poet declaimed one beautifully, which was very pleasing in its rhythm, but speechmaking in classical Arabic is not intended for the understanding of the vulgar. It was without shame therefore, that I asked the doctor[46] sitting next to me what it was all about. He said it was merely in honour of the Sayed's generosity, but I thought in the middle of this grand language, I had heard the word 'king' occur several times; whether symbolic or seditious I had no idea.

I thought however maybe I wouldn't clap anything more, just in case of accidents.

Suddenly while a speech was still going on, S.A.R. leant across to me. Would I stay and open the boys' school? I could catch the next train some three days later. I said I was sorry but I had work waiting for me in Khartoum. Well then, would I open it this afternoon on my way to the train? This, of course, I was very willing to agree to.

By this time a wild-eyed *sheikh* was making a most impassioned speech, which my neighbour, the doctor, said was in folklore language. The interesting part was that at one point the Sayed tried to stop the speaker with a most becoming show of modesty—'Ah, no, no' and hands up in protest, while the crowd roared with enthusiasm. A few lines later this pretty little comedy was enacted again and I could only think of Julius Caesar,

'You all did see that on the Lupercal[47]
I thrice presented him a kingly crown,
Which he did thrice refuse.'[48]

In the end we left before the speech was finished. Lunch had been laid for about thirty people and it seemed rather sad just the two of us among all these empty places. S.A.R.'s good temper was still unruffled, even though he ought to have known, that it was a risky time of year to arrange such a show, but it must have been disappointing, unless the acclamations of his people were success enough.

46. Dr Abdel Halim, probably Dr Ahmed Abdel Halim, D.K.S.M. 1.1.29 First appointment; 1944 Medical Officer, Malakal; 1946 Blue Nile, Medical Officer, Wad Medani or Dr Abdel Halim Mohamed, the first Sudanese to obtain the M.R.C.P. qualification. He succeeded R. McN. Buchanan, the last British Senior Physician in 1953. He was Director of the Khartoum Hospital and a Lecturer in Medicine.
47. Lupercal was a Roman festival on 15th February, connected with fertility rites.
48. Shakespeare, W., *Julius Caesar*, 3.ii.95.

I went to lie down for a little, having made all necessary precautions to get away at 4. At 3.30 a *wakil* [was] at the door.

I was summoned in the middle of the afternoon. The Sayed thought I ought to go at once and not stay to open the school, since the roads were very muddy and it might take me some time to get through.

> Far be it for me to delay or to enquire who would open the school. S.A.R. was going on with the daily blessings at this point and when I interrupted him to say goodbye it was rather a pretty picture with himself sitting at the head of the flight of steps and a bearded old man of venerable aspect sitting at his feet and pouring out some long tale ... I was beginning to feel very stifled and unreal.

I was not sorry to leave, since despite all the courtesy I was shown, there was a slight flavour of seclusion about my room. Not that I could go at once; there were all sorts of delays. The car arrived without any petrol; there was luggage to stow away, to take out and re-arrange several times. There were a number of visitors wanting a lift to the station.

Among these was a shrewd-looking little *sheikh* from the Hejaz.

> He was on his way to Dueim, an attractive fair-skinned old man with a bright, shrewd eye which missed very little.

While we waited for the car to be ready, chairs were brought and we sat and talked. He was evidently a great traveller, who had been in various parts of India, but I could not find out what exactly was the calling he followed. In any case S.A.R. was busy showing off to him the one distinguished guest he had managed to collect, for such was my rôle at this point. He expatiated on my experiences farther east, my academic qualifications and the scope of my present work, but to my disappointment laid more stress on my being a member of the Gordon College Council than the importance of girls' schools in general. 'Can she understand what we are saying?' enquired the *sheikh*. 'Of course', said S.A.R. 'Indeed', said the old man and volunteered no comment on women's education.

> I don't know if it was for his benefit that S.A.R. asked me to dinner on the following Thursday in a casual 'one of us' tone. I managed to plead my coming journey to Sinkat.

I could indeed thank the Sayed in all sincerity for his kind and generous hospitality and assure him truthfully, that I should never forget it all my life.

We did stick on the way to the train but arrived in good time and anyway the train was late. The Khartoum train with the 'one hundred and one' guests came in just as we were going and most of them, I gathered, just transferred to our train. I didn't see anyone really great and famous and not even anyone I knew.

The next day in Omdurman I felt less grateful, as I [thought I had] developed dysentery, which subsequently caused me much affliction.

After a day or two [suffering from a] fear of dysentery, I went to bed and didn't see anyone but the servant for two days. After which I was completely restored.

'What can you expect?' said my servant, who had accompanied me and been glad enough to bask in my reflected glory. 'After those dirty wells at Aba'.

As I lay in hospital[49] one of my visitors told me, there had been a public and official pronouncement to the effect that the Government had no intention of setting up a monarchy in Sudan. Feeling very low in mind and body I could not summon up much sympathy for the Sayed, however great a disappointment this might be to him. I had had plenty of time to look back over the strange muddliness in which I had lived, and the pretentiousness which clung to the old ways for its justification and yet wanted to compete with the new without a realisation of new standards.[50] Probably S.A.R. was content to be as muddled in his thinking as in his daily arrangements and could thus be in no way cynical about the religious power he wielded, although it might appear to outsiders that he used it for his personal advantage.

49. Dr Beasley went to hospital after her return from her Sinkat trip, to recover from the dysentery she contacted at Aba Island. By the beginning of September 1945 Dr Beasley had had two bouts in hospital. 'Somehow you would expect something long and lingering and insidious from Aba' (S.A.D. 657/7/19).
50. The Civil Secretary, (Sir) James Robertson, held a press conference to discuss the rumours about Sudan's political future. 'He assured them in no uncertain terms that there was not the slightest likelihood of a monarchy being set up in the Sudan' (S.A.D. 657/7/19). Yet S.A.R. continued to seek power. S.A.R. encouraged his supporters to take part in the Graduates Congress (inaugurated in 1938). He owned the newspaper *Haḍārat al-Sūdan* which was first edited by Hussein al-Khalifa Sherif (b.1888-d.1928), a grandson of the Mahdi, and later by Aḥmad 'Uthmān al-Qāḍī. He later owned the daily newspaper *An-Nīl*, whilst *Ṣawt as-Sūdān* was owned by the Mirghanists. In 1944 the Governor-General Sir Hubert Huddleston formed the Northern Advisory Council. In 1945 S.A.R.'s more sophisticated supporters were organised into the first political party in the Sudan, *al-Umma*. By 1947 a Legislative Assembly had been instituted with S.A.R.'s whole-hearted support. In 1953 came the Self-Government agreement by all Sudanese parties. In the elections in 1955 the N.U.P., not the Umma Party won, a bitter blow to S.A.R. In 1956, 'Abdallāh Khalil, Secretary-General of the Umma Party became Prime Minister when Sudan declared Independence, much to S.A.R.'s satisfaction.

Once I had recovered, however, I could discount all the political undertones and realise that I had been privileged to be accorded the sort of visit that would never come my way again.

> Somehow I find it difficult to believe that S.A.R. himself could be really dangerous politically, however great his admiration for Ibn Saud[51] and although we all know that the present Egyptian dynasty[52] is a bit upstart ... I wonder if now he ever does anything that means a real effort. The only danger could be an energetic and unscrupulous person or persons using him for their own ends. Cardboard and tinsel can be inflammable.

## 2. Sir Sayyid 'Alī al- Mirghanī

Beside S.A.R. no-one bulked quite so large in the public eye for, although Sir Sayed Ali Mirghani as a direct descendant of the Prophet had a large and devoted following, he had nothing of the same panache and flair for the dramatic as his rival. In person he was small and his health was far from good but a genuine inner dignity was revealed behind a quiet and unobtrusive manner. Roughly his support came more from the North and East and the apparent leaning towards Egypt was generally attributed to sheer opposition to the Mahdist party. As one old *sheikh* told me frankly, 'It isn't that we don't like the British. It isn't even that we like the Egyptians. But we aren't going to have that other chap as King.'

In our woman's world we were not much concerned with politics and the great tribal leaders, who lent their support to the opposing parties, only came my way in fleeting encounters, when, as conditions eased after the war, we were able to push our way into remoter places. There are plenty of tales of them elsewhere and no doubt much of their real attraction was that of an aesthetic satisfaction in dealing with strong men, whose attitude to life had an obvious wholeness, firmly planted in a tradition to which they belonged. Whatever political rifts he may have caused Sayed Ali does not fit into the story of girls' education in any outstanding way and he sometimes

---

51. After the advent of Independence S.A.R. maintained very close relations with most of the Arab heads of state and with King 'Abd al-'Azīz of Saudi Arabia in particular.

52. Sayyid 'Alī al-Mirghanī and his *Ashiqqā'* Party (later the National Unionists) favoured union with Egypt while S.A.R. strongly supported the Independence cause. This objective was resented and opposed by the Egyptian Government. In March 1954 the Independence Movement staged a demonstration declaring 'Long live Neguib, but no Union with Egypt' when General Neguib arrived for the opening of the first parliament. A riot led to the deaths of a number of people, including the Commissioner and Assistant Commissioner of Police. S.A.R. was placed under house-arrest, Neguib returned to Cairo, Parliament was postponed and a State of Emergency declared.

gave the impression, that he felt it part of the modern world, which would develop in any case, but that his concern was with other matters.

## 3. Mirghani Hamza[53]

All his[54] followers did not adopt this neutralist line and one of the most practical was Mirghani Hamza, who was determined that his daughter should not grow up to be like the former generation. Against strong family opposition he sent her to a Christian secondary school[55] in the days before Government education had reached that stage. His example was of much importance but still more his general enthusiasm was of the utmost value. As a member of the Municipal Council[56] and the Town Planning Board he would support and push through any demand we might make for land. As a senior official in the Public Works Department he was eager to ensure for us the best possible buildings. On one occasion he and a British architect came to breakfast with me and over the congealing eggs they encouraged one another to wonderful excesses of extravagance. For Mirghani Hamza nothing was too good for girls and the Domestic Science School he designed for us at Wad Medani later became something of a show place. We were delighted in 1949, when we were allowed to name our latest elementary school after him in recognition of his unflagging support. A tall, gaunt figure, who reminded me of reformers whose inner fire consumed their frame, he was unswerving in his belief both by example and precept. Happiness of the commonplace kind could never come to such men struggling towards the new order, in which he believed, but they had the force of a sense of purpose to co-ordinate their striving. He was not the only one but I knew him early and he made a deep impression.

In my more depressed moments I wondered whether in our efforts to spur on the women we might be removing from the educated Sudanese men their last bolt-hole for relaxation in the women's quarters, not for those like Mirghani Hamza, but for others less strong-minded and assured. Most

53. As a leading educated Sudanese, Mirghani Hamza was interviewed by the De La Warr Commission, 1937, as he held strong views on girls' education (Beshir, M.O., *Educational Development in the Sudan*, p. 113, 114); he was also a member of a committee who wrote a 'Note on education addressed to the Sudan Government', submitted July 1939. (See Beshir, M.O., *op. cit.*, p. 151). He was Chairman of a special committee on education, whose Report was submitted in May 1947, and was in fact the result of continuous work, research and consultation by him.
54. i.e. Sayyid ʿAlī al-Mirghanī's followers.
55. Unity High School?
56. Omdurman?

Sudanese have a real sense of humour but, once educated, the men appeared to an outsider to be always on duty and it must have been very wearing. They had been trying to catch up in thirty years, what it had taken Europe centuries to evolve. Whether or not they did read anything else I cannot say but they professed to read only what they had been told were good books, largely no doubt because the conception of an educated man was mixed up with memories of learned *ulema*, who discoursed at length and in fine language on the more obscure points of philosophy. Hobbies as we think of them were quite unknown. Most of us were quite sure that what was needed was a better balance in development between the sexes, but there were times, when I felt a little sorry for the educated men to whom culture was necessary but rather a strain. Small wonder that they found their relief in inflammatory politics and the sporting element in this deliriously exciting game. Somehow their education seemed to sit more easily on the women.

## 4. Encouraging sidelights on marriage

### 4.1 Amna and the Agricultural Inspector

Nevertheless it was still easy to make friends with them and to have at times encouraging sidelights on marriage made more promising by a modern outlook. I was invited one day to the wedding feast of a schoolmistress and a young agriculturalist. In defiance of established custom he sat at one end of the table and his bride the other. 'I don't like the old ways', he confided in me. 'I want to be friends with my wife. I want to take her with me and show her the things I am interested in.'

My heart warmed to him at once and it was an older schoolmistress, who had been married some years to an elderly official, who voiced the opposite point of view. 'Fast I call it', she commented. 'Both sitting down like that at the wedding and talking to one another. I never spoke a word to my husband until we had been married eighteen months.' Incidentally by that time she had borne him a child, who had died soon after.

The Agricultural Inspector was not daunted by such talk and caused more by taking his wife to Cyrenaica, when he was lent to the occupying Government there. As she worked in our schools, she went on with her teaching in this new circle, and managed also to run her house efficiently and produce two splendid children. So successful apparently was she, that the Director of Education in Cyrenaica wrote to me to ask, if I could second any more mistresses of her calibre. A few years later, when they came on leave, they brought the children to tea in our garden. It was the happiest of parties with the grown-ups all talking, while a beautiful little girl played contentedly on the lawn. 'Thank you for my wife Amna', said the husband to me, as they took their leave. It was a moment to make up for many disappointments.

## 4.2 The bridal dance

Such celebrations may have been less picturesque than the old-fashioned ones, which went on for days at vast expense, and to which I might be invited for a few hours, when it reached the stage of the bride dance. At one of these an obviously exhausted girl was sitting on the bed in the women's quarters, when we arrived, and was completely covered by her robes. After tea in the front yard she came out with her head uncovered and long plaits of silk woven into her short hair ready to flick at honoured guests. As she danced her groom criticised her until at last she snapped at him. He was flourishing a gaily coloured whip, which, he assured me, was purely symbolic, but, when he offered to present it to me, I readily accepted it. The men were watching from the back of the yard, where we had had tea, while the women pushed together at the entrance to their quarters, trying to see over one another's heads. At another similar party the dancing was more widespread with a number of girls other than the bride performing also. The remark of a boy here was illuminating. He pointed one of the girls out to me. 'Isn't she good?' he exclaimed in great admiration. 'But then she does not go to school, so she has plenty of time to practice.'

## 4.3 Marriage in Sheikh Babikr Bedri's clan

Among Sheikh Babikr Bedri's family there was one outstanding example of new ideas in practice. There were Bedri schoolmistresses everywhere, because the whole clan had to be educated and many of them joined the profession. They took it all as a matter of course, if an aunt should be taught by a niece much older than herself, or if there were some other intricate relationship, that it hardly seemed worthwhile to disentangle. But one of the Sheikh's daughters rebelled against this family tradition, when she was made to teach. She thoroughly disliked the job and, although intelligent enough and of a charming disposition, she was always bored and slack in the classroom. Once married, however, she changed from a reluctant teacher to a busy and cheerful housewife, who combined with great good sense what she thought appropriate from European ways with Sudanese habits. Her husband was a young pharmacist, who had qualified in Beirut, and was as good-looking as his wife. The appearance of a bridegroom was much discussed in the women's quarters, for, although they might marry an elderly partner, most spoke with approval, when a friend acquired someone handsome in this seeming lottery. To visit this particular household was a joy. We would be met at the door by both husband and wife together and the whole family would sit down to tea. Conversation would range over all sorts of topics with plenty of laughter and teasing between husband and wife. Two beautiful and healthy little boys would also form part of the company and add to everyone's pleasure. Sometimes an unexpected visitor might drop in without embarrassment.

Perhaps I was impatient at the time, because these examples were so few, but I shall always object to such a high priority being given to development in politics as a mark of advance, while life remained so one-sided in its domestic aspects. Changing views on marriage were very much bound up with the values, that the girls themselves began to set upon education.


## 5. Sitt Nafissa Awad al-Karim

At a tea party in my garden with a group of flower-like and desirable young women, one of them,[57] announced her distaste for the general idea, although we knew that she had had plenty of good offers. 'Men just think of us as cattle', she remarked. 'I am better as I am'. Indeed she enjoyed her independence and had, moreover, become one of the firm pillars round which girls' development had slowly taken shape. A Rufaa girl, she had early been accustomed to the thought of girls going to school and had been one of the second group of five students, who had come to the Girls' Training College in Omdurman at the beginning in 1921. A person like Nafissa Awad al-Karim was therefore not merely a representative of the new order but an individual in her own right. Her education had been a few years' elementary schooling and two years' training, after which at the age of about fifteen she started teaching. By 1939 she was a headmistress running an elementary school very competently.

When she was awarded a British Empire Medal for work which I shall describe later, it was a great moment, when she decided she would come to the Palace garden party to have her decoration presented, since Sudanese women never attended these functions. We hoped that it might set a precedent and that the Sudanese men would realise that the sexes could mingle without loss of modesty. After all the talk one heard about 'our customs', that women should not be seen by other men, the following incident was an encouraging pointer. As we stepped out of the car, a young

---

57. Sitt Nafissa Awad al-Karim; 1940 (possibly) headmistress in Ed-Damer school; Jan 1946 undertook a month's tour of Kordofan campaigning against 'female circumcision', with the backing of Babikr Bedri and Dr Ali Bedri. 1946/47 awarded the M.B.E.

Sudanese police officer noticed us. 'Why, it's Nafissa' he said and came across to greet her. They shook hands in an ordinary, friendly and unselfconscious way. Ten years before Nafissa even used to think she ought to cover her face and hang her head and mutter, if a father on school premises had occasion to ask her anything. Getting thoroughly interested in her work she found all this took too much time and it quickly disappeared. This may sound a trifle but normal, sensible relationships between the sexes even on this superficial level were a great relief. In small measure these attitudes on the part of both men and women were growing up everywhere and were especially important, because they evolved without any flourish.

Nafissa was outstanding, because she suggested an acceptable line of development. Her remarkable aptitude showed itself, when she was promoted to be the only Sudanese mistress at the first Girls' Intermediate School, opened in 1940. She was soon dealing with girls who were having an education beyond the level that she had attained, but by sheer force of character and innate intelligence she contrived to keep abreast of the new developments and to spur them on. It was too late for her to participate in these more advanced studies but her passionate belief in the future of women's education combined with her understanding of the old ways of thought made her able to help her pupils in this experiment, far more than she realised. Her enthusiasm was by no means exhausted by this first venture; it was on the contrary stimulated. When the idea of secondary classes for girls was first mooted, Nafissa, gossiping in my office one morning, remarked, 'And then there will be girls at the University. And then perhaps even to England ... ' Her eyes sparkled and her tone was vibrant. She had seen a vista shining without end and for the advancement of her pupils.

School work is generally and should be unspectacular. Teaching in the Sudan was probably less spectacular than elsewhere. If the schools had not been hidden behind high walls in the beginning the system for girls might never have taken strong roots. Nevertheless we all have our chances. When Nafissa's came, it was almost theatrical though of the utmost importance.

When the ordinance against 'pharaonic circumcision' was published in 1946, it was felt that sheer ignorance was one of the greatest obstacles to be overcome. The educated men said, 'It's only the women who hold things back.' The schoolmistresses laughed, when I passed this remark on to them, and their reply was, 'H'm. That's what they tell *you*.'

They agreed, however, that the women's attitude was largely conditioned by ignorance. Nafissa was asked if she would be prepared to undertake a campaign, teaching in the villages, and she accepted without demur. It was obvious that the idea was unexpected and startling to her. A small woman, delicately formed and not of robust health, she stood for a matter of seconds only, bracing herself as it were. Then she drew in a deep breath and the decision was finished, a decision of great importance for herself and others.

She had always been considered a guardian of respectability. Unmarried women did not travel about from place to place and most certainly not to address public meetings. Despite this she was prepared to brave censure for work in which she so firmly believed. She finished two tours in all, one in Kordofan and the other in her own district of the Blue Nile. Meetings were arranged first in the schools and then in the houses of the *omdah* or *sheikh* of the village. Hundreds of women attended. Nafissa's line of argument was based mainly on the point, that the practice is contrary to Mohammedan religion. Arabic is a language which readily lends itself to passionate rhetoric. Nafissa was a temperamental person with a keen sense of the dramatic and a quick wit. She was much respected as a woman of learning because, when she wished, she could indulge in the high-flown classical Arabic, which is much admired, even when not understood, but she knew well the mentality of the women to whom she wished to appeal. The result was, that she moved her audiences to enthusiasm at the time, but, as is the way of emotional response, the amount of practical benefit was not easy to estimate. 'You must talk to the men', said one old lady at a meeting. 'They are as hard and obstinate as this'. She slapped her hand on a wooden beam. 'Then we must be carpenters', replied Nafissa immediately. The women rose to her in a babel of merriment.

It was exhausting work, travelling in a lorry over long distances and she had her other duties in her school. Moreover once the novelty of the idea was over, it was time to think of something else. Now, however, that the notion had taken hold other headmistresses, such as Melk ed-Dar from El Obeid, followed it up at appropriate moments with tours, while an increasing number arranged private meetings locally.

Nafissa comforted me one day, when I was despondent, that we seemed to make so little headway. 'At least', she said, 'the women know now that it is wrong. Before no-one had ever told them.'

These tours added to her responsibility enormously and deepened the trust in which she knew she was held. Authority might not always take her advice but it realised, that her views, invariably shrewd, were always worth listening to. In this way she had power, which she enjoyed, as well as being in charge of one hundred and fifty girls. The growth of new ways meant that no-one frowned if he met Nafissa strolling across the square to visit some of her friends in her spare time, for she would be dressed with all the decorum suitable to a Sudanese woman.

She might, however, have been about some other ploy, for after 1946 she was allowed a fairly free hand in the running of women's night schools. A great part of the success of these was due to the way in which she took up the idea with enthusiasm, once it had been started. She encouraged the teachers, collected funds, arranged exhibitions so that the world might see what was happening, and obtained tremendous excitement from the steady growth of numbers in the various centres of the Three Towns. There were seven of them after three years' work and her great ambition was to have enrolled a thousand students.

Much to our surprise after more than twenty years of devoted service to the schools she married a man of substance in Government service, whose other wife she knew. Her marriage brought to her a new problem, since her family wished her to retire but so much of her life was bound up with the education of women and girls, that she could not slip easily into the anonymity of just being someone's wife. She enjoyed authority and it would be hard to think of giving it up. Nevertheless there were many changes at this time and the pace of development, particularly in Omdurman, was accelerating rapidly. It was going to become more and more difficult for the older teachers to keep up with younger girls, perhaps a little proud of their higher standards of academic learning. It would have been a dignified way of escaping such difficulties to have resigned on the crest of her success. For a long time she hesitated but could not bear to leave the life, where she had found so much happiness. Luckily a compromise could be arranged. Now that she was married, she could take on the duties of inspecting and tour the schools as a permanent job and not for the special excursions she had made on the 'Female Circumcision' crusade.

This, however, occurred in the months following my retirement and for my part I was glad not to have lost her from Omdurman, while I was there. To those of us who sighed nostalgically for the old days we knew must pass, she was part of a gentler tempo. I should have missed the immediate contact of her affectionate loyalty and the sight of her trim little person in a fresh white muslin *tobe*, delicate jewelled ear-rings and quantities of fine, gold bracelets.

## 6. Sitt Sekina Tewfiq

Much loved by us all was one of the pillars of the Girls' Training College, Sitt Sekina Tewfiq, who developed from a nice but rather ordinary teacher into a woman capable of taking considerable responsibility, and someone whose advice and sympathy were sought by both British staff and Sudanese girls. This latter characteristic was what will be most remembered about her but, although her ready compassion could be counted on, she was rock-like in matters of principle which she thought important. In manner and disposition she was quiet and had little of the expansive attitudes of many of her colleagues. When, therefore, the high moment of recognition arrived, its unexpected form was all the more striking.

Certain officials were to be sent to England as representatives of the Sudan Government for the Coronation in 1953. An enlightened Director of Education,[58] a British official, decided that, as it was a Queen to be crowned, a woman ought to represent the Education Department.[59] There was some gnashing of teeth among the men who hoped to go but Sekina, as one of the senior staff was selected for the honour. As I was working near London at the time, we were able to extend the visit by taking her to see some local schools and colleges. Although conversation was not possible, since she still spoke only Arabic, it was delightful to see how the children responded at once to her obvious warm affection for the young. Even before she had returned home, proposals of marriage were being pressed on her and eventually, as in Nafissa's case, she complied with her family's demand. In the same way an opportunity occurred for her then to extend her sphere by taking on the post of an Inspector in the provinces.

## 7. Sitt Medina Abdallah

I have already mentioned our first woman inspector, Sitt Medina Abdallah, and what a comfort I found her at Aba Island, when the extreme masculinity of the atmosphere began to seem unreal and fantastic. Alike in contributing to the development of the women of their country these friends made life richer for me personally by being such distinct individuals. It would be encouraging, if one could feel that many of the Sudanese had the same determination to grow so solidly from such small beginnings. Certainly if the women who have had far more chances than Sitt Medina can develop proportionately they have a great future in store. Her whole history showed considerable strength of character. She belonged to the household of S.A.R. and was married fairly young, bearing her husband a

---

58. Denys Heseltine Hibbert, C.B.E. (b.17.10.1905- ); Educated at Radley and Worcester College, Oxford; 2.9.29 First appointment; 1929-35 Education Department; 1935-39 Blue Nile (P.E.O.); 1939 transferred to Education Department; 1940 Inspector, Northern area, based in Khartoum; 1941-42 Khartoum Province, released to Political Service; 1943 returned to Education Department; 1943-45 Warden, Gordon Memorial College, based in Omdurman; 1945-50 Assistant Director, Southern Education, based in Juba; 1950-54 Director of Education, based in Khartoum; 1954 retired; 1954-65 Headmaster, Portsmouth Grammar School.
59. By then the Ministry of Education.

son[60] in 1924. Part of her value lay in the fact, that to her the set-up in S.A.R.'s household was by no means unreal and she managed to bridge the enormous gulf between that and the new order, which the girls' schools represented. I am not sure at what period the divorce came but in the late twenties she was attending one of the Government schools in Omdurman. 'My Arabic and Arithmetic were all right', she told me, 'but I very much wanted to learn some geography. So I went to school.'

We did not otherwise talk much about her early years, except about the progress of her much loved only son, and I was surprised therefore, when she was eager in a classroom one day to point out to me a girl about nine years old. 'That is Fakhr ed-Din's sister', she said and was pleased and interested in the child's work. As Arabic had plenty of words for the designation of such relationships as a half-sister, there was no need for elaborate explanations.

After the extra study which she had obtained for herself, the authorities had persuaded her to come into the Training College, though not as an ordinary student. Ten years later she was teaching there and the Education Department decided to promote her to be an Inspector. It was a bold step on everyone's part and most of all on hers, as there might have been the usual objections on the grounds of respectability. The fact that she had been married made it much easier and her poor old mother was dragged around as chaperone.

A year or so after her promotion she announced, that she was being married again, but that this would mean no alteration in her work. I never saw the husband, who was a cloth merchant in Omdurman, although I often met Sitt Medina's brothers. How much satisfaction he derived from the marriage I do not know except the glory of having a distinguished wife. The marriage contract was a remarkable document in which the husband agreed to pay one hundred pounds and to provide a house of specified dimensions, a very handsome dwelling in point of fact. Moreover a paper was attached on which he solemnly promised in no way to interfere with his wife's work and to put no obstacle in the way of her travelling wherever the Government wished to send her. In return for this he was the legal husband of the first Sudanese inspectress and one of the best paid Sudanese women in the country. After the war she was receiving upwards of £250 a year. No doubt the fact that S.A.R. approved all the arrangements helped our work considerably but at times I felt a little sorry for the husband. If I were to ask Sitt Medina, whether she could go on an extra long trek, perhaps down South, where we ran a school for Arab girls at Malakal, she would always say, 'I will ask the Sayed's opinion.' Never once did I hear from her, 'I will

60. Fakhr ed-Din.

see if my husband minds.' It seemed such a complete reversal of the tables, although there was nothing brazen or modern about Sitt Medina's behaviour. She veiled her face and presented a model of perfect manners in every respect. Her professional life was something apart.

At first it was a bit difficult fitting her into a regular programme and in the press of many affairs I was sometimes guilty of forgetting to make arrangements for her, when she was in Omdurman between outside visits. I would be in my office before breakfast as usual, when I would hear her heavy step across the yard, and would remember my remissness. That this state of affairs improved was small credit to me. Gradually Sitt Medina herself grew to understand the needs of the schools. 'Isn't it time', she would say, 'that someone went to see if things are in better shape at X?' '*Sitt Fulana*[61] was doing very badly [teaching] in First Year Arabic last week. Shall I look in on my way home?'

Then in the frequent dissensions and quarrels which occurred in the schools outside she began to play an increasingly useful part. From coming back with a simple report, not always unbiased, of what had happened and leaving action to higher authority, she would deal with the affair on the spot. After a time, as soon as a complaint came in, our immediate reaction tended to be, 'Oh, send Sitt Medina.' Originally my other trouble was, that there seemed so many mornings on which I went back to breakfast and sighed, 'Oh dear, Sitt Medina has been insulted again.'

Naturally in her new position she was extra sensitive to slights, for it took some years for the other schoolmistresses to accept her authority, and all the Sudanese officials, whom she met on her journeys, did not treat her with due consideration. It was easy for a British woman to see the amusing side of being provided with unsuitable transport. It did not damage my prestige in my own eyes, if I had to travel in a *suq* lorry, but these things appeared differently to a freshly promoted Sudanese offical. It is all very well for us to talk about people serving their country and putting up with hardships for further education, if they want it. The pace at which anyone like Sitt Medina was developing was in itself a strain, although it had its compensations. What I think this proves, is that we should not push people beyond the level of balance [of] understanding, which they have attained. That Sitt Medina did not 'crack' is not due to anything except her own innate worth but everyone does not possess her tenacity of purpose.

An interesting side-light on this is that most of the improper expressions in Arabic I have heard have come from this source, although not from her lips. I always insisted on knowing just what the insult had been, because I dislike vague charges, and our Syrian mistress or one of the masters at the

61. *Sitt Fulana*, 'Miss so and so'.

Training College would inform me. I have not, however, discovered anything novel about Sudanese mentality by this route. Insults seem to have a fairly international background, although there is variation in the animal favoured. I could never understand why *taht raqab[a]* meaning 'under supervision' should be so wounding. I found it easier to realise, why Sitt Medina had to be sent home in a state of jangled nerves one morning during a minor political disturbance. The school driver, who belonged to the other faction,[62] had called S.A.R. a *zeer* in a loud voice, purposely to offend her, she said. A *zeer* is a large earthenware water jar. Apparently it corresponds as a term of abuse to a 'whoring tosspot'. Certainly not what one would care to hear applied to the object of one's religious devotion.

But this phase passed too. A new generation of schoolmistresses grew up who accepted Sitt Medina's authority without question. She was awarded a British Empire Medal.[63] Then her son, who had completed his College course and obtained a post with the Publications Bureau, married one of our prettiest and brightest schoolmistresses and his mother felt that her anxieties on his account were over. Her sole complaint was that I acquired a grandson[64] before she did, but she was generous enough to go into raptures over the photograph of what, if we had both been truthful, was an ordinary fat baby on a cushion.

All the time I had known her, she had been a large and heavy woman but dignified and comely. Her eyes were fine but her jaw was too heavy for beauty of balance but it was a most interesting face, particularly when animated. The Sudanese admire plumpness in their women but Sitt Medina found her weight rather an encumbrance in an active life. She was the only one I met, who deliberately went in for banting. 'Very little lunch, no breakfast and nothing to eat for tea', she told me, 'and I still get fat'.

I could linger indefinitely over reminiscences of the schoolmistresses, so many different personalities, but yet sharing generally with such courage the same struggles and coming often to a fulfilment beyond anyone's earliest hopes. Most of all they were friends of mine.

---

62. Khatmiyya Mirghaniyya.

63. Miss Pode, the previous Controller, promoted Sitt Medina Abdulla to inspectress about 1939. 'She is regarded as rather progressive because she tours about the country, inspecting schools ... a very live wire. Now over 46 but has married again about 3 years ago [c.1942]. The husband, a merchant, gave a written understanding not to interfere with her work. He also paid £100 for her and a large house to be built for her use. He did not appear to figure hugely in her life' (S.A.D. 657/7/5). Sitt Medina Abdulla was awarded the British Empire Medal in March 1948. In 1970 she was decorated by the Sudan Government in recognition of her services.

64. By 1990 Dr Beasley had three grandchildren and three great-grandchildren.

# Chapter VII

# The South

These chapter headings may be geographically accurate and were administratively useful but there is a baldness about them, which in no way conveys the exciting differences and flavours of the various regions. I have put the South last, although for many people in England it is the one part of the Sudan, which most often makes headlines in the newspapers. For most officials, including myself, there was an accumulation of special and intricate problems, which bulked so largely in any consideration either of places or of work, that one could not respond with the same enthusiasm as to the more straightforward developments in the Arab North. From a spectacular point of view, Equatoria made much more showy sightseeing but this was not the object of my journeys and any subsidiary interest was overlaid by the depressing feeling of inadequacy about the necessary tasks and the limited ration of time in which to achieve even the bare minimum. I find that what I wrote in my diary in 1947 I can still endorse, namely that it 'was our business to provide the South as rapidly as possible with the tools of learning with which they may develop a way of life capable of adaptation to the world of the future, whether any of us like the particular shape of that world or not. There are forces outside their control and ours and all that we can do is to equip them, as best we may, for the contacts which they cannot indefinitely avoid.'

It was chiefly because of this urgency gnawing all the time, that it was hard to relax even in small measure and find the sort of enjoyment that I savoured elsewhere. The people were friendly enough but the points of contact were few. My own visits were of necessity so infrequent and brief, that I attributed much of this inadequacy to lack of time but more than one D.C., transferred from the North, felt similarly handicapped.

So different was all that concerned this enormous region, conveniently lumped as one and referred to as The South that it demands a short description. The dividing line[1] was roughly the parallel drawn near Kosti, north of which the homogeneity of religion and Arab culture offset the diversity of the various localities. Historically[2] it was the country from which strong, black slaves[3] could be taken, more specifically at one time for the armies of the Egyptian Khedives in the nineteenth century, and the memory of those days has been a long time dying among the tribes, however much the Moslems of the North may now try to explain away this grisly trade. When, therefore, the Anglo-Egyptian Condominium was set up in 1899 special arrangements were made for allaying the fears of these pagan peoples and allowing them an ordered government in which they might develop at their own pace.[4] Whether or not the pace was too leisurely can be debated endlessly. Haste is not a helpful factor in the evolution of primitive peoples and the climate just north of the Equator is no aid to hustling efficiency. Add to that the difficulties of communication and a long list of particularly nasty diseases prevalent in the area and some measure can be made of the size of the undertaking.

Only simplification of these issues can be mentioned here but there seemed to the Victorian administrators excellent reasons for keeping Moslems away from tribes who feared them as slave raiders. Moreover, after the defeat of the Khalifa,[5] the people of the North were occupied in their own rehabilitation and it is doubtful, if any of them were anxious to share the hardships of bringing law and order to pagans, whom they despised. The pagans themselves showed no signs of a religion with

1. The 10th parallel of north latitude roughly divides the North from the South. The South stretched to the southern borders, with Kenya, Uganda and the Belgian Congo. In 1903 the Sudan Government under Wingate allotted to each missionary society then applying for work in the Sudan a separate area for evangelisation to reduce rivalry between the missions (Wingate, F.R., *Wingate of the Sudan*, London, 1955, p.147). *Anglican Dioceses of the Sudan, a Handbook*, 1951, shows the zones assigned. Lord Cromer assured the Muslim northerners that no proselytism would take place north of Lat. 10°N (Zetland, Lord, *Lord Cromer*, London, 1935, p.250). In 1964 all foreign missionaries left Sudan.
2. Up until the end of the nineteenth century but perhaps even resuming today. The confidence of the Southerners in all foreign peoples, including British administrators, had been completely shattered by the slave trade. The Sudan Government felt that this confidence 'could only be won by building up a protective barrier against Northern merchants' (Sudan Government, *The Sudan, A Record of Progress, 1898-1947*, Khartoum, 1947, p.12). This policy is only valid as long as the North continues to think of the South as a pool of slaves.
3. Slaves were taken especially from the Nilotic tribes—Shilluk, Dinka and Nuer.
4. In the 1906 Mongalla Province Report it stated 'there is no need for education in this Province at present'. The southern districts were made 'closed districts' to which no Northerner was allowed access without a special permit, and were administered as a separate unit from the rest of the country. The 1924 Government Policy was deliberately aimed at keeping out Northerners. The mission schools took every opportunity to remind Southerners of their inheritance of slavery, through their teaching of religion and history.
5. In 1898.

fundamentals which could develop.[6] Officials reared in the Christian faith, therefore, were prepared to accept the offer of the missionary societies, who had laboured with much success in West Africa,[7] but similar obligations were laid on them. Evangelising was not enough; all institutions must include education efforts as well.

> They grumble that the Government thereby gets education on the cheap.[8] In 1938 the Government decided that the arrangement was not merely cheap in price but also in quality and, if the missionaries were going to run schools they should run better ones and bring out competent educationalists as they do in other countries such as Nigeria and Nyassaland. This did make a little difference and speeded up the work on the girls' side but it was still pitiably small.

Thus from my point of view this was not a tour of inspection of the service to which I belonged and all the friendly reception of mistresses trained in the system we had evolved and firmly under authority. I needed a different approach to[wards] English or Australian missionaries, to some of whom education was a secondary purpose, and to Italian nuns whose basic principles did not rest primarily on education.[9]

6. Anthropologists such as Evans-Pritchard have indicated how local beliefs were an integral if not essential part of existence for the Southern peoples.

7. The missionary societies began to establish themselves in the South immediately after 1898. The Roman Catholic Verona Fathers Mission (V.F.M.) (Bahr el Ghazal), the Anglican Church Missionary Society (C.M.S.) (Upper Nile and most of Mongalla Province) and the American Presbyterian Mission were the main organisations concerned, as well as the New Zealand and Australian branch of the Sudan United Mission and the Sudan Interior Mission. By 1926 there were 9 girls' schools, including Meridi, Yambio (C.M.S.), Melut (V.F.M., co-ed); 1933 11 schools, 1948 26 schools, with almost 92% in mission schools. In 1949 12% of pupils at C.M.S. schools were girls, with 584 girls attending schools in the South, including village schools (*ARDE*, 1949, see also S.A.D. 657/3/59(113)).

8. Before 1927 mission schools were free from government control. The Government took little interest in education in the South and then only through financial and professional co-operation with the Missions. From 1927 when Sir H. MacMichael became Civil Secretary, a regular system of subsidies was introduced and the mission schools came under the supervision of the Education Department. The missionary societies regarded closer association with the North and even economic development of the South as a challenge to Christianity.

9. In 1944 there were 731 girls in elementary mission schools (including village schools) in the South (C.M.S. 185, V.F.M. 482, Mill Hill Fathers 10, American Presbyterians 54), by 1948 there were 1,210 (C.M.S. 316, V.F.M. 864, Mill Hill Fathers 30) and by 1949 about 1,600. There were none in Government schools in the South (*ARDE*).

# 1. Equatoria Province

All the same my first trip[10] was most memorable despite all the recollections of despair and utter bodily fatigue.

> The man[11] in charge of Education there was rightly worried about the future of girls in the South and for one of those queer reasons, which affect men at times dealing with women, the men inspectors had an idea that they were not competent to inspect girls' schools and that there were hidden mysteries which only a woman could understand.

As a grade A official, I was allowed[12] one of the few places on an aeroplane flying to Juba. The experience of the river steamer I was sorry to miss. It has been described as the only transport in the world which proceeded deliberately by collision. At some places in the Sudd the steamer negotiated the curves by bumping off one bank for impetus to the next. There would have been the sense of understanding the country, always valuable, but the journey took three weeks each way and we were still very short of staff. Leaving Khartoum at dawn I was then in Juba by ten o'clock.

> I had stayed the night at the Grand Hotel in Khartoum where all the passengers stay, as I was sure that I could never manage to arrive at the airfield from Omdurman. It was all much more efficient than the last time I left, when I went to Fasher. Lord Trenchard[13] was on board ... About 8 o'clock we came down at Malakal for a cup of coffee.

I might not have had the 'feel' of the place but the pilot flew low and we had a magnificent view of it all with the river losing itself in all sorts of channels among the Sudd and its great patches of bright, rather evil, green vegetation and the plain stretching illimitably on both sides. I have always disliked talking about 'Africa and the Africans'. Sudden visions of its size as on this occasion make my heart sink. At this period I was bothered too by a

---

10. 8.4.46-22.4.46 (S.A.D. 657/7/30-54).

11. D.H. Hibbert.

12. Dr Beasley was allowed to fly by plane both ways by the Finance Department in Khartoum. The plane was a Lockheed (Lodestar) carrying ten passengers and the luggage hidden away underneath. Passengers also included 'a fiery engineer in the Irrigation Department'. The first planes started coming to Juba in 1930.

13. Lord Trenchard, Sir Hugh Montague, G.C.B., G.C.V.O., D.S.O. (b.3.2.1873-d.10.2.1956); 1893 Royal Scots Fusiliers; 1899-1902 South Africa; 1904-06 West African Frontier Force; 1908-10 Southern Nigeria Regiment; World War I commanded the Royal Flying Corps; 1916 Maj-Gen; Jan-Apr 1918, 1919-29 first British chief of air staff, principal organiser of the R.A.F., 1919 Air-Marshall, R.A.F.; 1921-25 Principal A.D.C. to H.M.; From 1927 first British Air Marshall of R.A.F.; 1931-35 Commissioner of the London metropolitan police. In a debate in the House of Lords (7.5.42), he criticised the slowness in progress of Africanisation of the colonial civil services, due mainly to the British fetish of efficiency.

pamphlet brought out by the Colonial Office on *Mass Literacy in Africa*.[14]
Looking out of the plane window on this morning I thought that only in
England could anyone make such glib generalisations.

Fortunately distraction arrived in more lively sights.

> We had been flying at about 8,000 feet and we came down lower to look for
> game ... It was hot and rather bumpy and I had considerable doubts as to
> whether this game seeing were really worthwhile. Suddenly I saw three
> elephants.

We were flying so low, that it looked almost as if we would hit the river, but
what we did was to skim above a big herd of elephants, who stood calmly
among the grass and took no notice of us. Later we saw one enormous beast
impressively alone and also flights of birds rising from a pond, scores of
what resembled red deer and black and white antelopes rushing up a little
hill.

## 1.1 Juba

Juba was not a picturesque place, although it was easier to manage gardens
there than in Omdurman.[15] I did not stay long, as an extensive trip had
been planned for me but this had had to be altered in one respect. The
[Assistant] Director of Education in the South was to have come with me
but the day before he had had news that his wife was arriving from Kenya
and he had to go to the frontier to meet her. It seemed fair enough after a
long separation but it meant going off on my own into strange country with
no language and a borrowed servant. He also took the new lorry, of which
more later. This was another of the occasions on which women officials had
to be over-scrupulous in not claiming rights. I tried not to blink an eyelid. I
certainly did not want to incur the possible wrath of a wife, who arrived
after a weary journey to find her husband gone out on trek with another
woman, even an official.

> I decided it would be preferable to go alone but I was a bit scared. A
> cockney-bred woman like me has not been brought up to go rushing round
> Africa unaccompanied. It did not seem bad in the North, where the people are
> more used to the Government, where Arab hospitality is a very real thing and
> the *sheikh* of a village takes responsibility and is often rather a person[ality].

14. Probably Colonial Office, *Mass Education in African Society*, London, 1943, no.186. See
also 'The Education and Welfare of Women and Girls in Africa', 1943. Reports by the
Advisory Committee on Native Education in British Tropical African Dependencies (later, on
Education in the Colonies).
15. 'D. [D.H. Hibbert] met me and took me to his house, a pleasant place with magnificent
views.'

Also there is a language I have at least been able to deal with for some time. I felt a bit more apprehensive about naked savages and no means of communication. However I suppose I am really rather lucky to have chances of adventure like this at my age but it all sounded very strenuous.

I was further saddened by the Governor of the Province[16] saying that my coming was a red letter day for the South, as no-one before had ever bothered enough about girls' education to make an effort to come and see it. This 'not bothering' was most lamentably true in all but a few corners. Both Protestant and Catholic missions would bring out one or two trained women teachers and then put them to work in the boys' schools.

### 1.2 Juba to Yei

Along the first stage of my journey I did have the company of a British education official,[17] who was most informative about the places we went through. I was interested to notice how well populated it all seemed but was told, that most people lived along the road. Some years before in an all-out campaign against sleeping sickness[18] the villagers had been forced to do this and now that the disease was sufficiently under control for the order to be rescinded, they had continued to live there. Compared with Tokar or Fasher to Nyala [roads] the district was almost thronged.

16. The Governor who came to dinner on this occasion was Bernard Vivian Marwood, C.B.E., 4N. (b.13.2.1899- ); Educated at Liverpool College and Wadham College, Oxford; 1917-19 R.E. Signals (France, Belgium); 19.11.23 First appointment; 1924-27 White Nile; 1927-30 Mongalla; 1930-33 Inspector, Finance Department; 1933-34 Halfa; 1935-38 Upper Nile; 1939 Kassala, Deputy Governor; 1.10.39-48 Equatoria, Deputy Governor, 1945-48 Governor, based in Juba; 1948 retired to Kenya; killed by the Mau Mau.
17. George E. Janson-Smith ('J.S', 'Janson'). (b.1907- ); Educated King's School, Canterbury and St Edmund Hall, Oxford; 1929-36 Served in Tanganyika, Zanzibar and India; 31.7.37 First appointment; 1937-55 Sudan Civil Service, Education Department; 1938-46 Inspector of Education, joining A.G. Hickson and J.A. Hartley and in 1944 a fourth inspector was appointed; 1946-50 Inspector (based in Yei) then Chief Inspector for Southern Education, based in Juba; 1950-55 Assistant Director, Southern Provinces.
18. A.C. Walker, D.C. Tembura area in 1923 (retired 1939) and Dr Derwish, a senior Syrian doctor, were responsible for the movement of villages to help control sleeping sickness between 1923 and 1928 (Squires, H.C., *The Sudan Medical Service, An Experiment in Social Medicine*, London, 1958, p.27).

**1.3 Loka**

We[19] went to Yei by way of Loka, where we saw the boys' [intermediate] school.[20]

> [The mission] has plans for technical education.[21] The school was a magnificent building, large, cool and airy. The teaching was all in English. The Headmaster[22] was an Englishman, now ordained, who had been a bank clerk ... The missionary had a nice wife and three delightful children. It was probably a very happy home life and they may not have been more lonely than in a remote parsonage in England ... the standard of work was not high again because the teachers were inadequate. Two Englishwomen had just been appointed to teach in the boys' school but had not yet arrived.[23]

My rather confused impressions were of splendid views, that have since blended into one another, of superb mountain chains through which we drove at an altitude of about 3,000 feet, and of still higher ranges all around backing the wide tree-covered valleys. At our feet the Spring rains had produced a sudden crop of vivid flowers, not perhaps an enamelled meadow but a definite profusion. One reminded me of a purple crocus, another of a forget-me-not, while a delightful salmon pink inflorescence grew out of a rosette like a cowslip and a feature which everywhere gave glory to the trip—banks of lilies; most common of these a medium sized one of tawny glow, a small one like pink china and less often a large white trumpet striped with red. To intensify this were gold *mohur* trees and a vivid flame-

---

19. G.E. Janson-Smith and Dr Beasley set off on trek on Tuesday 9.4.46.

20. The C.M.S. Nugent school, previously C.M.S. Juba High School (opened 1.7.20), was transfered to Loka in January 1929, due to the growing urbanisation (i.e. 'Northernisation') of Juba and was then able to provide a full intermediate course. In 1936 it had 84 pupils, including 1 girl. It became the C.M.S. educational showpiece of the South by 1944 (See also Sanderson, Lilian P., 'Educational development in the Southern Sudan: 1900-1948', *Sudan Notes and Records*, 1962, pp.110-112). In 1948 the girls' school was reorganised from Yei, with two Kakwa women teachers.

21. As early as 1930 the C.M.S. received an additional subsidy to its grant of 1,200 for the foundation of a trades school at Loka.

22. The Headmaster of the Nugent school was Rev. Geoffrey F. Earl from 1939 until 22.1.47; Educated at Monkton Combe and Birkbeck while clerk at the Bank of England, Classics 3rd class Hons; He worked in Children's Services and Crusaders in Islington and Hackney; 1935 obtained Education Diploma. His wife joined him in 1945. The Rev. Charles T. Sharland was in charge at Loka c.1942. Sharland worked in Sudan from 1931 to 1953 and was ordained in 1945. He married Miss F. Streatfield in 1951. Brian J.H. de Saram was headmaster in Rev. Earl's absence 1944-46.

23. Other staff at Loka Nugent School included Miss Joyce Beare (from 1946 to 1948) and Miss Iris Braine (1946) who arrived June 1946. Miss Iris Braine married Mr Lee in Khartoum in January 1947 (*The Torch*). John S. Parry (arrived in Sudan in 1941) and his wife (née Lines) also taught there from 1947 to 1951, as did Christopher L. Cook (arrived in Sudan in 1940, married in 1951) who was also Education Secretary of the C.M.S.

coloured one with soft green grass at their base. After the stony walks I dutifully plodded in Omdurman this was to be back with the romantic poets.

Less alluring were the occasional schools we saw in the villages. The people built these themselves, long erections with light coming in between the top of the wall and the thatched roof, and all the furniture mud benches. The buildings were also used for services and any other general gatherings of any kind. Classes were conducted by a local teacher in the vernacular, when the erratic habits of the local cultivation allowed. The result was that only two were functioning. In the one in which some teaching was actually in progress it was all so lifeless and desultory, that I wondered if the suggestion were really valid, that such simple institutions broke up the crust of indifference and introduced the concept of 'school'.

> There were three classes of rather less than a dozen in each ... They were learning to read in a rather desultory fashion. The youngest class just had a piece of cardboard on which were written some sentences in the vernacular with presumably actions attached. The children were learning these off by heart. Apparently 'the sentence method' of reading is fashionable here ... I incline myself to phonetics but agree there may be something to be said for words. I am still highly doubtful about this mere literacy value and feel there are no teacher-proof methods, so that inadequate teachers of this kind would ruin everything. It is all rather pathetic.

There are no teacher-proof methods of imparting literacy and I much doubted if any of the twenty odd children here would reach it anyway. There was one girl about fourteen or fifteen years old but I was informed, that schoolmasters did not encourage girls to come, as they found them a distraction. Some masters, whom I questioned, definitely shook their heads but would not elaborate their unwillingness. During this tour and subsequent ones I began to notice a withdrawn but not expressed irritation among Sudanese and some British. 'That woman! Always bleating about girls' schools.' Or so I imagined. I felt myself that it became rather a theme song, although amply justified.

## 1.4 Yei

> We went on after lunch and saw the country gradually opening out towards more heavily forested country ... We reached Yei about 3.30 p.m. It is the last place on the road to the Belgian Congo and therefore has customs with a bar across the road ... about 3000 feet up with magnificent views ... I was staying in Janson-Smith's pleasant house which again had a garden full of lilies.

At Yei, however, the girls' school[24] run by two trained and competent Englishwomen,[25] was more than a comfort.

> They took us down to watch the girls playing netball ... in charge of a teacher from Uganda, a well-educated girl of the Buganda tribe.[26]

It was inspiring in this desert of neglect and gave me definite standards for the rest of the inspection.

> The first year class was full and some had had to be turned away. There were over twenty in IA, II, III but IV was down to 14. About 70 boarders ... They were very short of apparatus ... There was a lot of writing on the ground ... They were rather behind one of our good *kuttub*s but the work on the whole was pretty thorough. The three native teachers were rather inadequate. If the school goes like this every day ... it should have some really good results.[27]
>
> The girls were most happy and friendly and, I should think, have a little order introduced into their lives. They are mostly Kakkwa but are taught in Bari.[28]

The children and one of the native teachers wore nothing but bunches of freshly picked leaves, fore and aft, and made a lovely colourful picture filing into assembly, their soft, brown bodies glossy as the green plants.

> I then listened to a scripture lesson by a native teacher, herself a large, well-developed girl with no dress but the leaves ... Part of the charm of the place was a well-ordered simplicity.
>
> ... Back to the house for tea [and mid-morning tea the next day] with a young parson who runs the divinity school. He has one pupil ... We dined with

24. Yei Girls' School was founded in 1929 initially with day girls only and with boarding facilities from 1941. This school maintained the largest regular attendance in its four-year course of any girls' school in the South and was probably the most successful C.M.S. school. The school was reorganised and rebuilt in 1941. In 1946 it had 123 girls.
25. Two missionaries, Miss A.M. Coombes (arrived in Sudan in 1941) and Miss Philippa Guillebaud (arrived in Sudan in 1945 or 1946), of the Gordon Memorial Sudan Mission with C.M.S. staff. They were both trained teachers. 'Miss Coombes had been in the place five years and Miss Guillebaud was new and seemed to get a lot of fever'. Miss Coombes married Rev. F.H.W. Crabb in September 1946 in Yei (*The Torch*) who was apppointed first Principal of C.M.S. Divinity School (Bishop Gwynne College at Mori) in 1945 and had previously been in charge at Yei school (See also Guillebaud, Philippa, *School Belts*, London, 1949).
26. Students were sent regularly to Uganda for teacher-training, from Loka Nugent School to Nabumale at the cost of the Education Department, for example, in 1942 and 1944.
27. 'An authentic school atmosphere' (Beasley, I., 'The education of Girls in the Southern Sudan', *Sudan Government Departmental Reports*, 18.5.46, S.A.D. 5/6/57).
28. According to Sanderson, L.P., *op. cit.*, p.116 the majority of the girls were Bari.

the D.C.[29] and his other guests were two agriculturalists. I played duets rather badly with the D.C.'s wife. All very civilised.

10th. I went out next morning about 6.30 to see P.T. at the school. it was quite useful and energetic. Then at 7 the girls went to hoe in the fields ... in charge of the school matron. Sometimes the English teachers hoe just to show that it is not degrading ... After this they had to clean up their houses and have breakfast, and dispensary. Lessons started at 10. It all seemed quite efficient ... The food was rather dull ... but in addition to the porridge they can grow fruit, vegetables and ground-nuts for their own use. No milk or eggs. As this is fly country there is no cattle and there is a taboo on eggs as making for infertility.

We had breakfast with the Archdeacon[30] and his wife in a lovely house with another garden whose views were magnificent. They have been there 25 years ... They had dug themselves in very comfortably and it all seemed very leisurely ... Visiting out-stations and bush schools must be strenuous[31] ... After breakfast I had an hour's talk with Christopher Cook, the Education Secretary.[32] I was told by him that the chief incentive to literacy was baptism, as the mission insisted on this before baptism ... We agreed that more literature is needed before organisation for literacy and that perhaps English is the best answer.

One thing pleased me very much. We had lunch with the two English girls.

Four of the older girls came on with us to Yambio, as the Headmistress[33] thought it a useful opportunity for them to see another school. It was all arranged with a minimum of fuss that was most laudable. The girls, with

29. Andrew Patrick Cullen, 4N. (b.4.7.1904- ); Educated at Christ's Hospital and Pembroke College, Oxford; 12.12.26 First appointment; 1926 Khartoum, Assistant Private Secretary to Governor-General, Civil Secretary's Office; 1927 White Nile; 1928-29 Upper Nile; 1929-31 Kordofan; 1931-36 Dongola; 1936-42 Khartoum, D.C.; 1.11.42-1946 Equatoria, D.C. Yei District, based in Yei; 1946-53 Blue Nile (1948-53 Deputy Governor, 1953-54 Governor), 1954 retired; 1955- H.M. Diplomatic Service.
30. Archdeacon Archibald Shaw (b.1879-d.1956); educated at Bromsgrove and Emmanuel College, Cambridge; 1905 C.M.S. missionary to the South. He set off with Pastor Gwynne and two other priests, Thom and William Haddow, in a boat up the Nile; 1907 helped establish the mission station at Malek; 1907-36 secretary of the Gordon Memorial Sudan Mission; 1922-40 Archdeacon, Southern Sudan; served until 1949 when he was succeeded by Canon Paul O'B. Gibson (Gibson arrived in Sudan 1916, Canon in 1936 and Archdeacon in 1946). He was apprehensive about receiving Government grants for specialised education experts at the expense of true evangelism. 'At times almost single-handed he created the C.M.S. Mission in the Southern Sudan in the face of appalling difficulties' (Vantini, Giovanni, *Christianity in the Sudan*, Bologna, 1981, pp.254-255).
31. 'J.S. told me that in the note asking us to breakfast the Archdeacon's wife had said she was sorry not to have asked us before but she had been so sure I should stay with the D.C.'s wife. A note that was to be repeated by the missionaries all through the tour.'
32. Christopher Cook, Education Secretary of C.M.S., though by 1947 this post was held by Rev. E.H. Philips (Rev. E.H. Philips or Phillips was in Sudan from 1927 to 1949; 1937-45 at Meridi mission).
33. Miss A.M. Coombes.

fresh cloths knotted over their shoulders were a credit to everyone concerned. Two or three years later, when I returned,[34] the school was still functioning successfully, but it had had to move on with the world. The girls had been learning needlework and were all arrayed in clean cotton frocks. It is not the sort of change that can or should be resisted but it makes problems for the educator.

### 1.5 Yei to Meridi

> We had to start at 1.45 p.m. because one of the agriculturalists was worried about his tyres. The drive to Meridi was tiring and bewildering ... Still there seemed quite a lot of people along the road with here and there a neat C.M.S. school, an occasional dispensary and one or two policemen ... light forest ... fine vistas ...

On the road I was surprised to see how many of the people we met had clothing of some sort, even if only a piece of barkcloth tucked into a girdle. This bark is stripped from a tree which has the accommodating knack of growing another layer to make good its loss. Then the piece of material is beaten soft by little hammers with heads made of ivory on one side and ebony on the other and the alternating rhythm of black and white is supposed to improve the quality of the stuff. Sometimes it was made into primitive-looking shorts [or] a loin cloth. Head coverings were also more in evidence than I expected and, although I have no data on this point, I was told[35] that it was a fallacy that Africans could expose their heads to the sun with impunity. Whatever the truth of the matter, a great number of men had little hats, either for use or ornament; these made of the local grasses into a wide variety of shapes, a favourite being an elementary sort of boater, while others looked like strawberry punnets. Add to a punnet a few feathers sticking out in all directions and little more than a loin cloth and a fierce sort of spear and the general effect is either intimidating or reminiscent of charades, according to one's mood.

### 1.6 Meridi

> It was just dusk when we came out onto what is called a main road and came to Meridi, our next overnight stop, about 7 o'clock. The house we arrived at was that of the Agricultural Inspector,[36] a very attractive place and most

34. 8.4.1949. In the same year C.M.S. re-organised their girls' teacher-training into a formal vernacular centre at Yei.
35. By Janson-Smith.
36. R.G. Laing, B.Sc.(Agric), N.D.D.; 10.1.38 First appointment; By 1.3.46 Inspector of Agriculture, Equatoria Province, based in Meridi.

carefuly netted against mosquitoes. In addition to Janson-Smith and myself, his guests were the other agriculturalist whose tyres had caused our early departure, yet another agriculturalist from Yambio and the D.C. from Yambio.[37] They had come to meet the D.C. from Amadi[38] who had not arrived. That had made them all a bit explosive but they were polite and nice to me. I learned afterwards, however, that the letters about my coming had not all arrived and apparently after I went to bed Janson-Smith got into trouble because of the inefficiency of his Department. In fact D.C. Yambio did not know who I was nor why this woman was wandering round making all this disturbance.

It was rather a disturbance. I had the spare bedroom. There were two men in the big bedroom, two on the verandah and Janson-Smith and the D.C. Amadi were to sleep in a resthouse at the bottom of the garden ... However we had an amicable game of bridge ...

At Meridi, our next overnight stop, there was both a boys' school[39] and a mission one for girls. The former was well housed in good brick buildings with adequate playing fields and competent local teachers all very anxious to improve their standards. Compared with this what was considered good enough for girls nearly reduced me to tears. I could only cling to the hope, that this belonged to a past epoch, for the Englishwoman in charge was the wife of the missionary[40] and they had returned to work after some years in retirement. She was a fearsome, old lady with a lovely head of grey, curling hair, which ruffled most prettily, as she chased round perpetually blowing a whistle for change of lessons. As most of the children had obviously been pressed into service for the morning and were not doing anything anyway, it seemed rather a needless exertion.

The school functioned from 6.30 a.m. to 8. I left the house at 6.40 a.m. [on 11th] and we went right into the middle of things. It had all the bad features I

37. Major J.W.G. Wyld, O.B.E., D.S.O., M.C., 4N.; 16.8.25 First appointment; 1.4.31- Equatoria; By 1.3.46 D.C. Zande District, based Yambio. He ruled the Azande autocratically from 1932 to 1951 and was in all but name the Zande paramount Chief. He refused to act on directions which he considered 'not applicable to Zande district' (See Sanderson, L.M.P. and G.N., *Education, Religion & Politics in Southern Sudan 1899-1914*, London, Ithaca Press, 1981, p.180, 229).
38. M.F.A. Keen.
39. Meridi mission was founded in 1901 with permanent buildings by 1921. The school was founded in 1924 by Rev. William Haddow and took girl boarders from 1929. By 1938 there were 36 girls at the school under the headship of Rev. E.H. Philips. By 1946 there were 83 girls. 'The headmaster had been in Uganda and had distinct possibilities.'
40. The missionaries were Rev. F.G. Laverick and Mrs H.O. Laverick, Gordon Memorial Sudan Mission, C.M.S. staff. They served in Sudan from 1926 to 1936 and from 1945 to 1947. They were posted to Meridi from Yambio from February 1927 and became experts in Avukaya and Western Moru languages. 'Definitely of the old regime and had just come back for a time after retiring in 1938.'

had expected ... all day girls and rather a scruffy lot ... The teaching was bad beyond belief.

The one woman teaching had her baby on her arm all the time and it was amazing that so small an infant should require such constant suckling and be able to make such large puddles. All this would not have mattered, if she had had a little more to teach her pupils.

> I could not help wondering what it was like when there was not an inspection. Some of the girls in her class could read a few words and could read 2 and 3 times table when written on the board but what their real knowledge of numbers might be I could only guess and at a hazard I should say nil. The top class could more or less read the Bible here and there and write a little.

After the solid and sensible lines on which the school at Yei had been functioning so admirably, it was strange that the missionary society should have contenanced this travesty. The four girls we had brought with us looked on in silence but the difference between them and the children here was most marked. It was a difference hard to define, as I could not talk to them, but it suggested a new kind of alertness and self-reliance.

> Mrs Laverick had not been at all pleased to see them the night before. She thought it all most inconsiderate ... eventually a teacher's wife took them in. Poor Mrs L. did not seem to realize the educational value of the trip.
>
> There were constant assurances that, having had no notice of my coming, no special arrangements had been made. I kept going into the classrooms to see what was going on.

As a visitor I must have been most unsatisfactory, because the poor missionary's wife kept suggesting, that I must be tired and would like to go back to her house, despite my assurances that this was the way I earned my daily bread and I was quite inured to the hardships of inspecting. I doubt, if she ever understood why I had come. She was entirely pre-occupied with some scandal about a school-boy and a girl, which was vaguely communicated to me by nudges and innuendoes

> ... but whether they were caught *in flagrante* I could not discover ... Mrs Laverick said it must be nice to have a fortnight's holiday in the mountains away from the heat of Khartoum [and also] how kind it was of me to spend my spare time looking at their schools. At which I got really uppish ... [Then] I felt they were too old to argue with ... There was no point in being uncivil to no purpose.

After breakfast and lengthy prayers,

> ... by a man teacher, probably sent over from the boys' school for the occasion and I was asked to say a few kind words and Mrs Laverick would translate,

she disappeared to deal with the culprits and I never saw her again.

> So Janson-Smith and I decided to go to the boys' school ... I went back to the Agricultural Inspector's house ... the D.C. Amadi arrived ... also another D.C. from Yambio[41] turned up ... There was quite a party for lunch.

## 1.7 Yambio

The heavens opened as we drove to Yambio in pouring rain with the road a torrent but usable, as the surface, fortunately, was hard. By this time we were in Zande land [Zande District] and in addition to the unending splendid mountain vistas, there were glimpses of great gallery forests not far away. Yambio itself was a large, clean, orderly station.

> There were clean, wide roads bordered with palm trees ... pleasant houses for officials at what the missionaries called the post and a big mission station at the foot of the hill. I was taken down to Mrs Bates[42] ... [After tea I] was taken to a resthouse about ten minutes walk away. Mrs Bates explained that as there was not a woman up at the post she thought I ought to be down here ... Bridge to repeat the night's before at the house of the Agriculture Inspector.

Yambio restored my faith somewhat by having a girls' school in the charge of two Englishwomen, which approximated to the manner of the one at Yei.[43]

> Miss Holt (in charge) who had been out about a year and (assistant) Miss Long ... genuinely interested in education and quite keen on their job ... There was another woman from Uganda, quite as good as the one at Yei and rather older, and a local woman about 40 ... a marvellous disciplinarian. Then there

41. Duncan Harkness Weir, O.B.E. (b.8.12.1913- ); Educated at Fettes and Glasgow University, Glasgow University Fives X, 1933 Scottish XX, National Match, Bisley; 9.5.37 First appointment; 1937-40 Kassala; 1940-41 Governor-General's Temporary Commission as Bimbashi in S.D.F.; 1941 seconded to O.E.T.A. (Eritrea and Cyrenaica); 16.5.44-47 Equatoria, by 1.3.46 A.D.C. Zande District, based in Yambio. By 1.9.46 D.C Zande District, based Yambio; 1947-51 Private Secretary to the Governor-General; 1951-53 Kassala; 1953-55 Assistant Financial Secretary; 1955 retired; 1955-73 Academic Registrar, London University.
42. 'Mrs Bates, wife of the headmaster of the boys' school at Yambio. She had been a teacher but gave it up upon marriage...with two girls.' Mr and Mrs J.S. Bates were in Yambio from 1938 to 1950. They married in 1938, he was ordained in 1947 and he died in 1950.
43. Yambio was run by the Gordon Memorial Sudan Mission with C.M.S. staff. Work started at Yambio in 1905. In 1921 the first classes for women and girls began in a permanent building. In February 1929 the girls' boarding school was opened by Miss L. Gore (in Sudan from 1927 to 1936), with 70 girls on the school roll). In 1938 and 1946 there were 54 girls, under the headship of Mrs G.B.M. Riley (in Yambio 1937-1938, wife of Rev. A.B.H. Riley) and then Miss N.J. Holt (in Sudan from 1943/4 to 1952). In 1947 third and fourth year classes were transferred to Lunjini, near Lui, as attendance in these classes in Yambio was poor (Sanderson, L.M.P., *op. cit.*, pp.115-116).

were four girls in training for teaching who took a number of classes under supervision ... About 40 boarders and some day girls ... boarding house pattern was the same as Yei. Standard of work (probably) lower than Yei ... I think perhaps here they would respond if more was expected of them. Lessons went on till 12.30, the last part being handwork ... good grass mats. Here the children do their gardening in the afternoons.

I went back to lunch with the two women[44] ... they assured me [the Zande] were the most immoral tribe in Africa. They kept talking about the infertility of the Zande which was due to their lax moral code (Morality to a missionary is of course sexual, as admittedly to many other people) and Mrs Bates did the same.

I was given much generous hospitality by the English officials and missionaries.

We all went to dinner with the D.C.[45] and a great deal of the evening ... pulling my leg about all that was going to happen to me when I set out on my own ... lions at Mabu, snakes coming up through the resthouse floor at Tambura, and leopards somewhere else. Then the number of days before the malaria would begin to show itself, to say nothing of bilharzia, ankylostomiasis and guinea worm.

I felt out of touch by not being able to talk to the Zande women and I thus missed the kindly social contacts with the villagers, that I was accustomed to in the North.

After tea we went to see the site of a new agricultural school which is part of the Zande scheme[46] ... looked very promising.

It was this lack, that made me feel a little forlorn the next morning, when I set out, because for the rest of the trip I was on my own and as I discovered later, not expected in some of the places, in what I believed was a carefully planned programme. My sense of insecurity was not lessened, when I saw the vehicle allotted to me for the journey.[47] It was undoubtedly a tribute to the skill of Mr. Henry Ford but its appearance filled me with the gloomiest foreboding, even though I was used by this time to elderly vehicles. In form it was a V8 truck without sides to the cab and with the hard bench of police

44. Under the '1938 Agreements' the C.M.S. agreed to post two women educationalists in each of their four centres, beginning with Yambio, under Miss N.J. Holt, headmistress and Miss M. Long (in Sudan 1945 to 1949/50).
45. Major J.W.G. Wyld.
46. It was part of C.W. Williams' proposed experiment in 'Village Crafts, Agriculture and Social Settlement Centre...preferably in Zande country' (Williams, C.W., *Educational Proposals*, November 1944, pp.37-38). By 1948, with only 67 pupils, it had become Yambio Agricultural Training School providing low-grade vocational training.
47. 'J.S. [Janson-Smith] lent me a servant and cook, bedding, trek box and all home comforts. Also maps.'

cars. Not a new car for the inspector-before-last away back in the early thirties, it had acquired an especially disreputable look by losing half its bonnet. I found out in transit, that the metal plates under our feet clanged together every time the driver let in the clutch and the mudguards flapped like an elephant's ears. All this somewhat wearing on a long drive.

A capable driver, however, had been assigned to me, I was assured, but I had been given his history the night before, which was again outside my Northern experience. He was, said my informants, a very reliable mechanic, as indeed he proved.

> [The car] turned up at 3 [the previous] afternoon having been five days on the road owing to a fault in the carburettor. Fortunately the mail lorry passed and the driver had sent to Wau for a new one but had had to sit two days on the road waiting for it to arrive.

The remarkable part of the tale was that his father had been hanged for cannabalism not so many years before and that not his first offence. The son had been dismissed from the police for torturing people, although perhaps not without provocation. As an important N.C.O. he had been in charge of the mail and staying overnight in his village, he found the bag had been stolen. Being the son of a big chief he managed to have the inhabitants tortured and by this means he recovered the bag, but lost his job. The Education Department now employed him and he served them well. Certainly I had no complaints, since he steered the scruffy truck over unspeakably rocky roads, with only one breakdown of about ten minutes towards the end of my trip. As we were setting off, the Agricultural Inspector came by in a shining green box, which I knew had been giving him trouble, in spite of its handsome appearance, because we had met on the road from Meridi the day before. At the sight of my ramshackle vehicle he looked half-concerned and half-amused. 'What happens if it rains?' he asked, indicating the bonnet. 'I suppose we get wet,' seemed to be the only possible, if fatuous, answer.

So with what I hoped was a wave and a bright smile we clattered off. It was the rain I feared as a far more likely mishap than hostile tribesmen or marauding leopards. To break down on some lonely road and have to wait maybe for a couple of days in the damp, while the trouble was rectified, would need more patience than the Sollum signal box. We did not have to contend with the sandy hindrances of so many of the Northern roads but the way was uneven and strewn with loose rocks of all sizes. At frequent intervals we came to dry water courses bridged by logs just overlaid with lumps of local stone or laterite and not too firmly pressed down. I wondered what happened, if we hit one of the larger pieces lying about but fortunately we never did.

### 1.8 Yambio to Mupoi

After Li Rangu, where we passed a spacious and efficient hospital and segregation camp for sleeping sickness, there was little but jungle and straw huts, until we suddenly came to an impressive clearing with large red brick buildings at Mupoi. Although we had halted for lunch by the road we had made better time than we had expected and arrived about half past one.

### 1.9 Mupoi

I found the Fathers[48] in an Italian style house, near an enormous church and was rather shaken to find that no-one had heard of my coming nor had the slightest idea who I was.

> As I was not expected in Wau until Monday afternoon, this meant that from Saturday morning until Monday night no-one would make enquiries about me, had I not arrived.

A message was sent to warn the Sisters and I was taken to see the church,

> ... a plain building with little chapels each side with figures in them ... There was a large bright altar with silver candlesticks of much magnificence and figures of angels on either side,

while they all recovered from the shock. The Sisters were most charming and, when they heard that I had already lunched, asked me back to tea at four o'clock.

> I had hoped they would ask me to stay partly because the jungle looked so lonely and partly because I had never had the opportunity of seeing the conventual life at first hand. I gathered, however, that I was not getting an invitation, so I went back to the resthouse ... We unpacked and I had a short rest on the camp-bed ... Then off again across the horrible bridge. One of the fathers took me down again to the Sisters' house through a great wide avenue of enormous trees.

The resthouse was about three miles back over a particularly nasty specimen of loose bridge above a pond. Boys from the school, who were bathing in it, cheered as I passed and called out 'Sister' in the friendliest tones. Our tea-party was thoroughly enjoyable despite the language strain of their having little English and I less Italian. Children swarming into the classroom, when we went to look at [the apparatus,] and women sitting or sauntering in the yard gave the place a pleasant, happy-go-lucky atmosphere, although the girls did not appear to be in such good physical

---

48. Verona Fathers Mission. Work started on a girls' school at Mupoi in 1913 and there was a permanent building by 1934.

shape as in the boarding schools at Yei, an impression increased by the bedraggled bunches of leaves they were wearing.

> Mother Superior was a sweet soul who had been out in Equatoria for fourteen years. We looked round the school ... There was a simple building where ... women came to be prepared for baptism. I did not gather they demanded the literacy test.

I could not stay very long, as I had to negotiate the bridge and three miles of road [to the resthouse] before the sudden darkness descended. Even in a trip overloaded with remarkable views the situation of this resthouse was striking. In itself it was merely a mud enclosure with a steep, thatched roof but no doors and windows, but outside the wall was lower, forming a covered verandah. Sitting here and writing my notes I looked out from the top of a slope to wide valleys in all directions filled with a tangle of splendid trees, that from my vantage point appeared almost solid. The sunset was rather veiled, not flaming with the theatrical grandeur that startles the desert skies but more in keeping with this softer landscape.

Until dusk fell, various Zande girls came and hung over the mud wall to watch what I was doing. It was very hard, that we could do no more than wave and smile and make friendly noises to one another. With their lithe, brown bodies adorned only with leaves they fitted into the scene, as if dryads from the forest close by. By the time the moon suddenly shot up over the ridge, they had all gone and my servant came to indicate, that he had put my bath outside the resthouse, because the canvas leaked. Indicate it had to be, as he had been lent to me for the journey, and we had no common language at all. His constant serious expression was probably due to over-anxiety about making the right arrangements. My bathing corner was shielded from the sight of any villagers but it was a novel experience to be standing in the moonlight as naked as any of them with the forest instead of bathroom walls to gaze on. Solitude settled soon, however, and I decided to go to bed early. I noticed that this had been set up inside under a mosquito net, and was likely to be stuffy. Unfortunately I could not enquire from anyone, whether there was any good reason against my sleeping outside, for even the driver had no more than a few words of pidgin Arabic. When he and the servant withdrew into a *tukl* across the road I watched them carefully draw a heap of brushwood to close up the entrance. I therefore put my folding chair across the gap in my wall. It would hardly keep out a determined intruder but it would allow me to hear any prowling animal. I did waken in the night and lay listening to the little noises that creep around even in apparent stillness. They were unfamiliar sounds in some indefinable way, not the dry voices of the desert, which is always a little restless even in its quietest moods. I very much wanted to know the time but the lamp was on the table across the room and I did not want to get out of bed to light it. Snakes are silent creatures and I did not fancy plodding about in the dark with the chance of one of these having slid in. My next awakening was to a welcome and familiar sound, the clink of a tea-cup on the verandah. I slipped on a dressing-gown and sat drinking my morning tea with this unending expanse of forest unrolled before me, fresh and soft, as the sun came up.

It was Palm Sunday.[49] When I arrived once more at the Mission, the church was overflowing with people, as far as I could see, happily taking part in some joyful activity, although how much they understood it would be difficult to say. Small boys in great numbers were wandering round very proud of their crosses made of palm and ornamented with frangi-pangi or gold *mohur*.

> Father Fortuna came to meet me ... The girls were by this time filing out of church and I went down to see the lessons. Class III, taken by a pupil teacher,[50] did a little elementary oral arithmetic. Class II taken by a teacher who was the wife of one of the masters, read Zande fairly well. Class V the Sisters were most proud of because they had some simple apparatus. [The teacher] did not seem to know as much as the class. The Sister in charge of the school came and took over. She was a good teacher ... I saw no timetables and thought the whole thing had rather a desultory air. Pleasant and friendly ... there is probably no incentive. I saw no signs of needlework or domestic science ... The dormitories were large rooms with straw mats, all carefully swept. The children prepared their own two meals a day in a simple fashion in a shed.

I tried to remember Bernard Shaw's words about the value of anything which increased people's faith, but I could not shut out the thought, that all this might be regarded as white man's magic and perhaps more powerful than the black man's. Such ideas seemed most unworthy in view of the obvious devotion of everyone at the Mission. One father had been there for over thirty years.

> The Father Superior was rather a dull-looking person with a swivel eye but pleasant ... There was also a very old man ... who had come to the place in

---

49. 14.4.46.
50. Mupoi was one of the designate teacher-training centres (for the Azande) set up by the V.F.M. under Cox's reforms in the '1938 Agreements'. The 23.12.44 memorandum from the Education Department suggested the conditions and details of the plan for setting up self-governing centres. Initially two were to be set up, one Catholic and one Protestant. Kwajok was opened for the Dinka, Busseri for the 'Wau conglomerate' and Palotaka for the peoples of Eastern Equatoria. Under the agreement the V.F.M. were also asked to post educationalist sisters at Kwajok, Mupoi and Palotaka.

1913, when it was first started.[51] There was a younger father about 40 who had gone to England in 1940 and spent the War in the Isle of Man. He seemed capable.

Their generous hospitality to me, such an unexpected visitor, was most warming. Nor had I expected it in Lent, but meals were thoroughly hearty for all of us and accompanied by a glass of pure grape juice, which made a welcome change from the taste of boiled water out of a *zamzamia*.

## 1.10 Mabu

> I managed to get away immediately lunch was over ... It was very hot driving ... Tambura was a biggish place with important looking brick stores. We had brought a lad from Mupoi who said he had money to take to Tambura. Mabu had a lovely situation among the hills.

My next stop at Mabu was at a similar resthouse [to that at Mupoi] but here I could see no village close by, nor a friendly mission for conversation and for sharing professional interests. I was too exhausted after a hot and stony road to explore the immediate surroundings, although I had been told the view might well include a pride of lions on the plain at the foot of the mound. We were leaving the shelter of the forests here and I was concerned by the prospect of rain, as the clouds began to pile up. It was difficult to explain this to the driver, who merely shook his head, when I pointed to the sky and declined to put the truck under cover. I did not want to hurt his professional pride by giving him orders and with the language barrier between us tactful explanations were definitely ruled out. We both shrugged therefore and I retired to the resthouse, which had been decorated by some local aspirant, with grotesque paintings mostly of Europeans in uniform. By the light of a single hurricane lamp the figures stood out eerily from the shadows. My worry this night, when I wakened, was in case I might detect the patter of rain among the rustling of the leaves. What could I do anyway, if I should hear it? Our luck held and we started off in the morning [8 o'clock from Mabu] in great style, with a slight haze over the sun to make driving less onerous than the day before.

51. Mupoi Mission was started towards the end of 1912 by F.X. Geyer (b.1860-d.1943), the Vicar Apostolic of Central Africa 1903-1913. By 1938 there were 54 pupils and the school was directed by Rev. Fr. Candido Mberti; by 1946 there were 100, under Sister Tonelli.

## 2. Bahr el Ghazal

These early morning starts never failed to bring a flutter of excitement as to what the journey might reveal and this was particularly so, when the road was new to me. By this time we were leaving the magnificence of the mountains behind and coming to the flatter country of the Bahr el Ghazal.

### 2.1 Raffili[52]

The surface did not improve and when we reached a mission station at Raffili [about 10.30 a.m.], I was glad to have the excuse to get out of the car to deliver a letter from Mupoi to one of the Fathers. It was a great relief after being so shaken and jolted, to sit in a chair, even if only for ten minutes, and chat with the Fathers[53] while drinking a lime juice and (to my wonderment) soda water. The Father for whom I had the letter was a newly ordained Jur, who was striking in his white robe, his very black head shining and almost polished-looking.

### 2.2 Wau

Despite the rough road, we made excellent time and before lunch came to the big sign with a stork on it, the [Bahr el Ghazal] Province badge announcing we had reached Wau.

> We went straight to the *Mudiria* where the Deputy Governor[54] shook hands with 'Dr Beasley I presume' and then started to say 'I wasn't expecting you' but finished to my great relief with 'till this afternoon'.

Here I was staying in comfort in the large, untidy bungalow of the Deputy Governor, who promptly took my truck in hand and refurbished it with a complete bonnet and an overhaul during the two days I was with him.

52. Raffili Mission was founded in 1913 by F.X. Geyer in the Bor and Belanda tribal areas as a half-way house between Wau and Mupoi.
53. Dr Beasley sat with the Fathers, 'A new one from Asmara, an ordinary little one and the Jur'.
54. Thomas Richard Hanby Owen, C.B.E., 4N. (b.23.5.1903-d.1982); Educated at Repton and Corpus Christi, Oxford; 12.12.26 First appointment; 1927 Bahr el Ghazal; 1928-32 White Nile; 1932-36 Kassala; 1936-39 Civil Secretary's Office; 1939-45 Kordofan; 1.10.45 Equatoria, 1946 Bahr el Ghazal Sub-Province, Deputy Governor; 1948-53 Governor, Bahr el Ghazal; 1953 retired; 1954- Assistant Warden, Game and Fisheries Department, Uganda; later lay-reader, Hereford Diocese.

There was much of interest in the history of the place but I thought it singularly uninviting despite its situation on the river,[55] then rather shrunken but later a broad, smooth stream. It may have been my imagination but I fancied a sinister 'feel' brooded over the town, as if it had never entirely dissipated the evil vapours of its position as a slave headquarters in the days of the Khedives. Even until the thirties it had an unwholesome reputation of sheltering a large number of undesirables among its inhabitants. In 1938 stern measures were taken to send back as many as possible to the districts from which they had originally come. With its present population reduced to about 3,000[56] it was a much more savoury place but I still disliked it. Its aspect could not become picturesque even with an odd Dinka or two swaggering down the road in all their graceful nakedness.

Professionally there was plenty to occupy me, [16th] for the Bishop of the Roman Catholic Mission[57] showed me round the boys' school[58] and the sensible and practical workshops training students for carpentry and mechanical jobs, and then left me in the charge of the Mother Superior. She was a woman to evoke the deepest liking and admiration, which strengthened as I came to know her more. Unluckily the girls' school was by no means up to the Yei standard and both she and the Bishop were obviously disappointed, that I did not say that everything was wonderful. I could not pretend, that the work was satisfactory, when it could manifestly have been improved.

The standards were really low. There was a kindergarten under a tree which I did not see. Class I was being taught by a native Sister, a Dinka, who was doing quite well but not sufficiently thorough ... Class IV took twenty minutes writing out the problem of 3 dresses at 12 P.T. each and only one worked the sum. Class III took longer to take 24 eggs from 135 and very few got the right answer. The same was true of reading. Class I was beginning well but II were learning their English books by heart. Class IV curiously enough read the Oxford Press version of *Snow White* quite well but Class III could hardly read at all. Apart from the [Dinka] Sister there were two very inadequate native

55. The Bahr el Ghazal River.
56. In the early 1930s the population of Wau was about 10,000.
57. Bishop Rudolf Orler; 1933-46 Vicariate Apostolic, Bahr el Ghazal based at Wau; His successor was Bishop E. Mason. By 1948 Bishop Mlakic was Prefect Apostolic of Bahr el Jebel.
58. Work started on the V.F.M. Wau Mission in 1905 and there was a permanent building there by 1938. In 1938 there were 33 girls and the school was directed by Rev. Fr. Santandrea; by 1946 there were 91, under Sister Germans.

girls. Two of the Sisters were supposed to teach in the school ... The Domestic
Science rooms were satisfactory but the needlework not up to the standard of
the syllabus. The kitchen was simple and sensible and looked as if it was used.

One nice touch I always recall. The Protestant missions were
uncompromisingly teetotal and complained, that some girls were not sent to
school because the brewing of beer was not included in the Domestic
Science syllabus. Here on the 'keep your men at home' principle making
*merissa* was always taught to the older girls.

### 2.3 Busseri[59]

I was very happy to fall in with the Bishop's suggestion, that the Mother
Superior should accompany me to Busseri, where there was a very
flourishing boys' school with a Father doing extremely good work in the
field of crafts.

> She was a nice person and very anxious for the welfare of the people and had
> done teaching, nursing and visiting ... Another bad road ... It may have been
> partly the personality of Father Simone who was in charge ... an excellent
> craftsman and certainly appeared a man of culture ... Vigour and cheerfulness
> seemed to radiate. They were most kind and welcoming.

Here I had the chance to talk to the Mission's education secretary,[60] who
appeared to me to have a rather fanatic gleam in his eye. We had an
enormous lunch in the Sisters' house and after their devotions set off again
to Mboro.[61] The only Sister teaching at Busseri worked in the boys' school
and the other [two] spent their time in cooking, laundering and mending for
the Fathers.

### 2.4 Busseri to Mboro

Being three in the small truck was not as uncomfortable as we might have
expected, because, no doubt, although the Mother Superior looked bulky,

59. By 1946 the Busseri Intermediate School was full to capacity, with some British
professional teachers on the staff. It was also a prrimary teacher-training centre.
60. Bishop Edoardo Mason (b.1903- ); Italian Catholic missionary, educationalist; 1927-30
Headmaster, Wau Intermediate School; 1930 Torit Normal school; 1932-38 Father Superior,
Wau Mission; 1939 education course in London. The *Report of the De La Warr Commission*
(1937) recommended that mission teachers be trained at the London Institute of Education or
other recognised Diploma course; 1940 Intermediate school, Busseri; 1940-47 Educational
Secretary, V.F.M., Bahr el Ghazal; 1947-60 Vicariate Apostolic of the Bahr el Ghazal; 1960-69
El Obeid.
61. Dr Beasley and the Mother Superior (probably Sister Germans) set off about 3.30 p.m. for
the drive of more than two hours to Mboro.

most of the girth was due to her voluminous petticoats, which crushed into cushions for both of us. The road surface was indescribably rugged but, as we bumped and clanged our way along, she managed to discuss all sorts of important matters shouting into my ears above the incessant din of the engine's racket.

> Her teaching, she complained, had had to be carried out in four successive languages owing to the changes of Government policy.

After her theories of education she began on her most heart- felt disappointment, her inability to persuade anyone to take action about the training of midwives in this district. All this she illustrated by the most horrible anecdotes of what she had actually seen in villages and while nursing in the hospital. She was a woman of wide experience and much energy, who had often gone into the villages in company with another Sister for any help they might offer to the women there. I was grieved that after this trip I never met her again but she was transferred shortly [after] to a position of greater responsibility.

## 2.5 Mboro

At Mboro we had a tremendous welcome, where a large girls' school[62] was in charge of a vigorous Sister,[63] who had been obliged to spend her war years in England and had used her time to good purpose.

> She attended courses at the Colonial Institute and elsewhere. She herself had run a course for Sisters at Busseri and her methods were used in Wau ... I got the impression that she would rather train teachers than do the actual teaching herself.

Contact with her was therefore easier than with most of these Italian Sisters, whose English was often scrappy and who were quite untrained as educators.

> [She] showed me all her records and syllabuses and timetables and I felt any school which lived up to them should do well. She had one Sister to help her with the teaching [as she] did not speak Ndogo. [This Sister] had been there many years and knew Ndogo fluently. Also there were two native teachers and occasional help from the boys' school.

62. V.F.M. opened in permanent buildings in Mboro in 1947. The Mission here was founded in 1912 in Gola country (though closed between 1914-16). By 1938 there were 62 girls with the school directed by Rev. Fr. Seri; by 1946 there were 110, under Sister Castricane. It was also a teacher-training centre.
63. Sister Inez.

After another ample meal we were given an entertainment by the girls, who marched round out of the darkness into the light of the Petromax lamp performing their native games and dances with much energy and no little skill. In my honour they finished with a version of 'God Save the King', which I only just recognised in time. Then they marched off still drumming with much zeal and excellent rhythm and singing heartily, until they were shoo-ed into their dormitories, unwilling to stop.

> They were disgracefully overcrowded. 87 girls in three ordinary sized rooms and more to come. The rooms were clean and the girls had white- washed the walls themselves. The girls, as at all the other schools, cooked their own food and had a careful scheme for their chores, which involved cleaning everything. Lessons were from 7 to 10.30 ... There was a new school building under construction.

Naturally I wondered what my accommodation would be, since the popular picture of conventual life conjours up a vision of clammy cells and straw pallets. I was allotted a room that was, I think, like all the others and except for the barred window there was no suggestion of restriction about it. It had furnishings that were simple but comfortable. The building was in the shape of a cross with rooms leading off the corridors. While I was undressing, I heard the Sisters at their devotions in the moonlight and they afterwards marched in procession, still chanting, to the little chapel next to my room. It was all rather impressive in this lonely and barren place so far away from the particular culture in which these ceremonies had evolved.

> I wanted to hear some reading in Class III but the results were not good. The attempt at sums was beneath contempt. The nuns were rather distressed ... admittedly the girls were just trickling back ready for Easter ... Fortunately Class II did them proud. A demonstration lesson on reading went well ... Things should be better when Sister Inez knows a bit more Ndogo ... the children were bright enough ... There is so much concentration in these three Catholic schools on the first year ... because the children are keen. Sister Inez [wanted my help to get the Government to pay] the teachers 20 P.T. per month.[64]
>     We then went to see the model house and I was very much surprised to see how much equipment there was in the way of furniture and utensils compared with an Arab *farikh* ... There was a large living room and a small bedroom, half of which was taken up by the baby's cot. The mother slept on a mat on the floor but what happened to father or any other children no-one seemed to know ... The Ndogo were good carpenters ... I was supposed to help get

---

64. From 1939 a grant of LS30 p.a. was paid by the Government for a girls' school where there was a minimum of 10 boarders. If 10 or more girls attended a boys' school, a grant of LS20 was allocated (Sanderson, L.P., *op. cit.*, p.115).

money for another [model house] from the Government [as] the house was
wanted by its owner ...

## 2.6 Mboro to Wau

This part of the country lacked the magnificent vistas which had been all
around me for the early part of my journey and the arid flatness of the
district near the school came closer to what I was accustomed to in the
North. We went back to Wau by a shorter route, which included the
notorious road to Raga. I had been told that it was the worst road in the
Sudan, a pretty strenuous claim, and I had always given my vote to the road
to Tokar. This was different, as in place of the fine, shifting sand, the
uneven surface was strewn with big chunks of ironstone and we endured a
terrific jolting. I was genuinely sorry to part with the Mother Superior and
still more so, that our mutual hopes of being able to work together were
never fulfilled.

## 2.7 Tonj

I set off after breakfast the next morning [19th] for Tonj, a mere 63 miles.

After this [Wau], the way took us through thick forest in the districts of the
Dinka[65] to Tonj, where the D.C.[66] [and his wife were] out hunting a lion,
that had eaten seventeen people.

He was not able to find it but he shot a leopard ... I enjoyed my stay ... They
were so kind and friendly ...
An extra tall man who had been a rowing blue ... In a district a little north
of this he had been holding forth in a village when a woman with some
unsolved grievance came up behind and dealt him a serious wound with a
spear. The villagers immediately made a litter and started to carry him to the
river to get a boat to a medical post. As they neared the next village came a
rush of men with spears, who had heard of this act of treachery and thought it

65. Jur River District.
66. John Hyrne Tucker Wilson (b.17.9.1914- ); Educated at Shrewsbury and Pembroke
College; 1934-36 Cambridge University Boat Club (President 1936), 1948 Gold Medal,
Olympic Games, Coxwainless Pair; 13.9.36 First appointment; 1936-39 Blue Nile; 1939-44
Upper Nile; 1944-45 Kordofan; 1.10.45-50 Equatoria (1945-48)/Bahr el Ghazal (1948-50),
A.D.C. (1945-46) later D.C. Jur River District, based in Tonj; 1950-53 Darfur; 1953-54 Bahr el
Ghazal, Deputy Governor; 1954 retired; 1955- Production Engineer, Stewart & Lloyds Ltd. *or*
    John Miller Hunter (b.15.2.1916- ); Educated at Glasgow Academy and Christ's College,
Cambridge; 26.12.38 First appointment; 1938-42 Blue Nile; 1.7.42-48 Equatoria/Bahr el
Ghazal, by March 1946 A.D.C. for Finance Department, Jur River District, based at Tonj, by
September 1946 D.C. Jur River District, based at Tonj; 1948-55 Kordofan, D.C.; 1955 retired
to farming in Aberdeenshire.

a good excuse for a scrap with the offending village. Despite pain and exhaustion the D.C. sat up and harangued the men until they went back to their village in peace. By good luck an Egyptian Irrigation launch happened to be on one of its rare trips and he was taken back to hospital where after a long and anxious period he recovered.

New buildings had recently been erected for the Government boys' school on a wonderful site perched on a high bluff overlooking the river, and sprinkled with huge trees.

It is now to have a British headmaster and work up to something better, like the intermediate school at Abwong.[67]

The boarding houses looked adequate and attractive but the temporary classrooms were in a converted cowshed. The Dinka were famed for their almost mystical devotion to their cattle, but this arrangement was probably pure chance.

A suggestion that the old buildings might be used to start a girls' school was greeted by the Dinka masters as merely fantastic. Even the matron, herself a Dinka, and a kind and sensible person did not favour the idea except for very small girls and a long way off from the boys' school. There was, I was told, a school at the Kajok Mission, where about thirty girls attended, each with her own cow, but some months before there had been a hasty withdrawal of pupils. A Dinka Sister at Wau had taken vows and celibacy, the parents felt, was much to be deprecated. In any case the [Kajok] school was on holiday and there would be nothing for me to see. Despite all this discouragement we did eventually start a Government girls' school at Tonj.[68]

From there I had my first glimpse of the *toitch*es, the flat grasslands on which the Dinka graze their cattle, as we drove across the wide, lonely stretch bordering the river, where the drab grass was dry with large burnt patches. No trees were in the foreground but mountains and forests stood out in the distance. It was a dull, grey morning with thick banks of cloud and *toitch* sounded an applicable word, admirably describing the feeling of desolation, reminiscent of dreary fen land. A little rain sprinkled down in a half-hearted way, until we came again to forests of some density and began to meet quite a number of people. One or two of the women wore

67. Tonj Boys' School had 129 boys by 1948 and had begun fifth year work. It was opened after 1944.
68. Tonj was the original pilot Government school, planned in 1938 and in the 1944 Williams Plan. It was a village school upgraded to elementary status with a British Headmistress, who arrived in 1949. The girls' school took its first pupils in May 1950 following Dr Beasley's recommendations in 1946 (*ARDE*, 1948-1951). It was the first Government girls' school to open, at the same time as the Malakal Girls' School.

occasional bits of clothing, mostly small, decorative effects and the aprons bordered with beads, which married women were supposed to put on, were on the whole decidedly ornamental. For the most part, however, the girls were as completely naked as the men. In one village just off the road a meeting of some kind was in progress, a most picturesque scene with the long, brown bodies sitting in easy postures or leaning elegantly draped against trees or supporting themselves on their spears. It could have been a native court but the driver's Arabic was insufficient for him to explain especially as he did not seem really interested.

## 2.8 Rumbek[69]

He was anxious to reach Rumbek, where we could obtain more petrol and have a safe pause for the engine. We found ourselves in a pleasant settlement with the official houses in good gardens and a square as centre to the town, which could have been matched in scores of places all over the Sudan. A lorry stood outside some small stores with Greeks and Syrians sitting on shaky wooden verandahs. The obvious difference was in the groups of Dinka standing about resting on their spears and immediately interested in the arrival of an unexpected traveller. As with the Zande women it was tiresome, that I could do no more than smile amicably and make friendly noises. Close to, these apparently fierce warriors had a much milder aspect. They laughed with much amusement pointing to the blue scarf with which I had tied up my hair, for some of them, although quite unclothed otherwise, had bits of blue cloth round their heads. Admittedly my ornament was a Paisley silk from Liberty's, and theirs rather faded muslin or fish net, but the resemblance took their fancy and made a bond between us, which we all acknowledged. Later I was told, that a former D.C.[70] had adopted this mark for distinguishing prisoners and, although the practice had now been dropped, the Dinka still retained a taste for blue cloth round their heads. We were all quite merry about it except for one solemn little boy in shorts, who spoke a little English, but could not bring us

---

69. In 1948 the government opened the first higher secondary school for boys in the South at Rumbek under the headship of K.O. Williams. From 1947 the C.M.S. Loka Nugent School also adopted secondary school status. As H.D. Hooper wrote to Christopher Cook, 'we therefore did not look with favour upon a system which proposed to reserve secondary education as a government sphere' (C.M.S. Archives, University of Birmingham, AF 35/49/G3.e3 (subfile 3)).

70. Possibly Edward Humphrey Nightingale, C.M.G., 4N. (b.19.9.1904- ); Educated at Denstone and Peterhouse, Cambridge; 12.12.26 First appointment; 1927-33 Blue Nile; 1933-42 Darfur; 1.1.42-47 Equatoria, by 1946 D.C. Lakes District based at Rumbek; 1947-48 Darfur, Deputy Governor; 1948-51 Assistant Civil Secretary (Departmental); 1952-54 Equatoria, Governor; 1954 retired to Kenya.

much further on this issue. Then arrived the postmaster to informed me that the [post] office was shut and I could not therefore wire my safe advent to anyone until the next morning, and certainly not indulge in any frivolous correspondence, such as sending postcards from the heart of Equatoria, even if I had had any. There was, however, a telegram for me from the D.C.[71] in Amadi, whom I had known suggesting that I should meet him at Mvolo for lunch and then go on with him.

### 2.9 Rumbek to Mvolo

In addition to the pleasure of meeting him again I liked the prospect of a vehicle, which might have some protection against the rain, which was definitely close at hand, and in my little truck I should have been very wet in any kind of shower. We pushed on therefore with determination, myself watching the clouds which still held up. By now we had left most of the *toitch*es behind and forests were coming down again on both sides of the road with glimpses of mountains near and far away. Some miles after Wulu[72] we were chaffing up a slope, when I suddenly noticed a great bulk in the middle of the road. My mind immediately flew to the tales of elephants I had heard, particularly in the Singa district, where they were very playful. But their idea of fun was tossing *tukl*s about and pushing lorries in all directions. My luck was still firm as this was nothing more formidable than a huge, piled-up lorry, a new, shining, green lorry, which had broken down. There also sitting by the road was the D.C. Amadi in a wet raincoat, lamenting that he had been reading there for the last two and a half hours and fretting that he could not get to Mvolo, where there was a great deal of official business for him to transact. Sitting in the road were two or three policemen, the driver of the mail lorry and several hangers-on all giving one another a lot of advice. Bits of engine had been removed and were scattered over the road with the men pouring petrol on them and unscrewing pieces here and there and tightening others up again. It looked a lovely game and my driver would have been only too delighted to join in but plans were quickly changed. We decided to use my old rattle-trap for, however noisy and uncomfortable, it was at least going for the time being. A few essentials and the cook were packed in the back and once more we were three up in front. Like so many of the Sudan Political Service, a disproportionate number of whom seemed to have been rowing Blues, the

71. Dr Beasley had known and stayed with M.F.A. Keen several times in the Northern Province. 'The D.C. seemed to me remarkably efficient and rapid' in his official transactions at Amadi.
72. 'The next settlement was a fair-sized place called Wulu, where there was a resthouse.'

D.C. was a big man and his bulk, unlike the skirts of the Reverend Mother, was not compressible.

> He was considered a most successful administrator by many ... Here, however he was not happy ... apart from the language question he could find no points of contact. In the North, he said, there was always someone to talk to ... a *sheikh* or a merchant ... who knew what was going on in the world near and far away and had opinions of their own and criticism to offer ... He was not very sympathetic to the missionaries either ... The D.C. also felt there was a lot of hypocricy about this Christianisation but we could not decide how to give an ethical base to our teaching in schools as the pagan beliefs seemed too difficult and unsuitable to build on. It was also a difficult and unsuitable subject to discuss in a noisy car.
>
> The numbered camps by the roadside interested me ... I was told they were for P.W.D. workers who mended the road.

## 2.10 Mvolo

Considering the load, we made surprisingly good time to Mvolo, where the cook and my servant produced lunch at record speed. Then while the D.C. went to the courthouse I had the pleasure of wandering round one of the most attractive villages I had come across. The sun had broken through to reveal the possibility of a lovely April sky even in these tropical latitudes. A winding road led gently up to a flat space like a village green of considerable size with houses grouped round it. As a background it had the magnificent views which were becoming almost commonplace on this tour and close by once again lines of gold *mohur* trees in full bloom and everywhere masses of tawny pink lilies, which had earlier won my heart. On a small mound to the north of the green the courthouse was perched, a large, open building with a great thatched roof, which reminded me of a [Burmese] *joss* house. Across the green a charming little house in much the same style, faced it. Actually it was the telephone kiosk but was just large enough for one person to sleep in, as it was protected by mosquito wire. Alongside was a large platform, the beginning of a resthouse, which had been planned in the same rather flamboyant style but the money allotted would not run to this and Mvolo could only boast the same utilitarian pattern as Mabu.

The people were friendly in a retiring way, but apart from a few, who could speak English, I could do little but smile greetings. I had learned the Zande expressions for 'good day' and 'good night' but these were pretty useless in these parts. Compared with the attractive, leaf-adorned Zande and the more glamorous Dinka in their slender elegance the Mvolo inhabitants were not so picturesque as their village. Most of them wore dull clothes and seemed on superficial evidence rather lumpish. As I strolled round this very pleasing quarter with neat square houses boasting verandahs complete with deck-chairs, I came upon a C.M.S. Dispensary, which was very clean and inviting. Then the schoolmaster sought me out, which was a cordial gesture, and we talked for some time about the twenty boys, who normally came to school. Inevitably I asked him about girls but here I drew an absolute blank. He simply shook his head and could not be persuaded to discuss the matter. From the way he looked at me, I suspected he thought me more than peculiar. It was a reaction I met so often, that it did not disappoint me but confirmed my belief, that the water dripping on stone technique was the only possible one for the time being.

### 2.11 Amadi

As there was still plenty of light, when all the official business was transacted, we decided to move on towards Amadi that night. Any hope that the D.C.'s lorry might have caught us up had been abandoned and I heard subsequently, that it was stuck on the road for another two days, until professional mechanics arrived with spare parts. It was a drizzly sort of evening but the way was full of interest, for there were far more animals crossing our path; plenty of squirrels, the occasional gazelle and a number of *dik-dik*; then red hussar monkeys scampered near and baboons ambled about, squatting, as I had seen them in Darfur, to watch us passing; after dusk four hartebeest moved quickly ahead; but dark came and the road was quiet.

> Soon after 6 o'clock we passed a small wooden building about four feet square, the last resthosue before Amadi ... [It was] possibly another one and a half hours to Amadi ... I was all for pushing on.

With terrific fuss we drove through large puddles left from the morning's rain but with daylight gone it was not wise to dodge them, and we were thus obliged to follow the ruts for fear of being stuck. Then there were the bridges of loose logs, that I had disliked so all the time, and on one of these over a deep gully the truck very nearly slipped off the edge and then embedded itself firmly on a wet slope on the opposite bank.

> The servants dismounted ... Remembering that this car had been overturned the previous summer and a servant thrown off and killed I was suddenly terrified and wished I had got off too.

No further trouble occurred and I was beginning to take a vicarious pride in my stalwart vehicle, when we pulled up in safety outside the D.C.'s front door.[73] My greatest relief was to be free of the continuing agony of sitting but I was really too exhausted to be able to rest well, although I lay in comfort on the softest of beds and listened to the rain pouring down. I had completed nearly 1,200 miles on that hard bench over those stony tracks but had only one more day to endure, even if it meant another 175 miles for my poor tail.

> I don't think I'm really an Empire builder ... I woke up in the morning [21st] with a splitting headache ... I went across to the house wondering how ill I looked ... The D.C. had just received a letter, which looked like cancellation of his leave ... I toyed with a lovely breakfast ... thereby eliciting a little genuine sympathy for the strain of my tour ... The worst was over by this time and the effort to cheer him up was probably the kindest thing he could have done for me.

The day began with some wonderful compensations. Starting uncertainly it cleared quickly to the soft April blue of the kind which had illuminated Mvolo. Even on a journey which had overwhelmed me by the grandeur of the scenery this was the most beautiful road of all. In the clear air the distant mountains stood out against a sparkling sky and the green of the trees, which softened their outlines, was fresh and clean in the general mass of colour. The great sweeps seemed gentle despite their strength, not repeating the cruel hostility that the Red Sea Hills suggested. Close to, were equal joys in the detail of the fine, soft grass and flowers everywhere, short and tall, yellow, pink, blue, white and purple.

### 2.12 Lui to Juba

My original intention in coming round by Amadi was not to rhapsodise over the views, but to call on the Mission[74] at Lui, which, as I passed, appeared a good-looking and well laid-out station. By ill chance, the British

---

73. 'The D.C.'s house was attractive—a great room with a sloping roof each end,' which they eventually reached at 8.45 p.m.
74. Gordon Memorial Sudan Mission with C.M.S. staff at Lui opened in 1937. By 1940 there was a small boarding school for Moru in a few grass huts. In 1946/47 the site was chosen for a C.M.S. primary teacher-training college at Mundiri near the Mundiri Bridge in Moru country on the Amadi-Meridi Road, a few miles from Lui and Amadi. In 1948 it had less than 20 students. Such an institution was tentatively suggested in 1939 by Bishop A.M. Gelsthorpe (C.M.S., Juba) as a joint Government-Mission project. In 1947 Roseveare, Janson-Smith, C.W. Williams and D.H. Hibbert were heavily involved in its implementation (Sanderson, L.M.P. and G.N., *op. cit.*, p.268). Major Eric Standish Jackson was recruited as Headmaster in 1947. He had previously been headmaster, St Thomas's C.E. School, Birmingham,

missionary[75] in charge was on extended sick leave and the girls' school had had to be closed.[76] The difficulties of obtaining staff meant, that there was never a reserve in such an emergency.

> This lack of continuity in the C.M.S. schools is distressing. It has [also] happened in Yambio.

To keep missionaries in a district long enough to learn the language and understand the local people was a task well-nigh impossible. Sorry though I was about the fate of the school, honesty forced me to confess, that I should have found a day's inspecting and general cordiality rather a strain.

> All through the trip I had been rather overwhelmed by the magnificence of the scenery but I think this was probably the most beautiful road of all ... flowers innumerable ... The villages here were still mostly grass houses ... the beaten earth round about them ... while a group of men sitting in deck-chairs dressed in shirt and shorts and smoking pipes gives quite a note of sophistication.

Here [at Lui] we caught up the mail lorry and then journeyed ahead of it. This was a comforting thought, for the roads were still slippery after last night's rain and there were signs at one point, that something had been stuck in the mud. It seemed also too good to be true, that our luck with my little lorry could hold indefinitely especially considering the extra load it had had to carry the day before through damp weather and rutted tracks. At one village we stopped for the driver to buy some mangoes and someone asked me to take a letter to Juba, which I readily agreed to do. Immediately this inspired another man to ask if he could travel with us, and he showed me his chits which suggested he was someone's cook. Still a little nervous about overturning the lorry, I said, yes, if he were quick and had not too much luggage. Within the prescribed five minutes he was back, but, as his luggage consisted of two wives, a sack of food under which he could hardly stagger and pots and pans and an enormous roll of bedding I retracted my permission. I felt rather mean about it but the mail lorry was not far behind. I asked my driver, why the man did not want to travel on it and he replied,

75. The school was established by Eileen Frazer for Moru girls and women in 1924. Her husband was K.G. Frazer, C.M.S. medical missionary (1877-1935), who founded and ran a school and hospital in Lui from 1921 until his death. They established dispensaries in the surrounding villages. He was also the first missionary in the South to possess a motor car. At least from 1939 to 1946 the headmistress was Miss Margaret Collard and the school had 85 girls in 1939 but only 70 girls by 1946. Miss Collard was on extended sick leave when Dr Beasley visited her as she had broken her arm.
76. In 1947 new buildings were erected at Lunjini, a mile from Lui. In 1947 the third and fourth year classes from Yambio were transferred to Lunjini. There was very stunted growth of C.M.S. village schools between 1944 and 1948, in sharp contrast to the V.F.M. schools (Sanderson, L.M.P. and G.N., *op. cit.*, p.288 (77)).

that it would take money, expressing his answer mostly by a gesture of the fingers, which suggested filching little by little.

As this was Easter Sunday it was obviously being observed as a real holiday. There were services in the schools and companies of boys and youths paraded everywhere with a grand display of clean shorts and shirts for the festival. Even if one could not call it colourful rejoicing there was certainly an atmosphere of relaxation. I meditated on the charge often brought against the missions, that they take all the fun out of people's lives in endeavouring to eradicate the evil. I had not enough knowledge to come to any conclusions; I could only let my mind float idly round the thought, as I sat under a shady tree on a sun-warmed boulder and ate a picnic lunch gazing out over the usual concomitants of this tour—majestic mountains and flowers around my feet.

> As a chair and table were produced, I did not even have to worry about ants ... I ate half a tin of warm sardines with some bread and butter and some lukewarm tea. Not a very appetising meal but the surroundings made up for it.

## 2.13 Juba

As we descended, the sticky heat enveloped us but the road surface improved, until we actually came to Juba, where it was so corrugated, that we rattled into town with a clanging, like a detachment of tanks. The hotel at Juba was the most unattractive of the four run by Sudan Railways, but it did provide a soft bed on which I could lie face downwards. I could enjoy the compensation of being a little magnanimous, when the [Assistant] Director of Education called [as] he had been rather perturbed, because the office had lost track of me for some days, and his conscience had been troubled, since he had not lent me his new lorry—as indeed he ought.[77] Everything was all right, I told him airily, except, that I should prefer to stand up while we discuss any practical plans for the future.

---

77. Dr Beasley drove up to D.H. Hibbert's's house on her arrival in Juba. 'As it was then about 3.15 the household was asleep. I left a message to announce my safe arrival and went to the hotel.' Janson-Smith and D.H. Hibbert called in the evening 'expressing great relief at my arrival, the latter in particular having been most worried as it had taken him two days to get any news from Wau ... However I have always felt very kindly to D. and now I was safely back bore him no ill-will. It might have been different, if we'd had a breakdown.'

**Problems facing Education in the South**

> [I had a] long talk with J.S. and D. next morning, although it was Easter
> Monday.

[D.H. Hibbert's] particular responsibility was for the South, but he had
always, when in the North, been a profound believer in the need for
spreading girls' education and had given much practical help. Therefore we
wanted to decide on some immediate action and agreed, that Government
schools at strategic places appeared to be the only answer and that we
would press for funds to start a school as a centre as soon as possible.[78] We
knew that there would be an outcry from the Missions about a breach of
faith but the matter was too urgent to wait longer for the action they were
unable to take.

> J.S. thinks that the missions are very badly done by but I don't think the
> Government can just hand out money without some guarantee of usefulness
> ... Even if they are obliged to teach in order to evangelise, it probably is not a
> bad thing to have something as concrete as ordinary education to work on ...
> also I still maintain that they do not make the most of what resources they
> have, time being one I noticed particularly as being wasted.

Meanwhile we would try at once for a woman inspector, whom in fact we
were able to appoint[79] not long after and who proved most valuable.

> J.S. very badly wanted a woman ... a flamboyant personality ... such as
> Uganda had acquired to bully the Central Government into giving the South
> lots of money ...

Also a small point but not irrelevant, we obtained for her especial use a
comfortable and well-maintained lorry to lessen the physical strain of much
trekking and thus to conserve her energy for the essentials of her task.

The saddest part of the story is that in the next two or three years it
became increasingly difficult to recruit staff of any sort. The partition of
India[80] in a blood bath of hatred and the unforeseen landslide to
Independence in Africa were probably powerful deterrents to people
seriously wanting to undertake work overseas. It might be argued, that it

---

78. The first centre was to be in Tonj. See Appendix V for further details on the aims of this
experiment.
79. Miss E.M. Golding appointed 29.1.48 to Juba as Superintendent of Girls' Education. She
had the special responsibility of helping to co-ordinate the standards of work in the South. 'A
nice girl and I think will work hard but she is young and has a soft blue eye' [November 1947].
This appointment was first proposed by C.W. Williams in 1944. She later married Dr A.R.
Hunt, Sudan Medical Service, who had previously been part of the Ethiopian military mission.
By 1953 she was Superintendent of Girls' Education; 1953 retired.
80. Partition of India took place in 1947.

had all been left too late. More vigorous action in the thirties might have encouraged a quicker rate of development[81] but the obstacles of finance, language and distances would still have been formidable, even if men's thoughts had not been mesmerised by Hitler and Mussolini. The recent tragic events in the South since the Sudan's assumption of Independence evoke much heart-searching. Were we right in thinking it was kinder not to hurry these people? As I said at the beginning, forces outside our control did take over. Had we made other decisions there might have been other forces equally unpredictable for good or ill. Viewed from afar the situation takes on the poignant inevitability of Hardy's vision of affairs. At this point, however, we were counting on at least twenty years of control and, having decided on our immediate plans as urgent, I had to hurry back to the world I knew better.

## 3. Return to Khartoum

> J.S. took me round the town that afternoon to see the dairy and the view downstream and the rapids. We talked shop most of the time for he is an enthusiast ... with just that look of an old world actor, which seems such a contradiction. More bridge [in the evening].

Odd transport was to be my destiny to the end. The regular service from Nairobi was full[82] and I was allowed to travel on an R.A.F. plane, an unconverted paratroop carrier. Fortunately there were not many men on it, and all the seating was broad canvas benches with not much back. I had the dubious satisfaction of being faced by a door covered with detailed instructions [for paratroops] about how to jump. We flew high, although not avoiding the bumps from the heat, and, as the machine was not pressurised, most of us were glad there was room to curl up and lie down. It was a great relief some five hours later to see Jebel Auliya, where even from a height the big dam looks very imposing. Still more of a relief was the familiar feel of ground level and the furnace blast from the airfield, when the door was opened [at Khartoum airport].

---

81. The *Report of the De La Warr Commission* (1937) recommended greater development within the existing missionary-government framework. *Education in the Northern Sudan: the Winter Committee Report* (1933) paid little attention to the South. The Director of Education, Christopher Cox, made several proposals for Southern education, including the '1938 agreements'.
82. 'Lord Trenchard's suite filled it up, I was told.'

### 3.1 Back in Omdurman

Familiarity was the keynote of the next few days not only from the pleasure of the ordinary routine of my own home but in being back in surroundings I understood with work, that was beginning to take shape. In the North we were gathering a few strands, that might be woven together, but the South was more like a vast jigsaw in which, if one hoped to find some bits that might interlock, there was always the fear, that the table might be overturned and the pieces swept into a muddle again. I was a bit stunned too by taking so many new experiences in quite such an undiluted form.

> I finished mentally in much the mood in which I started, rather appalled by the immensity of the problem and wondering how much damage one might do with the best of intentions. Viewed as a whole the missionary efforts must make a little ripple somewhere but is it of Value?

## 4. Later inspections in the South: East Bank[83]

Although not really adventurous in the sense that there were no desperate happenings, this first trip in the South always stands out in rather that light compared with later inspections. In the first place once the war was firmly behind us, for a time we managed to recruit more staff, including the British woman for inspection there, and the Missions also were able to increase their efforts. Thus even though the gains looked pitiably small[84] when listed, there was a whisper of hope.

### 4.1 Palataka

On a tour of the East Bank I talked to classes of young men in training as teachers and the idea of girls in school was not brushed aside as definitely peculiar but was seriously discussed with the very sensible realisation that it would be likely to disturb the domestic set-up as they knew it.

---

83. 1.4.49-13.4.49. Dr Beasley began a tour of the east bank of Equatoria, starting from Juba (1.4.49), then on to Liria, Okaru to visit the American Brothers (2.4.49) and then to Torit (3-4.4.49) to see [John] Owen's family. (The V.F.M. girls' school at Torit opened in permanent buildings in 1929. and had 28 girls in 1946, under Rev. Fr. Pazzaglia). After Loa, Dr Beasley visited Rejaf (V.F.M. girls' school opened in permanent buildings in 1945 with 45 girls by 1946, under Rev. Fr. Rosciano) on 7.4.49 and then returned to Juba before leaving for Yei.

84. In 1949 the number of trained Southern schoolmistresses was less than 20, and some of these were only trained to teach in village-school level in Mission elementary schools (see Sanderson, L.M.P. and G.N., *op. cit.*, p.304; 'Draft statement on Southern girls' education', *ARDE*, 1949).

Palataka[85] was one place, where the students were interested and wanted to know how an educated girl could look after a home and be in school at the same time. Some of the questions faced practical details. 'Would she cook for me? Would she bring a man's dinner to him in the fields? Could I beat her, if she did not obey me?'

There was also in Palataka a delightful [Catholic] mission[86] school in charge of a nun, who could not express to me, she said, how happy she had been when the Father had taken her from the boys' school two years before and put her in charge of girls. The result was a most successful centre with boarders and day pupils and mothers in the villages round all sure that here they would find a welcome. What impressed me also about this Sister was her extensive knowledge of the people of the district and an understanding of their habits and customs, that many an anthropologist might have envied.

## 4.2 Imatong Mountains

On the whole the tribes on the eastern side of the river lacked the picturesqueness of the Dinka and the Zande on the west [bank]. The Latuka were equally unclothed but they were also undernourished and had none of the photogenic quality of the long, lithe [Dinka] herdsmen leaning on their spears in the *toitch*es. As if in compensation, the scenery was even grander [on the east bank]. The Imatong Mountains towered up in magnificence with forests and streams in abundance. There was not time for exploration but on one or two evenings [3.4.49] I managed to snatch a quick walk amongst wide stretches of tall trees, where colobus monkeys could be glimpsed in the branches.

## 4.3 Loa

Everything was done in a hurry on this tour [of the East Bank], and, while remembering the overwhelming beauty of the background, professional impressions have lasted longest. There was, for example, a school, which delighted my heart, at Loa[87] near the border with Uganda, where the

85. 4-5.4.1949.
86. Palataka Verona Fathers' Mission School among the Acholi opened in permanent buildings in 1940. In 1946 there were 64 girls, under the headship of Rev. Fr. Del-Zotto. In Cox, C, *The Education of the Community in African Society*, Colonial Office Advisory Committee, 1935, and in the '1938 Agreements' (V.F.M.), the Verona Fathers were asked to post educationalist Sisters to Kwajok, Mupoi and Palataka.
87. Dr Beasley visited Loa on 6.4.49. This was a school run by V.F.M. which opened in permanent buildings in 1930. By 1946 there were 83 girls, under Rev. Fr. Bay.

experiment[88] of mixing the tribes had proved a great success despite all the jeremiads of the reactionaries. Supervised down to the smallest detail by the Mother Superior, a small, tireless woman who was constantly pushing her spectacles back on her nose, the training department was full of promise. Half in mockery, people said of her that her school was dearer to her than her salvation, which I only hoped would be accounted to her for righteousness [in Heaven].

True it was just an oasis in a vast emptiness but what encouraged us was the feeling that outright rejection [of girls' education] was no longer the order of the day.

## 4.4 Yei

At Yei[89] also not only were there teachers in training[90] but a short conference was held during my stay specifically to discuss girls' education.[91] Still prejudiced by my greater familiarity with the North I found the local chiefs unimpressive compared with the village councils of Northern *sheikh*s. No doubt they were admirable and worthy men but they did not look at ease in the orthodox shirts and shorts; yet I am not quite sure what I expected. Nevertheless they were asking for girls' schools and one schoolmaster even that there should be a full range of classes to the top.

That such a meeting should be serious and definitely heavy was not out of place but I was worried still more here than usual about the solemnity that surrounded both practice and theory. It was only natural that the girls in training would not talk freely to me, a stranger, but they did seem to be tackling their new responsibilities with undue gravity.

## 4.5 Music and dancing near the Belgian Congo border

This matter of taking all the fun out of life was brought home to me soon after, when I stayed the night in a village[92] near what was then the Belgian Congo frontier. It was a small place with a number of *tukl*s grouped round a little church with a cross and a bell. The resthouse, a primitive mud

---

88. As early as 1949 the Verona Fathers re-organised their girls' teacher-training in formal vernacular teacher-training centres at Mboro (Bahr el Ghazal), Mupoi (Zandeland) and Loa (Eastern Equatoria); see Sanderson, L.M.P. and G.N., *op. cit.*, pp.304-305.
89. Yei, in the heart of C.M.S. country; see Sanderson, L.M.P. and G.N., *op. cit.*, p.387.
90. Formal teacher-training C.M.S. centre at Yei serving the Bari and Kakwa tribes. The girls' training was shared with the boys; see Sanderson, L.M.P. and G.N., *op. cit.*, pp.304-305.
91. A most successful conference on girls' education was also held in June 1948 in Juba and was attended by representatives of C.M.S., V.F.M. and the Education Department.
92. 9-10.4.49 Dr Beasley stayed at Lugulu, which is probably this village.

construction like most, was perched on a bluff overlooking a deep valley with ranges of mountains stretching indefinitely far into the west. During the afternoon people began to appear over the rim of the valley and trudged along the roads singly or in groups. The drums started to beat insistently and appealingly and throughout the hottest hours men and women danced in a milling crowd in the open space under trees. Arrayed in all manner of garb and mostly sporting little feathers in their hair they shuffled untiringly and jogged with a variety of steps and movements, which the uninitiate cannot appreciate. Violent leaps and more dramatic movements of the body intervened from time to time according to individual fancy. A girl with the lithe grace of a born ballerina, decked only in her two bunches of leaves, slid from my side to mingle with the rest and face a tall man in most respectable slacks and cricket shirt. Throughout the long, warm afternoon the rhythm of the drums urged them on and the dancing never flagged but by the time the moon was high it was all over and they had gone away. The reason for the dance I could not discover, perhaps just a local variant of the worship of the great god Pan, but I have no doubt that it was vastly enjoyed. Authority in some parts has been known to frown on dances, liable to excite warlike passions, and missionaries often objected to them as a sexual stimulant after which couples retire into the bush in conditions of much promiscuity.

Dancing has so much significance in the life of African tribes, that it always seemed a pity there was so little time over from the utilitarian business of law and order and literacy to try and incorporate it into ideas of general development. Northerners too would drum in idle moments on an odd tin or any resonant article that came handy, as Europeans whistle in casual mood. In Fasher the great ceremonial drum about the size of a dining table was a show piece. The Northern dances, however, I personally did not find particularly inspiring but Southern rhythms were more varied and could fall into a definite aesthetic pattern. A dance I once saw by the Shilluk in the moonlight had this feeling of a definite pattern, which added much to the exciting quality of the performance, with these tall men in ceremonial belts and leggings with bells jingling energetically following the rules they understood.

> At [Khor] Atar I had seen them [Shilluk] dance by moonlight wearing their ceremonial belts and leggings with bells on. I felt they had come a long way ... The dance ... was quite the best I have seen. It was exciting enough to make me feel I could have joined in [November 1947].

Among the Zande too music can belong to the everyday life. There is a small instrument they make out of odd pieces of wood and metal, given the misnomer of a 'Zande harp'.[93] The relative lengths of the metal strips can be arranged for the instrument to be tuned to play a melody, as the strips are twanged. It was no uncommon sight to come across a lad strolling through the forest and making gentle music as he went. One Father at a mission station tried to collect some of the tunes to form an opera, while a Government Inspector also was anxious to encourage such an interest. He feared the art might be lost as something of no account compared with the prestige of European accomplishments.

All such admirable projects languished through scarcity of staff and the pressure of need for sheer literacy. This was probably much of the reason, that I never felt the same zest about tours in the South as elsewhere. The problems oppressed me with few flickers of relief and I did not have the same sense of identification as in the North. Darfur and the Nuba Mountains were equally remote from many aspects and yet I always enjoyed a visit there.


# 5. Upper Nile Province


## 5.1 Malakal[94]

Further downstream in the Upper Nile Province enthusiasm was possible on the boys' side but only in Malakal town itself did there appear to be much opportunity for girls. It was here that the Muslim North had really penetrated and all the familiar elements jostled with the conservative habits of the cattle-owning tribes. Dignified, robed merchants, who might have been at home in Omdurman, walked the streets alongside Nilotic tribesmen dressed in a cloth knotted on the shoulder or not dressed at all, and overtopping in height men, who were themselves tall by ordinary standards.

> The *suq* is not very impressive but what made it different was the array of odd Nilotes strolling about. The Shilluks have a ring of small circular scars just above the eyebrows, Dinka and Nuer have five to six straight lines graven in the forehead. I am told this is done with a six inch nail. The person operated on, while in his youth of course, must not cry out and if he moves the lines do not run straight.

An interesting meeting place it might be but it was all the same an unlovely place.

---

93. The Zande Harp is known generally throughout East Africa as the *sansa*.
94. Dr Beasley visited Malakal on her way by air to Juba in April 1946 and made an inspection there in November 1947.

The view from the air[95] ... a sort of kraal with broad, straight streets and good-looking cantonments with rather lush gardens.

One could sit by the river looking west in the evening and all impression was not of the glory of the sunset but of an all-pervading, damp monotony. Round about the country stretched unendingly flat and steamy and featureless. The one landmark which raised its head from the plain was the minaret[96] of an enormous mosque. Tales about this were flippant. The Egyptian Irrigation Department maintained a station here and sceptics said, that King Farouk looked at a map and ordered a mosque to be presented there, with his finger on the first settlement he saw. Possibly out of mischief, when it was offered to the Sudanese, they replied that it was not nearly large enough. This expensive stone building, well-proportioned, generously planned was the result. From the way it dominated the landscape it was reminiscent of those tall church steeples which are a feature of the East Anglian flatness.

It was from the demands of these Arab merchants that I was summoned to Malakal.[97] A most enterprising Headmaster had accepted a number of girls into the primary school[98] but was being assailed by the pressures of parents on two sides. Giving places to girls kept out a corresponding number of boys and he was therefore unpopular whomever he refused.[99] Plans being well ahead for the building,[100] we were fortunate also with regard to staff.[101]

I did not think that any mistresses would go and I was not sure what was the local reaction to Mohammedan strongholds in the South. Then the D.C.[102]

---

95. On 8.4.46 Dr Beasley saw the town from the air.

96. The mosque was under construction in November 1947 when Dr Beasley visited the town.

97. Dr Beasley went to Malakal to investigate demands for a girls' school in November 1947 by de-Havilland Dove, newly acquired by Sudan Airways in 1947. (See Bush, Simon, 'Sudan Airways: An Historical Outline' in *Sudan Studies*, no.7, January 1990).

'I left my bed in Omdurman at 4.30 a.m. and was in the Governor's house at Malakal by 8.30 a.m ... The British houses are built in a sort of cantonment but a number of them are right on the river front ... ' Dr Beasley felt that she gave 'an inspired address to the *effendis*' club in Malakal on spiritual values ... . It is a very sociable community in Malakal and I think I met them all at a drinks party in the evening, about 20.'

98. The Upper Nile government vernacular training centre was attached to this Northern style *kuttab* at Malakal.

99. On the Sunday Dr Beasley inspected the boys' school ... 'not too bad ... I am not sure how kindly the Sudanese take to being inspected by a woman'.

100. The building of a new girls' school in Malakal which was opened in 1948.

101. Trained Northern Sudanese schoolmistresses, unlike male teachers, could not be compulsorily posted to the South; Sanderson, L.M.P. and G.N., *op. cit.*, p.304.

102. J.C.N. Donald moved to Malakal in January 1947 and had previously met Dr Beasley in Talodi.

wrote rather sharply pointing out that Malakal was not as remote as Talodi.

One of the merchants had a daughter already in the service and to everyone's delight she and a friend volunteered to come. Another interesting feature of the enrolment was the keen determination of the pupils' fathers.

> The next morning[103] the headmaster and I had a list of the girls to be accepted for the school in January ... There were no mothers and the proceedings were comparatively orderly ... Crude demonstration of looking to see if the unfortunate brat has cut her second teeth. It was encouraging to have so many fathers turn up. While we were writing the names down, other children previously rejected managed to tack on to the end of the line and had to be rejected again.

Whereas in Berber some eight years before at my initiation into this harassing process of selection it had been the mothers who insisted on places for their children, here the girls were brought by equally resolute fathers.

> The morning[104] was spent in passing plans, seeing temporary buildings and a meeting with the Education Committee.

One old *sheikh* from the hinterland was vociferous in his demand for reservations for girls from the outlying villages, who would board with relatives in the town. Ten places he kept repeating was not nearly enough. Our hope was that a well-established and flourishing institution might have some influence among those of the tribesmen who had contacts with the town.[105]

To see this [*kuttāb*] bursting at the seams made by contrast its Egyptian counterpart sited in a sort of garden suburb a very dispirited affair.[106] Like all the houses round for the Irrigation staff good buildings had been set in a patch of green, but the place was half empty. Sudanese pupils would have been welcome as part of the Egyptian myth about the brotherhood of the Nile but their parents would not send them. Work was proceeding in a rather desultory fashion and the Headmaster spent most of my visit

103. The day after Dr Beasley arrived in Malakal in November 1947.
104. The day Dr Beasley arrived in Malakal in November 1947.
105. The school attracted mostly Arab merchants' children. The Malakal girls' school took 20 girls who had been attending the boys' schoool and was overwhelmed with demands for application for the First Year. A third mistress was sent down after the holidays. In 1949 they hoped to open Class IV there. (*ARDE*, 1948, 1949).
106. J.C.N. Donald took Dr Beasley to the Egyptian Irrigation Department School on her November 1947 visit. The Egyptian Irrigation Department school had about six children, in contrast to the fifty in the Government school. The headmaster was supposed to put out Egyptian propaganda by the Egyptian Government.

complaining of the iniquity of sending him to serve in this cultural slum. He did not seem a very good choice for furthering the aims of his political superiors.

## 5.2 Doleib Hill

Equally depressing but for other reasons was a visit to a mission[107] station at Doleib Hill. Here there was no thought of grumbling at the work or the place to which these two Englishwomen[108] had been assigned. I feel churlish in criticising the efforts of people so selfless and dedicated but I was concerned with educational standards and not the appreciation of personal devotion over twenty years. Much can be said in favour of the theory,[109] that it is wiser to introduce girls to schooling in their villages and not to divorce them from their background by taking them to board in the Mission compound.

> [Yet] the teaching in these village-schools is comparatively worthless. We went to two village schools ... then the boys were sent away and some girls dropped in ... The younger ones each had a baby to look after. There were two or three older girls who were able to cope with simple addition sums on bits of slate ... The next school was a rather larger building ... There is reading, writing and arithmetic about the place. The equipment is pathetic. There are two or three books in the vernacular in each school, one or two broken slates and bits of chalk. 2 blackboards.

In practice the village schools which I saw were so ineffectual, that they could only do harm to the idea of education in general. Moreover any intelligent villager who had been to Malakal could not fail to be struck by the contrast in enthusiasm between these and the Government School. One or two girls came into the classes in these village schools in a casual sort of way but I was told, that most were absent helping to build the boys' training college a few miles away. Schoolwork as so often seldom came first and girls always a long way second.

I was obviously disapproved of, since I was setting up a Muslim school in what was regarded as mission territory, and its progress would attract the

107. American (United Presbyterian Mission) began in 27.3.1902. The girls' school for Shilluk began in 1933. The same mission also established a girls' school at Nasr, Upper Nile Province, in 1932. It had 20 girls under Mrs P.J. Smith in 1938 and only 18 in 1946.
108. One of the two Englishwomen assigned to the Doleib Hill girls' school was Miss E.E. Grove 'so selfless and earnest' who was headmistress at Doleib Hill. 20 years previously she had worked in Khartoum North. By 1938 there were 45 girls at Doleib Hill. In 1946 it had 12 out-schools with 287 pupils and 7 teachers. Dr and Mrs Giffen, Dr and Mrs McLaughlin and Rev. and Mrs Laurie Anderson worked there at various times.
109. Miss Grove's theory.

tribesmen into the influence of Islam, where worldly success was more evident. I understood their fears and was sympathetic to their anxieties but I could not feel that girls, already Muslim, should thereby be deprived of schooling. Disagreement was still further increased, when over breakfast came a long condemnation of the unchastity of local girls. Admittance to school ought to be regarded as a prize for virtue, I gathered, but none of the girls in the neighbouring villages, I was assured [by Miss Grove], was a virgin. My tentative suggestion that that might be an extra reason for more energetic attempts to run schools was not well received.

> We have a race against time, which one would have expected the missionaries to have appreciated ... one would expect missionaries to be concerned about the souls unsaved and to hustle more than they do.

### 5.3 Khor Atar Intermediate School[110]

Happily one of my visits to Malakal included a trip to a vigorous and spirited Government institution run by professional educationalists, in other words trained teachers devoted first and foremost to education. My only discontent was that we had nothing comparable for girls but its very success gave impetus to the hope, that an experiment on similar lines might be tried at some point in the future. The Education Department had decided to attempt, once more against the advice of the pessimists, a men's training college in which a number of different tribes would be mixed together.

> From the bank Atar was not particularly prepossessing ... dormitories were dull red buildings of the two rooms-cum-*sala* type and bad workmanship all too evident ... It had rather a raw air but signs of hope.

The Englishman[111] and his wife, who were in charge, worked together with a unanimity of purpose, that had far-reaching effects on the whole scheme from the classroom through to all the details of the commissariat and called for an adaptability to large and small emergencies, which could never be

---

110. Khor Atar Intermediate School was officially opened 24.5.46 but started to function from 1944. In 1947 the first intake completed the four-year class. In 1948, 173 boys were in Khor Atar Intermediate School proper, with an additional 205 in the elementary section. In 1948 it began a secondary school class with 26 boys, the first in Southern Sudan, with an additional 17 boys sent to Uganda for secondary education from the South (see *ARDE*, 1948). In the South intermediate education for boys increased from 262 in 1944 to 467 (1946) and 506 (1948), due to the opening of Khor Atar (see Sanderson, L.M.P. and G.N., *op. cit.*, p.263).
111. K.O. Williams, appointed 26.6.41 as headmaster of Khor Atar Intermediate School, previously also Inspector until 1946 of Malakal District. His wife, Mrs P.M. Williams, appointed as mistress 1.3.45. He was later (c.1949-51) Headmaster at Rumbek Secondary School. J.E. Woodall (1.8.46 First appointment) succeeded K.O. Williams as Headmaster until c.1955.

foreseen or charted. It was all part of the day's routine for the wife to take off the large apron she had been wearing to help the servant cut up the meat, her husband having just shot the animal, and then go off to be in time to give a careful lesson in English. During a meal one or other might well be summoned to deal with a small boy bitten by a snake.

> The Williams are a successful married couple in the fullness of the term ... Professional educationalists ... principles and practice and the need for a plan for girls ... I managed to get one sketched out before I left ... When I got back I wrote a very vigorous note urging the Department [of Education] to go ahead with a school at Yambio at once and get some teachers trained.

An American missionary had been appointed as a full-time member of staff and for religious care chaplains visited at times from a range of denominations of Catholic and Protestant faiths.[112]

> There was the Intermediate section, teachers in training, under a missionary, who would go back to the mission schools, and the #Blue boys' for the teachers to practice on. There were Shilluks, Nuer, Dinka, Anuak (and others). I talked to the teachers' class about girls' education and found them interested and not at all hostile to the idea.

This experiment at Atar has been fully described elsewhere[113] but the school stands out for me as remarkable on many counts and especially so that amid that flat ugliness a venture had been established, that generated so much inspiration.


## 5.4 Malakal to Khor Atar

The flatness [of the countryside around Malakal] was emphasised the morning I set off on a small steamer, which had been tied up at the bottom of the Governor's garden.[114] It was pleasant to see tall grass on either bank with a few trees in the rear but otherwise nothing, since the ground by the river was too swampy for any kind of cultivation. In fact there had been some doubts as to whether the builders could find enough hard ground for

---

112. Probably Mr Webb (or C.J. Hunter, appointed as master 29.4.46). The idea of the Missions providing purely religious instruction within a system of state schools was discussed by C.W. Williams in his *Educational Proposals*, Sudan Government, Department of Education, November 1944, pp.5-6. It was actually adopted as a method in Khor Atar and Abwong as taught by the Rev. Laurie Anderson. While Dr Beasley was there 'the Prefect Apostolic visited with a group of Catholic priests'. The Prefect Apostolic was probably Monsignor Mlakic, Prefect Apostolic of Bahr el Jebel from c.1944.
113. Williams, K.O., 'The First Year' in *Oversea Education*, XVII, no. 3, April 1946, pp.306-15.
114. Dr Beasley went to Khor Atar from Malakal in November 1947 with the Governor, F.D. Kingdon, in his launch.

the school. The general aspect had none of the fascination of the Fung and although I was assured there were plenty, the crocodiles and hippopotamuses did not show themselves and there were far fewer birds. We had been steaming for about two hours and covered some ten miles when the *rais* sent a message to say, that a man had been running after us all the way from Malakal and was now very tired. Apparently he had cadged a lift [to Atar] and put his belongings on board. The launch was stopped and the man splashed through the reeds to climb aboard, looking remarkably fresh. Also on board was a D.C.[115] making a survey for the Jonglei Canal Scheme, which meant he had to make short treks into unmapped country among the swamps, where the great islands of the Sudd were constantly shifting. As a project it was of enormous significance but was being quietly and thoroughly studied without the fanfare, which so often jeopardises suggestions of this kind. If a canal could have been cut through the masses of wandering vegetation, it would have concentrated the water into one channel instead of allowing it to split into a number, from which an incredible amount of water was lost by evaporation. Properly regulated this would have had far-reaching effects downstream as far as Egypt and might have made unnecessary the building of the High Dam at Aswan and the flooding of Nubia. On the other hand it would most likely have drained the *toitch*es and upset the traditional ways of living of the Dinka. Unlike some European economists, who are prepared to state dogmatically, that under-developed countries must be industrialised in the shortest possible time, the administrators in charge were concerned with a lot of hard thinking about this question of changing the lives of pastoral peoples. Over breakfast in this little cabin I heard different aspects being carefully discussed but in the years to come politics for other reasons and certainly with no thought of the Dinka, Shilluk or Nuer altered the whole complexion of the problem and the Jonglei Canal Scheme has been lost in the glamour of the Aswan High Dam. No-one can pass judgement.

---

115. John Winder, 4N. (b.22.8.1905-d.1989). Educated at Oundle and King's College, Cambridge; 14.12.27 First appointment; 1927 Halfa; 1928 Red Sea; 1929-30 Port Sudan-Suakin Administration; 1930-33 Mongalla, D.C. Yei; 1933-36 Khartoum; 1936-42 Upper Nile; 1942-46 Northern, D.C. Shendi; 15.3.46-51 Upper Nile, 1946-48 D.C. Malakal, seconded to the Jonglei Scheme in 1946-47, 1948-51 Deputy Governor; 1951-53 Assistant Civil Secretary (Departmental); 1953-55 Upper Nile, Deputy Governor, then Governor; 1955 retired; 1956-60 Manager, Argyll Forestry Ltd; 1960-64 Land Agency, East Grinstead; 1967-71 Manager, Exporter and Importer, Crowborough.

## 5.5 Education in Upper Nile Province

My experience of the Upper Nile Province stretched no further and professionally Malakal was in essence an extension of our Northern organisation. But it was sad to know that girls in the districts round were not catered for in any way and therefore to look back on these visits with the same feeling of desolation, as I brought back from Equatoria. The pace had to be slow but practically nothing had really begun. Yet in those days it was that aspect which troubled us and not a complete despair, that nothing could ever be undertaken. The success of Atar had given the lie to that kind of gloom. That all should have turned out so differently is not the matter of this book, which is a chronicle of things past. There is no scope for any

# Chapter VIII

# History and Survey of Girls' Education in the Sudan

In the preceding chapters I have spoken often of encouraging girls' schools[1] and also of places, where the original enthusiasm faded to such an extent that a school had to be closed. By 1939[2] in the northern and Muslim part of the country the idea of education for girls had ceased to be a novelty but it was by no means universally accepted. There were in fact only 43 elementary schools over the whole country among a population roughly estimated at about 7 million. To those for whom compulsory education is an unquestioned part of everyday life it is not easy to appreciate all the implications of developing such a concept, especially as in recent years there has been so much clamour from emergent countries for more education for everybody.[3]

## 1. History of girls' education in the Sudan

The history of women's education in the Sudan therefore presents many facets of change where a society comes into contact with an alien culture. More straightforwardly it offers one of those tantalising speculations which depend on one particular and apparently remote happening. In this case the

---

1. Beasley, Ina, 'Girls' Education in the Anglo-Egyptian Sudan' *National Froebel Foundation Bulletin*, April, 1951. (Also *Colonial Review*, 1951, p.52).
2. Dr Beasley first arrived in Sudan in November 1939.
3. In the *Report of the De La Warr Commission* (1937) ' ... there appeared to be little doubt that the inadequacy of women's education was one of the main causes of backwardness in the Sudan and went on to recommend that this branch of education should be greatly expanded.' [This was] 'subsequently endorsed by Christopher Cox, in the paragraph upon Girls' Intermediate Schools in his 1938 Educational Submissions to Council he called attention to the fact that there were no Sudanese women sufficiently educated to be consulted on matters of social policy which intimately affected themselves and their homes, in marked contrast to Egypt and Uganda' (*The Future Development of Girls' Education in the Sudan*, 25.7.43, DE 9.1.1/3).

event which modified the possibilities was the slump in Egypt in 1907.[4]

## 1.1 Early beginnings

Prior to the reconquest of the country in 1898 there had been very little education of any sort, certainly none for girls,[5] but schools for boys were planned immediately with appropriate, if limited, objectives. In his first *Annual Report*,[6] the Director of Education,[7] states,[8]

' The duty of proceeding slowly, of avoiding expenditure on mere educational machinery, of setting nothing on foot that has no real vital connection with the economic needs of the country becomes plainer every day.'

With this cautious approach as Government policy[9] the tone of the following paragraph in a report of four years later is not surprising.

1905 'From Rufaa comes the most startling suggestion of all, no less a request for the establishment of a girls' school side by side with that for the boys. Matters are evidently progressing when such a proposal can be made. Whether it can or should be carried out remains to be seen'.[10]

The 'should' in the last sentence is not elaborated and one can only surmise what the implications might have been. Whatever the conversations not recorded, reactions were evidently favourable in the end, for by the time of the next *Annual Report* the school had been started and girls' education appears as a matter of course in every subsequent year. The authorities

4. 'The period of financial depression in Egypt has had its counterpart in the Sudan which has also been affected by the unfavourable trade conditions prevailing throughout the world' (Gorst, *General Report*, 1909 (S.A.D. 657/1/13)). For example, the establishment of Khartoum Girls' Elementary School had to be indefinitely postponed (*ARDE*, 1908, Khartoum, 1909).
5. See Appendix III.
6. Sudan Government, First *ARDE* of 1.11.1901 (S.A.D. 657/1/3).
7. Sir James Currie, K.B.E., M.G., 3O., 3M. (b.1868-d.1937); Educated at Fettes College and Edinburgh and Oxford Universities; 1900-14 Director of Education and Principal of Gordon Memorial College; 1911-14 member of the Governor-General's Council. Currie, J, 'The educational experiment in the Anglo-Egyptian Sudan 1900-1933', *Journal of the African Society*, XXXIII, 1934, pp.351-371 and XXXIV, 1935, pp.41-60.
8. The first part of this item reads '(3) in the creation of a native administrative class who will ultimately fill many minor posts'.
9. Holt, P.M., *Modern History of the Sudan*, London, 1961, pp.119-120. Also Currie, Sir James, *op. cit.*
10. *Report on the Finance, Administration and Condition of the Sudan*, 1905, Section III, Education, p.42.

acknowledge the venture[11] was due entirely to Sheikh Babikr Bedri[12] of whom I have spoken before as winning such a large place in my affections for his friendship and unfailing help. He was the Headmaster of the boys' school and the subsequent success of this parallel attempt, which was frequently commented on, was also attributed to his energy and interest. Its continued progress and all that followed is but another vindication of one man's foresight.

It is not here[13] but two years later that the breaking point occurred. More particularly the report mentions,—'the collapse of the educational programme settled in 1907'.[14] This programme included the buildings arranged in order of urgency, the whole to be spread over five years.

'VII. Girls' School, Training College and quarters for staff, furnishing etc. to accommodate 300, of whom 100 would be boarders. £20,000.'

Thinking of the way in which girls' education is so often starved, not only in African countries, one cannot fail to admire unreservedly the vision and courage of a Government which was less than ten years old, operating in a country renowned so short a time before for the barbarity of its manners. What would have been the result, the speculation runs, if this proposal for a Girls' Training College had been carried out in 1907 instead of being postponed by the slump for another fourteen years? Boys' education would not then have outrun girls', as in the event it was to do, and a more balanced society might have come about. Those early days of the Reconquest were crucial ones and through the velocity of change the lag in girls' education has been a great deal more than fourteen years in substance, with the result that the attempt to make up the leeway should have had proportionately greater efforts, as the men continued to hurry ahead.

Despite the stultifying influences of forces, on the surface so unconnected, this matter of girls' schools crops up again and again in these early years. By 1914 five Government institutions were in being[15] and the

---

11. For details on the establishment of Rufaa girls' school, see Appendix III. See also *Blue Nile Province Report*, 1910 (S.A.D. 657/1/6,13) and *ARDE*, 1911 (S.A.D. 657/1/19).

12. Sheikh Babikr Bedri (d.1954) was also a close friend of Bishop Gwynne. (Bedri, B., *Ta'rīkh ḥayātī* (The Story of my Life), 3 vols, Khartoum, 1961).

13. In 1905.

14. *ARDE*, 1907, Appendix B (S.A.D. 657/1/5).

15. In 1919 and 1921 there were schools at Rufaa, Kamlin, Merowe, Dongola and El Obeid (See Appendix III for further statistics on girls' education in the early years).

PLATE 9

Dr I.M. Beasley in Southern Sudan, c.1949. I.M. Beasley collection.

PLATE 10

Sitt Medina Abdulla, first school inspectress of girls' schools, 1940s. Taken by Mrs Sheila Connelly, from Dr I.M. Beasley's collection.

PLATE 11

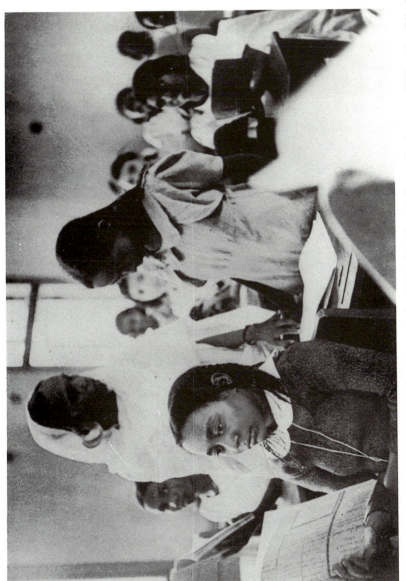

Sitt Nafissa Awad el-Karim giving an Arabic lesson at the Girls' Training College, Omdurman, 1940s. Mrs Elizabeth Hodgkin's collection.

PLATE 12

Sitt Batoul Mohamed Eisa, midwife and pioneer against 'female circumcision' in 1940s and 1950s. Bright collection, S.A.D. 729/22/9.

missionary societies were also doing useful work in the large urban centres.[16] Where Sudanese public opinion favoured schooling at all it was inclined to criticise a situation, in which Muslim girls in such places as Wad Medani, Atbara or the Three Towns could be educated only in Christian schools. Sir Reginald Wingate commented in 1914 'Much more ought to be done as soon as funds can be provided'.

Following these preliminary discussions[17] makes fascinating reading, despite the catastrophe of 1907.

### 1.2 1920s-1930s, Miss J. Dorothy Evans

The First World War retarded development in so many spheres, that it is not surprising that finally the date on which all future growth was pivoted was 1920,[18] when Miss J.D. Evans[19] was appointed by the Government to organise a system of elementary schools and teacher training for the Arabic

16. By 1911/12 the mission schools included American Mission in Khartoum North with 110 pupils, Halfa with 45 pupils who were mostly Syrians and Egyptians; Austrian Catholic schools in Khartoum (110 pupils) and Omdurman (53 pupils). There were 180 in the Austrian Mission schools by 1913. The Catholics also had schools in Atbara and Port Sudan. The C.M.S. girls' schools in 1911/12 were Khartoum (98 pupils), Omdurman (68 pupils) and Atbara (51 pupils). In 1912 a new school opened by C.M.S. in Wad Medani due to the exertions of Bishop Gwynne, under the care of Mrs Hall, with accommodation for 100 pupils.
17. 'The Sudan Government ought to make progress ... 3) by the institution of a good girls' school in Khartoum; as a preliminary to attempting something in the same direction throughout the country' (*ARDE*, 1908).
18. 'The attitude of the people towards girls' education had changed very much for the better but want of funds and staff has prevented the government from availing itself of this change; the Government has five elementary girls' schools in the provinces but the only higher girls' schools are managed by missionaries, English, American and Austrian' (Stack, Lee, *Egypt*, no.1, 1920).
19. Miss J. Dorothy Evans, M.B.E. A Welsh lady who had previously worked in Egypt; 13.11.1920 first appointment to organise a system of elementary schools and teacher-training for Muslim girls. 'A Girls' Training College has been opened in Omdurman and is proving a great success' (*Gordon College Report*, 1925 (S.A.D. 657/1/2)); 1920-31 Principal, Girls' Training College, Omdurman; 1932-1933 she was also Controller of Girls' Education. Later Controllers included 1934-35 her sister, Miss Dora Evans; 1935-42 Miss L.Y. Pode; October 1942-49 Dr Ina Beasley; 1949-56 Miss Sylvia Clark; Ahmed Mirghani from 1956. Babikr Bedri helped Miss J.D. Evans select the site for the Training College and suggested Khalifa 'Abd Allāhi's compound. (See Bedri, *op. cit.*, p.241 for his opinions of Miss J. Dorothy Evans).

half of the country.[20] Miss Evans and her sister,[21] who joined her five years later, had worked in Egypt but they seem from the first to have been determined to avoid the over-literary bias of the Egyptian schools and to lay the foundations of a practical curriculum with sufficient elasticity in the whole scheme for further development. One legacy above all they left for which their successors could never pay them adequate tribute. They created a tradition of friendliness and co-operation between staff and pupils, which always remained, and this spirit was of untold value in the development of the girls themselves, increasing their happiness far more than they perhaps realised.

Miss J.D. Evans gave over ten years' devoted service to this work and, although schools for girls had become no novelty by that time, she did not live to see the later tremendous and clamourous demands at all levels,[22] which might have been impossible without her original faith and patience.

## 2. The start of girls' teacher-training

The aim set for her, which she so brilliantly accomplished, was to train a nucleus of schoolmistresses to be responsible for all the teaching in the schools and to introduce a rather more enlightened curriculum for them to work on.[23] While doing this she had to be careful so as to arrange the external circumstances of their lives, that as little disruption as possible would be caused in the strongly entrenched Muslim prejudices about the seclusion of women and their place in the home. It must have seemed an

---

20. On Miss Evans's arrival, in December 1920, there were five Government *kuttāb*s for girls (*ARDE*, 1928. London, 1929). From 1922 girls' education was a separate section in *ARDE*s. Between 1925 and 1929 there was no significant educational development in the Sudan. There was a decade of stagnation until the mid-30s and the role of the educated Sudanese in administration was progressively reduced. After 1934 there were signs of recovery from the economic depression with new staff and methods bringing new life to the education service.

21. Miss J. Dorothy Evans was later joined by her sister Miss Dora Evans, a most able assistant and supporter. 11.10.1925 First appointment; 1925-33 Assistant Principal, Girls' Training College, Omdurman. From 14.10.34 she was succeeded by Miss E.M. Harvey; 1934-35 Controller of Girls' Education and Principal, Girls' Training College, Omdurman.

22. The *Report of De La Warr Commission* (1937) stressed the need for girls' education at all levels—higher, intermediate and secondary.

23. 'Concerning Kamlin and Rufaa girls' schools, the want of competent native mistresses is urgent. It is not proposed to attempt any scheme of advanced education for these girls, but merely to give them a sound knowledge of reading, writing and arithmetic, which the present mistresses, who are merely teachers of needlework, are not competent to impart, and such instructions as the girls get in these subjects is given by the headmasters of the boys' schools in any intervals they can spare from their own work' (*Blue Nile Province Report*, 1913 (S.A.D. 657/1/21)).

almost insuperable task at the time; now when the amount of freedom for girls seemed to increase every year without comment, they should be grateful for the trials she must have endured, and marvel at her belief that they would pass.

During her first years she toured[24] much in an endeavour to persuade parents to send their daughters to the Training College, opened in Omdurman in 1921. Despite all her efforts only five students were enrolled and of these one was a daughter and two were nieces of Sheikh Babikr Bedri. Six months later another five recruits were added.[25] These humble beginnings are of particular interest in our present world of large-scale planning, where it sometimes seems that in our desire to educate everybody at once, we obtain little but more educational machinery.

It was not only in her readiness to develop from small beginnings that Miss Evans showed her wisdom but in the way she was prepared to make concessions to public opinion until people's trust was won. That the Training College should have been surrounded by a high wall is not necessarily giving way to Sudanese prejudice. Girls in English institutions are frequently protected in this way and only allowed out in the care of visitors approved by their parents. That the boarding houses should be simple, conforming to the type of house to which the girls were accustomed is not surprising either. What must have been difficult to support was that in the beginning each student brought her own chaperone, and the chaperone would undoubtedly be an old and conservative relative long past any possibility of change. It was difficult enough in my time to struggle against the negativing of good habits by the elderly chaperones, who lived in the mistresses' quarters in elementary schools. At least the teacher had had by the time she was appointed, three years or in some cases more of boarding house life, where she had been impelled firmly into decent, cleanly ways of living. To have had the chaperone always on the premises in the Training College must have demanded considerable fortitude. Gradually the practice was discontinued but the compromise which allowed for it in the first place was amply justified.

The great objection put forward at first was that no-one would want to marry a girl who had so far broken the bonds of convention as to be a school teacher. Bribery was the method used to overcome this. Any schoolmistress who left the service to be married could have a dowry in proportion to the length of time she had worked.[26] Even this was later

---

24. Miss J.D. Evans spent some time visiting existing *kuttāb*s.
25. Sitt Sekina Tewfiq was among this group of students.
26. In 1925 the Government agreed to grant a bonus on marriage equivalent to one month's salary for every year of service, to any teacher who taught for four or more consecutive years.

discontinued and the supply of schoolmistresses increased steadily notwithstanding. Another sensible decision was the payment of generous salaries to them from the beginning. It should, however, in all fairness to the Sudanese be emphasised, that this would have been of no avail in forwarding the profession without the guarantee of respectability, which was so triumphantly achieved. Nursing, for example, despite financial inducements had a very much longer and harder struggle to be accepted, since it was so much harder to reconcile with this insistence on respectability.[27] It is easy to see that teaching can be made a much more sheltered task than hospital work. Schoolmistresses can be shut away behind high walls and still be capable of a reasonably good standard of work but it is difficult to prevent a nurse from coming up against the outside world in its more unpleasant aspects.

After a time parents began to realise not only that a girl's salary was a useful addition to the family income but that, still being regarded as respectable, schoolmistresses were asked in marriage just as much as other girls. Some twenty years later in many circles education was a distinct asset in the marriage market and the brideprice for a girl, who had had merely elementary schooling was higher than for her unlettered sister. For a schoolmistress the bridegroom might offer a dowry of up to £150.

It may seem strange to talk about schools shut up and away from the world, as obviously children must come to school and headmistresses have dealings with parents. Nevertheless it soothed the fears of relatives, that definite attempts were made from the first not to offend Muslim customs. It is sometimes argued that in many countries, British officials carried too far this respect for native sentiment. In some cases this was possibly true and opportunities for needed reform were allowed to slip out of regard for what was thought to be popular feeling. There was in the first place a great deal of opposition to girls' education but it was passive rather than actually hostile. It is pointless now to argue how much more pressure could have been safely applied. Also in a world where foreign aid floods vast sums of money in all directions one forgets how small were resources in the years before the Second World War and on a more concrete level, that motor transport was not so readily available, as it has since become, and in a country such as Sudan air travel had not begun. Whether one prefers the camel era or not is unimportant but its persistence must be remembered when evaluating the rates of development in the first quarter of the century. To some extent, therefore, this influenced the way in which girls' schools could be started but from the beginning a firm policy was adhered to, that

---

27. The Central Nursing Council was formed in 1948 in an attempt to put nursing training on a systematic basis but in 1960 there were only 11 students at the Nurses' Training College.

the towns should not have a monopoly of education, although it was very much simpler to staff schools there and inspect them.[28] That the first school should have been in Rufaa was a most fortunate augury for such an aim.[29] Moreover it set such a good example that the choice of places for schools was made on the application of the people in any particular district, who could show that there would be adequate support and a population to justify the foundation. A committee of notables of the village would make their request to the Governor of the Province and to the Education Department and would be asked to back this by the names of fifty to eighty girls of not less than seven years old. Sometimes local enterprise would provide an adequate building; sometimes this was left to the Public Works Department. In the early days philanthropists lent houses, unfortunately on occasion old and unsuitable ones, which the owners did not want but were thus kept in repair by the Government.

## 3. Opening Days

Of the opening days we have few descriptions but the Headmaster's report of the first morning of the El Obeid school in 1918 is still on record. It illustrated very amply the need for the Training College and Miss Evans' enlightened views of the way to teach small girls. The Governor[30] opened the school and twenty girls arrived. 'Every girl sat properly in her place with her books before her, and when all the speeches were delivered the Governor, British officials, ladies, parents of pupils and many others attended the buffet and then the girls in their class, which was a source of pleasure to all.'

28. '... The dominance of European peoples in Africa and Asia, whether presently waning or not, is bound to leave the impression that there is something in European education which helps peoples to power; that to impose some other type is to go on jealously guarding privilege in the interests of the ruling race ... development among human beings and human societies may take very different forms from those expected' (Sudan Government, Department of Education, *Notes from Extra-Departmental Conference on Girls' Education in Northern Sudan*, 8.11.43).
29. See Taha, Abdel Rahman Ali, 'Economic and Political Aspects of Education in the Sudan' in *Cultural Groups and Human Relations Conference on Educational Problems of Specific Cultural Groups*, New York, 1951, pp.127-39. See also 'Sudan Girls' Education' *Times Educational Supplement*, no.1911, 14.12.51, p.960, possibly written by Dr Beasley.
30. The Governor of Kordofan Province in 1918 was John Warburton Sagar, 4O. (b.6.12.1878-d.10.1.41); educated at Durham and Jesus College, Cambridge, represented England at Rugby Football, 1901; 27.5.1903 first appointment; 1903-04 Berber; 1905-08 Kordofan; 1909-10 Assistant Civil Secretary; 1911 Assistant Private Secretary to the Governor-General; 1911-14 Nuba Mountains; 1914-17 Blue Nile; 1917-22 Governor, Kordofan; 1922-24 Governor, Halfa; 1924 retired.

A respectable old *sheikh* had been appointed as a schoolmaster and he was assisted by an illiterate woman to teach needlework, most of which was very likely to be cross-stitch embroidery. Of the twenty eight periods in the timetable twelve were devoted to this subject; three were for instruction in religion; three for learning the Koran; three for a vague subject known as 'manners'.[31] In the remainder the children were expected to become literate. It was the sort of education that some Sudanese regarded for a long time as 'suited to the specific needs of the community' but fortunately the proportion holding this view gradually decreased.

Later the picture changes in many ways and after about 1935 the scene on an opening day would be something like this. News would have circulated in the village, that girls would be accepted on such and such a morning. Long before the prescribed hour the schoolyard would be filled by a crowd of women and girls.[32] As soon as the Headmistress appeared with a sheet of paper and a pencil, she was besieged by women, who pushed forward their own daughters, while shouting any kind of recommendation, that they thought might make them more quickly noticed. As they themselves would invariably be illiterate, have been shut away from the world and what we regard as its normal contacts, life for them would have been a confusing succession of other people's arbitrary decisions. Consequently their only reasoning was that they were begging a favour; *Allah* requites the dispenser of favours. Therefore they called down his blessings on the head of any official on the spot and hoped that the beggar's plea would move authority to mercy. 'I am poor and have many children' was the almost inevitable argument for the asking of any favour, whether relevant or not.

There was something disarmingly pathetic about these women which increased one's determination that their daughters should not be the

---

31. On the 1918 El Obeid girls' school timetable included Needlework for the second and third hour every day; Religion for the first hour on Saturday, Monday and Wednesday, with Koran on Sunday, Tuesday and Thursday for this period; Arithmetic at the fourth hour Saturday to Monday; Arabic was at the fourth hour on Tuesday and the fifth hour on Saturday, Sunday and Wednesday; Penmanship was at the fifth hour on Thursday; Manners (*adab*) was at the fifth hour on Monday and Tuesday and at the fourth hour on Wednesday and Thursday. Friday, the Muslim holiday was a holiday (S.A.D. 657/1/8).

32. 'Any real appreciation of learning even in its most rudimentary forms is probably non-existent ... more likely a vague recognition that a gift of value from the government may be had for the asking. The number of places in most girls' schools is sufficiently limited for it still to be a privilege to obtain one ... in the minds of the children is an overwhelming conviction that school is a thoroughly delightful place ... they find so little scope for development in their home life' (Sudan Government, Department of Education, *Note on Girls' Education in the Sudan*, December 1940).

same.[33] Nevertheless officialdom had to harden its heart. Provision was made in the schools for classes of forty girls. This would be reckoned a large class under any conditions and particularly so with the teacher a girl still in her teens, whose education had been no more than four or five years' elementary schooling and two or three years in the Girls' Training College. A school was started with two parallel classes. It would be unfair therefore to all concerned to increase the numbers still further and a line had to be drawn somewhere. The cry of 'Just one more. Just my daughter' was hard to refuse. We felt a keen bitterness when we wanted to be insisting on girls coming to school instead of denying them places.

The custom, therefore, was to take the older girls, since fortunately there was no shame for a big girl to be sitting learning her letters alongside others some years her junior. Then the younger girls could have another chance the following year. Reasonable though this might appear to authority, it was by no means acceptable to the disappointed mothers. They dragged forward their offspring and thrust them in the official's path, while opening the child's mouth for inspection. 'Look, Look! She has cut her second teeth. She must be old enough. I know she's a bit small and thin but look at her teeth!'

As the idea of birth certificates had only just begun to permeate in the large towns this rough and ready estimating had its points, but it did not meet the main difficulty, that once the eighty places had been allotted nothing more could be done immediately.

It needed a stern sense of duty to withstand the clamour of the rejected women and the heart-broken tears of the little girls who were urged so heartily to come again next year, when they were sure to be old enough.

On the other side of the yard were the proud, accepted ones, with mothers all smiles and the children in a state of tense excitement, too satisfied to give expression to their feelings but having that look of tightly compressed emotion, peculiar to all children. Naturally when the row of 'accepteds' was counted agin, there were always a few of the 'rejected', who managed to slip out of place and tack on at the end of the line. This was not from malice or cunning. The whole affair was very strange and bewildering and it was very easy to go to the wrong spot or be pushed there by some well-meaning relative, when no-one was looking. This confusion of queues might occur several times before the final sorting out was accomplished. It was the kind of trick, which can arouse great mirth from the stage or the screen but took another aspect on an occasion, which was after all very important. Having arrived at the final answer the Headmistress gave the

33. 'The children of educated women are sure to have more aptitude for education that those whose mothers are uneducated.' (*Red Sea Province Report*, 1908 (S.A.D. 657/1/12)).

girls a little speech admonishing them to come to school punctually and regularly and to be sure to be clean, as they were now lucky enough to be schoolgirls. After this the two schoolmistresses were expected to settle down to a steady round, until the same process was repeated for the new class at the beginning of the next school year.

It was later that enthusiasm began to wilt. The full course of schooling was for four years. Little enough by anyone's standards but all we could afford.[34] Even so it was impossible to count on all pupils finishing the fourth year, although happily the proportion rose every year.

## 4. Parental support

What moved parents to send their children to school and then be, to our way of thinking, so half-hearted about the continuity of it all is a matter for the sociologists. A mother might want a place for her little Nafissa because the woman next door had one for her little Sekina. There was a vague feeling that education was said to have some value. Anyway the Government provided elementary schools for girls free and it might be interesting to try and see what it was like. Then there were the schoolmistresses, who were better dressed, better looking and had become much more sought after in marriage. Perhaps little Nafissa might be like that one day and mother love and maternal pride were very strong forces in the limited world of secluded women. Most of all and most encouraging was the fact, that little Nafissa very earnestly desired to go to school. Being shut up in the women's quarters with nothing to do but look after the baby was not nearly so much fun as all the exciting things that happened along with a lot of other girls of her own age. One of the sad things about a Sudanese household was that there was not even a minimum of cultural background except for the very few. Certainly no trace of the arts, no books, newspapers, nor toys for the children. Think then what plasticine meant and coloured chalks and being allowed to make a little mat with bright embroidery thread.

---

34. Girls entered school at 6+ and left at 11+. 'The fear was always that they slip back into the ways of their grandmothers. 85% of girls who entered the first year now stayed until they had completed 4th year and there was often a strong desire to stay on after that. The Graduates Congress suggested a fifth year which would fill the gap but would mean better staff expertise at the intermediate level after teachers' training, or two fourth year classes running on alternative syllabuses' (Sudan Government, Department of Education, *Notes from a Meeting to discuss Girls' Education in 1942*, 29.3.41).

# 5. Absenteeism

This glowing description might suggest that education for girls would roll along without any of the difficulties, that beset administrations elsewhere. In fact there were all the usual troubles of absenteeism through the limited understanding of what schooling needed and because the habit of school belonged really only to that generation. There were from the start many parents who sent their children regularly to school and whose co-operation was all that could be wished and, as a generation grew up with mothers, who had themselves been to school, the improvement was marked. At first, however, in the villages everything went at a more leisurely pace. Mothers were really anxious to have their daughters considered educated but felt, that to have their names inscribed on the school register was the major part of the effort and, if they put in an appearance when convenient, that was what was meant by going to school. This business about washing Nafissa and getting her off by quarter to eight could not be intended for every day of every week. Perhaps that was almost too active an attitude. The good intention was always there but somehow the time faded away. It was Oblomovism in a rather extended and diluted form.

# 6. School closures

Neither of these extremes was universal and absenteeism gradually diminished but, as I noted in the case of Karkoj, very occasionally schools had to be closed, because the numbers fell away so much after the first year or so of enthusiasm. But this was regarded as a desperate measure, only to be resorted to, when the waste of public money seemed quite unjustified. The villagers would consider themselves much shamed and could generally be induced to rally round in face of such a threat. Also there was always the loss to the few girls who had been constant. One never knew if amongst them might be a Florence Nightingale, so badly needed, or perhaps an Elizabeth Garrett Anderson. The possibility of a Miss Beale or Miss Buss was not so far away but, in my opinion, militant suffragettes had outlived their usefulness and I never prayed for a Pankhurst.

# 7. Curriculum[35]

## 7.1 Literacy

An ordinary school, when complete, had four classes of about forty girls, each with four teachers, including the headmistress. The contents of the curriculum may be of interest, as it should be remembered, that they were set against the usual background of complete illiteracy in the women's quarters and in many cases in the men's also. Literacy therefore was a social problem and not merely a question of school methods. Arabic and arithmetic were imperative and systematically taught, since the 'three R's' are the tools without which no further progress is possible, and more effort is needed to instil these thoroughly, where there is nothing at all in life outside to reinforce the simplest operations. Very little actual money was needed in some of the more remote villages and there was nowhere for a child to go to run errands. The bigger villages might have general shops and most had a market perhaps once or twice a week but Nafissa was seldom sent out to fetch an odd purchase. Often the father was the person who did any marketing necessary, or at a slightly higher level in social status there might be a servant for such chores.

I am not prepared to say, whether becoming literate in Arabic is more difficult than in any other language, for those who have never heard anything else. As in most places the children responded readily to the first stages with the various simple toys and apparatus applicable to learning to read but it needed more than the usual effort to sustain this in a country, where nobody had been accustomed to read for the sheer enjoyment of so doing. Learning among the Arabs has always been reverenced; so much so in fact that one felt rather frivolous, almost blasphemous, in talking about reading for the fun of it. The wealth of books, which children in England enjoy, whether suitable or not, simply does not exist in Arabic speaking countries. We once asked an Egyptian professor, who had studied in Europe, for suggestions for reading material in Arabic for girls, who had finished elementary school, were about fifteen years of age and could read fluently. This was in 1940, not in the earliest days of girls' education. His list was divided into two parts; one was such tales as *Little Red Riding Hood* and *Beauty and the Beast*, the other *The Whole Duty of a Wife* and works on

---

35. Dr Beasley's comments on school syllabus included 'Not just literacy ... too narrow a viewpoint ... literacy is the most powerful method of making a child accessible to new ideas, but only one method and surprisingly ineffectual if practised in a vacuum ... school should not terribly clash with the atmosphere of the village ... need to teach people what they want not impose it from above ... nothing can make up for the moral and mental harm of inefficient or slipshod teaching.' (S.A.D. 657/1).

religion. This difficulty ran all through an Arabic education, when one tried to relate it to the needs of everyday life.

Determined efforts were made by the Education Department of the Sudan Government to overcome this defect but the restrictions of the war years delayed plans. In any case one cannot create a literature overnight, not even a children's literature. It is, however, indicative that, when in 1947 a sort of *Boy's Own Paper* (with a page for girls) was started,[36] its circulation grew to 10,000 within six months. It was known as *Al Sibyan* and published fortnightly at one piastre. This, it should be repeated, was among a population of about seven million, which would include the nomads and many illiterates in more settled places. The most depressing feature of this lack of ordinary books to buy is that large numbers of boys and girls, who may have been thoroughly competent at school, within three or four years relapse into the general illiteracy of their surroundings.

Personally I found it an absorbing hobby to write school stories for girls to be translated for *Al Sibyan,* and after many vicissitudes I induced a publisher to produce for the schools the sort of tale I used to enjoy as a child. *Nafissa fil Madresa* (Nafissa at School)[37] was not a Sudanised version of an English book but the narrative of a child based on what I had actually seen in the Sudan schools. Not long ago it was still being used and I hope someone will one day write a sequel.

So often all this about mass literacy for Africans blithely ignores the central fact, that once the pupil has learnt his textbook, which in pagan areas may often be a chapter or so of the Bible, there is nothing more for him to read. What is really needed is a blend of translators of the fifteenth century in England with the vision and acute business sense of the popular publishers of the nineteenth century. When people begin to discover an interest of reading, there will be no need for literacy plans as outlined in Whitehall but without teachers or material to put them into practice on the spot. Moreover, if we found this desperate lack of reading material in such an important language as Arabic, there would be a great deal of wasted effort, if literacy as such only were to be encouraged in the thousands of lesser tongues scattered all over Africa. I have touched on this question

---

36. *Al Sibyan* was started by the Publications Bureau in an attempt to maintain literacy. From small beginnings at Bakht er-Ruda, the Publications Bureau was opened in 1946. Under V.L. Griffiths' guidance, over 120 publications for the elementary schools had appeared by 1950 (Hodgkin, Robin A., 'The Sudan Publications Bureau beginnings', *Oversea Education*, XIX, no. 3, April 1948, pp.694-8; Sudan Government, Ministry of Education, *Publications Bureaux in the Sudan, 1946-51*, Khartoum, 1952).

37. Beasley, Ina, *Nafīsa fī'l-madrasa: qiṣṣa li'l-aṭfāl*, London/Cairo, 1949 (Tr. by N. Ibrahim, illustrations by her sister Mrs Sheila Connelly, who taught Art in the Sudan, just after the War, until she was invalided out with T.B.).

again in the last chapter but it is not irrelevant here to the problem of deciding of what elementary education should consist. As we could never have any doubts about the importance of literacy in the modern world, the later wastage had to be combatted by making these subjects as vital as possible in the schools; by an endeavour to increase post-school and adult education in various, preferably simple, forms and by stimulating the production of a literature, which was not ashamed to be homely and enjoyable.

## 7.2 Boys' versus girls' education[38]

All this was equally true for girls and for boys, although we were constantly battling against the attitude, that it was almost astonishing for a girl to be able to read. The more far-sighted Sudanese were genuinely anxious for their girls to reach the same standard as the boys, but the following little tale may illustrate a point of view, that was all too common. A Sudanese builder, English-speaking and excellent at his job, was walking across the yard of the Girls' Training College with the Principal to discuss some repairs. 'The yard is very tidy,' he remarked, 'much better than the boys' across the road'. 'It's part of the training', replied the Principal. 'The students have to learn to be tidy'. 'Oh, they'll soon forget', was the cheerful answer. 'Girls are so stupid'. Rather piqued, the Principal retorted that, when an Arabic Inspector had recently examined the Girls' Intermediate School, he had found their standard up to that of the boys. 'They'll get over that', said the builder. 'Girls are so stupid.'[39] He was, however, very sympathetic to girls' education, most helpful over the question of suitable buildings and was delighted, when he was able to lower the outer wall of a school by a metre, thinking that real progress was thus being made.

## 7.3 Domestic Science

It was indeed true that tidiness, although not an aim in itself, fitted in as part of the training. Much emphasis was laid on Domestic Science from the elementary school upwards. This was not solely in response to the 'better wives and mothers' demand but for the obvious reason, that many of these girls would be in charge of the household affairs later on and the more

38. Co-educational schools were possible in some areas e.g. Gala en Nahl, but there were difficulties of staffing, and the boys' curriculum was not suited to girls (Sudan Government, Department of Education, *Notes from a Meeting to discuss Girls' Education in 1942*, 29.3.41).
39. In 1932 a Committee chaired by R.K. Winter recommended a re- oganisation of boys' education more on the lines of girls' schools. This reflects the achievements of the Evans sisters (*Education in the Northern Sudan: the Winter Committee Report*, 1933).

competently they could perform their tasks the more satisfactory their lives. The result would most likely be better wives and mothers but we had the girls' own development as our starting point, realising also that it was in the interests of the whole community, that standards should be raised and that this was possible without much extra expenditure.

The syllabus, therefore, included native cooking by rather more orderly and less wasteful methods than in many homes with a striving after variety which could be obtained in most places. Sudanese husbands were most appreciative of this. Sewing was also important and all elementary schoolgirls had made themselves a set of clothes by the time they had completed four years' schooling and knew a little about mending. These garments were of a plain, stout calico supplied by the Government and paid for in instalments by the parents, except in some very remote districts, where money was scarce and we knew a family to be very poor. I have commented on the attitude of mothers in Shabarga, who would not send their children to school except in ordinary clothes. A whole treatise could be written about the effects of clothes in schools in emergent countries but this is no place for an African *Sartor Resartus*. Like school authorities everywhere we opted for sensible and appropriate dresses and tried to make them a method of instruction. Knitting also became very popular and the children were taught how to make simple garments such as a baby's vest from cotton they had themselves spun on a hand spindle. In some places, where the headmistress was especially interested in needlework, this went much further and the girls made themselves frocks of a smarter cut, produced remarkably fine embroidery and knitted jumpers and cardigans from the spun cotton, which they had dyed.

In one Omdurman school I even saw an elaborate but useful layette. 'This', said the headmistress, 'is the proper thing for an educated girl to make. You consider yourselves educated, don't you?' 'Certainly', chorussed the whole class. 'Then you should enjoy making beautiful things for your baby'. 'Of course', said the girls at that moment at any rate speaking with conviction.

More than any notions of vocational training these girls were to be encouraged to make things to be prised out of the distressing apathy of the generations of women, who spent their time 'just sitting', frequently slatterns amidst the squalor. So much has been written on the stimulating effect of clothes, that there is no need for a digression into elementary psychology here but it became more and more noticeable, how the girls benefitted from this dressmaking and taking a reasonable pride in their appearance. Self-respect had never entered into their conceptions before but in a society, where they were held of so little importance,it was a development very much needed. I do not pretend that this growth of self-esteem was due entirely to the cultivation of an interest in clothes but I have no doubt that it was of the greatest assistance.

As well as needlework housewifery in general figured largely in the syllabus with much insistence on personal and domestic hygiene. Teachers were incessantly reminded that practical everyday activities must not go unnoticed because of mere instruction in the classroom, since the most brilliant arithmetic lesson could not be weighed against unclean latrines or dirty heads. British staff, of course, had to assist in all these down to earth matters, partly because such supervision was at times necessary but mostly to emphasise, that no degree of learning absolved a woman from the combatting of dirt and the consequent unhealthy conditions.

It all sounds rather like 'the gods of the copy book headings' but such matters were not out of place in the particular stage the girls had reached as we thought it no shame to be simple and direct in trying for some measure of orderly progress in the daily round. Success might come slowly but husbands did begin to affirm that girls who had been to school made better housewives. There were even cases of a man with two old-fashioned wives taking an educated girl for his third for this very reason, not always, be it added, to the joy of the third. Important though it was Domestic Science did not take pride of place over the 'three R's', because the former is unsuited to very small girls in a really useful form and in any case the domestic subjects can be more easily taught to pupils who have mastered the processes of reading and writing.

Even though this side of schooling was an avowed favourite with most Sudanese parents, some tiresome reactions cropped up here and there. After the elementary stage the demand for a literary education was much greater than for a practical one. An Intermediate School was started at Wad Medani[40] with a domestic science bias, the aim being to prove that girls could be educated in this way as well as by more bookish methods, since there were girls who would profit more from such a course. The pupils did all their own work, except for the Friday holiday, but continued with a reasonable amount of ordinary studies. Many parents declared, that the idea was excellent but that they for their part preferred their daughters to go to Omdurman Intermediate School, where they could learn English.

Part of the strange cleavage between theory and practice was due to the fact that slavery was so near to the Sudanese in history, that they had not yet lost their consciousness of it, and their fear of being implicated in any work that bears a taint of it. People known to have slave ancestry were treated with a degree of disdain, which was quite inexplicable. They in turn reacted in the orthodox way. Housework came very near to this category.

40. About 1946.

For a woman to be able to direct a household was within the purlieus of education but to do housework herself was suspect. We always set our faces against the idea of 'little ladies', while regarding manners as essential and encouraging fineness of appearance, without extravagance. But the baser forms of cleaning had to be undertaken and understood also and this by practical methods. After a short period of doubt the idea was accepted with acclamation. The school was full, although fees were charged. Finally it took over the work of training Domestic Science teachers as well.

### 7.4 Other subjects taught in the curriculum

Even though the curriculum was based on these two aims, literacy and domestic order, it was not quite so austere as to include nothing else. Elementary schools managed to introduce a little geography, nature study, drawing, handwork, drill and religion. That none of this was taught with much thoroughness was due mainly to the limitations of the teachers' knowledge and the lack of any appropriate books in Arabic. As I mentioned at the beginning Bakht er-Ruda did produce some stimulating textbooks and the Girls' Training College brought out one on Physical Education,[41] but there was no hope of reference to material for lessons in the way that books are procurable in England. A subject such as nature study had obvious drawbacks, when the mistresses had to stay behind the school walls. I did, however, once see an energetic teacher with a live hen, cock and duck in a small room crammed with children. She was determined to make her lesson real; certainly it was spirited. Not so felicitous was a half-suffocated kitten produced from a table drawer. But the attempts to get away from mere talking were well intentioned.

## 8. School day

All this was easily fitted into working hours, which were comparatively short—8.00 a.m. to 1.00 p.m. with a break for food and two afternoons a week for needlework with Friday as a holiday.

There was then nothing very novel about the lessons, which took place in ordinary looking classrooms with desks and benches, blackboard and easel.

---

41. Sudan Government, Department of Education, *Al-Tarbiya al-badaniyya li'l madāris al-uliyya li'l-banāt*, [Physical education for girls' primary schools], Khartoum, 1943.

## 9. School buildings

The buildings fortunately were not exact replicas of one model, although a standard plan did exist as a guide for local authorities.[42] Most of the schools in Omdurman conformed to this and were solid, rather plain red-brick blocks with a verandah on the south side. They were convenient and comfortable and regarded by their headmistresses as a paradise, for the history of schoolbuildings in the town had not worked out well.[43] In the very early days well-meaning owners presented houses for use as schools, which did in fact prove adequate for the small number of girls using them. Education for girls grew in popularity here much faster than elsewhere and what would just accommodate fifty children could certainly not be stretched to make room for a full school of 160. The choice lay in one case between cutting down numbers or teaching forty children in a stable, which would not have housed two horses. Outside [the Three Towns] the local versions [of the plan] presented a pleasing variety. Kordofan provided two white-washed blocks with large thatched roofs, a very satisfactory divergence. The schools in the Fung were built of wood; the Northern Province, which seldom has any rain, could build cheaply in mud-brick.

## 10. Girls' Training College

### 10.1 Buildings

Even if such were not desirable for its own sake, simplicity had to be the keynote of it all, for in those days the country had a total budget of £11 million. The Girls' Training College had been deliberately started on a plan, which would make the girls feel, that they were not too far removed from home conditions. Although numbers were small originally, just before the war the demand for girls' education had begun to increase and within the next five years had swollen to unexpected proportions. After 1945,[44] when

---

42. By the 1930s there was a proper building plan.
43. On 3.3.40 'I went to Osman Saleh school to see if the teaching was as bad as I suspected. Admittedly the building is deplorable and must be disheartening ... the great disadvantage of the building is that the windows all give directly on to the street and that there is very little ground round the house. Of the four rooms, two lead out of the other two and exit and ingress is right through the middle of these outer classes. The rooms are in any case small and dark and the children crowded together. The verandah also too small for any kind of decent drill while the yard is so cut up with trenches (anti-aircraft precautions taken in all schools but not often necessary), that it is impossible to use ... '
44. At the end of the Second World War, a considerable expansion of the Government education system began.

building operations could be resumed, rather more dignified premises were decided upon in order that the College could house worthily the 150 students in residence. Now that the girls' education was beginning to develop, it was felt, that they would profit from the idea, that the centre of girls' education was considered important enough to merit buildings at least as impressive as the boys' secondary schools. As the old buildings were of no interest either archaeologically or architecturally and were not really suited to their purpose, it was with few regrets, that we saw them replaced by modern kitchens and a covered colonnade, which gave the effect of plain cloisters round a quadrangle.[45] We had never seen the ghosts of the Khalifa's women haunting their old precincts and now even their shades were forgotten among the fresh, red bricks. Whatever nostalgia sentimentalists might have felt about demolishing the past, the students and Sudanese mistresses were undivided in their praise of their fine new premises. They saw them as a symbol of promise for the future.

## 10.2 Examinations

This promise included a growing freedom, which was far more easily demonstrated in the case of schoolmistresses than in other walks of life and might help to account for the overwhelming popularity of the profession. It was a far cry from the days, when Miss Evans went seeking for students, persuading them to come in. In 1921 five girls came, not perhaps unwillingly, but probably rather tremulously.[46] In 1947 over 300 applied for 40 vacant places. Great was the chagrin amongst girls and parents at the necessary refusals. Retrograde though it may sound to many, a competitive examination including an interview seemed the only way to deal with the situation. The six northern provinces were each allotted a quota of places in proportion to the number of schools they possessed and every attempt was

45. 'The new buildings in the Girls' Training College, Omdurman have made the whole into a very dignified and worthy institution. Much of the merit of this construction is that it has not only given some pleasant cloisters, adequate classroom space including demonstration room, but also kitchens fit to be a model instead of a matter of shame.' The new buildings of the Girls' Training College were completed and came into use at the end of 1948 but the ceremony for their official opening by the Governor-General was not held, as there had been minor political disturbances in the streets at that time (*ARDE*, 1948).

46. Attendance at the Girls' Training College, Omdurman was 1921 5, 1930 61, 1938 60, 1939 80, 1940 80, 1941 60, 1944 58, 1943 73, 1946 131, 1947 c.125 students. 245 girls applied for 40 vacancies in 1946; by the end of that year 50 students qualified and were appointed as elementary school teachers. In 1949 there were 156 students, 56 in the final year. 1 Gordon College diplomat had been trained for the first time and 29 students with intermediate school education were taking the course (*ARDE*).

made to pick out the most suitable girls. Until 1943 girls came on the nomination of the Governor of the Province; it was because this system depended entirely on recommendation from Sudanese officials and thus came to savour too strongly of nepotism, that we feared we might be losing valuable recruits. A test was an unoriginal method but we could think of nothing equally satisfactory. I may note in passing that for three years we also found room for two students each year from Aden to help with a programme rather behind our own.[47]

Imperfect though the examination method may be, it definitely toned up the standard of entrants. The girls not only came from all parts of the country but from all ranks of society. They must have finished the four year course at an elementary school and, as these were free and open to all, there could be a chance for any girls with ability and character.[48]

## 10.3 Teacher-training

On the whole they took their training seriously, so seriously in fact that they were disturbingly cast down by adverse criticism, however kindly offered.[49] That criticism must be given to people who knew so little was manifest but their enquiry about a practice lesson was not 'Was it a good lesson?' but 'Are you pleased with me?'

The main trouble about their practice lessons was that the content was so thin. Many of the students and the teachers were surprisingly good at imparting what little they knew and, rather because of their ignorance than despite it, were staggeringly sure of themselves as instructors. Others, of course, showed depressingly little of either of these characteristics. In the beginning teaching [the trainee teachers] could only be on a sort of a Lancasterian method[50] in which the girls were taught lessons in the Training College, which they endeavoured to reproduce with degrees of

47. 1947, 1948 and 1949. In 1949 four girls from Aden were being trained for service in their own country (*ARDE*,1949).
48. By 1948 the examination for entry into the Girls' Training College and Girls' Intermediate School was an accepted feature of the organisation, but it was still experimental in its method of procedure. The number of failures remained large. Kassala Province sent 13 of whom 9 passed. Most candidates were from Khartoum (*ARDE*, 1948).
49. 'Training College is of paramount importance in the whole education scheme ... fountain head of knowledge ... needs to be more than ordinarily careful concerning the ideas implanted in the students under its care ... danger of sending them out satisfied with the little they know rather than wanting to pursue further enquiry. The very natural pride of the immature in attainment is not to be deprecated altogether but it will prove very mischievous if it becomes disproportionate and is not tempered with a becoming modesty' (Sudan Government, Department of Education, *Note on Girls' Education in the Sudan*, December 1940).
50. Lancasterian method, named after Jospeh Lancaster, the educationalist.

conscientiousness varying according to the individuals. Progress came gradually but the difficulty still remained, that with subjects such as geography and nature study there could be little individual work for the girls, who had no means of acquiring information except from a teacher at the Training College.[51]

## 10.4 Lecturers

For many years the teachers at the Training College had to be chosen from among the best women, that the College itself had produced and this scholastically tended to a rather dreary round.[52]

Men's education had for many years been at a much higher level. In 1942,[53] when an attempt to use the services of women teachers from Egypt[54] had come to a dismal end, a bold experiment was made. Without any unnecessary advertisement of the fact an English-speaking schoolmaster of the educated type, who wore European clothes, was appointed in order to raise the standards. He was, of course, very carefully chosen and the result was so successful, that others were employed and also in the intermediate school. No-one who mattered questioned the propriety of the proceeding. There had always been elderly *sheikh*s in robes to teach religion but public opinion was apt to suspect men in trousers more than men in skirts with, from the tales one heard, no justification whatever. Parents' confidence was maintained by the fact, that the posts of Principal of the Girls' Training

51. 'Teachers handicapped by being denied access to any of the normal channels through which ideas can expand ... little social intercourse, no libraries, nor reference books, the elementary benefits of travel denied them ... [had a] tendency to regurgitate lecture noted from College *ad infinitum*' (Sudan Government, Department of Education. *Note on Girls' Education in the Sudan*, December 1940). At the Girls' Training College, successful refresher courses (for example for 20 teachers in 1948 and another for two weeks in August 1949) were held for elementary school teachers and another for intermediate school teachers, to help reduce such problems (*ARDE*, 1949).

52. Between 1921 and 1924 the staff consisted of a *sheikh* who had been educated at Gordon College, a Sudanese woman who taught embroidery, and two Egyptian teachers. 'The wonderful success which is attending the efforts of the Ministry of Education in Cairo indicates clearly how much can be done. The bulk of the work must be done by women. Women teachers must be procured, at first from Egypt, and then native teachers trained. Opposition will be encountered alike from the conservative Sudanese and the sceptical official, but I have no shadow of doubt that after more than fifteen years of legitimate delay, a beginning ought to be made and that forthwith.' (*ARDE*, 1913 (S.A.D. 657/1/20)).

53. Dr Beasley meant 1924 not 1942. Senior Egyptian teachers were no longer used after 1924 following the murder of Sir Lee Stack.

54. 'The most satisfactory staffing is a combination of British and Sudanese. Egyptian mistresses as a stopgap are unsatisfactory ... Therefore there is a need for proper planning for next 20 years' (Sudan Government, Department of Education, *Notes from a meeting to discuss girls' education in 1942*, 29.3.41, File no. 9.1.1/3).

College and the Headmistress of the Intermediate School were still filled by British women.[55]

Also in 1943 we were enabled to begin an expansion plan which, although not large in absolute numbers, did show in proportion very rapid growth. Soon at least fifty students a year were qualifying and being appointed at once in the elementary schools. The other great gain of the plan was that in 1944 specialists from England could be appointed including some for the subjects I listed above as so unsatisfactory.[56] As all the instruction had to be in Arabic this still entailed working through Sudanese masters and mistresses but it quickly became possible to effect some improvement in the factual content of lessons and a great deal in the manner of their delivery. It was also remarkable how soon specialists in Domestic Science, Art, Handwork and Physical Education could conduct a lesson themselves in a foreign language.[57]

## 11. Intermediate schools

Another experiment, which helped the Girls' Training College and was bound to assist still more in the upgrading of the teachers' level, was the institution of intermediate schools for girls. The first one was started in

55. Dr Ina Beasley acted as Head of the Girls' Training College from 17-23.2.40, when Miss Harvey was visiting Bakht-er-Ruda and Miss P.J. Pellow was a chickenpox contact. 'It gave me an insight into the difficulties of the schools and gave me an idea of the quality of the teachers here ... the whole attitude seems to me that they are too easily satisfied. It is enough to have qualified as a teacher and be in a classroom ... some effort should be made to spur on the staff here. I feel that the first stage of girls' education is probably nearing its end and it would be as well to guide it towards an effort to further development before it crystallises at this very low level' [17.2.40].

56. 'There is a lack of specialists at the Training College ... there seems no understanding nor recognition of the reasons for teaching the various subjects in the curriculum ... i.e. more than one way of filling in school hours ... present danger of girls' education becoming on the one hand a very thin accomplishment and on the other a thoroughly respectable way for girls to make money until they are married ... teachers' outlook has to become something far deeper than a vague idea that little girls who can spell are nicer than those who cannot. Another year's training would be beneficial at college' (Sudan Government, Department of Education, *Note on Girls' Education in the Sudan*, December 1940).

57. Biographical details of men and women working in girls' education in this period are given in Appendix IV.

Omdurman in 1940[58] to be, as in the case of boys' schools, a stage between the elementary and secondary levels, since children straight from the elemetary schools were not ready to go directly to secondary work. There was a great deal of argument before it was started. Advice was asked from leading Sudanese and British men regarding its advisability and opinion was very sharply divided. A feminist may be forgiven for pointing out that masculine opinions only are recorded on file but everyone was grateful subsequently to the influential men who managed to carry the day and have the school established.[59]

A simple boarding establishment on the model of the Girls' Training College was therefore erected across the road from the parent institution. In January 1940 it was opened with much pomp and ceremony by the Governor-General[60] and all the leading Sudanese and British men of the district attended the inaugural tea-party. This would have been difficult to arrange otherwise, as Sudanese wives could not go to a public function and, because of the war, a ban had been placed on the entry of British wives into the country. Women officials[61] of the Education Department were present, three in number.

## 11.1 Official functions at school

This is not an important point in itself but I noticed it then and it worried me all through my service. A certain amount of panache is of inestimable value among the routine of ordinary teaching work. But, when one needed a ceremony connected with women, it was difficult to give it quite the right flavour. In England a girls' school can always find a woman distinguished in her own right to give away prizes or open new buildings and men and women can mingle in whatever party is arranged. We often had generous help from the wives of officials, when we had a women's audience for a prize giving, but it was not quite what we wanted to impress on girls and mothers, when the distinguished visitor was there by reason of her

---

58. 'There were 40 applicants for admission in end 1939 to the special class in the Training College, which had already been formed as a nucleus for the school. This one school has been the only avenue for further education for the girls of sixty or more *kuttāb*s in all parts of Sudan. 30 places a year are available in 1942 with 105 applicants. Five free places per annum through a special exam but majority are prepared to pay full fees.' (Sudan Government, Department of Education, *Notes from a Meeting to discuss girls' education in 1942*, 29.3.41, File 9.1.1/3). Within ten years Intermediate Girls' Schools could offer the same facilities as those offered to boys.
59. 1940 52, 1941 78, 1942 108, 1943 125 students.
60. The Governor-General in January 1940 was Sir George Stuart Symes; 1908-1919 Sudan; 1934-1940 Governor-General; later Governor of Tanganyika.
61. Miss L.Y. Pode, Miss Sylvia Clark and Dr Ina Beasley.

husband's position. If, however, it started to be a men's party, then the women and girls could not come. We occasionally asked such British officials as the Director of Education or the Principal of the Gordon Memorial College to such ceremonies. Once an ill-tempered vernacular newspaper made an unfavourable comment but on the whole no-one minded visitors like this. It seemed a pity that we could not have the pleasure of parents applauding together their daughters' success. We were never quite sure how deep was a man's distrust of other men looking on his womenfolk. We found in practice men and women did see more of one another than the strict theory suggested. While, however, the distrust was avowed, we could only refrain from flouting it and hope it would quietly disappear, as the natural contacts inevitable in school life proved it groundless.

This distrust had lain at the back of many of the arguments against starting the Girls' Intermediate School. Some fathers said, that once girls began to approach puberty and their figures began to develop, men would look at them with lustful eyes in the streets on their way to school. That it was the men's attitude which should be changed was a point they soon countered. The fathers were more realistic; they argued that men were in fact lustful and the only hindrance to their contaminating glances was to keep the girls inside high walls. Having a boarding house in the Girls' Intermediate School overcame this difficulty for some pupils but others were allowed to walk to school every day, braving public glare, although they might be as much as thirteen or fourteen years old.

A British headmistress[62] was in charge of the school and she taught English as a foreign language to the girls. A respectable old *sheikh* of retiring age assisted with Arabic and religion. The model of the Girls' Training College was followed by appointing one of the most outstanding elementary schoolmistresses to help with the boarding houses and to teach geography and history under the supervision of the Headmistress. An Egyptian mistress trained in Cairo taught arithmetic and elementary science but proved unadaptable, or at any rate unwilling to do anything else. Scholastically it was most unsatisfactory for the first year or two. The burden of preparing a subordinate's lessons and then explaining them in detail in Arabic had to be the unenviable lot of the Headmistress in this early stage. Two classes each of about twenty girls, who were experimented on in this way, responded incredibly well to their unorthodox instruction.

---

62. Headmistresses of the Intermediate school, Omdurman included Miss Sylvia Clark from 1940 to 1949; Mrs K.M.E. Wood from 1950 to 1954; Miss Lilian M. Passmore from 1955 to 1958.

Some did not complete the course but others reached a stage, when they sat with success in 1949 for the Cambridge School Leaving Certificate.

One of the experimental aspects was the payment of fees. Elementary education for girls in Government schools was entirely free. Parents were willing to make sacrifices to pay a boy's fees as the resultant success in life might be commensurate. It was quite a new idea to pay for a daughter. The school was heavily subsidised by the Government and the fees charged were £6 a year for day-girls and £8 a year for boarders. It is much to the credit of those forty fathers, that they were prepared to support their principles in hard cash, for it was with their daughters that post-elementary education began to take place in the general scheme. Some of the fathers did believe passionately, that more and more education for women was the country's salvation; some were lukewarm and felt that their daughters might as well stay at school a bit longer, as girls did not get married so young now. But whatever the reasons they did send their children and they did pay their fees, thus establishing a precedent which might have taken many weary years to establish, if this first effort had been a failure.

**11.2 Wartime disruptions**

Despite their support the school had many perils to surmount in its infancy. It had started in January 1940 in shining new buildings. By the time the children re-assembled after the summer recess the Italians were on and in some places over the frontier. The Army was laying claim to all sorts of educational buildings, although it already had a War Office very pleasantly situated on the embankment, in which we could comfortably have run four schools. Nevertheless through various requisitioning shuffles the Girls' Intermediate School had to leave its own premises and be doubled up with the Girls' Training College.[63] The war in our part of the world was brief and it was the Allies' first success. It caused us more discomfort and inconvenience than really acute suffering. We felt very much cut off,

63. 'Demand for secondary education was an entirely new feature and was not envisaged in 1940 ... largely taken for granted that secondary education is a natural development of the Government schemes for girls. 1943 some secondary education was provided for 2 girls who had completed the Intermediate course. 4 possibles in 1944 ... Parents willing to pay substantial fees ... even these demands are not satisfied due to cramped buildings and lack of staff. The conditions in which the Training College is working at present are such that we cannot provide enough teachers even for existing schools if we are to work at the normal distribution of 4 teachers to a full school. By sharing quarters with the Training College the present Intermediate School is cramped to such a degree which hinders proper development of this one institution ... therefore no provision can be made for real secondary work and the present temporary arrangements can be on a small scale only' (Sudan Government, Department of Education, *Notes from a Meeting to discuss girls' education in 1942*, 29.3.41, File 9.1.1/3).

especially as letters took months to arrive. The shops were emptied but real privation we never knew. Although the first few months were worrying, life was physically peaceful. Nevertheless I resented the Army's habits. I was never sure if in rescuing us from the enemy, they needed to have taken up quite so much room. It was a difficult point to argue, when Kassala, for example, was in enemy hands, since Kassala is only a few hours' drive from Khartoum.

I should have felt more resentful if the infant Girls' Intermediate School had been suffocated so early, but fortunately this did not happen.[64] In fact when a year later the Principal of the Girls' Training College[65] left to be married and the Headmistress of the Intermediate School[66] had to run both institutions there was a slight gain in having both in the same yard.

Everyone had difficulties of accommodation and equipment in those days and accounts of other peoples' are as boring as bomb stories. It proved important for girls' education, that this first Intermediate School was able to withstand these troubles, or it would have meant a much longer and more tedious road, before we could have even envisaged better education for the elementary mistresses and through this the general improvement in the quality of the whole.[67]

### 11.3 Other Intermediate schools

In August 1944, however, the Girls' Intermediate School was back in its own buildings in Omdurman and plans were afoot for more Intermediate schools in the provinces.[68]

---

64. By the end of 1943 there were 4 full classes in the Intermediate School and 107 girls competed for 30 places in the first year. At the beginning of 1944 and 1945 there was a double entry of 40 girls, bringing the total number of students to 120. By 1949 the desire for post-elementary schooling was increasing. 679 candidates took the entrance exams in March 1949 for admission to the Girls' Training College and in August for admission to the Girls' Intermediate School. 737 candidates took the exam for the 1950 intake in December 1949, to give them more time to sift for results (*ARDE*, 1949).
65. Principals of the Girls' Training College, Omdurman included 1923-33 Miss J.D. Evans; 1934-35 Miss D. Evans; 1935-39 Miss L.Y. Pode; 1939-43 Miss E.M. Harvey; Miss K.S.L. Clark and Dr I. Beasley (wartime temporary duty); 1946-47 Miss L.M. Witherspoon; 1947-49 Miss E. Hodgson later Mrs R. Hodgkin; 1950-54 Mrs H.M. Wibberley; from 1954 Ahmed El Bashir El Tayib.
66. Miss Sylvia Clark.
67. Entrance by 1948 was by examination for the Girls' Training College with 189 taken from Khartoum, 38 from Blue Nile, 25 from Kordofan, 9 from Darfur, 5 from Kassala. 10 free places were allotted to each intermediate school for entry to the Girls' Training College.
68. The intermediate school was something of a snob school, with a high proportion of its pupils from 'the best families'. In 1941 there was no immediate extension contemplated. 'Possibly Omdurman should carry a second school, but better in Provinces e.g. Medani or El

These were started in 1946, one in El Obeid[69] on the Omdurman model and the one in Wad Medani with the Domestic Science bias mentioned above.[70] These too had their vicissitudes in the beginning but settled down after a year or two each with a character of its own.[71] One of the great troubles, reflected all through the service, was early manifest here. This was the dislocation in staffing among both British and Sudanese mistresses. Just when a school seemed to be running smoothly someone would get married and leave. Marriage was in theory and in practice no bar to service but it did not always happen, that the individuals concerned wished to remain.

It seemed a far cry from the timidities of 1940 that, despite a world war, in seven years this post-elementary stage should have become so readily accepted. One of my most vivid impressions was the gain in spontaneity and cheerfulness among the pupils during those years. The intermediate schools had boarding facilities for practically all the children. They had expensive buildings set in wide grounds and it seemed as if the girls had an additional sense of freedom. They scampered about, particularly in Wad Medani, where there was enough water for lawns, and they found special interests and built up little traditions. In El Obeid they early developed a taste for netball, a game entirely new to them before, and a pride in talking English. This they would do to one another inside and outside the classroom, while visitors, always welcome, were doubly so, if they could be a help for the exercise of this new and exciting accomplishment.

In Wad Medani each girl had a small hanging locker for her clothes and personal possessions and there it early became a matter of pride, that these should always be in perfect order. It is easy to understand this sense of possession in girls who had practically all lived in rather cramped surroundings of varying degrees of tidiness. There would seldom have been any corner of the house which a girl could call her own and the joy of ownership soon stimulated a remarkable habit of neatness. Naturally in a

Obeid. They agreed that more intermediate schooling was needed. 5 places were reserved each year in the intermediate school for prospective trainees in teachers training.' (Sudan Government, Department of Education, *Notes from the meeting to discuss girls' education in 1942*, 29.3.41).

69. The headmistresses at El Obeid included Miss M. Beevers (c.1945-47); Mrs K.M.E. Wood (1947-1949); Miss M.D.G. Edwards (1949-51); Miss P. Ibbetson (1952-55); By 1953 Miss M.V. Baker was Headmistress of Atbara Intermediate School and Miss N.J. Holt was Headmistress at Meridi Intermediate School.

70. Wad Medani opened in 1946 under the headship of Miss M.P Burns (1944-46); Mrs Muriel McBain (née Irish) 1946-50; 1950- 55 Miss M.B. Brown, BSc. Household and Social Sciences, University of London (S.A.D. 658/5/1). 'The very large demand for admission quickly dispelled any doubts which may have been entertained as to their popularity.' (*ARDE*, 1946). In 1949 a training section opened at Wad Medani for 15 students (*ARDE*, 1949).

71. By 1952 there were 5 girls' intermediate schools, but by 1962 there were 32.

Domestic Science school needlework and handicrafts were very carefully taught. What had not been expected was that girls, who often came from homes where the women could not handle a needle, would find so much joy in stitching for its own sake. Much of their spare time was spent in making clothes for their small brothers and sisters or in elaborate embroidery. New designs in smocking or fresh ideas for knitting were seized on more eagerly than a story-book. It seemed sometimes as if the creative urge, dammed up in the women for so long, was coming out with extra intensity through this outlet, for in the other realms of art their opportunities were still very limited.

## 12. Secondary schools

What was rather heady about all this was that, although it had taken twenty years to get past the elementary stage, in some places the uprush was violent now that it had come. There were one or two fathers in 1942 and 1943 who, after the completion of the course in Omdurman, were not content with this addition to their daughters' schooling. Naturally Sheikh Babikr Bedri as the 'Father of Girls' Education' constantly urged us to [set up] a secondary school but our resources in personnel were too strained.[72]

### 12.1 Unity High School[73]

For the time being we were able to made use of a unique institution in

72. There was little demand for secondary education for girls until the mid-1940s. By 1952 there were 25 places in one Government secondary school. By 1962 there were 350 places in 5 Government secondary schools. Yet shortage of resources continued to be a problem even after attempts to meet the demands were made. For example, in 1954 the secondary school course was reduced from five to four years.

73. Unity High School was founded for the C.M.S. by Bishop Llewellyn Gwynne. In 1905 the C.M.S. built the school buildings. By 1909 there were 148 children. The headmistress, Miss Bewley, was mentioned with great respect in the *ARDE* (S.A.D. 657/1/12,19). In 1928 the school was taken over by a Fellowship of Christian Churches to be a secondary school for girls and the Unity High School was opened. Before 1928 Khartoum C.M.S. School just gave primary education (see L.H. Gwynne and others, *Unity High School for Girls, 1928-1949: Twenty-One Years of Progress*). In 1946 10 of the 12 candidates in the Cambridge School Certificate examination from Unity High School were successful (*ARDE*, 1946).

Khartoum.[74] Considering the girls' state of development at that time this was probably of more help to them than an extension of the type of Government schools they knew.

Away back in 1928 a private school for secondary education of Christian girls had been started under the aegis of the Anglican Bishop.[75] Its peculiar interest was that it arose from the banding together of all the various communities, who professed Christianity in any form, except the Roman Catholics who ran convent schools of their own.[76] Thus there were Syrians, Greeks, Copts, Armenians, Lebanese and girls of mixed origin all sharing in a type of education based on the English model of a day school. The language of instruction was English and as far as possible English mistresses were provided.[77] It was known as Unity High School, as its aim was union and not mission work, but its basis was Christian. To those of us, who have grown used to doctrines of secular education, it is a little hard to understand the courage that it needed for a Sudanese father not only to give his daughter more education than most people thought necessary for a girl, but to oppose the influential members of his family in sending a Muslim girl to an avowedly Christian establishment.[78]

The gain to the individual girls was, of course, enormous and through them to the circles of their acquaintance. They began to glimpse and taste a freedom of which they had formerly had no knowledge. Mixing with non-Arabic speaking girls with an entirely different home background broadened their horizons and gave them an aim, which they would have

74. In 1916 the Director of Education sent girls to Khartoum C.M.S. School (later called Unity High School) when they had finished the four year course at Rufaa, for a further two years' teacher-training. Um Selima Bedri, one of Babikr Bedri's family, was one of the first. Sitt Abuha Mustafa, another relative of Babikr Bedri's who was teaching at Rufaa, was the first teacher to go to Khartoum C.M.S. school for teacher-training. In 1944 the Sudan Government was sending 12 girls to Unity High School for secondary schooling.

75. Rt. Rev. Bishop Llewellyn H. Gwynne (b.1863-d.1957); Educated at Swansea Grammar school and St John's Hall, Canterbury; one of the earliest pioneers for girls' education in Sudan; arrived in Khartoum in 1899 accompanied by Dr Harper of C.M.S. Old Cairo Hospital to work for the Church Missionary Society; 1905-08 Archdeacon of the Sudan; 1908-20 Bishop of Khartoum; 1920-45 Anglican Bishop in Egypt and the Sudan.

76. For further information on private and Catholic schools see Appendices III and V.

77. Staff at Unity High School included the Principal (before 1938) Miss E.C.M. de Peyer, M.A.; Miss E.K.W. Maxwell, B.A. 27.12.38 brought from Egypt with two additional women teachers sent out by the C.M.S., Headmistress until 26.2.48. She continued to teach needlework, R.I. and other subjects at the school and in Omdurman from 1949; Miss Wilson, Principal from 26.2.48; Miss H. Elphinstone Junor, mistress around 1940.

78. 'Need to start secondary subjects in Omdurman Intermediate School. At present they live in the Intermediate School and go every day to Unity High School ... not very satisfactory with science and maths not up to standard and it is a Christian foundation unpalatable to many parents.' (Sudan Government, Department of Education, *Note from a meeting to discuss girls' education in 1942*, 29.3.41, File 9.1.1/3).

been much longer in seeking without this help. Naturally the experiment did not pass off without minor strains and stresses but the upshot of it all was another leap forward. Even when the Government began its own secondary classes[79] this contact remained. There were girls who had known another type of school and the interest in it had spread.

## 12.2 Secondary classes at Omdurman Intermediate school

There were still parents who could not bring themselves to venture so far afield. They had the same mistrust for schools of another religion, that is felt among different denominations in Europe. They knew and trusted the Government schools, since so far nothing cataclysmic had happened by reason of sending girls to school. Very tentatively these parents began to ask for more schooling but of the brand they were accustomed to.

After the recruiting of British staff from England in 1944 the difficulty of who was to teach a secondary class was resolved, as secondary work to be parallel with the boys had to be English. Room was found in the Omdurman Intermediate school for a class of twelve girls. They were some of our original pupils still anxious for further education. The position [of secondary classes] was to be reviewed at the end of two years. At the end of two years the class was still there; it had not melted away through apathy or marriage demands. Another small class was recruited and the following year a larger one. The school had laid hold on people's imagination; it appealed to parental pride but in part to a sense of wonder. 'I want my daughter to have the best education she can get.' And then there would come a look that was in a way slightly incredulous, the unvoiced, 'To think that I have a daughter with Secondary School education. To think that such a thing could happen in the Sudan.'

79. Secondary classes were begun at the Girls' Intermediate School in 1945 with a class of 12 fourth year girls in 1944-46 but contacts with Unity High School remained strong. Once 'the secondary section left the Intermediate School buildings in 1949 to separate quarters, undivided attention could be given in the Intermediate School to the improvement of the curricula, syllabuses and methods used' (*ARDE*, 1949).

## 12.3 Omdurman Secondary School for Girls[80]

By the beginning of 1949 there were huge piles of bricks and stone at the back of the Intermediate School in Omdurman. There had been heated arguments on various planning boards but no-one had really grudged what was felt to be due to the girls.[81] All the space between the Intermediate School and the river road, some 110,000 square metres of good building land in the best residential quarter of the town, which could have brought in a substantial revenue, was nevertheless reserved for the development of girls' institutions. No mere loaning of old houses. Some handsome buildings designed by the Public Works Department were begun forthwith.

It was an exhilarating feeling to walk all round this and survey our estate, exhilarating that is to say on most days. I can remember one, when a duststorm blew up suddenly and, looking round, I began to wonder what there was to rhapsodise about. The whole expanse was broken land, mostly gravel of an unpicturesque type and rather reminiscent of slag heaps; except that after a time dandelions and grass and willow herb may appear on a slag heap but nothing ever grew here. There were no trees, no mosses. The buildings were being erected on flat pieces of land and in between were great indentations, rugged and uneven. Yet on bright, fresh mornings, when the wind came down from the North and the Nile was blue, it was easy to remember the value of the river. Pumps and an irrigation scheme had been promised within the first year or two, to be completed in instalments. One lot of buildings to begin with, and room for others as required; netball pitches at first, then the uneven sides of the *khor* terraced for tennis courts; a gymnasium, a prayer room; space for hockey or cricket and last of all the large *khor* at the north to be turned into a swimming pool. It seemed a

80. The first secondary school for girls opened in September 1949 when the secondary section left the Girls' Intermediate School to separate quarters with 67 pupils, 27 in the first year. 9 girls took their School Certificate Examination in December 1949 (*ARDE*, 1949). Headmistresses at the Girls' Secondary School, Omdurman included 1949-52 Miss F.E.O. Gourlay; 1955-56 Mrs K.M.E. Wood.

81. 'Secondary education had now become a definite part of the system and public demand is insistent on the opening of a full secondary school as soon as possible' (*ARDE*, 1946). By 1948 there was no longer any doubt about demand for this school. Girls who had completed intermediate education in non-Government schools were coming in increasing numbers to enquire about the possibility of entry to secondary school and were prepared to work in Class IV Intermediate to increase their chances of acceptance (*ARDE*, 1948). Yet even in 1949 some British advisers doubted the wisdom of higher education for Sudanese girls (see Royston-Piggott, P.J., 'Higher Education for Sudanese Women', *Journal of Education*, vol 83, 1951, p.140).

worthy plan to bequeath to our successors,[82] if the British officials should
have left the country, before it was completed. For the women it marked a
stage in the growth of their dignity.[83]

## 13. Gordon Memorial College

The highest level reached by an educational institution in the Sudan at this
time was the Gordon Memorial College,[84] which had acquired University
College status and has since become a University.[85] Women students had
been admitted to this from Unity High School but although some of the
original Secondary class in the Government School were anxious to join,
none of them would be ready before 1950. The ambition and zest were
there, however, and this aim was in time fulfilled, since that date an
increasing number taking a full part in University studies.[86]

## 14. Adult education

Equal zest but ambition of a humbler sort was to be found at the extreme
other end of the scale. These were night schools for women in the towns and
adult classes in some villages. Just before the war there had been odd and

---

82. Although Dr Beasley advised against slow development of secondary education for girls,
the second girls' secondary school, the Khartoum Girls' Secondary School, did not start until
1958 (under the headship of Miss Lilian M. Passmore) so there were few women qualified for
careers at the time of Independence (see Passmore, Lilian M., 'Women's Progress in the
Sudan', (pseud. M. More), *African World*, April 1958; Sanderson, L.M.P., 'The Khartoum
Girls' Secondary School', *Oversea Education*, Jan 1963; Sanderson, L.M.P., 'Girls' Education
in the Sudan', *African World*, Feb 1963; Sanderson, L.M.P., 'Careers for Women in the Sudan'
*African Women*, June 1963; Beasley, Ina, *op. cit.*).
83. See also Geary, Dr C.L.H., 'The Education of Women and Girls in the Anglo-Egyptian
Sudan', *Gaskiya Corporation*, 1950, pp.5490-8.
84. Gordon Memorial College, 1902-1951. Dr Beasley was a member of Gordon Memorial
College Council.
85. University College of Khartoum in 1951, affiliated to the University of London taking
London external degrees; established as an independent university in 1956. Khartoum
University Act, June 1956.
86. The first woman was admitted to Gordon Memorial College in 1945. Faṭima Talib was the
first woman to gain a B.A. external degree from London University at Gordon Memorial
College. She was also the first feminist leader in Sudan and founded the Educated Girls'
Assocation, which was disbanded in 1949. There was one woman doctor, Khalda Zaher, who
had qualified from the Kitchener School of Medicine. She was also the first chairwoman of the
Association of Sudanese Women, which started in Omdurman about 1948. By 1957 there were
25 women graduates. (*The Times*, 20.11.53 (S.A.D. 658/5/5); Hall, Marjorie, and Ismail,
Bakhita Amin, *Sisters under the Sun*, 1981, pp.110-11).

unrelated instances of women's classes in girls' schools, which had depended entirely on the initiative and energy of the local elementary teachers. The latter had never been trained to teach anyone but young girls and their idea of adult classes was generally a repetition of things which had been taken from the elementary school syllabus with a concentration on cake-making. Rationing of sugar and of grain put an end to fancy cooking, and in any case classes tended to be of rather spasmodic growth. Anything approaching the Village Women's Institute idea was not practicable because the women had nothing of their own to contribute, having had no contact with any sort of craft. Even the simplest W.I. programmes would have been outside their scope. In Darfur there was grass-weaving but that and cotton spinning on a hand spindle was all that could be mustered and that not among many of the women, and only in some districts. Of other skills there was a complete lack, even to the extent that many who came to the classes had never held a needle. Obtaining materials for any sort of work, sewing, cookery, laundry, crafts was extremely difficult during the war and just after but the biggest hurdle of all was the want of informed direction.[87]

### 14.1 Rural adult education and the Um Gerr project

Among our British recruits to the Service in 1944 was a trained social worker[88] with a Domestic Science degree. After a year of preparation in Omdurman she went to the work, for which she had been appointed, in a district composed of a group of villages along the White Nile.[89] I have mentioned elsewhere the alternative livelihood schemes made necessary by the Jebel Auliya Dam.[90] Um Gerr was one of these, where only a few years before the villagers had been semi-nomadic. The important point here is that this small-scale social experiment was launched in such primitive conditions. Its connection with girls' education was that among the various

87. After 1950 adult education was controlled by a section of the Ministry of Education when the Department of Adult Education was created.
88. Miss G.E. Richards, Social Welfare Worker based at Bakht-er-Ruda, began work at Um Gerr in September 1945 (27.9.44 first appointment), when a girls' school was opened to serve as a centre for adult work; May 1948 passed Higher Standard Arabic exam.
89. Um Gerr, an island about 30 km south of Dueim (Nasr El Hag Amin and Amin, B.E., 'Mass Education in the Anglo-Egyptian Sudan', *Mass Education Bulletin*, Vol 1, no. 2, March 1950, pp.27-30; see also *ARDE*, 1948).
90. White Nile Alternative Livelihood Schemes Board (W.N.A.L.S.). See *Um Gerr Experiment* (mimeo pamphlet), Khartoum, 1948; Sudan Government, *First Progress Report on Um Gerr Experiments* (mimeo pamphlet), Khartoum, 1951; Mandour al-Mahdi, 'Adult education in the Rural Sudan', *Panorama*, IV, 2, 1962, p.23. Geoffrey Hawkesworth also gave a lecture 'An experiment in rural development (Um Gerr)'.

schemes for self-help in all phases of village life there had to be one for teaching hygiene to the women and helping in the ordering of their homes.

Meetings were arranged in the women's houses and rapidly became very popular. They were conducted by this British official and by a Sudanese ex-schoolmistress,[91] who had been given training in midwifery and nursing. It had been a rather difficult task to persuade her to undertake this training. She had recently been widowed and had to support a daughter and a niece. The opening was there and she had the courage to take it. Then after two or three years she had the satisfaction of feeling herself really a pioneer in the welfare of Sudanese women and a leader of others of the small band, who followed her example. The objections, which I listed above to the nursing profession, held back Sudanese women for a long time, although they were all ready to affirm the usefulness of the work.

Both she and the British official lived in one of the villages in a native style [mud-brick] house as headquarters but moved to other places for meetings. Physically it was most exhausting work and called for great resources of tact and patience. In the beginning the women who came to the meetings were encouraged to sew.[92] No doubt the educational value of little embroidered mats has been discussed by the psychologists in learned tomes but the demonstration of their value in this experiment was most marked. The women were taught sewing on the nursery principle with large stitches and brightly coloured silks. Their mats were things of tremendous joy and pride and induced in their owners a desire to keep them clean. This led gradually on to an increased interest in cleanliness generally. Despite the rationing, arrangements were made for soap to be sold at the classes and trade was brisk. When the group advanced to garment-making, this desire to look after things which they themselves had made continued and could be turned to good account. Cooking lessons came next, using materials which were easily obtainable locally. The women generally prepared a lunch for their own consumption but administrative difficulties began to arise, as the fame of these well-cooked lunches spread. Visitors tended to arrive in un-manageable numbers. A few had originally been welcome in order to scatter the gospel of better living, but it was disseminated rather more rapidly than had been expected.

91. Sitt Dar al-Gelaal, a trained teacher. In addition Mekki Abbas was Adult Education Officer, W.N.A.L.S. (Um Gerr) in 1944.
92. According to Miss G.E. Richards, most women asked to be taught to sew. Apart from embroidered cloths, they made *tagia*s, *tobe*s and sheets. They were also encouraged to bring their own handwork—*zaf* (fibrework), *birsh* (mat-making) or wool-spinning (Richards, G.E., 'Adult Education amongst Countrywomen: An Experiment at Um Gerr', *Sudan Notes and Records*, XXIX, 1948, pp.225-7).

In the informal gatherings there were boundless opportunities for talks about health in all sorts of practical ways. Later on a Health Visitor[93] from England was appointed and ordinary clinics and child welfare schemes introduced. After three years the team moved on to another district with the idea of going back after a year or so to see how the women had managed on their own.

By this time the difficulty of prestige, which had made the original worker hesitate, had been deflected by calling the helpers 'Teachers of Adults'. Then half a dozen schoolmistresses took part in a similar scheme in the Gezira,[94] the cotton growing area which had been settled for at least twenty years. Much the same plan was followed and was received with possibly even greater enthusiasm. It is difficult to give an impression of the concentration and determination of quite illiterate women over this matter of stitching a small cloth. They would sit on grass mats on the floor in a small mud-brick room and chat away, while they laboured with this unusual task of threading a needle and then putting it in the right place in the stuff. At frequent intervals a baby tucked in the folds of a *tobe* would be suckled. Some would wait patiently for help; others would be clamorous for attention; but in all the classes I saw there was no-one who gave up in despair, although there were many who seemed at first unteachable. The radiance of at last getting the needle in the right place and the excitement of moving on to a floral design, are, of course, parallelled in much educational work. Here, however, the attitude was uncomplicated and the setting unusual. Even if the first enthusiasm should wane, it showed the possibilities on which further developments could be suggested.

We were always very insistent that these were experiments and were very conscious, that the restricted area in such an ocean of illiteracy was bound to result in a quicker falling off, than if we had been able to strengthen one district by similar work in the neighbouring ones. The difficulty here even

93. Miss Hegan, a qualified Health Visitor, began working in January 1947, with the assistance of Sitt Um al-Hassan, to advise on and work out plans for Child Welfare aspects of adult education.
94. In September 1948 a three month training course began with four mistresses for the extension of Adult Education work to the southern Gezira. They were to be known as *mu'allimat al-kubar*. Two experienced elementary teachers were persuaded to take part. This was a great step forward as formerly they had regarded the work as too lowly for educated women. In the same year the first Literacy Campaign among adults was launched by the Publications Bureau (see Spelman, N.G., 'Women's work in the Gezira, Sudan', *Oversea Education*, Vol 26, 2, 1954, pp.66-69; see also *ARDE*, 1948; S.A.D. 658/5/6). In 1949 social welfare work in the Gezira was extended to include Wad Namaan, Remeitab and Hosh blocks. Classes were in needlework, cookery, reading and writing (*ARDE*, 1949). Fatima Zakariya, originally a school teacher from Omdurman, is to be noted for her contributions to adult education from 1961 to 1981, especially in the Gezira on similar schemes to this pioneer work.

more than in ordinary school work was one of personalities. We needed scores of workers from England to make any impression on the country as a whole but we had one. That no-one could have been more suited to the work or could have tackled it with such understanding and gusto was a piece of great good fortune. In all the plans for the development of Africa schemes of this sort recur and there can be no doubt, that they are of the utmost value, but they are expensive and they do not show immediate results. Moreover the strain on personnel is many times greater than in social work in England. To be a social worker on an island in the White Nile was to live in uncomfortable resthouses, never speaking one's own language and cut off by hundreds of miles and bad communications from anything approaching distractions.

I may have dwelt too long on this digression but, if the schools were not to lose a great deal of their value, steps had to be taken to stimulate the girls' mothers out of the tradition of just sitting. The response of the women was pathetic. They said openly how sorry they were, that they had not been educated and they seemed to acquire a small, queer pride in realising that the Government was prepared to take so much trouble over them. This was important, since increasing self-respect was really a large part of our job at all levels. It is an Arab custom to say to a visitor, 'You have honoured us'. In these cases it was no mere formality of expression. I think the women did regard these visits as an honour and grew a very little in stature for that reason. One group said to me in gratitude, 'Have you really come all the way from Khartoum just to see us?'

It seemed odd to go back to Khartoum immediately after such an inspection and find another experiment going on. In 1948 the first Legislative Assembly came into being and in some cases the members sitting in the House were husbands and relatives of the women with whom we had just been working. I am not suggesting that this is an argument against a Legislative Assembly but it does prove how necessary it is to adjust one's standard of values in these circumstances.

**14.2 Urban adult education**

We did not, however, confine our activities to village women. It is tempting in an agricultural country to talk only of rural life and make picturesque schemes for village communities. I have even known a few D.C.'s who wanted to educate the daughters of tribesmen only. Merchants do not perhaps make the same appeal to administrators as the sturdy cultivator or the dignified tribal *sheikh*. Fortunately we were only concerned with women and girls and we tried to educate them, wherever we could find them. Little girls were little girls to us and we were not concerned about their fathers' status. If anything, in towns the women's lives were more circumscribed than in the villages. There was some work in a rural household, which had to be done by the women. The theory was that they were shut away from other men but in practice there was a good bit more ordinary social intercourse than this theory suggests. There would not be mixed parties as a general rule but a decent, respected man could in matters of business exchange a few words with someone else's women-kind without scandal. Moreover in a village everyone was known to everyone else and the ties of kinship were widespread. Certainly a company of women seemed always to be able to come to a meeting in the morning in a village; in the towns they said that they could not come out until after dusk.

After the sporadic efforts, which I have touched on above, night schools for women were started in a fairly orderly way in 1946. They were under the guidance of a British official and some Sudanese schoolmistresses working voluntarily with later a senior Sudanese[95] having the main responsibility. A small class in one of the elementary schools seemed suddenly to take the popular fancy and by 1948 in the Three Towns the numbers attending were running into hundreds.[96] They were not organised by such a carefully handpicked team as the village centres and for this reason their success was all the more encouraging. When they became too much for two or three voluntary workers, small payments were made to women, who were either former schoolmistresses or professional dressmakers or mission-educated women who were not trained teachers. Very often for illiterate women, who wanted to learn to read, teachers of this type were not so terrifying as a brilliant, young woman, fresh from the Training College, rather sure and proud of herself.

The schools professed to teach anything which women wanted to learn. There must have been a very close bond between teachers and clients for the former to be so certain of what demands would be made. In the first place it was generally needlework and knitting, then cookery of rather a fancy kind, jams, cakes, puddings. A certain number wanted reading and writing, it might be in order to keep up with a daughter at elementary school.[97] Lectures on hygiene and child welfare were always popular, particularly when conducted by the Sudanese staff midwives of the Midwifery School.

95. Sitt Nafissa Awad al-Karim.
96. There was unexpected growth in the desire for education among women in the Three Towns. In January 1948 there were 2 night schools and 7 by the end of the year, with possibly over 600 attending. In 1948 adult education had a grant of £E1,400. In 1949 work at the night schools in Omdurman continued in 7 centres and some of the students were becoming literate (*ARDE*, 1949).
97. Even in 1956 only 4.4% of women could read and write in Sudan (S.A.D. 658/5/6) and by 1966-67 only 21% of girls (40% boys) aged 7 were in elementary schools.

Religion was occasionally asked for and one very old lady came and said, that she wanted to learn to say her prayers properly before she died.

The meetings were held in the elementary schools instead of the *sheikh*s' guest rooms as in the villages. It was equally humble and with the artificial light gave something of the impression one used to have from W.E.A. classes held in 'board school' buildings. It is the slightly depressing atmosphere of a classroom without children but filled in compensation with the spirit of people, who have, even if dimly, realised the blanks in their lives and are fumbling for a means to satisfy their hunger.

It would have been unkind to deny them, while we were able to spare the means whereby they could be given help. But neither these humble experiments for the mothers nor the grandeur of the Secondary School were the core of the education which we wanted for Sudanese girls. These were essential pieces of the structure but the main concentration of effort was in the spreading of elementary schools throughout the country and raising the standards of the work undertaken there.

I have set all this out in some detail, because, as I said in the first chapter, a time may come, when people may want to know our conscious aims, whether they approve of them or not. One point to be noticed is that these were deliberate decisions taken by the Government in the interests of the people of the country and we, as officials, were allowed considerable freedom in the interpretation of them within financial limits. Bound up with it all were some special problems outside the classroom, which I have illustrated in the next chapter.

# Chapter IX

# Special problems

To list inadequate finance and shortage of teachers as first problems is to invite the rejoinder, that there was nothing peculiar to the Sudan in those. What was different for us was the scale and the conditions in which these were felt. Firstly the Sudan was a poor country and tried in those years to live within its means.[1] Self-evident though this may be, it is often forgotten that because of this education had to receive such allocation of resources as the budget would permit, and, as this was naturally no vast sum, spending was restricted in proportion. The point to stress is that the choice did not lie between one type of schooling and another; there was no need for the passionate arguments which party politics in Europe engender. Decisions had to be made about the number of schools, that could be afforded and which places would have to wait, until they could be served.[2] That for this reason the system should develop gradually and not hastily was not always a disadvantage but the actual rate was dictated more by financial than educational considerations.[3]

1. £1,275,000 was allotted to education in the first development budget made by the British Government in 1946. Even if simplicity was not desirable for its own sake, it had to be the keynote, for in those days the country only had a total budget of £11 million.
2. 'The continued prevalence of war-time conditions ... makes it extremely improbable that any ambitious program of further expansion and reform can be undertaken before 1945 ... but need to plan and prepare ...'. There was Departmental discussion on girls' education at Headquarters in October 1943 with the Provinces Education Officers and senior staff from Bakht-er-Ruda ... leading to small committee to examine proposals in greater detail (*The future development of girls' education in the Sudan*, 25.7.43, File no. DE 9.1.1/3). Even in 1948 the lack of adequate buildings was the greatest setback to the general expansion plan (*ARDE*, 1948).
3. After 1946 when the Advisory Council for the Northern Sudan was established, there was more pressure to concentrate on boys' education to prepare them for imminent Independence, so funds were insufficient for the expansion of girls' education. The 1946 Ten Year Plan was designed to make more rapid advances in girls' elementary and intermediate education. A revised plan was submitted to the Government early in 1949.

# 1. Special grants

When such bodies as the Colonial and Welfare Development Fund began its distribution of aid,[4] to be followed after the war by other donating organisations, the tendency was to earmark gifts for definite projects to capture the public imagination. Possibly the rather showy nature of such a gesture as a university had a psychological value in addition to the actual benefit of conferring a centre for higher learning. I remember, however, the occasion, when the British Government made a grant of £1 million for the University College of Khartoum. It was a generous recognition of trust in the Sudan's future but I could not repress a tinge of envy. Even a few thousands would have provided the girls' elementary schools with a so much firmer basis. At the time, however, I was a member of the Council of the Gordon Memorial College and required in that capacity to keep my mind attuned to the needs of higher education. Nevertheless it was not easy to sit quietly round the table, while high-ranking officers from English Universities made resounding speeches, advising the Council not to spare money, to pay really large salaries to academic staff in order to ensure the best. Their arguments were flawless but they never visited the villages and saw how sparsely the schools were scattered, and from what foundations the students emerged. Where the emphasis should be placed brings a perennial debate but it was of moment in our endeavour, as we were most anxious not to encourage an unbalanced arrangement, especially with the object lesson before us of the unsatisfactory results of some of the Indian universities.

# 2. Shortage of teachers

Nevertheless better qualified teachers were badly needed at all levels[5] and the extension of facilities for higher education had to be part of the general

---

4. Sudan was not eligible for financial aid from the Colonial Development and Welfare Fund (Wieschoff, H.A., 'Education in the Anglo-Egyptian Sudan, British East Africa', *Journal of Negro Education*, Vol 15, 1946, pp.382-96).

5. The Sudan system could not rely on British teachers in the long term. In August 1942 there were 3 marriages in 6 months among the British staff. 'One has been nine years in the Training College [Miss Harvey] and has just got engaged to a man in the Department she has known all the time. A girl who came out in May was married last month to a man she met after she got here. Miss Clark and I are the only two left in the service—we ought to have 7 permanent British women' [Letter to her sister, Mrs Sheila Connelly, 8.8.42]. Again in 1947, they lost 6 British staff, including Miss Hodgson, which put a considerable burden on the staff who remained. Any extension of work in the Girls' Training College and in secondary sections restricted the amount of inspections possible by Omdurman staff. In the late 1930s new British Province Education Officers (P.E.O.s) were appointed. With their secondment in 1946 more inspections could be made locally (*ARDE*, 1946).

scheme.[6] It was the proportions, which needed to be carefully considered to ensure a firm basis for the whole structure. This basis we always envisaged as spread throughout the country in elementary schools, where definite standards should be insisted on. Rural districts were just as, if not more, important as the towns, although the difficulties in the rural areas were often considerable.[7]

Where girls were concerned, this problem of teachers presented one feature, which was in some ways a help to maintaining the desired quality of work. There was no reserve of women who could teach except for the cadre, which had been trained in Omdurman Girls' Training College.[8] When demands for expansion became really clamorous, it was an embarrassment in that there was no possibility of enlisting outside help. On the credit side it meant that there were never more than one or two women, who wanted to run unsatisfactory private schools. Except for the Government schools, described in the last chapter, and the few mission schools in the towns, there had been no chance of literacy even for most of the women. As I pointed out earlier, in a remote village it would take at least seven years to have a local girl ready to teach in the school.[9] By that time there would be other literate girls in the village but, if they aspired to teaching at all, they would probably make an effort to enter the Training College. Married women did sometimes return to the service, since there was no marriage bar, but their numbers were few in those days, certainly not enough to constitute a reserve force to assist any large scale plan.

6. Sudan Government, Director of Education, *Note by the Director of Education on the Government Plan for Educational Development in the Northern Sudan for the next ten years,* 1946; Ministry of Education, *Report of the Sub-Committee of the Advisory Council for the Northern Sudan,* set up to study and report on the Ten Year Plan, 1946-1956; Ministry of Education, *Proposals for the Expansion and Improvement of the Educational System in the Northern Provinces, 1946-1956.*
7. Teacher morale was low. The schools were supposed to be instruments of change and teachers needed a lot of support, but they were isolated in rural communities.
8. Only in 1960 was the Intermediate Teacher Training College for mistresses opened. In 1961 there were nine women at the High Institute, Omdurman, training to be secondary school mistresses.
9. 'Teachers-teaching life has now risen to about 8 years ... some problems of young Headmistresses ... Average age of new appointees in 1940 was 16.2 yrs; The Department was ready to deploy ex-teachers, and hoped that intermediate schoolgirls would enter the profession' (Sudan Government, Department of Education, *Minutes of meeting to discuss girls' education for 1942,* 29.3.1941). The opening of so many new schools often meant appointing teachers who were really too young for the responsibilities. For example 354 mistresses were needed in 1948 and with new appointments at the end of the Girls' Training College session in December it was possible to fill all the gaps (*ARDE,* 1948). In December 1949 there were 347 mistresses but 18 posts vacant in the East. By mid-1950 the situation was relieved somewhat by 71 students who finished their training (*ARDE,* 1949).

In describing the conditions in the Halfa Reach I touched on the difficulties of staffing in remote places. There was a plan behind it all, which everyone agreed to despite the perpetual arguments and attempts to obtain special consideration. Fathers willingly entered into a contract for their daughters to teach two years in any place to which the Education Department should post a girl. This was in return for free schooling and at the College free training, residence and uniform, in all at least seven years of free education. By Sudanese rates the mistresses' salaries were comparatively generous, especially as houses were provided, generally in the school-yard, and free travel for teacher and chaperone. This should be underlined, as although it was a major part of my duty to arrange these postings, there always remained the discomfort of being authoritarian. Since many of the Sudanese were apt to indulge in high-flown talk about education for everybody, it was logical to make whatever plans were most likely to spread the blessing [of education] and not let it pile up in the towns. Nevertheless there was a constant flow into my office of fathers demanding that their daughters should not be sent to teach away from home. 'But you signed a contract', I used to protest. 'I know I did, but you won't hold me to it, surely.' 'You said', I would go on, 'that you wanted girls educated all over the Sudan.' 'Of course I do. Education is a great blessing ... ' 'Then someone has to go and teach these children.' 'Of course, of course. But not my daughter.'

Always in the end the girl would go and I was able eventually to keep promises to arrange postings nearer home after a time. If we could have thought of a better way of providing teachers for these distant villages,[10] we should have preferred to do so, but, until more local girls were available, the system had to continue. It emphasised all too clearly the evident priorities. I can only remark again rather sourly, I wonder what ideas about staffing are envisaged by international bodies, who re-iterate that emergent countries must have more education.

## 3. Transport and Communications

True it was their country but the distances were so vast, that this alone was no small hindrance. As far as possible we tried to send girls to districts

---

10. 'Problems of ... the presence of so many chaperones in the school *hosh* ... most troubles traced to petty rivalries and jealousies of aunts, mothers and grandmothers ... if teachers came from same district sometimes one chaperone [can be used] for several teachers ... step in right direction ... in many cases their slovenly and dirty habits are obstacles in way of bringing about an improvement in ways of living' (Sudan Government, Department of Education, *Minutes of meeting to discuss girls' education for 1942*, 29.3.1941).

within their own provinces, not only because a Kordofan girl, for example, would be happier in the West than in the Northern Province, but also to avoid the exhaustion of longer journeys than necessary. There were some adventurous souls, who liked the excitement of seeing different places, even if they did not always want to stay many months. Most of the travelling, however, meant anything up to thirty six hours in a train or a spell on a lorry, or both, as in going to Darfur and, although this may in itself have had an educational value, it was tiring and meant at the end a certain amount of isolation. All things considered, the postal service in the Sudan functioned reasonably well but communication between a school and headquarters was not easy and all the business of stores was protracted and complicated by these factors of distance and transport. If the supply of pencils or chalk or sewing cotton ran out, because of a prolonged wash-out on the railway, there was no shop nearby to remedy the deficiency. At one point during the war such a contingency had occurred and an enterprising mistress was teaching the children their letters in the sand in the yard.

Such matters may seem the trivia of irritations rather than serious problems of education but they were the offshoot of the question of transport in a country of this size. They serve to bring out some of the reasons for the leisurely tempo of growth, especially in the early days. Before the First World War, for instance, motor transport was relatively unknown in these overseas territories.[11] It fact it was probably not until the thirties, that cars and lorries made any impact on methods of travel in the Sudan at all. Arguments can go on unceasingly about the comparative values of steady travel on the ground and 'nipping about' from point to point in an aeroplane. I can only record, that I once had to go to Geneina by plane and on the way back came down at Fasher, where I had matters to discuss with the Governor over breakfast, while later in the morning, when we stopped at El Obeid there was business of some kind to decide with the Headmistress of the Girls' Intermediate School there. I found it all most flurried and unsatisfactory but confess to not being attuned to haste.

The most evident disadvantage about these long distances was in the matter of inspection, because this was not thought of primarily as criticising of work but was essential for keeping in touch with teachers, who were immature and without much in the way of learning and were thus in need of as much help as we could give them. Making timetables for a round of visits, when one had to fit in with trains or steamers, that ran only once or twice a week, could have tested the most ardent of puzzle solvers. This improved as the years brought more inspectors, both British and Sudanese

11. Sir F.R. Wingate was testing the first motor-cars in the Sudan from 1904/5 (S.A.D. 234/3/28, 51, 55-56, 64-65).

women, who could be posted at focal points in the provinces and in some cases had lorries earmarked specifically for their work.

## 4. Problems of education in the South

### 4.1 Government grants to missions

I have already spoken of the British woman[12] who had the special responsibility of helping to co-ordinate the standards of work in the South, where the method of making Government grants to the various Christian missions in itself raised intricate problems, especially on matters of detail.[13] In a large measure this manner of financing would be quite straightforward but disputes did arise, when schools were not considered efficient enough to justify the expenditure of public money.[14] Moreover, although they might be rare, examples could arise, where a grant had been allocated for a school building. The school had died but meanwhile the money had already been spent to restore a church.[15] Exceptional though they might be, such occasions came more into prominence than the quiet, ordinary work going on steadily from day to day.

12. Miss E. Golding who took up her post in February 1948. She was succeeded by Mrs A.E. Everett in 1953.
13. For example in 1949 the C.M.S. was in serious financial difficulties. Between 1948 and 1949, when the C.M.S. educational expansion was negligible, the budgeted C.M.S. grant rose from c.£21,000 to c.£35,000. The Government increased the annual staff grants from £225 to £345 for each woman trained educationalist. To fail to support the C.M.S. would have been a serious educational (and political) disaster as the C.M.S. in 1948 was still providing over 25% of all mission education in Southern Sudan above village-school level. The newly appointed Minister for Education, Abdel Rahman Ali Taha, markedly increased Government aid to mission schools in an attempt both to expand Southern education and to control the missions (see Sanderson, L.M.P. and G.N., *Education, Religion and Politics in Southern Sudan 1899-1964*, London, Ithaca, 1981, pp.273-274, 278-279, 299, 308-310, 370; Trimingham, J.S., *The Christian Church in Post-War Sudan*, London, 1949).
14. In contrast the missionaries harped on about the danger of 'selling their birthright for a mess of Government grants' (Trimingham, J.S., *The Christian Church in Post-War Sudan*, London, 1949).
15. Lack of basic resources was the problem at Sallara where there were delays in building work from before 1946 and Miss Rachel Hassan was urged to take photographs to show any progress. On 24.6.47 an agreement was made to build two houses to develop a full elementary boarding school there (letter from Hooper, C.M.S. London to J.S. Trimingham). On 26.2.48 a report stated that Rachel [Hassan] and Jean's house was being built but was delayed because of lack of water. By 9.3.49 money granted for houses at Sallara had been used for two houses in Katcha (Note from Financial Secretary, C.M.S. to African Secretary).

## 4.2 Muslim investment in the missions

What made such a difficulty peculiarly complicated, especially as ideas of Independence began to grow, was that the vast bulk of the taxes was paid by the Moslem part of the population, whose leaders looked with no friendly eye on the evangelizing side of the work of the missions. That the obstacles, which in some places the missions had to overcome, were well nigh insuperable, could not be left as mere excuses, when the Moslem leaders began to enquire into the ways in which their money was being spent.[16]

There had been several good reasons, as I noted in the chapter on The South and another I describe below, for keeping Mohammedan influences out of the non-Arab districts in the early years of the Condominium and no doubt there was little overpowering zeal for living there, when the Northerners needed all their energy for the building up of their own part of the country after the depredations of the *Khalifat*. The question of providing education for the Southerners through the Christian missions thus became an increasing irritant,[17] as the North grew more self-conscious in the matter of nationalism. The aim, therefore, after Independence was Arabicisation of the South in the interests of unity. With this would be bound to come a great increase in the influence of Islam,[18] which would find favour in the eyes of simple people, not only by the definiteness of its creed and ritual, but also because it would appear as the mark of success as embodied in the officials, who adhered to its tenets. Against this blend of attitudes the Christian missionaries found the complications of their endeavours grow more tangled with the upsurge of national feeling in the North after the war.

16. Abdel Rahman Ali Taha, the first Minister of Education, was expected by Northern Sudanese to make rapid, fundamental changes in the Southern education system. The Northern Sudanese attributed the South's backwardness largely to the alleged inefficiency of mission education (Sanderson, L.M.P. and G.N., *op. cit.*, p.297). In 1948 a unified policy began to be adopted for the whole of the Sudan.

17. 'What is a highway for Christian penetration is equally an entrance for Moslem advance and for the inflow of materialism' (C.M.S., *The Southern Sudan Then and Now*, Adventure of Faith Series, no.12, London, 1950). Yet the South was financially wholly dependent on the North for the cost of its administration, including education.

18. Intensive Arabisation and Islamisation of the South was seen by most Northerners as the obvious road to national integration. The presence of missionaries was offensive to the Northerners (Sanderson, L.M.P. and G.N., *op. cit.*, pp.297-298).

### 4.3 Arabic as a *lingua franca*

There was manifest logic in the suggestion that one nation should have one language and there was much sense in the decision that that language should be Arabic, since it was spoken by the great majority of the population and, as one of the great languages of the world, it could link on to wide regions of thought and culture, both past and present.[19] Yet it confused still more the ubiqituous problem of education overseas with regard to the initial stages of literacy. In what tongue should children learn to read? Their mother tongue, however limited? If so, where are the books to come from? Where are the teachers to be found? Learned conferences[20] spend many hours, more than enough to teach whole classes of children to read, discussing what are the most appropriate ways of dealing with this problem and what are the psychological implications, and sometimes indeed reversing the decisions of a previous gathering. I noticed that in the Arabic North, where, as on the Dongola or Halfa Reach, there were small pockets of Nubian languages, the Sudanese mistresses gave short shrift to any fancy theories about literacy in the vernacular. I have seen a Headmistress separate a little group of girls in the playground for the sole reason, that they would talk in their own tongue. In her view all educated girls must speak Arabic and good Arabic at that. This same attitude to Arabic characterised the decisions of the Sudanese, when they took over the Government.

It plunged them, therefore, in the South into a situation, which resembled that of most British Overseas Territories, a welter of small vernaculars for the primary schools leading on to English at the later stages, and with some primary schools trying to start in English. To dislocate still further any theories about smooth progressing from one language to another some of the English was taught in the Southern missions by Italians, who had themselves a very imperfect grasp of the language. One week after seeing a number of classes, I had a sweeping vision of masses of children all over Africa saying, while suiting the action to the words, 'I am standing up, I am sitting down.' On the strength of this I feared they would claim 'to have done English'.

19. Just after his appointment Abdel Rahman Ali Taha called for the introduction within two years, of Arabic as a subject in all Sudanese secondary and intermediate schools. It was viewed as an important step towards cultural unification between North and South when the Executive Council and Legislative Assembly agreed in 1950 on the policy to introduce Arabic as the language of instruction in all government schools and mission schools above elementary level from 1951 (S.A.D. 658/5/10).

20. The Rejaf Language Conference, for example, held in April 1928 (*Report of the Rejaf Language Conference*, London, 1928); also the Mongalla Province annual conferences in the late 1920s and early 1930s. In 1933 the first conference on Southern education was held.

Some of the Southerners spoke excellent English, although their number was limited but by knowing no Arabic they hindered proceedings, when they were elected to the Leglislative Assembly, where many of the representatives spoke nothing but Arabic.[21]

There is no need to dilate further on this local Tower of Babel, but to record sadly, that we found no really satisfactory solution to it.[22] Many of the missionaries accomplished magnificent work in their studies of local languages, compiling grammars and dictionaries, which, as in the case of Zande, became standard works of reference.[23] Some Government officials also helped in this linguistic achievement. With a view to insisting on literacy among catechumens[24] translations were made of certain portions of the Bible. Unfortunately these might be all that there was to read in that particular district and such literacy for catechumens often led little further.

In the last chapter I discussed the trouble we found in providing suitable textbooks and reading material even in Arabic.[25] I repeat yet again that it is all too manifest, that such provision in the smaller languages is practically impossible. The experiments to obtain one language for education in, for example, Kenya and Malaya, had not begun in my time and their progress will be of the utmost importance. It may be that for the purposes of educating children only the great languages will be helpful. However

21. The argument that the South lagged far behind the North in political maturity had some truth but yet Southern representatives on the Legislative Assembly proved that they were a match for the Northerners. 'Although the senior British officials who are now members of the Assembly and the Executive Council (Cabinet) will have much influence at first, there is no saying what the Assembly will do when it has found its feet ... The Christian members have a hard and important task. Nearly all the others are Moslems, some of them intensely bent on spreading their faith. It requires only a little knowledge and imagination to guess at the pressure and strain that will arise, especially after Sudanese Independence is secured.' (C.M.S., *The Southern Sudan Then and Now*, Adventure of Faith Series, No: 12, London, 1950, p.16).
22. In the South there are around 48 major dialects and languages, with many regional differences (Sanderson, L.M.P., 'Educational development in the Southern Sudan: 1900-1948', *Sudan Notes and Records*, XLIII, 1962, pp.105-117). See Tucker, A.N and Bryan, M.A., *Linguistic Analyses, the non-Bantu Languages of North-Eastern Africa*, London, O.U.P. for International African Institute, 1966.
23. Many of the Missionaries became expert linguists, for example, Archbishop A. Shaw on Bor Dinka; Dr and Mrs E. Clive Gore who produced *A Zande and English Dictionary*, London, 1931 and translations of parts of the Bible; Dr Roland Stevenson (C.M.S.) on many Nuba and other languages, as is seen in references in Tucker, A.N. and Bryan, M.A., *Linguistic Analyses, The non-Bantu Languages of North-Eastern Africa*, 1966; Verona Fathers, Rev. Fr. Stephen Santandrea based at Wau and then Kayango (*S.N.R.*, 1933), Rev. Fr. Olivetti (R.C. Mission, Kajok); the American Presbyterian Mission especially Miss R. Huffman and Dr Müller; Rev. Harvey Hoekstra (Reformed Church of Holland in North America) who worked at Pibor and Boma and who translated the New Testament into Anuak.
24. This insistence on literacy for catechumens was found only in some missions.
25. A southern branch of the Publications Bureau started to produce literature for the South in 1948 (Hodgkin, Robin, *op. cit.*).

philologists may deplore the passing of the restricted vernaculars, the choice will have to be made.

### 4.4 Fear of Islamisation of the South

Educating children in a particular language is more than teaching them to repeat a number of words. Many people were apprehensive, that the introduction of Arabic among non-Muslim peoples would bring in its train conversion to Islam and an acceptance of all that belonged to that aspect of Arab culture. For the Christian missionaries, who had laboured to bring their faith to pagan tribes, such fear was logical and justified. For others it was only certain customs connected with the Muslim way of life that had to be restricted.[26] That devout Muslims should pray five times a day, give alms to the poor and shelter needy relatives should be a matter for admiration. The teaching and habits with regard to the position of women, however, raised very serious problems especially in matters of education. Where, as in the South and the Nuba Mountains, pagan women went untrammelled, it would have been iniquitous to have had them subjected to the practices from which Muslim women were themselves striving to be free. The very real danger for unsophisticated people was that success in the worldly sense was associated with the Arabic-speaking official and, if he shut up his women behind high walls and insisted on subjection explicitly set out in the Koran, this might be regarded as the appropriate model to follow.

## 5. Position of Women

From the educationalist's point of view in the North, the problem of the position of women had other facets than the straightforward confrontation of the last paragraph. At the beginning of girls' schools there was widespread apprehension, that this was a revolutionary development. Opposition took the form of non-participation rather than violent hostility. As always in this matter there was an underlying and generally unformulated doubt that, once girls were educated, things could never be the same again. It takes great courage to understand, that such a change will eventually be for the general good, quite apart from any matters of moral justice regarding individuals. For this reason, if for no other, the pace had to be slow. That this slowness was justified was evident from the fact, that the tender plant did take firm root. Where acute problems arose after that

---

26. For example 'female circumcision', associated with Northern Sudanese, had to be proscribed.

stage was in the attitude, that had to be combatted of 'so far and no further'. It was Hannah More all over again in her suggestions about the poor, although no-one was as niggardly as she. The idea lingered that it was all right for Sudanese girls to have just enough schooling to make them more orderly about the house; in fact, as I met the concept in my first few weeks, the sole aim was 'better wives and mothers'. It fitted smoothly into the utterances of the Prophet and, no doubt, would have satisfied the exponents of the doctrine, if the girls and their education could have been contained for ever behind the high mud walls.[27]

## 5.1 Property rights

Once the leaven began to act, however, the rate of change was cumulative. Most noticeable was the way in which the schoolmistresses became less biddable to their menfolk, when family squabbles about property took on a new complexion among women conscious of their earning power. A Headmistress with many years' service once married her sister's widower, a girl with a lot of character and great fun as a person,. They were married very soon after the funeral and, I was told, that it was not an uncommon custom, for a husband might say to his wife on her deathbed, 'I will not let your spirit go until you give me to your sister.' The Headmistress continued in her post but came to me one morning in a great state of annoyance with her husband, who was a very senior official in an accounting unit. 'I am not pleased with *fulan effendi*',[28] she exclaimed in a real fit of temper. 'All these years I have been putting my earnings into the Post Office Savings Bank. Now he wants me to give my salary to him. I say it is my money and I can do what I like with it. What do you think? And what is more, he has kept the gold which belonged to my sister. I want it to look after to save it for the education of her sons.'

This particular upset was fairly soon resolved but was followed by a series of similar outbursts in my office, which never led to any final break but apparently a satisfactory compromise.

## 5.2 Male power of life and death over women

It is not so much actual legal rights as the growth of custom, which has influenced the position of women in any Islamic community and in the

---

27. 'Yet in Sudan as elsewhere, a lack of formal education has not prevented women from acquiring a dominating position and profound influence in domestic and social life' (Holt, *op. cit.*, p.202).
28. *fulan effendi*, 'Mr someone'.

Sudan this question of male superiority was evident in every aspect of human relationships, sometimes brutally so. In its larger and pervasive form it appeared in the attitude, that women were of no real consequence in themselves. Women as individuals did not exist; any transitory importance they might possess was only in so far as it had a bearing on the lives of their men.

I recounted in the unhappy little tale in Wadi Halfa the claim of the Roman power of life and death over a daughter. A father here was an unlettered cultivator; therefore still more startling was to hear a similar sentiment from a young man with higher education, speaking perfect English and considered fit to train male teachers. It was a far more tragic story than the other. His sister, who was a schoolmistrees, complained that she had *zar* which corresponds roughly to the Biblical possession by an evil spirit. News came to me one day, that she had died suddenly and mysteriously the night before, while being treated by a *fikki*, and the descriptions of the treatment were alarming. I at once informed the D.C. and the body exhumed but by this time the *fikki* had disappeared never to be found. When a very charming young Sudanese officer came from the Police for confirmation of these reports, my informants were dumb and the officer disarmingly explained their reticence. 'None of us like these cases with *fikki*s', he explained. 'I suppose we haven't really got over our old superstitions and wonder a little what he may do to us.'

Some days later the brother came to see me and cut short my condolences by remarking brusqely, 'You shouldn't have gone to police about my sister. There was no poison found.' I reminded him that it was violence we had suspected, but he went on, 'Supposing she had committed adultery. My mother might have poisoned her.' 'All the more reason for going to the police', I suggested. 'But I might have poisoned her myself', he expostulated vehemently. 'And I should have been quite right to do so.' 'Would you poison the man too?' 'Ah, well, that's another matter.'

More angered than I can describe I told him, that if I found any brothers or fathers poisoning any of my girls I would see that they were hanged.

He did not argue this point and I really believe that such an attitude to male honour was quite startling to him. It is only fair to him to relate, that when he was transferred to teach science in the Girls' Training College, he proved to be one of the most helpful and likeable assistants we had. What is more, he was one of the few young men prepared to discuss thoughtfully 'female circumcision' as a problem and not shuffle it off for other people to deal with. He even went to the length of trying to persuade the Leader of the House to ask a question on the subject in the Legislative Assembly. That may be a slight digression from the theme of masculine superiority but a parade of honour carried to those lengths was just an illustration of the attitude towards women, which had to be overcome and as in this case evidently could be altered.

## 5.3 Seclusion of women

It was therefore the position of women in the general estimation that presented a more fundamental problem than the mere practice of seclusion. There is no need to tilt at the latter too strenuously, as it is fast breaking down in most Eastern countries, but a few misapprehensions still linger about it.[29] One can dismiss briefly the romantic illusions, that secluded women are always to be found in luxurious *harem*s, where life is a comedy played out on silken cushions to the accompaniment of muted strings with dusky eunuchs bringing cooling sherbet and scented sweetmeats. That there were places like this we have evidence in old Arab houses, such as some to be found in Cairo today, or in the Lebanese palace of the Emir Beshir at Beit-ed-Din. Here large, sunny rooms with raised divans and marble fountains still look down a fertile valley and give access to a blossoming garden, where the alabaster tomb of a favourite wife is flanked with cypress and orange trees. We are sufficiently democratic to know that such pleasures were only for the few and that, if the custom of the country was to shut women up, the majority would be shut up in anything but palaces.

In a country like the Sudan this was overwhelmingly the case. Large numbers of those I saw had nothing but a small mud room with a soft, sandy floor in a narrow court behind a high wall. It was hot, stuffy and squalid and the ignorance and apathy of the inhabitants generally increased the dirt and disorder. One of these dilapidated backquarters I visited in the town[30] near the Men's Training College. By contrast with this progressive institution[31] it was a district famed for its conservatism. There had been a long and boring teaparty of *sheikh*s in the front yard of a schoolmaster's house, where I had been the only woman. Just before it was time to go, I asked to pay my respects to his wife. This caused a certain amount of confusion but after a long interval I was escorted to a house at the back, where I tried to make conversation with a bewildered young woman wrapped in a rather grubby muslin *tobe*. There were several other women present and a surprising number of children pressed up to the windows. The room was not very well furnished and not particularly tidy but it is only in

29. The text was written before the development of the modern movement of Islamic fundamentalism. In the present day Sudan the Muslim Brotherhood have a strong influence in re-enforcing the seclusion of women.
30. Dueim.
31. Bakht-er-Ruda.

exceptional houses, that the women's apartments are up to the standard of the armchairs in the front. Conversation soon languished as, understandably enough, the wife was embarrassed and shy. Very much to my surprise she had a sudden, bright idea. 'Let's go and see the other wife.'

The three or four women there wrapped their *tobe*s round them and we started, only to cause a minor stampede outside. The way to the other wife's house led through the front yard where there were still men and a petromax lamp. The schoolmaster halted the women and bore the light into the farthest corner, where he stood shading it. The women all muffled their faces as thickly as possible, as we crept along in the shadow of the wall, while the men politely turned their backs.

In the next house a surprisingly cheerful old crone sat on a rumpled bed with a litter of household goods around her on the floor. She had not much more to talk about than her co-wife but she said everything several times over, which made the proceedings seem a little livelier. She spat frequently but purely, I think, from habit and not from disapproval. Most of all, of course, she was the most disturbing commentary on the elegant tea-party on the men's yard.

### 5.4 Polygamy

How far wives were really friendly under this system it was difficult to ascertain. Probably if they had to be shut up, it was more amusing to be shut up in company. In many cases they had separate houses and might perhaps live in different towns. They were so accustomed to the idea, that they never questioned it and, I doubt, if as a system they resented it. Where there was jealousy, it might well have been entirely on personal grounds. Certainly the children often made little distinction and had as much affection for half-sisters as for those wholly related. 'Yes', they would say, 'we are all sisters. Zenab and Fatma and I had one mother. Nafissa and Sekina and Medina had another mother. So, you see, we are all sisters.'

A schoolmistress once complained, because she could not go on teaching near her husband's house. 'But now that you have a husband to support you', I said. 'Ah, but he has three other wives', she replied, 'and I need to earn money.' Her grievance was not against the husband, not the wives, nor the system, only against the Government.

In actual practice few men could afford to keep four wives and one or two was the more general practice in the Sudan. With the coming of Western ideas the educated Sudanese felt that a *harem* would be regarded as old-fashioned and uncultured, especially as the new ways of living entailed more expense. A first marriage was generally made between cousins, an old survival of the need for tribal loyalty.[32] The fact the a man had only one wife did not necessarily mean, that he intended to stick to this first marriage indefinitely. There were, of course, a number of Sudanese who did remain loyal to their first wives but as the whole matter was regarded largely as a contract, it was based on rather different premises from that of ordinary European marriages. It is this instability rather than in polygamy itself that most people find the harm of Mohammedan customs; this lies not in the plurality of wives but in the ease and one-sidedness of divorce.

**5.5 The ease of divorce**

On this point too, education for girls made a noticeable impact, as, of course, it had in other countries. A woman able to earn an assured living did not need to think of marriage as the only possible means of subsistence. Moreover, if she should marry and be divorced, her position was not so precarious as that of her mother's generation. There were plenty of examples to underline this security, for the *Sharia* law provides for maintenance for a period only up to two years and appears to be based on the assumption that a woman will re-marry.

One of the most cynical divorces I remember among many was of a pretty, though rather feather-headed, schoolmistress,[33] whose earnings had been of much importance to her family, because she contributed to her brother's fees at the Secondary School, which was by no means an unusual proceeding. A sudden marriage was not unusual either but I did not expect it, while the brother was still needing help. Sitt Alawia was swept away in a hurry, decked with gold and very excited and pleased with her lot. A fortnight later she was back asking to be re-instated; the husband had tired of her and divorced her.

The change from her fluttering happiness to utter desolation was heartbreaking. She proved her desperation by asking to be sent to a remote village in the Northern Province, where no-one ever wanted to go. Not that she did much good there. She soon found that she was pregnant and spent most of her time miserably unwell. When I asked our Sudanese inspectress[34] who the husband was, she was forthright in her condemnation. 'A young merchant without sense. He made too much money during the War and he doesn't know what to do with it.'

---

32. For a discussion of endogamous marriage among the Amarar in the Sudan see Milne, J.C.M., *The changing pattern of mobility and migration of the Amarar tribe of Eastern Sudan*, S.O.A.S., M.Phil thesis, 1976, pp. 368-387; This is a common tradition in the Middle East.
Amarar.
33. Sitt Alawia.
34. Sitt Medina Abdulla.

Similar tales of hardship were frequent but what was more important was the way in which the girls began to take the measure of the situation. One very charming girl, who came back to teaching after being repudiated without cause by a young doctor appeared to me to have all that a husband could require. She was tall and slim with the willowy carriage associated with, but not always found in, Arab women, light-skinned and pleasing of feature; her voice was musical and her intelligence far above the average; her disposition was gentle and unquarrelsome. She had been a good teacher before and on her return she developed into one, who was quite outstanding. Although still retaining the prejudice of all schoolmistresses in favour of the academic subjects, she accepted the need for training on the domestic side and eventually specialised in this with much success. But there were other matters that she thought should be part of a girl's instruction and she came to me rather diffidently one day to discuss one of these, which she had been brooding over for some time. 'Could you', she asked, 'include in the religious lessons at the top of the schools, some authoritative information about a woman's real position? You see, for example, a husband may say to his wife, 'If you go out of this house to see your father, I shall divorce you.' Now, she ought to know, if he actually has the power to do that. She might be very much in need of her father's advice. It would help us, if we really knew where we stood. I don't want to go against the law of our religion but I should like to know.'

## 5.6 Contracts and marriage

It was an interesting development towards independent judgment. Other mistresses voiced their views, although not perhaps in such thoughtful ways nor after such unhappy experiences as the previous girl. Two girls, for instance, asked for new contracts long after their original one had expired. The first of these I have mentioned before, the energetic headmistress at El Obeid.[35] Soon after my first visit she had the initiative to take private lessons in English, in which she had made much progress, and her greatest ambition was to go to England to study. This extra work marked her out for promotion, when the Intermediate School was to be started in El Obeid, but at this point, her father brought forward this marriage proposal. The idea of leaving the life of schools with its endlessly exciting possibilities was more than she could bear. We therefore contrived to produce a contract requiring extra service in return for extra training. I doubt if it was legal but all she wanted was a piece of paper, looking official, to wave at her relations.

35. Melk ed-Dar.

Instead, therefore of settling down to the seclusion of women's quarters, she followed the example of Sitt Nafissa Awad al Karim and went out on trek to conduct more campaigns against Pharaonic circumcision. The first one she undertook in company with one of the Sudanese staff midwives[36] from the Midwifery Training School in Omdurman, and the combination of medical and religious points of view put over in this joint effort was very well received by the women to whom they talked. Her leave the following summer she spent accompanying a British Health Visitor, who had not been long in the country and found an interpreter of this status of inestimable help in her tour of the villages.

The second girl demanding a contract to show to her father for the same reason, was the daughter[37] of my old friend, S.A.R.'s cook. A plump, pale, pretty girl came into my office one morning in a great fluster. 'It's an old man', she explained, 'who belongs to the household (S.A.R.'s). He's married already. I don't want to sit at home and look after someone else's brats. I like teaching.'

An appeal to her father that Sitt Fatima was needed in her post staved off that misfortune without recourse to bits of paper but during the long vacation another and younger suitor was more successful. After the marriage Fatima still refused to give up her work and somehow the husband disappeared, when a son had arrived. Whether she persuaded him to divorce her or what happened, I was not told, but his wife seemed most unconcerned, although she adored the baby. 'Fatima didn't seem to care for him', his father confided to me. 'I don't understand it, because this one was young. But he was not very rich and, you know, she likes pretty clothes and ornaments.' 'I enjoy teaching', Fatima told me in private. 'I could not bear sitting at home.'

She passed unruffled through all these changes but for others the path was not easy. One mistress was transferred to Khartoum soon after her marriage to teach near her husband's house. A month or two only had passed, when she came to me in much distress. 'What shall I do? I cannot

---

36. Sitt Batoul Mohamed Eisa, who had some schooling at Sheikh Babikr Bedri's original girls' school in Rufaa; at an early age she married and was then left with a small son to bring up. She helped in her father's small business in Rufaa; In 1925 she was present at the confinement of a neighbour who was attended by a trained midwife from Omdurman. She was so impressed that she wrote to Miss G.L. Wolff, the Principal, offering to take the course at Omdurman Midwives' Training School; January 1926 she started the course; she undertook further training as a nurse in Omdurman hospital and was promoted to staff and then theatre nurse; 1930 Staff Midwife at Midwifery School; from 1944 campaigned against Pharaonic 'circumcision', for example from 19.9.46 she went with Sitt Melk ed-Dar to Blue Nile Province and Kordofan (Talodi, Kadugli, Muglad, el-Odeya, Nahud); by 1946 Senior Midwife at the Midwives' Training School; by 1953 Assistant Principal of the Midwives' Training School.
37. Sitt Fatima, daughter of Abdel Latif, S.A.R.'s cook.

bear it. My husband drinks. We quarrel continually. He brings strange women into the yard. They sing all night and I cannot sleep. Then in the morning I am not fit for work.'

As there was still a vacancy in the school from which she had come, I asked her if she would like to return to her home. Evidently she felt more at ease, after she had wept and poured out all her troubles, and she decided to try again. But a week later she was back reporting failure. 'Please may I go to Merowe after all? It is useless trying. I have packed my things and I am never going back to him.'

We gave her a railway warrant and sent her off at once. I expected an irate husband demanding reasons for this transfer but no-one came. His wife soon recovered her old zest and settled down happily and usefully. The only aftermath was a spate of anonymous letters making aspersions on her character but that sort of reaction was routine and the letters were burnt as usual.

### 5.7 Teaching versus marriage

The repercussions of these small tragedies were of increasingly wide significance, since in the Northern Sudan as in other places women who can earn their own living started to speculate on the advantages of professional as opposed to domestic life, as the latter appeared to them at that point. There is no evidence so far of any large scale desire to avoid marriage completely and it would be a disastrous outlook, if such were the results of education. There is no inconsistency in objecting to 'better wives and mothers' as the sole aim for education and realising that educated women are needed for the mothers of future generations. This, of course is not a problem for the administrator to investigate as a matter for formulating policy but it is part of an educator's task to be aware of rapidly changing customs and to decide how much education should attempt to influence the rate of development. Schools and colleges should be growing points everywhere and the special circumstances important in emergent countries are concerned with the suddenness of change in some directions and a need for development to be firmly rooted to avoid as far as possible, a disruption which may threaten the whole social fabric. This is no doubt a counsel of perfection but in helping the women of the Sudan to a fuller appreciation of life in general there were complications of this kind, which are more gradually resolved in more established educational systems.

It was clear by the middle of the 1940s, that women, even with the limited education of the schoolmistresses at the time, were already reaching out to 'the delights of the mind', although in small measure. They were tasting the satisfaction of exercising their faculties to an extent not dreamed of before, of knowing power, self-respect and a certain degree of independence.[38] They had contrived withal to stay within the charmed circle of respectability and most of the slanders brought against individuals were without foundation. What was most important was that as a class they stood high in popular esteem and it was to be within this class, that a very large number of schoolgirls aspired and the number was growing.

## 5.8 Outside the walls

These large issues moved but slowly and could then be considered little more than faint rumblings. The smaller superficial things could be seen more clearly and, if unimportant in themselves, they demonstrated the trend of affairs in that the women were taking their own way in the less fundamental conventions. But it was the trend that was significant. For example the canons of respectability used to preach that a woman should not go outside her yard until after sunset, when no man might see her. Naturally this was impossible for the very poor, especially in villages where the water at least must be fetched from the well. Gradually, however, this began to change amongst all classes of society. A party at the girls' school in mid-afternoon would be besieged by hundreds of women. Should there be need to ask an official for help with a daughter's education or for a favour of some sort, the mother would come to talk to a headmistress or a woman official, although at one time the father would have been more likely to appear. Journeys to strange towns had to be undertaken, when teachers needed chaperones or even if daughters had to travel any distance to boarding school. More and more women, themselves uneducated, pushed on their children rejoicing in their scholastic success.

## 5.9 Women and mass media

Even in the matter of amusement for themselves customs were altering. The value of films is not the issue here; the mere fact of going to the cinema made a decided advance in freedom, and, as time went on, women attended the commercial theatres in the towns and performances taken to the villages by the Public Relations Officer. It was not so many years before, that a most respected and progressive old *sheikh* took his wife to the pictures, all decorously veiled. People in the audience shouted, 'Why don't you bring your women out naked?' Soon after the war there was always an audience in

38. In the Sudan Elections of 1955 'there is no female suffrage, though women may present themselves as candidates and if suitably qualified, may vote in the senatorial and graduates' elections' (S.A.D. 658/5/7).

the gallery specially reserved for women and no-one noticed if a man should take his sisters in the more expensive seats.

By this time[39] the radio too was reaching out small tentacles. There were one or two wealthy families where the women were sufficiently interested to be well informed on such matters even as international news. This, however, preserved the requirement of being within the walls. Still more subversive of convention was the decision of some of the schoolmistresses to broadcast from the [radio] station in Omdurman.[40] The real conservatives say that it is against religious teaching for a woman's voice to be heard in public. Although anonymity was promised, it was some time before the mistresses eventually consented to take part. They were immediately acclaimed as an enormous success. With a little assistance they composed entertaining dialogues, useful household hints and read stories for children, which were much appreciated. They tried too to illustrate how beautiful a sound a woman's voice can be, for the loud shrill cries most often heard interspersed with the beggar's whine of suplication were an unlovely sign of the uneducated, which the schools strove hard to eradicate.

## 5.10 Veiling

That they should still veil their faces was an issue rather more complex. Firstly it was no particular loss to cover the nose and mouth in walking about in a hot and extremely dusty country. To the older women certainly unveiling would have required a disproportionate mental effort. There are few English women who would care to walk down Bond Street in a very scanty sun suit and that is about the level of comparison. [They] were wise too in retaining the *tobe* as the usual outdoor dress, because its graceful folds added much to the charm of slender beauty and was a help to dignify 'those with a fuller figure'. One might often see older schoolgirls unveiled in the streets of Omdurman as a rather daring gesture and the mistresses did not worry very much, when they were away from censorious eyes. At that time tearing off the veil in the spectacular way in which it was done in Egypt in the 1920s had no particular apppeal to the Sudanese. In this they were sensible, for it was going to avail them more to increase their growing awareness of responsibility and initiative before indulging in symbolic gestures. It was far more a sign of progress, that *tobes* were quietly discarded by teachers when in school, because they were found to impede

39. At the end of the Second World War.
40. By November 1942 Dr Beasley was one of the announcers for the Omdurman Broadcasting Station, reading the news in English and giving talks on education for girls in the Sudan, for example on 8.2.45.

work, than that there should be deliberate flouting of public opinion in unnecessary details.

Undoubtedly this must enter into girls' ideas after a time, as high spirits grow and the desire for experiment occurs. What matters most is not the outward show but the breaking up from within of restrictive practices. For in this matter of seclusion, with which the veiling of the face is linked, is more than the jealousy of possession; there is also the subtle harm of the snobbish vanity, which in Europe produced the ideal of the 'fine lady'. 'If my wife should work', said an impoverished clerk to me one day, 'people might think I couldn't afford to keep a servant.' He could not afford to keep a servant and his feckless wife and his undernourished children were a proof of his hopeless household.

### 5.11 'Stupidity of women'

It demonstrated a man's success in the world that he could maintain his wife locked away in luxurious idleness; it proved a woman's worth that he was content to keep her so. In a society without the refinements of art or civilisation to gloss over the devastating results of this the injury to all, and to the women in particular, was crudely manifested. I have inveighed several times against 'just sitting'; the evil of this was that, as they 'just sat' in all their ignorance, they atrophied. Small wonder that the men would say, 'Oh, but she's a woman. You can't expect her to understand.'

It made a wonderful excuse too, this stupidity of the women, and more especially, when it could be brought forward for the benefit of male officials, who were not likely to be able to ask the women concerned. 'Of course I wouldn't mind myself. I'm quite progressive in my opinions. It's my wife who won't hear of it. Well, you know what women are.'

The sad part was that so many of the women did justify these strictures. They had had so little opportunity to make use of their faculties; they had had no enlivening contacts; lack of exercise and fresh air made them often sick and frequently hypochondriac. They did become slow and stupid and tiresome. The marvel is that there were any who managed to retain an interest in life and betray occasionally a personality of some vigour. It was not that the flame never existed but that it was so soon damped down.

There seems every reason to hope that this will all be changed more quickly than anticipated. One can hope that there will soon be no more pathetic cases such as one I remember, that of a daughter of a very rich and religious merchant in Omdurman. She was allowed to finish an intermediate school course, as she could be brought every day in a closed car. At fifteen she made a 'good match'. Custom was followed and the bride thus kept in the house for the first three months and in the women's yard for the first year. Even then this habit was being rapidly discontinued but this family was strict and held to it in her particular case. At first the novelty of it all amused her. She showed visitors her large house, her sumptuous furniture, asked after schoolfellows and prattled happily along. Being a dutiful wife she produced a son before the first year was finished but the change in her was lamentable. She grew fat and rather sluttish, had no interest in her former companions, no questions to ask about what was going on, practically nothing to talk about at all. She did not even seem sad at being away from everything, nothing so definite as resigned, just dull.

One result of all this monotony was a frantic and ill-directed desire for a little excitement, wherever this could be found. Marriages, funerals, circumcision feasts, the wilder ceremony of exorcising the *zar* were eagerly seized upon as pretexts for gathering together and generally for feasting.

In old fashioned households marriages and funerals were lengthy and expensive. The nearest relative kept open house for some days and the main feature of the proceedings appeared to be that people just gathered together. Details of the old marriage customs can be found in *Sudan Notes and Records*[41] and these were still followed by some families. One modern development, often seen in Omdurman, was a procession of taxis dangerously overcrowded with women and girls uttering the regulation cries of joy, as the cars slowly perambulated the streets.

Funerals were on much the same lines with everyone calling to commiserate with the relatives and being given food and drink. The crowd of mourners were, of course, in proportion to the importance of the deceased. I thought a riot had broken out, when the wife of Sir Sayed Ali Mirghani died, but it was just the wailing of the guests. The women expressed themselves in another ululation rather difficult to distinguish from that of the noise of rejoicing, whilst the voices of the men could be heard in a chant. A *bikr* was the official name for a mourning and the participants indulged in an ecstacy of grief, which doubtless formed a most useful emotional outlet. One morning, when the school driver, a most respected old man, turned up to work with a voice so hoarse that he could hardly speak, I enquired sympathetically, if we could do anything for his cold. It was not a cold, he informed me, just that the night before he had been to a very good *bikr*.

41. See Zenkovsky, S., 'Marriage customs in Omdurman, *S.N.R.*, Vol 26, 1945, pp.241-256; 'Customs of the women of Omdurman, Part II, *S.N.R.*, Vol 30, 1949, pp.39-46; 'Zar and tambura as practised by the women of Omdurman', *S.N.R.*, Vol 31, 1950, pp.65-81; Beasley, Ina, *The Desert Rose*, London, Femina Books, 1969, a novel.

# 6. 'Female circumcision'

Parties for the circumcision of boys still continued but the matter of girls' 'circumcision' became rather complicated after the passing of a Government ordinance forbidding the practice in 1946.[42] This was to be enforced with discretion and resulted in children being sent often to outlying districts for the operation, since at home everyone would know about it. Details of the mutilation can be found in medical books and there is no need to set them out here.[43]

Distasteful though this subject may be, it would be cowardly not to explain, that it was indeed one of the special problems with which we were concerned.[44] Above all was the difficulty we experienced in trying to understand the mentality of people, who could practice this human cruelty and yet be first-rate individuals in other ways. Where the matter takes on a wider significance is that there might well be parallels among other African peoples, in that there are depths in their emotions and their thinking, that we cannot plumb. There seems considerable evidence that 'female circumcision' is now dying out in the Sudan but one cannot but expect that with increased contact with other and particularly Moslem countries it will cease entirely. But our difficulty was that we did not find educated men

---

42. Sir Douglas Newbold wrote to Canon E.S. Daniell, O.B.E. on 11.3.45 that that year's agenda for the Advisory Council included the subject of 'female circumcision'— 'a non-Islamic hangover from paganism and a scourge on girls' education' (Henderson, K.D.D., *The making of the Modern Sudan, the life and letters of Sir Douglas Newbold, K.B.E.*, London, 1953, pp.434, 447). The ordinance making 'Pharaonic circumcision' illegal became law on 30.12.45 at the 539th meeting of Council (*Legislative Supplement, Sudan Government Gazette*, no. 762, 15.1.46).
43. See S.A.D. 657/41 and in particular, Sanderson, Lilian Passmore, *Against the Mutilation of Women*, Ithaca, 1981, who outlines the struggle and the role played by Dr Beasley in the struggle against 'Pharaonic circumcision' in detail. See also Beasley, Ina, 'Female circumcision' in *Women Speaking*, London, July-Sept 1976, pp.21-23; Hellier, Mary, 'Female circumcision' *Journal of the Medical Women's Federation*, April 1951, pp.24-26, who collected notes from Lady Huddleston, the wife of the Governor-General; Muir-Leach, Alice I., 'Female circumcision, some after effects and other aspects', *Journal of the Medical Women's Federation*, Vol.43, No.3, July 1961, pp.111-122; Pridie, E.D. *et al*, *Female circumcision in the Anglo-Egyptian Sudan*, 1.3.45; Reid, J.A., 'Notes on tribes of the White Nile Province', *Sudan Notes and Records*, 1930, Vol.13; 'Behind Sudan's veil', *The Townswoman*, XXXVI, No.6, June 1969, London, National Union of Townswomen's Guilds, pp.205-207; Younis, N.Y., 'Report on tour of Kordofan 1922'; al-Maṣlaḥa al-ṭibbiyya al-Sūdāniyya, *al-khafaḍ al-fir'aūnī fi 'l-Sūdān*, [Pharaonic circumcision in the Sudan], Khartoum, 1947. (For further details about 'Pharaonic circumcision' see Appendix I).
44. D.R. Macdonald, M.B., Ch.B., 'Female circumcision in the Sudan', a lecture given on 9.3.36. This paper was also circulated to D.C.s in the provinces, by the Civil Secretary, Douglas Newbold. In June 1939 Sir Angus Gillan spoke to Sudanese notables against the practice on his retirement from his post as Civil Secretary (Sayyid 'Abd al-Hādī, article in *an-Nīl*, 25.7.39).

immediately and whole-heartedly condemning the practice and taking action to stop it even in their own families.[45] It was indeed one of the circumstances, which made some of us realise, that we had but a glimmer of understanding of the way in which the minds of another race work, and that there can be no key to the comprehension of the peoples of a whole continent. The urgent need, however, lies not only in getting rid of evil customs but in arriving at a juster estimate of the level of a people's development by balancing the fact, that such customs continue alongside growth in other fields.

What shocks (and I use the word in all shades of its meaning) most outsiders on hearing of this custom is that prior to 1946 the operation was performed on all Muslim girls in the Sudan in the six Northern provinces, whether of high or low degree, whether their parents were rich or poor, and, most startling of all, whether their fathers had been educated or not. The form used was the Pharaonic circumcision known only elsewhere in the South of Egypt round about Kom Ombo. For the greater part of Egypt a much lighter form was general, approximating to that allowed by the writings of the Holy Men and known as the *sunna* form but many educated families in Egypt and in the Hejaz had by this time given up any sort of operation. Nor is the custom known among Indian Muslims, or Pakistanis. That the term Pharaonic is in general use is because popular belief holds, that the custom originated in Egypt in the time of Pharaoh, who is regarded as the prototype of all evil.

I have mentioned already the tours undertaken by some of the

---

45. Eminent British and Sudanese doctors working against the practice of 'female circumcision' in the 1940s included E.D. Pridie, C.M.G., D.S.O., O.B.E., 3N., M.B., B.S., Director of the Sudan Medical Service; A.E. Lorenzen, 4N., M.R.C.S., L.R.C.P., D.P.M., also a Director of the S.M.S.; Dr A. Cruikshank, O.B.E., 4N., M.D., B.Ch., Senior Physician, S.M.S.; J.S. Howell, M.B., P.R.C.S.E, M.R.C.O.G., Obstetric Surgeon and Gynaecologist, S.M.S., D.R. Macdonald, M.B., Ch.B., Senior Medical Inspector, S.M.S.; Dr Ali Bedri; and doctors Abdel Halim Mohamed, Abdulla Omer Abu Shamma, El Tigani Mohamed El Mahi and Mansour Ali Hasib. The Governor-General Sir Hubert Huddleston, K.C.M.G., C.B., D.S.O., M.C. and his wife were also vigorous campaigners against the practice.

schoolmistresses[46] with their attempt to bring home to uneducated women the fact, that there was no basis in the idea of religious authority for the practice. For some years before the ordinance teaching on the subject was compulsory in the top classes of all girls' schools. Individual mistresses of their own accord made little speeches at Mothers' meetings and distributed specially designed posters and leaflets.[47] It is not an easy subject for which to obtain a quickly comprehended picture but, as most of the women at these meetings were illiterate, some sort of symbolic representation was needed. Posters illustrating the shadow of the old hag, Superstition, being driven away from little girls by the lovely maiden, Enlightenment, were the most successful.

The difficulty about propaganda was that, as no-one could find a valid reason for the continuance of the operation except the powerful phrase 'our custom', we did not know where to begin the attack and had to move where we could.[48] Psychologists may consider teaching of such a kind in elementary schools highly reprehensible but the need was to start somewhere and not wait for ever. Moreover as all the girls by that time would have undergone the operation, which took place at about eight or nine years old, they were not being confronted with horrors which were new to them. In addition to which some of them might themselves become

46. Senior Sudanese schoolmistresses including Sitt Nafissa Awad al-Karim and Sitt Melk ed-Dar Mohamed were among the pioneers making propaganda tours against 'Pharaonic circumcision' (*ARDE*, 1946). In 1945 107 Sudanese schoolmistresses signed a declaration against the practice, the names of whom are to be found in S.A.D. 657/41. Midwives such as Sitt Howa Ali El Beshir and Batoul Mohamed Eisa were also important figures in the campaign against the practice.

Sitt Howa Ali El Beshir, outstanding nursing pioneer. In her early years she was an elementary mistress; she married young and had two children; in the late 1930s she applied to Miss E. Hills-Young to train at the Midwives' Training School; after her training, an Omdurman merchant donated a house for Howa to set up the first Child Welfare Clinic; she then trained to be a nurse at Omdurman hospital; later she moved to El Obeid to establish the first Midwives' Training School there; from 1944 she campaigned against 'Pharaonic circumcision'; she then went to England to train as an S.R.N.; in early 1950s she went to England to study midwifery and public health; 1955 Principal Matron, Khartoum Hospital; from 1956 she was appointed Matron-in-Chief to Ministry of Health; 1960 Red Cross scholarship to continue training.

47. Propaganda included articles in the press such as 'Drastic laws to kill Sudan custom: Advisory Council talks on circumcision', *Sudan Star*, 7.11.45; 'Industry, liquor and circumcision', Advisory Council Progress Report, *Sudan Star*, 24.4.46.

48. Dr Beasley was a member of the Civil Secretary's Standing Committee on Female Circumcision. In 1942 Miss Hills-Young gave a course on the subject to Sudanese mistresses. From 1942 Sitt Negiba Kronfli, a Girls' Training College tutor, included lessons on the evils of 'female circumcision', with the help of Dr Campbell, Public Health Officer, and the Midwifery School.

mothers within a year or two of leaving school and we hoped that that part of their teaching at least might remain.

The obvious excuse that it was a guardian of chastity was not borne out by the facts. Talk and scandal were as current in the Sudan as elsewhere but still more revealing was an extract from the meeting of a Province Council Report in 1944.

'They attributed the high incidence of homicide in general to ignorance and lack of character training, which comes from education, and in particular to adultery and drunkenness.
To reduce the prevelance of adultery ...'

I may add that both these offences were explicitly forbidden in the Koran.

Another and more insidious obstacle was the masculine belief that thus could a man prove his virility. It is understandable that old men should cling to the beliefs of their youth but the danger lay in that the young men were loath to appear less virile than their fathers. Some were no doubt waiting for a lead and would have been glad to get rid of the custom, provided that they did not have to make an effort in what would have been a wearisome, exacting and disagreeable task. Meanwhile they could always shelve the responsibility for inaction by falling back on the ignorance of their women-folk and the pretence that this was entirely a woman's affair. Adam's excuse was frequently on the lips of the more educated Sudanese. 'It was my wife who did it. When I was away one time she had it done. She knew I didn't want it.'

The most harmful result of all this was the retaliatory accusations of the women, some of which I have mentioned before. As against stories of wives taking action behind the father's back, they told of incidents of mothers pleading for their children in the face of the husband's insistence.

That sort of mutual recrimination led nowhere. The young men might sulk and be resentful that their barbarous habits were being brought to the light of day just when they were beginning to claim their fitness to hold high office and achieve self-government. There was a danger too, that politics might be involved in a 'Hands off our native customs' attitude. But whatever the men's grievances, the women's were stronger; they had undergone the suffering; now they felt they had been 'put upon'. 'Why were we not born twenty years later?' some of the Girls' Training College students used to say. 'It is all very well', said the old women. 'We have always been told we are stupid and that men know all about religion. They told us this was part of our religion and we have undergone all this suffering. Now suddenly they say it is not our religion and we ought not to do it. That it is our fault that it goes on. All right. But first you must assure us that without it we shall get husbands for our daughters.' That assurance was not forthcoming.

The wider significance of this apparently internal wrangle lay in the disquieting thought, that the men who had been educated at so much labour and expense to be the leaders of their people would not accept a responsibility which was manifestly theirs. Does this in different aspects apply to other countries, which are hastening to control their own affairs? How much of reason has been inculcated, when superstition can lie so intermingled among the motives of both men and women? It is in ways like this that the gap between us and African peoples looms so wide, that in moments of despair we feel it can never be bridged.

Admittedly one can understand how difficult it is for a Sudanese suddenly to change his attitude to something, which has come down to him from the beginning of time and in his life has always been a part of the normal round of everyday, accepted and unquestioned. Before the superstition which is mixed up with this and more spectacular rites for different purposes in other countries we stand helpless. For superstition in Africa can be a black, brooding enemy, which lurks in wait in familiar places, hostile to man in his rational aspect and of unlimited power.

When oppression seemed to be settling too darkly over my spirits, I could find relief; it would be time to stop concentrating on 'female circumcision', to refuse to listen to the drums and the *zikr*s, and to turn my enthusiasm to the teaching of First Year arithmetic.

I have quoted in an earlier chapter Sitt Nafissa's remark, that the women of the country had never been told before that this practice was wrong.[49] That perhaps is the moral of it all, that in our plans for making a better world we have not realised sufficiently the evils of sheer ignorance. There has been a great deal of talk about moral rehabilitation, about political education and instruction in better techniques but not enough frontal attack on that prison of mind and body of which ignorance is the gaoler. The trouble is that it takes so long and everyone seems to be in such a hurry. Yet no amount of impatience can alter the fact, that education is a plant which must grow, not a structure which the planners can hustle into shape.

## 7. *Shillukh*, or scarring of the cheeks

As an instance of the way in which customs can be discarded through the appreciation of more enlightened ways is the decrease in *shillukh*, the

---

49. Sitt Nafissa Awad al-Karim.

scarring of the cheeks.[50] When I first went to the country this savage habit
was as extensively practised as Pharaonic circumcision. Some of the more
optimistic schoomistresses hoped that the sudden decline in face scarring
presaged a shift in public opinion, which might help to eradicate the more
serious operation. The origin of *shillukh*, unlike 'female circumcision', is
easily comprehensible. In a land of constantly warring tribes it is useful to
know friends and enemies at a glance. Different ways of scarring the face,
indicating various groups, belonged to an age that is gone, but it was only
towards the end of the 1940s that this cruel custom began to die out.
Happily there could be exact and proven evidence of this. Formerly by the
times the schoolgirls reached the top class they would all have been scarred.
In 1945 I counted half the girls in the Fourth year untouched; three years
later, in one school of 120 girls only six in the whole school had had the
operation and these were among the older pupils.

## 8. The South and 'female circumcision'

There is one other footnote to this. The Government were firmly
determined from the beginning of the Occupation that 'female circumcision'
should never be introduced into the South, where it was quite unknown as a
native custom.[51] One or two Arab merchants, who had been allowed to
trade there, were found to have had the operation performed on local
women and were punished accordingly. One cannot gauge the extent to
which the practice might have spread, had free access been allowed to
Northerners in the early days of the Condominium. With more enlightened
views prevailing now, the contacts between Northerners and Southerners
should not contain this peril.

I have dwelt at so much length on this unhappy question, because, as I
remarked earlier, this is a record of the past and for many good reasons it
has not often been discussed. Since one hopes that the practice has now
been banished for ever, it can be set down as one of the obstacles, which the
women of the country definitely have to overcome in the course of
development. From the above it is obvious that any description of their
growth to self-realisation would be incomplete without stressing this
handicap, which all of them have to endure.

50. For Dr Beasley's notes on *Shulūkh*, see Appendix II.
51. 'As regards its infiltration into the South, Fung, Nuba, Shilluk etc.,' by 1942 the tribal
courts were encouraged to punish cases, which they could legally do under their warrant. (See
letter from Sir Douglas Newbold to Mekkawi Suleiman, 24.9.42 in Henderson, K.D.D., *op.
cit.*, p.274).

How much women themselves have been instrumental in turning the tide we can never know but no doubt their growing sense of responsibility was of the greatest benefit. Instances of this could be multipied indefinitely and are important in the context of schools, because it is no light thing to jump in less than a couple of generations from being a chattel without understanding, expected to stay in the women's quarters, to being a person of influence in the village with a school of a hundred and fifty children in her charge and the power that must necessarily go with such a position. As it became an honour to be a headmistress, gradually in many cases it became too a matter of pride to run a really good school. It was also increasingly evident, that, as new tasks devolved on them, these girls could show considerable capability within their own sphere, and that this sphere was widening.

# 9. Expanding horizons

### 9.1 Schoolmistresses' centre[52]

Widening of scope did not mean that life was all work. In their social relations there was a movement from the mere gossiping in yards or wailing at a funeral to more directed ways of amusement.[53] In 1950 the schoolmistresses initiated a centre of their own in Omdurman, an entirely Sudanese creation planned by themselves. To the expert committee member their ways might appear muddled but the women proved themselves quite capable of starting the club, holding sensible meetings and thoroughly enjoying the new venture.[54] The Dramatic Society and the Library were the two most popular sections and some of the senior mistresses made handsome donations to the latter.[55]

---

52. See S.A.D. 657/3/105.
53. By 1949 the Girl Guides movement was gaining ground in elementary schools (*ARDE*, 1949).
54. Fawzi, Professor Saad al-Din, 'The Role of Women in a Developing Sudan', *Proceedings of the Institute of Differing Civilisations Conference*, Brussels, 1958.
55. The Federation of Women Teachers was founded in 1947 and the Association for the Advancement of Women was founded in 1948. Sitt Anisa Fatma Talib (probably the first Sudanese woman to gain a London B.A.) was President of the Sudan Women's Association. The formation by mistresses of an association for social and cultural purposes began in 1949 (*ARDE*, 1949). The first feminist movement booklet, *True Happiness* by Fatima S'ad al-Din came out in 1956. Dr Fatima Abdel Mahmoud, the former President of the Women's Union, became Minister of Social Affairs (Ministry established in 1976).

## 9.2 Changing leisure pursuits for women

This question of enjoyment is not unimportant, for it is so easy to plan and administer for people's good in what we call the necessities of life, while quite forgetting that these are dust and ashes if they are consumed in joylessness. It is true that in so harsh a country as Sudan the primitive needs bulk large and it would be wrong to talk about, for example, reading for pleasure to people who are hungry and thirsty. That is not the issue. What does matter is that in helping people to develop from the crude levels of existence, educators should not subtract all the old savage pleasures and give no lead towards 'doing things for fun'. Arabic admittedly has no exact equivalent of 'fun'[56] in this sense but the girls understood the idea.

## 9.3 Girls' Training College—Silver Jubilee

For long after many of the schoolmistresses talked rapturously about the celebrations held at the Girls' Training College for its Silver Jubilee.[57] Over three hundred of them attended and for three days they were encouraged to do nothing but enjoy their re-union. No lectures, no improving talks, no official business; nothing but expeditions and parties and the fun of meeting in a holiday spirit. It was an experiment but a tremendous success. It was a pity that distances in the Sudan made difficult such large scale festivals but no doubt smaller ones in districts will be encouraged, as the mistresses become more enterprising.

# 10. Conclusion

The enterprise and the initiative are there but until the last few years all women in the North were firmly locked within the code of Islam in which they as individuals did not matter; from which premise derived the second widely held belief that they were incapable. I have tried to point out how the women themselves were disproving all this but perhaps it is best summed up in the following words of Professor John McMurray. It was not a creed that we were constantly repeating to ourselves; in fact I doubt if we often formulated it in so many words. But I am convinced that it lay at the basis of our endeavours and that I shared it with other British colleagues, whose valued services there has been no room to describe in this book.

---

56. *Tasliya*, diversion, amusement, fun etc. would seem to be an equivalent.
57. Past and present students gathered at the Girls' Training College from 20.12.46 to 22.12.46 for the Silver Jubilee (*ARDE*, 1946).

'Women have increasingly insisted that they too are individuals, and must be permitted to stand upon their own achievement; to realise their own capacities as individuals ... And this is, I think, bound to continue and increase. We cannot do other than look upon it as a momentous advance in culture and civilisation; and to be afraid of it is surely to fail in faith and courage.'

After that there is nothing more to say. When my ten years were finished, it was time to leave but a tale like this has no ending.

# Appendix I

# 'Female circumcision'

## I.M. Beasley

The Pharaonic type of operations, taken from a pamphlet published by the Sudan Government[1]—

> 'This consists in the removal of a large part of the *labia majora* and the paring of the *labia minora* and the removal of the *clitoris*. This operation is usually carried out by an untrained midwife who uses for the purpose an unsterilised razor.
>
> The victim is usually about six years of age. These delicate parts of the child are pared away and a reed or match is inserted into the vaginal opening in order that after the wound heals a small hole may remain for the passage of urine and future flow of *menses*. The girl's legs are then strapped together for forty days to allow the wound in the two sides to heal by contact. In a few tribes thorns are used to suture the wound and these are held in place by thread wound round the projecting ends. The agonised shrieks of the victim are drowned by the cries of the crowd of female relatives who gather to attend the function and to hold the child down during the operation.
>
> The harmful results of this at the time are obvious.
> Shock to the child
> The danger of sepsis
> The possibility of complete occlusion and internal complications.'

Concerning later suffering the following is quoted from a paper read before the Sudan Branch of the British Medical Association in 1936.

---

1. The term 'female circumcision' may be misleading. It may involve clitoridectomy, labiadectomy and/or infibulation. 'Pharaonic circumcision' includes excision of the genital organs and infibulation. See Sanderson, Lilian Passmore, *Against the Mutilation of Women*, the struggle against unnecessary suffering, 1981, pp. 16-19). The editor has been unable to trace the source of the pamphlet, and other quotations given by Dr Beasley in Appendices I and II. The footnotes in Appendices are by the editor.

'When a woman marries sexual intercourse may be difficult or impossible. Nevertheless the husband does not immediately seek assistance because this is considered a disgrace. It is not uncommon for a husband to go on as long as a year trying to force a passage in spite of the torture thus inflicted on his unfortunate wife. Eventually should this prove unsuccessful the services of the midwife have again to be sought. A process of blackmail thus begins and large sums of money have to be paid by the husband before the midwife agrees to operate and the affronted wife consents not to give him away to his friends. Defibulation has to be carried out in childbirth in every case of Pharaonic circumcision ... After the confinement re-infibulation is almost invariably demanded by the husband.'

The following is taken from a report by a British woman doctor.

'The method of delivery of a child in normal labour of a woman who has been circumcised, Pharaonic type. ... proves in my opinion that Sudan women are incapable of delivering themselves normally as an uncircumcised woman is able to do as part of her normal bodily function. If these women had to deliver themselves alone and with no-one near, the child must either remain *in situ* and die from exhaustion with perhaps the mother later, or she may be able to deliver herself by tearing the *perineum* to such an extent that ... she would certainly be an invalid for the rest of her life, if she did not develop severe sepsis or die from shock or loss of blood.

Method. No anaesthetic. When the head is on the *perineum* and it is fully stretched the aperture for delivery would admit about two fingers ... A cut is made upwards towards the pelvis with a pair of long straight scissors ... an opening of four inches is thus made ... the child is then delivered through the open wound and also the *placenta* ... the lips of the wound are then sutured together ... The edges of the wound are then firmly squeezed together, and this leaves an opening that would admit two fingers, when the *perineum* joined up, later it would be less ...'

Sudanese women say that they feel most terrified when they hear the tinkle of the scissors. It should be borne in mind that the above operation has to be repeated for every child no matter how many a woman may bear. One last consequence:

'The resulting narrowing of the vaginal entrance is a cause of barrenness or sterility. In a series of cases of sterility it has been found that twenty to twenty five per cent were due to this cause. The necessity for cutting the scar at each confinement and the sewing up which is carried out after confinement cause repeated mental and physical shocks.'

With regard to the *sunna* form which the ordinance of 1946 permits, a *fetwa* by the *mufti*[2] contains the following among discussions on the subject by authoritative writers.

'Sheikh Mohamed Easa ... said ... that male circumcision was a *sunna* and female circumcision was merely preferable. He described the latter as the partial but not entire removal of the protruding skin at the top of the *vagina*. The Prophet's saying as handed down by Um Attiya, 'Circumcise but do not go too deep, this is more illuminating to the face and more enjoyable to the husband' is definitely intended to forbid excision of that organ as is being done in the Sudan.'[3]

As the law now stands it is not unlawful circumcision to remove the free and projecting part of the *clitoris*.

Unlawful circumcision is punishable under the Penal Code by imprisonment or fine or both.

Even as late as 1980 'female circumcision' has not died out. [It occurs] in more African and Middle Eastern countries than realised.

2. The *mufti* Abū Shāma 'Abd al-Maḥmūd made a *fatwā* on 2.12.39 on 'female circumcision' stating that Pharaonic circumcision is categorically forbidden by Islam. Between 1942 and 1945 British staff of the Department of Education on trek carried copies of this *fatwā*. The *mufti* and Deputy Grand *Kadi* of the Sudan, Sheikh Aḥmad al-Ṭāhir wrote a 'Foreword' in E.D. Pridie et al, *Female Circumcision in the Anglo-Egyptian Sudan*, Sudan Government Publication, 1.3.45.

3. On 17.7.44 Sayyid 'Abd al-Raḥmān al-Mahdī made a speech against 'female circumcision' at *mahraqam* in Omdurman. On 22.7.44 he wrote an article in *an-Nīl* advocating the role of education in combating Pharaonic circumcision with the view of replacement by *sunna*. After his pronouncement on 2.10.44 it was easier to spread propaganda to the villages (S.A.D,. 658/5/15). He also wrote a 'Foreword' in Pridie, E.D. et al, *op. cit.*, 1.3.45, including the statement 'I have enough information to convince people are giving thought to this vicious custom with a view to getting rid of it in a practical way'.

# Appendix II

# Shillukh, scarring of the cheeks[1]

**I.M. Beasley**

Ciciatrisation is practiced among many tribes in the Sudan both in the North and South. Much information on the subject can be found in *Sudan Notes and Records*.[2]

In the North until a few years ago [c.1960] both this operation and one for circumcision were performed on girls about the same time. The scars were generally three horizontal and three vertical lines, sometimes also three vertical lines and one horizontal. The cuts were made with a razor by the village midwife. Salt was rubbed in as an antiseptic. The wound was stuffed with cotton wool to keep it open wide enough to make a large scar.

There are plenty of stories of death from septicaemia or excessive bleeding, cases which were never reported.

It is an odd fact that after a time one becomes so accustomed to the scars that it needs an effort to remember with regard to individual women whether they have been scarred or not.

---

1. *Shillukh* [Col. Ar. *shalikh*, pl. *shulūkh*, also known as *faṣāda*], tribal scarring. *Shalikh*, the action of tribal marking, a single line of scarring; *shallakh*, verb, mark, scar; *mushallakh* (fem. *mushallakha*), a person with tribal scars. Tribal markings are a means of identity and are considered to be beautiful. The custom is probably dying out.

2. There appears to be no single article on the subject of *shulūkh* in *Sudan Notes and Records*. However, there are numerous articles in this journal about tribal customs which include some references to ciciatrisation. See Yūsuf Faḍl Ḥasan, *al-Shulūkh*, Khartoum, 1976.

# Appendix III

# Girls' education in the Condominium

**J.C.M. Starkey**

## 1. Demands for girls' education

With the establishment of the Condominium, and the development of schools for boys, came certain demands for girls' education. For example,

'42. A petition, numerously signed, was recently presented to the Government, with a view to establishment of a girls' school at Khartoum. The majority of the signatures were no doubt Egyptian officials anxious that means of education for their daughters should be brought within their reach, and at the same time preferring the non-sectarian atmosphere of a Government school to that conducted by missionary managers.'

43. ... In the meantime it may be noted as a singular and also, to some extent, as a satisfactory symptom, that whereas but a few years ago the whole of the Moslem population of Egypt were apathetic even if they were not hostile, to the education of girls, now it is regarded as a grievance—not merely by some Cairene Moslems, but also by some of the relatively backward population of Khartoum—that no facilities for female education are at once established in a country in which, as yet, only the rudiments of civilisation can be said to have been introduced.'[1]

### 1.1 Babikr Bedri's school at Rufaa

In 1906 Babikr Bedri had tackled J.W. Crowfoot (1873-1959), then Assistant Director of Education (1903-14) and later Director of Education (1914-26), on the subject of his private venture into girls' education. He had already raised the matter in 1904 and the Director had said that he was mad. Babikr Bakri had replied, 'Give me £10 and I'll build a classroom and open a girls' school. If it goes well, it can continue in it, and if not, it can be a room for the school watchman.'

---

1. *Reports of Departments*, 1906, Part 1, 39-42, p.223 (S.A.D. 657/1/11).

J.W. Crowfoot approved but Sir James Currie in Khartoum vetoed the plan, but said that if Babikr Bedri cared to open one in his own house, at his own expense, he would have no objection. Once Babikr Bedri received this letter from Sir James Currie, he began to sing the praises of having a girls' school to local people. He used the argument that a modern educated young man would be attracted to an educated young woman for a wife; otherwise there would be a danger of loosing them to foreign wives. The local people were utterly opposed on this matter. He did not give up but sought out a woman to teach embroidery and needlework on the basis that once they had seen something work in practice, they would be in favour of it. This led to the appointment of Nafisa Bint al-Makkawi, a local resident.[2]

Babikr Bedri unofficially added a girls' department to the elementary school for boys at Rufaa, at first for his own daughters, with 17 girls, nine from Babikr Bedri's household and the rest local citizens of Rufaa. It was 'staffed by a venerable *sheikh* who taught Koran, religion and the rudiments of reading, writing and arithmetic and a village woman who taught native embroidery.'[3] The Headmistress was Sitt Abuna Mustafa who was appointed in 1908. She was succeeded by Sitt Hanim 'an irresolute and poor manager'. The next Headmistress was Zahra bint al-Qabbani, wife of Muḥammad al-Amin 'Abd al-Halim, 'a good manager' who was sent for training to Unity High School under Miss Bewley.

'The question of constructing a Government school for girls at Khartoum is still under consideration but a school on a small scale has been established at Rufaa (17 girls).' Sir R. Wingate, in giving an account of a recent visit to the Blue Nile Province writes 'I was able to make an inspection at Rufaa of the first girls' school that has been opened under Government auspices in the country. The girls seemed bright and intelligent, and evidently very interested in their studies and anxious to work. I felt it to be a happy augury for the future.'[4] In the same year, 1907, Sir James Currie wanted to know whether Babikr Bedri's girls' school was worth supporting. J.W. Crowfoot inspected the school personally and then asked each parent individually why he had sent his daughter to school. He then decided to grant him a subsidy, with a note to the D.C. In 1910 his girls' school received official recognition. Sir Eldon Gorst, High Commissioner for Egypt, visited the school in 1911 and included a favourable report in his Annual Report.

2. See S.A.D. 657/1/8, also *Report of H.M. Consul General and Agent 1907* (S.A.D. 657/1/4).
3. See *Blue Nile Province Report*, 1910 (S.A.D. 657/1/6,13) and *ARDE*, 1911 (S.A.D. 657/1/19).
4. *Report of H.M. Consul-General and Agent*, 1907 (S.A.D. 657/1/4)).

## 1.2 Mission schools

While there were tentative moves in the Department of Education to establish girls' schools, the missions made more rapid progress in establishing several schools in Northern Sudan. St Joseph's School was opened in 1900 by the Verona Fathers Mission, who also established St Anne's School, Khartoum in the same year. In 1924 there were 140 girls in the Omdurman school and 300 in the Khartoum school. By 1930 there were Roman Catholic schools at Port Sudan and Atbara.

The Coptic School, Khartoum opened in 1902 and in 1903 this became the first Church Missionary Society school for girls. A second was opened in Omdurman in 1906. By 1909 the C.M.S. school in Omdurman had 60 children ' ... excellent work by Miss Bewley ... it is obvious that no school under such management can hope to meet the needs of a convinced Mohammedan population; but this particular institution is doing very fine work ...'[5] The American Presbyterian Mission School, Khartoum North opened 1.9.1908. It developed from an elementary to intermediate school and then later added secondary classes, and boarding facilities. A mission girls' school had also opened at Atbara with 25 pupils in 1908.[6]

'It was pointed out very strongly by Lord Cromer in 1907 that the Sudan Mohammedans had a distinct grievance so long as the only facilities for the education of their girls were thus provided by the various Christian bodies.'[7]

## 1.3 Government schools

Once the Rufaa school had proved to be successful, there was a gradual change in public opinion towards some Government provision for girls. For example, '... it has been definitely decided to build a girls' school in Khartoum and funds have been provided for the purpose. A site has been selected and I would hope that the building might be completed by October 1909 ... a couple of rooms specially for girls are in process of being added to the Khartoum Vernacular School.'[8]

It was not only in Khartoum that pressure was growing for some government provision of girls' education. Wad Medani inhabitants were anxious that a girls' school should be opened in the town and approached Sir James Currie in January 1909. 'It was found impossible to grant their

5. S.A.D. 657/1/13.
6. *ARDE*, 1908 (S.A.D. 657/1/12).
7. S.A.D. 657/1/13,19.
8. *ARDE*, 1907.

request ... as the number of pupils likely to attend the school was not sufficient to guarantee the necessary funds'.[9]

## 2. The expansion of girls' education: some statistics

By 1911 there were Government elementary schools at Rufaa (60), Kamlin (26), Kassala (6) and Dongola (37).[10] In 1912 Rufaa (60), Kamlin (50), Dongola (42), 1913 Rufaa (60), Kamlin (51), Wad Medani (private) 58. In 1919 and 1921 there were five elementary schools at Rufaa, Kamlin, Merowe, Dongola and El Obeid. By 1924 there were Government elementary schools for girls in Rufaa, Kamlin, Merowe, Dongola and El Obeid and there were private schools at Omdurman, Dueim and Geteina.

By 1928 there were 17 schools with an average attendance of 1000 girls.[11] In 1931 there were 23 schools with 2095 pupils. By 1939 43, and by 1946 five new elementary schools were opened and by 1948 there were 89, 12 new ones and two re-opened i.e. Goled (which had remained closed in 1946 as there was little local demand) and Tangassi island, with ten in preparation. 96 elementary schools were working in 1949 and additional classes were added to nine schools.[12] Yet even as late as 1961 the traditional *khalwa*s existed and Sudanese who receive formal education in the Western sense remain a minority.

According to 1941 projections, at the end of 1941, if the proposed new schools were opened, the position would be Darfur 2, Northern 11, Gezira 22, Kordofan 6, Kassala 4, Khartoum 14 (and the Girls' Training College and Intermediate school).[13] The number of schools by Province in 1943 was Khartoum Province 14 (Omdurman 9), Blue Nile Province 23 (Wad Medani 2), Kassala Province 4, Darfur 2, Kordofan 7 (El Obeid 2), Northern Province 13, Training College in Omdurman 1, Intermediate School in Omdurman 1. There were also two girls at Unity High school sponsored by the Government. There were 203 school mistresses, with a deficit of 13. The estimate of deficit on present schools 1944/45 was 27, in 1946 18 and by 1947 3.[14]

9. *Reports of Agents' Departments*, Blue Nile Province, 1909, Education for Girls, p.223 (S.A.D. 657/1/11).
10. *ARDE*, 1911 (S.A.D. 657/1/20).
11. *ARDE*, 1928, London, 1929.
12. *ARDE*, 1946, 1948, 1949. *Times Educational Supplement*, 27.11.48 (S.A.D. 657/5/3).
13. Department of Education, *Notes on a meeting to discuss girls' education in 1942*, 29.3.41.
14. Roseveare, R.V.H., *Notes on meeting about girls' education*, 17.10.43 (S.A.D. 657/1/74).
15. *ARDE*, 1960.

# Appendix IV

# Staff of the Education Department

**J.C.M. Starkey**

## 1. Sitt Melk ed-Dar Mohamed[1]

Sitt Melk ed-Dar (*Malikat ad-dār*) Mohamed was born in 1922 in El Obeid. She attended the boys' *khalwa* but she encountered strong opposition from her family. She used to disguise herself in her brothers' shirt and turban. After a year she went to al-Qubba Elementary School in El Obeid (then the only school for girls there) for 3 years; in 1932-33 she attended the Girls' Training College, Omdurman, a move which met with fierce opposition from her elder brother. He refused outright to allow her to attend and she was forced to set off secretly for Omdurman, without his knowledge. When she returned to El Obeid on holiday she suffered physical violence from him; 1934 graduated.

She taught at Kassala Girls' Elementary School with Headmistress Faṭima Muḥammad from El Obeid; for two years at Singa Girls' School, then she moved to El Obeid. She was extremely talented, wrote songs and put them to music; after 2-3 years in El Obeid she was promoted to Headmistress in 1940. She loved to give speeches at celebrations but this was strongly objected to.

Together with Sitt Hawa Ali el-Basir she organised a women's society to educate the illiterate and gave lessons in a building near the market, against her brothers' opposition. She taught Arabic to the wife of the Inspector in El Obeid who gave her English lessons in return. She pressed for the Intermediate School to be opened in El Obeid, with the help of this lady. Eventually (c.1945-46) she opened the Girls' Intermediate School in El Obeid with Khadiga Mustafa. An English woman was Headmistress (probably Miss Beevers) and Melk ed-Dar was the *ḍābiṭa* (entrusted with discipine). Problems arose between the Headmistress and Khadiga Mustafa, the latter supported by Melk ed-Dar. The pupils demonstrated in support of

---

1. Biographical details of Melk ed-Dar (1922-69) are found in the Sudan Archive, 27.12.1976 (S.A.D. 658/4/49-58). Information therein was given by her sister Aisha Mohamed Abdulla and also includes information from Ina Beasley's journal.

the headmistress and Melk ed-Dar left the school. She was promoted to Inspectress in the Education Office in El Obeid and was allocated a car. In 1946 she undertook a six weeks' tour against 'female circumcision', of Kordofan and Blue Nile Province to Talodi, Kadugli, Muglad, el-Odeya and Nahud, with midwife Sitt Batoul Mohamed Eisa.

She was the first Sudanese woman to learn typing at the Girls' Training College. She started writing in the 1940s. In 1947 she won first prize in a general short story competition with 'The Village Doctor'.[2] She was the first Sudanese woman novelist, with her book *Al-Farāgh al-'Arīḍ* 'The Great Vacuum'.[3] In the mid 1960s she started to write this in El Obeid and continued writing it in Omdurman. It was lost several times by the Publications Committee and the last part was lost by Hasan Najila.

She married Hakemdar Abu Shari who was in his mid-fifties and lived with him in Omdurman. She remained only one year with him, for, unbeknown to her, he forged her signature and collected her allowance from the Girls' Training College. He also disposed of her jewelry while she was in hospital having an operation. She then asked him to divorce her. A year later she married Yousif Mekki el-Sufi. The first five years of this marriage were happy until he took to drink. In 1969 she was posted to El Obeid, but after a violent quarrel with Yousif on the day she was to leave Khartoum, she died of a heart attack (S.A.D. 658/4/49-53).

To commemorate her work a new girls' elementary school was established in El Obeid and named after her.

---

2. Hall, Marjorie, and Ismail, Bakhita Amin, *Sisters under the Sun*, 1981, pp.110-11.
3. *al-Farāgh al-'arīḍ*, was submitted to the Publications Bureau, c.1948, unpublished and not yet traced.

## 2. Women recruited to the Education Department

The following list includes some of those women employed by the Department of Education before, during and just after Dr Beasley worked in the Sudan. In the 1940s, appointments to Girls' Education were termed 'British Mistresses'. They all spent a period in the Girls' Training College, Omdurman being briefed and acquiring some basic Arabic, before being posted elsewhere. Those working, at that time, in the Northern Sudan had to learn Arabic on the job. Expatriate staff only received confirmation to permanent appointment after passing the Lower Arabic Examination, and many of them also took the Higher Arabic Examination.

As many of the women concerned married and changed their names, it has been particularly difficult to follow their careers. Information has been gleaned from a variety of sources, including Government staff lists from 1914 to 1956, and also through personal communications with Dr Beasley, Mrs K.M.E. Wood, Miss E. Jackson, Mrs Grizelda El Tayeb, Mrs Suzanne Abdel Karim, G.E. Janson-Smith, Mrs E.M. Hunt and many others who were involved in girls' education in the Sudan. In particular, Dr Lilian Passmore Sanderson has been most helpful in enabling me to compile this list. The spellings of names are taken from the *Sudan Government Lists*. Further details of many are available in footnotes in the main text. Due to the great interest expressed by many of those who served in the Sudan, the editor is planning to undertake further research on this topic.

Agil Ishag (Sitt). One of the two first women graduates from Gordon Memorial College; pursued a career in girls' education and teacher training; mistress, Girls' Secondary School, Omdurman.

Agil Tadros (Sitt). One of the two first women graduates from Gordon Memorial College; pursued a career in the field of linguistics; 1989 two year Fulbright scholarship.

Mrs M. Ann Amin. 1956 mistress, Girls' Intermediate School, Omdurman; taught in Wad Medani, based at Hantoub.

Mrs Rhoda Amin. 1960s taught mathematics, mistress, Girls' Secondary School, Omdurman.

Miss Shirley Appleby. (Mrs S. Hadi). 1958-65 taught English, Girls' Secondary School, Omdurman.

Miss Asma Mowgood. 20.8.54 First appointment; 1955-56 mistress, Girls' Training College, Omdurman.

Miss Aziza Mohamed Ahmed Khalil. 9.9.54 First appointment; 1956 mistress, Girls' Intermediate School, Omdurman.

Miss Badiha Mustafa. 16.9.53 First appointment; 1954-56 mistress, Girls' Intermediate School, Atbara.

Miss Badia' Hakeem. 20.8.54 First appointment; 1955-56 mistress, Girls' Secondary School, Omdurman.

Miss M.V. Baker. 15.8.51 First appointment; 1951-53 mistress, Girls' Secondary School, Omdurman; 1954-55 headmistress, Girls' Intermediate School, Atbara; 1955 resigned.

Mrs J.M. Barbour. 12.7.54 First appointment; 1955-57 mistress, Girls' Secondary School, Omdurman (temporary appointment); (Spelt Barber on *Government Lists*).

Mrs F. Barratt see Miss M.B. Brown.

Miss Vera M. Barrett. 8.53 First appointment; 1953-55 mistress, Intermediate School, Meridi; resigned on marriage.

Dr Ina M. Beasley. For full details see Editor's Preface.

Miss M.W. Beevers. 22.12.43 First appointment; 1943-c.45 mistress, Girls' Training College, Omdurman; late 1945 headmistress, newly opened Girls' Intermediate School, El Obeid; Nov 1947 transferred to Omdurman owing to breakdown; March 1948 resigned; now deceased.

Miss M.B. Berry. 18.2.52 First appointment; 1952-56 Social Welfare Officer, Adult Education, based in Gezira.

Mrs A. Bothwell. 1.8.53 First appointment; By 1962 Dept of Girls Sectretarial Training, Asst. Grade A.

Mrs E. Bright (Polly). 16.12.42 First appointment; 1942-44/45 mistress, Girls' Training College, Omdurman; a maths teacher; married to John A. Bright of Bakht-er-Ruda.

Miss M. Brown. 12.1.51 First appointment; 1951-52 mistress, Girls' Secondary School, Omdurman; 1953 mistress, Girls' Training College, Omdurman; 1953 resigned.

Miss M.B. Brown, B.Sc. (Mrs F. Barratt). 16.1.47 First appointment; 1947-50 mistress, Girls' Training College, Omdurman and Girls' Intermediate School, Omdurman with responsibility for the teaching of Domestic subjects, including Needlework; 1950- 55 Headmistress;; 1950-55 headmistress, Girls' Intermediate School, Wad Medani; 1956 returned briefly as mistress, Girls' Training College, Omdurman; 1956 left Sudan.

Miss M. Patricia Burns. (Mrs J.S. Owen). 27.9.44 First appointment; 1944-46 headmistress, Wad Medani Intermediate School; 1946 resigned on marriage.

Miss M. Butcher. 26.8.46 First appointment; 1946-50 mistress, Girls' Training College, Omdurman; 1950-51 Vice-Principal, Girls' Training College, Omdurman.

Miss Kathleen M.E. Challis. (Mrs G.C. Wood). 27.12.46 First appointment; 1946-47 mistress, Girls' Training College, Omdurman; Jan 1948-Jul 1949 headmistress, Girls' Intermediate School, El Obeid; Jul 1949-Jan 53 headmistress, Girls' Intermediate School, Omdurman; Jan 1953-Apr 57 headmistress, Girls' Secondary School, Omdurman; Apr 1957-Apr 1958 officially Assistant to Ahmed Mirghani, Controller Women's Education, but worked at Girls' Secondary School, Omdurman until Oct 1957; April 1958 left Sudan.

Miss K. Sylvia L. Clark. 13.9.38 First appointment; 1938-39 mistress, Girls' Training College, Omdurman; 1940 opened Omdurman Girls' Intermediate School, Omdurman as headmistress. Miss Clark was responsible for starting this school, and for its subsequent development. She was headmstress there until August 1949. Also opened two classes for post-intermediate education; these were housed in the Girls' Intermediate school, Omdurman; 1943-44 Acting Principal, Girls' Training College, Omdurman; 1949 succeeded Dr Beasley as Controller of Girls' Education; (spelt Clarke in *Government List* from Sept 50 to Sept 51); March 1955 retired from the service and was succeeded by Ahmed Mirghani.

Mrs L. Coleman. 1.1.42 First appointment; 1942-44 mistress, Girls' Training College, Omdurman; 1944-45 mistress (temporary), Girls' Training College, Omdurman; 1945-46 mistress, Girls' Training College, Omdurman; 1946-47 Vice-Principal, Girls' Training College, Omdurman; domestic science teacher; c.1948 left Sudan.

Mrs Sheila Connelly. 10.11.48 First appointment; Appointed as mistress, Girls' Training College, Omdurman to be resonsible for the teaching of art there and to advise on art in schools; Dr Beasley's sister; Unfortunately, ill health obliged her to resign in 1950.

Miss M.M. Cooper. 7.9.48. First appointment; 1949 mistress, Girls' Training College, Omdurman; taught Domestic subjects; advised and inspected teaching of these subjects in Omdurman Schools and in the provinces; 1950-51 headmistress, Girls' Intermediate School, El Obeid; 1951-1953 headmistress, Girls' Intermediate School, Kerreri; 1953 left Sudan.

Mrs R. Corrick see Miss M.D.G. Edwards.

Mrs Joan Disney. wife of Anthony Disney, a senior D.C. Mrs Disney worked unofficially, or on a temporary basis, during the war years, at Girls' Training College, Omdurman. Always maintained an active interest in womens' education throughout her time in Sudan.

Miss Mary D.G. Edwards. (Mrs R. Corrick). 5.4.46 First appointment; 1946-47 mistress, Girls' Training College, Omdurman; assistant P.E.O. Northern Province; 1947-Apr 1949 Province Education Officer for Girls, Kordofan; Illness necessitated period of sick leave. Returned to work late 1949; 1949-51 headmistress, Girls'Intermediate School, El Obeid; 1951 resigned on marriage.

Miss Esther Bakhit Hanna. 16.9.53 First appointment;. 1954-56 mistress, Girls' Intermediate School, El Obeid.

Miss Dora Evans. 11.10.25 First appointment; 1925-34 Asst. Principal, Girls' Training College, Omdurman; 1934-35 Controller of Girls' Education and Principal, Girls' Training College, Omdurman.

Miss J. Dorothy Evans. 13.11.20 First appointment; 1920-31 Principal, Girls' Training College, Omdurman; By 1932-33 Controller of Girls' Education and Principal, Girls' Training College, Omdurman.

Mrs A.E. Everett. 29.4.53 First appointment; 1953-54 Assistant Superintendent Girls' Education (South) based in Wau, then Juba; 1954 resigned.

Miss Fawzia Adham. 20.8.54 First appointment; 1954-1955 mistress, Girls' Secondary School, Omdurman.

Miss Fawzia El Sayed. 20.8.54 First appointment; 1955-56 mistress, Girls' Training College, Omdurman.

Miss Foreman. 15.3.53 First appointment; 1953-56 mistress, Girls' Intermediate School, Wad Medani.

Miss Phyllis I. Fretwell. 29.1.48 First appointment; 1948-50 mistress, Girls' Intermediate School, Omdurman; 1950-55 Kordofan, Province Education Officer (Girls), based in El Obeid; 1955 resigned.

Miss J. Gibson, 9.6.52 First appointment; 1952-54 Health Worker, Adult Education, Gezira.

Miss M. Ailie Glancy. (Mrs Roy Lauder). 29.1.48 First appointment; for a very short time misstress, Girls' Secondary School, Omdurman; 1948-1949 mistress, Girls' Intermediate School, Wad Medani; resigned on marriage, residing in Medani.

Mrs G. Glass see Miss H.M. Thomson.

Miss E.M. Golding. (Mrs A.R. Hunt). 27.1.48 First appointment; Sept 1948-53 Superintendent Girls' Education (South) based in Juba, then Wau; c.1950 Married Dr A.R. Hunt, Sudan Medical Service but continued in her post under her married name; Oct 1953 resigned.

Miss E.A. Gordon. 1.8.52 First appointment; 1952-54 mistress, Girls' Secondary School, Omdurman.

Miss G.T. Gordon. 1.8.52 First appointment; 1952-54 mistress, Girls' Secondary School, Omdurman.

Miss Ann M. Gorse. (Mrs A. Osley). 4.1.51 First appointment; 1952-55 Vice-Principal, Girls' Training College, Dilling, set up Home Economics in Dilling College; 1955 resigned; now deceased.

Miss F.E.O. Gourlay. 26.11.49 First appointment; 1949-52 headmistress, Girls' Secondary School, Omdurman; resigned while on leave 1952.

Miss Suzanne G. Gumbrielle. (Mrs Mahmoud Abdel Karim). 17.8.53 First appointment; 1953-4 mistress, Girls' Intermediate School, Meridi; worked with Yusuf Bedri at his Intermediate School; reappointed 12.7.54; 1954-56 mistress, Girls' Secondary School, Omdurman; 58-60 mistress, Khartoum Girls' Secondary School; worked at some time at Girls' Intermediate School, Kerreri; 1962- 65 mistress, Girls' Secondary School, Wad Medani; geography teacher; worked two years with Radio Omdurman.

Mrs S. Hadi see Miss Shirley Appleby.

Mrs Harcourt. 1956 mistress, Girls' Secondary School, Omdurman; left Sudan c.1958.

Miss E.M. Harvey (Betty). (Mrs W.B. de la M. Jamieson). 14.10.34 First appointment; 1935-38 Assistant Principal, Girls' Training College, Omdurman; 1939-43 Principal, Training College, Omdurman; 1943 resigned on marriage to Education Inspector W.B. de la M. Jamieson, who also encouraged girls' education in the Sudan (see Chapter I, p.21 [73]).

Miss S.E. Higgs. 5.7.42 First appointment; 1942-44 mistress, Girls' Intermediate School, Omdurman; 1945 resigned.

Miss Vera Hitchcock. (Mrs V. Lesley). 1960s taught Art, Girls' Secondary School, Omdurman.

Mrs R.A. Hodgkin see Miss E.M. Hodgson

Miss E.M. Hodgson. (Mrs R.A. Hodgkin). 27.9.44 First appointment as British Mistress; 1945-46 mistress, Girls' Training College, Omdurman; 1946 worked as the first P.E.O. (Girls) in Kordofan and Darfur; 1947-48 Principal, Girls' Training College, Omdurman; Dec 1947 resigned on marriage and moved to Bakht-er-Ruda in August 1949; after that time she was not involved in girls' education.

Miss N.J. Holt. 30.6.52 First appointment; 1953-57 headmistress, Girls' Intermediate School, Meridi; By 1958 mistress, Teachers' Training College, Meridi.

Miss B. Howard. 6.53 First appointment; 1953 mistress, Girls' Secondary School, Omdurman.

Mrs A.R. Hunt see Miss E. Golding.

Miss D. Phyllis Ibbetson. 29.1.48 First appointment; 1948-49 mistress, Girls' Intermediate School, Omdurman; 1950-52 mistress, Girls' Secondary School, Omdurman; 1952-55 headmistress, Girls' Intermediate School, El Obeid; wrongly listed under two names some in *Government Lists*.

Miss Muriel Irish. (Mrs F.C.A. McBain). 5.4.46 First appointment; 1946 mistress, Girls' Intermediate School, Omdurman; 1946-50 headmistress, Girls' Intermediate School, Wad Medani.

Miss D. Jackson. 10.9.51 First appointment; 1951-53 mistress, Girls' Intermediate School, Wadi Halfa.

Miss Edith Jackson. (b.1915); educated at Herts and Essex High Schools, and St. Hugh's College, Oxford; 29.1.1948 First appointment; 1948-1949 mistress, Omdurman Girls' Training College; 1949 served briefly in El Obeid; Jan 1950 headmistress, Tonj, Bahr el Ghazal, to open Girls' Elementary School for Dinka; early June 1950 school opened, with 4 boarding houses, each for 6 to 8 girls; kitchen, pounding shed, lavatories etc., provided and classes held on verandah until classrooms ready; the post was Sudanised in March 1955; later served in Nigeria, in Sokoto and subsequently in Kaduno; headmistress, Queen Elizabeth Girls' Government Secondary School, Ilorin, Nigeria.

Mrs W.B. de la M. Jamieson see Miss E.M. Harvey

Miss K.S. Jays. 12.2.49 First appointment; 1949-50 mistress, Girls' Training College, Omdurman; 1951-52 mistress, Girls' Training College, Dilling; 1952-55 Principal, Girls' Training College, Dilling; 1955 resigned.

Mrs A.R. Jole see Miss N.B. Stewart.

Mrs D. Kelly. 1.7.54 First appointment; 1954-55 mistress, Girls' Secondary School, Omdurman.

Mrs E. Kennedy see Miss Elizabeth Saville.

Miss Kowthar Mustafa. 20.8.54 First appointment; 1955-56 mistress, Girls' Training College, Omdurman.

Mrs V. Lesley see Miss Vera Hitchcock.

Mrs Roy Lauder see Miss M. Ailie Glancy.

Miss L.T. Lloyd-Jones. 1942 mistress, Girls' Intermediate School, Omdurman.

Mrs F.C.A. McBain see Miss M. Irish.

Miss H.M. McGinn. 16.10.49 First apppointment; 1949-51 mistress, Girls' Secondary School, Omdurman.

Mrs L.G. McNeil see Miss Muriel S. Reed.

Miss Sylvia M. McNeil. (Mrs S.S. Richardson). 16.2.48 First appointment; 1948-49 mistress, Girls' Intermediate School, El Obeid; 1949 resigned on marriage.

Miss Madeleina Girgis. 16.9.53 First appointment; 1954-56 mistress, Girls' Intermediate School, Wad Medani.

Mrs Mahmoud Abdel Karim (spelt Kareem on *Government Lists*) see Miss S.G. Gumbrielle.

Miss A.M. Mead. 21.8.52 First appointment; 1952-54 mistress, Girls' Intermediate School, El Obeid.

Miss M.E. Meston. 1.9.50 First appointment; 1950-53 mistress Girls' Training College, Omdurman.

Mrs E. Mordecar. 30.6.53 First appointment; 1953-55 mistress, Intermediate School, Meridi.

Miss T.B. Muir. (Mrs T.B. Ross). 4.10.49 First appointment; 1949- 50 mistress, Girls' Intermediate School, Omdurman; 1950-51 mistress, Girls' Training College, Omdurman; 1951 mistress, Girls' Intermediate School, Wad Medani; 1952 mistress, Girls' Intermediate School, Omdurman; 1953-54 mistress, Girls' Training College, Omdurman.

Mrs J. Mullan. 17.11.50 First appointment; 1953-54 mistress, Girls' Training College, Omdurman; 1955 P.E.O. (Girls), Khartoum Province; 1955 resigned.

Sitt Nafissa Awad El Karim. 1.9.27 First appointment; By 1962- 63 Inspectress (Girls' Education); for further details see text.

Mrs A. Ossley see Miss Ann M. Gorse.

Mrs J.S. Owen see Miss M. Patricia Burns.

Miss Hilda M. Parkin. (Mrs N. Wibberley). 16.1.47 First appointment; 1947-48 mistress, Girls' Training College, Omdurman; 1949 Vice-Principal, Girls' Training College, Omdurman; 1950-54 Principal, Girls' Training College, Omdurman; married c.1947-48; 1954 resigned and left Sudan in 1954/55.

Mrs Parry of the C.M.S. who acted as Adviser (one of several) to Ahmed Mirghani (for a short time in 1956) on schools in the South.

Miss Lilian M. Passmore. 30.6.53 First appointment; 1953-54 mistress, Girls' Secondary School, Omdurman; 1954-58 headmistress, Girls' Intermediate School, Omdurman; 1958-62 headmistress of new Girls' Secondary School, Khartoum; married Professor G.N. Sanderson in May 1960; 1962 part-time teaching, University of Khartoum; 1963-64 educational research; Nov 1964 left Sudan.

Mrs J.K. Petrie. 21.7.52 First appointment; 1952 mistress, Girls' Intermediate School, Omdurman; 1952-55 seconded to Ahfad schools; 1955 resigned.

Miss P. Joan Pellow. 21.10.39 First appointment; 1939-42/3 mistress then Assistant Principal, Girls' Training College, Omdurman.

Miss D.M. Penson. 18.8.50 First appointment; 1950 mistress, Girls' Secondary School, Omdurman; 1952 resigned on marriage.

Miss L.Y. Pode. 1.10.35 First appointment; 1935-39 Controller of Girls' Education and Principal, Girls' Training College, Omdurman; 1939-42 Controller of Girls' Education.

Miss A.M. Rae. 6.8.50 First appointment; 1950-53 mistress, Girls' Training College, Omdurman; 1953-54 Vice-Principal, Girls' Training College, Omdurman.

Miss A.M. Ravaisou. 5.2.44 First appointment; 1944-46 mistress, Girls' Training College, Omdurman; 1946-55 Province Education Officer (Girls), based in Wad Medani, Blue Nile Province, seconded from the Education Department; Mar 1955 left Sudan.

Miss Muriel S. Reed. (Mrs L.G. McNeil). 29.1.48 First appointment; 1948-50 mistress, Girls' Intermediate School, Omdurman; 1950-51 headmistress, Girls' Intermediate School, Atbara; 1951 resigned on marriage.

Mrs S.S. Richardson see Miss Sylvia M. McNeil.

Mrs Ridler. 1956-58 mistress, Girls' Secondary School, Omdurman.

Miss J. Riley. 10.9.51 First appointment; 1951-52 mistress, Girls' Training College, Omdurman; not on Sept 52 list.

Mrs T.B. Ross see Miss T.B. Muir.

Miss M.P.H. Roy. 21.6.52 First appointment; 1952-53 mistress, Girls' Secondary School, Omdurman; 1954-55 Superintendent Girls' Education, Southern Education, based in Juba.

Miss I.K. Russell. 13.10.50 First appointment; 1950-52 mistress, Girls' Secondary School, Omdurman; Mar 1952 resigned; (spelt Russel on *Government Lists.*

Miss Elizabeth Saville (Mrs E. Kennedy). 1960s taught History, Girls' Secondary School, Omdurman.

Mrs J.R. Shaw see Miss A.M.D. Trollope.

Miss L. Skinner. 7.9.48 First appointment; 1948-49 mistress, Girls' Intermediate School, Omdurman; 1950-54 mistress, Girls' Secondary School, Omdurman; 1954 resigned.

Miss Sowad Mohamed Sadig. 9.9.54 First appointment; 1954-56 mistress, Girls' Intermediate School, El Obeid.

Miss N.G. Spelman. 2.3.50 First appointment; 1950-56 Social Welfare Officer, Adult Education, Gezira.

Miss Margery W. Stanton. 21.6.52 First appointment; 1952 mistress, Girls' Secondary School, Omdurman; 1953-56 deputy headmistress, Girls Secondary School, Omdurman; taught geography; 1956 left Sudan.

Miss N.B. Stewart. (Mrs A.R. Jole). 26.8.46 First appointment; 1946-49 mistress, Girls' Intermediate School, Omdurman; married by Sept 1948.

Mrs Grizelda El Tayeb. 1956-61, mistress, Girls' Training College, Omdurman and at Girls' Secondary school, Omdurman; from 1961 mistress, Khartoum Girls' Secondary School and at the two- year training school, the Intermediate Teachers' Training College, Omdurman. She set up Art departments and designed the art syllabus for Sudan; wife of Arabic lecturer (later Professor) Abdulla El Tayeb.

Mrs F.I. Thomas. 17.11.50 First appointment; 1950-53 mistress, Girls' Training College, Omdurman; 1953-54 Province Education Officer (Girls), Khartoum Province, based in Omdurman. Miss Sylvia Clark relied on her to 'hold the fort' at headquarters when Miss Clark herself was on trek; 1954 resigned.

Miss S.A.E. Thompson. 18.8.50 First appointment; 1950-51 mistress, Girls' Intermediate School, El Obeid; 1952-53 mistress, Girls' Secondary School, Omdurman; 1952-53 Province Education Officer (Girls), Northern Province, based in Ed-Damer; 1954-55 headmistress, Girls' Intermediate School, Kerreri; 1955 resigned.

Miss H.M. Thomson. (Mrs G. Glass). 5.4.46 First appointment; 1946-48 mistress, Girls' Intermediate School, Omdurman; 1948 resigned on marriage.

Miss A.M.D. Trollope. (Mrs J.R. Shaw). 27.9.44 first appointment; 1944 mistress, Girls' Training College, Omdurman and mistress, Girls' Intermediate School, Omdurman; 1946 resigned on marriage.

Miss W.E. Tucker. 4.1.50 First appointment; 1950-51 mistress, Tonj.

Miss Wasima Abu Bakr. 1956 mistress, Girls' Secondary School, Omdurman.

Mrs N. Wibberley see Miss Hilda M. Parkin.

Miss M.E.A. Wickham. 17.6.52 First appointment; 1952-54 mistress, Girls' Training College, Omdurman; 1955 Vice-Principal, Girls' Training College, Omdurman; 1955 resigned.

Miss E.D. Williams. 18.12.38 First appointment; 1939 Superintendent Girls' Education, Omdurman (post vacant by Oct 1939).

Miss L.M. Witherspoon. 27.9.44 First appointment; by 1946 Principal, Girls' Training College, based in Khartoum; March 1947 resigned.

Mrs G.C. Wood see Miss K.M.E. Challis.

## 3. Masters in Girls' Education

Apart from masters listed in the footnotes, such as Abdel Rahman Ali Taha and Osman Mahgoub, the following list includes men who were involved in girls' education up to 1956.

Sheikh Abdalla Abdel Mahmoud. 1.11.12 First appointment; by Sept 1946-47, master, Girls' Training College, Omdurman.

Abdalla Mohammed Ahmad Awad. 1.3.47 First appointment; By 1951 master, Girls' Secondary School, Omdurman; 1951-53 editor, Publications Bureau, Khartoum; 1954-55 master, Girls' Training College, Omdurman.

Sheikh Abdalla Mohamed Omer El Banna. 1.10.12 First appointment; by January 1944 Arabic master at Bakht-er-Ruda; by 1946 lecturer, Gordon Memorial College; 1946 retired.

Abdalla Omer. 15.2.41 First appointment; By 1956 master, Girls' Intermediate School, El Obeid.

Abdalla Suleiman El Manoufli. 11.1.50 First appointment; By 1954-55 master, Girls' Training College, Omdurman.

Abdel Aal Hammour. — ; By 1952-54 master, Girls' Training College, Omdurman; 1954 retired.

Abdel Gadir Hussein. 1.9.53 First appointment; By 1953 master, Girls' Training College, Omdurman.

Sheikh Abdel Gader Abdalla. 1956 Principal, Girls' Training College, Dilling.

Abdu El Megid. In 1940 at Bakht-er-Ruda and was sent by Miss Pode to help Sitt Medina Abdulla examine in Arabic at Wad Medani C.M.S. School.

Ahmed Abdalla Sami. 4.6.46 First appointment; by 15.3.55 master, Girls' Training College, Omdurman; 1956 Vice-Principal, Girls' Training College, Omdurman.

Ahmed Beshir El Abbadi. 1.1.31 First appointment; 1960 took over as Controller (Girls' Education) from Ahmed Mirghani; By 1962 Asst. Director (Girls' Education).

Sheikh Ahmed El Bashir El Tayib. 25.9.16 First appointment; 1946 on temporary duty for Northern Province, from post based at Bakht-er-Ruda as a Province Education Officer; 1947-51 P.E.O., Northern Province; 1953-54 master, Girls' Secondary School, Omdurman; 1955-56+ Principal, Girls' Training College.

Ahmed Mirghani. 2.9.28 First appointment; By 1946-47 headmaster Shendi Intermediate School; By 1948 headmaster, Omdurman Secondary School; 1949-51 headmaster, Bakht-er-Ruda School, Dueim; 1952-53 Supervisor, Dilling Teacher Training Centre; 1954 Supervisor, Shendi Teacher Training Centre; 1955 Supervisor, Bakht-er-Ruda; 1956-1960 Controller of Girls' Education, succeeeded by Ahmed Beshir El Abbadi; 1962 Asst Director (P. and C.), Ministry of Education.

Sheikh Ahmed Mohamed Ibrahim. 8.1.37 First appointment; By 1948-54 master, Girls' Intermediate School, Omdurman; 1955-56 master, Girls' Training College, Omdurman; from 1956 for some years he taught religion in Girls' Intermediate School, Omdurman.

Ahmed Mohamed Nur. 1.1.41. 1956 master, Girls' Intermediate School, Kerreri.

Ahmed Mohamed Salih, M.B.E. 1.10.14 First appointment; By 1944 master, Gordon Memorial College; By 1946 master, Omdurman Secondary School; Sept 1946 master, Hantub Secondary School, Wad Medani; 1947 assistant headmaster, Hantub; 1947-48 Supervisor, Omdurman Junior Secondary School; By Dec 1948-51 Assistant Director of Education.

Ahmed Musa Yacoub. 15.2.43 First appointment; 1953-54+ master, Girls' Intermediate School, Kerreri.

Ali Salih Dawood. 2.9.44 First appointment; 1952-54 master, Girls' Training College, Omdurman.

Bushra Abdel Rahman Magboul. 1.1.29 First appointment; 1946-47 master, Girls' Intermediate School, Omdurman; 1948-49 headmaster, Intermediate School, Berber; 1950-51 headmaster, Bakht-er-Ruda, based at Dilling; 1951-53+ headmaster, Bakht-er-Ruda; 1956 P.E.O. (Girls), Blue Nile Province.

Geili Babiker. 1.1.42 First appointment; 1950-52 master, Dilling, Bakht-er-Ruda; 1952-53+ master, Girls' Secondary School, Omdurman.

Hussein Khogali. 1.1.41; 1956 master, Girls' Intermediate School, Atbara.

Ibrahim Omer El Nahas. 1.8.55; 1956 master, Girls' Training College, Omdurman.

Sheikh Ismail Abu el Gasim. 1.10.41 First appointment; 1949-52 master, Hantub Secondary School; 1952-56+ master, Girls' Secondary School, Omdurman.

Ismail Omer. 1.9.32 First appointment; 20.8.50 P.E.O. (Girls), Kordofan Province.

R.W. Jeffery. 8.7.51 First appointment; 1955-56 master, Girls' Secondary School, Omdurman.

Khalid Musa. 1.1.31 First appointment; By 1946 master, Girls' Training College, Omdurman; 1947-51 master, Wadi Seidna Secondary School; Mar 1949 study course in U.K.

Khogali Omer. 1.7.33 First appointment; 21.8.55-56+ P.E.O. (Girls), Khartoum Province.

Mahmoud Abdel Karim. 1961 started Girls' Secondary School, Wad Medani; 1962-65 headmaster, Girls Secondary School, Wad Medani; married Miss S.G. Gumbrielle (see above).

Mahgoub Makawi. 1956 master, Girls' Intermediate School, Wad Medani.

Mekki Abbas. 1.1.31 First appointment; by 1944 working on the Um Gerr project; by 1946 Adult Education Officer, Bakht-er-Ruda; 1947 on Advisory Council for the Northern Sudan, representing Blue Nile Province Council; 1947-48 Gordon Memorial College Council; 1950-53+ Sudan Gezira Board. Author.

Sheikh Mohamed Ali Hamad/Ahmed. 1.1.46 First appointment; 1950-52 master, Girls' Training College, Omdurman; Ahmed not Hamed on Sept 51 list; 1952 resigned.

Mohamed Ali Osman. 15.2.42 First appointment; By 1953-56 master, Girls' Intermediate School, Wad Medani; By 1959 Vice-Principal Girls' Training College, Wad Medani.

Mohammed El Hassan El Amin. 1956 master, Girls' Training College, Omdurman.

Mohamed Yousif Abu Turki. 15.2.43 First appointment; By 1954 master, Girls' Training College, Omdurman.

Mubarak Idris. 1.1.43 First appointment; 1955-58 master, Girls' Training College, Omdurman; By 1959-63+ Vice-Principal, Girls' Training College, Omdurman.

El Nur Ibrahim. 1.1.31 First appointment; By 1946-53 master, Girls' Training College, Omdurman; 1954-55+ P.E.O. (Girls), Northern Province.

Osman Ibrahim. 1.1.17 First appointment; By 1946-49 master, Bakht-er-Ruda; 1950-54 master, Girls' Training College, Omdurman.

Salih Adam. 12.4.33 First appointment; 1948-49 master, Girls' Intermediate School, Omdurman; 1950-52 headmaster, Wad Medani Intermediate

School; 1953 headmaster, Goled Intermediate School; By 1963 Senior Technical Inspector, Khartoum Province.

El Tayeb Shibeika. 4.2.39 First appointment; 1955-56 P.E.O. (Girls) Northern Province.

Sheikh Yousif El Khalifa. By Sept 1951 master, Girls' Secondary School, Omdurman; not on Sept 52 list.

# Appendix V

# Extracts from Dr Beasley's journals on girls' education

## selected by J.C.M. Starkey

The following impressions of Dr Beasley's visits to schools in the Three Towns and later in the Provinces, and to the Girls' Training College, Omdurman have been selected from her diaries[1] to show the wide range of facilities available when Dr Beasley first arrived in Sudan. Additional comments are provided by the editor.

## 1. School inspections in the Three Towns

Even in 1939 there were very few Government schools for girls although several mission schools existed. In Omdurman girls' education was in the hands of the Church Missionary Society.[2] Dr Beasley made some schoolinspections                                                                 and visited the following schools shortly after she first arrived in the Sudan;-
22.11.39 St Joseph's School, Khartoum; 23.11.39 C.M.S. School, Omdurman; 25.11.39 Wad Nubawi School, Omdurman and Siddig Eisa School, Omdurman; 26.11.39 Al Abbassia School, Omdurman; 27.11.39 American Presbyterian Mission School, Khartoum North;[3] 28.11.39 Unity High School; 2.12.39 Khartoum North School; 18.12.1939 Coptic School, Khartoum; 2.1.40 St Joseph's School, Omdurman.[4]

1. S.A.D. G//S 968.
2. In 1940 Miss A.K. Hunter was Assistant, Girls' Schools, C.M.S. Northern Sudan Mission, based in Omdurman, with whom Dr Beasley would have had contact.
3. The headmistress at the Khartoum North American Mission school was Miss N.M. McClellan in 1939, with Miss Turk as a teacher with Miss V. Pillow running the American Presbyterian Mission Library in Khartoum.
4. Appropriately Dr Beasley started at St. Joseph's, one of the earliest of the mission girls' schools.

## 1.1 St Joseph's School, Khartoum

Her first inspection was at St Joseph's School, Khartoum on 22.11.39. Dr Beasley found a school copying a European model rather without adaptation. Her first impressions were:-

1. Neat, orderly and this particular morning discipline seemed excellent and I don't think the girls were subdued.
2. Certain amount of show kept for visitors
e.g. Drill—a few exercises learnt off by heart and repeated by rote.
Sewing—shown a few pieces of good embroidery of Victorian type.
[Art]—excrucable paintings—copies of particularly uneducational postcards for the most part. No imagination.
Singing—extremely bad singing, just learning by heart—was not shown a singing lesson in progress, merely bad results in Italian, French and English.

Syllabuses seemed reasonable. No opportunity of judging how far instruction kept to syllabus. The books in use, apart from a deplorable effort on religious instruction, were comparatively well chosen e.g. Piers Plowman Series for History. French also looked a trifle old-fashioned.

A round of the classes in progress suggested that there was much reading out of books but not a great deal of explanation or questioning. This probably due to fact that much of instruction in English and teachers' proficiency possibly inadequate.

Apparent difficulties of polyglot instructions did not appear to worry the Mother Superior when asked about it. So many languages among staff and pupils that probably always an interpreter at hand. Sisters seemed to converse in a blend of English, French and Italian.

In History, French and Religious Instruction (English) girls were simply reading aloud. A certain glibness but accuracy doubtful. Should imagine results somewhat superficial. Too much work of copying variety. Dressmaking exercise books showed neat results but identical notes and patterns. Results in one or two garments shown good as far as execution was concerned, standard of taste open to criticism.

The three girls in examination class talked intelligently and were bright and interested. Probably provide good material for exam results.

Kindergarten seemed to be badly run. Did not see any apparatus of normal type. Children were just sitting in desks but many were merely scribbling on slates and unable to understand the making of English letters which a few were attempting. A little rather dull paperwork was produced but doubtful if the children found the routine anything but dreary.

I feel it quite right and natural that it should be thought proper for me to see the school at its best but the mere fact that I had this feeling of best behaviour made me wonder how different a normal day would be. I realise that a prejudice against the whole system may have influenced me. Possible that it is a solution of the education problem for the odd bits of communities in a place like this but not perhaps a very happy one.

**1.2 Wad Nubawi School**

The first Government school Dr Beasley visited was on 25.11.39. Her
impressions make an interesting contrast with those on St Joseph's and
highlight the problems of cramped buildings[5] and sloppy teaching which
she later did so much to overcome.

> Went with Sitt Negiba to visit Wad Nubawi School. On the way stopped at
> Siddiq Aissa School to leave a mistress. A very small building tucked away in
> a back street. The rooms were abominably overcrowded, and there was little
> space outside for the children to play. Did not stay to watch the teaching but
> under those conditions any teaching must be difficult. Only advantage of a
> mud hut with earth floors that probably a number of the children live in such
> and it it is possible to inculcate tidy habits in this place, they might be really
> useful.
>
> The Wad Noubawi School was a larger mud building and with a bigger
> yard. Not quite so compressed and obviously unhealthy but really fit for
> condemnation ... Possible this may have had an effect on the school but the
> sloppy atmosphere could not be attributed entirely to that except that the
> better teachers would doubtless prefer to go elsewhere if possible.
>
> Should be inclined to ascribe much of the slackness to the headmistress.
> Must remember that it is unfair to judge on such slight data but she did not
> make a favourable impression. She was very ornate and had a face like a
> painting from an Egyptian tomb. The other teachers seemed lazy also.
> Speaking in soft voices was carried to the length of not so much as rousing the
> children.
>
> There was a lack of order about the usual disposition of things, changing of
> classes and giving out of books.
>
> The lessons were conducted in a slack way. The children, according to
> Negiba, did not understand many of the words in their reading books. Some
> of the books were neat ... most striking thing to me the way in which the
> children in the first class answered up brightly but other classes deteriorated
> until the top classes just muttered. Were capable of standing up and going on
> reading so that no-one could hear, the teacher doing something else and most
> of the rest of the class reading to themselves.
>
> Standard of handwork low. Too much copying apparent in the drawing
> books. Clay modelling might possibly have been made more use of. I thought
> it rather poor that the first class should sit and pull wool for stuffing
> pincushions throughout a whole lesson. Again the native embroidery was
> good and the needlework on the whole was neat. The headmistress insisted on
> showing me piles of it.

5. Dr Beasley pursued problems of overcrowding with vigour throughout her career in Sudan.
In the early days she discussed the problems with the Director of Education, R.V.H. Roseveare
[13.2.40], Tom Brown [14.3.40], Denys Hibbert [23.3.40] at a P.E.O. meeting, and the
Controller, Miss L.Y. Pode [5.4.40] as well as the Public Health Department [13.4.40 seq.].

The whole place wanted pulling together and even with the unfavourable surroundings something a little more vigorous would have been possible.

## 1.3 Siddiq Issa School

By 1940 there were often inequate buildings as Dr Beasley found in her early inspections. For example

I have been to Siddiq Issa before and thought then it was a deplorable place. I am still of that opinion. The headmistress was not necessarily incompetent but she must be working under tremendous difficulties. The place was very cramped and the various classes must have interfered with one another considerably in the way of noise [12.2.40].

## 1.4 El-Murada School

In contrast at El-Murada (C.M.S. School) ;-

A delightful little place. There were only two classes but both were working hard and the whole place was quiet and well under control ... the headmistress[6] was intelligent and we were able to understand one another, which was encouraging [15.2.40].

## 1.5 El-Abbasiya School

Dr Beasley found El-Abbasiya School, Omdurman a very much better school on 26.11.39.

A brick building, with clean tiled floors and a large verandah where drill could be taken at all times.
    The headmistress seemed able and efficient. It was easy to keep the place clean and tidy and everything was extremely orderly ... Sitt Negiba said that the standard of work was higher as far as actual substance went ... There was much more vigour in the teaching generally. I saw a reading class, taught by a Copt which did not mumble—a lesson in Quran where the babes chanted very attractively. The drill was very poor. The student retained her *tobe* and did not attempt to show the girls anything.

6. From 11.7.39 the Headmistress was Sitt Henaina Tadros, her predecessor being Sitt Hanim Goubrial.

... saw a good lesson in arithmetic by one of the older Sudanese teachers. It was valuable as a standard, showing what can be done by an able teacher with a firm grip on her class.

In comparison Dr Beasley saw the same class being given an Arabic lesson on 15.11.39. 'The student was young, ineffectual and by the end of the lesson completely overwhelmed' and the class was 'bored, noisy and inattentive'. Dr Beasley conducted English lessons herself

... with rather unsatisfactory results. Two or three of the girls knew a good bit more than the others and were interested. Some went to sleep. This variation is exactly on the same lines as an English class [16.11.39].

Dr Beasley watched Miss Harvey taking a drawing class, invigilated at exams and even acted as head in Miss Harvey's and Miss Pellow's absence.


## 4. Blue Nile Province

### 4.1 Bakht-er-Ruda *kuttāb*

The classrooms for the students were quite normal, but in the *kuttab* the boys have to sit on mats on the floor and write at low desks. This was due to an idiosyncrasy on the part of a Governor here. I doubt its wisdom. The boys may not be used to chairs at home but neither are they in the habit of sitting at desks doing much writing.

Much care has been expended on the drawing up of the syllabus and the writing of the arithmetic textbook ... the general level was far above the girls' schools.

The project lessons are avowedly an experiment ... Mr Griffiths has not yet made up his mind as to their real educational value. Projects included making cheese, growing flowers, making calendars and running a stall [1940].

Dr Beasley visited the *kuttāb* again 22.1.1941, where she felt that discipline is easier in girls' schools. She observed students and later the headmaster, giving an arithmetic lesson.


### 4.2 Ed Dueim

On 16.1.40 Dr Beasley visited two lessons at Ed Dueim Girls' school and thought it

rather scrappy. There were four mistresses. The headmistress ... is new, seemed an attractive girl and able. Of the others there was one tall, bad-tempered looking girl, who might do well with careful handling or who might just turn into a shrew. Of the other two one was just tolerable and the other a definitely bad teacher ... I saw a very bad geography lesson but the girl had to keep two classes going. She was making one class write in copybooks while she discussed the earth and the sun with another ... although the girl had gone to the trouble of lighting a lamp, she waved the lamp round the globe ... The writing was being done with shaped wooden sticks ... writing letters for forty minutes is dulling and a number of the children were inclined to idle ... the domestic science rooms were scrubbed clean and in good order ... Somehow I did not like the general tone of the school and I understand that it is not regarded with favour in the town [16.1.40].

### 4.3 Gulli

There is a big difference between the girls at Kosti and Gulli. The girls in Class IV in Gulli were noticeably healthier, brighter and better-looking ... There were no new entrants in January because of the cotton harvest and the first year were a sorry remnant left down from last year. It seemed incredible that they had could have been in school a year and have learned nothing.

Sitt Amna seems rather lost. She had been foolish about the arrangement of classes, putting I and II in a smaller room than III or IV, leaving too many benches in IV and leaving 6 on a bench in I ... why was this school left without readers last year? ... I imagine they must have spent a large proportion of time last year sewing. An interesting school but probably needs frequent inspections. Hafiza apparently liked the life there and she and Halima have far more possibilities than Mariam Abdel Basit, who is probably responsible for neglect of class I ... Could be such an attractive school. Decent building with a feeling of openness about it [20.1.41].

Attendance at Gulli on this visit (20.1.41) was good, with Class I 12/17 Class II 15/16 Class III 14/14 and Class IV 15/15.

### 4.4 Kosti

I was not able to see the school on 18.1.40 because it was the *'Id*.

I went, however, to see the headmistress, who had just been installed in her new house and who showed me over this and the new school building with justifiable pride. It is a brick building, distempered in white and doors and windows painted in a pleasing shade of pale green. the mistresses house was spacious and contained a bathroom with an ordinary long bath. The headmistress seemed a capable person but it was impossible to formulate any criticism of the school [18.1.40].

In 19.1.41 Dr Beasley stayed at the rest-house, furnished and with attendance and found it quite comfortable, but the town was still 'most unlovely'.

The school buildings are good and as usually happens, the school is living up to them. Not as many children as I expected but a well-balanced lot .... The headmistress Mariam's character may tell against the school in time. She has been good and is still very capable and probably awe-inspiring to the children. But she is getting fat and 'bad on her feet'. I noticed she taught no arithmetic but a lot of Koran .... this does not matter as the younger girls may quite well teach arithmetic better ... it shows a certain laziness ... but a considerable degree of wisdom. I liked Effendia and her work. She will probably get out of the habit of talking so much. Nur and Nafissa Musa are good girls and intelligent. Nafissa ran a little to seed by hanging about the college but should do well with a little prodding ... Nafissa's lessons on tens and units without apparatus bored the tinies but with a coloured chart they were all keen to take part ... a crime to leave children sitting without anything to do, even if the needlework stores haven't come. The children are too well-behaved. They are ordinary and noisy in their play, however, and show a healthy interest in food. I was interested to see that some of them were walking around the playground reading their new readers aloud. A very pleasant school to be in and the only one I remember that has a good bed of flowers—zinnias, also trees, and a *henna* hedge just coming up [19.1.41].

In 1946 'I intended to go to Kosti and Tendelti but was unwell again.'

### 4.5 Deims Rufaa school

9-10.4.40 Dr Beasley preferred it to the other school in Rufaa.

It has not the same 'tone' but there is a much more energetic undercurrent and I felt the teachers, (especially the Headmistress and Sitt Khitma) were more efficient ... the whole note suggested more efficiency and less reliance on the good name of the school [9.4.40].
    ... Was pleased in Class I when I set children some fresh sums to find that they could do them. Was not so pleased to find Sheikh Lutwi standing impressively in middle of room looking down on me [10.4.40].

On 20.1.41 Dr Beasley went to Deims Rufaa school.

The school in good working order. Was delighted with recitations in II and IV because the children enjoyed it so ... I was also delighted that the women's class was such a success ... about half of them had attended school before marriage.

In January 1942 'one of my primary concerns was to see the Adult Education Centre which I tried to start in 1941'.

## 4.6 Hassaheisa

Hassiheissa is as unattractive as Rufaa except that the D.C. has a lovely garden. It is about ten acres ... laid out like an English park ... a rose garden and sweeping drives.

The school has been badly built and the doors and windows are all loose ... half the mistresses' quarters was being used for the pupils. The result was most reprehensible overcrowdiing. One of the mistresses here an interesting case. Christian family, with a sister working for C.M.S. The brother living on their earnings and parents dead. He was angry because the sister was not allowed to teach in Omdurman where he could live on her salary.

## 4.7 Welfare Worker at Rufaa

In February 1941 Dr Beasley was actively seeking a suitable Sudanese to be a welfare worker based at Bakht-er-Ruda, but had some difficulties. Both Griffiths and the Governor of Kordofan were interested in the idea.

It was very difficult to find the right type of woman.

Dr Beasley felt that it would be

better for all in the long run if she were Sudanese, but is it possible to find one with the right amount of initiative [18.1.1941].

Dr Beasley and Miss Betty Harvey interviewed Salwa Idris, a relative of Babikr Bedri, ex-schoolmistress, divorced and with a boy of seven, but she did not want to have anything to do with confinements. Dr Beasley had further discussions with Griffiths [2.2.41] and felt that the difficulties were still tremendous, as it was doubtful if they could find a girl sufficiently imaginative to know what is wanted and not be afraid of work of a slightly unpleasant kind. The list of duties looked rather formidable. On 18.3.41 Dr Beasley investigated the possibility of a widow who professed herself willing to do anything. [21.3.41] Sheikh Lutwi and Osman Mahjoub came to see her in Rufaa to say they approved of Dar al-Gilaal as woman welfare worker at Bakht-er-Ruda. In addition [26.11.41] Miss E. Hills-Young went to Rufaa to initiate the work of the welfare worker, as Dr Beasley had a chill at that time and could not go herself.

I want the women to run it for themselves. The centre is under the charge of the former Headmistress of the Deims school. I think she had a conscience but it needs a degree of sophistication to pass from a job planned by headquarters to make a job for oneself without a model. Being a married woman has helped her in establisheing contacts but it does not solve the problem of material for the school ... It is all so nebulous ... I need to think out something to give fresh impetus ... The contact with the ante-natal work of the midwives should be valuable ...

By 27.9.44 Miss C.G. Richards was appointed Social Welfare Officer at Bakht-er-Ruda.

## 5. The West

### 5.1 Government Policy in the Nuba Mountains

The area presented the Government with a tricky problem. The British Empire was supposed to be tolerant of all religions and creeds. The Northern Sudan was firmly Muslim, but the Nubas were not Muslim. The British Government was fairly sure that once their country was opened up, there would be plenty of Arab traders and so on going in and what with that and the contact that was bound to occur, this vague paganism would be bound to give in to the strength of a religion such as Islam, a positive religion with a terrific force behind it in numbers, history, wealth and tradition. It has a definite set of rules which are by no means difficult for the underdeveloped to follow, without attempting to cope with the more abstruse doctrines, in which the *sheikh*s at Muslim universities delight as much as the good old scholiasts.[9]

Meanwhile contacts were growing between the Nuba and the Sudanese in the ordinary everyday way and the Nuba were going to lose very heavily if no one was going to bother about their education at all. The Government started some schools of its own in which, of course, it taught in Arabic. Copts as far as possible, were employed as being a type of Christian.[10] One or two Muslim teachers and the learning of Arabic made another link between Nubas and the Muslim world round about. The missionaries were furious and went around shouting about the dishonesty of the Government, and a breach of faith—but someone had to teach the wretched people.[11]

Practically nothing was done for the girls.[12] I protested, or they would be getting too far behind their menfolk and we should have just the same trouble again that they had in Sudan proper, where the educated Sudanese man complains that he cannot find a fit mate.

In September 1944 Mr Kingdon's proposal to send all girls to El Obeid was condiered by Dr Beasley as an unmixed evil, leading to their arabisation and

9. See Dr Beasley's letter to the Director of Education, September 1944 (S.A.D. 657/3/1-2); Dr Beasley's Report of July 1945 to the Director of Education (S.A.D. 657/3/8-11).
10. At Heiban, for example, Coptic mistresses were sent at the request of the local Mission. Apart from religious instruction, the school was conducted along the usual lines (*ARDE*, 1948).
11. See S.A.D. 657/6/1-11.
12. There was a proposal by Mr Kingdon (Deputy Governor, Kordofan 1935-44) to send ten to El Obeid (September 1944, S.A.D. 657/3/1-2).

the accompanying seclusion and circumcision. Dr Beasley felt that they would not fit into a normal boarding school and that it was better to educate them in the Nuba mountains alongside the boys.

> The missionaries, during the twenty years in which they have had a free hand have not managed to develop education within the framework of their evangelisation. It is therefore better to have a secular framework of education in which religious values would be encouraged to flourish even if no deliberate bias were given to either Islam or Christianity.[13]

In November 1944

> a fine missionary[14] had to return home because of ill-health. His wife was a doctor who had been at college with me. He had believed it was impossible to convert the Nubas to Christianity until they were educated. He therefore set about educating them. I thought it rather a sin to let him go without picking his brains. Trimingham,[15] the C.M.S. Secretary asked me to tea. I said it seemed a pity to let the boys get too far ahead of the girls. At the end of the year, out of the blue came a request from the Church Missionary Society for a grant for a girls' school which they were setting up in the Nuba Mountains, to be run by a woman,[16] who had quite satisfactory qualifications. Obviously the C.M.S. were afraid we might get in first. They were given a grant for a year but were warned that an inspection and satisfactory report would be necessary for a grant for the next year. Thus I was on my tour of inspection[17]

## 5.2 Sallara

> I didn't think much of the Arithmetic. Although the children were learning their letters in Arabic satisfactorily, that is an easy stage which even the most indifferent of our teachers can cope with. They also had one lesson a day in spoken English ... confused thinking on Miss Hassan's part. She said the Colonial Section of the Institute of Education had recommended it. But she did not know if the recommendation was made where there was a language like Arabic. I suspect the missionaries in their hatred of Arabicisation also recommended it. It seemed to me rather a lot to be teaching children with no literate background, 2 new languages at the same time.
>
> There was a drill lesson in English because Miss Hassan said she had to be spontaneous. From a plain woman well in her thirties this sounded a little forced ... a dull lesson ... with certain limitations of communication.
>
> The handwork was poor—mostly sewing which, as the theory was not to encourage the use of clothes, seemed a little contradictory ... there had been a

13. S.A.D. 657/3.
14. Rev. R.S. Macdonald and wife, Dr Catherine Macdonald, a medical officer.
15. Canon J. Spencer Trimingham. By 1940 Secretary, C.M.S., Khartoum. Author.
16. Miss Rachel Hassan.
17. Ina Beasley in a letter to her sister Mrs Sheila Connelly, April 1945.

bit of difficulty in enforcing this naked simplicity. Parents thought it a step backward and the local *mek* had removed his daughters. Boys in Government schools were given shorts so they thought the girls should be given something. Therefore in the classroom they had doled out to them little bits of nasty cheap cloth like an apron.

Gardening was on the programme ... a very small sandy patch near the well ... Mr Martin told us [it] was generally a hollow scooped out of a hill ... the children had planted a *zareeba* around it but when I went to look, most of this had blown away.

She had a lesson in Arabic every morning, while Miss Norton took a Scripture lesson with the girls, in really rather painful Arabic. Miss Hassan's Arabic was really very limited and she acknowledged that she couldn't go on teaching it much further. Then what? She was going to ask for an Arabic speaking teacher. Where from? The Lord would provide.

## 6. The South

### 6.1 Comments on missionaries

In the eyes of some missionaries bad teaching is not a deadly sin since school is chiefly a method of conversion. In consequence something which is half-baked to us seems quite normal to them. Our picture of a school eventually means producing self-reliant children, accessible to new ideas but capable of rejecting bad ones, prepared to work for a higher standard of living and prepared to teach their own children something of what they have learnt. Missionaries just see themselves with a group of children grouped around learning the life of Christ. [The] Catholic sisters [are] somewhat different ... often conscientious in their work but incapable of any adaptation to local needs. The mission is an output of Christianity and children who come into it come into a beleaguered fortress and must be separated from their heathen background.[18]

### 6.2 The experiment at Tonj

[We were] regarding it [the Tonj school] as an experiment to find out what could really be done in the South. I don't think I should like to be the woman who lived at Tonj but everyone is not as cowardly as I am ... It would be a simple, uninterrupted life and would need someone with a very strong professional conscience.

[The aims of the experiment would be]

(a) to discover whether it is possible to fit schooling into the present framework of the tribe so that the girls return to their homes after school to lead lives of the same pattern with perhaps more order induced into them—an

18. S.A.D. 657/1/92.

accretion, which will show its value after several generations. This I feel, at a superficial glance is unlikely to be possible, as the ferment of going to school and learning to read and write is liable to be more upsetting than we can calculate.

(b) To recognise honestly that detribalisation has to come and to attempt to make some thoughtful plan whereby our education may replace the older—and in our judgement—less worthy values. It may be argued that this has already been thought out but it might be well before starting a girls' school to review the position very carefully and attempt to hazard a guess at the sort of girls, which the school would produce and the future we think she should help to make for her people. As the process of schooling become more thorough we are bound to shake her belief in her tribal gods and we should be ready to offer something of substance as guides. As far as ethics is concerned it would probably be best to base our teaching on Christianity as that is a system we understand and can probably most helpfully apply to the children's needs but it would have to be completely unsectarian and undoctrinal. Any girl who had been to school would be likely to eschew her tribal gods also from a social point of view. That we should raise up a race of 'little ladies' is a pernicious result to be fought against wherever the signs appear but we must in all common fairness instil into girls a large measure of self-respect, which may fit ill with the present social system whereby so much drudgery comes to the women ... these difficulties ... should be thoroughly discussed and intelligently recognised, as half the value of the school will lie in its attempts to find the solutions.

# Select Bibliography

### compiled by J.C.M. Starkey

In the original text Dr Beasley gave no complete references or bibliography. The list below includes references given in the footnotes, and complete references for any items given in the text, as well as relevant items used for background research. Of particular use were all the articles listed below by Lilian Passmore Sanderson, for which I was grateful. [Bell, G] and [Dee, B.D.], *The Sudan Political Service, 1899-1956*, Oxford, [1958?] was extremely useful for biographical details, but only for British officials who served with the Sudan Political Service. Other biographical footnotes have been gleaned from a variety of sources, especially Sudan Government half-yearly lists. Many of these sources are available at the University of Durham Library or in the Sudan Collections at the University of Khartoum, but are otherwise difficult to find. I have divided the material into (1) Archival material, (2) Government reports and official papers, and (3) other publications (including unpublished theses), although there is inevitably considerable overlap between these categories.

## 1. Archival material

### Church Missionary Society Archives

Church Missionary Society Archives, lodged at University of Birmingham Library. Relevant material was found in the following files:-

(SN G1 1936-49) Atbara
(SN G3 1934-35) Nuba Mountains
(AF 35/49/G3 SN e2) Omdurman Girls' Central School
(AF 35/49/G3 SN e3) Wad Medani Girls' School
(AF 35/49/G3 SN e4) Unity High for Girls; Wad Medani
(AF 35/49/G3 SN G4 1937-54) Omdurman
(G3 SN G5 1945-54) Sallara
(SN1 G3 1932-59)
(S G3 g2,5,7,8,10,11; Se G3 files 1,3,5-9; S1 G3 1935-59)
(S7 G3 1956-59) Islamic teaching in Sudan schools
(AF 35/49 G3 Se1) Juba

(AF 35/49 G3 Se3) Loka Nugent school (two files)
(AF 35/49 G3 Se3 subfile 4,6-8) Loka
(AF 35/49 G3 Se4) Bishop Gwynne College
(AF 35/49 G3 Se5) Elementary teacher-training Mundri

**Sudan Archives**

The Sudan Archives are lodged at the Library, University of Durham. Sources consulted include the following:-

S.A.D. 234/3/28, 55-56, 64-65 Wingate, F.R., personal papers, 1904/05.

S.A.D. 606/7/34, S.A.D. 606/8/1-11, 97 Balfour, E.A., correspondence to his mother Lady Grace Balfour, 1940s.

S.A.D. 631/3/36-39 Hills-Young, E. 'Female circumcision in the Sudan: surgical seal of chastity', Nov-Dec 1944, typescript.

S.A.D. 657/1/1-85 Beasley, I.M., Administrative Papers, 1898-1946 including items listed above; also Notes on Early Education, Rufaa etc. (S.A.D. 657/1/10).

S.A.D. 657/2/1-49 Beasley, I.M., Administrative Papers, 1943-62.

S.A.D. 657/3/1-108 Beasley, I.M., File of administrative papers re girls' education in the Nuba Mountains and Equatoria Province, 1944-53, including her Report to the Director of Education re Nuba education and the College in the West, July 1945 (S.A.D. 657/3/8-29, 57-58); The South (S.A.D. 657/3/59-103) including a paper entitled 'The education of girls in the Southern Sudan', *Sudan Government Departmental Reports*, 18.5.46 (S.A.D. 657/3/57); Teacher's Association and women's clubs in Omdurman, 1953 (S.A.D. 657/3/104-108).

S.A.D. 657/4/1-274 Beasley, I.M., File of papers re female circumcision, 1936-49.

S.A.D. 657/5/1-134 Beasley, I.M., Letters from Ina Beasley to her mother Mrs A.B. Girdwood, 5.4.1941-28.3.1948, including progress of the war, developments in Burma, publication of her novel *The Desert Rose*, her stay with S.A.R., leave and treks to Kordofan 18.9.41 (S.A.D. 657/5/28-31), to Gezira and Kassala 29.10.41 (S.A.D. 657/5/32-34), to Kassala 21.11.41 (S.A.D. 657/5/35-37), to Blue Nile Province 28.1.42, 19.3.42, 31.10.42 (S.A.D. 657/5/41-43, 46-48, 64-66), to Malakal 12.12.47 (S.A.D. 657/5/128), to the West 26.2.48 (S.A.D. 657/5/131-133).

S.A.D. 657/6/2-59 Letters from Ina Beasley to her sister Mrs Sheila Connelly, 8.6.-10.8.1945, taking the form of trek diaries re Nuba Mountains (including Sallara) and Kordofan and the West.

S.A.D. 657/7/1-94 Beasley, Ina. M., Personal Correspondence including information on S.A.R. and her visit to Aba Island, 10.8.1945 (S.A.D.

657/7/1-19); her visit to Equatoria 8.4.1946 (S.A.D. 657/7/30-54); tour of inspection to Kassala Province, including Tokar 7.3.1947 (S.A.D. 657/7/55-94).

S.A.D. 658/2/1-376 Beasley, Ina M., *Before the Wind Changed: People and Places in the Sudan*, typescript, n.d.

S.A.D. 658/3/1-226 Beasley, Ina M., *Shambat Ferry*, novel, typescript, n.d.

S.A.D. 658/4/1-11 Beasley, Ina M., 'Education for girls in the Sudan', copy of a broadcast in Omdurman, c.1942.

S.A.D. 658/4/12-19 Beasley, Ina M., 'Education of girls in the Sudan during the last two years', copy of a broadcast in Omdurman, 8.2.1945.

S.A.D. 658/4/39-44 Beasley, Ina M., 'Girls schools in the Anglo-Egyptian Sudan: 25 years of progress' and 'The Girls' Training College, Omdurman', unpublished papers, [1948].

S.A.D. 658/4/49-58 Biographical details of Malakat al-Dar (1922-69). Information from her sister Aisha Mohamed Abdulla and Ina Beasley's journal, 27.12.1976.

S.A.D. 662/11/1-2 Cox, C.W.M., Administrative papers, educational submissions, listing proposed Girls' Elementary Schools, 1947-56, 1946.

S.A.D. 662/11/6-9 Cox, C.W.M., Administrative Papers, Note by R.A. Hodgkin on 'Prliminary work in mass literacy in the Sudan' with covering letter from C.W. Williams, Director of education, 5.1.1948.

S.A.D. 664/10/1-22 Cox, C.W.M., Administrative Papers, report of the Commission appointed by the Sudan Government and the C.M.S. on 'Education of Women and Girls in the area occupied by the Church Missionary Society in the Southern Sudan', with comments by C.W.M. Cox, March 1939.

S.A.D. 665/7-11, 666/1-10 Teachers' handbooks used at Bakht-er-Ruda (Cox, C.W.M. Collection).

S.A.D. G//S 968 Beasley, Ina M., *The Verandah at Suakin*, unpublished typescript.

S.A.D. G//S 968 Beasley, Ina M., two volumes of her journal covering her stay in Sudan from 1939 to 1949, unpublished.

S.A.D. G//S 992 Allison, O., C.M.S. Mission Nuba Mountains file.

## 2.Government Reports and Official papers

Ainley, N.E. and Warburton, M.C., *Report on Women's Education in the Southern Sudan*, E.D.A., 1939.

Ali, Nasr el Hag, *Education in the Northern Sudan*, mimeo., Khartoum, Publications Bureau, Ministry of Education, 1954.

Brown, Lewis W., *Brown Plan for Education, 1946-56*, Khartoum, Department of Education, 1946 (repr. Khartoum, Educational Planning Unit, 1969).

Cox, C.M.W., *The Education of the Community in African Society*, Colonial Office Advisory Committee, 1935.

Pridie, E.D., *et al*, *Female Circumcision in the Anglo-Egyptian Sudan*, Sudan Government Publication, McC 285, 1.3.45.

Sudan Government, *Report of the Rejaf Language Conference*, London, 1928.

——————, *Sudan Almanac*, an official handbook, Khartoum, Central office of Information, 1941.

——————, *The Sudan, A Record of Progress 1898-1947*, Khartoum.

——————, *First Progress Report on Um Gerr Experiment*, mimeo pamphlet, Khartoum, 1951.

Sudan Government, Advisory Council for the Northern Sudan, *Second Report of the Sub-Committee of the Advisory Council for the Northern Sudan, set up to study and report on the Ten Years [1946-56] Programme of Education*, Khartoum, c. 1946 (Cox, C.W.M., Education Reports, S.A.D. 663/3/1-17).

Sudan Government, Department of Education, *Annual Reports of the Department of Education*, [*ARDE* in footnotes], 1900-1914, 1928-1948.

——————, *Gordon College Report*, 1925 (S.A.D. 657/1/2).

——————, The Winter Committee Report, *Education in the Northern Sudan*, report of a committee appointed by his Excellency the Governor General (1933, under the chairmanship of R.K. Winter), 1934.

——————, Williams, C.W., 9.2.1936 'Report on Education in the Southern Sudan', S.G.A./Equatoria/ File E.P./S.C.R./17.A.3.

——————, Director's Office, Proposals for the expansion and improvement of the Education System in the Sudan, 27.5.38.

——————, Beasley, Ina M., Note on Girls' Education in the Sudan, Dec 1940 (S.A.D. 657/1/53-62).

——————, Notes from a meeting to discuss girls' education in 1942, 29.3.41 (File DE9.1.1/3) (S.A.D. 657/1/67-73).

——————, The future development of girls' education in the Sudan, 25.7.43, (File DE9.1.1/3) (S.A.D. 657/1/67-73).

—————, Agenda and Minutes of an extra-Departmental Conference on Girls' Education in Northern Sudan, 8.11.43 (S.A.D. 657/1/82-85).

—————, *al-Tarbiyyat al-badaniyya li'l-madaris al-uliya li'l-banat*, [Physical education for girls' primary schools], Khartoum 1943.

—————, *The future development of girls' education in the Sudan*, [Reports of discussion at the Department of Education], typescript, Khartoum, 1943, typescript.

—————, Roseveare, R.V.H., 'Proposals for the expansions of educational facilities for girls', 24.2.1944 (Cox, C.W.M., Education Reports, S.A.D. 662/16/23-26).

—————, Williams, C.W., Educational proposals, Nov 1944, pp.37-38.

—————, *Proposals for the expansion and improvement of the educational system in the Sudan, 1947-56*, Part I, Northern Sudan, 26.5.1946 (Cox, C.W.M., Education Reports, S.A.D. 663/2/1-86); Part II, Southern Sudan, 1946-50, 31.5.46 (Cox, C.W.M., Education Reports, S.A.D. 663/1/7-54).

—————, Beasley, Ina M., Annual Report, 1947 (Cox, C.W.M., Education Reports, S.A.D. 663/3/21-27).

Sudan Government, Department of Interior, *Sudan Government List*, half-yearly, 1926-64.

Sudan Government, Department of Interior, *Sudan Government List*, quarterly, 1900-1956.

Sudan Government Gazette, *Legislative Supplement*, no.762, 15.1.46.

Sudan Government, Ministry of Education, *Annual Reports*, [*ARDE* in footnotes], 1949-57/58.

—————, *Guide to Bakht er Ruda Institute of Education*, Khartoum, 1949 (typescript, 1944, S.A.D. 665/4/19-23; typescript, 1949, S.A.D. 665/4/24-34).

—————, *Proposal for the expansion and improvement of the educational system in the Southern Provinces, 1951-56*, Khartoum, McCorquodale, 1950.

—————, *Revised plan for education in the Southern Provinces 1951-56*, Khartoum, [1951].

—————, *Proposals for the expansion and improvement of the educational system in the Northern Provinces, 1949-56*, Khartoum, Sudan Survey Department, 1951 (Cox, C.W.M., Education Reports, S.A.D. 663/4/1-66).

—————, *Educational statistics for the academic year 1959-60*, Ministry of Education, Khartoum, April 1961.

—————, *Girls' Education in the Sudan* (repr. Khartoum, Educational Planning Unit, 1970).

Sudan, Ministry of Education, Institute of Education, Bakht-er-Ruda, *Bakht er Ruda: Twenty years Old*, Khartoum, Publications Bureau, 1954.

Sudan, Ministry of Education, Publications Bureau, *Publications Bureaux in the Sudan, 1946-51*, Khartoum, Publications Bureau, 1952.

Sudan Government Archives (S.G.A.), GENCO/3/42; DAKHLIA/17/5/File B8; CIVSEC 20/29/141.

United Kingdom, *Report of H.M. Consul-General and Agent on the Finance, Administration and Conditions of Egypt and the Soudan*, Khartoum, The Governor General, Section III, Education, 1905; *Report of Agents' Departments*, Part I, 1906 (S.A.D. 657/1/11); 1907 (S.A.D. 657/1/4, 8); *Red Sea Province Report*, 1908 (S.A.D. 657/1/12); Gorst, Sir Eldon, 1909 (S.A.D. 657/1/7, 13); 'Education for girls', 1909, p.223 (S.A.D. 657/1/11); Wingate, F.R., 1910 (S.A.D. 657/1/12); *Blue Nile Province Report*, 1910 (S.A.D. 657/1/6, 13); 1913 (S.A.D. 657/1/21).

————, Colonial Office, *Mass Education in African Society*, London, Government White paper, no: 186, 1943.

————, Ministry of Information, *The Abyssinian Campaigns*, London, 1942.

Warr, Lord De La, *Report of the Education Commission*, Khartoum, Department of Education, 28.12.1937 (repr. Khartoum, Educational Planning Unit, 1969).

## 3. Publications

Abbas, Mekki, *The Sudan Question*, London, O.U.P. and Faber and Faber, 1952 (repr. 1962).

Abdel Hadi, Sayed, article against female circumcision in *al-Nīl* newspaper, 25.7.39.

Abdel Magid, Abdel Aziz Amin, *al-Tarbiya fī al-Sūdān fī al-qarn al-tāsi' 'ashar*, [History of Education in the Sudan in the nineteenth century], Cairo, 1949.

'Abd al-Rahim, Muddathir, *Imperialism and Nationalism in the Sudan, A Study in Constitutional and Political Development 1899-1956*, Oxford, Clarendon Press, 1969.

*Ahfad College Magazine* (in Arabic), Omdurman, 1955 and 1961.

Amery, H.F.S., *English-Arabic Vocabulary for the use of officials in the Anglo-Egyptian Sudan*, Cairo, Egyptian Army, Intelligence Department, 1905.

Amin, Nasr el Hag and B.E., 'Mass Education in the Anglo-Egyptian Sudan', *Mass Education Bulletin*, Vol 1, no.2, March 1950, pp.27-30.

Arkell, A.J., 'Fung origins', *S.N.R.*, XV, pt.2, pp.201-250.

Arkell, A.J., 'The history of Darfur, 1200-1700', *S.N.R.*, XXXII, pt.1, 1951, pp.37-70; XXXII, pt.2, 1951, pp.207-238; XXXIII, pt.1, 1952, pp.129-155; XXXIII, pt.2, 1952, p.244-275.

Arkell, A.J., *A History of the Sudan from the earliest times to 1821*, New York, 1955.

Atiyah, Edward, *An Arab Tells his Story*, London, 1946.

——————, *Black Vanguard*, London, 1952.

Bacon, G.H., 'Agricultural Education', in Tothill, J.D. *Agriculture in the Sudan*, London, 1948, pp.222-247.

Bakheit, G.M.A., *British Administration and Sudanese Nationalism 1919-39*, unpublished PhD thesis, Cambridge, 1965.

Barbour, K.M., *The Republic of the Sudan, a Regional Geography*, London, University of London Press, 1961.

Beasley, Ina M., *Book of English Grammar*, O.U.P., 1939.

——————, *Nafīsa fī 'l-madrasa: qiṣṣa li 'l-aṭfāl*, [Nafisa at school, children's textbook] (Tr. by N. Ibrahim), London/Cairo, 1949.

——————, 'Girls' Education in the Anglo-Egyptian Sudan' *National Froebel Foundation Bulletin*, April 1951 (also *Colonial Review*, 1951, p.52).

——————, *The Desert Rose*, London, Femina Books, 1969.

——————, 'Female circumcision', *Women Speaking*, July-Sept 1976, pp.21-23.

——————, 'Women and Colonial Development', *The Contemporary Review*, offprint, n.d.?

Bedri, Babikr, *Ta'rīkh ḥayātī*, [The story of my life], in 3 vols, [?Khartoum], 1959-61.

Bedri, Yusuf and Scott, George (ed. and trans.), *The Memoirs of Babikr Bedri*, with an introduction by P.M. Holt, Vol 1, London, O.U.P., 1969.

Bedri, Yusuf and Hogg, Peter (ed. and trans.), *The Memoirs of Babikr Bedri*, Vol 2, London, Ithaca Press, 1980.

[Bell, G] and [Dee, B.D.], *The Sudan Political Service, 1899-1956*, Oxford, [1958?].

Bell, G., *Shadows on the Sudan*, London, 1983.

Beshir, Mohamed Omer, *The Southern Sudan: Background to Conflict*, London, Christopher Hurst, 1968.

——————, *Educational Development in the Sudan 1898 to 1956*, Oxford, Clarendon Press, 1969.

Bloss, J.F.E., 'The story of Suakin', *S.N.R.*, (I) XIX, 1936, pp.271-300; (II) XX, 1937, pp.247-280.

Bruce, James, *Travels to Discover the Source of the Nile*, London, 1790.

Bush, Simon, 'Sudan Airways: An historical outline', *Sudan Studies*, no 7, January 1990.

Cave, Francis O. and MacDonald, James D., *Birds of the Sudan: Their Identification and Distribution*, Edinburgh, Oliver and Boyd, 1955.

Churchill, Winston, *The River War: an Account of the Reconquest of the Soudan*, London, Eyre and Spottiswoode, 1899 (repr. 1933, 1951).

Church Missionary Society, *The Torch*, 1947.

——————, *The Southern Sudan, Then and Now*, Adventure of Faith Series, no 12, London, 1950.

Cloudsley, J. Anne, *Women of Omdurman, Victims of Circumcision*, London, Fawcett Society, 1981.

——————, *Women of Omdurman. Life, Love and the Cult of Virginity*, Ethnographica, 1983.

Corbyn, E.N., 'Bakht er Ruda Institute of Education in the Sudan', *Times Educational Supplement*, 1599, Dec 22, 1945, p.504.

Coulson, N.J., *A History of Islamic Law*, Islamic Surveys, 2, Edinburgh University Press, 1964.

Currie, Sir James, 'The Educational Experiment in the Anglo-Egyptian Sudan, 1900-1933', *Journal of the African Society*, XXXIII, 1934, pp. 351-71 and XXXIV, 1935, pp. 41-59 (repr. Khartoum, Educational Planning Unit, 1969).

El Dareer, Asma, *Woman, Why do you Weep? Circumcision and its Consequences*, London, Zed Press, 1982.

Ḍayfallāh, Muḥammad wad, *Kitāb al-ṭabaqāt*, ed. Yūsuf Faḍl Ḥasan, Khartoum, 1971. [Biography of notables of the Funj kingdom of Sannār c.1800].

Daly, M.W., *British Administration and the Northern Sudan, 1917-1924. The Governor-Generalship of Sir Lee Stack in the Sudan*, Leiden, Historisch-Archaeologisch Institut te Istanbul, 1980.

——————, *Empire on the Nile, The Anglo-Egyptian Sudan, 1898-1934*, Cambridge, C.U.P., 1986.

Davis, R., 'The Masalit Sultanate', *S.N.R.*, VII, 1924, pp.49-62.

Doughty, C.M., *Arabia Deserta*, Vol II, 1888.

Drabble, Margaret (ed.), *The Oxford Companion to English Literature*, London, O.U.P., 1985.

Duncan, J.S.R., *The Sudan: A Record of Achievement*, Edinburgh, Blackwood, 1952.

——————, *The Sudan's Path to Independence*, Edinburgh, 1957.

Earl, G.F., 'Some educational ideals and progress in the Southern Sudan', *East and West Review*, Vol 5, 1939, pp.34-43.

Evans-Pritchard, E.E., *The Nuer*, Oxford, 1940.

——————, *The Divine Kingship of the Shilluk*, Cambridge, 1948.

——————, *The Azande*, Oxford, 1971.

Fabumni, L.A., *The Sudan in Anglo-Egyptian Relations, 1800-1956*, London, Longman, 1960.

Fairman, H.W., 'Preliminary Report on the Excavations at Amara West', *Journal of Egyptian Archaeology*, XXXIV, 1948.

Fawzi, Saad el-Din, *The Labour Movement in the Sudan, 1946-55*, Oxford, Clarendon Press, 1957.

——————, 'The role of women in a developing Sudan', *Proceedings of the Institute of Differing Civilisations Conference*, Brussels, 1958.

Geary, C.L.H., 'The Education of Women and Girls in the Anglo-Egyptian Sudan', *Gaskiya Corporation*, 1950, pp.5490-8.

Gelsthorpe, A.M. (ed.), *Anglican Diocese of the Sudan, A Handbook*, London, 1951.

Gore, E.C. and Mrs, *A Zande and English Dictionary*, London, 1931.

Griffiths, V.L., 'A Teacher Training and Research Centre in the Sudan', *Oversea Education*, Vol 16, no 1, 1944, pp.1-6.

——————, *An Experiment in Education: An account of the attempts to improve the lower stages of boys' education in the Moslem Anglo-Egyptian Sudan*, London, Longmans, 1953 (repr. by London Institute of Rural Life, 1957).

——————, 'An experiment in education in the Sudan', *Overseas Quarterly*, 1958, pp.1-6.

——————, *Teacher-centred: Quality in Sudan Primary Education 1930 to 1970*, Longman, 1975.

Griffiths, V.L., and Taha, Abdel Rahman Ali, *Character Training: an explanation of the principles of character training for parents*, (trans. by Derdiri Osman and Ahmed El Tayeb), Khartoum, 1945.

——————, *Character, its Psychology: an Introduction*, (Arabic and English) (trans. into Arabic by Abdel Rahman Ali Taha), Khartoum, 1949.

——————, *Character Aims: Some Suggestions on Standards for a Rising Nation*, London, 1949.

Guillebaud, Philippa, *School Belts*, London, 1949.

Gwynne, L.H. and others, *Unity High School for Girls, 1928-49, Twenty-one Years of Progress*, Khartoum, Middle East Press, 1950.

Hall, Majorie and Ismail, Bakhita Amin, *Sisters under the Sun: the Story of Sudanese Women*, London and New York, Longman, 1981.

Hamilton, J.A. de C. (ed.), *The Anglo-Egyptian Sudan from Within*, London, Faber and Faber, 1935.

Hasan, Yūsuf Faḍl, *The Arabs and the Sudan, from the Seventh to the early Sixteenth Century*, New York and Edinburgh, 1967 (repr. Khartoum, K.U.P., 1973).

Ḥasan, Yūsuf Faḍl, *al-Shulūkh*, Khartoum, 1976.

Hawley, D.F., 'Law in the Sudan under the Condominium', *The Condominium Remembered, Proceedings of the Durham Sudan Historical Records Conference 1982*, Vol 1, The Making of the Sudanese State, (ed.) Lavin, D., Durham, CMEIS, 1991, pp.39-53.

Hellier, Mary, 'Female circumcision', *Journal of the Medical Women's Federation*, April 1951, pp.24-26.

Henderson, K.D.D., *The Making of the Modern Sudan, The life and letters of Sir Douglas Newbold, K.B.E.*, London, Faber and Faber, London, 1953 (repr. Connecticut, Greenwood, 1974).

——————, *The Sudan Republic*, London, Benn, 1965.

Hill, Richard [L.], *A Biographical Dictionary of the Anglo-Egyptian Sudan*, Oxford, Clarendon Press, 1951 (repr. 1967).

——————, *Egypt in the Sudan, 1820-1881*, London, O.U.P., 1959.

——————, *Sudan Transport*, London, O.U.P., 1965.

Hillard, R.J., *Survey of the Sudan's mercantile and economic position, 1948-49*, being the text of a speech delivered in the Sudan Chamber of Commerce on 7th April 1949, Khartoum, Sudan Government, 1949.

Hodgkin, Robin A., 'The Sudan Publication Bureau beginnings', *Oversea Education*, XIX, no.3, April 1948, pp.694-8.

——————, *Education and Change: a book mainly for those who work in countries where education is part of a process of rapid social change*, London, O.U.P., 1957.

Holt, P.M. and Daly, M.W., *A History of the Sudan: from the Coming of Islam to the Present Day*, 4th ed. London, Longman, 1986 (supercedes Holt, P.M., *Modern History of the Sudan*, London, 1961 which is quoted in footnotes).

Jackson, H.C., *Sudan Days and Ways*, London, 1954.

——————, *Behind the Modern Sudan*, London, 1955.

——————, *Pastor on the Nile*, London, 1960.

Kirk-Greene, A.H.M., *The Sudan Political Service: a Preliminary Profile*, Oxford, 1982 and 1989.

Lampen, G.D., 'History of Darfur', *S.N.R.*, XXXI, 1950, pp.177-209.

Lewis, B., *the Arabs in History*, New York, 1967.

Lewis, D.J., 'The Simuliidae of the Anglo-Egyptian Sudan', *Trans. Royal Ent. Soc.*, London, Vol 99, 1948.

MacDonald, D.R., 'Female Circumcision in the Sudan', paper given at the B.M.A., Sudan Branch, mimeo., 1936.

MacKinnon, E., 'The Blue Nile Province' in Tothill, J.D. *Agriculture in the Sudan*, London, 1948, pp.789-809.

MacMichael, Sir Harold [A.], *The Anglo-Egyptian Sudan*, London, 1934.

——————, *The Sudan*, London, 1954.

El Mahdi, Mandour, 'Adult Education in the Rural Sudan', *Panorama*, 14.2.1962, pp.23.

Mahjoub, Mohamed Ahmed, *Democracy on Trial: Reflections on Arab and African Politics*, London, Deutsch, 1974.

al-Maṣlaḥa al-Ṭibbiyya al-Sūdāniyya, *Al-Khafaḍ al-Fir'aūnī fī 'l-Sūdān*, [Pharaonic circumcision in the Sudan], Khartoum, 1947.

Milne, J.C.M., *The Changing Pattern of Mobility and Migration of the Amarar Tribe of Eastern Sudan*, unpublished M.Phil thesis, University of London, S.O.A.S., 1976.

Muir-Leach, Alice I, 'Female circumcision: some after effects and other aspects', *Journal of the Medical Women's Federation*, Vol 43, no.3, July 1961, pp.111-122.

Myers, D.H., 'Excavations in the Second Cataract area', *S.N.R.*, Vol XXIX, 1948, p.129.

Nadel, S.F., *The Nuba*, London, 1947.

al-Nagar, 'Umar, *The Pilgrimage Tradition in West Africa*, Khartoum, 1972.

O'Fahey, R.S., *State and Society in Dār Fūr*, London, C. Hurst, 1980.

O'Fahey, R.S. and Spaulding, J.L., *Kingdoms of the Sudan*, London, Methuen, 1974.

Okeir, Abdel Gader, 'Education amongst the Beja', *Oversea Education*, Vol 23, no.1, Oct 1951, pp.194-196.

*Panorama*, 'Khartoum Technical Institute', no 1, Spring 1962, p.26.

Passmore, Lilian, (pseud. M. More), 'Women's Progress in the Sudan', *African World*, April 1958.

Passmore, Lilian *see also* Sanderson, Lilian Passmore.

Paul, A., *A History of the Beja Tribes of the Sudan*, London, Frank Cass, 1954.

Philosophical Society of the Sudan, *Proceedings of the Annual Conference*, 11th Conference, 10-11.1.1962, *Education in the Sudan*, convenor and editor Yusuf Bedri, Khartoum, 1963.

Reid, J.A., 'Notes on tribes of the White Nile Province', *S.N.R.*, Vol XIII, 1930, pp.149-210.

Richards, G.E.R., 'Adult Education amongst Country Women; an Experiment at Um Gerr', *S.N.R.*, XXIX, 1948, pp.225-7.

Robertson, J., *Transition in Africa: From Direct Rule to Independence*, London, Christopher Hurst, 1974.

Royal Institute of International Affairs, *Middle East: A Political and Economic Survey*, London, 1950.

Royston-Piggott, P.J., 'Higher Education for Sudanese Women', *Journal of Education*, Vol 83, 1951, p.490.

Sanderson, Lilian Passmore, 'Some Aspects of the Development of Girls' Education in the Northern Sudan', *S.N.R.*, XLII, 1961, pp.91-101.

——————, *A History of Education in the Sudan with Special Reference to the Development of Girls' Education*, unpublished M.A. thesis, London, 1962.

——————, 'Educational Development in the Southern Sudan, 1900-1949', *S.N.R.*, XLIII, 1962, pp.110-112.

——————, 'A Survey of Material Available for the Study of Educational Development in the Modern Sudan, 1900-1963', *S.N.R.*, XLIV, 1963, pp.69-81.

——————, 'The Khartoum Girls' Secondary School', *Oversea Education*, January 1963.

——————, 'Careers for Women in the Sudan', *African Women*, June 1963.

——————, 'Educational Development and Administrative Control in the Nuba Mountains Region of the Sudan', *Journal of African History*, IV, no 2, 1963, pp.233-247.

——————, 'University Education for Sudanese Women in African Perspectives', *Sudan Society*, 2, 1964.

——————, *Education in the Southern Sudan, 1900-1948*, unpublished PhD thesis, London, 1965.

——————, *Against the Mutilation of Women: the Struggle against Unnecessary Suffering*, London, Ithaca, 1981.

——————, *Female Genital Mutliation—Excision and Infibulation: A Bibliography*, Anti-Slavery Society, 1986.

Sanderson, L.M. Passmore and G.N., *Education, Religion and Politics in Southern Sudan 1899-1964*, London, Ithaca Press, 1981.

Santandrea, Stephen, 'The Belanda, Ndogo, etc. in the Bahr el Ghazal', *S.N.R.*, XVI, 1933, pp.161-180.

Shaw, W.B.K., 'Darb al-arba'īn; the forty days' road', *S.N.R.*, XII, 1929, pp.63-71.

Shinnie, P.L., 'Archaeological Discoveries during Winter 1947-48, Amara West', *S.N.R.*, Vol XXIX, 1948, p.128.

Slatin, Rudolf C. von, *Fire and Sword in the Sudan*, ed. by Wingate, F.R., London, Arnold, 1896.

Spelman, N.G., 'Women's work in the Gezira, Sudan', *Oversea Education*, Vol 26, 2, 1954, pp.66-69.

Squires, H.C., *The Sudan Medical Service: an Experiment in Social Medicine*, London, 1958.

Steevens, G.W., *With Kitchener to Khartoum*, London and Edinburgh, Blackwood, 1898.

*Sudan Star*, 'Drastic laws to kill Sudan Custom', Advisory Council talks on Circumcision, 7.11.45.

—————, 'Industry, Liquor, Circumcision', Advisory Council Progress Report, 24.4.46.

Symes, S.G., *Tour of Duty*, London, 1946.

Taha, Abdel Rahman Ali, 'Economic and political aspects of education in the Sudan', in *Cultural Groups and Human Relations Conference on Educational Problems of Specific Cultural Groups*, New York, 1951, pp.127-39.

Theobald, A.B., *The Mahdīya, a history of the Anglo-Egyptian Sudan 1881-1899*, London, Longmans, 1951.

—————, *'Alī Dīnar, last Sultan of Darfur 1898-1916*, London, Longmans, 1965.

Thomas, Graham and Ismay, *Sayed Abdel Rahman al-Mahdi, a Pictorial Biography*, Lama Publishing, 1986.

*The Times*, article on Girls' education in the Sudan, 20.11.53 (S.A.D. 658/5/5).

*Times Educational Supplement*, 'Girls' education in the Sudan', 27.11.48 (S.A.D. 658/5/3-4).

*Times Educational Supplement*, 'Sudan Girls' Education', no: 1911, Dec 14, 1951, p.960.

Toniolo, E.F., 'The First Centenary of the Roman Catholic Mission to Central Africa, 1846-1946', *S.N.R.*, XXVII, 1946, pp.98-126.

Tothill, J.D., (ed.), *Agriculture in the Sudan*, London, O.U.P., 1948.

*The Townswoman*, 'Behind Sudan's Veil', XXXVI, no.6, London, National Union of Townswomen's Guilds, June 1969, pp.205-207.

Trimingham, J. Spencer, *The Christian Approach to Islam in the Sudan*, London, O.U.P, 1948.

—————, *Islam in the Sudan*, London, O.U.P., 1949.

—————, *The Christian Church in Post-war Sudan*, [pamphlet], London, World Domination P., [1949].

—————, C.M.S., Mission Policy in the Northern Anglo-Egyptian Sudan, 7.11.1945.

—————, C.M.S., Southern Sudan: Government Education Policy as affecting the C.M.S., 160/3.

Tucker, A.N., *Primitive Tribal Music and Dancing in the Southern Sudan (Africa) at Social and Ceremonial Gatherings*, London, William Reeves, n.d.

—————, *The Eastern Sudanic Languages*, Vol I, London, O.U.P. for International Institute of African Languages and Cultures, 1940.

Tucker, A.N and Bryan, M.A., *Linguistic Analyses: the non-Bantu Languages of North-Eastern Africa*, London, O.U.P. for International African Institute, 1966.

Vantini, Giovanni, *Christianity in the Sudan*, Bologna, 1981.

Voll, John O., *A History of the Khatmiyya Tariqa in the Sudan*, unpublished PhD thesis, Harvard, 1969 (University Microfilms International, Ann Arbor, Michigan, 1978).

Wieschoff, H.A., 'Education in the Anglo-Egyptian Sudan and British East Africa', *Journal of Negro Education*, Vol 15, 1946, pp.382-96.

Williams, C.W., *Note by the Director of Education on the Government Plan for Educational Development in the Northern Sudan for the next ten years [1946-56]*, Khartoum, Department of Education, 1946 (repr. Khartoum, Educational Planning Unit, 1969).

Williams, K.O., 'Education in the Sudan', *School and Society*, 48, 1938, p. 520.

——————, *A Brief Summary of Girls' Education in the Anglo-Egyptian Sudan based on Sudan Education Reports, 1928-38*, mimeo pamphlet, 1941.

——————, 'The First Year', *Oversea Education*, XVII, 3, April 1946, pp.306-315.

Wingate, F.R., *Wingate of the Sudan*, London, John Murray, 1955.

Woodward, Peter, *Sudan 1898-1989: The Unstable State*, London, Rienner and Lester Crook, 1990.

Yunis, N., 'Notes on the Baggara and Nuba of western Kordofan', *S.N.R.*, V, 1922.

Zenkovsky, S., 'Marriage customs in Omdurman, *S.N.R.*, Vol XXVI, 1945, pp. 241-256.

——————, 'Customs of the women of Omdurman, Part II, *S.N.R.*, Vol XXX, 1949, pp.39-46.

——————, 'Zar and tambura as practised by the women of Omdurman', *S.N.R.*, Vol XXXI, 1950, pp.65-81.

Zetland, Lord, *Lord Cromer*, London, 1935.

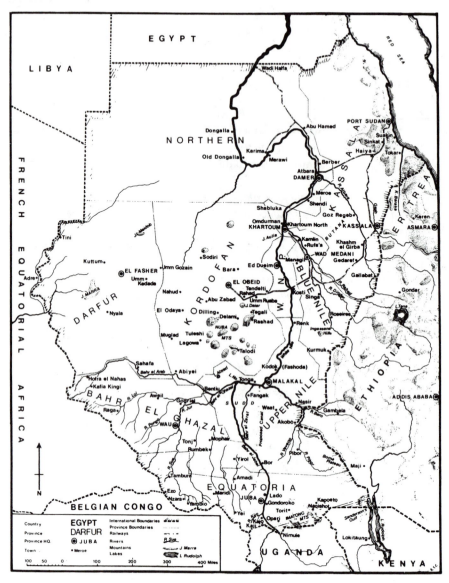

**Map 1.** The Anglo-Egyptian Sudan during the Condominium, by Rosalind Caldecott

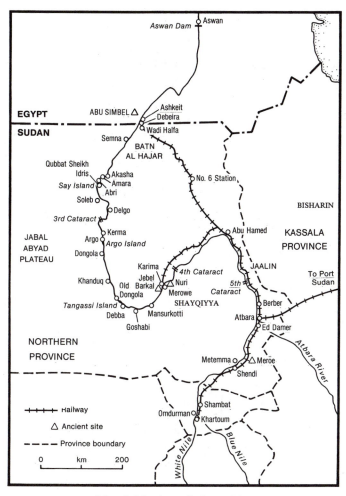

**Map 2.** Northern Sudan, 1940s

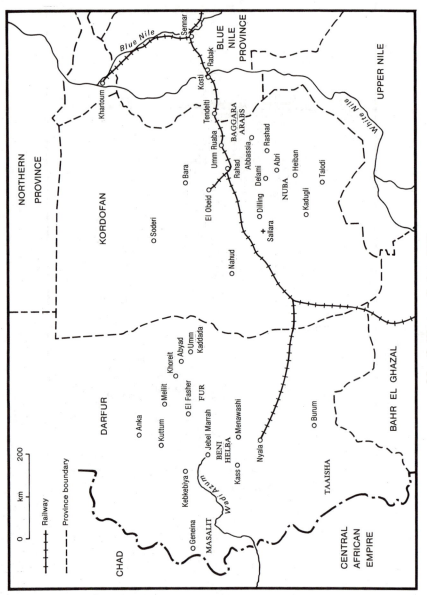

**Map 3.** Western Sudan, 1940s

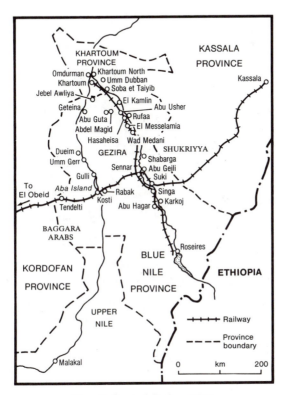

**Map 4.** Central Sudan, 1940s

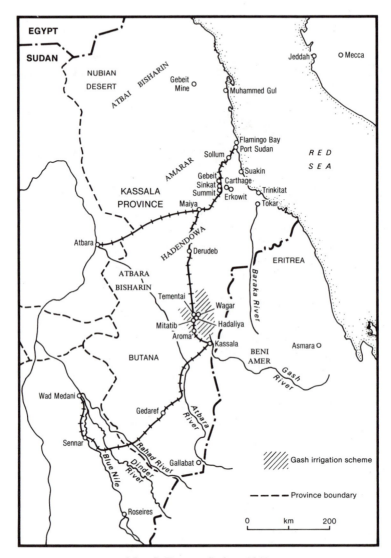

**Map 5.** Eastern Sudan, 1940s

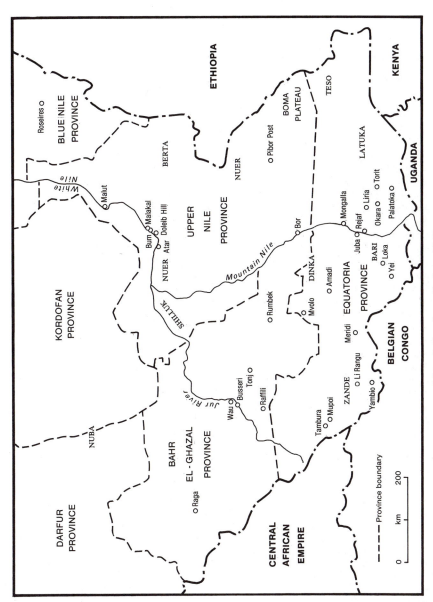

**Map 6.** Southern Sudan, 1940s

ETHIOPIA

KENYA

Roseires O

BLUE NILE
PROVINCE

BERTA

BOMA
PLATEAU

TESO

White Nile

Pibor Post O

NUER

LATUKA

Malut

UPPER
NILE
PROVINCE

Bum Malakal
Atar Doleib Hill

NUER

Mountain Nile

Bor

Mongalla

Rejaf
Juba

Liria
Okara O Torit

Palatoka O

KORDOFAN
PROVINCE

SHILLUK

DINKA

Amadi

Rumbek

Mvolo

BARI
Loka
Yei

EQUATORIA
PROVINCE

Jur River

Meridi

BELGIAN
CONGO

NUBA

Busseri
Tonj O

Raffili

Li Rangu O

ZANDE

Wau

BAHR
EL - GHAZAL
PROVINCE

Tambura

Mupoi

Yambio O

DARFUR
PROVINCE

Raga O

CENTRAL
AFRICAN
EMPIRE

UGANDA

Province boundary

0    km    200

# Index of places and groups

# Index of people

Names are given as cited in the text and footnotes, with those spellings used by Dr Beasley and Sudan Government Lists, except for religious and historical figures. Footnote numbers are given after the page number, where relevant.